D0454896

Software Product Lines

Software Product Lines

Practices and Patterns

Paul Clements

Linda Northrop

Addison-Wesley

Boston • San Francisco • New York • Toronto
Montreal • London • Munich • Paris
Madrid • Capetown • Sydney • Tokyo
Singapore • Mexico City

The SEI Series in Software Engineering

The publisher offers discounts on this book when ordered in quantity for bulk purchases and special sales. For more information, please contact:

U.S. Corporate and Government Sales
(800) 382-3419
corpsales@pearsontechgroup.com

For sales outside of the U.S., please contact:

International Sales
(317) 581-3793
international@pearsontechgroup.com

Visit Addison-Wesley on the Web: www.awprofessional.com

Library of Congress Cataloging-in-Publication Data

Clements, Paul C.
Software product lines : practices and patterns / Paul Clements, Linda Northrop.
p. cm. — (The SEI series in software engineering)
Includes bibliographical references.
ISBN 0-201-70332-7
1. Computer software—Development. I. Northrop, Linda. II. Title. III. Series.
QA76 76.D47 C58 2001
005.1—dc21 2001035285

Text printed on recycled and acid-free paper.

ISBN 0201703327

4 5 6 7 8 9 CRW 07 06 05

4th Printing November 2005

Contents

Foreword

The Promised Land of Product Lines

A number of economic analyses of software productivity (including some of mine) have identified software reuse as the biggest opportunity area for improving software productivity, quality, and cycle time. The initial concept sounds so easy and attractive: you just save all your components and reassemble them to make new applications.

If you try to do this, as I first found out in 1966 when I tried it with the Rand Computer Program Catalog, you quickly gain a great appreciation for how many ways one software component can be incompatible with another. They can have different invocation conventions, units, dimensions, coordinate systems, formats, control assumptions, business assumptions—the list goes on. Even now, however, organizations continue to assemble ad hoc collections of components in the vain hope that they will fortuitously fit together.

The clear next step in capitalizing on reuse is to define and follow rules for composable components. Again, there were a number of unsuccessful attempts to do this in a completely general context. Eventually, we found out that reuse went much better if we defined different domain-specific software architectures for each domain and developed components to interoperate within these architectures.

At this point, a number of organizations climbed the hill of domain engineering and domain architecting, expecting to find the promised land of product line reuse in easy sight, just a simple matter of programming down the hill.

Instead, what they found was another hill to climb; this one also a function of software economics. Jeff Poulin's landmark book, *Measuring Software Reuse* (Addison-Wesley, 1997) shows across a dozen studies that reusable components cost about 50 percent more to develop than one-off components. If, as in many organizations, software projects are budgeted just to get their own job done, there are not enough resources to do a good job of making the components reusable.

And when organizations climbed this hill, they found another hill on the horizon—this one more a matter of culture. This is primarily due to two factors:

- **Not Invented Here.** Lots of software developers still liked building their own stuff. A classic response we got in our first reuse initiative at TRW was, "That stuff's not reusable. If you want *really* reusable components, let *me* rebuild them for you."
- **Risk Aversion.** You may be pretty sure you can build a component in the six weeks allocated for developing it. If you're presented with a reusable component which requires some adaptation, you may assess it as having an 80 percent chance of needing only 2 weeks to adapt, but a 20 percent chance of needing 10 weeks to adapt. From an expected value standpoint, the expected time to adapt the component is (.8)(2) + (.2)(10) = 3.6 weeks, which is a good deal better than the 6-week build-it-yourself option. However, if the component is on the project's critical path, even a 20 percent chance of being responsible for a 4-week project slip will generally be enough to have you reject the reuse option.

These economic and cultural factors can generally be surmounted by two more critical success factors for successful product line reuse. One is an empowered product line manager who has the authority and responsibility to invest in reusable components and to provide incentive to people and projects to reuse them. The other is to develop well-certified plug-and-play components with a low risk of requiring major adaptation effort.

Once atop this hill, though, you still may not see the promised land of product line reuse. Some other hills that may get in your way are mismatches between product line choices and business value, operating successful reusable-asset libraries with good search capabilities and configuration management, and mobilizing to cope with architecture and component obsolescence.

All of this may sound pretty discouraging. You probably don't want to wander in the wilderness for 40 years before catching sight of the promised land of product lines. And that's where this book by Paul Clements and Linda Northrop comes to the rescue. It distills the results of many organizations' product line successes and difficulties into a good map of the mountains and valleys of software product line practices. It provides integrated product line strategies that enable you to surmount problems concurrently rather than sequentially and to avoid the steeper slopes. And it provides good examples of product line success stories that can serve as role models for you and evidence for your managers that the promised land of product line success can be much more than a promise.

BARRY BOEHM, USC

Preface

From subroutines in the 1960s through modules in the 1970s, objects in the 1980s, and components in the 1990s, software engineering has been the story of a continuously ascending spiral of increasing capability and economy battled by increasing complexity. Now, at the dawn of the new millennium, comes the next great turn of the cycle. Software product lines promise to revolutionize the way that organizations, large and small, conceptualize and carry out their software development activities. Software product lines enable companies to field entire families of systems—perhaps containing dozens or even hundreds of members—for little more than the cost of building two or three the old way. This relatively straightforward concept is bringing about breathtaking improvements in productivity, time to market, cost, and quality; and it can be applied to software in every application area and deployed on every kind of platform, regardless of size.

For us, the story began in 1995, when two fortuitous events aligned at exactly the right juncture. First, we quite accidentally stumbled onto a software product line that would forever fuel our thinking; and second, our organization funded an effort dedicated to improving the practice of software product lines.

As researchers at the Software Engineering Institute (SEI), we were scouring our sources looking for case studies in software architecture, a topic just blossoming into the software engineering community's consciousness. We wanted to show that architectural drivers (for example, the need for high performance, security, or modifiability) could be consistently described across different applications and that the same architectural solutions to these drivers would probably surface again and again. This kind of thinking is what motivates the design pattern and architectural style communities. So we wanted to start a "butterfly collection" of architectures, categorized by the problems they solved. Off we went with our nets. One of our colleagues, Lisa Brownsword, mentioned that she knew of an architecture constructed to achieve a quality not in our list. In fact, this quality was not to be found in any of the usual lists of "ilities" that often describe the goals for a software architecture. And yet, Lisa told us, this quality was so important that a company had gambled its whole existence on it.

We were intrigued.

That company was CelsiusTech Systems AB, a Swedish defense contractor supplying shipboard command and control systems to navies around the world. In 1985, CelsiusTech faced a monumental crisis: they were compelled to build two systems much larger than anything the company had ever attempted, and although they had an excellent reputation in their market, CelsiusTech had had trouble meeting schedules and budgets before. Their only hope was to build one solution that would satisfy the (very different) requirements of both customers *and*—and this was their key insight—would also satisfy customers that they hoped would come after these two. The overriding quality that drove the CelsiusTech architecture was its applicability across a wide (but planned) range of products—that is, its suitability to serve as the architecture for a software product line.

So Lisa and one of the authors (PCC) flew off to Sweden, butterfly nets in hand. As we listened to the CelsiusTech story, it became clear that we were onto something much bigger than just an interesting architecture. Yes, the software architecture was the critical foundation for the product line, but it was only one part of a broader story. In some ways, the architecture had been the easy part compared to changing the way the company did business. Adopting the product line strategy required reorganization (more than once), copious training, and an adjustment in the very way that people thought about carrying out their jobs. Architecture and reuse were the technical keys—but by no means the only keys—to adopting a software product line strategy.

And what had this strategy wrought? Not only did it allow the company to deliver both pilot systems, but on subsequent projects (more than 50 of them, in fact), it took years off delivery schedules, allowed a smaller staff to produce more systems, and sent their software reuse levels into the 90 percent range. As an example of their productivity gains, the integration testing of one of these enormous (1.5 million lines of Ada) real-time, safety-critical, highly distributed systems can be routinely handled by one or two people at most. Porting one of these systems to a whole new computing environment and operating system takes less than a month.

When we returned home and reported our findings, we described the architecture. It was, after all, what we had gone to investigate. It was layered and multiprocess, with a blackboard to mediate between data consumers and data producers—it was, in short, just what one would expect. One of our colleagues remarked how uninteresting it was and, I'm sure, didn't think it justified a trip to Sweden—but he didn't grasp the big picture. What we learned was that even a vanilla architecture, if embellished with judiciously planned extension and variation points and created in the context of an overall shift in the way a company does business, can save an organization from oblivion if the organization is willing to reshape itself.

What a discovery and how fortunate for us that it occurred right at the time the SEI's interest in flexible systems was coming into focus with the creation of the Product Line Systems Program, under the direction of one of the authors (LMN). This new program, like the other three technical programs at the SEI, was launched to carry out the mission of the SEI: to provide leadership in advancing the state of the practice of software engineering to improve the quality of systems that depend on software. But this program had a unique charter: to build on earlier SEI work as well as both commercial and government software product line efforts to enable the widespread efficacy of software product lines. We agreed on two strategies to fulfill our mission: (1) we would codify and establish best practices for organizations wishing to undertake that reshaping to become skilled at producing software product lines; and (2) we would build and equip a community of people interested in working on software product line issues. We set out with enthusiasm to effect those strategies.

In that process, we've worked to gather information and identify key people in the field. We've held nearly a dozen workshops attended by experienced product line practitioners from all over the world. They've told us how they've solved problems in all areas of product line production, and they've let us know about areas where they've stumbled and made the wrong choices as well. We've participated in many other conferences and workshops with software product lines in the agenda (sometimes as a result of our prodding or initiation). We sponsored and held the First Software Product Line Conference in August 2000. (We expect that there will be many more such conferences.) There, almost 200 people gathered to discuss and learn about software product lines. Finally, we work with organizations directly to help them adopt the product line paradigm as a way of doing business. This puts us in the trenches with the people who must undergo the changes precipitated by the shift. Our customer collaborations have two effects. First, they give us the best seat in the house from which to judge and record what works and what doesn't. Second, they put everything we think and counsel about product lines through a trial by fire. If these things are not right—or if they are right but unimportant—our customers/collaborators will let us know in a hurry.

What we've learned is that software product lines represent a powerful paradigm for software that can and does achieve remarkable improvements in time, cost, and quality. Systems turned out in days instead of years. Order-of-magnitude productivity gains. Smaller staffs producing more projects that are larger and of higher quality. Mass customization wherein 20 software builds are parlayed into a family of over a thousand specifically tailored systems. These and other stories are what we've discovered.

This book is the distillation of all that we've learned about software product lines. We describe the essential activities, which are (1) the development of a set of core assets from which all of the products will be built, (2) the development of products using those core assets, and (3) strong technical and organizational management to launch and coordinate both core asset development and product development. We delve beneath the surfaces of these three broad essential activities. To be more prescriptive about what an organization must do, we describe 29 *practice areas* that must be mastered. The practice areas are divided into the categories of software engineering, technical management, and organizational management according to what types of skills are required to carry them out. For example, defining the architecture is a software engineering practice area; configuration control is a technical management practice area; and training is an organizational management practice area.

The essential activities and the practice areas have constituted the pivotal output of the SEI's product line practice work and are continually updated in a Web-based document. Parts I and II of this book are derived from that document, which is called *A Framework for Software Product Line Practice* [Clements 00b]. This work has been used by organizations, large and small, to help them plan their adoption of the product line approach as well as to help them gauge how they're doing and in what areas they're falling short. We use it to guide our collaborations with customers. We have also used it as the basis for conducting product line technical probes, which are formal diagnostics of an organization's product line fitness. It represents our best picture of sound product line practice as described to us by its many reviewers and users—practitioners all.

In addition to the practice areas and essential activities, which offer "what to do" guidance, this book provides *software product line practice patterns* as "how to" guidance. These patterns give common product line problem/solution pairs in which the problems are product line work to be done and the solutions are the groups of practice areas to apply in concert to accomplish the work. We also chronicle three detailed case studies (and short takes of several others) that show how different organizations have overcome product line hurdles in their own unique ways. Cummins Inc., the U.S. Government's National Reconnaissance Office, and Germany's Market Maker AG all made deliberate decisions to go down the product line path, and each has a compelling story to tell about its experiences. (The CelsiusTech story is chronicled elsewhere [Bass 98a].)

The book includes discussion questions throughout, so that a study group (maybe a brown-bag lunch discussion group or a university class) can explore the subtleties of the issues together. We have also added numerous sidebars that tell stories, relate the experiences or viewpoints of others, or simply underscore significant points. Anecdotes in the sidebars are all true and come from first-hand knowledge, although confidentiality occasionally prevents us from naming sources. Many of the sidebars form a series we call "Other Voices." In them we have borrowed (with permission) from product line practitioners' experiences that have appeared in the open literature. They provide a set of first-person war stories that we hope will resonate with readers.

Software Product Lines: Practices and Patterns is the culmination of our efforts to grow and nurture a community of people interested in software product lines. As a reader of this book, you are also a member of this growing community. Welcome.

PCC
Austin, Texas

LMN
Pittsburgh, Pennsylvania

Acknowledgments

This book would not have been possible without the efforts of many people.

Our sponsors, both in the Department of Defense and at the Software Engineering Institute (SEI), have believed in the value of our product line work and have continued to fund the SEI's Product Line Practice Initiative. In the early years, Larry Druffel and Julia Allen, as SEI directors, and Peter Feiler, a program manager, were instrumental. The current directors, Stephen Cross and Clyde Chittister, are strong proponents of this initiative and have been highly supportive. John Goodenough, the SEI's Chief Technical Officer, helped shape the early vision and strategies and has been tireless in his efforts to promote and add value to our efforts.

Many of our colleagues at the SEI contributed their creativity and insights, not to mention their written words, to make the practice areas in Part II first take form. They contributed the early descriptions of each practice area. They also contributed to the evolution of the basic concepts, to the focusing of the key ideas, and to the conceptual integrity of the work as a whole. We recognize the profound contributions of Felix Bachmann, Len Bass, Joe Batman, John Bergey, Grady Campbell, Gary Chastek, Sholom Cohen, Patrick Donohoe, Matthew Fisher, Brian Gallagher, Lawrence Jones, Robert Krut, Reed Little, John McGregor, William O'Brien, Dennis Smith, Albert Soule, Scott Tilley, Nelson Weiderman, Steven Woods, and Dave Zubrow. Many helped by attending the SEI's product line practice workshops and capturing the wisdom and experience shared by our expert guests. And many provided comprehensive, insightful, detailed reviews of the material. We appreciate the reviews of David Carney, Priscilla Fowler, Kyo Kang, and Robert Nord. Special thanks to Larry Jones for his work in helping to craft the Product Line Technical Probe and for his stewardship of the sidebar "Software Process Improvement and Product Line Practice." We thank Robert Fantazier, who created all of the diagrams and illustrations that help to visualize the product line concepts. Robert Krut installed a previous version of some of this material on the SEI's Web site, and in doing so uncovered and helped us correct numerous errors. Laura Novacic and Melissa Kacik provided invaluable secretarial support throughout the effort.

Many external reviewers helped to improve the work, including those anonymous reviewers engaged by the publisher, but also Dave Bristow, T.W. Cook, Krzysztof Czarnecki, Bob Ferguson, Emil Jandourek, Jean Jourdan, Gregor Kiczales, Philippe Lalanda, Ron Lannan, Henk Obbink, Fabio Peruzzi, Rick Randall, and David Sharp. Thanks to Ben Northrop, who provided the candid comments that only someone who is both a software engineer and a son could give.

Klaus Schmid provided useful insights into the problem of product line scoping and the PuLSE-ECO method. Ulrike Becker-Korns kindly supplied helpful comments on the Process Definition practice area. Thanks to Michalis Anastasopoulos for making available his splendid work on variation mechanisms applied to component development. Thanks to Sholom Cohen and Patrick Donohoe for their contribution to the case study on the Control Channel Toolkit, to John McGregor for his work on the sidebar "Components as Products," and to John Vu for his help with the sidebar "Process Improvement Gains with a Product Line Focus." Thanks to Patrick Donohoe, Grady Campbell, Stuart Faulk, David Weiss, and Audris Mockus for providing key information and references for the sidebar "It Takes Two." Thanks to Charles Krueger and Ira Baxter for their respective help with the sidebars "A Tool for Software Product Line Production" and "A Tool for Mining" and especially for making their software tools available to us. Charles Krueger also carried out and made available to us the market study mentioned in the sidebar "E Pluribus Unum." Special thanks to Cristina Gacek, Peter Knauber, and Klaus Schmid for making the Market Maker case study possible, and for their superb help in carrying it out and writing it up. Thanks to Joe Batman for pointing us to the "Ying-tsao fa-shih" building codes mentioned in the sidebar "Product Lines Everywhere."

Much of the information in this book comes from people who have actually built software product lines, occasionally with our help. Confidentiality prevents us from naming all of our collaborators, but without those people allowing us to peer over their shoulders, our knowledge would have been just informed speculation. We are sincerely grateful to them. We thank the people who have participated in our software product line workshops over the past few years and the organizations that supported their participation. They generously shared their knowledge and experience with us and with each other for the overall advancement of the community. They taught us a lot.

Perceiving the competition's hot breath on the backs of their necks, companies are understandably reluctant to see anything published that might give away an advantage. Hence, it is almost impossible to get a representative of a software product line organization to sit still for an open-literature case study.

With this prelude, we acknowledge the extraordinary cooperation of all of our case study participants. Market Maker's chief architect, Martin Verlage, answered our questions patiently and painstakingly. Even better, he answered important questions that we hadn't thought to ask. The authors deeply appreciate his insight, thoughtful analysis, and good humor. At Cummins Inc., Joe Gahimer put together a remarkable multiday agenda of interviews and presentations, all cast in terms of our 29 practice areas. We are extremely grateful for his hard work and willingness to share the Cummins experience. We thank everyone at Cummins who gave of their time to speak with us, especially Jim Dager and Ron Temple, whose participation was above and beyond the call of duty. At the U. S. National Reconnaissance Office and Raytheon we are deeply indebted to Mike Grier, John Ohlinger, Kevin Payne, Jeff Shaw, and Cliff Stockdill. They provided us with an opportunity to work on a first-class software product line effort and to write about it.

The "Other Voices" sidebars that include material from *Software Product Lines: Proceedings of the First Software Product Line Conference* (edited by Pat Donohoe, published by Kluwer Academic Publishers, 2000) do so with the kind permission of Kluwer and the authors whom we quoted. We take pleasure in acknowledging P. America, M. Ardis, W. Chae, B. Choi, D. Coleman, J. Dager, M. Dehlin, L. Dor, P. Dudak, S. Faulk, R. Harmon, K. Kang, C. Kaveri, B. Kim, E. Koh, K. Lee, W. Leu, F. van der Linden, A. Mili, L. Nakatani, H. Obbink, J. Ohta, B. Olsen, R. van Ommering, F. Peruzzi, P. Pontrelli, B. Pronk, D. Raffo, S. Thiel, P. Toft, A. Walker, T. Wappler, S. Yacoub, and J. van Zyl.

Thanks to the staff at Addison-Wesley Professional for their customary smooth professionalism. Peter Gordon was, as always, a taskmaster with a velvet whip.

And thanks to our families, friends, and colleagues who had to put up with our long hours, endless fact-finding trips, and offsite writing marathons.

We consider a set of programs a family if they have so much in common
that it pays to look at their common aspects
before looking at the aspects that differentiate them.
This rather pragmatic definition does not tell us what pays,
but it does explain the motivation for designing program families.
We want to exploit the commonalities . . . and reduce . . . costs.

David Lorge Parnas, 1979

Reader's Guide

This book is a work in three parts.

Part I is called "Software Product Line Fundamentals," and its three chapters lay out the conceptual groundwork for software product lines. Chapter 1 covers the background and basic ideas. Chapter 2 describes the benefits of a software product line approach from a variety of points of view throughout an organization. Chapter 3 lays out the three essential activities for product lines: development of a reusable base of core assets, development of products that utilize those core assets, and management to orchestrate the entire affair.

Part II is called "Software Product Line Practice Areas." It defines 29 skill areas in which an organization needs to be adept in order to achieve a software product line capability. All of these practice areas will be familiar to every reader experienced in software development; they are pockets of expertise that must be present in any software development organization. They include architecture definition, component development, testing, configuration management, market analysis, training, and the like. However, each one takes on a new dimension and needs to be applied in different ways in a software product line context. The practice areas are organized into three groups: software engineering practice areas (Chapter 4), technical management practice areas (Chapter 5), and organizational management practice areas (Chapter 6).

Part III is called "Putting the Practice Areas into Action." Its goal is to provide the reader with the tools necessary to apply the practice areas in a way most beneficial to a specific organizational context. Chapter 7 shows how the practice areas can be applied in software product line practice patterns, a powerful mechanism by which organizations can bring the practice areas into play according to their own situations and goals. Chapter 8 introduces the Product Line Technical Probe, a diagnostic instrument that lets an organization discover where it is lacking necessary practice area skills. Chapters 9 through 11 present three case studies of organizations that adopted the software product line approach, and they take the reader along for the ride as they explain how these organizations worked to skirt the pitfalls, solve the problems, and eventually reap the benefits of software product line practice.

Different readers may wish to use this book in different ways.

If you're seeking to persuade upper management of the viability of the software product line approach, you should point them to Chapters 1, 2, and 3, with special emphasis on Chapter 2. You should also show them the case study chapters (Chapters 9–11); odds are that something in those success stories will resonate.

If you're a new product line manager, you should read Part I (Chapters 1–3) carefully and make sure to grasp the fundamentals given there. Read Part II to comprehend the scope of the product line activities that will be required. The extent to which you need to master the practice areas depends on the extent to which you will delegate responsibility for them to others. The patterns in Chapter 7 in Part III will provide key guidance for helping with the delegation, and you should study those patterns carefully. Patterns will also help you launch the product line effort, as will the Product Line Technical Probe in Chapter 8, and the case studies in Chapters 9–11 can increase your confidence and help you remember the end game. You might also encourage (or require) others in your organization to read the case studies, for the same two reasons: to show that success is possible and to reinforce the reasons for adopting the approach.

If you've been given responsibility for part of a software product line, you should read Part I (Chapters 1–3) to grasp the big picture, and in Part II (Chapters 4–6) concentrate on those practice areas that fall within your purview. Pay attention to Chapter 7 to see how your practice areas interact with others in patterns, and examine the case studies (Chapters 9–11) to see how those organizations put your practice areas into play; they may give you ideas for doing the same.

If you work for a small organization interested in software product line concepts, start by reading the basics in Part I and strive to gain a passing familiarity with the practice areas in Part II, but then pay special attention to Part III. Chapter 7, which discusses the software product line practice patterns, will help you apply the practice areas in a way tailored to a small organization, and the Market Maker case study in Chapter 11 shows how a small organization can enjoy unparalleled success with software product line ideas.

Discussion questions designed to stimulate thought about the material appear throughout the book. These questions can be assigned as essay questions for homework in a university class, but they can also guide the discussion if this book is used as the basis for a brown-bag seminar or reading group in a company setting.

A glossary of vocabulary terms appears at the end of the book.

PART I

Software Product Line Fundamentals

Imagine that you are responsible for turning out a 1.5-million-line Ada command and control system for a Navy frigate. The system is hard real-time, fault-tolerant, and highly distributed, running on 70 separate processors on 30 different local area network nodes scattered all over the ship. It must interface with radars and other sensors, missile and torpedo launchers, and other complicated devices. The human-computer interface (HCI) is complex and highly demanding. In a safety-critical application such as this one, quality is everything: the system must be robust, be reliable, and avoid a host of performance, distribution, communication, and other errors.

Now suppose that you have not one but several of these systems to build. Your marketing department has succeeded beyond your wildest dreams. Navies from all over the world have ordered your command and control system. Now your software must run on ships of almost a dozen different classes, including a submarine, and these are really separate systems. The end users speak different languages (and hence the HCI requirements are wildly different), and the ships are laid out differently and have different numbers of processors and nodes, different fault tolerance requirements, different weapons systems and sensors, and even different computers and operating systems. But quality remains crucial in all of them.

How do you manage? Do you quadruple your work force? Do you turn down the new business? Do you panic? Do you resign?

What if you could produce each one of the systems for a fraction of the cost and in a fraction of the time that one would normally expect, using only the staff you currently have? And what if you could do it so that quality was improved and reliability and customer satisfaction increased with each new system? What if creating a new ship system was merely a matter of combining large, easily tailorable components under the aegis of a software architecture that was generic across the entire domain (in this case, of shipboard command and control systems)?

Is this a fantasy? In fact, it is not. It is the story of CelsiusTech, the company mentioned in the Preface. In the mid-1980s, CelsiusTech was in trouble. The systems they were delivering were becoming more complex and technology was changing quickly. Ada was on the scene. Microprocessors were replacing minicomputers. Object-oriented design was displacing older methodologies. Just before Christmas that fateful year, its marketing staff landed not one but *two* contracts to build systems much larger than anything the company had ever attempted, and CelsiusTech had had trouble meeting schedules and budgets before. Their management realized they had no hope of fulfilling the contracts using two teams; there weren't that many software engineers in all of Sweden.

Their only hope was to build one solution that would satisfy the (very different) requirements of both customers *and*—and this was their key insight—would also satisfy customers that they hoped would come after these two. The first two systems were to serve ships of different classes in two different navies. The human-computer interfaces, security protocols, weapons and sensor types, algorithms, hardware platforms, and performance requirements would all be different. Subsequent members of this product family would differ even more and would even include a system for a submarine. And yet CelsiusTech recognized that among these systems (the two they were building, plus the ones they envisioned) there were more similarities than differences. With their extensive background in the domain, they believed they could engineer a single system and software architecture that would suffice for the first two systems, and more. Where there needed to be accommodations for differences among the family members, extension or variation points would be built in.

In short, CelsiusTech launched a *product line* effort to build their software. A product line is a set of products that together address a particular market segment or fulfill a particular mission.

Product lines are, of course, nothing new in manufacturing. Boeing builds one, and so do Ford, Dell, and even McDonald's. Each of these companies exploits commonality in different ways. Boeing, for example, developed the 757 and 767 transports in tandem, and the parts lists for these very two different aircraft overlap by about 60%. But *software* product lines based on interproduct commonality are a relatively new concept and are rapidly emerging as a viable and important software development paradigm. Product flexibility is the new anthem of the software marketplace, and product lines fulfill the promise of tailor-made systems built specifically for the needs of particular customers or customer groups. A product line succeeds because the commonalities shared by the software products can be exploited to achieve economies of production. The products are built from common assets in a prescribed way.

Companies are finding that this practice of building sets of related systems from common assets can yield remarkable quantitative improvements in productivity, time to market, product quality, and customer satisfaction. They are finding that a software product line can efficiently satisfy the current hunger for mass customization. Organizations that acquire, as opposed to build, software systems are finding that commissioning a set of related systems as a commonly developed product line yields economies in delivery time, cost, simplified training, and streamlined acquisition. In Parts II and III, we provide snippets and full case studies of actual software product line efforts. Each of these efforts, like CelsiusTech's, boasts remarkable benefits. However, each also provides direct evidence that along with the gains come risks. Using a product line approach constitutes an entirely new technical strategy, and the technical issues in software product lines are formidable, but they are only one part of the entire picture. Organizational and management issues constitute obstacles that are at least as critical to overcome and may in fact add more risk because they are less obvious.

Our goal is to equip you with comprehensive knowledge that will jump-start your ability to achieve the benefits and navigate the risks associated with software product lines. We begin in Part I by laying the necessary conceptual foundation. Chapter 1 presents the basic ideas and terms. Chapter 2 expounds on the benefits of software product lines. We discuss benefits to the organization as a whole, but we also consider a variety of viewpoints across an organization and describe the benefits of a software product line approach from each. We also examine some of the costs and risks because, as we said, the benefits are only part of the picture. We will learn in Parts II and III that there are dozens of practices that are needed to achieve the benefits of software product lines and to prevent the inherent risks from unraveling the effort, but they all stem from a very simple triad. Chapter 3 lays out these three essential activities of software product line development: development of a reusable base of core assets, development of products that utilize those core assets, and the management to orchestrate and support the entire operation. Additional reading sources for Part I are located at the end of Chapter 3.

Part I begins your orientation to software product lines. Let's get started.

1

Basic Ideas and Terms

We trumpeted software product lines in our introduction to Part I, raving about the benefits that were possible and hinting about some potential risks. In this chapter we will go beneath the surface and examine the associated ideas and terms more closely. We begin by answering the question: What is a software product line?

1.1 What Is a Software Product Line?

A *software product line* is a set of software-intensive systems sharing a common, managed set of features that satisfy the specific needs of a particular market segment or mission and that are developed from a common set of core assets in a prescribed way.

This definition is consistent with the definition traditionally given for any product line—a set of systems that share a common, managed set of features satisfying the specific needs of a particular market segment or mission. But it adds more; it puts constraints on the way in which the systems in a software product line are developed. Why? Because substantial production economies can be achieved when the systems in a software product line are developed from a common set of assets in a prescribed way, in contrast to being developed separately, from scratch, or in an arbitrary fashion. It is exactly these production economies that make software product lines attractive.

How is production made more economical? Each product is formed by taking applicable components from the base of common assets, tailoring them as necessary through preplanned variation mechanisms such as parameterization or inheritance, adding any new components that may be necessary, and assembling the collection according to the rules of a common, product-line-wide architecture. Building a new product (system) becomes more a matter of assembly or generation than one of creation; the predominant activity is integration rather than programming. For each software product line there is a predefined guide or plan that specifies the exact product-building approach.

Certainly the desire for production economies is not a new business goal, and neither is a product line solution. If you look carefully, you will find plenty of examples all around you.

Product Lines Everywhere

In his bestseller, *Chaos: Making a New Science,* James Gleick relates how some of the pioneers of chaos theory would, while relaxing in their favorite coffeehouse, compete to find the nearest example of a certain kind of chaotic system [Gleick 87, p. 262]. A flag whipping in the breeze, a dripping faucet, a rattling car fender—they seemed to be everywhere.

I can relate. Lately it seems that no matter where I turn I see a product line. At airports I see product lines of airliners (such as the Airbus A-318, A-319, A-320, and A-321, a family of aircraft that range from 100 to 220 seats but clearly share production commonalities) powered by product lines of jet engines and equipped with product lines of navigation and communication equipment. When I arrive at my destination, I rent an American midsize car that is always pretty much the same except for cosmetic factors and features, even though it could have any one of four nameplates on it. I wonder how much more expensive the cars would be if they had nothing in common. The hotel leaves a copy of the local newspaper at my door: the morning edition of the citywide version. Someone else will get the afternoon edition of the upstate version, but it will have most of the same stories, will have all of the same comics, and will come off the same presses. On my way to work I pass residential subdivisions where the houses are all variants on a few basic designs. Even the street signs are the same except for the names of the streets. While the actual street name is fundamental to a street sign's function, it is inconsequential to its fabrication and is just a variation point.

We know that product lines have been around in manufacturing almost since manufacturing began. Remember Eli Whitney's idea of interchangeable parts for rifles in the early 1800s? This idea made it possible to build a product line of firearms that shared components. Remember the IBM System/360 family of computers? From the Principles of Operation:

> *Models of System/360 differ in storage speed, storage width (the amount of data obtained in each storage access), register width, and*

> *capabilities for processing data concurrently with the operation of multiple input/output devices. Several CPU's permit a wide choice in internal performance. Yet none of these differences affects the logical appearance of these models to the programmer. An individual System/360 is obtained by selecting the system components most suited to the applications from a wide variety of alternatives in internal performance, functional ability, and input/output (I/O).*

This was clearly a product line, and the operating system that powered it was a software product line. And town plans in which the buildings look like each other predate post-War suburbia by at least eight centuries. During the Pei Sung dynasty of northern China (960–1127 A.D.), a book called the "Ying-tsao fa-shih" was written by Li Chieh, the state architect of the emperor Hui-tsung, in 1100 A.D. and published in 1103 A.D. This was a set of building codes for official buildings. It described in encyclopedic detail the layouts, materials, and practices for designing and building official buildings. It listed standard parts and standard ways of connecting the parts as well as recognizing and parameterizing variations of the parts such as allowable lengths, load capacities, bracketing, decorations, allowed components based on the building's purpose, and the options available for various component choices. The book also included design construction details that provided a process for building design and implementation of that design. While it was influential in spreading the most advanced techniques of the time of its first publication in 1103, by codifying practice it may also have inhibited further development and contributed to the conservatism of later techniques. Some scholars even claim that because of it, Chinese architecture remained largely unchanged until the beginning of the twentieth century. (In a product line, you've got to know when your architecture has outlived its usefulness.)

However, like Gleick's scientists, I find some of the best examples of product lines in places where I go to eat. Here's something I saw on the menu at a little Mexican restaurant recently:

> *#16. Enchiladas verdes: Corn tortillas baked with a zesty filling, covered with a green tomatillo sauce. Your choice of chicken, beef, pork, or cheese.*
>
> *#17. Enchiladas rojas: Corn tortillas baked with a zesty filling, covered with a red ancho chile sauce. Your choice of chicken, beef, or pork.*

See what I mean? This restaurant clearly produces an "enchilada" product line. (Well, all right, "clearly" applies only to those of us who have been thinking about this for too long.) While admittedly a cheesy example (sorry), it actually provides a pretty good analogy with *software* product lines and the central concepts they embody.

The enchilada product line consists of seven separate products, differentiated by filling and sauce. This defines their variabilities. The corn tortillas are core assets because they're used in every product. The red and green sauces are also core assets because they're used in four and three products, respectively. And the meat fillings are also core assets, used in two products each. But the cheese is a product-specific asset, used only in the enchiladas verdes.

Some of the core assets have attached processes that indicate how they are to be instantiated for use in products. Here, the beef, pork, and chicken have attached processes that dictate how they're chopped, seasoned, and cooked. The processes call for different spices to be added depending on the sauce.

All of the products share an "architecture"—tortillas wrapped around a filling, covered with sauce. And they also share a "production plan": prepare filling, wrap filling in tortilla, cover with sauce, bake at 350 degrees for 15 minutes, garnish, serve.

This little product line provides economies of scope; the common ingredients let the restaurant stock a small number of food items delivered from a small number of suppliers. They provide personnel flexibility: the same person who makes the pork enchiladas rojas is, I would bet my house, the same person who makes the cheese enchiladas verdes. And because the choices are limited, many of the ingredients can be pre-prepared, allowing for rapid time-to-market, which in this case means time-to-table.

As a family, the products define a clear scope that leaves little doubt what's in and what's out. Chicken enchiladas are in. Beef enchiladas are in. And if you wanted cheese enchiladas with the red sauce instead of the green, well, that's probably open for discussion. As we'll see, a scope definition with a pronounced gray area is a healthy thing—but duck enchiladas with a white sauce are definitely out.

Finally, because the commonalities and variabilities are exquisitely clear, it's easy to see how this product line's scope could be expanded, by offering new fillings and new sauces and perhaps new combinations. You could even see how this efficient production capability could be used to launch an entirely new product line to capture a new market segment: replace the corn tortillas with flour tortillas, lose the sauce, add lettuce and tomato and other condiments, and open a new restaurant chain that sells "wraps."

If you already had a strong grasp of the concepts underlying software product lines, this little culinary diversion probably had no effect on you, except possibly to make you hungry. If you didn't, perhaps the concepts are now a bit more palpable for you. In either case, the next time you're at a coffeehouse or restaurant, try looking around to see how many product lines you can spot.

¡Buen provecho!

—PCC

But a software product line is a relatively new idea, and it should seem clear from our description that software product lines require a different technical tack. The more subtle consequence is that software product lines require much more than new technical practices.

The common set of assets and the plan for how they are used to build products don't just materialize without planning, and they certainly don't come free. They require organizational foresight, investment, planning, and direction. They require strategic thinking that looks beyond a single product. The disciplined use of the assets to build products doesn't just happen either. Management must direct, track, and enforce the use of the assets. Software product lines are as much about business practices as they are about technical practices.

Other Voices: Beyond Technology

The primary thesis of this book is that software product lines, although enmeshed in the highly technological field of software, rely on much more than technology to succeed. Martin Griss, a reuse expert at Hewlett-Packard and co-author of the highly regarded *Software Reuse: Architecture, Process, and Organization for Business Success* [Jacbobson 97], put it this way [Griss 95]:

> *. . . In almost all cases, a simple architecture, a separate component group, a stable application domain, standards, and organizational support are the keys to success. Correct handling of these (largely non-technical) issues is almost always more critical to successful reuse than the choice of specific language or design method, yet too many . . . experts choose to ignore these factors.*
>
> *. . . Over the last 10 years, software reuse researchers and practitioners have learned that success with systematic reuse requires careful attention be paid to both technical and nontechnical issues. Furthermore, the nontechnical issues are more pervasive and complex than was realized at first. Without a systematic and joint focus on people, process, and product issues, a project will not succeed at managing the scope and magnitude of the changes and investment necessary to achieve reuse. Simply creating and announcing a reusable class library will not work. Without a "reuse mindset," organizational support, and methodical processes directed at the design and construction of appropriate reusable assets, the reuse investment will not be worthwhile.*
>
> *. . . Often, sweeping changes in the software development organization are needed to institute large-scale, systematic reuse. These include business, process, management, and organizational changes . . . .*

Software product lines give you *economies of scope,* which means that you take economic advantage of the fact that many of your products are very similar—not by accident, but because you planned it that way. You make deliberate, strategic decisions and are systematic in effecting those decisions.

Other Voices: Japanese Software Factories and Economies of Scope

In 1991, Michael Cusumano's *Japan's Software Factories* [Cusumano 91] burst onto the scene, revealing the "secrets" of the Japanese software companies that, at the time, it was feared were going to bury American and European firms with their sky-high productivity rates. And what was their secret? Largely it was what we would call today a software product line approach, based on that feeling of déjà vu that all eventual product line managers share: "You know, I could swear we've built this product already." The driving concept of economies of scope was born. Cusumano wrote:

> *The Japanese software facilities discussed in this book differed in some respects, reflecting variations in products, competitive strategies, organizational structures, and management styles. Nonetheless, the approaches of Hitachi, Toshiba, NEC, and Fujitsu had far more elements in common than in contrast, as each firm attempted the* strategic management and integration *of activities required in software production, as well as the achievement of* planned economies of scope—*cost reductions or productivity gains that come from developing a series of products within one firm (or facility) more efficiently than building each product from scratch in a separate project. Planned scope economies thus required the deliberate (rather than accidental) sharing of resources across different projects, such as product specifications and designs, executable code, tools, methods, documentation and manuals, test cases, and personnel experience. It appears that scope economies helped firms combine process efficiency with flexibility, allowing them to deliver seemingly unique or tailored products with higher levels of productivity than if they had not shared resources among multiple projects.*
>
> *Japanese managers did not adopt factory models and pursue scope economies simply out of faith. Detailed studies concluded that as much as 90 percent of the programs they developed in any given year, especially in business applications, appeared similar to work they had done in the past, with designs of product components falling into a limited number of patterns. Such observations convinced managers of the possibility for greater efficiencies, in scope if not in scale, and set an agenda for process improvement. Companies subsequently established facilities focused on similar products, collected productivity and quality data, standardized tools and techniques, and instituted appropriate goals and controls. As the factory discussions demonstrate, Japanese firms managed in this way not simply one or two special projects for a few years. They established permanent software facilities and research*

and development efforts, as well as emphasized several common elements in managing across a series of projects [not the least of which was a commitment to process improvement].

1.2 What Software Product Lines Are Not

There are many approaches that at first blush could be confused with software product lines. In fact, you might be asking: "Isn't software product line just a new name for *x*?" Though we certainly want you to build on previous knowledge and experience, we want to ensure from the outset that you don't erroneously equate software product lines with something they are not. Describing what you don't mean is often as instructive as describing what do you mean. When we speak of software product lines, we don't mean any of the following:

1.2.1 Fortuitous Small-Grained Reuse

Reuse, as a software strategy for decreasing development costs and improving quality, is not a new idea, and software product lines definitely involve reuse—reuse, in fact, of the highest order. So what's the difference? Past reuse agendas have focused on the reuse of relatively small pieces of code—that is, small-grained reuse. Organizations have built reuse libraries containing algorithms, modules, objects, or components. Almost anything a software developer writes goes into the library. Other developers are then urged (and sometimes required) to use what the library provides instead of creating their own versions. Unfortunately, it often takes longer to locate these small pieces and integrate them into a system than it would take to build them anew. Documentation, if it exists at all, might explain the situation for which the piece was created but not how it can be generalized or adapted to other situations. The benefits of small-grained reuse depend on the predisposition of the software engineer to use what is in the library, the suitability of what is in the library for the engineer's particular needs, and the successful adaptation and integration of the library units into the rest of the system. If reuse occurs at all under these conditions, it is fortuitous and the payoff is usually nonexistent.

In a software product line approach, the reuse is planned, enabled, and enforced—the opposite of opportunistic. The asset base includes those artifacts in software development that are most costly to develop from scratch—namely, the requirements, domain models, software architecture, performance models, test cases, and components. All of the assets are designed to be reused and are optimized for use in more than a single system. The reuse with software product lines is comprehensive, planned, and profitable.

1.2.2 Single-System Development with Reuse

You are developing a new system that seems very similar to one you have built before. You borrow what you can from your previous effort, modify it as necessary, add whatever it takes, and field the product. What you have done is what is called "clone and own." You certainly have taken economic advantage of previous work; you have reused a part of another system. But now you have two entirely different systems, not two systems built from the same base. You need to maintain two systems as entirely separate entities. This is again ad hoc reuse.

There are two major differences between this approach and a software product line approach. First, software product lines reuse assets that were designed explicitly for reuse. Second, the product line is treated as a whole, not as multiple products that are viewed and maintained separately. In mature product line organizations, the concept of multiple products disappears. Each product is simply a tailoring of the core assets. It is the core assets that are designed carefully and evolved over time. It is the core assets that are the organization's premiere intellectual property.

1.2.3 Just Component-Based Development

Software product lines rely on a form of component-based development, but much more is involved. The typical definition of component-based development involves the selection of components from an in-house library or the marketplace to build products. Although the products in software product lines certainly are composed of components, these components are all specified by the product line architecture. Moreover, the components are assembled in a prescribed way, which includes exercising built-in variability mechanisms in the components to put them to use in specific products. The prescription comes from both the architecture and the production plan and is missing from standard component-based development. In a product line, the generic form of the component is evolved and maintained in the asset base. In component-based development, if any variation is involved, it is usually accomplished by writing code, and the variants are most likely maintained separately. Component-based development alone also lacks the technical and organizational management aspects that are so important to the success of a software product.

1.2.4 Just a Reconfigurable Architecture

Reference architectures and object-oriented frameworks are designed to be reused in multiple systems and to be reconfigured as necessary. Reusing architectural structures is a good idea because the architecture is a pivotal part of any system and a costly one to construct. A product line architecture is designed to support the variation needed by the products in the product line, and so making it reconfigurable makes sense. But the product line architecture is just one asset, albeit an important one, in the product line's asset base.

1.2.5 Releases and Versions of Single Products

Organizations routinely produce new releases and versions of products. Each of these new versions and releases is typically constructed using the architecture, components, test plans, and other features of the prior releases. Why are software product lines different? First, in a product line there are multiple simultaneous products, all of which are going through their own cycles of release and versioning simultaneously. Thus, the evolution of a single product must be considered within a broader context—namely, the evolution of the product line as a whole. Second, in a single-product context, once a product is updated there's often no looking back—whatever went into the production of earlier products is no longer considered to be of any value. But in a product line, an early version of a product that is still considered to have market potential can easily be kept as a viable member of the family: it is, after all, an instantiation of the core assets, just like other versions of other products.

1.2.6 Just a Set of Technical Standards

Many organizations set up technical standards to limit the choices their software engineers can make regarding the kinds and sources of components to incorporate in systems. They audit at architecture and design reviews to ensure that the standards are being followed. For example, the developer might be able to select between two identified database choices and two identified Web browsers but must use a specific middleware or spreadsheet product if either is necessary. Technical standards are constraints to promote interoperability and to decrease the cost associated with maintenance and support of commercial components. An organization that undertakes a product line effort may have such technical standards, in which case the product line architecture and components will need to conform to those standards. However, the standards are simply constraints that are inputted to the software product line, no more.

1.3 A Note on Terminology

Now that we have covered what we don't mean, the following terms lay out what we do mean:

A software product line is a set of software-intensive systems sharing a common, managed set of features that satisfy the specific needs of a particular market segment or mission and that are developed from a common set of core assets in a prescribed way. This is the definition we provided in Section 1.1.

Core assets are those assets that form the basis for the software product line. Core assets often include, but are not limited to, the architecture, reusable software components, domain models, requirements statements, documentation and specifications, performance models, schedules, budgets, test plans, test cases, work plans, and process descriptions. The architecture is key among the collection of core assets.

Development is a generic term used to describe how core assets (or products) come to fruition. Software enters an organization in any one of three ways: the organization can build it itself (either from scratch or by mining legacy software), purchase it (buy it, largely unchanged, off the shelf), or commission it (contract with someone else to develop it especially for the organization). So our use of the term "development" may actually involve building, acquisition, purchase, retrofitting earlier work, or any combination of these options. We recognize and address these options, but we use "development" as the general term.

A *domain* is a specialized body of knowledge, an area of expertise, or a collection of related functionality. For example, the telecommunications domain is a set of telecommunications functionality, which in turn consists of other domains such as switching, protocols, telephony, and network. A telecommunications software product line is a specific set of software systems that provides some of that functionality.

Software product line practice is the systematic use of core assets to assemble, instantiate, or generate the multiple products that constitute a software product line. The choice of verb depends on the production approach for the product line. Software product line practice involves strategic, large-grained reuse.

Some practitioners use a different set of terms to convey essentially the same meaning. In this alternate terminology, a *product line* is a profit and loss center concerned with turning out a set of products; it refers to a business unit, not a set of products. The *product family* is that set of products, which we call the product line. The core asset base is called the *platform*. Figure 1.1 shows the mapping between our terminology and this different set of terms.

To us, the terminology is not as important as the concepts. That having been said, you might encounter both sets of terms in other places and should be able to translate between them. You might also use an entirely different set of terms that are equivalent to the ones we use. In that case you will probably want to do your own mapping, akin to that shown in Figure 1.1, before you proceed with the rest of the book. Although we have tried not to invent vocabulary, as you read on you may find other terms we use that you may call by different names, and you may want to expand your map.

The next chapter discusses the benefits (and the risks) of software product lines.

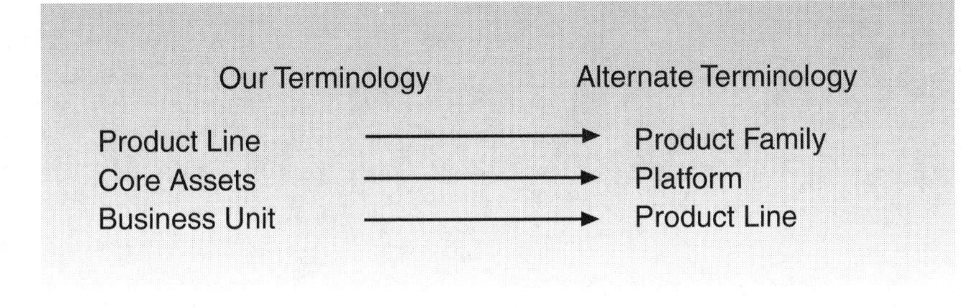

Figure 1.1 Alternate Terminology

1.4 For Further Reading

See Section 3.6.

1.5 Discussion Questions

1. Some would argue that a software product line is just the group of products produced by a single business unit (profit/loss center). What distinguishes this definition from the one we gave in Section 1.3?
2. What is the difference between software product line practice and domain engineering? What is the difference between software product line practice and application engineering?
3. Suppose your organization has a library of components *and* a reconfigurable architecture to support a family of products that have many common features. Do you have a software product line? If not, what is missing?
4. Describe an experience you have had with software reuse. Identify the similarities and differences between software product line practice and your experience.

2

Benefits

The terms and ideas discussed in Chapter 1 give us a foundation on which to explore further the benefits of software product lines. We begin with a closer examination of the organizational benefits of software product lines. Then we consider a variety of viewpoints across an organization and describe the benefits from each. We balance our treatment of the benefits of software product lines with an examination of some of their inherent costs and general risks.

2.1 Organizational Benefits

The organizations that we have studied chose a software product line approach in order to realize not only benefits that they desired but also benefits that they absolutely needed to ensure their organizational health and in some cases their very existence. Here are the reasons they have given:

- To achieve large-scale productivity gains
- To improve time-to-market
- To maintain market presence
- To sustain unprecedented growth
- To improve product quality
- To increase customer satisfaction
- To achieve reuse goals
- To enable mass customization
- To compensate for an inability to hire software engineers

These business goals could be attributed to just about any modern business. The last one—inability to hire—has become most compelling in recent times and resonates across almost all software-producing organizations.

In Good Times and in Bad

It is January 2000. The world has survived the highly feared "Y2K Crisis" with only a few minor blips. Dot.coms are flourishing and software jobs are abundant. The job pool can't even come close to meeting the need for software developers. College students who graduate with undergraduate degrees in computer science are getting signing bonuses, company perks (cars, ski vacations), flexible work conditions, and in some cases six-figure starting salaries. Those with experience are getting even higher wages, bonuses, shares of stock, and their pick of geographic location. The competition for software talent is keen. Times are good for everyone in the software industry.

You happen to manage an avionics company based in the midwestern United States. Your company is renowned for its high-quality products. You have a strong engineering talent base, but many are baby boomers nearing the age of retirement, and most aren't software experts. Your software has become increasingly more complex and a more and more pervasive part of your products. The truth is, you are in dire need of software developers. Times are good and you have the money to hire scores of new people, but you are working on safety-critical systems, and you can't hire just any programmer. You need people who are current in computer science *and* savvy about real-time programming *and* who know something about avionics *and* about engineering systems made up of hardware and software. And, oh by the way, you *are* in the Midwest. How can you compete?

You can't. You have to change your way of doing business. You simply cannot tolerate any redundant effort because you simply can't squander your human resources that way. You have to consolidate separate projects that have separate teams but build very similar software products. The times may be good, but you need a software product line to succeed in an industry you have been leading. You take comfort in the fact that you have the advantage of a solid reputation and a robust legacy base. There are others who have less established foundations and who, given the lack of employable talent to do the job any other way, also need to embrace a software product line approach in order to survive.

Now it is November 2000. Dot.coms are folding; their stocks are going through the floor. The whole economy has slowed down. The number of available software developers has increased, and you can actually be selective. Perhaps you can go back to business as usual. Perhaps you don't need a software product line after all. But alas, times aren't good for you either. Your stock is down and you no longer have the money to hire more developers. You have to make do with the staff you currently have, regardless of the increase in the software load they will have to handle.

There is even pressure to increase your software output to bring earnings back in line. You are faced with the same dilemma as before. You have to make better use of the people you have. They simply cannot work on separate projects (what in the Midwest might be called silos), building similar products. You still need a software product line to stay buoyant.

In good times and in bad, organizations are realizing that they need software product lines, if for no other reason than to make better use of scarce resources.

—LMN

But how does a software product line approach achieve such business goals? Benefits are derived from the reuse of the core assets in a strategic and prescribed way. Once the product line asset repository is established, there is a direct savings *each* time a product is built, associated with *each* of the following:

- **Requirements:** There are common product line requirements. Product requirements are deltas to this established requirements base. Extensive requirements analysis is saved. Feasibility is assured.
- **Architecture:** An architecture for a software system represents a large investment of time from the organization's most talented engineers. The quality goals for a system—its performance, reliability, modifiability, and so on—are largely allowed or precluded once the architecture is in place. If the architecture is wrong, the system cannot be saved. The product line architecture is used for each product and need only be instantiated. Considerable time and risk are spared.
- **Components:** Up to 100% of the components in the asset base are used in each product. These components may need to be altered using inheritance or parameters, but the design is intact, as are data structures and algorithms. In addition, the product line architecture provides component specifications for all but any unique components that may be necessary.
- **Modeling and analysis:** Performance models and the associated analyses are existing product line assets. With each new product there is extremely high confidence that the timing problems have been worked out and that the bugs associated with distributed computing—synchronization, network loading, and absence of deadlock—have been eliminated.
- **Testing:** Generic test plans, test processes, test cases, test data, test harnesses, and the communication paths required to report and fix problems

have already been built. They need only be tailored on the basis of the variations related to the product.

- **Planning:** The production plan has already been established. Baseline budgets and schedules from previous product development projects already exist and provide a reliable basis for the product work plans.
- **Processes:** Configuration control boards, configuration management tools and procedures, management processes, and the overall software development process are in place, have been used before, and are robust, reliable, and responsive to the organization's special needs.
- **People:** Fewer people are required to build products, and the people are more easily transferred across the entire line.

Product lines enhance quality. Each new system takes advantage of all of the defect elimination in its forebears; developer and customer confidence both rise with each new instantiation. The more complicated the system, the higher the payoff for solving the vexing performance, distribution, reliability, and other engineering issues once for the entire family.

2.2 Individual Benefits

Given these organizational benefits, product lines might also be a winning approach for your organization. But what's in it for you personally? How can product lines help you? The answer depends on what your role is in your organization.

If you are the *chief executive officer,* software product lines can help you achieve large-scale productivity gains and greatly improved time-to-market. You will be building products from a common set of predetermined assets that are assembled in predetermined ways; you will be taking economic advantage of the commonality in your software products. If you are already in the market, it will be easier to maintain market presence, because a large portion of future products in the product line will have already been developed. If you have a product line that has signaled unprecedented growth for your company, you will be better able to sustain that growth if you can capitalize on the assets that got you there by using a product line approach to build future products. Software product lines offer a systematic and highly economical way to capture a market niche.

If you are the *chief operating officer,* software product lines offer a more efficient approach to utilization of your work force. Currently there is an overwhelming shortage of software engineers, and yet many organizations squander their software talent by staffing individual project teams to build single systems that have a great deal in common. By taking a product line approach, product-building teams can be greatly reduced. The case study in Chapter 9 shows almost a four-to-one improvement, while the case study in Chapter 10 shows an order-of-magnitude reduction. Therefore you can have a leaner product development work force, or you can staff other product lines or explore new markets, new technologies, and/or new products. Also, because of the commonality of the applications, personnel can be fluidly transferred among projects as required. Their expertise is applicable across the entire line.

If you are the *technical manager,* software product lines spell predictability. The generic schedules and estimates for building and fielding products have already been established, and there is an established track record for meeting them using predefined processes and assets. Roles and responsibilities among the product line team members are well engrained; your staff members communicate and collaborate in predictable and efficient ways. Building products in pretested ways from validated assets yields increased and more predictable product quality, which then yields increased and more predictable customer satisfaction.

Imagine, however, that you are far away from boardroom discussions. Suppose you are the software *product developer*. Do product lines take all the creativity and challenge out of your job? How satisfied can you be following a plan to use someone else's design and software? Developers working on software product lines have higher morale and greater job satisfaction than they did when they were building stand-alone products. Why? Listed below are reasons given in interviews we held with product developers in a software product line environment. They told us that they

- get to focus their time on the truly unique aspects of products rather than redoing the same pedestrian development for each product
- do not have to suffer through painful software integration phases because they are using a validated architecture with components whose integration has already been tested
- have fewer stressful schedule delays because they are following a proven production plan
- are part of a team building products with an established quality record and reputation
- are more marketable in the software work force because of their knowledge of product line practices
- have greater mobility within their organization because their knowledge is more global
- have more time to get involved in new technology

Some of these benefits, of course, depend on organizational circumstances, but product developers universally echoed many of these refrains.

And what if you are the *architect* or the *core asset developer*? Software product lines afford you the opportunity to work on design and software that will be used in multiple products. The challenge is greater: you need to design and build high-quality, robust, and extensible assets that will endure longer and support more users than any single system. But the rewards are commensurate with the greater challenge. Your work will affect many systems, not just one. Your work will have a profound impact on the success of your organization in the marketplace. If you are successful, you will have a position of technical prominence that will put you on the leading edge of software designers. You will become as marketable as your product line.

Perhaps you are neither a manager nor a software engineer. Maybe you are in *marketing and sales*. If so, your role will change when a product line approach is taken. Instead of selling single systems that aim to meet the desires of individual customers, you will be selling products of higher quality and more predictable delivery, and usually at greater profit for your organization. Suppose you market information systems for commercial banks. With a product line you will know the basic features that are non-negotiable, such as loan, savings, checking, and credit accounts. You will be able to predict with confidence the security, availability, and performance of the system. You will also know the features that can vary among individual bank customers, such as account packaging. You will be confident about the time to integrate and field a product that will meet the needs of an individual bank customer, and you will have a track record that will help you sell customers. You will feel satisfaction not only at the time of the sale but also after the sale when the customer is satisfied. For you, product lines will equate to greater confidence that the needs of the customer will be met. You will become an expert in the product line and on how it can fit customers' needs rather than on how you can bend your organization to build to the whim of the customer. Organizations with mature product lines market pedigrees that customers associate with quality.

And what if you are the *customer*? What's in it for you? What benefit can you derive from buying a software-intensive system that was built using a product line approach? The system will be of higher quality. You will encounter fewer defects, which may equate to fewer service calls and costly delays in your business. You will be able to count on the predicted delivery date and the quoted price. You will be able to understand the costs of unique requirements that are beyond the standard features of the product line. Most of your desired variations and extensions will be accommodated because the assets were engineered carefully to support variability. Well-tested training materials and documentation will be available. You may be able to share maintenance costs for much of your system with other customers of the product line. There might even be a users' group that will enable you to benefit from the experiences of other customers of the product line and will provide you with a powerful influence on future enhancements of the product line. (We have seen situations in which customers of products in the product line sit on the configuration control board for the core assets.)

Finally, what if you are the *end user* but not the paying customer for a system in the product line? You might be a teller at the bank that bought from the product line of bank systems. Fewer software defects will make your life easier, too. Better training materials and documentation and a network of others who have used similar systems will shorten your learning curve when the system is installed or when you are new to the job.

2.3 Benefits versus Costs

We have established that the strategic reuse of assets that defines product line practice represents an opportunity for benefits across the board, but the picture is not yet complete. Launching a software product line is a business decision that should not be made randomly. Any organization that launches a product line should have in mind specific and solid business goals that it plans to achieve through product line practice. Moreover, the benefits given above should align carefully with the achievement of those goals because a software product line requires a substantial start-up investment as well as ongoing costs to maintain the assets. We have already listed the benefits associated with the reuse of particular assets. Usually a cost and a caveat are associated with the achievement of each benefit. Table 2.1 gives a partial list of core assets with the typical additional costs. We repeat the benefits for the sake of comparison. For each of these assets, the investment cost is usually much less than the value of the benefit. Also, most of the costs are up-front costs associated with establishing the product line. The benefits, on the other hand, accrue with each new product release. Once the approach is established, the organization's productivity accelerates rapidly and the benefits far outweigh the costs. However, an organization that attempts to institute a product line without being aware of the costs is likely to abandon the product line concept before seeing it through.

It takes a certain degree of maturity in the developing organization to field a product line successfully. Technology change is not the only barrier to successful product line adoption. For instance, traditional organizational structures that simply have one business unit per product are generally not appropriate for product lines. Who will build and maintain the core reusable assets—the architecture, the reusable components, and so forth? If these assets are under the control of a business unit associated with one product or one large customer, the assets may evolve to serve that business unit, that product, or that customer, to the exclusion of all others. And on the other hand, establishing a separate business unit to work on the core assets, but not on any individual products, carries the danger that this unit will produce assets that emphasize beauty and elegance over practicality and utility. In either case, producing and managing the reusable assets means establishing

Table 2.1 Costs and Benefits of Product Lines

Asset	Benefit	Additional Cost
Requirements: The requirements are written for the group of systems as a whole, with requirements for individual systems specified by a delta or an increment to the generic set.	Commonality and variation are documented explicitly, which will help lead to an architecture for the product line. New systems in the product line will be much simpler to specify because the requirements are reused and tailored.	Capturing requirements for a group of systems may require sophisticated analysis and intense negotiation to agree on both common requirements and variation points acceptable for all the systems.
Architecture: The architecture for the product line is the blueprint for how each product is assembled from the components in the asset base.	Architecture represents a significant investment by the organization's most talented engineers. Leveraging this investment across all products in the product line means that for subsequent products, the most important design step is largely completed.	The architecture must support the variation inherent in the product line, which imposes an additional constraint on the architecture and requires greater talent to define.
Software components: The software components that populate the asset base form the building blocks for each product in the product line. Some will be reused without alteration. Others will be tailored according to prespecified variation mechanisms.	The interfaces for components are reused. For actual components that are reused, the design decisions, data structures, algorithms, documentation, reviews, code, and debugging effort can all be leveraged across multiple products in the product line.	The components must be designed to be robust and extensible so that they are applicable across a range of product contexts. Variation points must be built in or at least anticipated. Often, components must be designed to be more general without loss of performance.
Performance modeling and analysis: For products that must meet real-time constraints (and some that have soft real-time constraints), analysis must be performed to show that the system's performance will be adequate.	A new product can be fielded with high confidence that real-time and distributed-systems problems have already been worked out because the analysis and modeling can be reused from product to product. Process scheduling, network traffic loads, deadlock elimination, data consistency problems, and the like will all have been modeled and analyzed.	Reusing the analysis may impose constraints on moving of processes among processors, on creation of new processes, or on synchronization of existing processes.

Asset	Benefit	Additional Cost
Business case, market analysis, marketing collateral, cost and schedule estimates: These are the up-front business necessities involved in any product. Generic versions that support the entire product line are built.	All of the business and management artifacts involved in turning out already exist at least in a generic form and can be reused.	All of these artifacts must be generic, or be made extensible, to accommodate product variations.
Tools and processes for software development and for making changes: The infrastructure for turning out a software product requires specific product line processes and appropriate tool support.	Configuration control boards, configuration management tools and procedures, management processes, and the overall software development process are in place and have been used before. Tools and environments purchased for one product can be amortized across the entire product line.	The boards, process definitions, tools, and procedures must be more robust to account for unique product line needs and for the differences between managing a product line and managing a single product.
Test cases, test plans, test data: There are generic testing artifacts for the entire set of products in the product line with variation points to accommodate product variation.	Test plans, test cases, test scripts, and test data have already been developed and reviewed for the components that are reused. Testing artifacts represent a substantial organizational investment. Any saving in this area is a benefit.	All of the testing artifacts must be more robust because they will support more than one product. They also must be extensible to accommodate variation among the products.
People, skills, training: In a product line organization, even though members of the development staff may work on a single product at a time, they are in reality working on the entire product line. The product line is a single entity that embraces multiple products.	Because of the commonality of the products and the production process, personnel can be more easily transferred among product projects as required. Their expertise is usually applicable across the entire product line. Their productivity, when measured by the number of products to which their work applies, rises dramatically. Resources spent on training developers to use processes, tools, and system components are expended only once.	Personnel must be trained beyond general software engineering and corporate procedures to ensure that they understand software product line practices and can use the assets and procedures associated with the product line. New personnel must be much more specifically trained for the product line. Training materials that address the product line must be created. As product lines mature, the skills required in an organization tend to change, away from programming and toward relevant domain expertise and technology forecasting. This transition must be managed.

processes for making the assets satisfy the needs of all of the business units that use them. This is a role requiring staff skilled in abstraction, in design, and in negotiation and creative problem solving. The question of funding the core asset development is also nontrivial. As we continue our study of software product lines, we will see many other management and organizational practices that are involved. Successful adoption of software product line practice is a careful blend of technological, process, organizational, and business improvements.

Past, Present, and Future

Besides saving the company from disaster by allowing it to deliver two promised products, what results came from CelsiusTech's software product line? Just these:

- System cost due to software reduced by about half
- Fewer than 50 workers doing the work of more than 200, all while turning out more systems
- Delivery time slashed from years to months
- Software reuse ranging from 70% to over 90%
- Higher product quality
- Higher customer satisfaction

The last point was illustrated when the Swedish navy declined a source-code-level bug fix from CelsiusTech, saying they would wait until the entire product line was updated so they wouldn't be running unique software.

These results are ones that any company would be proud of, but there are two kinds of benefits that a software product line imparts to a company. The first benefit, exemplified by numbers such as the ones in the list above, is that the product line allows a company to carry out its *current* business with ruthless efficiency. But the second benefit, and in some ways the more exciting one, is that the product line lets companies move into *new* businesses quickly and effectively. After the ship system product line was up and running, CelsiusTech realized that there was a market opportunity nearby. A ground-based air defense system is a radar-guided antiaircraft gun on wheels. But in CelsiusTech's eyes it is a very simple ship system—but without the ship. CelsiusTech realized that such a system could use the same architecture, many of the same components (such as those responsible for target tracking), the same production process, and many other of the core assets of their ship system product line. At the instant they decided to take a foray into this new business area, CelsiusTech had 40% of their new product line in place. As of the time of our case study, they were also exploring the possibility of a larger and more complex application area for which their product line architecture and other assets would allow them fast and effective entry. They asked us not to reveal what it was, but the next chapter in the CelsiusTech story could be as interesting as the last ones. We look forward to hearing it.

—PCC

Organizations of all stripes have enjoyed quantitative benefits from their product lines (for CelsiusTech's results, see "Past, Present, and Future" sidebar). Product line practitioners have also shared with us examples of the costs, such as

- canceling three large projects so that sufficient resources could be devoted to the development of core assets
- reassigning staff who could not adjust to the product line way of doing business
- suspending product delivery for a year while putting the new practices into place

Companies that bore these costs and made the successful transition to product line practice all agree that the payoff more than compensated for the effort, but these costs underscore the point that product line practice is often uncharted territory and may not be the right path for every organization. The remainder of this book is intended to be a map through the new territory of product lines with guidance about essential activities and practices, patterns, case studies and anecdotes about others who have made the trip, advice that you should heed, and risks that you should mitigate. We begin in the next chapter with an examination of how software product lines work.

2.4 For Further Reading

See Section 3.6.

2.5 Discussion Questions

1. We covered the roles of several types of individuals and the benefits they would enjoy in product line operations. There are individuals we left out. Discuss what might be the benefits for the members of the tool support group, for documentation experts, for training specialists, and for the chief financial officer. Identify still other individuals who might be

stakeholders in a software product line effort and the benefits they would enjoy.

2. Identify ways in which software product lines might benefit you in your software development efforts.
3. Why would organizations see software product lines as a way to maintain market presence?
4. Explain what is meant by "mass customization" and why software product lines would enable mass customization.
5. The costs we listed in Table 2.1 all relate to start-up costs for the assets listed. Create an additional column for this table that presents additional maintenance costs for the listed assets. Then indicate the benefits that would be accrued at the time of maintenance as a result of using the product line approach.
6. Product lines clearly benefit the developing organization, but they also benefit acquirers of software systems. List ways in which you might benefit if you were to commission the building of a software product line.

3

The Three Essential Activities

Organizations that span a wide and diverse range have reaped the benefits we have described by using a software product line approach for their systems. Each organization is different, varying widely in terms of

- the nature of their products
- their market or mission
- their business goals
- their organizational structure
- their culture and policies
- their software process disciplines
- the maturity and extent of their legacy artifacts
- the geographic distribution of their work force

No doubt your organization will differ in large or small respects from the example organizations we describe. Nevertheless, we have distilled universal and essential software product line activities and practices that apply in every situation. At the highest level of generality are three essential activities.

3.1 What Are the Essential Activities?

At its essence, fielding of a product line involves *core asset development* and *product development* using the core assets, both under the aegis of technical and organizational *management*. Core asset development and product development from the core assets can occur in either order: new products are built from core assets, or core assets are extracted from existing products. Often, products and core assets are built in concert with each other. Core asset development has also been called domain engineering. Product development from core assets is often called application engineering. Figure 3.1 illustrates this triad of essential activities. Each rotating circle represents one of the essential activities. All three are linked together and in perpetual motion, showing that all three are essential, are inextricably linked, can occur in any order, and are highly iterative.

The rotating arrows indicate not only that core assets are used to develop products, but also that revisions of existing core assets or even new core assets might, and most often do, evolve out of product development. The diagram in Figure 3.1 is neutral in regard to which part of the effort is launched first. In some contexts, already existing products are mined for generic assets—perhaps a requirements specification, an architecture, or software components—which are then migrated into the product line's asset base. In other cases, the core assets may be developed or procured for later use in the production of products.

There is a strong feedback loop between the core assets and the products. Core assets are refreshed as new products are developed. Use of assets is tracked, and the results are fed back to the asset development activity. In addition, the value of the core assets is realized through the products that are developed from

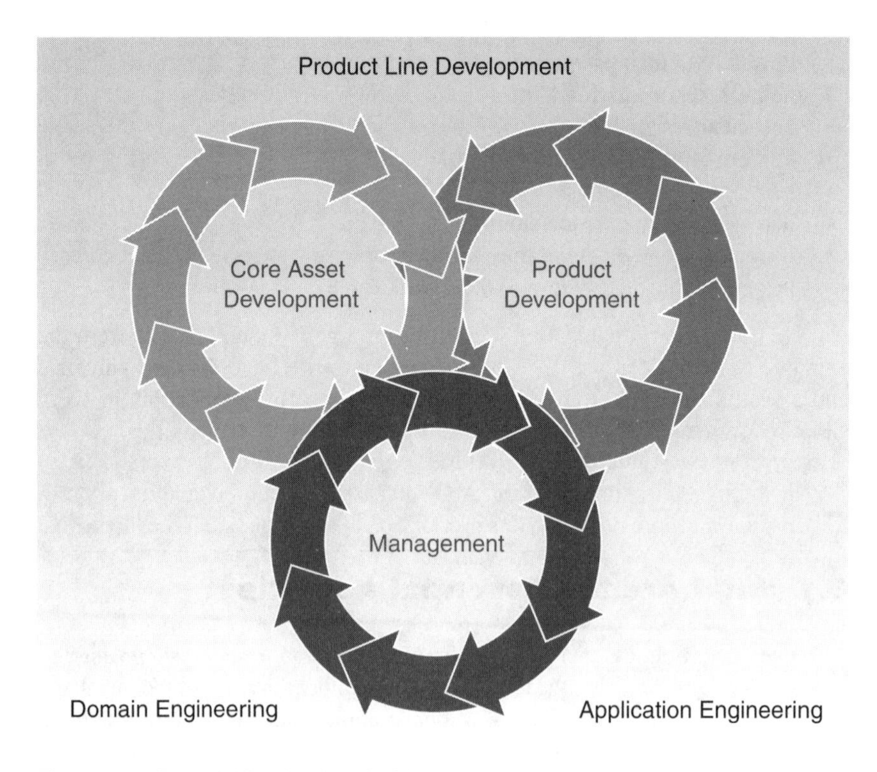

Figure 3.1 Essential Product Line Activities

them. As a result, the core assets are made more generic by considering potential new products on the horizon. There is a constant need for strong, visionary management to invest resources in the development and sustainment of the core assets. Management must also precipitate the cultural change to view new products in the context of the available assets. Either new products must align with the existing assets, or the assets must be updated to reflect the new products that are being marketed. Iteration is inherent in product line activities—that is, in turning out core assets, in turning out products, and in the coordination of the two. In the next three sections we examine the three essential activities in greater detail.

3.2 Core Asset Development

The goal of the core asset development activity is to establish a production capability for products. Figure 3.2 illustrates the core asset development activity along with its outputs and necessary inputs. This activity, like its counterparts, is iterative. The rotating arrows suggest that there is no one-way causal relationship from inputs to outputs; the inputs and outputs of this activity affect each other. For example, slightly expanding the product line scope (one of the outputs) may admit whole new classes of systems to examine as possible sources of legacy assets (one of the inputs). Similarly, an input production constraint (such as mandating the use of a particular middleware product) may lead to restrictions on the architectural styles and patterns (other inputs) that will be considered for the product line as a whole (such as the message-passing distributed object style). This restriction, in turn, will determine which preexisting assets are candidates for reuse or mining (still other inputs).

Three things are required for a production capability to develop products, and these three things are the outputs of the core asset development activity.

1. **Product line scope:** The product line scope is a description of the products that will constitute the product line or that the product line is capable of including. At its simplest, scope may consist of an enumerated list of product names. More typically, this description is cast in terms of the things that the products all have in common and the ways in which they vary from one another. These might include features or operations they provide, performance or other quality attributes they exhibit, platforms on which they run, and so on.

   Defining the product line scope is often referred to as *scoping*. For a product line to be successful, its scope must be defined carefully. If the scope is too large and product members vary too widely, then the core assets will be strained beyond their ability to accommodate the variability,

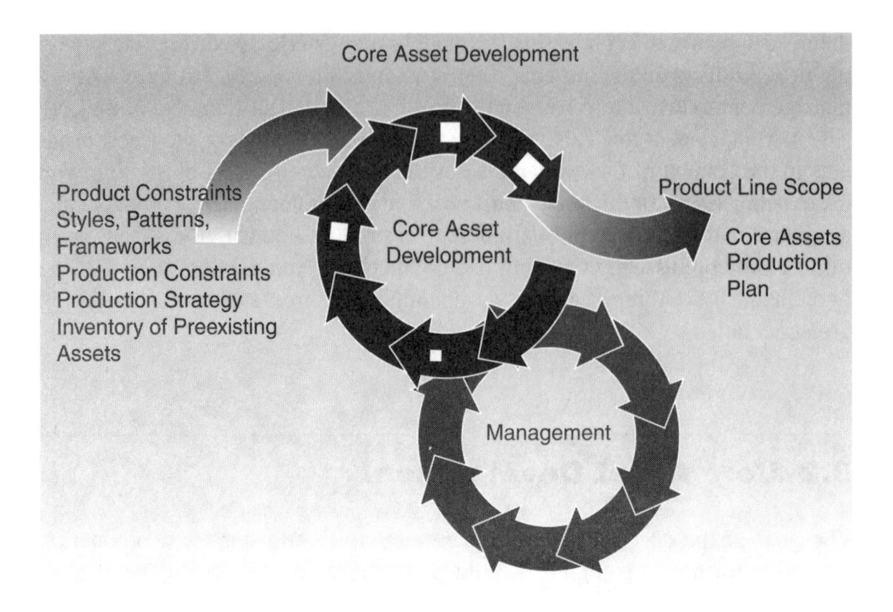

Figure 3.2 Core Asset Development

economies of production will be lost, and the product line will collapse into the old-style one-at-a-time product development effort. If the scope is too small, then the core assets might not be built in a generic enough fashion to accommodate future growth, and the product line will stagnate; economies of scope will never be realized, and the return on investment will never materialize.

The scope of the product line must target the right products, as determined by knowledge of similar products or systems, the prevailing or predicted market factors, the nature of competing efforts, and the organization's business goals for embarking on a product line approach (such as merging a set of similar but currently independent product development projects).

The scope of the product line evolves as market conditions change, as the organization's plans change, as new opportunities arise, or as the organization quite simply becomes more adept at software product lines. Evolving the scope is the starting point for evolving the product line to keep it current.

2. **Core assets:** Core assets are the basis for production of products in the product line. As we have already described, these assets almost certainly include an architecture that the products in the product line will share, as well as software components that are developed for systematic reuse across

the product line. Any real-time performance models or other architecture evaluation results associated with the product line architecture are core assets. Software components may also bring with them test plans, test cases, and all manner of design documentation. Requirements specifications and domain models are core assets, as is the statement of the product line's scope. Commercial off-the-shelf (COTS) components, if adopted, also constitute core assets.

Among the core assets, the architecture warrants special treatment. A product line architecture is a software architecture that will satisfy the needs of the product line in general and the individual products in particular by explicitly admitting a set of variation points required to support the spectrum of products within the scope. The product line architecture plays a special role among the other core assets. It specifies the structure of the products in the product lines and provides interface specifications for the components that will be in the asset base. Producing a product line architecture requires the product line scope (discussed above); a knowledge of relevant styles, patterns, and frameworks; and any available inventory of preexisting assets (all discussed below).

Each core asset should have associated with it an *attached process* that specifies how it will be used in the development of actual products. For example, the attached process for a set of product line requirements would give the process to follow when expressing the requirements for an individual product. This process might simply say: (1) use the product line requirements as the baseline requirements, (2) specify the variation requirement for any allowed variation point, (3) add any requirements outside the set of specified product line requirements, and (4) validate that the variations and extensions can be supported by the architecture. The process might also specify the automated tool support for accomplishing these steps. These attached processes are themselves core assets that get folded into what becomes the production plan for the product line. Figure 3.3 illustrates this concept of attached processes and how they are incorporated into the production plan.

There are also core assets at a less technical level—namely, the training specific to the product line, the business case for use of a product line approach for this particular set of products, the technical management process definitions associated with the product line, and the set of identified risks for building products in the product line. Although not every core asset will necessarily be used in every product in the product line, all will be used in enough of the products to make their coordinated development, maintenance, and evolution pay off.

Finally, part of creating the core asset base is defining how that core asset base will be updated as the product line evolves, as more resources become available, as fielded products are maintained, and as technological changes or market shifts affect the product line scope.

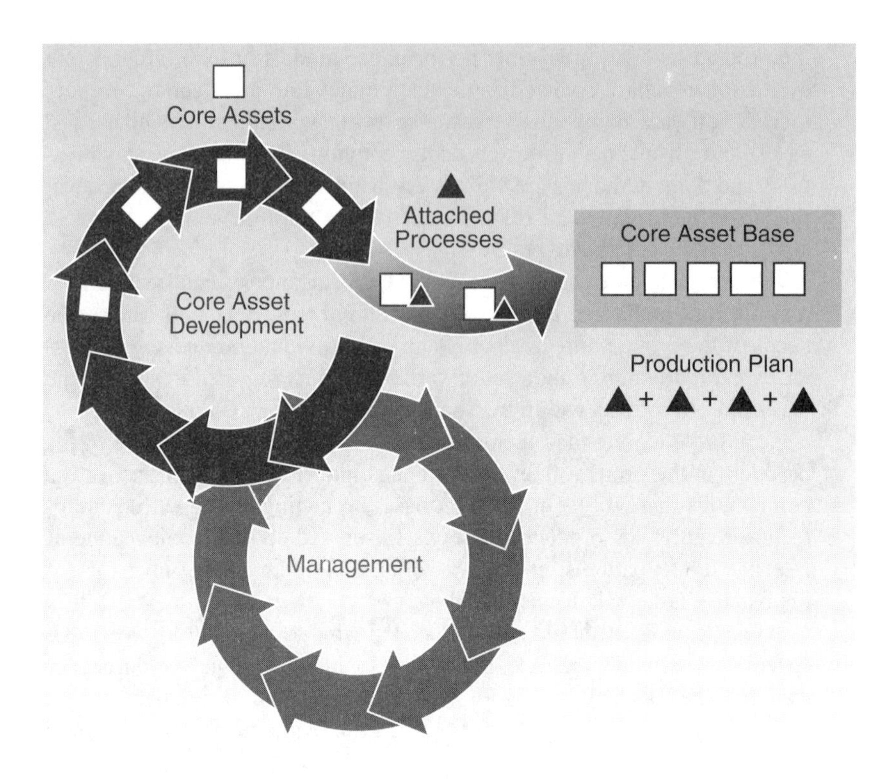

Figure 3.3 Attached Processes

3. **Production plan:** A production plan describes how the products are produced from the core assets. As noted above, core assets should each have an attached process that defines how it will be used in product development. The production plan is essentially a set of these attached processes with the necessary glue. It describes the overall scheme for how these individual processes can be fitted together to build a product. It is, in effect, the reuser's guide to product development within the product line. Each product in the product line will vary, consistent with predefined variation points. How these variation points can be accommodated will vary from product line to product line. For example, variation could be achieved by selecting from an assortment of components to provide a given feature, by adding or deleting components, or by tailoring one or more components via inheritance or parameterization. It could also be the case that products are generated automatically. The exact vehicle to be used to provide the requisite variation among products is described in the production plan. Without the production plan, the product builder would not know the linkage among the

core assets or how to utilize them effectively and within the constraints of the product line.

To develop a production plan, you need to understand who will be building the products—the audience for the production plan. Knowing who the audience is will give you a better idea how to format the production plan. Production plans can range from a detailed process model to a much more informal guidebook. The degree of specificity required in the production plan depends on the background of the intended product builders, the structure of the organization, the culture of the organization, and the concept of operations for the product line. It will be useful to have at least a preliminary definition of the product line organization before developing the production plan.

The production plan should describe how specific tools are to be applied in order to use, tailor, and evolve the core assets. The production plan should also incorporate any metrics defined to measure organizational improvement as a result of the product line (or other process improvement) practices and the plan for collecting the data to feed those metrics.

These three outputs are the necessary ingredients for feeding the product development activity, which turns out products that serve a particular customer or market niche. But what are the inputs necessary to create these outputs?

The inputs to the core asset development activity are as follows.

1. **Product constraints:** What are the commonalities and variations among the products that will constitute the product line? What behavioral features do they provide? What features do the market and technology forecasts say will be beneficial in the future? What standards must they follow? What performance limits must they observe? With what external systems must they interface? What physical constraints must be observed? What quality requirements (such as availability and security) are imposed? The core assets must capitalize on the commonalities and accommodate envisioned variation with minimal trade-off to product quality drivers such as security, reliability, usability, and so on.
2. **Styles, patterns, and frameworks:** These days, architectures are seldom built from scratch but rather evolve from solutions previously applied to similar problems. Architectural styles represent a current approach to reusing architectural design solutions. Architectural style catalogs exist that explain the properties of a particular style, including how well suited each style is for achieving specific quality attributes such as security or high performance. Design patterns occupy the same role at a finer granularity of design. Whereas architectures prescribe how large-grained components (subsystems) interact with each other, patterns usually suggest ways to

implement individual (or groups of finer-grained) components. So, a product line architect must ask: What are the relevant architectural building blocks that can be applied toward meeting the product and production constraints? What are the coordination protocols and patterns? Application frameworks, vertical architectures, and architectural patterns and styles are all inputs that can shape the pivotal core asset—the product line architecture—and in turn the production plan for utilizing the core assets to build products. Although these are really inputs to architecture definition, they are purposely elevated to this level of discussion to underscore the importance of the architecture to software product line practice.

3. **Production constraints:** What commercial, military, or company-specific standards apply to the products in the product line? Is there an underlying infrastructure on which these products must be built? What are the time-to-market or time-to-initial-operating-capability requirements for each? What off-the-shelf components should be used? Which legacy components could/should be reused? The answers to these questions all have dramatic impacts on the construction of the core assets and hence on the core assets themselves.
4. **Production strategy:** The production strategy is the overall approach for realizing the core assets. Will the product line be built from the top down (starting with a set of core assets and spinning products off from them) or from the bottom up (starting with a set of products and generalizing their components to produce the product line assets)? What will the transfer pricing strategy be—that is, how will the cost of producing the generic components be divided among the cost centers for the products? Will generic components be produced internally or purchased on the open market? Will products be automatically generated from the assets, or will they be assembled? How will production of core assets be managed? The production strategy dictates the genesis of the architecture and associated components and the path for their growth.
5. **Inventory of preexisting assets:** Legacy systems embody an organization's domain expertise and/or define its market presence. The product line architecture, or at least pieces of it, may borrow heavily from proven structures of related legacy systems. Components may be mined from legacy systems. Such components may represent key intellectual property of the organization in relevant domains and therefore become prime candidates for components in the core asset base.

   What software and organizational assets are available at the outset of the product line effort? Are there libraries, frameworks, algorithms, tools, and components that can be utilized? Are there technical management processes, funding models, and training resources that can be easily adapted for the product line? The inventory includes all potential preexisting assets. Through careful analysis, an organization determines what is most appropriate to utilize.

Of course, the next question is how these inputs will be utilized to produce the identified three outputs. The real answer is more involved than would be appropriate to cover at this stage. We will defer a more detailed description until Parts II and III.

3.3 Product Development

Mature product line organizations prioritize the health of the overall product line over that of individual products (see "E Pluribus Unum" sidebar), but in the end, the activity of turning out products is the ultimate product line goal. The product development activity depends on the three outputs described above—the product line scope, the core assets, and the production plan—plus the requirements for individual products. Figure 3.4 illustrates these relationships. Once more, the rotating arrows indicate iteration and intricate relationships. For example, the existence and availability of a particular product may well affect

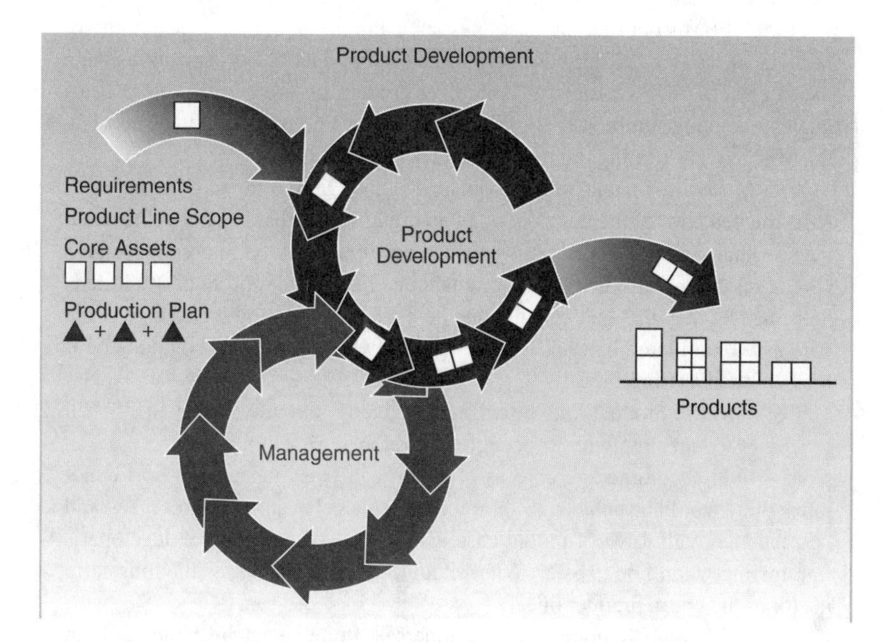

Figure 3.4 Product Development

the requirements for a subsequent product. As another example, building a product that has previously unrecognized commonality with another product already in the product line will create pressure to update the core assets and provide a basis for exploiting that commonality for future products.

E Pluribus Unum

The title of this sidebar is Latin for "out of many, one." It is the motto of the United States and expresses the vision of its founders that out of a group of loosely related states would emerge a unified nation. This motto is part of our culture. Culture is what binds a group of people together and gives them a common identity. Culture is the name we give to our habits, our values, our history, our likes and dislikes. Culture is a lens through which we view the world.

Product line organizations have a culture, also. After years of pulling back the covers and peeking inside companies that do this for a living, some aspects of that culture have become startlingly evident. Successful product line organizations employ people who are very comfortable working under the auspices of strong, documented processes. They have long and deep expertise in their application areas. They have an identifiable champion who lobbied tirelessly to turn the organization to product lines.

And it turns out that the best ones have an unofficial motto, which might fairly be phrased as "e pluribus unum." The best product line organizations view their business, their mission, as building a product line—singular. Other companies, including those still climbing the product line mountain, tend to view their business as turning out individual products—plural.

How does this manifest itself operationally? Quite often, a good barometer is the behavior of the developers. In an organization that has not yet reached the spiritual plateau of e pluribus unum, a developer will be likely to change a core asset unilaterally if it's not quite what he needs and a product deadline is looming. He may feel bad about it, and he may intend to send the change to the core asset team later, but he'll do it. After all, where would his company be if he didn't sell any products?

In a mature product line organization, covertly circumventing established processes would simply never occur to a developer. First of all, the processes in place would accommodate core assets that need tweaking under short deadlines; there would be no need to shortcut the process because the process would be robust enough to work in that case. But more to the point, the developer's first instinct would be to ask, "What should I do that is best for the long-term health of the entire product line?"

Each of these hypothetical developers is doing what he believes is in the best interest of his organization. And each is probably operating under the reward and incentive structures that are in place. The first developer believes that the product line approach is a luxury that can be afforded only after the company's "real" business has been taken care of. The second developer knows that the product line *is* the company's real business. How did they each come to these conclusions? What messages has management sent about what really counts when the pressure's on?

Out of many, one: the Zen of product lines if there ever was one. We first observed it when writing the CelsiusTech case study [Brownsword 96]:

> *Externally, CelsiusTech builds ship systems. Internally, it develops and grows a common asset base that provides the capability to turn out ship systems. This mentality—which is what it is—might sound subtle, but it manifests itself in the configuration-control policies, the organization of the enterprise, and the way that new products are marketed.*

It emerges over and over. From a 1999 case study of the software product line of an avionics manufacturer whom we visited (the case study remains unpublished to preserve confidentiality):

> *We shared with this group [of senior technical managers] that we hypothesized that one difference between a mature product line organization and an immature one is that the mature organization sees their business as maintaining and nurturing the product line, where as the immature one sees their business as turning out products via reuse. "I can tell you," said one of them immediately, "that is not just a hypothesis." (He meant it was true.) It is exactly how they view themselves—their primary responsibility is to the product line.*

And from a report on an engine control software product line at Cummins Engine Company, the world's largest manufacturer of large diesel engines [Dager 00]:

> *The software product line program slashed development costs and cycle time across these highly varying products and launched many successful products over the past four years . . . Cummins now has a group dedicated to the study and improvement of software architecture. No longer is Cummins concerned with the separate delivery of software products, but has turned its focus to the delivery of integrated product lines and taking advantage of all the benefits that come with a product line engineering concept.*

The difference was put to us in stark relief recently when we urged a company struggling to adopt the product line approach to devote more resources to their core asset team. The senior manager, in a moment of keen frustration as a result of too much business and too few people, lost his composure. "You don't seem to understand," he erupted, "we have products to get out!"

We do understand. But we also understand the difference between a short-term and a long-term view. We suspect this company will continue to get products out, because that's what their management holds to be important. And so their developers will continue to take shortcuts (and be rewarded for it), and their product line efforts will continue to falter. By "getting products out" they are not making the investment to exploit fully what those products have in common. As they contract to build more and more products, they are in more and more need of the product line paradigm and are less and less likely to achieve it.

I spoke recently with someone who just finished a market study of 12 organizations that are producing e-commerce software. "Mass customization" is the order of the day; they produce many versions of their products, tailored to individual customers. Or at least, they would like to. The market study asked about their ability to manage the different versions effectively. Seven of the organizations responded that they had already "hit the wall"—that the complexity of keeping track of the deployed versions, and the assets that went into the building of each, was already consuming vast amounts of time and intellectual capital, and they were on the verge of losing control completely. Four of the organizations avowed that they weren't yet to that point, but they could all see that wall fast approaching. And one organization was so intimidated by the problem of tracking multiple versions that it actually refused to deploy more than one version of its product. If a customer wanted something different, well, sorry, that's not possible. My contact asked all of them if they thought they could use technology that would let them manage their software as a set of variations off of a single product, rather than so many unrelated products. "It was amazing," he said. "You could see the light go on above their heads. It was a way of thinking about their business that had never occurred to them before." It was an e pluribus unum epiphany.

Out of many, one. For the mature product line organizations we have observed who have this motto, it also describes their position relative to their competition.

—PCC

The inputs for the product development activity are as follows:

- the requirements for a particular product, often expressed as a delta or variation from some generic product description contained in the product line scope (such a generic description is itself a core asset) or as a delta from the set of product line requirements
- the product line scope, which indicates whether or not the product under consideration can be included in the product line
- the core assets from which the product is built
- the production plan, which details how the core assets are to be used to build the product

A software product line is, fundamentally, a set of related products, but how they come into existence can vary greatly depending on the assets, the production plan, and the organizational context. From a very simple view, requirements for a product that is in the product line scope are received, and the production plan is followed so that the core assets can be properly used to develop the product. If the production plan is a more informal document, the product builders will need to build a product development plan that follows the guidance given. If the production plan is documented as a generic process description, the product builders will instantiate the production plan, recognizing the variation points being selected for the given product.

However, the process is rarely, if ever, so linear. The creation of products may have a strong feedback effect on the product line scope, the core assets, the production plan, and even the requirements for specific products. The ability to turn out a particular member of the product line quickly—perhaps a member that was not originally envisioned by the people responsible for defining the scope—will in turn affect the product line scope definition. Each new product may have similarities with other products that can be exploited by creating new core assets. As more products enter the field, efficiencies of production may dictate new system generation procedures, causing the production plan to be updated.

An interesting twist on product development occurs when the products are actually components used to build other products.

Components as Products

Products in a software product line are software products for internal use or for sale. Common components for the software product line are parts of the core asset base. But what if you are in the software component business? Then each product you build *is* a software component. If you have a family of components that share many common features but vary in some distinct and predictable ways, could you have a product line of components? Is this a silly idea? Not at all silly, just confusing. In fact, today a product line of components makes a lot of sense (and for many, a lot of money).

But before we explain, let's first define what we mean by "component." Szyperski gives the following definition [Szyperski 98]:

> *A software component is a unit of composition with contractually specified interfaces and explicit context dependencies only. A software component can be deployed independently and is subject to composition by third parties.*

A component is therefore opaque, and it is this opaqueness that allows one company to use proprietary information and algorithms from another company without detailed access that would compromise the intellectual property rights of the providing company. The using company must be able to compose the component with other components easily and without special environments or tools. The increased standards for specific purposes, such as the Enterprise Java Beans and CORBA models, provide market strata and architectural constraints that guide and facilitate the component selection process.

Providing individual software components as products is a rapidly growing business; however, it is not a new business. Software libraries for domains such as numerical analysis and graphics have been available for more than 30 years, but a number of changes have occurred in the last few years that have reshaped the component marketplace.

An increased focus on defining interfaces and component models that are defined via interfaces has made it simpler to identify candidates for a particular use. These candidate components "almost" fit, and the amount of rework required to use them has decreased dramatically. When you couple this opportunity to eliminate some of the in-house development work with the ever-growing demand for software—more complex and more challenging software—using some prefabricated components makes sense. And many have reached this conclusion: the market demand for components is strong. Moreover, the granularity of commercial components has grown from small, low-payoff components such as stacks and queues to components that provide more comprehensive functionality, such as a complete voice recognition engine. These new, larger, more sophisticated components command healthy prices, which result in attractive returns on development investment—an incentive for the component developer. In response, electronic marketplaces such as flashline.com have made it possible to offer small individual components for sale at affordable but profitable prices.

Consider a hypothetical (but close to real) example from the domain of telecommunications protocols. Our hypothetical company, Protocols-R-Us, is a company founded by a small group of managers and developers who all worked for the same multinational telecommunications corporation. The company has begun production of "protocol stack" software components, which are used to parse signals coming into a communications device, to do error detection and retry, and to deliver the signal to the platform software.

As a small company, Protocols-R-Us moves carefully to define their market. Their original business plan is narrowly scoped to address only their first product. The company begins by supplying an implementation of a communications protocol to both their former employer and one other company. As the first product nears release, the managers begin to consider other products. Given the depth of technical knowledge of the company founders, they explore products that can be leveraged from the work done so far. The team determines that their market consists of companies that are developing the broad array of communications devices and add-ons that are being introduced into the consumer market. Each of these devices is capable of receiving a variety of signals, including voice conversations and data transmissions. Each device will actually need to "understand" numerous protocols. Which protocols are useful is information that is changing rapidly, as are the specifications of many of the newer protocols.

The company team sees the rapid increase in the creation and release of new protocol standards as a business opportunity. They can capitalize on this business opportunity only if they can design and produce implementations of several protocols that can coexist in a single device and if they can do so in a way that can keep pace with the release of standards updates as protocols are revised and expanded. The company will also have to be able to keep costs low because the "shelf life" of a given implementation is extremely short. Client companies will want each new version of their device to have the latest implementation in order to provide the widest array of services to their clients. Protocols-R-Us sets the goal of meeting the protocol processing needs of customers by providing high-quality implementations of telecommunications protocols and doing so as quickly and efficiently as possible.

The company's small staff will need to be enlarged, but given current job market conditions, the new hires will not have a depth of experience in either software development or telecommunications. There will have to be a significant increase in productivity among the experienced personnel or the company will miss most of the benefits of the current telecommunications explosion.

How can they succeed? They can take a software product line approach. And what will their products be? A *product line of components*.

As the team begins planning for the product line, they have to identify the products that will constitute the product line (the product line scope). The initial product is an implementation of the HyperText Transfer Protocol (HTTP) and a HyperText Markup Language (HTML) translator. If they are to build on their existing client base, it makes sense to include protocols that are related to either the Transfer Control Protocol/Internet Protocol (TCP/IP) or HTTP. However, these are well-known protocols for which many implementations exist. A new, but somewhat related, area is the Wireless Application Protocol (WAP) used to provide Internet access from a mobile phone. This is an emerging area in which it should be possible to establish a presence. As an initial scope, the team identifies the following pieces that will be needed for a complete protocol stack from signal reception to screen presentation:

- Wireless Application Environment (WAE)
- Wireless Session Layer (WSL)
- Wireless Transaction Protocol (WTP)
- Wireless Transport Layer Security (WTLS)
- Wireless Datagram Protocol (WDP)

To offer a "complete solution," the company will also have to provide an implementation of the Wireless Markup Language (WML). The protocol stack accompanied by the language will provide support for accessing HTML-based content on the mobile phone.

The team recognizes that their most important asset will be the basic architecture from which all of the products are derived. Since the products will be components, they actually have to consider two architectures: the architecture of the systems into which the components are intended to fit and the architecture for the protocol components—their product line architecture. They know that the product line architecture for the components must provide a link between the standard organization for communications protocols and the individual components to permit clients, who are familiar with the network model, to understand easily how the Protocols-R-Us components will fit into their architecture.

The architecture will have to be updated to anticipate the evolution of those components with which it must interoperate. The company forms strategic alliances with a number of companies that produce related products. Through these partnerships, Protocols-R-Us hopes to keep up with the latest design changes and receive advance releases. It will test its products with these new releases to identify any unintended interactions. The architecture must also be maintained to remain current with the latest versions of the applicable standards.

And how will the final products be packaged? Each component will be packaged with a test component that contains the test cases used to test the protocol component. The component will also contain technical documentation that includes specification of both the *provides* and *requires* interfaces for the component. Finally, the shrink-wrapped package will also contain sample designs for integrating sets of the components into different configurations that provide support for different types of products.

Protocols-R-Us shows that the basic principles of product line development apply regardless of the nature of the products—even if the products are components. In the case of our component product line, the main changes in practices are the result of the size of the products and the need to manage the requirements with limited effort. The major impact on the architecture development is the need to pay more attention to the architecture of the environment into which the components will be integrated. There is always some integration between an application and its operating environment; however, the interface between an individual component and an application architecture is not as standardized as the OS interface. On the positive side, the interfaces implemented by a single component are smaller and can be more completely specified than the interface of an entire application.

And so you can have a software product line in which the components are products. In fact, a product line approach is a promising development paradigm for the component industry for the same reasons that made sense for Protocols-R-Us.

—LMN with JOHN MCGREGOR

3.4 Management

Management plays a critical role in the successful fielding of a product line. Activities must be given resources, coordinated, and supervised. Management at both the technical (or project) and organizational levels must be strongly committed to the software product line effort. That commitment manifests itself in a number of ways that feed the product line effort and keep it healthy and vital. Technical management oversees the core asset development and the product development activities by ensuring that the groups that build core assets and the groups that build products are engaged in the required activities, follow the processes defined for the product line, and collect data sufficient to track progress.

Organizational management must set in place the proper organizational structure that makes sense for the enterprise and must make sure that the organizational units receive the right resources (for example, well-trained personnel) in sufficient amounts. We define organizational management as the authority that is responsible for the ultimate success or failure of the product line effort. Organizational management determines a funding model that will ensure the evolution of the core assets and then provides the funds accordingly. Organizational management also orchestrates the technical activities in and iterations between the essential activities of core asset development and product development. Management should ensure that these operations and the communication paths of the product line effort are documented in an operational concept. Management mitigates at the organizational level those risks that threaten the success of the product line. The organization's external interfaces also need careful management. Product lines tend to engender different relationships with an organization's customers and suppliers, and these new relationships must be introduced, nurtured, and strengthened. One of the most important things that management must do is create an adoption plan that describes the desired state of the organization (that is, routinely producing products in the product lines) and a strategy for achieving that state.

Both technical and organizational management also contribute to the core asset base by making available for reuse those management artifacts (especially schedules and budgets) used in developing products in the product line.

Finally, someone should be designated as the product line manager, and that person must either act as or find and empower a product line champion. This person must be a strong, visionary leader who can keep the organization squarely pointed toward the product line goals, especially in the early stages when the going gets rough. Leadership is required for software product line success. Management and leadership are not always synonymous (see "Only Leaders Need Apply" sidebar).

Only Leaders Need Apply

In 1981 Jack Welch assumed the position of CEO at General Electric (GE). He quickly unveiled an aggressive strategic redirection that transformed GE into 14 distinct businesses focused on three "strategic circles": core manufacturing, technology-intensive businesses, and services [Tichy 89]. He coupled his business overhaul with an initiative to revitalize the work force. He was passionate about his vision, and he relentlessly drove it to completion. But he didn't stay at the vision and strategy level of organizational management; he got involved in GE daily operations. In fact, he never hired a chief operating officer (COO) despite the enormity of the enterprise he ran. He interacted directly with GE workers at all levels. He believed in his staff, listened to them, and gave them abundant feedback. He made them part of his solution, and he embraced their good ideas. He broke down the walls between managers and subordinates. He was interested not only in his own success, but also in GE's success. He spent years selecting, nurturing, and pruning a set of candidate successors. Welch's innovative strategies and management style transformed GE into a "highly productive, labor-efficient powerhouse with a staggering $200 billion-plus market capitalization" [Slater 1998]. Under Welch, GE soared to the top of the Fortune 500. Tom Brokaw, anchor and managing editor of "NBC Nightly News with Tom Brokaw," characterized his boss this way:[1] "Jack Welch is a genius at making all who work for him raise the level of their game."[2]

My brother has been a high school football coach for over 35 years. His teams have amassed 19 championships and five unbeaten seasons. The high school even named its football stadium after him. He has encyclopedic knowledge of football and athletic ability to match, but it's more than his knowledge and skills that have made him a legend. He does all of the workouts with his team and keeps the training rules he sets for them. He gets to know each player and relentlessly drives them to achieve their potential, and then some. He is always in the game, not just directing it. One season he "fired" more than half of his first-string players for breaking in-season training rules. Despite vehement pressure from parents, the school board, and administrators, he refused to reverse his decision. As a result, the team was purged of its finest talent, and some of the remaining players had to play both offense and defense. He worked tirelessly with the skeleton squad, challenging them and spurring them on. He believed they could succeed, but more important he made *them* believe they could succeed. And they did; they went to the championship playoffs.

---

1. General Electric owns NBC.
2. http//www.leadershipnow.com/leadershop/8104-5.html

Now what could Jack Welch and my brother possibly have in common? Simple: they are both leaders. And what do leaders have to do with software product lines? Everything: you can't just manage a software product line operation, you have to lead it. Managers control. Leaders spur an emotional energy that fuels an organization to succeed despite downturns and obstacles. Ron Temple led Cummins Inc. boldly through turbulent waters to success with their product line approach for engine control software (see Chapter 9). Jaak Urmi did the same for CelsiusTech. In fact, there is a leader behind each story of successful product line adoption that we have studied. And of the failed product line efforts we have seen, most either lacked a leader or lost one.

If product line management must lead to succeed, then we ought to take time out to describe the qualities of a leader. We have only to study role models such as Welch, my brother, Temple, and others. Leaders are

- **intelligent:** They know their business. They can quickly assess a problem and arrive at a solution.
- **self-assured:** They are confident in their abilities and don't need continual gratification. They surround themselves with top-notch talent and are not threatened by good ideas and brilliance.
- **visionary:** They can see the whole picture and can project it into the future. They see trends and can imagine solutions beyond what exists or what others think can exist.
- **enthusiastic:** They have an unquenchable, contagious zest for their work and their organizations.
- **competitive:** They are hungry; they push and push to make things happen.
- **decisive:** They are not afraid to make decisions and do so quickly.
- **committed:** They believe in their goals and focus to achieve them.
- **flexible:** They can change gracefully if a change is needed.
- **articulate:** They are good communicators.
- **people-focused:** They have a deep interest in people, and they care about the people in their organizations.
- **realistic:** They can recognize when things are not working or when a change in approach is needed. They strive for the maximum effort but not the impossible.
- **externally focused:** They are in tune with the world around them.
- **open:** They don't need to hide behind a cloak of secrecy.
- **honest:** They tell the truth and expect the same of others.
- **trusting:** They empower and have faith in others.
- **action-focused:** They get things done.

Leaders have what CEO coach Ram Charan calls "emotional strength" [Charan 99].

Given these qualities, what do leaders in product line settings do that sets them apart? They

- Pave the way.
- Understand what it takes to succeed with product lines.
- Know their business and their competition.
- Establish a product line vision and tangible product line goals; communicate both clearly and often.
- Take risks but have mitigation strategies in their back pockets.
- Garner support (including stable funding) from their superiors, from customers, and from boards of directors; and they keep their superiors informed and enthused about product lines.
- Know their people, assign them to jobs that match their talents, and hold them accountable.
- Train their people so that each is knowledgeable in his product line role.
- Are the product line champions or recognize and support those who are.
- Take an active role in the journey.
- Execute their plans and deliver on commitments.
- Make decisions quickly and communicate them openly.
- Use process to drive decisions and accomplish work, not to delay it.
- Drive the organization to succeed, but reward achievements along the way.
- Link pay directly to performance that supports the product line goals.
- Keep track of all critical assignments.
- Know what's going on in their organizations. They pay spontaneous visits to workers at all levels. They listen to the undercurrent and pay attention to morale signs.
- Confront reality. If a strategy isn't working, they change it. If people aren't performing, they coach, reassign, or fire.
- Believe in their people. They listen and provide feedback.
- Don't get discouraged by the inevitable backlash to a technology adoption.
- Know that they are there to support their people, not the other way around.

This is a tall list that goes beyond what most people would call management. Jack Welch refused to call himself a manager. He preferred the term "business leader." To him, a leader is a teacher, a cheerleader, and a liberator, not a controller [Tichy 89]. If you are choosing the individual to be at the helm of a product line effort, choose a leader. If you are the person in charge, take heed.

—LMN

3.5 All Three Together

Each of the three activities—core asset development, product development, and management—is individually essential, and careful blending of all three is also essential—a blend of technology and business practices. In Part II you will learn about the specific practices that relate to each essential activity and that accomplish the necessary blending.

3.6 For Further Reading

The collection of publications that addresses software product lines is not voluminous, but it is growing.

Meyer describes a hardware product line in *The Power of Product Platforms* [Meyer 97]. Michael Cusumano's *Japan's Software Factories* [Cusumano 91] describes early efforts at what we call software product line practice. This book is wonderful background for any study of software product lines. Jan Bosch's *Design and Use of Software Architectures* [Bosch 00] gives a solid software product line overview in addition to its specific treatment of architecture. Weiss and Lai present their software product line processes in their book, *Software Product-Line Engineering* [Weiss 99]. Jacobson et al.'s *Software Reuse: Architecture, Process, and Organization for Business Success* [Jacobson 97] provides a holistic description of the technical and business elements of strategic reuse.

The SEI's Product Line Practice Initiative has produced a number of documents and reports [SEI PLP] that augment our discussion in Part I. The most comprehensive of these is *A Framework for Software Product Line Practice* [Clements 00b], which was described in the preface of this book. *A Case Study in Successful Product Line Development* [Brownsword 96] details the complete CelsiusTech case study.

And finally, you will find 27 technical papers that describe software product line experience and current research in the proceedings from the First Software Product Line Conference, *Software Product Lines: Experience and Research Directions* [Donohoe 00]. Excerpts from some of these papers appear in the "Other Voices" sidebars that pepper the chapters of this book.

3.7 Discussion Questions

1. Production strategy was listed as an input to the core asset development activity. Under what circumstances would you choose a top-down production strategy? Under what circumstances would you choose a bottom-up production strategy?
2. An inventory of preexisting assets was listed as an input to the core asset development activity. Suppose an organization has no relevant existing assets. How will this affect core asset development, product development, and management?
3. Describe what might be included in the attached process for each of the following assets: a product line architecture, a component, a test case, and a product development estimate.
4. Some of the responsibilities of technical management were given in Section 3.4. Augment that list to include other responsibilities that you think would be appropriate.
5. Schedules and budgets are listed as example core assets that management creates. Name others.

PART II

Software Product Line Practice Areas

A functioning product line engine requires a blend of skillful engineering as well as technical and organizational management. By gathering information and identifying key people with product line experience, through surveys, workshops, conferences, and direct collaboration with organizations on product line efforts, we have built and categorized a reservoir of practical information that will help you fuel your own product line engine.

In Part I, we introduced three essential activities that are involved in developing a software product line. These are (1) core asset development, (2) product development, and (3) management. Now we define in more detail what an organization must do to perform those broad essential activities. We do this by defining *practice areas*. A practice area is a body of work or a collection of activities that an organization must master to successfully carry out the essential work of a product line. Practice areas help to make the essential activities more achievable by defining activities that are smaller and more tractable than a broad imperative such as "Develop core assets." Practice areas provide starting points from which organizations can make (and measure) progress in adopting a product line approach for software.

So, to achieve a software product line, you must carry out the three essential activities. To be able to carry out the essential activities, you must master the practice areas relevant to each. By "mastering," we mean an ability to achieve repeatable, not just one-time, success with the work.

Almost all of the practice areas describe activities that are essential for any successful software development, not just software product lines. You'll see practice areas such as architecture definition, configuration management, and training—all integral aspects of standard product building. However, these and the other practice areas all either take on particular significance or must be carried out in a unique way in a product line context. Those aspects that are specifically relevant to software product lines, as opposed to single-system development, will be emphasized.

Describing the Practice Areas

For each practice area we present the following information:

- An introductory overview of the practice area that summarizes what it's about. You will not find a definitive discourse on the practice area here because, in most cases, there is overlap with what can be found in traditional software engineering and management reference books. We provide a few basic references if you need a refresher.
- Those aspects of the practice area that apply especially to a product line, as opposed to a single system. Here you will learn in what ways traditional software and management practice areas need to be refocused or tailored to support a product line approach.
- How the practice area is applied to core asset development and product development, respectively. We separate these two essential activities; although in most cases a given practice area applies to both of these broad areas, the lens that you look through to focus changes when you are building products versus developing assets.
- A description of any *specific practices* that are known to apply to the practice area. A specific practice describes a particular way of accomplishing the work associated with a practice area. Specific practices are not meant to be end-to-end methodological solutions to carrying out a practice area but approaches to the problem that have been used in practice to build product lines. Whether or not a specific practice will work for your organization depends on context.
- Known risks associated with the practice area. These are ways in which a practice area can go wrong, to the detriment of the overall product line effort. Our understanding of these risks is borne out of the pitfalls of others in their product line efforts.
- A list of references for further reading, to support your investigation in areas where you desire more depth.

There are other kinds of information associated with each practice area, although these are not called out in the description. When planning to carry out the practice area, be sure to keep the following in mind:

- For each practice area, make a work plan for carrying it out. The work plan should specify who is the plan owner, what are the specific tasks, who is responsible for doing them, what resources those people will be given, and when the results are due. More information about planning for product lines can be found in the "Technical Planning" and "Organizational Planning" practice areas (Sections 5.6 and 6.8).
- For each practice area, define metrics associated with tracking its completion and measuring its success. These metrics will help an organization identify where the practice areas are (or are not) being executed in a way that is meeting the organization's goals.
- Many practice areas produce tangible artifacts. For each practice area that does so, make a plan for keeping its produced artifacts up to date and identify the set of stakeholders who hold a vested interest in the artifacts produced. Collect organizational plans for artifact evolution and sustainment, and for stakeholder definitions, in your product line's operational concept, which is discussed in the "Operations" practice area.
- Many practice areas lead to the creation of core assets of some sort. For those that do, define and document an attached process (see Section 3.2) that tells how the core assets are used (modified, instantiated, and so on) to build products. These attached processes together form the production plan for the product line. The "Process Definition" practice area describes the essential ingredients for defining these (and other) processes. The "Operations" and "Architecture Definition" practice areas describe documents for containing some of them.

Starting versus Running a Product Line

Many of the practice areas are written from the point of view of describing an in-place product line capability. Of course, we recognize that ramping up to a product line is in many ways different from running one on a day-to-day basis. We felt it was important to describe the end or "steady state" so that readers could understand the goals. To address the issues of starting (rather than running) a software product line shop, refer to the "Launching and Institutionalizing" practice area.

Organizing the Practice Areas

Since there are so many practice areas, we need a way of organizing them for easier access and reference. We divide them loosely into three categories:

1. *Software engineering* practice areas (Chapter 4) are those necessary to apply the appropriate technology to create and evolve both core assets and products.
2. *Technical management* practice areas (Chapter 5) are those management practices necessary to engineer the creation and evolution of the core assets and the products.
3. *Organizational management* practice areas (Chapter 6) are those necessary for the orchestration of the entire software product line effort.

Each of these categories appeals to a different body of knowledge and requires a different skill set for the people needed to carry them out. The categories represent disciplines rather than job titles.

There is no way to divide cleanly into practice areas the knowledge necessary to achieve a software product line. Some overlap is inevitable. We have chosen what we hope to be a reasonable scheme and have identified practice area overlap where possible. After we present the practice areas, Part III will show how to put the practice areas into play for a particular organization's context and goals.

4

Software Engineering Practice Areas

Software engineering practice areas are those practice areas that are necessary to apply the appropriate technology to the creation and evolution of both core assets and products. They are carried out in the technical activities represented by the top two circles in Figure 4.1. In alphabetical order, they are

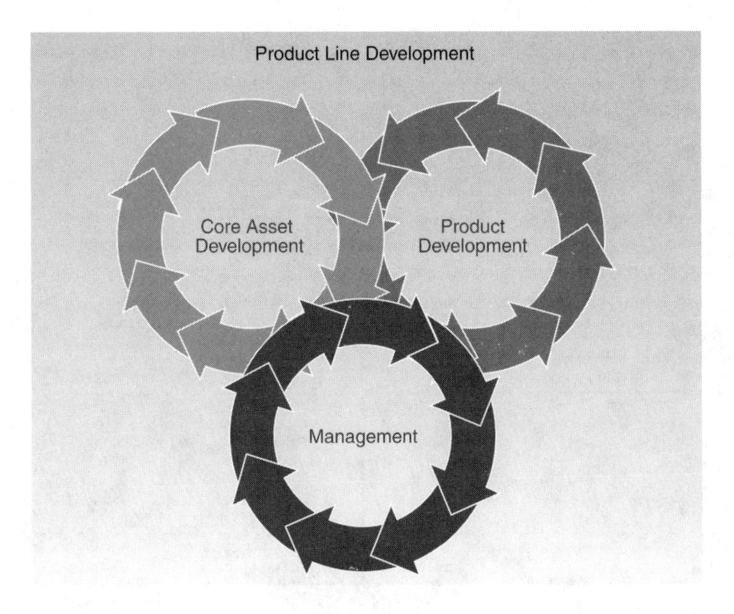

Figure 4.1 Essential Product Line Activities

- Architecture Definition
- Architecture Evaluation
- Component Development
- COTS Utilization
- Mining Existing Assets
- Requirements Engineering
- Software System Integration
- Testing
- Understanding Relevant Domains

All of these practice areas should sound familiar because all are part of every well-engineered software system. But they all take on special meaning when the software is a product line, as we will see. How do they relate to each other in a software product line context? Figure 4.2 sketches the story.

Domain understanding feeds requirements, which drive an architecture, which specifies components. Components may be made in-house, bought on the open market, mined from legacy assets, or commissioned under contract. This choice depends on the availability of in-house talent and resources, open-market components, an exploitable legacy base, and able contractors. The existence (or nonexistence) of these things can affect the requirements and architecture for the product line. Once available, the components must be integrated, and they and the system must be tested. This is a quick trip through an iterative growth cycle, and it oversimplifies the story shamelessly but shows a good approximation of how the software engineering practice areas come into play.

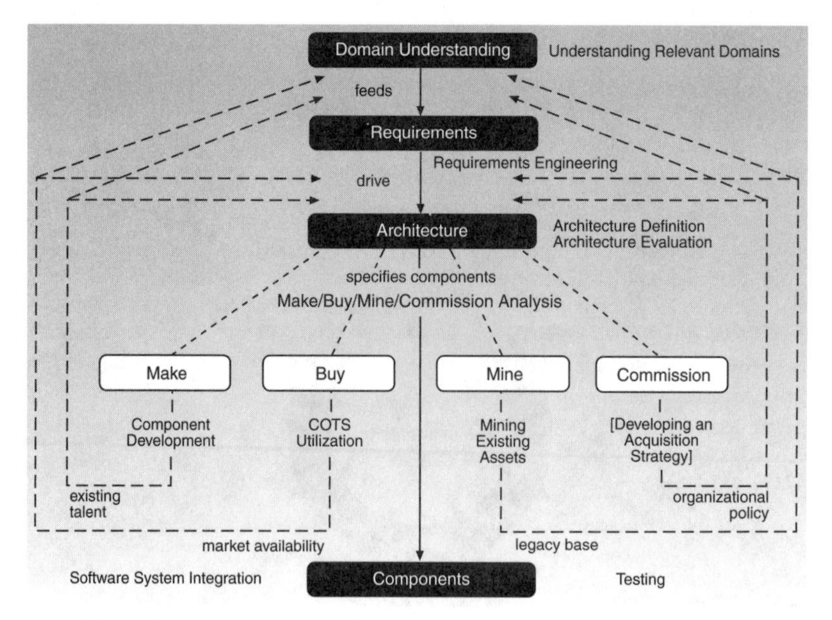

Figure 4.2 Relationships among Software Engineering Practice Areas

We begin, fittingly, with architecture definition. Perhaps more than any other core asset, the architecture will determine how well an organization can field products that are built efficiently from a shared repository of core assets.

4.1 Architecture Definition

This practice area describes the activities that must be performed to define a software architecture. By software architecture, we mean the following [Bass 98a]:

> *The software architecture of a program or computing system is the structure or structures of the system, which comprise software components, the externally visible properties of those components, and the relationships among them. By "externally visible" properties, we are referring to those assumptions other components can make of a component, such as its provided services, performance characteristics, fault handling, shared resource usage, and so on.*

By making "externally visible properties" of components part of the definition, we intentionally and explicitly include component interfaces, including their behaviors, as part of the architecture. We will return to this point later.

Architecture is key to the success of any software project, not just a software product line. Architecture is the first design artifact that begins to place requirements into a solution space. Quality attributes of a system (such as performance, modifiability, and availability) are in large part permitted or precluded by its architecture—if the architecture is not suitable from the beginning for these qualities, don't expect to achieve them by some miracle later. The architecture determines the structure and management of the development project as well as the resulting system, since teams are formed and resources allocated around architectural components. For anyone seeking to learn how the system works, the architecture is the place where understanding begins. The right architecture is absolutely essential for smooth sailing. The wrong one is a recipe for disaster.

Architectural requirements: For an architecture to be successful, its constraints must be known and articulated. And contrary to standard software engineering waterfall models, an architecture's constraints go far beyond implementing the required *behavior* of the system that is specified in a requirements document (see "Other Voices: Requirements They Didn't Teach You in Software Engineering Class" sidebar). Other architectural drivers that a seasoned architect knows to take into account include:

- the quality attributes (as mentioned above) that are required for each product that will be built from the architecture.
- whether the system will have to interact with other systems.

- the business goals that the developing organization has for the system. These might include ambitions to use the architecture as the basis for other systems (or even other software product lines). Or perhaps the organization wishes to develop a particular competence in an area such as Web-based database access. Consequently, the architecture will be strongly influenced by that desire.
- best sources for components. A software architecture will, when it is completed, call for a set of components to be defined, implemented, and integrated. Those components may be implemented in-house (see the "Component Development" practice area, Section 4.3), purchased from the commercial marketplace (see the "COTS Utilization" practice area, Section 4.4), contracted to third-party developers (see the "Developing an Acquisition Strategy" practice area, Section 6.3), or excavated from the organization's own legacy vaults (see the "Mining Existing Assets" practice area, Section 4.5). The architecture is indifferent as to the source. However, the availability of preexisting components (commercial, third-party, or legacy) may influence the architecture considerably and cause the architect to carve out a place in the architecture for a preexisting component to fit, if doing so will save time or money or play into the organization's long-term strategies.

Other Voices: Requirements They Didn't Teach You in Software Engineering Class

It is a savvy architect who knows that not all of the constraints on an architecture are to be found by paging through the requirements document. Ben Pronk of Philips Medical Systems has written about a family of medical imaging devices, the software of which is developed as a product line [Pronk 00]. The nature of their products imposes some interesting, if not esoteric, obligations on the architecture that may well not be on the inevitable list of "-ilities" found in most software engineering texts. Does your product line architecture carry with it such a well-expressed rationale? Moreover, can your architecture evaluation method help you make sure that your product line architecture satisfies requirements such as the following?

> *The architecture of a medical device is very much driven by the fact that such equipment is actively maintained for many years (more than 10). This means that, starting from the original code base for one product, many, sometimes even up to 10, releases are delivered, each featuring large functional extensions. Furthermore, over the lifetime of a*

product many versions or types of peripherals with different capabilities must be supported. It is important to note that not only new deliveries contain these new features; many systems are upgraded in the field to new releases, while retaining at least some of the original hardware configuration. Contrary to the practice of some software manufacturers, the medical industry cannot afford to force their clients to upgrade to the newest hardware every two or three years. The reason is simple: the real costs in medical imaging equipment are in the peripherals. At the same time, while providing an upgrade, customers who are not willing to upgrade are still running older releases. From a commercial viewpoint, this makes delivery of new functionality in the context of these old releases interesting. Over time this leaves product development with a series of releases, each of which has to support the sum of all functions on a combinatorial set of hardware configurations. In reality this is often impossible to handle. Consequently the industry resorts to commercial solutions such as reducing the amount of supported combinations and forcing (sometimes even giving away) upgrades to the latest versions.

The main requirements for any architecture in the medical imaging area are, therefore,

- *Support for flexible integration of new functions and peripherals during the life cycle of the architecture.*
- *Extension of the system with new (more powerful) peripherals without the need to update all application software.*
- *An efficient testing approach that avoids the need for testing a function for all possible configurations . . . .*
- *The most trivial requirement is of course the ability to support the variation as described above while maximizing efficient software reuse. This is not necessarily identical to sharing as many lines of code as possible. The organizational overhead of reusing a small library developed at one site at several other sites may exceed the gain.*
- *It must be possible to develop in parallel, at various locations around the world, derived products based on the same platform release.*
- *The various system groups that implement end-user products based on the platform need the ability to react fast upon market changes. This mainly concerns features like a new processing algorithm or support for a new printer. Since the platform will be released at regular intervals that are much larger than the required market response time, this implies that additional variation points in the platform are needed to support this. System groups must be able to add certain classes of features without the need of new platform release.*
- *There are thus two categories of variation requirements for the product family architecture: support for the variation inherent*

in the supported applications, and support for the variation imposed by the need for fast market reaction (see previous point). Both aspects should preferably be covered by one mechanism.

- *User interface aspects. To allow for discrimination in the marketplace, and for application reasons, variations in user interaction have to be supported.*

By the way, notice how nicely the first paragraph makes the case for a particular configuration management capability: "a series of releases, each of which has to support the sum of all functions on a combinatorial set of hardware configurations."

Architectural approaches: There are many activities that are necessary to design a complete system (including documenting rationale, identifying and specifying coordination protocols, partitioning functionality, and defining interfaces), but these activities can be ordered in many ways because architects use a wide variety of techniques and processes. Architects usually take one of the following paths when laying out an architecture:

- **Top down:** Start from requirements and then define an architecture as a series of refinements. Prior to beginning the next refinement, the current step must be completed and verified. This is an approach that results in a design for a completely working system without intermediate demonstrations. The resulting design can be checked for consistency and completeness at each stage, but it is slow to realize a working system or a system that can be viewed by the users to test usability.
- **Focus on the infrastructural aspects of the system prior to designing for application functionality:** The infrastructure of a system comprises those portions without which no application functionality can execute. The operating system, communication protocols, middleware, and system-specific supporting functionality are all portions of the infrastructure. This approach results in a system in which the application functionality can be implemented incrementally since even the smallest function will run. A risk is a system infrastructure that has elegance but doesn't work well for the applications.
- **Focus on the application functionality prior to investigating the infrastructure:** The application functionality can be implemented in components from which many infrastructure assumptions have been abstracted. This approach assumes that the architect knows that the infrastructure can be constructed without risk, but the risk lies in the achievement of the application functionality. It results in a system where application functionality can be demonstrated early but without the performance, reliability, or generality that comes from the implementation of the actual infrastructure.

Architectural styles: Architects do not start from scratch when setting out to craft the solution to a problem. A growing body of trade knowledge exists in the form of architectural styles—the architectural equivalents of design patterns. An architectural style defines a set of component types, specifies a topological pattern for their interconnection, and imposes semantic constraints on their runtime interaction. Styles are not complete architectures, but rather they are protoarchitectures, and each has known quality properties. If you are familiar with systems that can be described as n-tier client-server or layered or pipe-and-filter or data-repository-centric, then you already know something about architectural styles. Today it is incumbent on any professional software architect to be familiar with the styles and patterns used in similar systems and with architectural styles and patterns in general.

Component interfaces: As we alluded to in the opening of this section, architecture includes the interfaces of its components. It is therefore incumbent on the architect to specify those interfaces (or, if the component is developed externally, to ensure that its interface is adequately specified by others). By "interface" we mean something far more complete than the simple functional signatures one finds in header files. Signatures simply name the programs and specify the numbers and types of their parameters, but they tell nothing about the semantics of the operations, the resources consumed, the exceptions raised, or the externally visible behavior. As Parnas wrote in 1971, an interface consists of the set of assumptions that users of the component may safely make about it—nothing more, but nothing less [Parnas 71].

Interfaces are often specified using a contractual approach. Contracts state pre- and postconditions for each service and define invariants that express constraints about the interactions of services within the component. The contract approach is static and does not address the dynamic aspects of a component-based system or even the dynamic aspects of a single component's behavior. Additional techniques such as state machines [Harel 98] and interval temporal logic [Moszkowski 86] can be used to specify on the component constraints that deal with the ordering of events and the timing between events. For example, a service may create a thread and assign it to do work that will not be completed within the execution window of the service. A postcondition for that service would include the logical clause for "eventually this work is accomplished."

A complete contract should include information about what will be both provided and required. The typical component interface specification describes the services that a component provides. To document a component fully so that it can be integrated easily with other components, the specification should also document the resources that the component requires. In addition to making it easy to determine what must be available for the component to be integrated successfully, this documentation provides a basis for determining whether there are possible conflicts between the resources needed for the set of components comprising the application.

A component's interface provides only a specification of how individual services respond when invoked. As components are integrated, additional information is needed. The interactions between two components needed to achieve a specific objective can be described as a protocol. A protocol groups together a set of messages from both components and specifies the order in which they are to occur.

Each component exhibits a number of externally visible attributes that are important to its use but are often omitted (incorrectly) from its interface specification. Performance (throughput) and reliability are two such attributes. The standard technique for documenting the performance of a component is the computational complexity of the dominant algorithms. Although this technique is platform-independent, it is difficult to use in reasoning about satisfying requirements in real-time systems because it fails to yield an actual time measure. Worse, it uses information that will change when algorithms (presumably encapsulated within the component) change. A better approach is to document performance bounds, setting an upper bound on time consumed. The documentation remains true when the software is ported to a platform at least as fast as the current one—a safe assumption in today's environment. Cases in which the stated bounds are not fast enough can be resolved on a case-by-case basis. If the product can in fact meet the more stringent requirement on that product's platform, that fact can be revealed. If it cannot, either remedial action must be taken or the requirement must be relaxed.

Connecting components: Applications are constructed by connecting components to enable communication and coordination. In simple systems that run on a single processor, the venerable procedure call is the oldest and most widely used mechanism for component interaction. In modern distributed systems, however, something more sophisticated is desirable. There are several competing technologies, discussed below, for providing these connections as well as other infrastructure services. Among the services provided by the infrastructures are remote procedure calls (allowing components to be deployed on different processors transparently), communication protocols, object persistence and the creation of standard methods, and "naming services" that allow one component to find another via the component's registered name. These infrastructures are purchased as commercial packages; they are components themselves that facilitate connection among other components. These infrastructure packages are called middleware and, like styles, represent another class of already solved problems (highly functional component interactions for distributed object-based systems) that the architect need not reinvent. There are, at the time of this writing, three leading contenders in the race for middleware market dominance:

- **Common Object Request Broker Architecture (CORBA):** The Object Management Group (OMG) has defined a core element, the Object Request Broker (ORB), which is used to enable communication between components [OMG 97]. The interface of the ORB was an initial structuring element that shaped the interfaces of the components that use the ORB. The OMG has gradually expanded the scope of its approach to specify more of the system's pieces. The Object Management Architecture (OMA) specifies several categories into which a component can be placed. The OMA includes CORBA services, CORBA facilities, and application objects. The services and facilities will most often be provided by a commercial vendor and incorporated into a product. The application objects provide the domain-specific behavior. Even for the application objects, groups such as the Business Object Domain Task Force of the OMG are working to standardize specifications. The object model defined by OMA is a source-code-level standard that defines standards in a number of areas including language bindings. This model provides a very flexible environment with support for multiple languages and platforms and provides the flexibility needed to integrate components from a wide variety of sources.
- **Distributed Object Component Model (DCOM):** This model began as a "standard" defined by Microsoft Corporation for simple component-based systems, Component Object Model (COM). This standard was extended to support distribution, DCOM. More recently, COM+, a new version of DCOM, was released to support the more dynamic runtime environment of languages such as Java. An "interface" is the standard means of specifying expected behavior in a COM program. The COM model defines its standard interfaces at the binary level, so it does not address how a component implements the interface, nor does it discuss the differences in programming languages.
- **JavaBeans:** This model also began as the effort of a single company, Sun. This model does not define a source code or binary standards. The "standard" is defined largely through design patterns and tool conventions. The design patterns include a "listener" approach to the notification of significant events and the definition of properties that parameterize key aspects of the component. The tool conventions include the assumption that if an attribute named "X" is defined in the component, methods "getX" and "setX" will also be defined. A second assumption is the availability of a "BeanInfo" class defined in parallel to each "Bean" class. Unlike the other two component models, JavaBeans doesn't have any standard interfaces that are assumed or expected. In fact, it does not assume a single model for distribution either. Both Remote Method Invocation (RMI), a Java-specific approach, and CORBA can be used. The most recent implementations of RMI are IIOP-compatible and support the more general-naming service approach to finding other components with which to interact.

4.1.1 Aspects Peculiar to Product Lines

All architectures are abstractions that admit a plurality of instances; a great source of their conceptual value is, after all, the fact that they allow us to concentrate on design while admitting a number of implementations. But a product line architecture goes beyond this simple dichotomy between design and code; it is concerned with a set of explicitly allowed variations, whereas with a conventional architecture almost any instance will do as long as the (single) system's behavioral and quality goals are met. A product line architecture is concerned with which variations are instantiated because those are products. Thus, identifying the allowable variations is part of a product line architecture's responsibility, as is providing built-in mechanisms for achieving them. And those variations may be substantial. Products in a software product line exist simultaneously and may vary from each other in terms of their behavior, quality attributes, platform, network, physical configuration, middleware, scale factors, and a myriad of other ways.

In a conventional architecture, the mechanism for achieving different instances almost always comes down to modifying the code. But in a software product line, support for variation can take many forms (and be exercised at many times; see "Other Voices: Architectural Binding Times from Philips" sidebar). Variation can be accomplished by introducing build-time parameters to a component, subsystem, or collection of subsystems, whereby a product is configured by setting a collection of values. This type of variation assumes that all variants have been envisioned, a priori, and accommodated in the existing code. Conceptually, each combination's parameter values should correspond to a different product in the software product line's scope. Of course, in practice it doesn't really work that way. Some parameter combinations may be disallowed as semantically meaningless or outside the scope.

In object-oriented systems, another type of variation comes from specializing particular classes. Classes can be written to admit a variety of specializations that can be written for various products as necessary. In this way, variants can be constructed incrementally. Inheritance and delegation are object-oriented techniques that can also be used to allow for variants.

Other Voices:
Architectural Binding Times from Philips

Hand-in-hand with what variations an architecture should provide goes the question of when each variation is designed to be exercised. Implicit in that decision is who will exercise it. Most product lines have variation mechanisms that can be set at system-build time, but many have features that can be bound by the installers in the field or even by customers long after the installers have all gone home. Here are the binding times available in the software product lines of Philips' consumer electronics and medical imaging devices [America 00]:

> *Binding time concerns the moment of making decisions. This is a relevant issue only when dealing with families of products: if a product dependent decision is made when designing a component, this component may become unusable in other products. Late binding techniques allow postponing product decisions until product time.*
>
> *In our professional [medical] systems, we distinguish between platform time, product time, and installation time. At platform time, a large collection of plug-in components is created; at product time a selection of these is made. Many platform units and components can still be configured (using long lists of parameters); this configuration can be done both at product time (by defining default values) and at installation time (by defining the actual values).*
>
> *In our consumer systems, we recognize component time, subsystem time, product time, factory time, dealer time, and customer time. Decisions that cannot be made at component time are handled through (long lists of) component parameters. Components are selected and bound at subsystem time and their parameters are assigned values. Whatever selection, binding and value decisions cannot be made at subsystem time are handled through subsystem parameters and postponed to a later time. This process is repeated at product time. Up to then, significant code optimizations can be obtained by recompiling all source code. Decisions that are postponed to factory, dealer, or customer time are handled through parameters stored in non-volatile memory.*

It is also possible to achieve variation by replacing components with different components embodying the particular variant desired. Similarly, products with less capability may be achieved by leaving out entire components. Or, high-capacity variants might be turned out by using more of certain components (such as servers) whose precise number is left intentionally unbound by the product line architecture.

Integration may assume a greater role for software product lines than for one-off systems simply because of the number of times it's performed. A product line with a large number of products and upgrades requires a smooth and easy process for each product. Therefore, it pays to select a variation mechanism that allows for reliable and efficient integration when new products are turned out. This means some degree of automation. For example, if the variation mechanism chosen for the architecture is component selection and deselection, you will want an integration tool that carries out your wishes by selecting the right components and feeding them to the compiler or code generator. If the variation mechanism is parameterization or conditional compilation, you will want an integration tool that checks the parameter values for consistency and compatibility and then feeds those values to the compilation step. Hence, the variation mechanism chosen for the architecture will go hand-in-hand with the integration approach (see the "Software System Integration" practice area, Section 4.7).

For many other system qualities, such as performance, availability, functionality, usability, and testability, there are no major peculiarities that distinguish architecture for product lines relative to one-of-a-kind systems.

There must be documentation for the product line architecture as it resides in the core asset base and for each product's architecture (to the extent that it varies from the product line architecture). Documentation carries two obligations. The first is to document the product line architecture. Here, architectural views come into play. A view is a projection of the architecture that includes certain kinds of information and suppresses other kinds. For example, the process view will show the processes in the software and how they communicate or synchronize with each other, but it will not show how the software is divided into layers (if it is). The layered view will show this, but it will not show the processes. And a view that shows data flow among major modules will not show either. There are many views of an architecture; choosing which ones to document is a matter of what information you wish to convey. Commonly used views include the process view, the logical or module view, a layered view, a deployment (or process to processor) view, a physical view that shows the hardware computing environment and network topologies, a "uses" view that shows how parts of the software employ each other, a data flow view, a class view, and others. Each view has a particular usefulness. Performance tuning, for example, is often achieved by manipulating processes or how those processes are allocated to software; hence, performance engineers tend to be interested in the process and deployment views. A computation's accuracy is a function of the data flow that the inputs traverse before being transformed into output, so an accuracy tester will want to see the data flow view. Someone interested in deploying a subset of the system (not an unusual situation in a product line, when one of the products offers low-end service) will want to work with the "uses" view. For a software product line, the views will need to show the variations that are possible.

The second documentation obligation is to describe the architecture's attached (instantiation) process—that is, the part of the production plan that deals with the architecture. It should describe the architecture's variation points, how to exercise them, and a rationale for the variation. In practice, the attached process for the architecture is often bundled with the attached processes for requirements engineering, component development, software integration, and testing into an operational document that serves as a product builder's guide. This builder's guide should explain how to build a product, from requirements to testing, whether it involves tailoring, extracting from a library, setting parameters, using configuration files, or some other technique. The product builder's guide will be discussed in more detail in Section 4.1.4.

4.1.2 Application to Core Asset Development

The product line architecture is an early and prominent member in the collection of core assets. The architecture is expected to persist over the life of the product line and to change relatively little and relatively slowly over time. The architecture defines the set of software components (and hence their supporting assets such as documentation and test artifacts) that populate the core asset base. The architecture also spawns its attached process, which is itself an important core asset for sustaining the product line.

4.1.3 Application to Product Development

Once it has been placed in the product line core asset base, the architecture is used to create instance architectures for each new product according to its attached process. If product builders discover a variation point or a needed mode of variation that is not permitted by the architecture, it should be brought to the architect's attention; if the variation is within scope (or deemed desirable to add to the scope), the architecture may be enhanced to accommodate it. The "Operations" practice area (Section 6.7) deals with setting up this feedback loop in the organization.

4.1.4 Specific Practices

Architecture definition and architecture-based development: As the field of software architecture has grown and matured, methods of creating, defining, and using architecture have proliferated. Many specific practices related to architecture definition are defined in widely available works [Kruchten 98, Jacobson 97, Hofmeister 00, Bachmann 00]. The Rational Unified Process (RUP) is the most widely used method for object-oriented systems. An explanation of RUP is beyond the scope of this book, but there is a plethora of resources under no such constraint.

Architecture styles and patterns: An architecture style is a description of component types and a pattern of their runtime control and/or data transfer [Shaw 96, Bass 98a]. Styles are becoming a de facto design language for software architectures. People speak of pipe-and-filter styles, an n-tier, a client-server style, or an agent-based architecture, and these phrases immediately convey complex and sophisticated design information. Using a previously cataloged style shortens the architecture definition process because styles come with pedigrees: what applications they work well for, what their performance properties are, where they can easily accommodate variation points, and so forth. For example, the layered architectural style is well known for imbuing a system with portability, the ability to move the software to a new operating environment with minimal change. Portability is a desirable characteristic for a product line architecture if different products are expected to run on different platforms, or if the entire product line may migrate to a new platform one day. Thus, a product line architect designing for portability may start out by considering a layered architecture. Product line architects should be familiar with well-known architectural styles as well as styles (well known or not) used in systems similar to the ones they are building.

Aspect-oriented programming (AOP): AOP is an approach to program development that makes it possible to modularize systemic properties of a program such as synchronization, error handling, security, persistence, resource sharing, distribution, memory management, replication, and the like. Rather than staying well localized within a class, these concerns tend to crosscut the system's class and module structure. An "aspect" is a special kind of module that implements one of these specific properties of a program. As that property varies, the effects "ripple" through the entire program automatically. Like object-oriented programming, AOP works by allowing the programmer to cleanly express certain structural properties of the program and then take advantage of that structure in powerful ways. In object-oriented programming, the structure is rooted in notions of hierarchies, inheritance, and specialization. In AOP, the structure is rooted in notions of crosscutting. As an example, an AOP program might define "the public methods of a given package" as a crosscutting structure and then say that all of those methods should do a certain kind of error handling. This would be coded in a few lines of well-modularized code. AOP is an architectural approach because it provides a means of separating concerns that would otherwise affect a multitude of components that were constructed to separate a different, orthogonal set of concerns. The AOP work at Xerox PARC is described on its Web page [Xerox 99].

Product builder's guide: A product line architecture is instantiated as a product architecture each time a product is turned out. The product architecture may be the same as the product line architecture, or it may be the result of preplanned tailoring or binding. For example, install *four* servers, *52* client workstations, and *two* databases; configure the network routers accordingly; use the *high-speed, low-resolution version* of the graphics component, and turn encryption in the message generator *off*. The steps that product builders must take to create this product architecture constitute its attached process and should of course be documented. However, many organizations collect the attached processes for requirements engineering, architecture definition, component development, software integration, and testing into a single operational document that is the "how-to" manual for product builders. One organization we have worked with adopted the following organization for its product builder's guide:

- **Introduction:** goals and purpose of the document; intended audience; basic common assumptions; applicable development standards.

- **Sources of other information:** references to documents containing the product line architecture definition (which is maintained separately from the product builder's guide because its stakeholders include more than product builders) and associated information such as terms and terminology, the architecture's goals, architecture training materials, development standards, and configuration management procedures and policies.
- **Basic concepts:** What is a variation point? What mechanisms for realizing variation points have been used in this architecture? What is the relation between the product line architecture and the architecture for a particular product? What is an architecture layer, and how is the concept used? What is a service (in this case, the basic unit of reuse provided by the architecture)? And so forth.
- **Service component catalog:** This organization's product line architecture contained some preintegrated units of functionality called service components that product builders could utilize to construct products. This section cataloged those service components, defined their interfaces, and explained how service components related to each other.
- **Building an application:** This section gave code templates and examples for building applications. It proceeded incrementally. First, how do you build the most trivial application possible, one that perhaps does nothing but start a process running? Then, how do you build the most trivial application that actually does something observable, the domain's equivalent of the ubiquitous "Hello, world!" program that was the first computer program many of us ever wrote? Then, how do you build an application that contains the functions common to many of the products in the product line? Then, how do you build an application that runs on a single processor? Distributed across multiple processors? And so forth. The examples showed how to instantiate the architecture's variation points at each step along the way.
- **Performance engineering:** This section presented guidelines on how to build a product when performance was a concern.

Mechanisms for achieving variability in a product line architecture (1): Mikael Svahnberg and Jan Bosch have crisply staked out the landscape of architecture-based support for variability in product lines [Svahnberg 00]. Their list includes the following mechanisms:

- **Inheritance:** used when a method needs to be implemented differently (or perhaps extended) for each product in the product line.
- **Extensions and extension points:** used when parts of a component can be augmented with additional behavior or functionality.
- **Parameterization:** used when a component's behavior can be characterized abstractly by a placeholder that is then defined at build time. Macros and templates are forms of parameterization.

- **Configuration and module interconnection languages:** used to define the build-time structure of a system, including selecting (or deselecting) whole components.
- **Generation:** used when there is a higher-level language that can be used to define a component's desired properties.
- **Compile-time selection of different implementations:** The variable *#ifdefs* can be used when variability in a component can be realized by choosing different implementations.

Code-based mechanisms used to achieve variability within individual components will be discussed further in the "Component Development" practice area (Section 4.3).

Mechanisms for achieving variability in a product line architecture (2): Philips Research Laboratories uses *service component frameworks* to achieve diversity in their product line of medical imaging systems [Wijnstra 00]. Goals for that family include extensibility over time and support for different functions at the same time. A framework is a skeleton of an application that can be customized to yield a product. White-box frameworks rely heavily on inheritance and dynamic binding; knowledge of the framework's internals is necessary in order to use it. Black-box frameworks define interfaces for components that can be plugged in via composition tools. A service component framework is a type of black-box framework, supporting a variable number of plug-in components. Each plug-in is a container for one or more services, which provide the necessary functionality. All services support the framework's defined interface but exhibit different behaviors. Clients use the functionality provided by the component framework and the services as a whole; the assemblage is itself a component in the products' architecture. Conversely, units in the product line architecture may consist of or contain one or more component frameworks.

Planning for architectural variation: Nokia has used a "requirements definition hierarchy" as a way to understand what variations are important to particular products [Kuusela 00]. The hierarchy consists of design objectives (goals or wishes) and design decisions (solutions adopted to meet the corresponding goals). For example, a design objective might be "System shall be highly reliable." One way to meet that objective is to decree that the "System shall be a duplicated system." This in turn might mean that the "System shall have duplicated hardware" and/or the "System duplicates communication links." Another way to meet the reliability objective is to decree that the "System shall have self-diagnostic capacity," which can be met in several ways. Each box in the hierarchy is tagged with a vector, each element of which corresponds to a product in the product line. The value of an element is the priority or importance given to that objective, or the endorsement of that design decision, by the particular product. For example, if an overall goal for a product line is high reliability, being a duplicated system might be very important to Product 2 and Product 3, but not at all important to Product 1, which will be a single-chip system.

The requirements definition hierarchy is a tool that the architect can use as a bridge between the product line's scope (see the "Scoping" practice area, Section 5.5), which will tell what variations the architecture will have to support and the architecture, which may support the variation in a number of ways. It is also useful to see how widely used a new feature or variation will be: should it be incorporated into the architecture for many products to use, or is it a one-of-a-kind requirement best left to the devices of the product that spawned it? The hierarchy is a way for the architect to capture the rationale behind such decisions.

4.1.5 Practice Risks

The biggest risk associated with this practice area is failing to have a suitable product line architecture. This will result in

- components that do not fit together or interact properly
- products that do not meet their behavioral, performance, or other quality goals
- products that should be in scope, but which are unable to be produced from the core assets at hand
- a tedious and ad hoc product-building process

These in turn will lead to extensive and time-consuming rework, poor system quality, and inability to realize the product line's full benefits. If product teams do not find the architecture to be suitable for their products and easy to understand and use, they may bypass it, resulting in the eventual degradation of the entire product line concept.

Unsuitable architectures could result from

- **Lack of a skilled architect:** Although maturing rapidly, architecture definition is still more dependent on an experienced architect than it is on a well-defined set of rules, practices, and patterns. The practice is even less well defined for product lines. In the five workshops that have been held by the SEI on commercial product line practices, there has been general agreement that architecture is an important factor, but it is not often mentioned as a difficult problem. When questioned about this apparent anomaly, the participants responded that architecture is not a problem because they employ high-caliber architects that make the process look straightforward, if not easy. While this may be true in leading-edge organizations, there is little evidence that architecture definition is a solved problem in the wider community. A product line architect must be skilled in current and promising technologies, the nuances of the application domains at hand, modern design techniques and tool support, and professional practices such as the use of patterns and styles. The architect must know all of the sources of requirements and constraints on the architecture, including those (such as organizational goals) not traditionally specified in a requirements specification (see "Other Voices: Requirements They Didn't Teach You in Software Engineering Class" sidebar).

- **Lack of sound input:** No architecture can be successful if the information it depends on is not reliable. The product line scope and production strategy must be well defined and stable. The requirements for products must be articulated clearly and completely enough so that architectural decisions may be reliably based on them. Forthcoming technology, which the architecture must be poised to accept, must be forecast accurately. Relevant domains must be understood so that their architectural lessons are learned. Of course, real-world exigencies often preclude complete requirements specifications, crisp scope definitions, and clairvoyant technology forecasts. To the extent to which the architect is compelled to make guesses, the architecture poses a risk. In any case, the architect is obligated to document the assumptions he or she made about the information that was lacking.
- **Poor communication:** The best architecture is useless if it is documented and communicated in ways that its consumers—the product builders—cannot understand. An architecture whose documentation is chronically out of date is effectively the same as an undocumented architecture. Hand-in-hand with the architect's responsibility to craft a suitable architecture is the obligation to document it and keep its definition current. There must be clear and open two-way communication channels between the architect and the organizations using the architecture. Mentoring product developers until they are sufficiently familiar with the architecture and product line operation is a good way to ameliorate this risk. The two-way communication will benefit both sides.
- **Lack of supportive management and culture:** To be successful, there must be a culture of architecture-based development that is institutionalized in the developing organizations and their management and marketing organizations. Management that fails to create and sustain this culture will create risks for this practice. There must be management support for the product line architecture, especially if the architecture group is separate from the product development group. Failing this, product groups may "go renegade" and make unilateral changes to the architecture or decline to use it at all, when they turn out their systems. There are additional risks if management does not support the strong integration of system and software engineering. The exploration and definition of software architecture cannot take place in a vacuum separate from system architecture.

- **Poor tools:** There are precious few tools for this practice area, and the tools that exist can often be counterproductive rather than helpful. There are, of course, tools that help document, design, and evolve an architecture, but practically none that help with designing, specifying, or exercising an architecture's variability mechanisms—a fundamental part of a product line architecture. Documentation tools, especially, are lacking, and documentation remains largely an ad hoc process. Tools to test the compliance of products to an architecture are virtually nonexistent.
- **Poor timing:** Declaring an architecture ready for production too early leads to stagnation, while declaring it too late may allow unwanted variation. Discretion is needed when deciding when and how firmly to freeze the architecture. The time required to develop the architecture fully also may be too long. If product development is curtailed while the product line architecture is being completed, developers may lose patience, management may lose resolve, and salespeople may lose market share.

Unsuitable architectures are characterized by

- **Inappropriate parameterization:** Parameterization is a valuable tool for building variation points into the architecture, but beware: overparameterization can make a system unwieldy and difficult to understand. (See "A Tool for Software Product Line Production" sidebar.) Underparameterization can eliminate some of the necessary customizations of the system. The early binding of parameters can also preclude easy customization, while the late binding of parameters can lead to inefficiencies.
- **Inadequate specifications:** Components may not integrate properly if their specifications are limited to static descriptions of individual services. This risk is very likely to occur even in a product line effort because current component specification technologies do not have notations for expressing temporal relationships or interactions. This risk can be mitigated by supplementing standard contractual notations with techniques, such as interval temporal logic and protocol specifications that specify explicitly how components that implement interacting interfaces must behave.
- **Decomposition flaws:** A component may not provide the functionality needed to implement the system correctly if there is not an appropriate decomposition of the required system functionality. This risk ought to be less likely to occur in a product line effort because there should be a strong emphasis on the definition and evaluation of the product line architecture. The risk is mitigated by a robust architectural definition that includes the definition of interfaces. These interfaces represent the division of functional responsibilities. This decomposition should be checked for completeness, correctness, and consistency. (See the "Testing" practice area, Section 4.8.)

- **Wrong level of specificity:** A component may not be reusable if the component is too specific or too general. If the component is made so general that it encompasses multiple domain concepts, the component may require complex configuration information to make it fit a specific situation and therefore be inherently difficult to reuse. The excessive generality may also tax performance and other quality attributes to an unacceptable point. If the component is too specific, there will be few situations in which it is the correct choice. Component specification and design should be analyzed carefully to fend off the possible development of components that are at the wrong level of specificity for a reuse environment.
- **Excessive intercomponent dependencies:** A component may become less reusable if it has excessive dependencies on other components. The analyses described in the "Architecture Evaluation" and "Understanding Relevant Domains" practice areas (Sections 4.2 and 4.9) are mitigation strategies for this risk. The practices they entail result in a clearer delineation of the division of responsibility between components.

4.1.6 For Further Reading

Software architecture has become a software engineering field of study in its own right. As of this writing, there are three books that could be considered foundational for their introduction and exposition of the relevant concepts. *Software Architecture in Practice* by Bass et al. [Bass98a] emphasizes architecture's role in system development and provides several case studies of architectures used to solve real problems. One is an architecture for the CelsiusTech ship systems product line. It also includes an extensive discussion of architectural views. *Software Architecture: Perspectives on an Emerging Discipline* by Mary Shaw and David Garlan [Shaw 96] provides an excellent treatment of architectural styles and their ramifications for system building. *Applied Software Architecture* by Hofmeister et al. [Hofmeister 00] emphasizes views and structures and provides a solid treatment of building a system from an architecture and its views.

Jan Bosch's *Design and Use of Software Architectures* [Bosch 00a] brings a dedicated product line focus to the mix and is required reading for the product line practitioner.

For treatments of software architecture from a strictly object-oriented point of view, several resources are available. Booch's *Object-Oriented Analysis and Design with Applications* [Booch 94] is a good start. Jacobson et al.'s *Software Reuse: Architecture, Process, and Organization for Business Success* [Jacobson 97] devotes an entire section to architectural styles for object-oriented systems designed with strategic reuse in mind. Kruchten's *The Rational Unified Process: An Introduction* [Kruchten 98] is a good reference for the preeminent development process in the object-oriented realm. Buschmann et al.'s *Pattern-Oriented Software Architecture: A System of Patterns* [Buschmann 96] raises the design pattern phenomenon to the arena of software architecture and is a good staple of any architect's toolbox. Smith and Williams's *Software Performance Engineering for Object-Oriented Systems* [Smith 01] contains three chapters of principles and guidance for architecting systems (object-oriented or not) in which performance is a concern.

While architectural styles and design patterns arm an architect with solution strategies, at least as important is a deep understanding of the problem that is being attacked. Michael Jackson's *Problem Frames and Methods: Structuring and Analyzing Software Development Problems* [Jackson 00] classifies, analyzes, and structures a set of recurring software development problems, organized according to how the software will interact with the outside world.

An architecture is only as good as its ability to be communicated, which brings us to architecture documentation. Although Rational's Unified Modeling Language has been criticized for its inability to represent architectural constructs straightforwardly, it is the de facto standard for languages to express design. Rational's Web site (http://www.rational.com/uml) is the starting point, and there is no shortage of UML books available.

Finally, the SEI's software architecture Web page [SEI ATA] provides a wide variety of software architecture resources and links.

4.1.7 Discussion Questions

1. What distinguishes an architecture for a software product line from an architecture built for a system designed to be easily modified?
2. What design patterns or styles do you believe might be especially relevant to a product line architecture? For example, what kind of quality attributes important to a software product line are imparted by a layered software architecture? How about a client-server architecture?
3. What qualities do you believe are important for a product line software architect to possess? Why? How high on the list of qualities did you put good communication skills? Why?
4. Architecture description languages (ADLs) are popular research topics. They let an architect specify, evolve, and evaluate a software architecture (often by simulating it). What features would you want an ADL to have if you wanted to use it to represent an architecture for a software product line? Which of those features does UML offer, and which does it lack?
5. Must all products in a software product line share the same architecture? If the products have different architectures but share other core assets, is that or is that not a product line?

4.2 Architecture Evaluation

"Marry your architecture in haste, and you can repent in leisure." So admonished Barry Boehm in a recent lecture [Boehm 00]. The architecture of a system represents a coherent set of the earliest design decisions, which are the most difficult to change and the most critical to get right. It is the first design artifact that addresses the quality goals of the system such as security, reliability, usability, modifiability, and real-time performance. The architecture describes the system structure and serves as a common communication vehicle among the system stakeholders: developers, managers, maintainers, users, customers, testers, marketers, and anyone else who has a vested interest in the development or use of the system.

With the advent of repeatable, cost-effective architecture evaluation methods, it is now feasible to make architecture evaluation a standard part of the development cycle. And because so much rides on the architecture and because it is available early in the life cycle, it makes utmost sense to evaluate the architecture early when there is still time for midcourse correction. In any nontrivial project, there are competing requirements and architectural decisions that must be made to resolve them. It is best to air and evaluate those decisions and to document the basis for making them before the decisions are cast into code.

Architecture evaluation is a form of artifact validation, just as software testing is a form of code validation. In the "Testing" practice area (Section 4.8), we will discuss validation of artifacts in general—and, in fact, prescribe a validation step for all of the product line's assets—but the architecture for the product line is so foundational that we give its validation its own special practice area.

The evaluation can be done at a variety of stages during the design process. For example, the evaluation can occur when the architecture is still on the drawing board and candidate structures are being weighed. The evaluation can also be done later, after preliminary architectural decisions have been made but before detailed design has begun. The evaluation can even be done after the entire system has been built (such as in the case of a reengineering or mining operation). The outputs will depend on the stage at which the evaluation is performed. Enough design decisions must have been made so that the achievement of the requirements and quality-attribute goals can be analyzed. The more architectural decisions that have been made, the more precise the evaluation can be. On the other hand, the more decisions that have been made, the more difficult it is to change them.

An organization's business goals for a system lead to particular behavioral requirements and quality-attribute goals. The architecture is evaluated with respect to those requirements and goals. Therefore, before an evaluation can proceed, the behavioral and quality-attribute goals against which an architecture is to be evaluated must be made explicit. These quality-attribute goals support the business goals. For example, if a business goal is that the system should be long-lived, modifiability becomes an important quality-attribute goal.

Quality-attribute goals, by themselves, are not definitive enough either for design or for evaluation. They must be made more concrete. Using modifiability as an example, if a product line can be adapted easily to have different user interfaces but is dependent on a particular operating system, is it modifiable? The answer is yes with respect to the user interface, but no with respect to porting to a new operating system. Whether this architecture is suitably modifiable or not depends on what modifications to the product line are expected over its lifetime. That is, the abstract quality goal of modifiability must be made concrete: modifiable with respect to what kinds of changes, exactly? The same is true for other attributes. The evaluation method that you use must include a way to concretize the quality and behavioral goals for the architecture being evaluated.

4.2.1 Aspects Peculiar to Product Lines

In a product line, architecture assumes a dual role. There is the architecture for the product line as a whole, and there are architectures for each of the products. The latter are produced from the former by exercising the built-in variation mechanisms to achieve instances. Both should be evaluated. The product line architecture should be evaluated for its robustness and generality, to make sure it can serve as the basis for products in the product line's envisioned scope. Instance architectures should be evaluated to make sure they meet the specific behavioral and quality requirements of the product at hand. In practice, the extent to which these two evaluations are separate exercises depends on the extent to which the product architecture differs from the product line architecture. Evaluating both the product line and product architectures is a prudent, low-cost, risk-reduction method.

Some of the business goals will be related to the fact that the architecture is for a product line. For example, the architecture will almost certainly have built-in variation points that can be exercised to derive specific products having different attributes. The evaluation will have to focus on the variation points to make sure they are appropriate, offer sufficient flexibility to cover the product line's intended scope, can be exercised in a way that lets products be built quickly, and do not impose unacceptable runtime performance costs. Also, different products in the product line may have different quality-attribute requirements, and the architecture will have to be evaluated for its ability to provide all required combinations.

Often, some of the hardware and other performance-affecting factors for a product line architecture are unknown to begin with. Thus, the evaluation of the product line architecture must establish bounds on the performance that the architecture is able to achieve, assuming bounds on hardware and other variables. Use the evaluation to identify potential contention problems and to put in place the policies and strategies to resolve contention. The evaluation of a particular instance of the product line architecture can verify whether the hardware and performance decisions that have been made are compatible with the goals of that instance.

4.2.2 Application to Core Asset Development

Clearly, an evaluation should be applied to the core asset that is the product line architecture. As the requirements, business goals, and architecture all evolve over time, there should be periodic (although not frequent) mini-evaluations that discover whether the architecture and business goals are still well matched. Some evaluation methods produce a report that summarizes what the articulated, prioritized quality-attribute goals are for the architecture and how the architecture satisfies them. Such a report makes an excellent rationale record, which can then accompany the architecture throughout its evolution as a core asset in its own right.

An architecture evaluation can also be performed on components that are candidates to be acquired as core assets, as well as on components developed in-house. In either case, the evaluation proceeds with technical personnel from the organization that developed the potential acquisition. An architecture evaluation is not possible for "black-box" architecture acquisitions where the architecture is not visible. The quality-attribute goals to be used for the evaluation will include how well the potential acquisition will (1) support the quality goals for the product line and (2) evolve over time to support the intended evolution of the products in the product line.

4.2.3 Application to Product Development

An architecture evaluation should be performed on an instance or variation of the architecture that will be used to build one or more of the products in the product line. The extent to which this is a separate, dedicated evaluation depends on the extent to which the product architecture differs in quality-attribute-affecting ways from the product line architecture. If it doesn't, then these product architecture evaluations can be abbreviated because many of the issues that would normally be raised in a single product evaluation will have been dealt with in the evaluation of the product line architecture. In fact, just as the product architecture is a variation of the product line architecture, the product architecture evaluation is a variation of the product line architecture evaluation. Therefore, depending on the architecture evaluation method used, the evaluation artifacts (scenarios, checklists, and so on) will certainly have reuse potential, and you should create them with that in mind. Document a short attached process for the architecture evaluation of the product line or product architectures. This process description would include the method used, what artifacts can be reused, and what issues to focus on. The results of architecture evaluation for product architectures often provide useful feedback to the architect(s) of the product line architecture and fuel improvements in the product line architecture.

Finally, when a new product that falls outside the scope of the original product line (for which the architecture was presumably evaluated) is proposed, the product line architecture can be reevaluated to see if it will suffice for this new product. If it will, the product line's scope is expanded to include the new product. If it will not, the evaluation can be used to determine how the architecture would have to be modified to accommodate the new product.

4.2.4 Specific Practices

Several different architecture evaluation techniques exist and can be modified to serve in a product line context. Techniques can be categorized broadly as either questioning techniques (those using questionnaires, checklists, scenarios, and the like as the basis for architectural investigation) or measuring techniques (such as simulation or experimentation with a running system) [Abowd 96]. A well-versed architect should have a spectrum of techniques in his or her evaluation kit. For full-fledged architectures, software performance engineering or a method such as the ATAM or the SAAM is indispensable. For less fully worked out designs, a technique such as Active Reviews for Intermediate Designs (ARID) is handy. For validating architectural (and other design) specifications, active design reviews (ADRs) are the approach of choice. A bibliography of software architecture analysis, available from the journal *Software Engineering Notes* [Zhao 99], provides more alternatives.

ATAM: The Architecture Trade-off Analysis Method (ATAM) is a scenario-based architecture evaluation method that focuses on a system's quality goals. The input to the ATAM consists of an architecture, the business goals of a system or product line, and the perspectives of stakeholders involved with that system or product line. The ATAM achieves its evaluation of an architecture by utilizing an understanding of the architectural approach that is used to achieve particular quality goals and the implications of that approach. The ATAM utilizes stakeholder perspectives to derive a collection of scenarios giving specific instances for usage, performance requirements, various types of failures, possible threats, and a set of likely modifications. The scenarios are used for the evaluators to understand the inherent architectural risks, sensitivity points to particular quality attributes, and trade-offs among quality attributes. Of particular interest to ATAM-based evaluations of product line architectures are the sensitivity points to extensibility (or variation) and the trade-offs of extensibility with other quality-attribute goals (usually real-time performance, security, and reliability).

The output of an ATAM evaluation includes

- the collection of scenarios that represent the stakeholders' highest-priority expression of usage and quality-attribute goals for the system and its architecture.
- a utility tree that assigns specific scenarios to a location in the "space" of quality attributes that apply to the system(s) whose architecture is being evaluated.

- specific analysis results, including the explicit identification of sensitivity points, trade-offs, and other architectural decisions that impact desired quality attributes either positively or problematically. The latter constitute areas of risk.

The ATAM can be used to evaluate both product line and product architectures at various stages of development (conceptual, before code, during development, or after deployment). An ATAM evaluation usually requires three full days plus some preparation and preliminary investigation time. The ATAM is described fully by Clements et al. [Clements 01] and on the World Wide Web [SEI ATA].

SAAM: The Software Architecture Analysis Method (SAAM) is a predecessor of the ATAM that has also been used to evaluate architectures for product lines. The SAAM also elicits stakeholder input to identify explicitly the quality goals that the architecture is intended to satisfy. Unlike the ATAM, which operates around a broad collection of quality attributes, the SAAM concentrates on attributes of modifiability, variability (suitability for a product line), and achievement of functionality. A SAAM exercise typically requires two full days. The SAAM is defined more completely on the World Wide Web [SEI ATA], by Bass et al. [Bass 98a], and by Clements et al. [Clements 01].

SPE: Software performance engineering (SPE) is a method for making sure that a design will allow a system to meet its performance goals before it has been built. SPE involves articulating the specific performance goals, building coarse-grained models to get early ideas about whether the design is problematic, and refining those models along well-defined lines as more information becomes available. Conceptually, SPE resembles the ATAM, in which the singular quality of interest is performance. Connie Smith has written both the definitive resource for SPE and its concise method description [Smith 90, Smith 99].

ARID: Active Reviews for Intermediate Designs (ARID) [Clements 00a] is a hybrid design review method that combines the active design review philosophy of ADRs with the scenario-based analysis of the ATAM and SAAM. ARID was created to evaluate partial (subsystem, for example) designs in their early or conceptual phases, before they are fully documented. While such designs are architectural in nature, they are not complete architectures. ARID works by assembling stakeholders for the design, having them adopt a set of scenarios that express a set of meaningful ways they would want to use the design, and then having them write code or pseudocode that uses the design to carry out each scenario. This will wring out any conceptual flaws early, plus give stakeholders an early familiarity with the design until it is completely documented. An ARID exercise takes from one to two days.

Active Design Reviews: An active design review (ADR) [Parnas 85] is a technique that can be used to evaluate an architecture still under construction. ADRs are particularly well suited for evaluating the designs of single components or small groups of components before the entire architecture has been solidified. The principle behind ADRs is that stakeholders are engaged to review the documentation that describes the interface facilities provided by a component, but the stakeholders are asked to complete exercises that compel them to actually use the documentation. For example, each reviewer may be asked to write a short code segment that performs some useful task using the component's interface facilities, or each reviewer may be asked to verify that essential information about each interface operation is present and well specified. ADRs are contrasted with unstructured reviews in which people are asked to read a document, attend a long meeting, and comment on whatever they wish. In an ADR, there is no meeting; reviewers are debriefed (or walked through their assignments) individually or in small informal groups. The key is to avoid asking questions to which a reviewer can blithely and without much thought answer "yes" or "no." An ADR for a medium-sized component usually takes a full day from each of about a half dozen reviewers who can work in parallel. The debriefing takes about an hour for each session.

4.2.5 Practice Risks

The major risk associated with this practice is failing to perform an effective architecture evaluation that will prevent unsuitable architectures from being allowed to pollute a software product line effort. Architecture evaluation is the safety valve for product line architectures, and an ineffective evaluation will lead to the same consequences as an unsuitable architecture; these were listed in the "Architecture Definition" practice area (Section 4.1).

An ineffective evaluation can result from the following:

- **Wrong people involved in the evaluation:** A cardinal rule for architecture evaluations is to have the right people participate in the exercise. The architect(s) must be involved, of course, but so must the architecture's stakeholders. An architecture must respond to the requirements and goals of a broad community. Their stakes must be represented in the evaluation, because their views will surface eventually; however, eventually may be too late to address their needs economically. Stakeholders should include representatives from the development team, the customer community, support groups, tools groups, and domain experts.
- **Wrong time in the life cycle:** If the review is too early, not enough decisions have been made, so there isn't anything to evaluate. If the review is too late, little can be changed as a result of the evaluation.

- **No time for evaluation:** The major reason that most organizations don't do an architecture evaluation or don't do a thorough evaluation is a perceived lack of time. But omitting an architecture evaluation because of time pressures is no more defensible than omitting software testing. If time is not planned for the evaluation, the people who need to be involved will not be able to give it their attention, the evaluation will not be conducted effectively, and the results will be superficial at best.
- **Wrong interpretation of evaluation:** The results of any architecture evaluation should not be seen as a complete enumeration of all of the risks in the development. An architecture evaluation process may fail to uncover some second-order problems. Process deficiencies, resource inadequacies, personnel issues, and downstream implementation problems are all risks unlikely to be exposed by an architecture evaluation. (However, the practice areas on risk management offer more help in this regard.) Above all else, remember that the fidelity of the results is a function of the quality of the participants.
- **Failure to reevaluate:** As the architecture inevitably evolves, or the criteria for its suitability inevitably evolve, it should be reevaluated (perhaps using a lightweight version of the original evaluation) periodically to give the organization confidence that they are on the right track.

4.2.6 For Further Reading

Clements et al.'s *Evaluating Software Architectures: Methods and Case Studies* [Clements 01] is a primer on software architecture evaluation, containing a detailed process model and practical guidance for applying the ATAM and comparing it with other evaluation methods. The SAAM and ARID methods are also treated in depth. Bass et al.'s *Software Architecture in Practice* [Bass 98a] devotes two chapters to software architecture evaluation: Chapter 9 describes the SAAM, while Chapter 10 discusses best industrial evaluation practices.

Evaluating an architecture for its ability to deliver satisfactory performance is at least as important in product lines as in single-system developments. Connie Smith's *Performance Engineering of Software Systems* [Smith 90] remains the definitive treatment of that subject. It should be accompanied, and not replaced, by its superb sequel: Smith and Williams's *Software Performance Engineering for Object-Oriented Systems* [Smith 01].

For validating architectural (and other design) specifications, active design reviews (ADRs) are essential. The original description by Parnas and Weiss [Parnas 85] remains the most comprehensive.

The home page for the Software Engineering Institute's Architecture Tradeoff Analysis initiative contains publications about the ATAM and the SAAM, as well as other software architecture topics [SEI ATA]. Finally, Jianjun Zhao has compiled a bibliography on software architecture analysis [Zhao 99]. His Web site, where the list is kept up-to-date, is cited on the SEI's ATA page.

4.2.7 Discussion Questions

1. For a software product line in your organization, who are or would be the stakeholders? What are their roles? What would they expect from the product line architecture? What concerns would you expect them to raise at an evaluation? Which ones would you expect to raise conflicting goals?
2. Think about (or hypothesize) a software product line. What are some of the more important quality attributes its architecture should enable? What means might the architecture use to achieve them?
3. Craft about a dozen scenarios that precisely express the quality attributes of security, performance, and reliability (respectively) for a system or some systems in your organization.
4. Craft about a dozen scenarios that precisely express the quality attribute of modifiability for a product line architecture. Think about different flavors of modifiability—portability, maintainability, extensibility, and variability—and how each of these comes into play in a software product line.
5. Argue why or why not this practice area should have been written as part of (a) the "Testing" practice area (Section 4.8) and (b) the "Technical Risk Management" practice area (Section 5.7).

4.3 Component Development

One of the tasks of the software architect is to produce the list of components that will populate the architecture. This list gives the development, mining, and acquisition teams their marching orders for supplying the parts that the software system will comprise. The term "component" is about as generic as the term "object"; definitions for each term abound. Simply stated, components are the units of software that go together to form whole systems (products), as dictated by the software architecture for the products. Szyperski offers a more precise definition that applies well [Szyperski 98]:

> *A software component is a unit of composition with contractually specified interfaces and explicit context dependencies only. A software component can be deployed independently and is subject to composition by third parties.*

By component development, we mean the production of components that implement specific functionality within the context of a software architecture. The functionality is encapsulated and packaged and then integrated with other components using an interconnection method.

Software components trace their heritage back to the subroutine, which was the first unit of software reuse. Programmers discovered they could invoke a previously written segment of code and have access to its functionality while being blissfully unconcerned with its implementation, development history, storage management, and so forth. Soon, very few people ever again had to worry about how to code, say, a numerically stable double-precision cosine algorithm. Besides saving time, this practice elevated our thinking: we could think "cosine" and not about storage registers and overflowing multiplications. It also elevated our languages: sophisticated subroutines were indistinguishable from primitive, atomic statements in the programming language.

What we now call component-based software development flows in an unbroken line from these early beginnings. Modern components are much larger, are much more sophisticated, carry us much higher into domain-specific application realms, and have more complex interaction mechanisms than subroutine invocation, but the concepts and the reasons we embrace the concepts remain the same. In the same way that early subroutines liberated the programmer from thinking about details, component-based software development shifts the emphasis from *programming software* to *composing software systems*. Implementation has given way to integration as the focus. At its foundation is the assumption that there is sufficient commonality in many large software systems to justify developing reusable components to exploit and satisfy that commonality. Today, we look for components that provide large collections of related functionality all at once (instead of a cosine routine, think *Mathematica*) and whose interconnections with each other are loose and flexible. If we have control over the decomposition into components and the interfaces of each, then the granularity and interconnection is determined by our system's software architecture. If the components are built externally, then their granularity and interfaces are imposed on us, and they affect our software architecture.[1]

The practice area of component development is concerned with the former case and how to build the components so that the instructions given to us in the architecture are carried out. (One type of instruction carried out by the architecture is what other parts of a system a component is allowed to use. A layered view of an architecture, for example, is highly concerned with this. Allowed-to-use information is not part of the component's interface or of its functionality, but it is nevertheless architectural and must be honored by the implementation.) Very complex components may have substructure of their own and be implemented partially by employing smaller components, either built or acquired.

---

1. The nature of a component differs from the source of a component. As we will see in the "Mining Existing Assets" practice area (Section 4.5), components can be recovered from existing legacy software. This practice area is about developing a component in-house. Subsequent practice areas will cover purchasing COTS components from the open market and contracting to have components built by outside sources. Finally, a technical management practice area will cover making the economic decision about whether to make, buy, mine, or commission the components that populate a product line's asset base and individual products.

4.3.1 Aspects Peculiar to Product Lines

For the purposes of product lines, components are the units of software that go together to form whole systems (products), as dictated by the product line architecture for the products and the product line as a whole. If we appeal to the Szyperski definition of components given above, "deployed independently" may simply mean installed into a product line's core asset base where they are made available for use in one or more products. The "third parties" are the product builders, who compose the component with others to build systems. The contractually specified interfaces are paramount, as they are in any software development paradigm with software architecture at its foundation.

The component development portion of a product line development effort focuses on providing the operational software that is needed by the products and that is to be developed in-house. The resultant components either are included in the core asset base and hence used in multiple products in the product line or are product-specific components. Components that are included in the core asset base must support the flexibility needed to satisfy the variation points specified in the product line architecture and/or the product line requirements. Needed functionality is defined in the context of the product line architecture. The architecture also defines those places at which variation is needed.

The singular aspect of component development that is peculiar to product lines is providing required variability in the developed components via the mechanisms that are described in the specific practices for this practice area.

4.3.2 Application to Core Asset Development

If a developed component is to be a core component, it must have attached with it an associated process that explains how any built-in component-level variability can be exercised in order to produce an instantiated version for a particular product. Developed components and their related artifacts (interface specifications, attached processes for instantiating built-in variability, test support, and so on) constitute a major portion of the product line's core asset base. Hand in hand with the software architecture that mandated them into existence, the core components form the conceptual basis for building products. Consequently, component development, as described above, is a large portion of the activity on the core asset development side of product line operations.

4.3.3 Application to Product Development

If a developed component is not to be part of the core asset base, this suggests that it is specific to a particular product and therefore probably does not have much variability built into it. While the development task must obey the architecture as strictly as it must for core components, noncore development is likely to be simpler. Nevertheless, developers of noncore components would be wise to look for places where variability could be installed in the future, should the component in question ever turn out to be useful in a group of products.

Components for a product are (1) used directly from the core asset base, (2) used directly after binding the built-in variabilities, (3) used after modification or adaptation, or (4) developed anew. Because the first two cases are pro forma, we will discuss the last two.

Adapting components: Components that are being used in a context other than the one for which they were originally developed often do not exactly fit their assigned roles. There are a couple of techniques for accommodating these differences. The adapter design pattern [Gamma 95] imposes an intermediary between two components. The adapter can compensate for mismatches in number or types of parameters within a service signature, provide synchronization in a multithreaded interaction, and adjust for many other types of incompatibilities. Scripting languages can often be used to implement the adapter.

The second technique is to modify the component to fit its new environment. This may be impossible if the source code is not available. Even if it is possible, it is usually a bad idea. Cloning an existing component creates a new asset that must be managed and creates a dependency that cannot be expressed explicitly. It can vary independently of its parent component, making maintenance of both pieces a difficult task. Object-oriented notations provide a semantic device to express this type of relationship by defining the dependent class in terms of an extension of the original class. Although similar devices do not exist at the component level, a new component may be implemented by deriving objects from those that implement the original component.

Developing new components: New development should occur only after a thorough search has been made of existing assets. In some organizations, the product team may have to "contract" with a component development organization to build the needed component. If it is built in the product organization, there should be product line standards to follow for the creation of the assets supporting the component.

Whether a product component is adapted or built from scratch, it should be reviewed ultimately for "promotion" to the core asset base (and, it fact, should be developed with that in mind). To help with that review, robustness analysis [Jacobson 97] can be applied to determine how flexible the product is with respect to future changes in requirements. By examining change cases (use cases that are not yet requirements), the team identifies points in the system that would need changes in order to support the new requirements. This provides a feedback loop to the component developers. Specifications for new components and modifications to existing ones are the outputs of this analysis.

4.3.4 Specific Practices

All of the specific practices in this practice area deal with component-level variability mechanisms.

Variability mechanisms (1): Jacobson et al. discuss the mechanisms for supporting variability in components, which are shown in Table 4.1 [Jacobson 97]. Each mechanism provides a different type of variability. The variation of functionality happens at different times depending on the type. Some of these variation types are included in the specification implicitly. For example, when a parameter is used, the specification is taken to include the specific type of component mentioned in the contract or any component that is a specialization of that component. In the template instantiation example in Table 4.1, the parameter to the template is Container, which permits variation implicitly via the inheritance style. The Container parameter can be replaced by any of its subclasses, such as Set or Bag.

Variability can also be shown explicitly, but that is more cumbersome than the implicit approach. The javadoc tool in Java lists all of the known subclasses of the class whose documentation is being created. This requires that the documentation for the parent class be regenerated every time a new subclass is declared. Any explicit listing of variants will require this type of maintenance. The variations may also be captured in an activity diagram that maps alternative paths.

One aspect of variability that is important in a product line effort is whether the variants must be identified at the time of product line architecture definition or can be discovered during the individual product's architectural phase. Inheritance allows for a variant to be created without the existing component having knowledge of the new variant. Likewise, template instantiation allows for the discovery of new parameter values after the template is designed; however, the new parameter must satisfy the assumptions of the template, which may not be stated explicitly in the interface of the formal parameter. In most cases, configuration further constrains the variation to a fixed set of attributes and a fixed set of values for each attribute.

Variability mechanisms (2): Anastasopoulos and Gacek expound a somewhat different set of variability options [Anastasopoulos 00]. Their list includes

- Aggregation/delegation, an object-oriented technique in which functionality of an object is extended by delegating work it cannot normally perform to an object that can. The delegating object must have a repertoire of candidates (and their methods) known to it and assumes a role resembling that of a service broker.
- Inheritance, which assigns base functionality to a superclass and extended or specialized functionality to a subclass. Complex forms include dynamic and multiple inheritance, in addition to the more standard varieties.

Table 4.1 Types of Variation [Jacobson 97]

Mechanism	Time of Specialization	Type of Variability
Inheritance	At class definition time	Specialization is done by modifying or adding to existing definitions. Example: LongDistanceCall inherits from PhoneCall.
Extension	At requirements time	One use of a system can be defined by adding to the definition of another use. Example: WithdrawalTransaction extends BasicTransaction.
Uses	At requirements time	One use of a system can be defined by including the functionality of another use. Example: WithdrawalTransaction uses the Authentication use.
Configuration	Previous to runtime	A separate resource, such as file, is used to specialize the component. Example: JavaBeans properties file
Parameters	At component implementation time	A functional definition is written in terms of unbound elements that are supplied when actual use is made of the definition. Example: calculatePriority(Rule)
Template instantiation	At component implementation time	A type specification is written in terms of unbound elements that are supplied when actual use is made of the specification. Example: ExceptionHandler<Container>
Generation	Before or during runtime	A tool produces definitions from user input. Example: Configuration wizard

- Parameterization, as described above.
- Overloading, which means reusing a named functionality to operate on different types. Overloading promotes code reuse but at the cost of understandability and code complexity.
- Properties in the Delphi language, which are attributes of an object. Variability is achieved by modifying the attribute values or the actual set of attributes.
- Dynamic class loading in Java, where classes are loaded into memory when needed. A product can query its context and that of its user to decide at runtime which classes to load.

- Static libraries, which contain external functions that are linked to after compilation time. By changing the libraries, one can change the implementations of functions whose names and signatures are known.
- Dynamic link libraries, which give the flexibility of static libraries but defer the decision until runtime based on context and execution conditions.
- Conditional compilation puts multiple implementations of a module in the same file, with one chosen at compile time by providing appropriate preprocessor directives.
- Frame technology. Frames are source files equipped with preprocessor-like directives that allow parent frames to copy and adapt child frames and form hierarchies. On top of each hierarchical assembly of frames lies a corresponding specification frame that collects code from the lower frames and provides the ready-to-compile module that results.
- Reflection, the ability of a program to manipulate data that represents information about itself or its execution environment or state. Reflective programs can adjust their behavior based on their context.
- Aspect-oriented programming, which was described in the "Architecture Definition" practice area (Section 4.1).
- Design patterns, which are extensible, object-oriented solution templates cataloged in various handbooks (for example, [Gamma 95]). The adapter pattern was mentioned specifically as a variability mechanism earlier in this practice area.

4.3.5 Practice Risks

The overriding risk in component development is building unsuitable components for the software product line applications. This will result in poor product quality, the inability to field products quickly, low customer satisfaction, and low organizational morale. Unsuitable components can come about by

- **Not enough variability:** Components not only must meet their behavioral and quality requirements (as imposed on them by the product line's software architecture) but also must be tailorable in preplanned ways to enable product builders to instantiate them quickly and reliably in the correct forms for specific products.
- **Too much variability:** Building in too much variability can prevent the components from being understood well enough to be used effectively or can cause unforeseen errors when the variabilities conflict with each other.
- **Choosing the wrong variation mechanism(s) for the job:** The wrong choice can result in components that cannot be tailored at the time they need to be.
- **Poor quality of components:** Components of poor quality will set back any effort, but poor core asset components will undermine the entire product line. Product builders will lose confidence with the core asset builders,

and pressure to bypass them will mount. The "Testing" practice area (Section 4.8) should be applied to ameliorate this risk.

4.3.6 For Further Reading

Szyperski's *Component Software: Beyond Object-Oriented Programming* [Szyperski 98] is a comprehensive presentation on components. It provides a survey of component models and covers supporting topics such as domain analysis and component frameworks.

The two references cited under Specific Practices (Section 4.3.4) [Jacobson 97, Anastasopoulos 00] provide a superb compendium of component-level variability mechanisms that are available to a product line component developer.

4.3.7 Discussion Questions

1. Besides the code, what artifacts associated with a component do you think belong in the core asset repository?
2. Should every component be designed with the same variation mechanism, or is there a case to be made for different components using different mechanisms to achieve their variability?
3. Add "time of specialization" information, given in the table of mechanisms in [Jacobson 97], to the list of mechanisms cataloged in [Anastasopoulos 00].
4. Pick a small number of variation mechanisms and, for each one, describe when you would choose that one over the others in your list.

4.4 COTS Utilization

The software for any system may be derived from a number of different sources, one of which is the commercial marketplace. COTS (commercial off-the-shelf) software plays a pivotal role in almost all systems developed today. COTS products exist independent of a specific system and are developed by a commercial organization for commercial purposes. COTS products are available for purchase or licensing to the general public through a catalog or price list; they are commodities in the marketplace [Oberndorf 98].

For years, operating systems have been the best examples of COTS software running in products. Commercially supplied compilers, environments, and tools have pervaded the development realm. During the last decade, however, the explosion of middleware technologies and standards has seen the use of COTS components mushroom in large-scale system development. Now, not only operating systems but also communication infrastructures, network management software, databases, and a host of domain-specific utilities are available for purchase. You're building an accounting system? You can buy any number of complete accounting packages. An on-line auction Web site? You can buy packages to manage the auctions, take credit cards for payment, and implement personalized search and notification functions for your customers. The list is endless. In many cases, entire architectures are now available in the marketplace. The utilization of COTS products is reported to cut costs, take advantage of common architectures, and enable large-scale reuse. However, when COTS products are used as components in a system, there is far less control over both the ways in which the components fit into the architecture and the evolution of the components. The utilization of COTS components introduces a new set of issues, concerns, and trade-offs, many of which are listed in the Practice Risks section of this practice area.

Although specific practices vary, COTS product utilization always necessitates the following steps:

1. **Analyze the architecture in detail.** Determine the ways in which the components will fit into the architecture, paying particular attention to points of flexibility and variability, as well as areas that can't be compromised. Conversely, recognize that the availability of COTS components may represent an advantage of such magnitude (over in-house development) that it might pay to modify the architecture to make a place for those components.
2. **Understand the requirements of the organization.** Some organizations have specific technical constraints or standards to which all software must conform; this is particularly true in government organizations. These constraints may rule out otherwise acceptable COTS products. On the positive side, such constraints will quickly narrow the search for suitable candidates. In any case, the constraints need to be written down so they can be reviewed for completeness, be occasionally revisited for relevancy or revision, and be given to someone to guide the product search.
3. **Study the marketplace in detail.** New products are being developed all the time; be alert to those that can be relevant. For large-scale efforts, it will pay to dedicate resources to keeping up-to-date on new technologies, middleware products, and relevant COTS components that are available in this rapidly changing field. Try following relevant standards groups and products conforming to standards. Determine subsets of the marketplace that are important, subscribe to newsgroups and lists that advertise new components, and maintain a list or database of potentially relevant components for when it's time to make a purchase decision.

4. **Develop requirements in a flexible manner.** COTS products are written to the vendor's expectations about the market, not to your organization's specifications. The vendors hope they meet your needs, but they probably won't do so exactly. Instead of traditional requirements that specify "must" and "should" needs, requirements for COTS-based systems articulate broad categories of needs and possible trade-offs, in addition to the critical or nonnegotiable requirements. These flexible requirements can be used to narrow the field of candidates; if none is found and the fall-back is in-house development, then the requirements can be tightened as usual to drive that development. But the bottom line is that you need to keep an open mind about what it was that you thought you needed, so you can take advantage of what's available.

5. **Develop an approach for the evaluation of products and technologies.** The approach should prescribe not only the evaluation steps but also the evaluation criteria. Include things such as price, vendor stability, level of support required and provided, ease of replacing the component with a competitor's product should the need arise, simplicity of integration, and ease of use. Make sure to include the important quality attributes that you expect the products to have: performance, security, reliability, and so on.

6. **Select viable products and technologies.** Use the evaluation approach to qualify potential product candidates and make selections based on the evaluation criteria.

7. **Buy the products.** Buying software may not be simple. Organizational purchasing policies and guidelines must be followed. In some cases, you may want to test the products in prototypes before committing to a full purchase. In other cases, a commitment can be made immediately.

8. **Integrate products into the architecture.** Don't underestimate the task of integrating the COTS components with each other and with the rest of the system. Don't assume that a COTS product can simply be plugged into an existing architecture without modifications (to either the architecture or the product). Plan for adaptation with wrappers, middleware, or other software "glue." See the "Software System Integration" practice area (Section 4.7) for more advice on this topic.

9. **Test the products and the configuration of products.** The inclusion of COTS products requires testing of the products' interfaces: remember, the components are essentially black boxes. It also requires testing any potential interactions with other components that may have an unpredictable impact. This is especially true for the quality-attribute requirements. Because COTS products are developed by someone else according to a set

of requirements unknown to you, quality attributes need to be considered, specifically if there are stringent needs for such factors as security, performance, and availability.

10. **Manage the system on an ongoing basis.** Monitor the current configuration of products and scan the horizon for new products or potential replacements. Write guidelines for making decisions about upgrading and replacing components. Maintaining COTS products means incorporating new releases into an existing set of assets; therefore, maintenance requires attention to different upgrade cycles, potentially incompatible data sets, conflicting naming conventions, and new conflicts between different COTS components. In addition, decide who will be the point of contact with the COTS vendors for issues, problems, and upgrades.

The discussion so far has related to the purchase of COTS components. It is also possible to adopt whole architectures and application frameworks off-the-shelf. A framework is a template for systems within a particular domain [Jacobson 97]. In the object-oriented world, a framework is often provided in the form of a set of class definitions. If a commercial or open-source architecture is selected, that architecture must be analyzed carefully to determine whether it is appropriate for the desired system. Perform an architecture evaluation just like you would for a home-grown architecture. The evaluation can likely be abbreviated, since many of the architecture's quality and behavioral attributes should already be known. An off-the-shelf architecture often admits the use of whole sets of available off-the-shelf components that are compatible with it.

Using an application-standard architecture brings about a subtle but significant change in focus. Instead of designing an architecture, specifying components, and then going to the marketplace to see what is available, evaluating the choices, and so on as described above, the marketplace is scoured for existing architectures and components and for systems built from both. The architecture is then selected or defined on the basis of the available COTS components. From this perspective, COTS products are utilized as product constraints that get factored into the requirements and early architectural activities and greatly influence or even dictate the architecture.

4.4.1 Aspects Peculiar to Product Lines

COTS products can populate the core assets of a product line, or they can be relevant for the development of specific products in the product line. If they are core assets, then COTS components, like other product line components, must be flexible enough to satisfy the variability needs inherent in a product line. Variability, then, must be added to the selection criteria. When selecting a COTS component, the variety of products in which it will find itself must be used to help evaluate it for fitness. Pay particular attention to the variation points and the requirements that can't be compromised.

Because of the central importance of the architecture for product lines and because of the need to fit a potentially large family of systems, a product line solution using COTS products needs to be generalized, involving general-purpose integration mechanisms that span a number of potential products. As a result, the range of potentially qualifying products may be reduced, and the use of wrappers and middleware needs to focus on generalized solutions rather than on some of the more opportunistic solutions that may be appropriate for single-product systems. The evolution strategy for making updates is now more complex because the range of affected systems is greater.

4.4.2 Application to Core Asset Development

COTS products are certainly a viable choice to become core assets. Commercial components such as databases, graphical user interfaces, graphics components, World Wide Web browsers, Java-based products, and other middleware products based on such approaches as DCOM or CORBA can represent an important part of the asset infrastructure. Application- or domain-specific components or subsystems are also available. Because core assets need to be dependable over a long period of time, you'll need to pay attention to stability factors such as

- **maturity and robustness of the products.** Do they have a track record in the field, or will you be the first organization to use them?
- **expected product update schedule.** Will the vendor be issuing new releases every month? Every year? Every five years? Will the new versions be backward-compatible, or will incorporating them require changes to other software in your system?
- **interoperability with a wide variety of products.** Do they work and play well with other components, or do they make self-centered assumptions such as that they are the sole owner of the software's main timing loop?
- **stability of the vendor.** Is the vendor a trusted name in the field, or is it a new venture that is struggling to get off the ground and might be out of business in a year?

When COTS products are evaluated for adoption as core assets, consider their interfaces and the relevant protocols and standards to which the products conform. These will determine how well (or if) components will work within an infrastructure. Be aware that the mechanisms by which a product conforms to a standard may be idiosyncratic or inconsistent. In addition, since core assets can apply to a potentially large class of products, focus their testing on issues of generality and extensibility.

Licensing issues may be more complex with a COTS product used as a core asset. Ordinarily, a license would be granted to use the product in multiple copies of a single system. But if the COTS product is a core asset, it will be used in multiple copies of many different systems, and the vendor is likely to want a different legal arrangement.

4.4.3 Application to Product Development

An individual product in a product line may contain product-specific code that applies only to that product. If that code corresponds to a full component, there is no reason why that component cannot be a COTS component. Of course, the economics of such a decision will have to be weighed; in that case, the decision will be the same as for COTS use in a single-system development. Beyond that, the technical factors for choosing a COTS component are the same as for a core asset.

4.4.4 Specific Practices

COTS-based systems practices: The COTS-Based Systems (CBS) initiative at the SEI has developed a set of practices to help with COTS product and technology evaluation, COTS acquisition and management, design and software engineering using COTS products, business-case analysis, and COTS policy and planning [SEI CBS].

In work that is part of this initiative, Carney [Carney 98] suggests the following three-step approach for evaluating commercial products and technologies to see if they present a viable option for your development:

1. Plan the evaluation.
   - Define the problem, considering the entire context of the product line assets (functional, technical, quality attributes, platform, resources, alternatives, and business issues).
   - Define the outcomes of the evaluation.
   - Assess the decision risk.
   - Identify the decision maker.
   - Identify the resources.
   - Identify the stakeholders.
   - Identify the alternatives.
   - Assess the nature of the evaluation context.
2. Design the evaluation instrument.
   - Specify the evaluation criteria.
   - Build a priority structure.
   - Define the assessment approach.
   - Select an aggregation technique.
   - Select assessment techniques.

3. Apply the evaluation instrument.
- Obtain products (for evaluation).
- Build a measurement infrastructure.
- Aggregate data.
- Form recommendations.

Other Voices: COTS Certification Criteria from the National Product Line Asset Center

The National Product Line Asset Center is an independent software testing facility sponsored by the U.S. Air Force Electronic Systems Center. From their experience in evaluating COTS components comes a comprehensive set of COTS selection criteria [Yacoub 00], many of which concentrate on the vendor:

> *As opposed to certification of in-house, off-the-shelf component, COTS certification involves commercial aspects that pertain to the component vendor. The worthiness of a component is measured by its vendor credentials. Certification criteria based on vendor and market attributes include assessment of the following:*
>
> - *the vendor business stability, for instance how long the vendor has been in business and the risks of the vendor's going out of business.*
> - *the development process that is followed in developing the component, including testing and certification process at the vendor site.*
> - *obsolescence of the component (i.e., what happens if the vendor goes out of business or the component becomes obsolete?).*
> - *the maintenance contract. In COTS development the maintenance of COTS products is the responsibility of the vendor usually because of the unavailability of source code.*
> - *stability of the component, which includes assessment of the versioning history of the component, frequency of upgrades, and the reasons for upgrade (e.g., more functionality, fewer defects, etc.).*
> - *marketing trends, including assessment of technology issues and market trends and considerations for alternative COTS components in the market.*
> - *the availability of customer support and the form of the support (on-line, phone-based, etc.).*

The services provided by a component must, of course, be functionally adequate, but moreover,

> *. . . the quality of these services is a property of the component that deserves further certification. Quality-of-Service (QoS) attributes include: tolerating failures, such as masking failures and failure recovery; performance attributes, such as response time; security attributes,*

such as immunity to viruses or access constraints; and reliability attributes, such as the failure history of the component over its operational period.

The criteria conclude by addressing a component's understandability, the ease with which a consumer can apply adaptations to it, and the quality of its documentation.

4.4.5 Practice Risks

Ineffective COTS utilization can lead to schedule breakdowns during initial development as well as throughout the life cycle of a software product line. If a product is unsuitable to begin with or loses vendor support and becomes unsuitable, then the result will be a sudden hole in the architecture, with a concomitant hole in the schedule while it is repaired. Major risks can be divided into issues relating to the COTS product in question and issues relating to the vendor and vendor policies. Product-related risks include

- **Unknown interactions:** There may be unknown interactions between the COTS components and other components that could result in a system that does not behave as intended. The mitigation to this risk is to study the COTS product and its interactions thoroughly and to make specific tests during integration testing. (See the "Testing" practice area, Section 4.8.)
- **Poor COTS product quality:** Similar to the previous risk, COTS products without extensive track records pose the risk of failing to meet the reliability standards for the system. Failure to adequately qualify or test a COTS product can admit an unacceptable product into the system.
- **Inappropriate product for the job:** Failure to comprehensively qualify a COTS product for its intended use may result in the selection of a COTS product that fails to meet the behavioral requirements or (more likely) the quality requirements such as performance and security.
- **Lack of adaptability:** COTS products often need to be adapted to fit within an architecture and an environment. Since COTS products are usually black boxes, this adaptation may be costly and may result in unpredictable behavior because the internal workings and assumptions of the COTS products are unknown. Changing (or persuading the vendor to change) a COTS component is a risky move in any case because the result will be an untested one-of-a-kind piece of software that won't track with future releases or other products in the vendor's inventory.
- **Replacements for COTS components:** Replacements or substitutions for COTS products will not represent one-for-one substitutions. Sometimes a new COTS product that will perform most of the functions of an existing product will be available. On the other hand, a COTS product may overlap

partially with several components. Decisions on replacements need to be made within the context of the evaluation criteria for the selection of COTS products.

Vendor-related risks include

- **Inopportune updates to COTS products:** COTS product updates will almost certainly not be synchronized with updates to the product line, and they may conflict with the technical direction of the product line. Make sure to develop an update strategy for making decisions about when to update COTS products, as well as when to forego updates.
- **Lack of support for COTS products:** The support for COTS products will vary by product and vendor. Some products will be withdrawn by a vendor, and some vendors may go out of business. It is important to include specific evaluation criteria based on the vendor's stability, product strategy, support record, and update policy for specific COTS products.

4.4.6 For Further Reading

The Software Engineering Institute's COTS-Based Systems (CBS) World Wide Web site provides a host of papers and monographs on COTS utilization and pointers to further resources, including courseware [SEI CBS]. The viewgraph presentation "Gotchas of COTS" is a good myth-shattering introduction to the issues.

4.4.7 Discussion Questions

1. When would you choose *not* to accept an upgraded version of a COTS product that is installed in a system? What are the dangers of refusing upgrades?
2. Theoretically, COTS components should be very reliable because they have been used across a broad range of applications. When might this not be true? How can you protect yourself from situations in which it is not true?
3. What factors other than the quality and applicability of their software might lead you to choose one COTS vendor over another?
4. Describe an example in which the availability of a COTS component would compel you to change the architecture of your system or product line in order to accommodate it.
5. What would it mean to buy an architecture from a vendor?

4.5 Mining Existing Assets

Mining existing assets refers to resurrecting and rehabilitating a piece of an old system to serve in a new system for which it was not originally intended. Often it simply refers to finding useful legacy code from an organization's existing systems portfolio and reusing it within a new application. However, the code-only view completely misses the big picture. We have known for years that in the grand scheme of things, code plays a small role in the cost of a system. Coding is simply not what's difficult about system/software development. Rich candidates for mining include a wide range of assets besides code—assets that will pay lucrative dividends. Business models, rule bases, requirements specifications, schedules, budgets, test plans, test cases, coding standards, algorithms, process definitions, performance models, and the like are all wonderful assets for reuse. The only reason so-called "code reuse" pays at all is because of the designs and algorithms and interfaces that come along with the code.

Other Voices: Reuse beyond Code in the Software Factories

One of the American software factories tracked by Michael Cusumano in his book *Japan's Software Factories* experienced the fabled cost reduction brought about by strategic reuse. To their credit, they realized that while code reuse was a bonus, it was not by any means necessary for a big win [Cusumano 91, p. 140]:

> *[The factory manager] tracked reuse rates and cost for four functionally equivalent air defense systems built after SAGE [a large air defense command and control system built for the U.S. Strategic Air Command]. The first was SAGE's immediate successor, the BUIC system, the second an air defense system for Spain contracted to Hughes Aircraft, the third a system for Morocco (contracted to Westinghouse), and the fourth a similar system for Thailand:*
>
> *"The first time we didn't use a lot of the code, but we used an awful lot of the design . . . and we came in on cost. SAGE cost in excess of 100 million dollars for the computer programs. BUIC cost about 30 million dollars for the computer programs. The Hughes system cost about 12 million dollars. Morocco cost about 3.5 million dollars. And the new one we are building today for Thailand is zero million dollars, because we are basically using all the existing code. The reason Morocco was cheapest, for instance, in our line to BUIC, is because we used a lot of design and knowledge . . . . We didn't have to spend all the time working out what the dynamics were for interceptors and what the equations of motion were and all the database functions and structures . . . . [d]esign is about 40% of the cost of a system and test is about 40% of*

the cost of the system. If you reuse the design, you can reuse a lot of your test, so it cuts a lot of that 80% of the cost of the system out . . . . [i]t talks to the fact that . . . when the programmers really do understand the problem, they have a much better chance of doing it right and cheaper, as opposed to bringing in a new pro to do it."

When mining your organization's legacy assets, make sure you include noncode artifacts in your search and recovery operations.

Whole or partial architectures, and the design decisions they embody (captured by documented rationale), are especially valuable. And if a mined architecture is suitable, then probably the components that originally populated it can be migrated along with it. But to determine fitness for reuse of either the architecture or its components, it is necessary to obtain a thorough architectural understanding of the legacy system. And, of course, the architect may be long gone. If good documentation does not exist, the process of architecture reconstruction may need to be employed. Reconstruction will reveal the interactions and relations among the architecture's components. It will illuminate constraints for how, if mined, the components can interact within the architecture of the new or updated software. It can also help to understand the trade-off options available for reusing components in a new or improved way. Once the architecture has been extracted, it can be evaluated for suitability using the techniques described in the "Architecture Evaluation" practice area (Section 4.2).

The reuse of any legacy assets, software or otherwise, in a new application is constrained by cost, schedule, and capability. Reuse is valuable only when a project that uses those assets can be completed on time at lower cost and can produce capability equal to or greater than that of comparable freshly developed assets. Any calculation of reuse cost must include the total cost of use over the lifetime of the new product or products, not just the cost of mining/restoring a particular set of assets. In practice, improvements on one of the scales (at a cost to the other two) may produce a significant tactical advantage. For example, if mining and restoration gain time, but lose cost and functionality (relative to building from scratch), they could still provide a significant advantage if time-to-market is a primary driver.

Because the mining of assets is resource-intensive, the reuse of small-grained software assets such as subroutines or individual small programs is seldom economical. The most desirable software assets for mining are those that make up large patterns of interoperation in the legacy architecture and that satisfy specific requirements in the new architecture. Thus, reuse of software assets is not restricted to single components. Entire assemblies of components and their predefined and supported interactions or patterns can often be mined for reuse.

Mining involves understanding what is available and what is needed and rehabilitation. Both require support from analysts who are familiar with both the legacy system and the new system. For software assets, rehabilitation usually requires the support of the new system's architect, who will direct how the assets will be integrated into the new architecture.

Once the existing software assets have been organized and understood and candidate assets for mining have been identified, the rehabilitation of these assets can begin. Focus first on large-grained assets that can be wrapped or that will require only interface changes rather than changes in large chunks of the underlying algorithms. Determine how the candidate asset can fit into the architecture of the targeted new system. Don't forget to consider the requirements for performance, modifiability, reliability, and other nonbehavioral qualities. Also, don't forget to include all the nonsoftware assets associated with the software: requirements, design, test, and management artifacts. Then weigh the cost of developing the asset from scratch versus the cost of the required changes that will be made in the mined assets.

Mining undocumented software assets requires tool support, in lieu of spending hours (if not months) hunched over source code listings trying to ascertain what a piece of software does and how it interacts with other parts of the system. Tools that automatically chart interconnections of various kinds among software modules can be brought to bear. More valuable than tools, however, are the people who worked on the legacy software. Find them if you can. They can tell you the software's strengths and weaknesses that weren't written down, and they can give you the "inside story" that no tool can hope to recover.

4.5.1 Aspects Peculiar to Product Lines

Mined assets for a product line must have the same qualities as newly developed core assets. Mined assets must be (re)packaged with reuse in mind, must meet the product line requirements, must align with the product line architecture, and must meet the quality goals consistent with the goals of the product line. Product lines must focus on the strategic, large-grained reuse of the mined assets. The primary issues that motivate large-scale reuse for a product line are schedule, cost, and quality. The mined and rehabilitated assets must meet the needs of the plurality of systems in the product line. A product line accommodates a longer and wider view of future system change; any mined asset must be robust enough to accommodate such change gracefully.

When mining an asset (software or otherwise) for a software product line, consider

- its alignment with requirements for immediate products in terms of both common features and variation points
- its appropriateness for potential future products

- the amount of effort required to make the asset's interface conform to the constraints of the product line architecture
- the extensibility of the asset with respect to its potential future based on the future evolution that will be required of the architecture
- its maintenance history

When mining software assets for single systems, we look for components that perform specific functions well. However, for product line systems, quality attributes such as maintainability and suitability become more important over time. Thus, we might accept mined assets for product lines that are suboptimal in fulfilling specific tasks if they meet the critical quality-attribute goals. An asset's total cost of ownership across the products for which it will be used should be lower than the sum of similar assets mined for one-time use.

Mined software assets that do not require extensive renovation and rehabilitation can be added to the core asset library in a cost-effective way. However, don't underestimate the rehabilitation cost. In many ways, reengineering a software asset resembles a development project in its own right. Technical planning (as in the "Technical Planning" practice area, Section 5.6) can help.

4.5.2 Application to Core Asset Development

The process of mining existing assets is largely about finding suitable candidates for core assets of the product line. Software assets that are well structured and well documented and have been used effectively over long periods of time can sometimes be included as product line core assets with little or no change. Software assets that can be wrapped to satisfy new interoperability requirements are also desirable. On the other hand, assets that don't satisfy these requirements are undesirable and may have higher maintenance costs over the long term. Depending on the legacy inventory and its quality, an assortment of candidate assets is possible, from architectures to small pieces of code.

An existing architecture should be analyzed carefully before being accepted as the pivotal core asset—the product line architecture. See the "Architecture Evaluation" practice area (Section 4.2) for a discussion of what that analysis should entail.

Candidate component assets must align with the product line architecture, meet specified component behavior requirements, and accommodate any specified variation points. In some cases, a mined component may represent a potentially valuable core asset but won't fit directly into the product line architecture. Usually, the component will need to be changed to accommodate the constraints of the architecture. Sometimes a change in the architecture might be easier, but of course this will have implications for other components, for the satisfaction of quality goals, and for the support of the products in the product line.

Once in the product line asset base, mined assets are treated in the same way as newly developed assets.

4.5.3 Application to Product Development

It is possible and reasonable to use mined assets for components that are unique to a single product in the product line, but in this case the mining activity will become indistinguishable from mining in the non-product-line case. The same issues discussed above (paying attention to quality attributes, architecture, cost, and time-to-market) will still apply. And it will be worth taking a long, hard look at whether the mined component really is unique to a single product or could be used in other products as well, thus making the cost of its rehabilitation more palatable.

4.5.4 Specific Practices

Options Analysis for Reengineering (OAR): OAR is a method that can be used to evaluate the feasibility and economy of mining existing components for a product line. OAR operates like a funnel in which a large set of potential assets is screened out so that the effort can most efficiently focus on a smaller set that will most effectively meet the technical and programmatic needs of the product line. OAR prescribes the following steps [SEI REENG]:

1. **Establish mining context:** First, capture your organization's product line approach, legacy base, and expectations for mining components. Establish the programmatic and technical drivers for the effort, catalog the documentation available from the legacy systems, and identify a broad set of candidate components for mining. This task establishes the needs of the mining effort and begins to illuminate the types of assets that will be

A Tool for Mining

If you're going to build a software product line by corralling a herd of already built, separately developed products, each one running off in its own direction, mining is certainly going to be high on your list of activities. You'll need to populate your core asset base with, among other things, software components that manifest the essential common aspects of your products. And you won't want to code them from scratch; you'll probably want to recover them from your legacy base.

What should those components be? Your software architecture will eventually answer that question with authority, but the existence of recoverable assets can and should influence the architecture. All other things (such as the ability to achieve necessary function and qualities) being equal, why shouldn't the architecture start with componentry that matches what you have at hand?

Where do you begin? In the absence of expert knowledge about the legacy code—often the case in a mining operation—how do you extract common functionality from what may be nothing more than some directory listings of suggestively named but otherwise anonymous source files?

Consider clone detection. Clone detection is the process of finding identical or almost-identical code segments in two different places (either in the same file or across thousands of different files derived from the same source code base or from source code bases that once shared a common history). A company called Semantic Designs, Inc. (http://www.semdesigns.com) markets a product called CloneDR designed for exactly this purpose. Doing clone detection directly on program text makes it difficult to recognize clones in terms of the programming language structure. Worse, clone detection in general is a computationally expensive process. But CloneDR uses compiler technology to construct and compare the programs' abstract syntax trees to help control the cost and recognize clones in terms of language phrases. This allows program segments that vary in the use of variable names or expressions, or in other nonessential ways, to be identified as clones of each other.

Clone detection is a fruitful approach in mining a legacy base for a product line because cloning (the copying and modifying of code segments) is probably how the legacy base of separate-but-similar code was grown in the first place. In the interim, knowledge about who copied what and how they changed it is invariably lost, and clone detection can bring the unmanageable hordes into line by helping you identify and then factor out commonality.

CloneDR does both clone detection and factoring. It can replace segments identified as clones of each other with a reference (usually a procedure call) to a single version of the code, parameterized as necessary. The figure below

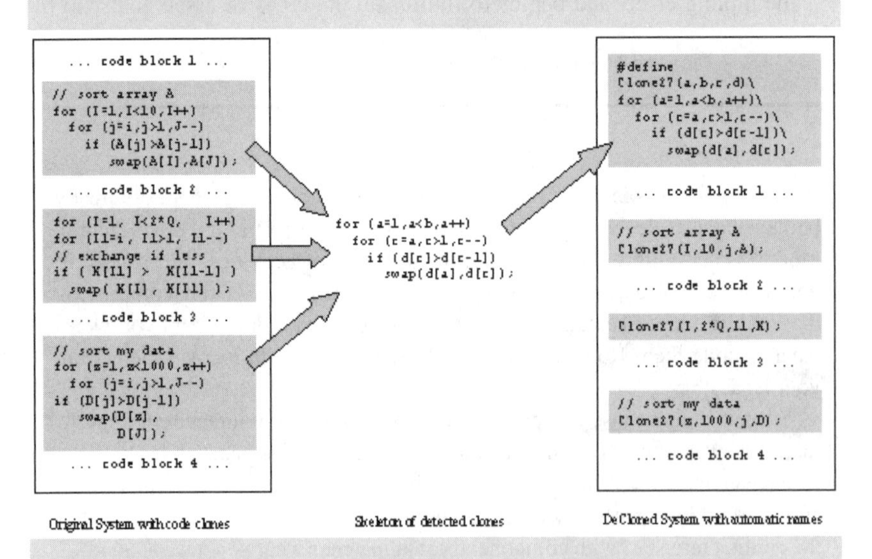

Identifying Clones with CloneDR

shows a simple example of identified clones and how CloneDR would replace them with calls to something more general.

Ira Baxter, the CTO of Semantic Designs, Inc., says that automated clone detection works extremely well; automated clone removal works well but does better when an engineer can provide meaningful names for removed clones. "Almost always," Baxter says, "we'll show a cloned segment to a programmer and he'll immediately be able to tell us what it is and what it does, in a clear concise fashion." In other words, he may not remember what he cloned, but he'll recognize the intent of a clone when he sees it. "Oh, yes," the programmer will say. "That's a routine that normalizes the data with respect to the reference frame," or some other such pronouncement. His recollection can then be used to document the extracted, generic version quickly.

Baxter says that CloneDR has been used on programs from small to very large. The tool will work on source code in any language as long as the tool is taught the syntax of the language. In a typical case, the tool was applied to a 77,000-line suite of Cobol code. It found 95 pairs of like segments, including a 1015-line segment used in five places. More than 15,000 lines of code, or almost 20%, were eliminated. Results such as this can give you a good leg up on commonality analysis: programmers clone code fragments that have an integral purpose that is semantically meaningful with respect to the problem or the solution domain. Clones thus represent both useful conceptual ideas about the applications and useful ways to implement those ideas.

—PCC

most relevant for mining. It also identifies the documentation and artifacts that are available, and it enables focused efforts to close gaps in existing documentation.

2. **Inventory components:** Next, identify the legacy system components that can potentially be mined for use in a product line core asset base. During this activity, identify required characteristics of the components (such as functionality, language, infrastructure support, and interfaces) in the context of the product line architecture. Review legacy components at a gross level to determine if they meet the required characteristics on the basis of the identified criteria, such as language or complexity. This activity creates an inventory of candidate legacy components together with a list of the relevant characteristics of those components. It also creates a list of those needs that cannot be satisfied through the mining effort.
3. **Analyze candidate components:** Next, analyze the candidate set of legacy components in more detail to evaluate their potential for use as product line components. Screen them on the basis of how well they match the required characteristics. Separate candidate components in terms of whether they

will require black-box or white-box changes. Analyze each candidate component to determine the changes that will be required, how variability can be accommodated, the level of granularity, and the level of difficulty and relative costs of the changes. This activity provides a list of candidate components, together with estimates of the cost and effort required for rehabilitating those components.

4. **Analyze mining options:** Next, analyze the feasibility and viability of mining various aggregations of components on the basis of cost, effort, and risk. Assemble different aggregations of components and weigh their costs, benefits, and risks. This will result in a set of mining options—that is, aggregations of components—that are feasible and are compatible with the product line or target architecture.
5. **Select mining option:** Finally, select the mining option that can best satisfy the organization's mining goals by balancing the programmatic and technical considerations. First, establish drivers for making a final decision, such as cost, schedule, risks, and difficulty. Trade-offs often can be established by this activity. For example, schedule may be the most critical driver, regardless of cost. On the other hand, it may be most critical to establish a low-risk option, regardless of cost or schedule. Evaluate each mining option (component aggregation) on the basis of how well it satisfies the most critical driver. Select an option, and then develop a final report to communicate the results. Have the final report detail the option selected, the options not selected and why, the changes that will need to be made, how the assets to be mined will fit into the product line or target architecture, and the product line needs that will not be satisfied through the mining effort.

Architecture recovery/reconstruction tools: Some tools that are available to assist in the architecture reconstruction process include Rigi [Muller 88], the Software Bookshelf [Finnegan 97], DISCOVER [Tilley 98b], the Code-Base Management System (CBMS) [Reasoning 00], and the Dali workbench [Kazman 98].

The Dali workbench is a flexible, lightweight integration skeleton into which various tools can be plugged to accomplish architecture reconstruction. Using Dali involves five steps:

1. View extraction, which uses the existing design and implementation artifacts to construct different views of the system. The extraction activity uses tools such as parsers to extract the source code.
2. Database construction, which stores a set of extracted views in a database for future analysis.
3. View fusion, which augments the extracted information by combining information from several related views.

4. Architecture reconstruction, which performs a visualization of the system's architecture and enables the user to explore and manipulate views.
5. Architecture analysis, which evaluates the conformance of the as-built architecture obtained from reconstruction to an as-designed architecture.

Wrapping: Wrapping involves changing the interface of a component to comply with a new architecture but not making other changes in the component's internals. In fact, pure wrapping involves no change whatsoever in the component, but only interposing a new thin layer of software between the original component and its clients. That thin layer provides the new interface by translating to and from the old. There are enormous advantages to reusing existing assets with little or no internal modification through wrapping. As soon as any modification takes place, the associated documentation changes, the test cases change, and a ripple effect that influences other associated software takes place. Wrapping prevents this and allows the "as-is" reuse of many of the assets associated with the software component, such as its test cases and internal design documentation. The idea is to translate the "as-is" interface to the "to-be" interface. Weiderman et al. discuss some of the available wrapping techniques [Weiderman 98].

4.5.5 Practice Risks

The major risks associated with mining are (1) failure to find the right assets and (2) choosing the wrong assets. Both will result in schedule slippage and opportunity cost in terms of what other productive activities the staff could have been carrying out. A secondary risk is inadequate support for the mining operation, which will result in a failed operation and the (misguided) impression that mining is not a viable option.

Specific risks associated with the operation include

- **Unsuccessful search:** The search for reusable assets may be fruitless, resulting in a waste of time and resources. Or, relevant assets may be overlooked, resulting in time and resources being wasted on duplication of what already exists. A special case of the latter is when noncode assets are shortsightedly ignored. To minimize both of these risks, build a catalog of your reusable assets (including noncode assets), and treat that catalog as a core asset of the product line. It will save time and effort next time.
- **Overly successful search:** There may be too many similar assets, resulting in too much effort spent on analysis.
- **Fuzzy criteria:** The criteria for what to search for need to be crisp enough so that an overly successful search is avoided, yet general enough so that not all viable candidates are ruled out.
- **Failure to search for nonsoftware assets:** Failure to consider nonsoftware assets in your search, such as specifications, test suites, procedures, budgets,

work plans, requirements, and design rationale, will reduce the effectiveness of any mining operation.

- **Inappropriate assets:** Assets recovered from a search may appear to be usable but later turn out to be of inferior quality or unable to accommodate the scope of variation required.
- **Bad rehabilitation estimates:** Initial estimates of the cost of rehabilitation may be inadequate, leading to escalating and unpredictable costs.

Organizational issues leading to mining risks include

- **Lack of corporate memory:** Corporate memory may not be able to provide sufficient data to utilize the software asset effectively.
- **Inappropriate methods:** The wrong reengineering methods and tools may be selected, leading to schedule and cost overruns.
- **Lack of tools:** Tools required for the mining effort may not be integrated to the extent necessary, leading to risky and expensive workarounds.
- **Turf conflicts:** Potential turf conflicts may undermine the decision process in selecting between similar candidate assets. Or, a repository of assets may be off limits for political or organizational reasons.
- **Inability to tap needed resources:** There may be an inability to free resources from the group that originally created the component to rehabilitate or renovate it.

4.5.6 Discussion Questions

1. Sketch out a simple cost/benefit model that you can use to determine when a software asset is worth mining and when it's probably more cost-effective to design and implement anew. How would your model differ for a nonsoftware asset?
2. For a product line you know about or can hypothesize, write a checklist that you would use to qualify a candidate software asset for reuse, and write a checklist that you would use to qualify a candidate nonsoftware asset for reuse. Where do these checklists overlap?
3. It is said that fixing an error during the requirement phase is one to two orders of magnitude less expensive than fixing the same error in acceptance testing. Assuming this is true—and there is an abundance of evidence that it is—can you make an argument that reusing requirements and other precode documentation is correspondingly more cost-effective than reusing code?
4. What testing assets would be reasonable candidates for mining and reuse? What design assets? What management assets?

4.6 Requirements Engineering

The hardest single part of building a software system is deciding precisely what to build. No other part of the conceptual work is as difficult as establishing the detailed technical requirements . . . . No other part of the work so cripples the resulting system if done wrong. No other part is as difficult to rectify later.

So wrote Fred Brooks in 1987 [Brooks 87], and so it remains [Davis 90, Faulk 97]. "The inability to produce complete, correct, and unambiguous software requirements is still considered the major cause of software failure today" [Dorfman 97].

Requirements are statements of what the system must do, how it must behave, the properties it must exhibit, the qualities it must possess, and the constraints that the system and its development must satisfy. The IEEE defines a requirement as

1. a condition or capability needed by a user to solve a problem or achieve an objective
2. a condition or capability that must be met or possessed by a system or system component to satisfy a contract, standard, specification, or other formally imposed document
3. a documented representation of a condition or capability as in definition 1 or 2 [IEEE 90]

Requirements engineering emphasizes the utilization of systematic and repeatable techniques that ensure the completeness, consistency, and relevance of the system requirements [Sommerville 97]. Specifically, requirements engineering encompasses requirements elicitation, analysis, specification, verification, and management, where

- **Requirements elicitation** is the process of discovering, reviewing, documenting, and understanding the user's needs and constraints for the system.
- **Requirements analysis** is the process of refining the user's needs and constraints.
- **Requirements specification** is the process of documenting the user's needs and constraints clearly and precisely.
- **Requirements verification** is the process of ensuring that the system requirements are complete, correct, consistent, and clear.
- **Requirements management** is the process of scheduling, coordinating, and documenting the requirements engineering activities (that is, elicitation, analysis, specification, and verification) [Dorfman 97].

Requirements engineering is complex because of the three roles involved in producing even a single requirement: the requester (referred to as the "user" in the IEEE definition), the developer (who will design and implement the system), and the author (who will document the requirements). Typically, the requester understands the problem to be solved by the system but not how to build a system. The developer understands the tools and techniques required to construct and maintain a system but not the problem to be solved by that system. The author needs to create a statement that communicates unambiguously to the developer what the requester desires. Hence, requirements address a fundamental communications problem.

The communications problem is further compounded by the number and diversity of system requesters. In practice, any system stakeholder has needs and expectations (that is, requirements) for the system. System stakeholder is a role played by any of the various people or systems involved in or affected by a system development. This includes executives (who know the organization's business goals and constraints), end users (who know how the products will be used), marketers (who know the market demands), technical managers (who know the available personnel), and developers (who know the available tools and technology). It can potentially include legal experts, government agencies, and insurance experts. Successful requirements engineering depends on the identification and solicitation of the appropriate community of stakeholders.

Reconciling the diverse needs and expectations of the various system stakeholders necessitates trade-offs—that is, decisions between potentially conflicting requirements from different stakeholders. Trade-offs require mechanisms for capturing and analyzing the different stakeholder requirements, for recognizing the conflicting requirements of different stakeholders, for deciding among those conflicting requirements, and for recording the results of those decisions. Trade-offs are captured as system decisions that are linked to the affected requirements.

Requirements are pervasive, continuously affecting all development and maintenance phases of a system's development by providing the primary information needed by those phases. The requirements form a trigger mechanism for the development and maintenance efforts. Testing, for instance, depends on a precise statement of quality and behavioral requirements to define the standard of correctness against which to test. Requirements engineering is not just an upfront activity but rather has ramifications over the entire development and maintenance effort.

The longer the system's lifetime, the more it is exposed to changes in the requirements resulting from changes in the needs and concerns of the system stakeholders. For example, the end user's demands can change as a result of new features offered by a competing organization's products. The organization's business goals and constraints can change as a result of market demands, new laws, or new insurance regulations. New technologies and software tools such as operating systems can change the way the system is constructed. This requires mechanisms for managing the changes—that is, a requirements-change management process. That process is based on the traceability links between the requirements and the system work products and between the requirements and the related decisions and trade-offs.

4.6.1 Aspects Peculiar to Product Lines

Product line requirements define the products and the features of the products in the product line. Requirements common across the entire family constitute an important and tangible core asset and should be maintained separately from requirements that are particular to a subset of the products (or to a single product), which must be maintained and managed as well. Requirements common to the entire product line are written with variation points that can be filled in or exercised to create product-specific requirements. These variation points may be small, such as replacing a symbolic name such as "max_nbr_of_users" with a value such as "150," or may be substantial, such as leaving a placeholder for an entire specification of part of the behavior. Sometimes the variation point will map to null for a product, corresponding to a feature that the product does not have. And there must be some mechanism by which the complete set of requirements for a particular product (common plus unique) can be produced quickly and easily, implying that the product-specific requirements are stored as a set of deltas relative to the product-line-wide requirements specification.

The product line scope bounds the products included in the product line: the product line requirements refine the scope by more precisely defining the characteristics of the products in the product line. The scope evolves not only because of changing user, customer, business, and marketing needs, but also as a result of system decisions made over the development, design, implementation, and maintenance lifetime of the product line. The product line requirements map the stakeholders' needs to the evolving scope; the scope and the product line requirements are tightly coupled and evolve together. (See "What's the difference between product line scope and product line requirements?" sidebar.)

Requirements engineering for a product line differs from requirements engineering for single systems, as follows:

- **Requirements elicitation** for a product line must capture anticipated variations explicitly over the foreseeable lifetime of the product line. This means that the community of stakeholders is probably larger than for single-system requirements elicitation and may well include domain experts, market experts, and others. Requirements elicitation focuses on the scope, explicitly capturing the anticipated variation by the application of domain analysis techniques, the incorporation of existing domain analysis models, and the incorporation of use cases that capture the variations that are expected to occur over the lifetime of the product line (e.g., change cases [Ecklund 96] and use-case variation points [Jacobson 97]).

- **Requirements analysis** for a product line involves finding commonalities and identifying variations. It may also involve a more vigorous feedback mechanism to the requesters, pointing out where a particular system might achieve economies if it were able to use more common and fewer unique requirements. And requirements analysis has the product line scope as one of its inputs: an artifact that does not exist outside the product line context. Requirements analysis performs commonality and variability analysis (a technique used frequently in domain analysis) on the elicited product line requirements to identify the opportunities for large-grained reuse within the product line. Two such techniques are feature-oriented domain analysis (FODA) [Kang 90] and use cases [Jacobson 97].
- **Requirements specification** now includes preparation of a product-line-wide set of requirements and product-specific requirements. The product-line-wide requirements will include symbolic placeholders that the various product-specific requirements documents would fill in, expand, or instantiate.
- **Requirements verification** now includes a broader reviewer pool and occurs in stages. First, the product-line-wide requirements must be verified. Later, as each product comes on the scene (or is updated), its product-specific requirements must be verified. But the product-line-wide requirements must also be verified to make sure that they make sense for this product.
- **Requirements management** must now make allowances for the dual nature of the requirements engineering process and the staged (common, specific) nature of the activity. Change-management policies must provide a formal mechanism for proposing changes in the product line and for supporting the systematic assessment of the impact of the proposed changes on the product line. Change-management policies govern how changes in the product line requirements are proposed, analyzed, and reviewed. The coupling between the product line requirements and the core assets is leveraged by the use of traceability links between those requirements and their associated core assets. Changes in the requirements can then trigger the appropriate changes in the related core assets [Sommerville 97]. The "Configuration Management" practice area (Section 5.1) describes change management in more detail.

4.6.2 Application to Core Asset Development

First of all, the requirements artifacts produced by requirements engineering are important core assets in their own right. Beyond that, requirements engineering creates the product line requirements that feed the development and acquisition of other core assets. The requirements artifacts will help to

- determine the feasibility and refine the scope and business case of a product line. The initial version of the business case is frequently based on an informal notion of the scope. Requirements engineering refines the scope, and hence the business case, by determining more precisely the requirements for the product line. That more precise definition of the product line provides input to the business-case activity for a correspondingly more precise determination of that product line's feasibility.

- lay the groundwork for the product line architecture, which must accommodate the commonalities and variabilities identified in the requirements.
- ensure that the other core assets support the anticipated variations.
- determine schedules and budgets for the product line and products.
- create the test cases and other test artifacts for products in the product line.

A significant difference in requirements engineering for product lines involves a rapid initial pass through the requirements for key stakeholders to initiate early design work, capturing the high-level requirements that affect the initial design (that is, the architecturally significant requirements [Jacobson 97]). The purpose of this pass is to compress the time to initial delivery and to demonstrate the feasibility of and to establish the credibility of the product line approach—in short, to provide an early justification of the investment [Graham 98].

4.6.3 Application to Product Development

Requirements engineering plays a key role in

- determining the feasibility of producing a particular product as part of the product line. You can use a statement of the requirements specific to that candidate product to help estimate the cost of developing the product.
- the production, testing, and deployment of the particular product. Requirements play a role in these activities just as they do for single-system development.
- the evolution of the product line (that is, the incorporation of changes) that results from product development. Product-specific requirements often "grow up" to become product line requirements if they can be slightly generalized or if they pop up in more than one product. This is the primary mechanism for the evolution of software product lines over time.

To expand on the first point, determining the feasibility of a particular product in a product line is an ongoing activity that is part of building the business case for that product. The initial version of that business case is frequently based on an informal description of the prospective product. Requirements engineering—particularly elicitation and analysis—supports the business case for the product by determining more precisely the requirements for that product. The product line requirements guide the elicitation of the specific requirements for that product. Requirements analysis determines the variance between the product line and the product-specific requirements. That variance provides input to the business-case activity for a correspondingly more precise cost estimate for building the specific product as part of the product line (that is, determination of that product's feasibility).

4.6.4 Specific Practices

Domain analysis techniques: These techniques can be used to expand the scope of the requirements elicitation, to identify and plan for anticipated changes, to determine fundamental commonalities and variations in the products of the product line, and to support the creation of robust architectures. (See the "Understanding Relevant Domains" practice area, Section 4.9). One of these techniques, FODA, has been incorporated recently in a newer approach to requirements engineering for product lines. Product Line Analysis (PLA) combines traditional object-based analysis with FODA feature modeling and stakeholder-view modeling to elicit, analyze, specify, and verify the requirements for a product line. Feature modeling facilitates the identification and analysis of the product line's commonality and variability and provides a natural vehicle for requirements specification. Stakeholder-view modeling supports the completeness of the requirements elicitation, while the PLA work products (the object model, use-case model, feature model, and product line terminology dictionary) provide incremental verification of the requirements modeling [SEI PLA, Chastek 01].

Stakeholder-view modeling: This technique can be used to support the prioritized modeling of the significant stakeholder requirements for the product line. Viewpoint modeling is based on the recognition that a system must satisfy the needs and expectations of the many system stakeholders, who all have their own perspectives (views) of the system. Each stakeholder view can be modeled separately as a set of system requirements. These models are core assets that support the explicit identification of conflicts, and determination of trade-offs, among the needs of the system stakeholders [Sommerville 97].

Feature modeling: This technique can be used to complement object and use-case modeling and to organize the results of the commonality and variability analysis in preparation for reuse. Features are user-visible aspects or characteristics of a system and are organized into a tree of And/Or nodes to identify the commonalities and variabilities within the system. Feature modeling is an integral part of the feature-oriented domain analysis (FODA) method [Kang 90] and the feature-oriented reuse method (FORM) [Kang 98]. In the latter, requirements for a family of related systems are organized according to that family's features. The commonalities and variabilities within those features are then exploited to create a set of reference models (that is, software architectures and components) that can be used to implement the products of that family. Feature modeling has also been integrated into the reuse-driven software engineering business (RSEB) [Jacobson 97, Griss 98].

Use-case modeling: This technique can be used with variation points to capture and describe commonality and variability within product line requirements. A variation point is a location within a use case where a variation (that is, variability) occurs. That variation is captured in a variant that describes the context and mode of the variation. The mechanisms supported for capturing and describing different types of variation within use cases include inheritance, uses, extensions and extension points, and parameterization [Jacobson 97].

Change-case modeling: This technique can be used to identify and capture anticipated changes in a system explicitly, and ultimately to incorporate those changes explicitly in the design to enhance its long-term robustness. Change cases are use cases that describe potential future requirements for a system. They are linked to the existing system use cases that will be affected if and when the future requirements are adopted. The inclusion of change cases allows the designers to plan for and more effectively accommodate anticipated changes [Ecklund 96].

Traceability of requirements to their associated work products: This technique can be used to ensure that the design and implementation of a system satisfy the requirements for that system. Requirements traceability links the requirements backward to their sources (a stakeholder, for example) and forward to the resulting system development work products (a component, for example). In addition to assisting with the elicitation and verification of requirements, requirements traceability is critical in determining the potential impact of proposed changes in a system [Ramesh 97, Sommerville 97].

4.6.5 Practice Risks

The major risk associated with requirements engineering is failure to capture the right requirements over the life of the product line. Documenting the wrong or inappropriate requirements, failing to keep the requirements up-to-date, or failure to document the requirements at all puts the architect and the component developers at a grave disadvantage. They will be unable to produce the systems that will satisfy the customers and fulfill the market expectations. Inappropriate requirements can result from the following:

- **Failure to distinguish between product-line-wide requirements and product-specific requirements:** These different kinds of requirements have different audiences in a product line. The core asset builders need to know the requirements they must build to, while the product-specific software builders must know what is expected of them as well.
- **Insufficient generality:** Insufficient generality in the requirements leads to a design that is too brittle to deal with the change actually experienced over the lifetime of the product line.

- **Excessive generality:** Overly general requirements lead to excessive effort in producing both core assets (to provide that generality) and specific products (which must turn that generality into a specific instantiation).
- **Wrong variation points:** Incorrect determination of the variation points results in inflexible products and the inability to respond rapidly to customer needs and market shifts.
- **Failure to account for qualities other than behavior:** Product line requirements, as is the case for software requirements in general, should capture requirements for quality attributes such as performance, reliability, security, and the like.

In addition, requirements engineering for a product line is subject to the risks enumerated in the "Understanding Relevant Domains" practice area (Section 4.9).

4.6.6 For Further Reading

Two good textbooks for requirements engineering are Davis's *Software Requirements: Analysis and Specification* [Davis 90] and Sommerville and Sawyer's *Requirements Engineering: A Good Practice Guide* [Sommerville 97]. Of particular value in the latter is a table that describes the basic, intermediate, and advanced requirements engineering guidelines.

Two good tutorials are also available. Faulk's "Software Requirements: A Tutorial" [Faulk 97] provides an excellent brief introduction to requirements engineering, describing such techniques as functional decomposition, structured analysis, operational specification, and object-oriented analysis. Dorfman and Thayer's *Software Requirements Engineering* [Dorfman 97] is a tutorial in book form based on the most significant requirements engineering papers of the last two decades.

4.6.7 Discussion Questions

1. For a software product line that you know or can imagine, list as many common requirements as you can think of. Use whatever notation is standard in your organization. List some of the variations. Are you able to use the same notation to express variations? What properties of the notation or specification language do you need in order to express variation conveniently?
2. What is the difference between requirements analysis for a product line and a domain analysis? How are they similar?
3. Software requirements are, for better or worse, often documented using an ordinary natural language such as English. Discuss how this makes building a generic requirements document (with built-in variation points) for a

product line easier or more difficult. How would you go about it? What guidelines or constraints would you propose?

4. Suppose your organization was considering building a new member of an already existing product line. How would you use the product line's generic requirements specification to help determine whether or not that decision was cost-effective? What information would the requirements specification need to contain in order to help make that determination?
5. How might a requirements specification for a member of a product line feed back to affect the product line's scope definition? How might a requirements specification for a member of a product line feed back to affect the product line's domain model?
6. Given the relationship among requirements engineering, scoping, and understanding relevant domains, would you put the same people or different people in charge of each of these activities? What would you do in theory, and why? What would you do in your organization? Would it be different? Why?

4.7 Software System Integration

Software system integration refers to the practice of combining individual software components into an integrated whole. Software is integrated when components are combined into subsystems or when subsystems are combined into products. In a waterfall model, software system integration appears as a discrete step toward the end of the development life cycle between component development and integration testing. In an incremental model, integration is an ongoing activity; components and subsystems are integrated as they are developed into multiple working miniversions of the system. An incremental approach to integration decreases risk because problems encountered during software integration are often the most complex. Object technologists are proponents of incremental development, and object-oriented development methods are based on the principle of ongoing integration practices.

Integration is bound up in the concept of component interfaces. Recall from the "Architecture Definition" practice area (Section 4.1) that an interface between two components is the set of assumptions that the programmers of each component can safely make about the other component [Parnas 71]. This includes its behavior, the resources it consumes, how it acts in the face of an error, and other assumptions that should be documented as part of a component's interface. This definition is in stark contrast to the simplistic (and quite insufficient) notion of "interface" that merely refers to the "signature" or syntactic interface that includes only the program's names and parameter types. This definition of "interface" may let two components compile together successfully, but only the Parnas definition (which subsumes the simpler one) will let two components work together correctly. When interfaces are defined thoughtfully and documented carefully, integration proceeds much more smoothly because the interfaces define how the components will connect to and work with each other.

4.7.1 Aspects Peculiar to Product Lines

In a product line effort, software system integration occurs during the installation of core assets into the asset base and also during the building of an individual product. In the former case, preintegrating as many of the software core assets as you can will make product-building a much more economical operation. In either case, you need to consider integration early on in the development of the production plan and architecture for the entire product line. The goal is to make software system integration more straightforward and predictable.

Other Voices:
Large Preintegrated Chunks at CelsiusTech

We've said (over and over) that a software product line involves the disciplined planned reuse of artifacts and processes far beyond simple code. Code reuse is to a software product line what icing is to a cake—a welcome addition, but not the main attraction. You shouldn't be surprised, then, to hear that integration is an activity that can be reused—and thus amortized—across all members of a software product line. One of the finest examples of this we've seen, which was mentioned in the preface, was the ShipSystem 2000 (SS2000) software product line of CelsiusTech Systems [Brownsword 96]. Their secret was in engineering large, preintegrated segments for their asset repository.

> *Several types of components exist in the SS2000 architecture. Each serves a particular purpose. Functional requirements are embodied in system functions. A system function is a collection of software that implements a logically connected set of requirements; it may be thought of as a subsystem. A system function is composed of a number of Ada code units, which are the basic unit of work for a program, and the unit of combination for the Ada compiler and environment. System functions comprise roughly 5–25K lines of Ada. An example is a component that handles all the ballistic calculations for a gun.*
>
> *A system function group comprises a set of system functions and forms the basic work assignment for a development team. System function groups, primarily organizational units for management, are*

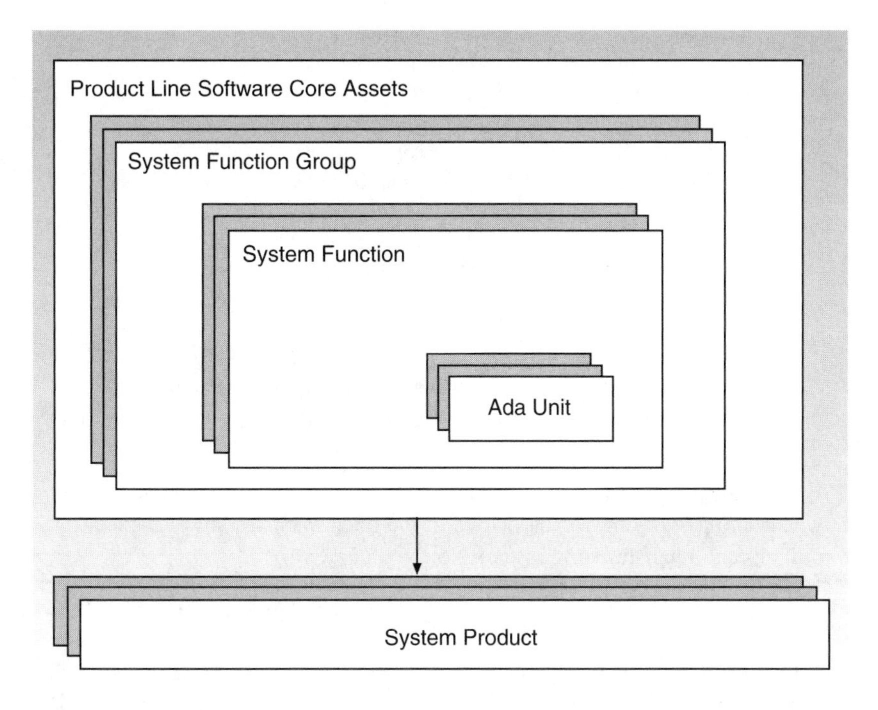

Units of Software at CelsiusTech

clustered around major functional areas [such as weapons control, the user interface, or intrasystem communication].

System function groups may (and do) contain system functions from more than one layer. They correspond to larger pieces of functionality that are more appropriately developed by a large team. For example, a separate software requirements specification (SRS) is written for each system function group.

System functions, not the Ada code units, are the basic units of test and integration for systems in the product line. This is a crucial point. The primacy of system functions and system function groups allows a new member of the product line to be treated as the composition of a few dozen high-quality, high-confidence components that interact with each other in controlled, predictable ways as opposed to thousands of small units that must be regression tested with each new change. Assembly of large components without the need to retest at the lowest level of granularity for each new system is a critical key to making reuse work . . . .

SS2000 consists of about 30 system function groups, each comprising up to 20 or so system functions.

. . . In the classical literature on software reuse repositories, the unit of reuse is typically either a small, fine-grained component (such as

an Ada package, a subroutine, or an object) or a large-scale, independently executing subsystem (such as a tool or a commercial stand-alone product). In the former case, the small components must be assembled, integrated, configured, and tested after checking out; in the latter case, the subsystems are typically not very configurable or flexible.

CelsiusTech took an intermediate approach that makes much more sense. The unit of reuse is a system function, a thread of related functionality that comprises elements from different layers in the architecture. System functions are pre-integrated—that is, the components they comprise have been assembled, compiled together, tested individually, and tested as a unit. When the system function is checked out of the asset repository, it is ready for use. In this way, CelsiusTech is not only reusing components, it is also reusing the integration, component test, and unit test effort that would otherwise have to be needlessly repeated for each application.

Recall from our preface that CelsiusTech faced the enviable dilemma of whether to assign one person or two to the integration testing of their latest million-and-a-half-line Ada system. Now you know why.

In a product line, the effort involved in software system integration lies along a spectrum. At one end, the effort is almost zero. If you know all of the products' variabilities in advance, you can produce an integrated parameterized template of a generic system with formal parameters. You can then generate final products by supplying the actual parameters specific to the individual product requirements and then launching the construction tool (along the lines of the Unix "make" utility). In this case, each product consists entirely of core components; no product-specific code exists. This is the "system generation" end of the integration spectrum.

At the other end of the spectrum, considerable coding may be involved to bring together the right core components into a cohesive whole. Perhaps the components need to be wrapped, or perhaps new components need to be designed and implemented especially for the product. In this case, the integration more closely resembles that of a single-system project.

Most software product lines occupy a middle point on the spectrum. Obviously, the closer to the generation side of the spectrum you can align your production approach, the easier integration will be and the more products you will be able to turn out in a short period of time. For example, in Chapter 9 we'll see that it used to take Cummins Inc. about a year to bring new engine-control software to the point of acceptance testing. Now, after adopting a product line approach, they can do it in about a week.

However, circumstances may prevent you from achieving pure generation. Perhaps a new product has features you have not considered. Perhaps your application area prevents you from knowing all of the variabilities up front. Or perhaps the variabilities are so numerous or complex or interact with each other in such complicated ways, that building the construction tool will be too expensive. And it may be that you do not want to turn out many products in a short amount of time, but fewer products spread out over even periods. In that case, the construction tool may be less appealing.

In software system integration for product lines, the cost of integration is amortized over many products. Once the product line scope, core assets, and production plan have been established in the asset base and a few systems have been produced from that base, most of the software system integration work has been done. The interfaces have been defined, and they work predictably. They have been tested. Components work with one another. In subsequent variations and adaptations of the product, there is relatively little software system integration effort when the variations and adaptations occur within components. Even when new components are being added with new interfaces, the models from previous interfaces can and should be followed, thus minimizing the work and the risk of integration. So, in a very real sense, products (after the first one or two) tend to be "preintegrated" such that there are few surprises when a system comes together.

In the past (and this is still true in many cases today), the interfaces between subsystems or components were described in a natural-language document, often called an Interface Description Document (IDD). These documents would describe the data, process calls, and timing-and-performance constraints between two components. These components were then often written by separate groups that used the IDD as the "contract" between the two pieces of software. When it came time to integrate these components, several types of errors occurred, including errors of omission, misinterpretation, and implementation. These sources of errors have in the past made software system integration a very rocky and error-prone process. Like most modern development practices, product line practices tend to be concerned with software system integration early and continuously in the development life cycle. This is consistent with traditional incremental development policies; however, in the case of product line development, there is a conscious and purposeful effort to maintain large, integrated components as part of an asset library. The integration is done according to the plan for each product; hence the integration occurs according to a preordained and tested scheme. These plans generally call for the use of modern technology and tools that keep large chunks of code "continuously integrated."

The "continuous integration" of first products and "preintegration" of subsequent products alleviate many of the errors that ordinarily come late in the development process. With "continuous integration," the rules of software system integration are often enforced by automated tools rather than by natural-language documents. The error-prone nature of human language has for the most part been replaced by the unforgiving strictness of programming languages and their associated tools. With "preintegration," the integration effort is reduced in two ways. First, the components in the core asset base have been tested and integrated in previous systems. While the first attempt at integration may be difficult, subsequent attempts will be by assembly of large components that have been assembled and tested before. Second, the components are designed for assembly. Just as Lego components fit together, components from a core asset base fit together. The core assets were built to have a prescribed interface described in a language more formal than in the past, precluding a whole range of errors.

4.7.2 Aplication to Core Asset Development

When core assets are developed, acquired, or mined, remember to take integration into account. Try to specify component interfaces not solely in natural language but in machine-checkable form. Using languages such as Interface Description Language (IDL), the syntactic or "signature" part of the interfaces can be specified early and kept current continuously throughout the development process. Early on, the bodies for these specifications can be stubbed out so that the code can be compiled and checked by a machine for consistency. Absence of consistency errors does not guarantee smooth integration—the components might assemble smoothly but still fail to work correctly together—but it's a good start.

Evaluate any components you mine or acquire for their integrability and their granularity. A component is "integrable" if its interfaces (in the Parnas sense) are well defined and well documented so that it can potentially be wrapped for commonality with other components (if not used with assurance as is). Finally, remember that it is generally easier to build a system from small numbers of large, preintegrated pieces than from large numbers of small, unintegrated components.

4.7.3 Application to Product Development

A big benefit of product line practice is that software system integration costs tend to decrease for each of the subsequent products in the product line. If the production plan calls for the addition of components or internal changes in components, some integration may be required depending on the nature of the changes. Finally, in the system generation case, integration becomes a matter of providing values for the parameters and launching the construction tool. The key in all of these cases is that the integration occurs according to a preordained and tested scheme.

4.7.4 Specific Practices

Interface languages: Programming languages such as IDL allow you to define machine-independent syntactic interfaces. Programming languages such as Ada allow you to define a compilable specification separate from the body.

Ada programmers have found that keeping a continuously integrated system using full specifications and stubbed bodies decreases the integration time and costs dramatically. These languages and others do not allow specification of the full semantic interfaces of components, but catching signature-level integration bugs early is a win.

This practice applies primarily to the development of new components but retains the leverage for subsequent products in a product line. One of the principal aspects of CelsiusTech's product line solution was the institutionalization of continuous integration using Ada rather than the more traditional all-at-once approach [Brownsword 96]. Most object-oriented design techniques prescribe the development of architectural frameworks and the use of patterns; both have been proven to support product lines and facilitate software integration.

Wrapping: Wrapping, described as a specific practice in the "Mining Existing Assets" practice area (Section 4.5), involves writing a small piece of software to mediate between the interface that a component user expects and the interface that the used component comes with. Wrapping is a technique for integrating components whose interfaces you do not control, such as components that you have mined or acquired from a third party.

Middleware: An especially integrable kind of architecture employs a specific class of software products to be the intermediaries between user interfaces on the one hand and the data generators and repositories on the other. Such software is called "middleware" and is used in connection with Distributed Object Technology (DOT) [Wallnau 97]. There are three prominent examples of middleware standards and technology. One is the Common Object Request Broker Architecture (CORBA) and its various commercial implementations [OMG 97]. The second is the Distributed Component Object Model (DCOM). The third is the proprietary middleware solution that has grown around the Java programming language. Middleware is discussed in more detail in the "Architecture Definition" practice area (Section 4.1).

System generation: In some limited cases, a new product in a product line can be produced with no software system integration at all. These are cases in which all (or most) of the product line variability is known in advance. In these cases, it may be possible to have a template system from which a computer program produces the new products in the product line simply by specifying variabilities as actual parameters. Such a program is called a "system generator." One example of such a family of products would be an operating system in which all of the variabilities of the system are known ahead of time. Then, to generate the operating system, the "sysgen" program is simply provided with a list of system parameters (such as processor, disk, and peripheral types and their performance characteristics), and the program produces a tailored operating system rather than integrating all the components of an operating system.

FAST generators: In *Software Product-Line Engineering* [Weiss 99], Weiss and Lai describe a process for building families of systems using generator technology. The Family-Oriented Abstraction, Specification, and Translation (FAST) process begins by explicitly identifying specific commonalities and variabilities among potential family members and then designing a small special-purpose language to express both. The language is used as the basis for building a generator. Turning out a new family member (product) is then simply a matter of describing the product in the language and "compiling" that description to produce the product.

4.7.5 Practice Risks

The major risks associated with software system integration include

- **Natural-language interface documentation:** Relying too heavily on natural language for system interface documentation and not relying heavily enough on the automated checking of system interfaces will lead to integration errors. Natural language interfaces are imprecise, incomplete, and error-prone. Carrying forward in the face of undetected interface errors increases the cost of correcting such errors and increases the overall cost of integration. Automated tools, however, are more oriented to syntactic checking and are less effective at checking race conditions, semantic mismatch, fidelity mismatch, and so on. Some interface specifications must still be done largely with natural language and are still error-prone.
- **Component granularity:** There is a risk in trying to integrate components that are too small. The cost of integration is directly proportional to the number and size of the interfaces. If the components are small, the number of interfaces increases proportionally, if not geometrically, depending on the connections they have to each other. This leads to greatly increased testing time. One of the lessons of the CelsiusTech case study was that *CelsiusTech found it economically infeasible to integrate large systems at the Ada-unit level* [Brownsword 96]. Although the component granularity is dictated by the architecture, we capture the risk here because this is where the consequence will make itself known.
- **Variation support:** There is a risk in trying to make variations and adaptations that are too large or too different from existing components. When new components or subsystems are added, they must be integrated. Variations and adaptations within components are relatively inexpensive as far as system integration is concerned, but new components may cause architectural changes that structure the product in ways that cause integration problems.

4.7.6 For Further Reading

Software Product-Line Engineering [Weiss 99] describes the Family-Oriented Abstraction, Specification, and Translation (FAST) process, which includes a generator-building step that essentially obviates the integration phase of product development. Although readings on middleware and particular middleware solutions abound, a nicely digestible overview is provided in a technical report by Wallnau et al. [Wallnau 97].

4.7.7 Discussion Questions

1. What other kinds of "glue code" besides wrappers are there? When would you use each kind? What assets do you think you should build to accompany glue code, such as documentation or test assets?
2. When is the glue code (such as a wrapper) associated with a core asset itself a core asset?
3. Having an automatic product generation capability brings certain advantages but also certain disadvantages. What might those disadvantages be? Might this capability cause an organization to turn down lucrative business it would otherwise accept? Might it lead to complacency and stagnation?
4. How might an automatic product generation capability affect building of a business case or the product line's scope? How might it affect the organizational structure? Do you think an organization with this capability would be more or less likely to maintain a separate core asset team? Why?
5. What measurements might you want to take to see if your product line's integration process is a good one or to find ways in which it could be improved?

4.8 Testing

Testing traditionally has been used for two basic purposes within a project. First, during development, testing is used to assist developers in identifying faults that lead to failures so they can be repaired. Second, testing is used to determine whether a product can perform as specified by its requirements. Recently, the role of testing has been expanded in many organizations to provide techniques for estimating the reliability of pieces of software.

If a program could be executed with all possible inputs, all possible failures would be revealed so all the faults would be found and could be repaired. However, since it is almost always impossible to use all possible inputs, testing is really a search process. During development, the developer tests by looking for those inputs that are most likely to result in failures. After a piece of code has been constructed, the system tester searches for those failures that the user is most likely to encounter. Not all failures have the same impact on the user.

The amount of effort that is expended in searching for these failures should be proportionate to the impact on the quality of the program.

Testing is a continuous activity within a software development process. It is also a labor-intensive activity: estimates for the resources expended for writing code for testing purposes range from 40% to as high as 300% or even 500% of the amount expended for all other effort on the application under development [Pressman 98, p. 595].

Different types of testing are carried out during the development process. Each testing task is organized around three basic activities:

1. **Analysis:** The material to be tested is examined using specific strategies to identify appropriate test cases. Performing test analysis will actually detect some defects such as poor testability. The output from this activity is a detailed test plan.
2. **Construction:** The artifacts needed to execute the tests specified in the test plan are built. These artifacts usually include test drivers, test data sets, and the software that implements the actual tests.
3. **Execution and evaluation:** The tests are conducted, and the results are analyzed. The software is judged to have passed or failed each test, and decisions are made about the next process step in the development process to be executed. For example, if a large number of failures occur during integration testing, the development team may return to the component specification phase rather than just repairing identified faults.

All testing activities should be carried out under the following desiderata:

1. **Testing is objective.** The process by which criteria are determined should be guided only by the satisfaction of requirements specified for the asset.
2. **Testing is systematic.** Criteria are selected according to an algorithm that describes the reason for selecting each criterion.
3. **Testing is thorough.** The criteria used should achieve some logical closure that can be argued as being complete by some definition.
4. **Testing is integral to the development process.** Before an artifact is produced, plans are made as to how best to assess it.

Testing has many forms and flavors, but the following overview will provide the basis for our discussion.

Analysis and Design Model Validation

In the development process, each phase that includes a model creation step should include a testing step that verifies the syntax of the model and validates it against the required system. We use "model" in a broad sense to refer to nonsoftware assets that either make predictions or prescribe constraints for other assets. A business case for a product line is a model; it predicts how profitable the product line will be. Software design documents are models; they predict behavior and also impose constraints on implementations. Each of these models has its own "syntax" (rules for completeness and well-formedness) and constraints. Test cases are constructed from the requirements and constraints. Preeminent among the models is the software architecture; software architecture evaluation (see the "Architecture Evaluation" practice area, Section 4.2) is how it is validated.

For most nonsoftware model assets, few tools are available to assist in this validation, but sometimes prototyping tools can be useful (for example, to help test requirements by examining a prototype system they describe). Most of the model assets in this category are early-life-cycle artifacts, and we know how much easier and cheaper it is to weed out errors in those assets than in later assets. Validating these nonsoftware assets is sufficiently important that even if you have to resort to manual validation, the effort is worth the return.

The remainder of this overview refers to software testing.

Unit Testing

Testing for implementation defects begins with the most basic unit of development. This unit may be a function, class, or component. This kind of testing occurs during coding; therefore, the intention is to direct the testing search to those portions of the code that are most likely to contain faults. As each unit is constructed, it is tested to ensure that it (1) does everything that its specification claims and (2) does not do anything it should not do. Conducting these unit tests is particularly productive because the visibility into the code under test is at its maximum. The degree of visibility is related directly to the testability (the ease with which the code under test can be tested).

Complex control structures such as deeply nested IF statements are more likely to contain faults than a series of unrelated lines of code. Recognizing this, a *directed test* approach requires more test cases per line of code for complex statements than for simple code, but the technique treats all bugs as having the same importance. A test case associates a set of input values with the result that should be produced by a correctly functioning system. The test inputs for a test case are selected according to a strategy. The *functional testing* strategy uses the specification of the unit to determine which inputs to use. If the unit passes the functional tests, our confidence that the unit does what it is supposed to do is increased. A second strategy, termed *structural testing,* selects test inputs on the basis of the structure of the code that implements the functionality of the unit. If the unit passes the structural tests, our confidence that the implementation will operate safely—that is, the code will not abort, destroy files, or lock up the system—is increased. By using both testing strategies on a system, the testing activity attempts to determine that the unit will do everything it is supposed to do and nothing it is not supposed to do.

Subsystem Integration Testing

As basic units are integrated into subsystems, even units that have received adequate unit-level testing may produce failures when used in connection with the other units that comprise the subsystem. Specifications, written by component developers, do not describe behavior in sufficient detail to define how the component will interact with every other component. The directed tests are constructed from the interactions between units as specified in the architecture. These representative tests search for those failures that users of the system are most likely to encounter. The representative tests are constructed from the use cases used to represent the product's requirements.

The integration test plan should describe tests that cover each protocol between pairs of components. A protocol is a complete sequence of messages going back and forth between two components. Each protocol must be consistent with the state machines in both components. Test cases should include instances in which the protocol is violated with the expected result that one of the two components will recognize the violation and raise an exception.

System Integration Testing

The final round of integration yields the completed application. At this time, the focus shifts completely to representative tests of the system. Even if the code operates correctly according to its detailed specifications, it may not perform the correct tasks. The test coverage is measured in terms of "uses" of the system—that is, how many of the possible ways in which the system can be used have been tested. Thus system integration testing (also known as *system testing*) determines whether a product does what it is supposed to do. These *representative tests* are selected to cover the complete specification for the portion of functionality that has been produced. The amount of testing a specific function receives is based either on its frequency of use (operational profiles) or on the criticality of the function (risk-based testing).

Special forms of system testing include *load testing* (to determine if the software can handle the anticipated amount of work), *stress testing* (to determine if the software can handle an unanticipated amount of work), and *performance testing* (to determine if the software can handle the anticipated amount of work in the required time).

Regression Testing

Regression testing is used to make sure that things that have worked before will continue to work in the face of some change. Regression tests are constructed to determine periodically whether a large set of components remains correct and consistent over time. Hence, regression testing is apropos to a product line or reuse situation. Predefined levels of change, as identified by the version control system, activate the regression testing activity. The actual test cases used in regression testing are no different from any other test cases. The regression test suite is a sample of the functional tests for all of the components.

Conformance Testing

Conformance testing is an essential activity in determining that a component can be used in a specific role in an application. The conformance test set should cover all required interactions between the component and the other components that will participate in the application. Whereas regression testing focuses on change over time, conformance testing focuses on an initial validation. A subset of the conformance test cases is used in the regression test suite.

Acceptance Testing

To validate the claims of the manufacturer or provider, the consumer performs acceptance testing. The acceptance test is more realistic than the system test because the application being tested is introduced into the consumer's actual environment. An acceptance test should play a critical role in the acquisition process for software products, including development tools and software that are all or part of a needed application.

Deployment Testing

Deployment testing is, in some respects, both an extension of, and a precursor to, acceptance testing. Deployment testing is conducted by the development organization prior to release of the software to customers for acceptance testing. Whereas acceptance testing focuses on the functionality of the delivered product, deployment testing covers all the unique system configurations on which the product is to be deployed. This testing focuses on the interaction between the product and platform-specific libraries, device drivers, and operating systems. During the deployment testing phase, the application's ability to deploy or install itself is also tested. With runtime environments becoming more complex and dynamic, there is an increased possibility that required library files may not be present, that permissions may be incorrect on a directory, or that one version may interfere with another. In deployment testing, not only is the new application executed, but other applications are exercised as well to determine whether the new application has caused them any problems.

Reliability Models

Testing can be used to estimate the reliability of a software component or system [Musa 99]; however, establishing the reliability of a piece of software through testing is a costly process. The cost can be justified for applications that require high levels of reliability, but the effort can be hard to justify for ordinary applications.

4.8.1 Aspects Peculiar to Product Lines

Testing in a product line organization must examine the core asset software, the product-specific software, and the interactions between them. Unlike single-system development projects, responsibilities for testing may be distributed across different parts of the organization (see "Other Voices: Software Product Line Testing at Philips" sidebar). Also unlike single-system development projects, testing represents an activity (and a producer of artifacts) whose efforts are reused across a multitude of products. Planning is necessary to take full advantage of the benefits that reuse brings. The following guidelines should help.

Other Voices: Software Product Line Testing at Philips

Philips is a worldwide leader in electronic systems; in addition to their well-known consumer electronics products, they also build a family of medical imaging devices. Their research arm has helped both divisions produce their software in product line form. Here is how they divided the testing responsibilities within their organization to balance rigor and safety against flexibility [America 00]:

> *As in the case of family engineering, the internals of the platform and product engineering process also depend on the business and organizational context. For example, in the medical imaging area, the complexity of the products and the high safety demands from the market necessitate a large and well-organized testing effort. Because of this, it makes sense to do the main part of integration and testing within the platform engineering process, so that all the product engineering processes can reuse a strongly integrated and well-tested platform. In consumer electronics, where the necessary testing effort is considerably less, the product engineering processes can do more integration and testing. This also gives them more freedom in combining platform components with product-specific components to build a product.*

Structure the testing software for reuse: The structure of the test software should support traceability from the test code to the code that it tests. In iterative, incremental development, and, in fact, in any development process that corrects its mistakes, the test code will be executed many times over the span of development. As changes are made in the product code, corresponding changes may be required in the test code. So, to maximize traceability, the test software should reflect the product line architecture wherever possible. Grouping the test code for a software unit from the application in a single unit of test software creates the mapping from test code to source code. For example, in an object-oriented development effort, the test software for a class is grouped within a single class. Where two parts of the product line architecture have a particular relationship, the test code for each of those parts is also related. For example, where one class in the application software inherits from another, the test class for that class inherits from the test class for the parent application class. In object-oriented software, the inheritance relation defines a hierarchy of definitions from abstract to specific in which each subclass adds more specific information to what it inherits. Test plans should be established at each of these levels, and test cases should be designed to have increasing specificity at each level of the hierarchy. The abstract test cases are not applied directly any more than abstract class definitions are used directly; however, they provide support for the reuse of definitions.

This approach reduces the cost of maintaining the test software because it is easier to identify where to make changes. The development environment already contains tools that work with the application's units and can just as easily be applied to the units of test software.

The test software should include common utilities that developers of test cases can share. These utilities provide complete solutions for certain services such as logging test results or providing reliability computations. The utilities also provide building blocks such as timers and prebuilt GUIs that can be used in the construction of test cases.

Include architectural support for testing: The product line architecture can provide support for testing. This support takes forms such as special test interfaces that allow a self-test functionality to be invoked and special access to certain state types that are stored (maintained internally) by the program. These types of interfaces and functionality are often too resource-intensive to be provided in a one-off system but are cost-effective in a product line environment.

The self-test functionality provides the system user with the capability to determine whether the system is currently operational. This capability is particularly useful in systems that are configurable, systems that dynamically incorporate resources into the program, and systems that have significant hardware components. The basic support for self-testing can be defined in the product line architecture and then elaborated by specific products. The self-test functionality can run a set of regression test cases that are designed to exercise those parts of the program that dynamically load and link functionality and those parts that rely on information from configuration files and other external resources.

Reuse assets for system integration testing: The "Requirements Engineering" and "Architecture Definition" practice areas (Sections 4.6 and 4.1) discuss various views of producing use cases or scenarios that describe how the system is intended to work. Select test inputs for system integration based on these descriptions.

Employ regression testing: The sampling should be weighted toward testing of components that are used at the points of variability in the product line architecture. These are the points at which the most changes, and probably the most errors, will occur.

Keep track of acceptance testing: In a product line development process, some of this responsibility can be shifted from the customer to the developer. That is, in a product line environment, it is more cost-effective for the development organization to create testing laboratories that closely model the deployment environment. The product development group should maintain close contact with the purchaser because information provided by the acceptance test is useful to other clients. The result is more effective system testing and a reduced possibility of failures in the field. Stress and performance testing are also carried out in a more realistic environment.

4.8.2 Application to Core Asset Development

Testing concepts are applied to core asset development in two ways. First, testing itself produces reusable core assets. There are three categories of such assets:

1. **Documents:** Test plans and test reports are the two fundamental types of test documents. The sampling strategies, coverage criteria, and other results of the analysis of the product to be tested can be arranged in a hierarchical fashion that parallels the relationships among the products in the product line. An "abstract" or skeletal test plan that addresses much of the commonality identified among products can be created. This ensures that common features are tested in basically the same way for every product.
2. **Test data sets:** The data needed for a test include all the inputs required to establish the preconditions for a test case and the actual test step. The construction and verification of these data sets require a significant resource investment. Careful test design based around the identified commonalities can produce savings in these resources.
3. **Test software:** Test harnesses can be as complicated as the production software. For example, there may be a need to time a component's response to determine whether it has met real-time requirements or a need to populate a large database, execute a test case, and then restore the database to its initial state for the next test case. These harnesses can be defined incrementally, sharing those things that address points of commonality and being parameterized by variation points.

The second way in which testing concepts are applied to core asset development is by testing other core assets; this is a key activity in satisfying the quality and reuse goals in a product line effort. Building a component to be reusable is widely recognized to be more costly than a one-off implementation targeted at a specific application because the component must be designed to handle a wide range of inputs and encompass a more complete set of states. (This applies to nonsoftware assets as well.) This results in additional tests being necessary to achieve adequate test coverage; however, the scale of reuse in a product line effort keeps this testing cost-effective.

Testing nonsoftware core assets: Every asset should be validated as it is created. This includes the business case, the scope definition, and the requirements model, and carries on to the analysis, architecture, and detailed design models. To make the validation of these models more objective, use personnel who did not create the model as the testers. For example, the process for testing an analysis model would specify that a group of domain experts who did not contribute to the original requirements capture would participate in the model's validation. The process remains subjective to the extent that the reviewers evaluate the quality of the model in addition to the other attributes. The testing process is made more systematic by defining a technique that selects test cases according to a specific algorithm, such as selecting a test case for each "very high priority" requirement. The validation process is made thorough by defining techniques for measuring the adequacy of the tests that have been selected so far. Finally, the testing process is integrated into the development process by tying it to the exit criteria for the development step that creates the asset.

For models built using a nonexecutable notation, the process described above is a review process that requires some way of determining whether or not the model produces correct answers. One technique is to have reviewers manually trace through the model (with the help of those who created it) to determine the answer that would result if the model could be executed. An alternative is to actually build an executable version of the model.

Testing software core assets: Software core assets are components, or even complete applications, that are intended to be integrated to produce products. Subject each component to a rigorous test during its construction. Examine the component against its specification, but also examine the behavior of the component in integrated situations. This unit test activity is the assessment procedure for the process step that produces the basic product code.

Product line assets have variation points implemented perhaps by providing a parameterization mechanism or by providing multiple implementations of an interface. The test plan for an individual component is divided into functional and structural test suites. Functional tests can be used for all of the variations. The structural tests must be modified for each different variation, as shown in Figure 4.3. For example, in object-oriented systems, the multiple

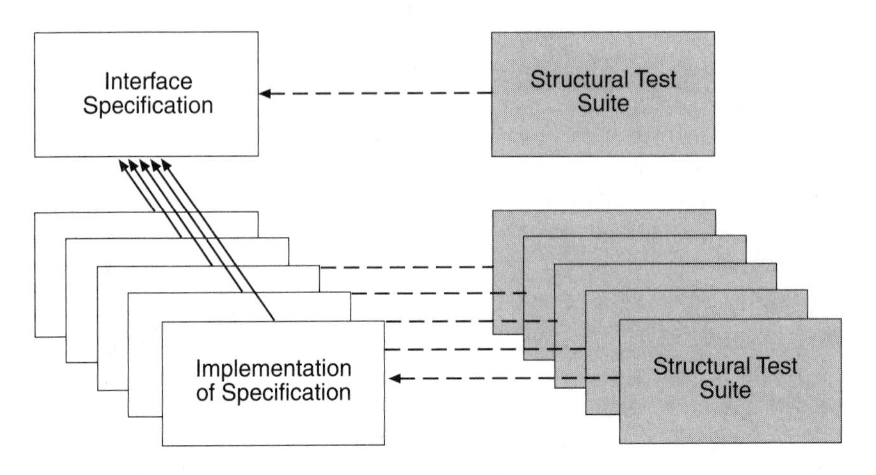

Figure 4.3 Multiple Implementations Lead to Multiple Test Suites

implementations are related to some abstract definition via an inheritance relationship.

An acceptance test is performed on all the assets being acquired. Designing the acceptance test includes identification of the desired attributes, definition of acceptable levels of those attributes, and evaluation of the asset to see if it exhibits those attributes. Assets such as compilers, other modeling tools from which code will be generated, and component libraries should be tested before being deployed to the technical staff.

4.8.3 Application to Product Development

Testing is used in two fundamental ways for products. Test between phases in the development process to *verify* that what was produced in the last phase is correct and suitable as input to the next phase. Test to *validate* a product against its requirements. Validation tests are intended to evaluate correctness relative to requirements.

In a product line effort, the main product development activity is assembly of products from core assets. The majority of each product's specification will be defined in a document generic to the product line. Define a complete set of functional tests for that specification. Some portion of each product's implementation will also be created at the product line level. Even if the functionality has been tested by means of some mechanism at the product line level, when it is integrated into a specific product, interactions with product-specific functionality can lead to failures. Define a set of interaction tests that will ensure that the additions made by the product developers do not cause failures. The tests used at the product level can be derived from the functionality tests, or possibly test templates, created at the product line level. The mapping between product assets and testing assets facilitates the reuse of these test assets. The mapping associates the test cases, as well as the test drivers and test data sets, with those requirements that are common across the product line. Taking advantage of this commonality results in a reduction in the amount of effort associated with (re)testing a product.

There is a trade-off between saving resources through the reuse of testing assets and improving quality by expending some of the saved resources. When more resources are devoted to those products created early in the product line effort, the quality of early deliverables is improved. Since these are the assets that will be reused, this improved quality will be propagated to future versions of the product being constructed and to future products.

4.8.4 Specific Practices

For analysis and model reviews, guided inspection is a technique that combines the checklist of an inspection with the thoroughness of testing [McGregor 99]. The inspection process is "guided" by the test cases. Specific methods for evaluating architecture and design models are discussed in the "Architecture Evaluation" practice area (Section 4.2).

McGregor describes testing practices designed specifically for product lines [McGregor 00].

4.8.5 Practice Risks

The major risks in testing are not doing enough of it and not doing it in high-payoff ways. Inadequate testing will result in low software quality, which will undermine the product line. Inadequate validation of nonsoftware artifacts will result in loss of trust in those artifacts and a decaying of the process-based or documentation-based practices they were intended to support. Specific testing risks include

- **Inadequate unit testing:** Component quality will be low if the unit-level testing is inadequate. Technical staff often will decide to "save time" by performing little or no unit-level testing. This may actually take more time because it will require an unexpected amount of integration and system testing. Additional time may be lost because it is well established that repairing errors found late in the development cycle is more costly than repairing those found early. The probability that this will occur is less in a product line environment that fosters a culture of reuse. However, if the risk becomes a problem, the cost will be far greater. The increased cost is directly attributable to the propagation of poor-quality components across the larger number of reuse sites. A well-defined software development process that specifies a unit test activity and defines a level of adequate coverage mitigates this risk.

- **Inadequate unit testing due to inadequate tool support:** The automation for unit testing will be inadequate if the testing is conducted only on application program interfaces (APIs). Few of the automated testing tools work on APIs, and those that do work usually require some amount of custom programming or comprehensive specifications. The risk is that if tools are not available, more resources will be expended to achieve an acceptable level of coverage. The probability that this will occur is less in a product line environment, where the cost of building special tools can be amortized over multiple products for which resources will be made available. However, if the risk becomes a problem, the cost will be far greater, owing to the propagation of poor-quality components across the larger number of reuse sites. A tools group at the product line level that provides testing support to all products mitigates this risk.
- **Inadequate specifications:** The testability of components will be low if inadequate specifications make it impossible to design tests. The probability that this will occur is about the same in a product line environment. However, if the risk becomes a problem, the cost will be far greater. The cost to the product line effort if this risk occurs is increased resource requirements to ensure adequate quality. Training developers to write complete, consistent, and correct specifications mitigates the risk.
- **Insufficient integration testing:** The flow of products will be slower than expected if sufficient integration testing is not conducted. The probability that this will occur will be higher in a product line environment if appropriate linkages are not established. The product line team and the product teams must be linked in a feedback loop. Internally, the product line team should use the product line architecture as a blueprint for communication links between component development teams to ensure that the interactions between components will be complete and correct.
- **Inadequate test infrastructure:** The anticipated high level of reuse of test assets will not be realized if sufficient resources are not devoted to the test infrastructure. If developers are allowed to test in ad hoc ways, or the test software architecture is not maintained properly, new tests will not be derived from existing ones. The resulting loss may be a reduction in quality and available resources.

4.8.6 For Further Reading

Beizer's *Software Testing Techniques* [Beizer 90] is a comprehensive survey of testing techniques applied at the unit, integration, and system levels. Beizer describes basic techniques regardless of the process or development paradigm. This book serves as a good general background.

McGregor's tutorial, "Building Reusable Test Assets for a Product Line" [McGregor 00], provides a jump-start for personnel charged with establishing the testing process for a product line environment. It presents techniques for taking advantage of the personnel organization and software architectures to reduce the effort required for adequate testing. The techniques organize unit-level testing assets in a manner that directly reflects the architecture of the product software. The techniques also associate the requirements, in the form of use cases, with the system test cases.

Musa's *Software Reliability Engineering* [Musa 99] ties the amount of testing to measures of reliability. It describes the computation required to determine the levels of tests that are necessary to "prove" specific levels of reliability.

4.8.7 Discussion Questions

1. Testing is easier for a product line core asset because the effort applies to a large number of products. At the same time, testing is more difficult for a product line core asset because more test cases are needed to ensure that the core asset is sufficiently general across its (broad) range of intended use. Resolve this apparent paradox.
2. Sketch a validation plan for several nonsoftware core assets. How will you make sure that such assets satisfy their stakeholders' needs?
3. Discuss how software testing concepts such as unit testing and regression testing might have analogies in the process of validating nonsoftware assets such as design documents or domain models.
4. There are metrics that apply specifically to testing. Coverage metrics have been identified for several of the testing techniques discussed above. They measure how completely an artifact has been exercised by the tests that have been applied to it. The productivity of a testing technique, termed the *yield,* can be expressed as the number of faults found per hour of developer time or per hour of machine time. These measures can be used to compare different testing techniques. Some projects use these measures as stopping criteria. When the productivity falls below a certain threshold, this type of testing may be terminated. Try to define some coverage and yield metrics for various core assets in a software product line you are familiar with. What is a "fault" in a nonsoftware asset?

4.9 Understanding Relevant Domains

One of the constants we've observed in successful software product line organizations is that they have at their disposal a deep and broad understanding of the domains that are relevant to their software endeavors. This practice area is about achieving that understanding. Domains are areas of expertise that can be applied to the creation of a system or set of systems. Domain knowledge is characterized by a set of concepts and terminology understood by practitioners in that area of expertise. It also includes an understanding of recurring problems and known solutions within the domain. Knowledge from several domains is usually required to build a single product. For example, to build a distributed banking application you would need knowledge of banking practices, commercial bank information systems, workflow management, database management systems, networking, and user interfaces, just to name a few. The point is, you would never attempt to build a distributed banking application (or any other nontrivial system) without first making sure you knew enough about the relevant business and technical areas to impart at least a reasonable hope for success. "Knowing enough" to make good product decisions comes from understanding the relevant domains.

The practice of understanding the relevant domains imparts the following responsibilities:

- Identifying the areas of expertise—domains—that are useful for building the product or products under consideration
- Identifying the recurring problems and known solutions within those domains
- Capturing and representing this information in ways that allow it to be communicated to the stakeholders and used and reused across the entire effort

How does an organization achieve this understanding? Typically, an organization builds up its store of expertise from its prior experiences with delivering products. An organization can also hire outside experts who provide or augment the organic level of understanding. In addition, it can employ domain analysis methods to gather, organize, and communicate domain information in a form known as a domain model.

Understanding relevant domains is initiated by eliciting domain information from various sources. This elicitation includes the investigation of current products and interviews with domain experts and product marketers, developers, and users to identify the current and potential future capabilities for the product(s) being considered. The elicitation also captures the needs and expectations of the various stakeholders and helps in the assessment of the technical maturity and stability of the relevant domains. The extent of the elicitation activity depends on the availability of sources and the amount of domain knowledge already known in-house.

It should be incumbent on whoever is selected to be the repository of your organization's domain expertise to document the key domain information in the form of a domain model that can be used as the vehicle for analysis and reasoning. The domain model should capture the different views of the product(s) from the perspectives of relevant stakeholders. In the absence of a documented domain model, your organization is vulnerable to the loss of the experts. Furthermore, documentation will refine and sharpen the understanding of the experts themselves; writing a thing down requires a deeper understanding of it than carrying it around in one's head. And finally, a documented domain model can be reviewed and improved by stakeholders who can make a contribution to it not otherwise possible by adding to it their anticipated future needs.

The extent to which a formal analysis is performed depends on two factors:

1. **The depth of the organization's domain experience:** Organizations that have deep domain expertise frequently opt not to invest in a full-blown "formal" domain analysis to model their understanding of the relevant domains. (For example, they may use a hybrid approach that combines requirements gathering with use-case modeling and commonality and variability analysis.) This allows them to move into designing more quickly or to perform some initial design activities (such as the investigation of architectural styles) in parallel with the analysis.
2. **The amount of resources that can be devoted to analysis:** The time, money, and people allocated to the analysis will determine the duration and scope of the analysis activities. However, this is not to suggest that more analysis is always better. In fact, "analysis paralysis," discussed in Section 4.9.5, is a risk associated with this practice area.

Regardless of its formality or comprehensiveness, the purpose of having a domain model at all is to be able to document the expertise needed to serve as authoritative criteria for making product and design decisions. You need to have enough information to make sound business decisions without necessarily undertaking an extensive analysis of all of the applicable domain knowledge. An organization has achieved a sufficient understanding of the domains relevant to a product or products when it can successfully apply that understanding toward

- reasoning about the technical and business implications of a proposed design
- making informed decisions about features, capabilities, and technologies to offer in proposed products
- creating a set of artifacts that exploits the understanding of the relevant domains

4.9.1 Aspects Peculiar to Product Lines

Understanding the relevant domains is the first step to understanding the commonality and variability that can be expected to occur among the products identified in the product line's scope. What you need to know to build a product line is distinguished from what you need to know for single-system construction by its emphasis on capturing and representing the common and variant capabilities of multiple systems encompassing multiple domains. That is, when gathering domain knowledge, look for the ways in which systems in those (or using those) domains are alike and the ways in which they differ from each other. A domain model for a product line will thus identify commonalities and variations present in a domain explicitly, whereas a domain model for a one-of-a-kind system probably will not, focusing instead perhaps on how systems evolve once fielded.

A domain model will be especially useful to help you determine

- which capabilities tend to be common across systems in the domain(s) and which variations are present. This information will inform the process of scoping, in which the commonality and variations for *your* product line will be established.
- which subsets of capabilities might be packaged together as assets for the product line. This information begins to inform the architecture creation effort for the product line by suggesting potential subsystems that have occurred in other systems in the domain(s).
- what constraints (such as standards, legal restrictions, business constraints, specific hardware platforms) apply to systems in the domain(s).
- which assets typically constitute members of the domain(s). This suggests a list of assets that an organization could begin to search for in its own legacy inventory or on the open market.
- whether to continue with the product line development effort.

The last item is important; the ability to reason about a product line can help management gain confidence in the soundness of the decision to adopt a product line approach. Reasoning also grounds the design decisions in a firm experiential basis (even if the experience is not the organization's own), which reduces technical risk and also has a soothing effect on nervous managers. Even a rudimentary and informal domain analysis, for example, that examines at a high level the potential domains and their interactions within a product line, can help refine both the scope of the product line and the initial estimates for resource allocation. And it can show the organization and its management that they are not exploring uncharted territory.

The level of detail and degree of formality of the models for a product line depend on the depth and distribution of an organization's domain knowledge as well as on the kind of reasoning about the product line that the organization wishes to support by modeling. Some organizations have such a thorough understanding of their domains and their reuse potential that they can move very quickly from identifying a business opportunity to creating core assets. Organizations less experienced in exploiting reuse need to approach the problem more deliberately, analyzing commonality and variability in order to understand the technical implications for assets and products and analyzing the business implications for the product line as a whole. Additionally, they may have to hire domain experts if the requisite domain expertise isn't already present or isn't mature enough. Whatever the degree of understanding, each organization has some model of the product line that evolves as the development effort progresses. The model may be an informal, shared understanding of the product line, with minimal documentation, or it may be a more formal abstract characterization of the product line, complete with its own representation schemes and automated support. If the purpose of the analysis is to obtain insights into the technical feasibility and potential scope of the product line quickly, the analysis does not need to model the commonality and variability exhaustively.

In summary, understanding relevant domains is about systematically capturing and utilizing knowledge of systems similar to the ones that you are about to build. This knowledge provides you with an informed world view from which you can then make specific decisions about your product line, especially regarding its scope, shared and unique requirements, and architecture.

4.9.2 Application to Core Asset Development

Understanding relevant domains is applied to core asset development to identify and model the opportunities for large-grained reuse across a product line early in the product line's life cycle. It has a profound influence on the architecture for the product line, which is the definitive design statement about the commonalities and variabilities that will be supported across the product line. It also supports the business case for the product line and feeds the "Scoping" and "Requirements Engineering" practice areas (Sections 5.5 and 4.6).

Other Voices: Commonality Analysis at Lucent Technologies

In 1994, Lucent Technologies launched the Domain Engineered Configuration Control (DECC) project to try to standardize software written to help engineers manage the hardware components installed in Lucent's flagship 5ESS telephone switch. The DECC team adopted a product line approach, which began by understanding the domain [Ardis 00].

> *The first step of the DECC project was to perform a domain analysis of [5ESS hardware] configuration control software. The main task was to compose a* commonality analysis *document as a group activity. A recorder transcribed the document during the meetings, with all team members present. A moderator facilitated the process, and helped the group find appropriate representations of their knowledge. (In fact, the same person often performed the moderator and recorder roles.) This style of group writing is unusual, but it emphasizes the importance of consensus amongst experts. Each member of the team was an author of the final document and was responsible for its accuracy.*

Disputes between experts were resolved through further analysis and discussion . . . .

A commonality analysis document primarily consists of definitions of technical terms, commonalities of family members, variabilities between family members, and parameters of variation, which are refinements of the variabilities . . . .

Definitions captured the common vocabulary of the domain, an area of surprising controversy. Experts would occasionally misunderstand one another, because they were using the same words in different ways. In fact, experts would sometimes be in "violent agreement" with one another, all the while expressing the same idea in different terms. Only after defining terms precisely did they discover their common ground . . . .

Commonalities captured what was essentially the same among all family members. Often the commonalities were obfuscated by different implementations of the software. The difficulty of domain analysis lies in abstracting the commonalities from the details of their implementations. This was often done by starting with common examples and then considering possible exceptions to the norm. Reviews performed by additional domain experts helped to ensure that all possible cases were considered . . . .

Variabilities described the possible differences between family members. For configuration control that meant different attributes of hardware units and different relationships between those units. Discovering the variability of hardware attributes was relatively straightforward, but occasionally tedious. The main job was to pare down all of the possible attributes to those that affected configuration control. In the final analysis the units were distinguishable on about forty attributes . . . .

Once the variabilities had been described, the team refined them into parameters of variation. *These were precise specifications of the ranges of variabilities, binding times of values, and default values. Creation of the parameters took only a few sessions, but it provided a review of the variabilities for internal consistency . . . .*

Throughout the analysis effort issues would occasionally arise that prevented the team from making progress. Whenever this occurred the team would write the issue as a question to be resolved and assign an owner to the issue. It was the owner's responsibility to research the issue and propose a set of alternative solutions. The team would consider the solutions and try to reach consensus. If they could not come to consensus they would leave the issue unresolved and seek more research. Most issues were resolved after one round of research, but a few were revisited several times.

The team met once or twice a week over six months to complete the document, with each meeting lasting about 3 hours. Although this may seem like a lot of work, the total effort for this phase was only about one staff-year. Team membership varied over the duration of the project.

Some experts came for a few meetings and then dropped out. The core of the team consisted of four experts who were present for almost all meetings.

Other domain experts reviewed draft versions of the commonality analysis document. This provided two main benefits. First, it helped ensure the accuracy of the analysis by employing the knowledge of more experts. Second, it began the socialization of the ideas in the analysis throughout the community of eventual users of the resulting technology. Domain experts outside the team were also consulted on issues identified for research. These informal contacts helped to educate the outside experts in the mission and direction of the DECC team. This process also made those experts better reviewers, as they had a better understanding of the purpose of the analysis

Clarifying terminology is a recurring theme in domain analysis experience reports, especially in efforts that bring together (as they should) a diverse group of experts and stakeholders. Plan for your domain analysis work to produce a glossary that explains key terms and concepts relevant to your product line effort, and make that glossary a core asset. You might want to release it as part of the production plan or the product line concept of operations document (see the "Operations" practice area (Section 6.7).

4.9.3 Application to Product Development

A customer request for a new product or for new capabilities in an existing product triggers a business decision. That decision can and should be supported by domain understanding. The simplest case is when the requested capabilities have already been modeled and analyzed as part of core asset development. If they have not, a decision has to be made about the effects of the request on the product line.

- Should the new product or capabilities be developed as a one-off customer-specific solution?
- Should the requested capabilities be incorporated into the product line because of their potential reuse in future products?

The understanding of the relevant domains facilitates this kind of decision making by providing information that supports the assessment of customer-specific requests for new product line capabilities. This assessment, in turn, may broaden the understanding of the relevant domain knowledge. In fact, such decision-making opportunities represent one form of feedback between asset consumers and asset producers, and they have the potential to expand the scope of the product line by challenging previously held assumptions about commonality and variability. Any such feedback from products to assets should be documented so that it can be evaluated and, if necessary, incorporated into any models of the relevant domains.

Similarly, understanding the relevant domains can also be used as the basis for analyzing the effects of a proposed change in the requirements for the product line and for recommending a course of action. For example, a business decision to switch to a different operating system can be checked against the operating system capabilities assumed for the product line. At a minimum, there could be a checklist of features whose presence or absence in the new operating system will either shorten or lengthen the product development schedule. A more detailed model of assumed operating system capabilities would provide a greater ability to quantify the effects of the proposed change on the product development process.

4.9.4 Specific Practices

The main practice is having the right people in the product line organization—those with long, deep experience in the relevant domains. (This has been a recurring theme at the annual Software Engineering Institute (SEI) product line practice workshops [Bass 98b].) The specific practices for eliciting and representing relevant domain information are embodied in the analysis processes described below.

Other Voices: Domain Analysis for Elevator Control Systems

LG Industrial Systems Co. Ltd. is one of Korea's leading suppliers of elevator control systems. Here is their experience with domain analysis for their software product line [Lee 00]:

> *Domain analysis, which exploits commonality and variability in a domain, is a key requirement for a product line organization . . . . The (elevator control software) feature model is composed of 490 features (157 capability, 22 operating environment, 291 domain technology, and 20 implementation technique features). For about 3 months, 8 domain experts, 2 methodologists, and 1 moderator were involved in the modeling activity. It is our experience that clarifying the domain boundaries and standardizing domain terminology must come before feature modeling as different perceptions of domain boundary and domain terminology often lead to wasteful discussions between modelers and may produce a complicated feature model with redundant information . . . . In our experience, the feature-oriented domain analysis method is effective in identifying commonality and variability and in modeling reusable and adaptable components in a product line . . . . We often found that engineers working on the same product line did not agree on*

what specific features meant. It would be difficult to develop a feature model for a product line without a common understanding and an agreement of the semantics of features.

Scope, commonality, and variability (SCV) analysis: The SCV approach, from Lucent Technologies, gives software engineers a systematic way of thinking about the product family they are creating. It identifies, formalizes, and documents commonalities and variabilities. SCV is the commonality analysis portion of the Family-Oriented Abstraction, Specification, and Translation (FAST) approach, also from Lucent Technologies. The FAST method includes the dual life cycles of domain engineering and application engineering. It uses the results of a commonality analysis to create a language for both specifying domain members and generating members from the specification [Coplien 98, Weiss 99].

Domain analysis and design process (DADP): DADP is a process model for domain analysis and design created by the Defense Information Systems Agency (DISA). It is based on an object-oriented approach to analysis and design. The domain analysis process focuses on identifying commonalities and determining common object adaptation requirements (the differences among domain common objects are not described in terms of variability but rather in terms of tailoring the information to particular needs) [DISA 93].

Feature-oriented domain analysis (FODA): The FODA method defines the process and products of a domain analysis, with an emphasis on the commonality and variability of the features that users commonly expect in domain applications. The analysis process creates models of the domain that describe its relationship to other domains, the common and variant features of the domain, and the behavior of applications in the domain [Kang 90, Cohen 92].

Other Voices: Domain Analysis at Cummins Inc.

Cummins Inc. is the world's largest producer of large diesel engines, which are laden with embedded software. Cummins launched a successful software product line to produce this software with impressive results described elsewhere in this book. Here, they describe their experience with domain analysis for the product line [Dager 00]:

Cummins encountered the concept of product-line-specific domain analysis during its search for industry best practices. Two people were assigned part-time to perform this analysis over a four-week period. Several others provided additional information and reviewed the results.

Performing this domain analysis quickly put to rest concerns about the nonoperational expectations of Cummins products not being fully understood. Domain analysis helped Cummins complete its requirement space.

Until domain analysis was completed, Cummins had always driven its software architecture and reuse concept based on the functionality common across each market in which its products were sold. This allowed the uncommon elements to be designed outside the common architecture team. The requirements generated by different markets were not being analyzed or compared against the existing requirements and designs of the core software asset. If two features of the system simply had different marketing names, they were often developed separately. Domain analysis allowed Cummins to begin seeing similarities rather than assuming differences. This allowed Cummins to truly see the gaps in its products and begin designing around the true differences and similarities. It is noted that truly understanding the differences has proven as beneficial to the architectural development as understanding the similarities.

You can read more about Cummins's software product line for engines in Chapter 9.

Synthesis process of the reuse-driven software processes (RSP) approach: Synthesis is a methodology for creating software systems as instances of a family of similar systems. It was developed by the Software Productivity Consortium in recognition of a need to produce improvements in software productivity, product quality, manageability, and customer responsiveness. A Synthesis process consists of two subprocesses: domain engineering and application engineering. The domain engineering process includes an explicit domain analysis process that captures commonality and variability for a product family [SPC 93].

Domain analysis process of organizational domain modeling (ODM): ODM is a highly tailorable and configurable domain engineering process model. The process model is organized hierarchically as a tree of processes, and although the term "domain analysis" is not used, all the elements of a domain analysis process are present at various levels within the process tree. In particular, there are subtrees of processes for domain identification and scoping, domain modeling, and model refinement. ODM was created by Organon Motives, Inc. and Lockheed Martin under contract to the Department of Defense's STARS (Software Technology for Adaptable Reliable Systems) program [STARS 96].

There are documented cases of organizations that have employed and adapted these methods successfully. Several books contain chapters that summarize and compare the characteristics of these and other domain analysis methods [Arango 94, Wartik 92]. There are also cases in which organizations have employed domain analysis practices successfully in the creation of product lines, even though they did not use a documented domain analysis method [Bass 98b].

The elicitation, representation, and validation of relevant domain information and the techniques employed (such as object-oriented technology, use-case modeling, and state-transition diagrams) vary across the different domain analysis methods and are not described using the same vocabulary. In a product line context, organizations perform these practices to varying degrees of completeness and rigor. In particular, organizations with deep domain knowledge and considerable expertise in applying it to building products often opt for an abbreviated form of analysis that proceeds very quickly to the design.

4.9.5 Practice Risks

Inadequate domain understanding in the organization will jeopardize the product line effort. Without a detailed (not just basic) understanding of the precise commonalities and variabilities that need to be accounted for, the architect's hands are tied, the business case will be weak, and the scope definition will be unrealistic. The result will be a set of products that do not adequately address the applications they were intended to work for. Inadequate domain understanding can result from

- **Analysis paralysis:** The "analysis paralysis" phenomenon occurs when an inordinate amount of time is devoted to the creation of one or more very detailed analysis models. A strategy for mitigating this risk is to perform a relatively quick, broad exploration of commonality and variability to gain an understanding of the issues and their effects on the product line. This allows for early input to management decision makers, who can then assess the value of proceeding further with the analysis and allocate resources accordingly. It also allows some of the design work to proceed in parallel—for example, the initial architecture exploration. Ideally, this approach would be part of an overall iterative and incremental process for the development of the product line. An alternative risk-mitigation strategy is to narrow the scope of the analysis.
- **Lack of access to the necessary domain expertise:** It is essential to be able to elicit domain information from the domain experts. However, the domain experts are usually coveted organizational resources who are in high demand and may not be in the same geographic location as the rest of the analysis team. Therefore careful planning is needed to ensure that the domain experts' time is not wasted. Such planning might include scheduling of specific meetings with the experts, circulation of elicitation questionnaires in advance, and use of videoconferences or teleconferences

when face-to-face meetings are not possible. In all cases, there must be management commitment to ensure that the domain experts are available for participation.

- **Inadequate documentation and sharing of relevant domain information:** If the understanding of the relevant domains is in the heads of a few key people and not shared with the rest of the product line team, there is a great and obvious risk should any of these key people leave the organization. There is the more subtle risk of false assumptions and time wasted rediscovering what is already known. Hence, the "mental model" carried by the key people should at least be recorded so that it can be shared. The level of rigor and the amount of detail in the documentation should be driven by the need to make such information robust enough for the long haul of a product line effort. At a minimum, assumptions and decisions about what is common, what is variable, and what is excluded from the product line should be documented, plus some justification for these assumptions and decisions that ties to the business case. Recording this information will also mitigate the risk of having key people leave the project, taking their domain understanding with them.
- **Lack of understanding of an analysis process:** The naïve application of an analysis process can be evidenced by a premature focus on design and implementation issues or too much time spent in the analysis. Proper training in both the analysis method and its role for the product line is essential here; the analysis should be performed in the context of the organization's overall reuse and process improvement goals and the specific goals established for the product line.
- **Lack of appropriate tool support for process and products of domain analysis:** Organizations typically use existing commercial object-oriented analysis and design tools to support a product line analysis effort. Such tools may not support the kind of conceptual modeling required by product line analysis; care must be taken to avoid being driven by the tool into a premature design process masquerading as an analysis process.
- **Lack of management commitment:** If management either does not appreciate the value of domain understanding or does not understand the need for an analysis process that could be time-consuming and does not culminate with the production of any marketable products (or executable code), the effort will likely lose requisite management support. The documentation of a domain model and any analysis that is initiated should be grounded in issues that are key to management; they support specific business goals established for the product line. Management needs to be made aware of the importance of having documented domain understanding not only as essential to subsequent decisions about the product line but also as a powerful way of mitigating the technical and product risks associated with the product line effort.

4.9.6 For Further Reading

For a comparative survey of published domain analysis methods that also maps each method onto a common domain analysis process, see Chapter 2 in Arango's *Software Reusability* [Arango 94]. For a comprehensive description of a best-of-breed domain analysis method, see Kang's 1990 report on feature-oriented domain analysis (FODA) [Kang 90] or the STARS report on organization domain modeling (ODM) [STARS 96]. The Software Productivity Consortium's Synthesis methodology incorporates domain analysis into the construction of families of systems having similar descriptions [SPC 93b]. Commonality and variability analysis is an important part of Weiss and Lai's Feature-Oriented Abstraction, Specification, and Translation (FAST) process for product lines [Weiss 99].

4.9.7 Discussion Questions

1. Think about a software product line that is or could be produced by your organization or a software product line that you know about.
   - What are the relevant domains? How would you go about constructing a domain model for the most important ones?
   - What are some of the commonalities shared by products? What are the variations?
   - In your organization, where does the expertise for these domains reside? How did the experts come by their knowledge?
2. Suppose you are responsible for building the relevant domain models for a product line.
   - Suppose a colleague of yours is responsible for defining the scope of the product line. What information do you suppose he or she will need from you? What information will you need from him or her?
   - What information do you suppose the product line's architect will want from you?
   - What information do you suppose the person responsible for the product line's business case will want from you? What information will you want from him or her?

5

Technical Management Practice Areas

Technical management practices are those management practices that are necessary to engineer the creation and evolution of both core assets and products. Technical management practices are carried out in the technical activities represented by the core asset and product development parts of Figure 5.1. In alphabetical order, the practice areas in technical management are as follows:

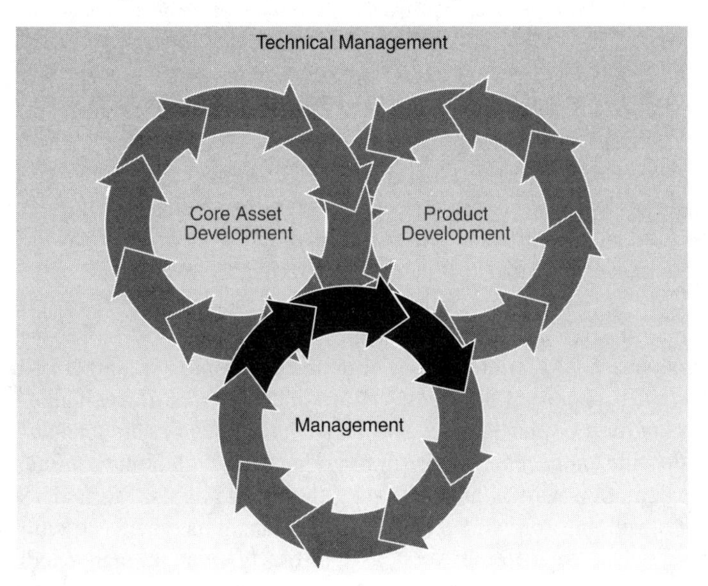

Figure 5.1 Technical Management

- Configuration Management
- Data Collection, Metrics, and Tracking
- Make/ Buy/ Mine/Commission Analysis
- Process Definition
- Scoping
- Technical Planning
- Technical Risk Management
- Tool Support

These are skills that any project manager will be familiar with, but, like the software engineering practice areas, they take on special forms and shades of meaning in a software product line. All of these skills support and pave the way for software development activities. Scoping and Technical Planning lay out what is to be built and how. Data Collection, Metrics, and Tracking as well as Technical Risk Management establish "health" measures for the software development efforts and help assess their current conditions. Make/Buy/Mine/Commission Analysis, Tool Support, Configuration Management, and Process Definition all contribute to the smooth running of the development efforts.

5.1 Configuration Management

> *The purpose of Software Configuration Management is to establish and maintain the integrity of the products of the software project throughout the project's software life cycle. Software Configuration Management involves identifying configuration items for the software project, controlling these configuration items and changes to them, and recording and reporting status and change activity for these configuration items [SEI 00].*

Configuration management (CM) refers to a discipline for evaluating, coordinating, approving or disapproving, and implementing changes in artifacts that are used to construct and maintain software systems. An artifact may be an item of hardware, software, or documentation. CM enables the management of artifacts from the initial concept through design, implementation, testing, baselining, building, release, and maintenance.

At its heart, CM is intended to eliminate the confusion and error brought about by the existence of different versions of artifacts. Artifact change is a fact of life: plan for it or plan to be overwhelmed by it. Changes are made to correct errors, provide enhancements, or simply reflect the evolutionary refinement of product definition. CM is about keeping the inevitable change under control. Without a well-enforced CM process, different team members (possibly at different sites) can use different versions of artifacts unintentionally; individuals can create versions without the proper authority; and the wrong version of an artifact can be used inadvertently. Successful CM requires a well-defined and institutionalized set of policies and standards that clearly define the following:

- the set of artifacts (configuration items) under the jurisdiction of CM
- how artifacts are named
- how artifacts enter and leave the controlled set
- how an artifact under CM is allowed to change
- how different versions of an artifact under CM are made available and under what conditions each is allowed to be used
- how CM tools are used to enable and enforce CM

These policies and standards are documented in a CM plan that informs everyone in the organization just how CM is carried out.

5.1.1 Aspects Peculiar to Product Lines

CM is, of course, an integral part of any software development activity, but it takes on a special significance in the product line context. As illustrated in Figure 5.2, CM for product lines is generally viewed as a multidimensional version of the CM problem for one-of-a-kind systems. The core assets constitute a configuration that needs to be managed; each of the products in the product line

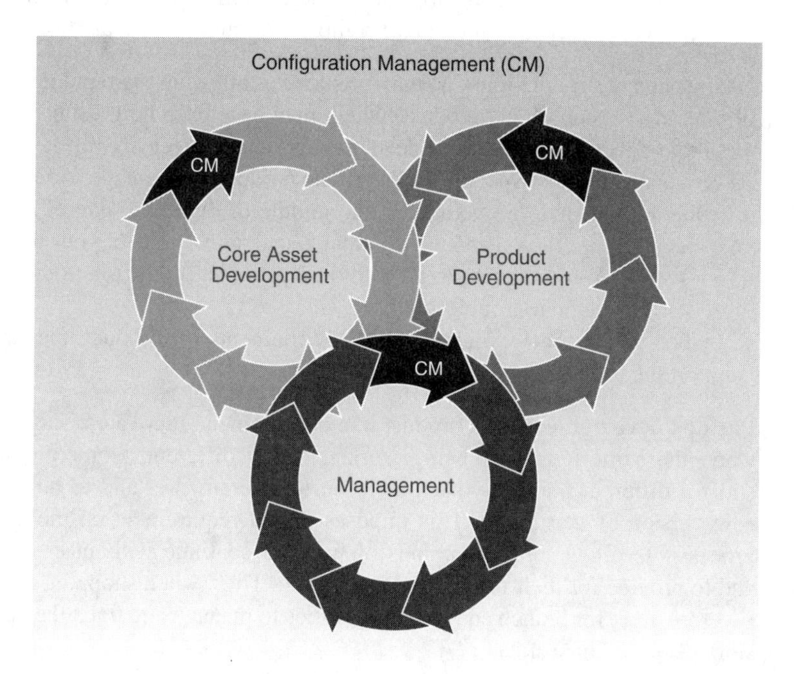

Figure 5.2 Configuration Management and Software Product Lines

constitutes a configuration that must be managed; and the management of all of these configurations must be coordinated under a single process.

CM for product lines is therefore more complex than it is for single systems. In particular:

- In single-system CM, each version of the system has a configuration associated with it that defines the versions of the configuration items that went into its production. In product line CM, there must be a configuration maintained for each version *of each product.*
- In single-system CM, each product with all of its versions may be managed separately. In product line CM, this is untenable because the core assets are used across all products. Hence, the entire product line is usually managed with a single, unified CM process.
- Product line CM must control the configuration of the core asset base and its use by all product developers. It must account for the fact that assets are usually produced by one team and used in parallel by several others. Single-system CM has no such burden: the component developers and the product developers are the same.
- Only the most capable CM tools can be used in a product line effort. Many tools that are adequate for single-system CM are simply not sufficiently robust to handle the demands of product line CM. (See the "Tool Support" practice area, Section 5.8, for a more complete discussion of tools.)

The mission of product line CM may be stated as allowing the rapid reconstruction of any version of any product, which may have been built using various versions of the core assets and development/operating environment *plus* various versions of product-specific artifacts. One product line manager summed up the problem this way: "Sometime, in the middle of the night, one of your customers is going to call you and tell you that his version of one of your products doesn't work. You are going to have to duplicate that product in your test lab before you can begin to troubleshoot."

To elaborate, the tools, processes, and environments for product line CM must support the following capabilities:

- **Parallel development:** In a product line development, there are occasions when the same items are being worked on by different people/groups and for different purposes (such as to customize an asset and to build a new version of that asset). This imposes a dual requirement on the CM process—to allow separate strands of work to continue without conflict and to provide for their ultimate consolidation. Thus, when shopping for a CM tool, look for branch and join capabilities to manage and track the version history of an artifact.
- **Distributed engineering:** Organizations that develop product lines might have more than one development/maintenance site. This requires CM to

support distribution, possibly via a network. Depending on the speed of the network connection, this may imply replication of configuration items, which would require the CM to keep replicated configuration items consistent over the network. In a distributed development/maintenance environment, it is also likely that the different groups will be working in different development environments. In that case, CM will need to support heterogeneous environments, which will require import/export features.

- **Build and release management:** Build management enables developers to create a version of a product, which can be anything from a single component to a complete customer solution for the purpose of testing and/or integration. Release management builds the final customer solution, which also includes instantiation of the developing and testing environment. In a product line context, release management includes the release of core assets to product developers. When shopping for CM tools, make sure the one you buy can help you build releases.
- **Change management:** An authorized group must analyze carefully any changes proposed to artifacts that are under configuration control. The resolution of the proposals must be communicated, and any resultant changes must be planned, assigned, tracked, and broadcast. Changes in core assets need to be weighed carefully for their impact on the entire product line. Requests for changes in core assets can come from any product team or from the core asset team.
- **Configuration and workspace management:** The individual handling of artifacts is also important to manage. Configuration and workspace management specifies what a configuration is; this includes the testing and support environment (for instance, a compiler and a debugger) and how users can create their own workspaces or views when working on a configuration. Whether or not your CM tool helps you with this, remember to carry along the environmental information with each artifact.
- **Process management:** Defined processes are essential for a mature CM capability. Especially in a product line environment, the CM must define the process life cycles for the configuration items and set up appropriate change control and authorization policies for product element modifications. CM processes need to be reviewed and improved as the product line effort matures. Any changes in the CM process need to be managed and rolled out carefully to the entire product line organization. The defined process must address:
  - **life-cycle management:** The life cycle is defined for every type of configuration item, assigning states and possible transitions to it. Changes in any item need to be analyzed, authorized, planned, implemented, documented, reviewed, tracked, and communicated. Also included are a list of actions (such as notifying a set of interested parties) that need to occur when an item transitions from one state to another; change

authorization policies that define how changes are authorized for an item; and closure rules that specify when an item (such as a change request) is closed.

- **roles and responsibilities:** There are roles and responsibilities associated with each configuration item. For example, roles include owner (who has the responsibility for the artifact), reviewer (who analyzes changes in the artifact), implementer (who makes the changes), and so on. CM must support the definition and management of product line roles, many of which are nontraditional.
- **configuration item identification and attributes:** Specific configuration items need specific names and information (labels). The information needed for a core component (for example, the products in which the core asset is currently used) differs from that needed for product-specific components. There might also be a requirement within a particular product line development to assign special attributes (for instance, has a proxy). The product line CM system has to have a means of applying this kind of attribute customization.

- **Repository management:** This facilitates the storage of the configuration items with version management and branching, and their attached information, as well as providing a comprehensive query capability for accessing all the information in the repository.

Product line CM must also support the process of merging results either because new versions of assets are included in a product or because product-specific results are introduced into the asset base. Finally, since introducing changes may affect multiple versions of multiple products, you'll want your CM system for a product line to deliver sound data for an impact analysis to help you understand what impact a proposed change will have.

5.1.2 Application to Core Asset Development

The entire core asset base is under CM, with support for all of the tasks described in the preceding section. Core assets, after all, may be developed in parallel by distributed teams, may need their builds and releases to be managed, and so forth. Beyond this support, however, core asset development requires other features of the organization's CM capability. First, it requires a flexible concept of assets, which can be hardware, software, and documents of all varieties. One of the more useful features of a CM tool is the ability to report the differences between two versions of an artifact, but this often requires fluency in the language in which the artifact is represented. (Have you ever tried to execute a DIFF command on two binary files? If so, you get the point.) Thus, a tool's difference-reporting capabilities may weigh heavily in the selection process.

5.1.3 Application to Product Development

The CM process should make it easy to set up the initial configuration of a new product. Every time a new product is developed (which can occur very often in a healthy and robust product line), the task of determining the appropriate core assets and how to make them available must be supported.

CM also has to keep track of all the versions of configuration items that are used. This includes the version of the tool environment (compilers, test suites, and so on) used to create the configuration. Incorporating new versions of assets to build a new version of a product is a task that requires an impact analysis that must be supported by CM. Changes in core assets must be communicated via the CM process to the core asset development organization.

5.1.4 Specific Practices

IEEE/ANSI standard for CM plans: There is a finely detailed IEEE/ANSI standard on CM that contains a comprehensive outline for a CM plan as well as several fully worked out examples of CM plans for different kinds of systems and organizations [IEEE 87]. These plans contain change control policies, describe organizational roles, define artifact life cycles, and in general make a fine starting point for an organization wishing to craft its own CM plan. One sample plan, called "Software Configuration Management Plan for a Product Line System," is of particular interest. This plan is for a hypothetical organization that produces many versions of a product for a myriad of customers, some of whom are internal to the organization itself. This plan hypothesizes an engineering group (that would seem to mirror our notion of a core asset group) as well as several product groups. This, as well as other similarities to our concept of a product line built as a product family, make this plan an excellent place to start.

Other Voices: CM at HP

Hewlett-Packard has enjoyed long success with the software product line approach, particularly in their family of printers. Here is how they approach the configuration management task for a project they call "Owen" [Toft 00]:

> *Owen uses the "change-set" (c-set) methodology [see www.truesoft.com] for software configuration management (SCM). This is a third-generation SCM approach that manages each single, complete, logical change to the code base as a c-set. A single, logical change could be an added feature, a defect fix, a performance enhancement, and so on. A single c-set can include changes to many discrete files, can include or exclude files, can alter the location of files in the file hierarchy, and so on. The c-set,*

not the file, is the fundamental unit of version management. C-sets are considered to be orthogonal to one another, in that they represent discrete, (hopefully) noninteracting changes.

Each Owen component is composed of a "set of c-sets"—that is, the original version of the code for the component, plus the application of some or all of the c-sets created for that component. So the firmware for an Owen product is generated from the code base by specifying which components are part of the version and which versions of those components.

The c-set approach differs from the traditional "branch/merge" and "branch/deviate" approaches in that it allows the engineering team to choose which c-sets to take and which not to take. For example, an engineer might choose to take all c-sets related to defect fixes for a component but reject all c-sets related to feature extensions, perhaps until the next version of the product. This is consistent with the product-focused approach as it allows projects to manage the risk associated with their product.

This SCM approach is very well aligned with Owen's principles and development paradigm. It allows engineering teams the freedom to make a change to a component in the shared code base where the change might be needed only by their product. They know that other teams have the option of including or rejecting the c-set representing the change so the effect of their decision is decoupled from other teams. They are empowered to make the changes they need to develop their product and do not have to rely on other teams to do anything.

By reflecting the component-based approach in the SCM system, rapid leverage of the code base is also facilitated; engineering teams can quickly determine which versions of which components they need in order to begin development, and they can easily pull these from the asset base.

CMMI steps for CM: The SEI's Capability Maturity Model (Integrated) for System and Software Engineering lists the following practices as instrumental for a CM capability in an organization [SEI 00]:

1. Identify the configuration items, components, and related work products that will be placed under configuration management.
2. Establish and maintain a configuration management and change management system for controlling work products.
3. Create or release baselines for internal use and for delivery to the customer.
4. Track change requests for the configuration items.
5. Control changes in the content of configuration items.
6. Establish and maintain records describing configuration items.
7. Perform configuration audits to maintain the integrity of the configuration baselines.

5.1.5 Practice Risks

Configuration management imposes intellectual control over the otherwise unmanageable combinations involved in updating and using a multitude of versions of a multitude of artifacts, both core assets (of all kinds) and product-specific resources. Without an adequate CM process in place, and without adequate adherence to that process, developers will not be able to build and deploy products correctly, let alone re-create versions of products produced in the past. Inadequate CM control can result from the following:

- **Process not sufficiently robust:** CM for product lines is more complex than CM for single systems. If an organization does not define a robust enough CM process (that takes into account the features listed in Section 5.1.1), CM will fail, and the product line approach to product building will become less efficient.
- **CM occurs too late:** If the organization developing the product line does not have CM practices in place well before the first product is shipped, building new product versions or rebuilding shipped versions will be very time-consuming and expensive, negating one of the chief benefits of product lines.
- **Multiple asset evolution paths:** There is a risk that an asset may evolve in different directions. This can happen by design to enable the usage of an asset in different environments (operating systems, for example) or by accident when an asset evolves within a specific product. The first case increases the complexity of the CM but might not be avoidable. Attention should be directed to the second case. If this cannot be avoided, the usefulness of the asset base will be degraded. (See "A Tool for Software Product Line Production" sidebar for an example of a tool that helps ameliorate this problem.)
- **Unenforced CM practices:** Owing to the complexity of the total product line configuration, not enforcing a CM process can result in total chaos (much worse than for a single system).
- **Tool support not sufficiently robust:** CM sophisticated enough to support a nontrivial product line requires tool support, and there is no shortage of available commercial CM systems. However, most of them do not directly support the required functionality to be useful in a product line context. Many of them can be "convinced" to provide the necessary functionality, but this convincing is a time-consuming task requiring specialized knowledge. If the organization fails to assign someone to customize the CM system to the needs within the product line development, the CM tool support is likely to be ineffectual. Such a person needs to have both a good understanding of the product line processes and a solid grounding in CM.

5.1.6 For Further Reading

Rigg et al.'s *Ovum Evaluates: Configuration Management Tools* [Rigg 95] contains a thorough comparison of commercially available configuration management tools. It is a must for anybody who plans to buy a tool; even if it is a bit dated by now, its list of criteria remains helpful. Relevant industrial standards from IEEE and ISO on configuration management should also be on every project manager's bookshelf [IEEE 87, IEEE 98b, ISO 95b].

A good starting point for a World Wide Web literature search is WWW: <URL: *http://www.stsc.hill.af.mil/crosstalk/1999/mar/cmsites.asp*>, which contains links to other CM-related sites.

5.1.7 Discussion Questions

1. What artifacts in a product line would you put under configuration management? Of the ones you listed, how many are software, and how many are not?
2. For each artifact you named in the preceding question, whom would you appoint to the committee to approve/disapprove changes in it, and why? What qualities does someone who is asked to serve on a change control board need?
3. Does your organization have a CM plan? What aspects does it have, or does it lack, from the list given earlier in this practice area for a product line CM capability?
4. Think about a product line organization that produces about 30 or so very large products, each of which goes to a small number of known customers. Now think about an organization that produces about 30 or so small-to-medium products, each of which goes to thousands of anonymous customers. Would the CM capabilities for these two organizations need to be different? If so, how?
5. What are the advantages and disadvantages of saving changes in an artifact and then handling them all as a batch? What are the advantages and disadvantages of releasing groups of artifacts affected by a single change simultaneously, as opposed to releasing the individual artifacts as each one is changed?

5.2 Data Collection, Metrics, and Tracking

The purpose of measurement is to guide management decision making [Grady 92, Park 96]. The manager of an effort sets goals, defines objectives that satisfy those goals, and then creates a plan and applies resources to achieve those objectives. In order to determine whether the goals are being achieved as time passes (that is, whether the plan is working), the manager has to have data that indicate the state of the effort. By tracking and analyzing relevant, measurable attributes of the effort's process and product as metrics, the manager has a window on the progress toward the effort's goals. The manager can also detect issues that indicate when the effort has diverged from expectations. The manager can then revise the effort's goals, plan, or resources to address these issues—or recalibrate everyone's expectations.

In general, the measurement activity comprises two phases: an initiation phase and a performance phase. The steps in the performance phase are repeated until the effort's goals have been achieved. You may need to revise the goals along the way.

Initiation Phase

The initiation phase is a planning activity that involves the following steps:

1. Designate the goals that will be tracked.
2. Define the metrics that will be used to track the progress toward those goals.
3. Identify the data that must be collected in order to derive those metrics.
4. Characterize the expected results and issues that may be discovered, based on any foreseen risks.
5. Specify how the data will be collected, when the data will be collected, and by whom it will be collected.

Performance Phase

The performance phase carries out the plan and involves the following steps:

1. Collect the specified data.
2. Analyze and translate the collected data into metrics and compare them against the expectations that were characterized during the initiation phase.
3. Determine the actions that are needed to remedy any discovered issues.
4. Confirm whether those actions were appropriate for addressing those issues.

5.2.1 Aspects Peculiar to Product Lines

The techniques for collecting and tracking data are the same for a product line as for a single system; both situations require an initiation phase and a performance phase. But in a product line, data collection needs to provide information from three perspectives, not just the single perspective of product development. Recall the three essential activities of product line development:

1. Core asset development, comprising efforts to produce reusable assets and the supporting infrastructure for their use
2. Product development, comprising efforts to produce individual products for customers
3. Management of the overall product line, including the strategic planning and direction of a total product line enterprise

Collecting and tracking appropriate metrics supports each of these activities. A product line manager is concerned with tracking whether the overall multiproduct effort is efficient and effective and is progressing properly toward achieving its strategic goals. Managers of core asset development are concerned with the quality and usefulness of the assets they produce and the productivity of those producing them. And individual product managers are concerned with the efficiency of their staff and the quality of the products they turn out.

These differing concerns are complementary in that the metrics required to track the progress of the overall product line effort are mostly aggregated from the metrics required to track the progress of its constituent core asset and product efforts. For example, a product line goal of better quality (as might be indicated by fewer errors after delivery) across all products is tracked in terms of the level of quality (errors after delivery) determined in each of the individual products and how those levels compare and change over time. The quality level of the individual products is influenced heavily by the quality of the core assets from which they are built. So detecting fewer errors in core assets after their delivery to the product developers becomes a local goal of core asset development and is also tracked.

As another example, consider a product line goal to improve the profitability of product development. The profitability is tracked by metrics that are reported while component assets are assembled according to the production plan. The cost metrics associated with the development and evolution of the core assets also need to be factored into the profitability measurement.

Over and above the specifics of which metrics to track and which data to collect for software product lines, this practice area has another dimension that makes it highly relevant. The ability of an organization to collect and analyze data and track metrics about itself *at all* makes a strong statement. Data collection marks an organization as comfortable with disciplined processes, accustomed to taking a long-term view and interested in self-improvement—all of which are the hallmarks of successful product line organizations.

5.2.2 Application to Core Asset Development

The core asset manager has two concerns: the efficiency of the core asset effort and its effectiveness in benefiting the associated product efforts that are its clients.

To meet efficiency goals, the manager should focus on tracking the cost and time required to develop the core assets. Satisfying efficiency goals means that core assets will have a minimum investment cost, requiring a lower payback from product efforts, and will be available sooner for product efforts to use. These benefits mean that the overall product line effort will spend less on both assets and products, permitting it either to lower prices or to increase profits as the company's business strategy and market conditions dictate.

To meet effectiveness goals, the manager should focus on providing assets that offer the greatest opportunities for product efforts to avoid work. Metrics for effectiveness will indicate

- which assets are used by product efforts and how often, to determine whether the available core assets are useful
- how many bugs are found in core assets by the product developers, to determine the quality of the core assets
- how much product efforts expend in finding, tailoring, and integrating assets, to identify needed improvements in supporting infrastructure
- where product efforts spend time otherwise, to identify opportunities for future asset or infrastructure work

5.2.3 Application to Product Development

The measurement activity for product development efforts has two facets: one conventional and the other specific to product lines. The conventional facet involves the collection and analysis of metrics needed for the management of any product development effort. For example, managers of product development efforts in general need to track the time and cost of their work activities, the quality of the products developed, and customer satisfaction. These particular metrics are not unique to whether or not products are developed from core assets.

The facet specific to product lines involves the collection of metrics that are needed by product line and core asset development managers to be effective managers but that can come only from product development. The metrics needed for the management of core asset development relate to the quality and usability of core assets from the perspective of the product efforts. Only the product efforts can provide the data that are necessary for core asset management to evaluate whether the efforts' results are satisfying management's primary goal: more effective and efficient product efforts. The metrics needed for product line management are generally a subset of those needed to manage core asset and product efforts but are aggregated across all of the product line's efforts. Product line management will use these metrics to determine whether resources are allocated properly between core asset and product efforts and whether these efforts are achieving the intended market results for the business.

5.2.4 Specific Practices

Choosing metrics: The most difficult aspect of measurement is deciding what to measure. The Goal-Question-Metric method is a good technique for deciding which metrics are appropriate to the goals of a specific effort [Basili 84]. First, the goals are articulated. For a product line, goals typically include increased productivity, shorter time-to-market, higher product quality, and the like. For each goal, a manager identifies a set of questions whose answers would indicate whether or not the goal is being met. For each of these questions, a set of metrics that indicates the data needed to answer the question with sufficient accuracy is identified. This approach ties the required metrics to the goals of the effort, to ensure that needed data are collected and that resources are not expended collecting data unrelated to those goals. In some cases, the needed measures are not directly obtainable but may be derived from other measures that are.

Another good starting point for choosing metrics is from Zubrow et al. [Zubrow 00]. They catalog lists of indicators that are of interest to a product line manager, an asset development manager, and a product development manager, respectively (see Table 5.1). Under each category is defined a broad set of metrics returning information about performance (measuring cost, schedule, and quality of product efforts), compliance (measuring the adherence of the product line effort to established procedures and processes), and effectiveness (characterizing how the overall product line effort is meeting its goals).

Collecting data: Different types of metrics require different data collection techniques. Common techniques include:

- the direct measurement of observable attributes of a process or product, such as the date that a baseline was created or the size of a core asset
- the indirect measurement of objective attributes, such as the time spent by a developer in creating a core asset or a work product
- surveys for the measurement of subjective attributes, such as how easy or pleasant an automated product is to use (this would help measure customer satisfaction with a product line)
- the derivation of implicit attribute measures as computations from other measures, such as the cost of a work product as a function of its size and the cost of the developer's time or the usability of an automated product as a function of the number of user mistakes

Each of these techniques can be applied manually or with the assistance of automated tools, depending on the size of the effort being undertaken and whether time or money is the more limited resource.

Reuse metrics: A higher level of software reuse is not in itself an end goal of a product line effort but merely a strategy for achieving goals such as shorter time-to-market. But because it is such a cornerstone of the product line strategy,

Table 5.1 Product Line Indicators and Measures [Zubrow 00]

Goal	Product Line Manager	Asset Development Manager	Product Development Manager
Improved Performance	• total product development cost • productivity • schedule deviation • time-to-market • trends in defect density • number of products (past, current, future) • time spent on life-cycle activities	• cost to produce core assets • cost to produce infrastructure • schedule deviation • defect density in core assets • number and type of artifacts in asset library	• direct product cost • defect density in application artifacts • percent reuse
Compliance	• mission focus • process compliance	• mission focus • process compliance	• process compliance
Increased Effectiveness	• return on investment • market satisfaction	• core assets utility • core assets cost of use • percent reuse	• customer satisfaction

it is a useful quantity to measure. Beyond that, it is useful to have a metric-based model of what the reuse is buying you, in terms of cost avoidance, return on investment, or some other goal-related quantity. Poulin provides several such models [Poulin 97]. Some of the proposed models also have associated tools that support the appropriate analyses and presentation of results.

5.2.5 Practice Risks

A poor data collection and metrics program will be a waste of time and resources, will impose an opportunity cost in terms of what productive work the staff could have been doing, and will cause resentment and mistrust of future metrics efforts. It will also fail to inform management of where the organization stands with respect to meeting its product line goals. This failure can in turn lead to uninformed management decisions that can undermine the product line efforts. Potential causes of inadequate data collection and metrics are as follows:

- **Metric mismatch:** Metrics that are not based on product line, subordinate core asset, or product development goals will result in wasted effort spent collecting data that do not contribute to management decision making.
- **Goals without metrics:** Goals that have no associated metrics will result in managers being unable to detect any issues that hinder the achievement of those goals until an unacceptable expenditure of work or time has been incurred.
- **Measurement not aligned:** Any measurement activities that is not integrated into the product line process will result in data collection that does not mesh properly into other product line activity and leads to inaccurate results that either hide legitimate issues or raise false issues.
- **Costly metrics:** Metrics that are too costly or difficult to obtain will result in failure to track progress, which in turn will result in failure or delays in detecting problem issues or interference with the effort's primary work.

5.2.6 For Further Reading

Park's *Goal-Driven Software Measurement—A Guidebook* [Park 96] is an extensive guide to establishing measurement activity based on business goals. Poulin's *Measuring Software Reuse: Principles, Practices, and Economic Models* [Poulin 97] treats measurement from the point of view of a reuse organization and contains a good suite of reuse-based metrics and models.

5.2.7 Discussion Questions

1. Reduced time-to-market is a premier goal of product line organizations, but it can be tricky to measure because of the difficulty of determining when to start and stop the clock. How would you define time-to-market for your organization? When would you start measuring? When would you stop? Are there circumstances that would cause you to take a "time out" along the way?
2. Increased productivity is another premier goal of product line organizations. This goal usually translates into doing more work with the same number (or a smaller number) of people. Again, like time-to-market, it's hard to measure precisely, and especially so for product lines when many products (and people) are involved. How would you do it?
3. Rewards based on metrics can be fraught with peril. Reuse metrics are notorious for this, but they are not the only ones. When a character in the comic strip "Dilbert" heard that his company was paying people to find errors in

their code, he went happily off to his cubicle to "write myself a new car." Think of some metrics that, in the hands of the devilish, could backfire by encouraging behavior detrimental to product lines.

4. Suppose your organization is one in which core assets are built not by a separate unit but by individual product units that then export them to other product units. Would this arrangement change the metrics you might want to collect about the quality, utility, and efficiency of core asset production? How would you measure the time a developer spent working on the core assets as opposed to the product assigned to that developer's unit?
5. It is said that product quality is not as important as the customer's perception of product quality. How would you measure each? Suppose your product line organization sold its products to thousands of anonymous customers as shrink-wrapped software. How would you measure these things in that case?
6. Your organization is trying to adopt a product approach, but management is hesitant to make a full commitment to it. As the product line champion, you have asked management to pull a half dozen people off of their current assignments so that they can form a product line architecture and core asset team. Management balks, pointing out that each person you have named is important right where he is, turning out products (the old-fashioned way), and the loss of the six or so people will cripple their teams. "How do we know," they ask, "that the company isn't better off keeping those people right where they are?" The products involved will be part of the new product line, but the deadlines are tight and the customers important. What do you say?
7. Maintenance in a product line should be less expensive because each fix automatically applies to many products. On the other hand, maintenance should be more expensive because each fix needs to be robust and generic across the entire family. What data would you collect to settle this apparent paradox? Would you try to normalize the changes somehow? If so, why and how? If not, why not?

5.3 Make/Buy/Mine/Commission Analysis

Earlier, we pointed out that software enters an organization in one of three ways: it can be *built* in-house, *purchased* from a commercial vendor, or *commissioned* through a third party to be built especially for the organization. Software that is built in-house can actually be constructed anew or *mined* from software already in the organization for use in a new effort. Every piece of software that is part of a development effort arrived as the result of this unavoidable four-way choice, which we dub "make/buy/mine/commission." Organizations that build software systems all make this choice—it cannot be avoided—but almost always without a conscious rationale for the alternative they select. The purpose of this practice area is both to underscore the necessity of making a conscious and reasoned choice and to describe some of the analyses that are appropriate for helping to make this choice.

Techniques from the discipline of decision analysis apply well here. Decision analysis is the process of applying analytical methods to decision making in situations where there is uncertainty, multiple conflicting objectives, or dynamic change [Clemen 91, Hammond 99]. When an organization is deciding the most appropriate way to get a piece of software, business, technical, and political factors have to be weighed. So the decision is often beset with uncertainty, multiple conflicting objectives, and dynamic change. Making the decision requires both qualitative and quantitative analysis.

For some organizations, all the software assets are developed in-house for proprietary (or political) reasons. For other organizations, all the assets are commissioned because of organizational policy or because of unique requirements and a lack of in-house development resources. (In the United States, most government organizations fit into this category.) More commonly, however, some of the software will be built from scratch, some will be mined, some will be purchased, and some will be commissioned.

The make/buy/mine/commission decision for software is, first of all, based on quality and fitness of purpose that each alternative would produce. If no other organization but yours has the necessary expertise in a component's realm, then "buy" and "commission" are going to receive short shrift. Conversely, if you have neither the skill nor the history to build a component, then "make" and "mine" are going to be nonstarters. But beyond these factors, cost, staff availability, and schedule are the determinants. Assume for a moment that each alternative would yield a product of acceptable quality and fitness. Then the decision factors revolve around the opportunity costs and the benefits of each alternative. The direct cost of each alternative is a factor, but so is the opportunity cost: what could your staff be doing if you relieved them of the responsibility for the component by buying or commissioning it? If you developed it in-house, what could you do with the funds you would save by not employing an expensive contractor? If the staff is underutilized, the "make" and "mine" options get more weight. If the staff is overutilized and the schedule is tight, the "buy" and "commission" options get more weight.

However, the assumption that all options would yield the same quality and fitness for purpose is tenuous and would need to be verified through analysis. The "COTS Utilization" practice area (Section 4.4) will help with analyzing the "buy" alternative, whereas the "Architecture Evaluation" practice area (Section 4.2) contains practices that will help with the "make" and "mine" options. To carry out the "commission" choice, you must rely on past performance of the contractor to provide insight into the likelihood that it can deliver as promised.

Here, vendor reliability and stability are key, as for a COTS component; see the "Developing an Acquisition Strategy" practice area (Section 6.3).

Secondary criteria include a frank assessment of an organization's own capabilities. Establishing working relationships with contractors can be tricky, and the legalities of drawing up an ironclad contract can be formidable for those without experience. If your organization does not have a standing legal department for which such relationships are pro forma, you might be better off on the "make/mine" side of the equation—that is, unless it is to your strategic advantage to build such a capability for the future. Conversely, if your development capabilities are weak, then letting others tackle the technical complexities may be the best approach—again, unless you are trying to improve your organization's development skills or domain expertise. In either case, start your venture into the unknown with small steps, relying on the new approaches for the least critical components. And have contingency plans to handle major missteps along the way.

Also keep in mind that the four options are not always mutually exclusive—for a given asset, you might do a little of each. For example, a component can be built largely from scratch, but with some percentage derived from a legacy system. Commissioned software is sometimes based at least partially on legacy assets. And how much alteration of a commercial off-the-shelf (COTS) system is allowed before it falls into one of the other three categories? The make/buy/mine/commission decision analysis can be complex, which is why making the decision consciously is a good idea.

5.3.1 Aspects Peculiar to Product Lines

The analysis approach for a product line is similar to the analysis approach for single systems. However, the weighting factors are different—primarily for the following reasons:

- Costlier options that would be ruled out for single systems may be acceptable for product lines because the cost can be amortized over a number of products. For example, in a single system you might be willing to use a COTS component because it would be cheaper than building your own, but in a product line you may be willing to pay the higher cost of in-house development so that your entire group of products is not held hostage by a vendor's version release and upgrade schedule.
- The "make," "mine," and "commission" options are usually more expensive because the assets have to be more robust so as to be reusable across the entire family of products.
- The "buy" option, on the other hand, may not be any more expensive a single-system case because COTS components tend to be built for generic usage. Of course, you still have to find an off-the-shelf component in the commercial marketplace that has the required variability and quality.

The search for such a component and its subsequent qualification may be more expensive than if it were going to be used in only one system.

- Product lines tend to be built on a legacy foundation; the realization that a company is building many similar products is often the impetus for the product line approach. Hence, "mine" is a more viable alternative in a product line because of the likely existence of a rich legacy base.

The decision analysis for a product line must also look further into the future for multiple products that will be spawned, each having its own lifetime. In a product line, much more is riding on the decisions about how and where to obtain software. Analysis is essential, and rigorous analysis is warranted.

5.3.2 Application to Core Asset Development

Because all core assets have to come from somewhere, make/buy/mine/commission analysis is at the root of core asset development, and the analysis applies to nonsoftware as well as software assets. The possibility of commissioning entire swaths of product line development (such as domain analysis, scoping analysis, market analysis, requirements engineering, and testing) should not be dismissed without consideration. Requirements and designs, as we saw in the "Mining Existing Assets" practice area (Section 4.5), are superb candidates for recovery and rehabilitation from previous systems. The criteria to factor into the analysis include:

- quality
- cost (including opportunity cost)
- alignment with the product line requirements
- alignment with the product line architecture
- flexibility sufficient to support requisite variation among the products in the product line
- maintainability
- schedule
- ability of your organization to prosecute each of the four options successfully

The decision regarding the source of the product line architecture must be made prior to, or at least concurrent with, the decisions for obtaining individual component assets. The architecture, by definition, specifies constraints for the component assets, constraints that must be factored into any analysis about how they will be obtained.

5.3.3 Application to Product Development

Individual products in the product line may need additional software components not contained in the asset base. The same decision analysis process should be used to determine how to obtain these components. The criteria may be less demanding if the component in question will not be a candidate for inclusion in the asset base. Although it would still need to align with the product line architecture, it wouldn't have to support the variability potentially needed to support other products. On the other hand, cost may be more of a consideration because the cost of obtaining the component has to be absorbed by a single product rather than being amortized over a family of products.

For example, if there isn't a human-computer interface (HCI) component or subsystem in the asset base and a specific product needs one, the product builder can select the HCI component that is optimal for the needs of that particular product and the allowable budget. On the other hand, if an HCI component would be a viable candidate for addition to the asset base, the decision analysis would rely on the same criteria used for core asset development, as described above.

5.3.4 Specific Practices

The starting point for defining a specific practice is to use standard "make or buy" techniques and then to tailor these practices for a product line approach. One realistic approach is to adopt a breadth-first strategy in which each of the four options for obtaining software is considered and explored before any of them is eliminated. For some options, the consideration may be trivial. For example, if organizational policy dictates commissioning of all software systems, the "make" choice requires no consideration: it's not an option.

Examples of questions for make/buy/mine/commission decision analysis are given below. First, there is an umbrella set of questions for the breadth-first strategy. These questions are followed by four sets of specific questions, one for each of the four options. Because each organization is unique, these sample questions should be viewed as a starter set to be customized and augmented as appropriate.

The initial question set is as follows:

- What are the time constraints for obtaining the asset? What external factors drive those time constraints? How reliable are the external predictions?
- How well defined is the asset that must be obtained? Have the product line requirements been defined? Have the required software commonalities and variabilities of all the products in the product line been defined? Has the system architecture into which the software will fit been defined completely? (If any or all of these items are not well defined, it will be hard to hand off the responsibility for developing the asset, either software or non-software, to an outside party.)
- Is there a market for the asset separate from the market for the product line? (If not, odds are that the asset will not be found on the open market as COTS.)

After this initial analysis, the choices may be narrowed to two or three, or even to one, of the four major options. A more detailed analysis for each option still in the running could include questions such as the following:

Sample questions for the "make" option:

- Are developers with appropriate expertise available?
- How would the developers be utilized if not on this project?
- If additional personnel need to be hired, will they be available within the needed time frame?
- How successful has the organization been in developing similar assets?
- What specific flexibilities are gained by developing products in-house as opposed to purchasing them?
- What development tools and environments are available? Are they suitable? How skilled is the targeted work force in their use?
- What are the costs of development tools and training, if needed?
- What are the other specific costs of developing the asset in-house?
- What are the other specific benefits of developing the asset in-house?

Sample questions for the "buy" option:

- What assets are commercially available?
- How well does the COTS software conform to the product line architecture?
- How closely does the available COTS software satisfy the product line requirements?
- Are small changes in COTS software a viable option?
- Is source code available with the software? What documentation comes with the software?
- What are the integration challenges?
- What rights to redistribute are purchased with the COTS software?
- What are the other specific costs associated with purchasing the software?
- What are the other specific benefits associated with purchasing the software?
- How stable is the vendor?
- How often are upgrades produced? How relevant are the upgrades to the product line?
- How responsive is the vendor to user requests for improvements?
- How strong is the vendor support?

Sample questions for the "mine" option:

- What legacy systems are available from which to mine assets?
- How close is the functionality of the legacy software to the functionality that is required?
- What is the defect track record for the software and nonsoftware assets?
- How well is the legacy system documented?
- What mining strategies are appropriate?
- How expensive are those strategies?

- What experience does the organization have in mining assets?
- What mining tools are available? Are they appropriate? How skilled is the work force in their use?
- What are the costs of mining tools and training, if needed?
- What are the other specific costs associated with mining the asset?
- What are the other specific benefits associated with mining the asset?

Sample questions for the "commission" option:

- What contractors are available to develop the asset?
- What is the track record of the contractor in terms of schedule and budget?
- Is the acquiring organization skilled in supervising contracted work?
- Are the requirements defined to the extent that the asset can be subcontracted?
- Are interface specifications well defined and stable?
- What experience does the contractor have with the principles of product line development?
- Who needs to own the asset? Who maintains it?
- What are the other specific costs associated with commissioning the asset?
- What are the other specific benefits associated with commissioning the asset?
- What are the costs of maintaining the commissioned asset?
- Does commissioning the asset involve divulging to the contractor any technology or information that it is in the acquiring organization's interest to keep in-house?

These question sets are meant to be starter sets. Weigh these factors according to your organization's needs and experience and augment them with factors of your own.

Tool support: Although spreadsheets are the most common tool used in decision analysis, more sophisticated tools are also available on personal computers. For example, TreeAge Software offers tools called DATA and DATA Interactive [TreeAge 99]. With DATA, an analyst can build sophisticated decision models as decision trees, influence diagrams, or Markov processes and then analyze them utilizing analysis tools including sensitivity analysis, cohort simulation, and Monte Carlo simulation. A companion product, DATA Interactive, provides a model customization and delivery system for accessing and analyzing the decision models created in DATA. These tools require knowledge about decision analysis principles, the problem domain, and the tools' functionality for building and analyzing models.

5.3.5 Practice Risks

Do not confuse the risks of this practice area with the risks of the practice areas associated with each of the four options (component development, COTS utilization, mining existing assets, and developing an acquisition strategy). The risks here are involved in choosing among these options. The major risk specific to this practice area is, of course, choosing the *wrong* option, which can result in inappropriate assets and undue direct (or opportunity) costs. This could arise because of any of the following reasons:

- There are not enough data on which to base decisions.
- The data are inaccurate.
- Political pressures force the decision.
- There is no process for the decision analysis.
- There is not enough time to execute the process.
- There is a failure to consider all the options. Normally, all four options should be kept on the table for the initial analysis steps.
- There is no established or documented product line architecture to factor into the decision.
- There are poor estimates of the probabilities of projected outcomes.
- The product line requirements have not been defined adequately.
- There are hidden interactions between alternative choices which may produce unpredictable consequences.
- There is a lack of documentation to support decision analysis.

5.3.6 For Further Reading

The best background reading for make/buy/mine/commission analysis is a text in decision analysis. Books by Clemen [Clemen 91] and Hammond [Hammond 99] are good choices.

5.3.7 Discussion Questions

1. We have asserted that deep domain expertise is essential for successful building of a software product line, and so, on the face of it, commissioning a domain analysis might seem to be a bad idea. When might you consider doing this? Are there parts of a domain analysis that would be less risky to outsource than others? What exactly would you task the contractor with delivering?
2. Make a table of the software engineering, technical management, and organizational management practice areas. For each area, list the major artifacts that applying it produces. Then try to envision buying, mining, or commissioning those artifacts. For example, what might it mean to "commission" an organizational structure? Now go back and circle each option for each artifact that would be viable in your organization. Are there more or fewer circles than you would have imagined?
3. Make cases for and against commissioning your product line's testing activities.
4. Make cases for and against commissioning your product line's requirements engineering activities.

5.4 Process Definition

The process definition practice area is about an organization's capability to define and document processes. An essential aspect of software engineering is the discipline it requires for a group of people to work together cooperatively to solve a common problem. Defined processes set the bounds for each person's roles and responsibilities so that the collaboration is a successful and efficient one. Processes crop up throughout software engineering efforts in general and product line development in particular. This practice area is about the skill required to clearly define and document those various processes so that they can fulfill their purposes.

The related term *software process modeling* is used to describe the production of models of defined software development processes. A process model is an abstract description of an actual or proposed process that represents selected process elements that are considered important to the purpose of the model and can be enacted by a human or a machine [Curtis 92].

Whether or not a formal model is built from a defined process, its definition should be represented in a form that is understandable by humans and should be clear and complete enough to satisfy the following goals:

- Facilitate human understanding and communication
  - Enable communication about and agreement on the software process.
  - Provide sufficient information to allow an individual or team to perform the intended process.
  - Form a basis for training individuals to follow the intended process.
- Support process management
  - Develop a project-specific software process to accommodate the attributes of a particular project, such as its product or organizational environment.
  - Reason about the attributes of software creation or evolution.
  - Support the development of plans for the project.
  - Monitor, manage, and coordinate the process.
  - Provide a basis for process measurement, such as the definition of measurement points within the context of a specific process.
- Support process improvement
  - Reuse well-defined and effective software processes on future projects.
  - Compare alternative software processes.
  - Estimate the impacts of potential changes in a software process before putting them into actual practice.
  - Assist in the selection and incorporation of technology (tools, for example) into a process.

5.4.1 Aspects Peculiar to Product Lines

If software engineering is about a group of people working together to solve a problem cooperatively, then product line software engineering requires cooperation in spades. Because of the plurality of products and of groups cooperating to develop those products, the entire apparatus will work only if everyone does his or her job within agreed-upon parameters. For example, no one is allowed to change core assets unilaterally. Core asset developers are not allowed to change them before understanding how the changes will affect the products in (or already out of) the production pipeline. Product developers are certainly not allowed to change them because "clone and own" is a poor form of reuse that is the antithesis of product lines. Core assets do indeed change but only as the result of all parties adhering to an agreed-upon process for making the changes.

Besides configuration management, two other prime examples of product line processes are

- the operational concept for the product line, such as the one embodied in a product line concept of operations (see the "Operations" practice area, Section 6.7). The concept of operations is essentially the expression of a process, and process definition skills must be brought to bear to build an operational definition that everyone can follow, that can be improved, and that will serve the goals of the product line.
- the attached processes that help product builders instantiate core assets for specific products. These processes must account for a wide variety of assets and variabilities and accommodate the different role-players who are going to carry them out.

Other product line activities also rely on process definition to achieve their required fidelity. Launching a product line, carrying out technical and organizational risk management activities, collecting and analyzing metrics, performing make/buy/mine/commission analysis, and maintaining the correct customer interface all rely on adherence to processes that must be defined and specified. But not all practice areas require process definitions of the same weight. Whereas CM needs an industrial-strength, no-nonsense process definition that everyone must follow, an activity as exploratory as, say, market analysis does not.

Because product lines call for the repeated, ongoing, disciplined interaction of separate organizational entities, they rely heavily on the adherence to a process. Process definition represents an area of expertise that enables many other practice areas to be executed successfully. In fact, organizations that do not have a strong process culture will find deploying a successful product line a perilous proposition (see "Software Process Improvement and Product Line Practice" sidebar).

5.4.2 Application to Core Asset Development

Every core asset has an attached process associated with it that explains how the asset is used to build products in the product line. Together, these attached processes form the product line's production plan, which shows how core assets are turned into products. Process definition is the vehicle by which these processes are specified.

The attached processes differ across assets. For example, the way in which the product line requirements are used to express the requirements for a specific product differs from the way in which the product line architecture is instantiated to architect the specific product. Since the people who create an asset are usually not the people who use it, the attached process communicates the intended use.

In addition, there are processes (specified typically through "Operations" practices) that explain how core assets are created, evaluated, maintained, and evolved over the lifetime of the product line. Again, process definition is the mechanism by which these processes are defined and improved.

5.4.3 Application to Product Development

A core asset's attached process is the bridge between the core asset developers and the product developers; it is a way for the asset builders to speak across the gulf to the product builders and tell them how the assets should be used to create systems. Therefore, the attached processes have implications for product development as well as for core asset development. Process definition provides the skills by which easy-to-use, effective, and efficient attached processes are created; processes that are cumbersome or unwieldy will probably be discarded by product builders in favor of ad hoc, nonrepeatable approaches.

Products, like core assets, also have rules for evolution and maintenance, and these rules are captured in a process definition (usually created within the "Operations" practice area).

5.4.4 Specific Practices

Specific practices for process definition include the following:

- Electronic process documentation for the user of a process, such as a Web-based process handbook or an electronic process guide. These documents allow process definitions to be focused or presented in different ways to shield the process user from scores of unnecessary details. Instead, the electronic documentation displays a narrowed view that describes at any specific time the process steps that should be performed. In general, role-specific views of a process decrease the complexity of process definition and allow one to focus on those aspects of the process that are relevant to a specific user. Finkelstein gives a fairly comprehensive overview of various modeling and documentation techniques [Finkelstein 94].

- Integrated process support environments utilize computer systems to automate some of the required process steps, such as informing a quality assurance organization that a document is ready for review or sending a change request to core asset developers [Finkelstein 94].
- A generic process definition will obviate the need to define a comprehensive product line process that would take into account all the possible variabilities—a daunting task. A generic process represents a class of processes for building a class of products. In other words, a product line process represents a family of processes [Huff 96]. The variations in the processes within a family reflect the variations in the products.

5.4.5 Practice Risks

Poor process definition will lead to processes that are inappropriate, vague, unclear, overconstraining, or ineffective. As a result, the staff will choose not to follow them and will carry out their work in an ad hoc manner, or they will follow them but will not achieve the results the processes were intended to deliver. In either case, the result will be resentment and mistrust of the processes and poor quality results in the product line development. Potential causes of poor process definition are as follows:

- **Process mismatch:** There is a possibility of a process mismatch among a number of factors, such as the organizational structure, the organizational culture, the process that is employed, the experience and expertise of the employees, and the market to which the process is applicable. For example, the defined process may be too complex for the organization, resulting in detailed practices that are not followed. On the other hand, the process may be too simplistic and thus too general and at too high a level to provide practical guidance.
- **Process doesn't address product line needs:** The process may not accommodate a bidirectional flow between core asset development and product development processes. This flow is necessary for product line success.
- **Inadequate process support:** Processes have to be supported within an organization, especially newly introduced ones. Lack of support (such as training, motivation, templates, and examples) will lead to rejection of the process.
- **Uneven process quality:** Because of divergent goals, skills, and backgrounds, there may be uneven quality in the contributions of the core asset teams and product development teams. This may also result in a lack of harmonization in the processes for the different teams.
- **Lack of buy-in:** The organization may not buy into process definition, resulting in failure to adopt it.

- **Dictatorial introduction:** One organizational unit mandating the processes that another must follow is likely to result in resentment and failure to adopt them.

5.4.6 For Further Reading

The paper probably most referenced in the software process modeling community is Curtis and Kellner's "Process Modeling" [Curtis 92]. It is a must for anyone who wishes to understand software development processes and process modeling. Humphrey and Feiler's *Software Process Development and Enactment: Concepts and Definitions* [Humphrey 92] helped to create the basis for the process community by publishing sound definitions for process terminology. It is an excellent source for definitions. Finkelstein's *Software Process Modeling and Technology* [Finkelstein 94] is a fairly comprehensive overview of process-centered environments. It shows the different approaches and techniques and suggests tools for enacting defined processes.

5.4.7 Discussion Questions

1. The most elegantly defined process will be of no use if the people for whom it was intended fail to adopt it. What measures should you take to increase buy-in of a defined process? Who should be in charge of defining processes, what should their background be, and what qualities should they exhibit to help make the defined process a success?
2. For your organization, do you think there should be a centralized process definition group or should process definition responsibility be farmed out to different teams or should a solution be sought somewhere in between?
3. What metrics would you put in place to gauge how well a process is working?
4. Integrated process support environments (mentioned in the specific practices) are considered by some to be too restrictive for widespread use. Automating small, repetitive parts of a process makes sense, but a complex process such as that for building product line software is too unpredictable in its detail to be supported by a process automaton. Discuss. Which parts of the process do you think would lend themselves to this kind of technology, and which would not?

5.5 Scoping

Scoping is an activity that bounds a system or set of systems by defining those behaviors or aspects that are "in" and those behaviors or aspects that are "out." All system development involves scoping; there is no system for which everything is "in." The Rational Unified Process (RUP) includes an inception phase to establish "the project's software scope and boundary conditions, including an operational concept, acceptance criteria, and descriptions of what is and is not intended to be in the product" [Kruchten 98]. Kruchten defines scoping as "capturing the context and the most important requirements and constraints so that you can derive acceptance criteria for the end product."

In conventional system development, Kruchten's explicit treatment notwithstanding, scoping is usually done informally, perhaps as an unofficial prelude to the requirements engineering activity. In systems designed with ease of change in mind, the activity of scoping helps determine the set of modifications the design will accommodate and those it need not accommodate.

In product line development, however, scoping is a fundamental activity that will determine the long-term viability of the product line.

5.5.1 Aspects Peculiar to Product Lines

Like scoping in general, product line scoping is the activity that determines what's "in" and what's "out." The result is a scope definition document, which itself becomes a product line core asset. The scope definition identifies those entities with which products in the product line will interact (that is, the product line context), and it also establishes the commonality and bounds the variability of the product line.

The scope definition will almost always commence as a broad, general document that is refined as more knowledge is brought to the table and more analysis is performed. For example, for a product line of World Wide Web software, we would start by declaring that browsers would definitely be "in," aircraft flight simulators would definitely be "out," and e-mail handlers would . . . well, we wouldn't be sure until the scope was refined further. Hence, the product line scope may not come into sharp focus all at once; that's fine. The market analysis for the product line will usually contain a fuzzy description of the scope. A refined version emerges as domain understanding increases. Finally, the detailed modeling of user-visible services during a product line requirements stage completes the product line scope. Scoping does not end here, but is refined as the product line architecture and components are developed.

What's the Difference between
Product Line Scope and Product Line Requirements?

Setting the proper scope of the product line is a step of fundamental importance. Make it too large, and the core assets will have to be too hopelessly generic ever to work; make it too small, and the market demand for your product suite will be too small to recover the up-front investment. Make it the right size but encompassing the wrong systems for your market, and you'll have no customers.

What does the representation of a product line scope look like, exactly? That is, how do you write one down? It can be very vague, or very precise—any statement that will let a decision maker decide whether a proposed product is in or out will do. In practice, to make such a decision requires a fairly precise statement of what the "in" systems will all have in common. One product line scope definition that we once saw talked about systems for special-operations helicopters. These systems were supposed to do three things: "aviate" (that is, fly), "navigate" (move from point A to point B), and "communicate" (talk to other systems). While this description ruled out, say, software for toasters, it was clearly insufficient to tell whether the software for another kind of aircraft would be in or out of the product line. Something more detailed was needed. During the next round, some specific behaviors and features were articulated, and this began to position the product line squarely in the realm of special-operations helicopters.

This is usually how it goes. Scope starts out as a vague description of a set of systems by naming some functions they provide. After that, it's refined to be written in terms of the products' observable behaviors and their exhibited quality attributes such as performance or security.

But now that you mention it, that is also how writing down requirements for a system goes. So why are the scope and the requirements covered in two separate practice areas? Aren't they in fact the same activity? The answer is "theoretically, yes," but "theoretically, yes" is often a euphemism for "not really."

In Part a of the figure below, the rectangle represents every possible software system that ever has been, ever will be, or ever could be built. This is the starting point, albeit a not very useful one, for determining the scope of a product line. Typically, a product line manager is able to start describing systems that are definitely outside the product line (toasters) and a few products that are definitely in (a small list of specific special-operations helicopters). Part b of the figure shows the system space divided into three parts: systems that are out (mottled), systems that are in (white), and systems we aren't sure about yet

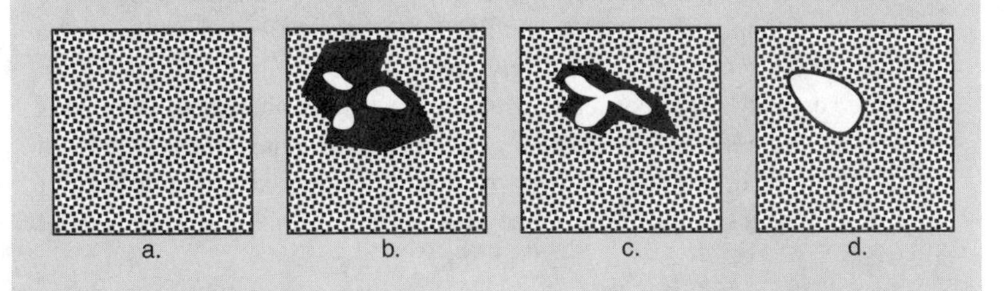

The Evolution of a Product Line Scope

(black). The process of defining the product line scope is the process of narrowing down the "not sure about" space by carefully defining more of the "out" and "in" spaces, until conceptually it resembles Part c.

Now think about requirements. A good requirements specification should tell us everything that must be true about a system for it to be acceptable, and no more. The "no more" part means that many systems could be built to satisfy a given requirements specification, since a statement of requirements does not and should not mandate a particular implementation. Requirements for a product line specify things that are true about every system in the family and specify a set of allowable variations exhibited by individual systems. Given any system, we should be able to compare it with the requirements specification and see whether or not it conforms—that is, whether or not it satisfies all of the common requirements and an allowable combination of the variable requirements. Either it does or it doesn't: there is no "in between." Part d is a visual rendition of this situation, which is just Part c pursued to the point where the "not sure about" space has been squeezed to nothingness. This is why we said that requirements engineering was theoretically akin to product line scoping—a completely precise scope is, in fact, a requirements specification for the product line.

At least theoretically. Often, the scope includes aspects of the system that would not appear in even the most complete requirements specification—aspects related to business goals or construction constraints. For example, "any reasonable system commissioned by our most important customer" might appear in a scope definition as something you're willing to build, but it would not appear in any requirements spec because it's not a testable condition of the software.

In addition, the scope and the requirements are defined at different times. The scope is defined early enough so that a business case can be built and used to see if the product line is economically viable. The requirements are specified as a prelude to actual development. The two products have different consumers. The scope is written for people such as marketers, who need to see what they will be asked to sell but do not require full statements of product behavior. The requirements spec is used by the architect and the developers of core assets and products that *do* need to know exact behavior. (The scope definition is also used by the architect to begin planning architectural means to provide the commonality and variability defined there.) Finally, there is no mandate for the scope to be completely precise—the situation in Part c is just fine. The vast majority of systems is ruled out; a useful number of systems is ruled in; and a class of systems remains on the cusp, meaning "If asked to build one of those, we'll think about it." If, over time, you're asked to build a *lot* of those, it may be a sign that your scope missed the target a bit and needs to be adjusted.

In fact, the situation in Part c is *more* desirable for a scope than the one in Part d. If you're asked to build a system that lies oh-so-close-to but just outside the anointed set of "in" systems, then "I'll think about it" is probably a better response than a flat "no." Rejecting it out of hand might cause you to miss a good business opportunity that you had not previously considered.

So if you thought that setting the scope and setting the product line requirements sounded like similar activities, you're right—they are. In practice, however, scoping and requirements engineering are done by different people, stop at different points, and are used for different purposes by different stakeholders.

—PCC

The goal of the scope definition is to draw the boundary between in and out in such a way that the product line is profitable. If the scope is too large, the core assets will have to be so generic that they will be useless. If the scope is too small, the product line may not have enough customers to recoup the investment in the core assets. And if the scope bounds the wrong products, the product line will not find a market. Getting the scope right is important.

Driving the scope definition are the following:

- the prevailing or predicted market drivers, obtained through "Market Analysis" practices (see Section 6.6)
- the nature of competing efforts, obtained through "Market Analysis" or "Understanding Relevant Domains" practices (see Sections 6.6 and 4.9)
- business goals that led to embarking on a product line approach, obtained through the "Building a Business Case" practice area (see Section 6.1). An example of a scope-setting goal is the merging of a set of similar, but currently independent, product development projects to save cost.

Scoping identifies the commonality that members share and the ways in which they vary. Identifying commonalities and variabilities is a theme that pervades virtually every product line practice area; it is the essence of the product line concept, and it is the essence of scoping. Because the scope describes the characteristics of a class of systems, and not specific systems, the scope will apply equally well to existing products and products that have not yet been built or defined completely. The descriptions of scope are essential for determining whether a planned system can be built within the product line and from product line assets. In most cases, scoping activities must continue after the initial scope has been defined because new market opportunities may arise, and new opportunities for the strategic reuse and merging of projects may make themselves known.

Scoping may occur in a variety of contexts other than a start-from-scratch product line. For example, an organization may be building (or commissioning) several systems that are similar to each other but do not presently take advantage of their similarity. The organization may wish to merge the efforts to gain economies of scope. In this case, the initial set of systems is defined by the list of products that are planned currently, and the scope must be broad enough to cover them. In another case, the organization may aim to capture or penetrate a market segment by establishing a flexible, quick-response capability for launching new products in that product's market area. In this case, the set of systems may be defined on the basis of marketing projections obtained through "Market Analysis" practices (see Section 6.6).

In short, scoping answers the question: "What products should be in my software product line?" This question is asked at product line launch, but it is also asked as new product opportunities arise. By passing a candidate product over the scope definition, you can decide whether that product is "in" or "out" of the product line. If it is "out," you can judge by how much. At this point, you can decide (via business case practices) whether to expand the product line's scope to include the new project, to develop the new project as a stand-alone system, or to abandon it entirely. The candidate project may be a new one brought to the table by a customer or your marketers, or it may be an already existing system being maintained separately by your organization, and you hope to achieve economies by merging it with your product line. In all of these cases, the scope lets you decide: is it in or is it out?

The scope delivers a technical decision, but business case factors might override its verdict. For example, you may agree to develop a product that is nominally outside the product line's scope if the customer who wants it is a very important one or (as we will see in the next paragraph) it represents an entrée into a desirable new business area. Or, you may decline to build a product that is in scope if the market for it is small or the opportunity cost for it is high.

Scoping, as described up to this point, is a reactive exercise: given a product opportunity, the scope will help inform the decision whether or not to bring it into the product line family. But mature product line organizations know how to use their scope to make their own product opportunities. A scope defines an organization's product line area of expertise—the set of systems that it can efficiently build. Thus, scoping can be wonderfully proactive, by providing a basis for discovering products for which an untapped market may well exist. These new products might be squarely within the defined scope, or they might be outside but "nearby." The experience of CelsiusTech is an example of the latter [Brownsword 96]:

> *Although CelsiusTech's largest business area is naval applications, it has expanded its business into the ground-based air defense systems market. . . . The current project is a new C3 system for the Swedish Air Force. By reusing the abstractions inherent in the SS2000 architecture, CelsiusTech was able to quickly build the new architecture, lifting 40% of its components directly from the SS2000 asset base. Other business opportunities are being explored in new domains where the architecture and other product line assets are likely to prove a good fit.*

Just by understanding their scope, and then shrewdly expanding it, CelsiusTech was able to enter an entirely new (but related) business area in very short order. We have seen other examples of proactive scoping: for example, one company we know parlayed their expertise (and software product line) in two-way pagers into a software product line powering digital cellular telephones. All three case studies in this book (Chapters 9, 10, and 11) contain different flavors of product line companies that intentionally expanded their scope into new market areas, with excellent results.

5.5.2 Application to Core Asset Development

The scope definition is a core asset for the product line, one that will be consulted extensively and revised as necessary as the product line grows and evolves. The scope definition informs the requirements engineering process, so the requirements-related core assets must be consistent with the scope. We have already shown that market analysis (another core asset) can influence the scope definition. The scope definition can also influence the market analysis by identifying places where a new product variant can be produced very efficiently. Perhaps the market for such a variant would not justify its construction from scratch; however, it may be robust enough for a product line member to fill the niche nicely.

5.5.3 Application to Product Development

The scope definition is used during product development to gauge whether a product (in your legacy base, in development, or merely being considered) would make a viable member of the product line. That is, the scope lets you decide whether it would be economically advantageous to develop that product using the product line's core assets. Sometimes a product will be clearly in scope, and sometimes it will be clearly out of scope. The interesting case, of course, is when the product is on the cusp. In this case, a revised market analysis may help to determine whether the organization should produce the product, after which the scope can be adjusted to reflect the decision. If many on-the-cusp products crop up, it may be an indication that the scope should be expanded slightly to include them, assuming that the concomitant expense of fortifying the core assets to accommodate them is deemed to be economically sound.

One Product Line or Several?

Suppose your company builds a broadly related group of product sets, each of which is a group of closely related products. Should you build a single product line or a group of product lines?

This can be answered by making a business case for each alternative and weighing the costs and benefits. It also depends on the amount of commonality that can be extracted from the broadly related group. For what it's worth, where we've seen this situation in practice, the choice has always been to go with the single, large product line. Examples come from avionics, missile software, embedded engine controllers, and shipboard command and control systems.

However, a dissenting view can be found in the experience of Philips, the Dutch electronics giant [America 00].

> *A diverse company like Philips must develop several, widely different product families, ranging from consumer electronics (TV, VCR, DVD, audio, telephones, etc.) to professional systems (among others for medical imaging, electronic component mounting, and digital video communication). For each of these families a specifically tuned family engineering method is necessary because the business and organization constraints differ. . . .*
>
> *It is useful to point out why we did not . . . organize the different product families into one larger family or population subsuming them all. The reason for this is that such a large population only makes sense if the products have enough in common to make it profitable to develop them as a population and the organization is able to coordinate the marketing, development, and other aspects of a large population. At this moment these two conditions are not fulfilled, but the similarities between our product families are growing and our organizations are learning to deal with larger families and populations, so that we may see them in the future. In the meantime, [our] method family allows us to share knowledge about developing product families, even though the product families themselves do not share other assets.*

A business case will help you decide if you are better off with one, or more than one, product line. Even if you adopt the pluralistic approach, you can still share knowledge across the product lines, just as Philips has done. Training, methodologies, tool instruction, plans, risk management programs, organizational structure—all of these are exemplary (albeit nonsoftware) core assets that can be shared across a wide spectrum. Whether the result is a single product line or several is of interest to purists and philosophers; the important thing is to share what it makes sense to share.

—PCC

5.5.4 Specific Practices

Examining existing products: Conducting a thorough study of existing products helps identify commonality across a potential product line and identifies the types of differences that are likely to occur. A survey of each group that is developing these products will likely identify future plans, market strategies, and context. In many cases, existing products will contain potential product line assets that can be mined and used in the future. The set of steps in this process will include the following:

1. Identify existing products similar to those that will be part of the product line.
2. Gather any available documentation and conduct product demonstrations.
3. Conduct oral or written surveys of the current developers, users, and maintainers of these products and product experts.
4. Identify the products' capabilities, structure, and evolution, and any other relevant factors about them.
5. Determine which elements of these products should be considered part of the product line.

Other Voices: The Product Portfolio

When planning your stable of products, how do you decide which are in and which are out? These authors from South Africa prescribe a strategy that includes value maximization and balancing the portfolio, all the while staying in concert with the company's strategic direction [van Zyl 00]:

> ***Value maximization:*** *Expected economic value is a method used to maximize the commercial worth of the portfolio. It takes into account factors such as the following: expected commercial value of the product, probability of commercial success, probability of technical success, development costs of the projects that make up the product, commercialization costs that include marketing and launching the product, [and] the net present value of the product's future earnings.*
>
> *It is not always feasible to follow this approach where up-front financial calculations determine a product's future. There must be times when management will continue with projects because of an intuition. Many organizations have built world-class products even though they were seen initially as being losers.*
>
> *Organizations should build their own scoring models whereby the factors that are most important to them will be considered. A checklist might look like this:*

- *expected economic value, including the assumptions that accompany the ratios and values*
- *core competencies in the organization that can be exploited in such a way that innovations will occur that can yield major returns*
- *trends in the market that can play a major role in deciding what to build and when to build it*
- *competitive advantage and market perception that influence all decisions*

Balanced portfolio: *It is not always possible to reach a balance between product lines and projects. Information might not be available, or environmental conditions might influence decisions. Customers play a major role in decisions made about what gets built. Product management needs to make decisions that balance existing customer value vs. what is needed to generate new customers in the future.*

Having a portfolio with breakthrough products only, for example, presents a major risk, as there will be maturity and deployment problems. It is advisable to have a balance of different products at various stages of maturity in the product family.

Conducting a workshop to understand product line goals and products: It is important to gather the potential product line stakeholders to set the direction for the product. The stakeholders include management, marketing, developers, users, testers, tool developers, technology researchers, and domain experts. The market analysis and business case will also explore goals; during scoping, however, the activity examines the product line more from the perspective of the user than of the organization. The workshop should produce a product line strategy that identifies the following:

- the business goals to be satisfied by the product line
- the mapping of product line business goals to the organization's business goals and to users' needs
- descriptions of current and potential future products that will constitute the product line
- essential product line assets that may include platforms, standards, protocols, and processes

The workshop should also establish a coarse-grained schedule that aligns product line development with marketing or overall mission strategies.

Other Voices:
Scoping at Robert Bosch GmbH

Robert Bosch GmbH is a large German electronics manufacturer of automotive equipment. This equipment ranges from motor control units and automatic braking systems to airbag controllers, various sensor-based applications, and car multimedia systems. Here is how they approached the scoping problem for their software product line [Thiel 00]. Notice how it combines aspects of traditional scoping with business case and domain analysis to produce a complete picture of the bounding constraints.

In our context, the objective of performing a PLS [product line scoping] phase was to identify the functional, technical, political, legal, and business constraints that are characteristic to the product line. Typical inputs for scoping a product line include existing product descriptions, marketing analyses, expert knowledge as well as business visions and strategies for introducing the company's new products into the market. For scoping our product line, we applied the following practices. . . .

Business investigation: *To understand the business goals and constraints of the product line development effort, we had to gather information from the executives' point of view. In our case, this was mostly done by interviewing marketing and business personnel responsible for selling and developing the company's products. The investigation resulted in a collection of baseline information including the description of the coarse functional range of the envisioned members of the product line as well as the product line's long-term vision, the market segment that was to be addressed, and the organizational constraints on the development of future products.*

Product space examination: *The goal of this step was to mine the set of legacy and competitors' products (product space). The product space had to comply with the envisioned market segment previously outlined by the executive stakeholders. Mining the product space also included the consideration of future products and extensions to current products as expected by potential product line users or customers.*

When we conducted a description of the product space for the product line of interest, we found it helpful to concentrate on two aspects: the products' functionality and the interfaces to other products/systems. We specified the coarse functionality of the products by looking at typical usage modes and use cases. Interfaces could be identified by examining and describing the products' external actors, that is, the environment in which the products are typically embedded. For illustrating the interface relationships we used context diagrams. . . .

Modeling the (available) product space helped us to better understand the capability spectrum that will have to be provided by product members of the product line. Although our focus was, as described above, on defining the functional capabilities of the products, we also assessed other characteristics—for example, the coarse architectural mechanisms used in the current realization of the products to fulfill essential quality attributes (i.e., reliability, availability, and performance). . . .

Standards and technology investigation: *Besides investigating business aspects and the product space, we also spent some time in documenting standards and technologies related to the product line under consideration. For this purpose, we interviewed product experts. In addition, we examined the product space models created before. Finally, we came up with a short categorization and description of the most important standards and technologies. The document also contained a reference list with pointers to more detailed information.*

Context diagramming: A context diagram places the product line in the context of other systems and of product users. This diagram depicts the important entities that affect the product line or are affected by the product line (for example, people, physical environment, and other systems). The diagram is a generalization across the product line; not every system in the product may connect with all systems or types of users shown in the diagram. Similarly, the context diagram may not show all the interactions of all the potential systems. And even if some product line systems have interactions that are unique to one system, they should still be included in the product line. In addition to highlighting the common context, the context diagram and accompanying documentation should describe possible options and variations. A rationale for the selection of options or variants should also be included. Figure 5.3 illustrates a context diagram for the software in a personal sound system.

Developing an attribute/product matrix: An attribute/product matrix sorts, in order of priority, the important attributes by which products in the product line differ. Typically, the attributes that drive the market are listed vertically on the left side of the matrix, and the different products are listed horizontally across the top of the matrix. For example, in Table 5.2, attributes include radio tuner, displays, and audio control; products include low-cost model, mid-priced model, and high-end model. The value for the attribute of each product (analog, for example) is listed where the attribute column (radio tuner) and product row (low-cost model) intersect. In practice, of course, software attributes are often less tangible. The

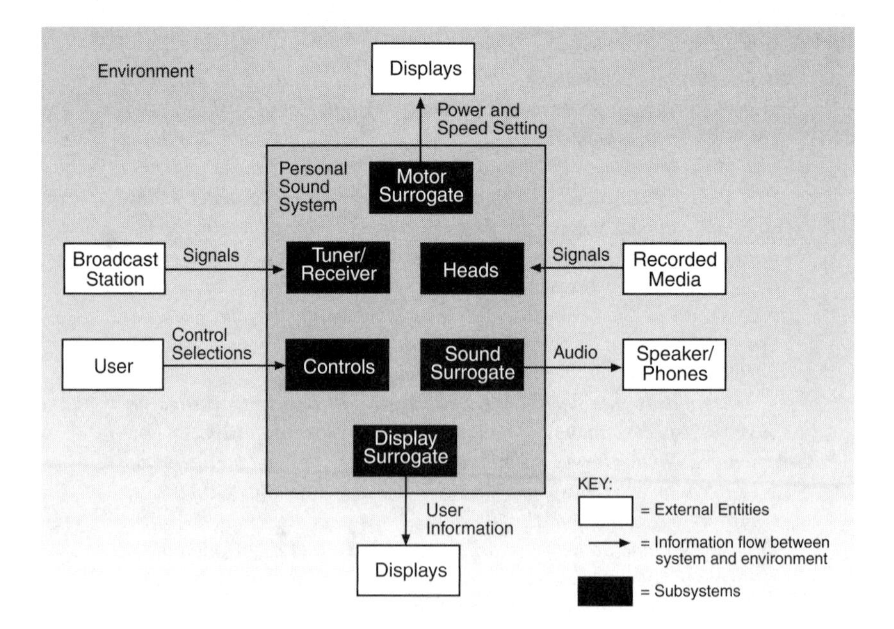

Figure 5.3 Context Diagram of a Personal Sound System

Table 5.2 Attribute/Product Matrix for Personal Audio System

	Low-Cost Model	Mid-Priced Model	High-End Model
Radio Tuner	analog	digital presets	digital presets
Displays	none	frequency	frequency, graphical equalizer
Audio Control	volume	bass-added	full-spectrum equalizer

matrix is used in scoping to define the variability of the product line. By sorting in order of attribute priority, the cluster of the most important attributes that are common across the product can be identified readily.

Developing product line scenarios: Product line scenarios are key to defining a product line's scope. They describe user or system interactions with products in the product line. They identify interactions that are common to all products in the product line, as well as those that are unique to a subset of products in the product line. The purpose is to test the context for the scope of the product line. Are there entities that affect the systems that are not included in the context diagram? If so, must new domains be identified? Along with creating the scenarios, it is important to conduct scenario walkthroughs. These walkthroughs help us understand the support that will be needed to realize the scenarios in product line products.

PuLSE-ECO: DeBaud and Schmid write about a method for determining the scope of a product line [DeBaud 00]. The method is called PuLSE-ECO. First, product candidates are mapped out, based on input about the system domain and stakeholders. Candidates include existing, planned, and potential systems. The result is a list of potential characteristics for products in the product line. Products and characteristics are combined into a product map, a kind of product/attribute matrix as described above. In parallel, evaluation functions are created, using stakeholder and business goals as input. These evaluation functions will enable the prediction of the costs and benefits of imbuing a particular product with a particular characteristic (such as a feature). Next, potential products are characterized, using product maps and the evaluation functions. Finally, benefit analysis gathers the characteristic and evaluation information and determines the scope of the product line.

5.5.5 Practice Risks

The major risk associated with product line scoping is that the wrong set of products will be targeted. In particular,

- **Scope too big or too small:** For a product line to be successful, its scope must be defined carefully. If an attempt is made to encompass product members that vary too widely, the core assets will be strained beyond their ability to accommodate the variability; economies of production will be lost; and the product line will collapse into the old-style, one-at-a-time product development effort. If the scope is defined too narrowly, the core assets might not be built in a generic enough fashion to accommodate future growth, and the product line will stagnate.

- **Scope includes the wrong products:** Commonalities and variations across current and future systems will include functional requirements, user concerns, and interactions with external systems. In addition, these commonalities and variations will include system qualities, performance issues, and technology evolution. The scoping effort must define a scope that reflects both what is desired for the product line from a marketing perspective and what is feasible from a design perspective. The focus must consider issues that span both the problem and solution spaces. The risk is that, short of this, the scope will either fail to achieve the goals for product line development or be impossible to achieve given the design and technology constraints.
- **Essential stakeholders don't participate:** The specific practices in scoping require participation from a wide range of stakeholders. These stakeholders will include management, developers, customers, users, methodologists, and subject-matter experts. The risk is that without sufficient participation in planning the product line scope, the buy-in necessary to achieve the desired downstream results (the product line architecture and other assets) will not exist. Stakeholders' input is required to reduce the obvious risk that the scope is inappropriate for the product line. More important, the involvement of a wide range of stakeholders increases the awareness of product line efforts, obtains their critical input, and builds momentum for the long-term investment in asset development and use.

5.5.6 For Further Reading

DeBaud and Schmid's PuLSE-ECO is perhaps the most comprehensively documented method for scoping a software product line [DeBaud 00], but it is not the only one. Cohen and Northrop have written about product line scoping in the context of object technology [Cohen 98]. The use of object-oriented approaches such as scenarios, use cases, and frameworks can contribute to our understanding of a product line and the development of a scope for that product line. Their article also offers an example product line scope, context diagram, and use cases. Jandourek has described an approach for platform (or product line) development that was used at Hewlett-Packard [Jandourek 96]. The first step in the approach is product portfolio planning to establish a product lineage chart. This chart defines the organization's product needs and scopes the platform in terms of the products it must support. Robertson's article in *Sloan Management Review* discusses platform planning as a method of achieving software product lines [Robertson 98]. The planning process uses concepts that are used in product line scoping: (1) identifying the concepts, variants, and options to be embodied in products; (2) determining elements in the products that are common and unique; and (3) listing attributes that will differentiate products. Finally, Withey's investment analysis technique assesses the worthiness of investing in software assets [Withey 96]. An initial step in the analysis is scoping the product line that will use the assets. The author suggests methods of developing and analyzing the financial effectiveness of scoping decisions.

5.5.7 Discussion Questions

1. Where should scoping be assigned in a product line organization? Who should do it? Who should be involved in its validation? What qualities, talents, and experience should the person in charge of scoping have?
2. Think about a software product line that is or could be produced by your organization, or one that you know about.
   - Sketch a product/feature matrix for it.
   - Suppose your organization becomes very adept at producing all the products within that scope. What new but related business area does that scope suggest you might be readily prepared to enter?
   - Describe a system "on the cusp" of the scope or just outside the scope. Now adjust your scope definition to include it.
3. How does domain knowledge inform the scope definition? How does the information uncovered during scoping inform the domain model?
4. One organization we know began its scoping effort by attempting to complete the following four sentences:
   - "Products in our product line must . . ."
   - "Products in our product line should . . ."
   - "Products in our product line must not . . ."
   - "Products in our product line should not . . ."

   How would you complete these sentences for a product line in your organization?
5. As a product line grows and evolves, what are some good indications that its scope has been defined too narrowly? Too broadly? What measurements (or at least what checks) could you put in place to detect these conditions?

5.6 Technical Planning

Planning is one of the fundamental functions of management at any level. It provides the basis for the other management functions, particularly tracking and controlling. This practice area is concerned with the planning of projects. By "project," we mean an undertaking typically requiring concerted effort that is focused on developing or maintaining a specific product or products. Typically, a project has its own funding, accounting, and delivery schedule. In a product line context, a project might be responsible for developing specific core assets or for developing a specific product from the core assets. A companion practice area is "Organizational Planning" (Section 6.8), which focuses on the strategic planning that transcends projects.

It is useful to distinguish between the process by which plans are created (the planning process) and the product of that process (the plans). Most planning processes are very similar regardless of the organizational level at which the plan is applied. Differences among processes are primarily limited to differences in personnel and in the scope of the effort to be planned. The process of planning should include:

- establishing the plan and its contents
- establishing commitments to the plan
- establishing estimates of the resources required to carry out the plan
- reviewing the plan for feasibility by those who will be bound by it

The planning process needs to be iterative and ongoing—after all, plans change. Plans should be updated and revised as appropriate throughout their lives.

There are different types of plans for addressing different purposes. Examples of project-oriented technical management plans include project plans, software development plans, quality assurance plans, configuration management plans, test plans, and technical risk management plans.

Although the exact contents of a plan should be tailored to fit its particular use, there are some fairly standard plan contents. Allowing for differences in terminology, typical plans include the following:

- **Goals:** A goal is a statement of a desired state that will be achieved by the successful execution of the plan.
- **Strategies:** A strategy is a description of a way to achieve plan goals.
- **Objectives:** An objective describes a significant, measurable, time-related intermediate state that will be achieved as the plan is executed.
- **A set of activities to perform:** An activity is an assignable, discrete step that contributes to the achievement of objectives.
- **Resources allocated:** The plan should include an assessment of the resources that the planned activities are allowed to consume (chief among which is time).

Other potential plan contents include responsibilities and commitments, work breakdown structures, resource and schedule estimates, risks, progress measures, relationships, and traceability to other plans.

The most usable plans have a particular focus. To plan a task of any complexity often requires a set of interrelated plans. Relationships among plans might include:

- **Temporal relationships:** Some plans might cover a time period preceding or following other plans.
- **Hierarchical relationships:** Some plans contain subordinate details.
- **Relationships involving critical dependencies:** Some plans depend on the execution of other plans.
- **Relationships based on supporting infrastructure:** Some plans depend on the existence of an organizational function—for example, a quality assurance group or a process group.

5.6.1 Aspects Peculiar to Product Lines

There is nothing fundamentally different about a planning process for a product line. However, there are certain types of technical management plans that are unique to product lines. These plans include:

- **Core asset development and maintenance work plans:** These plans describe not only how assets will be created initially, but also how the asset base will grow and evolve.
- **Production/reuse plans:** These plans describe how products will be developed from a set of core assets.

Project plans will have a richer set of dependencies in a product line approach. Project plans will have external dependencies among different groups and other plans, possibly at the organizational level, with relation to the core assets. Examples of project plans that may have dependencies include configuration management plans, funding plans, software integration plans, testing plans, and risk management plans.

The Man with the Plan

In October of 1999 I went to visit the software core asset manager for a product line project we were helping to get off the ground. It had been a few months since my last visit, and in the interim the product line project had undertaken a massive and detailed planning effort. The manager wanted to show me the results. "I have to give my manager credit," he said, referring to the overall product line manager. He began unrolling a cylinder of paper on a conference table, spreading out a sheet roughly the size of a queen-size bed, to reveal an enormous PERT chart. "He asked me if it would be worthwhile to hire a management consultant to help us build this project plan for the core assets and keep it up to date. I said 'Sure, why not?' Since then, the guy has worked full time on-site for a week every other week for several months."

A full-time management consultant hired to help with planning sounded expensive, if not extravagant. Had it paid off?

"I can't believe what a difference it's made," he said. "Just this week, I've had four or five product managers come to me and say they needed to have a particular task moved over here"—and with a sweeping motion of his hand he indicated the left side of the huge chart, home to the earliest tasks—"and they needed it now." He smiled—rather serenely, I noticed. "I said, 'Well, there are about 2,000 tasks in the plan. Yours is one. We can move it, but it's going to affect everything else. We'll have to see if that's what management wants.'"

This resonated immediately. Almost three years earlier we had performed a risk evaluation at this organization, and one of the most critical risks to their ambitions of launching a product line was a lack of planning. Project engineers intent on getting a particular product out the door as soon as possible would make heated demands on the newly formed, embryonic, and hopelessly overworked core asset team. When they balked, the project engineer could point to a deadline, whether real or invented, whereas the core asset team could point to nothing. One of the risk evaluation participants lamented, "We never had enough information to be able to justify a 'no' answer."

Not that a "no" answer was anyone's goal, but some good, well-placed "nos" will keep an organization focused on the long-term product line goals and not let the organization get trodden over by short-term, single-project concerns. Learning how and when to say "no" is a big part of product line culture.

And that wasn't all. The manager went on to explain that his consultant would visit the product development, systems engineering, and hardware engineering groups to study the intergroup dependencies and account for them in the core asset software plan. Groups that had poor plans of their own could not justify the arbitrary deadlines they once were able to impose on the core asset group. The message was, "When you understand what you really need and why you need it, come see us and we'll see what we can do to help you. Until then, poor planning on your part does not constitute an emergency on our part." It was a message that was never delivered explicitly; it never had to be.

As we went through the plan, I noticed something I hadn't heard before. The manager told me he thought that the software core assets were going to be ready sometime in 2001.

"Really?" I said. "The last I heard, you were on the hook to deliver those this spring."

He nodded and said, "April 2000." That was only six months hence.

"And now not until 2001?"

"Yep."

"What happened?"

With another sweep of his hand, he indicated, at the leftmost edge of his furniture-sized PERT chart, a column of blue boxes indicating dependencies on external projects such as the systems engineering group or the hardware selection group. "These won't be ready in time," he said, trying very hard to suppress a grin.

I thought a minute. "There's no way that you would have been allowed to slip your schedule almost a year without this plan, is there?"

"Nope," he said, the grin no longer suppressed. "Now we're going to get to do it right."

The point, as we both knew, was not that a year's delay in the product line was a thing to be smug about, but because the dependencies really did exist, the delays would have occurred anyway. However, they would have occurred maybe a month at a time, each time precipitating unpleasant surprise, finger-pointing, hand-wringing, disappointment, and (more than likely) management pressure that would have intensified each time, to no good end. The plan had bought the core asset group the additional time it would have gotten anyway, but without planning, that time would have arrived in jerky four-week chunks and would not have been used to best advantage.

If the truth will set you free, then I was looking at a very liberated software core asset manager.

Besides uncovering the truth, planning had had another ironic side effect. Considered to be a way to let the core asset group say "no," planning had now let them avoid having to say it. The message is one of cooperation, not confrontation. They could respond to requests along the lines of the following:

- "We'll happily move your task up—after all, we're here to serve—but here are the ramifications. Let's see if the product line manager agrees with those effects wrought on other development groups and the product line itself."
- "We'll happily move your task up. Show me in your plan where it feeds into a critical path so we can agree on the timing."
- "We're all ready to produce the core assets in the amount of time we promised, but we can't make progress until we get the following information from the following groups."

"That consultant makes a lot of money," the manager volunteered, rolling up the chart. I knew the manager was talking in terms of an hourly rate, and consultants being consultants, I had no doubt that the rate was breathtaking. But if we were measuring the serenity that this information imparted to the core asset group, a serenity that I had not observed heretofore in this manager, then I got the distinct impression that the manager thought the consultant was not overpaid at all. I was inclined to agree.

—PCC

5.6.2 Application to Core Asset Development

A product line effort requires work plans for core asset development and maintenance. These plans correspond to standard project plans, except that the "project" in this case is the development and maintenance of core assets. In addition to the generic plan contents identified earlier, these plans should also answer the following questions:

- What is the set of core assets?
- How will core assets be created initially?
- How will core assets be tested (or, in the case of the architecture, evaluated)?
- How will the core asset base be expanded and maintained, and how will components be certified for incorporation?
- How will core asset development and maintenance be funded? This should include the identification of funding sources and over time a funding profile that addresses initial creation as well as sustainment. Because of the scope, planning for core asset funding is likely to occur at the organizational level. In this case, project and organizational planning would work in close concert. Project planning might determine funding needs. How to satisfy these needs could be planned at the organizational level.
- How might these plans interact with product development plans? Core asset development and maintenance plans and product development plans might have mutual dependencies illuminated by questions like the following:
  - What core assets must be available to support particular product development needs? When must they be available?
  - Are any product development projects providing components to the core asset base? When are they needed? How are they to be incorporated?
- How will the configuration of and changes in the core assets be controlled?

Whether you opt for a separate plan for each core asset or for an overall "master" plan for the entire core asset effort depends on your context and culture. While the preceding list may appear daunting, it is mostly just a restatement of the plans we've discussed elsewhere in the software engineering and technical management practice areas. There, we've admonished you to include an architecture evaluation in your project planning, to write CM and test plans for your core assets, to write a COTS plan for finding and acquiring off-the-shelf components, to make a plan for any mining you expect to carry out, to plan for risk management and data collection and tool support, and to make an adoption plan for any processes you define.

Don't overlook the fact that the plans themselves (or parts of the plans) make splendid reusable core assets. Ideally, reusable plans should be tailorable in the same fashion as other core assets—that is, they have defined points of commonality and variability. Cost, effort, and schedule estimates may be particularly useful candidates for reuse. So are work breakdown structures, goals, strategies, and objectives.

5.6.3 Application to Product Development

Each product development effort needs a plan to describe how a specific product will be produced using the core assets. We call it a *production plan;* others sometimes call it a *reuse plan*. In addition to the generic plan contents identified earlier, a production plan should also answer the following questions:

- What processes must be followed to utilize and adapt the core assets for use in each product?
- How will any necessary tailoring of the core assets be accomplished?
- How will any product-unique development be accomplished to supplement the core assets?
- How will products be tested?
- How might these plans interact with core asset development/maintenance plans? Production/reuse plans and core asset development and maintenance plans might have the following types of mutual dependencies:
  - What core assets must be available to support particular product development needs? When must they be available?
  - Are any product development projects providing components to the core asset base? When are they needed? What product development team actions are necessary to add components to the core asset base?

In the "Architecture Definition" practice area (Section 4.1), we suggested packaging a large part of the production plan with the architecture. Note that this subsumes the integration plan we described in the "Software System Integration" practice area (Section 4.7).

5.6.4 Specific Practices

Production plans: One method of constructing a production plan uses the concept of associating specific reuse processes with specific core assets. In this approach, each core asset has an attached process that explains how it is to be reused. Thus, the production plan for a specific product describes how to sequence these attached processes and also describes the planning of any product-unique development.

Improvement plans: Jones and Northrop [Jones 99] offer general lessons that apply to product line planning—lessons learned during technical and strategic planning for process improvement. These lessons apply to both the *process* of planning and the *plans* themselves.

These authors list the characteristics of a good planning process as *modularity, iteration, validation, consensus,* and *adaptation*. For complex activities, a focus on *modularity* leads to a divide-and-conquer approach, which recognizes that it may be appropriate to create a set of interrelated plans. A modular planning process separates concerns so that appropriate groups can create and execute plans with the appropriate scope and focus. An *iterative* planning process recognizes that a one-pass approach to planning is not generally realistic. As more is learned about the details of a particular plan, it is useful to return to previously drafted portions (iterate) and revise them in light of what has been learned. A good planning process also includes *validation* steps to confirm that previously drafted portions are correct as more details are learned. Validation steps are an effective way to drive the iteration. It is important to achieve *consensus* on the content of a plan among those who will implement it. This is achieved most easily if the team that will execute the plan also developed it. Finally, a good planning process is flexible to allow the *adaptation* of the plan's contents to the particular needs of a project or group.

Regarding the plans themselves, Jones and Northrop list the following, sometimes competing, characteristics of good plans:

- **Appropriateness for purpose:** A good plan is focused on the correct things in order to accomplish identified goals.
- **Clarity:** Good plans communicate unambiguously *what* is going to be done and *why, how* it will be approached and *when, who* will be responsible, and *what* resources will be required.
- **Brevity:** If a plan is too lengthy, it will be difficult to use and maintain.
- **Sufficient detail:** A plan should be brief but not so brief as to sacrifice clarity.
- **Internal modularity:** Supporting details should be separated from the body of the plan. Volatile information should be separated from information that will be relatively stable throughout the life of the plan.
- **Internal and external consistency and traceability:** A good plan should not contradict itself. The refinement of detail should be logical, and its source should be apparent. Dependencies must be identified and traceable.
- **Usability:** A good plan is usable; a usable plan has an appropriate balance of the previous characteristics.

5.6.5 Practice Risks

Poor-quality technical plans can fail to plot the needed tasks and provide adequate resources for product line efforts. The result will be a lack of confidence in the planners, missed deadlines, and poor quality due to desperate shortcuts. In particular, plans can suffer from the following:

- **Lack of product line support:** If the additional coordination and commitments required for product line planning are not accomplished effectively, the result will likely be a poorly coordinated effort in which product line benefits are lost.
- **Shelfware plans:** If plans are not updated as changes occur, the plans become useless and the process becomes unmanageable.
- **Inappropriate plans:** If plans are too aggressive, too detailed, or too abstract, they will not be followed. Plans need to be realistic to the organization and the goals. They need to provide sufficient direction but leave some flexibility.

- **Stakeholders not involved:** Product line plans typically have more stakeholders than typical project plans. Unless all the appropriate stakeholders (or at least a representative set of them) are involved in the creation of product line plans, the plans may not be viable for all concerned.

5.6.6 Discussion Questions

1. In this section we read that product line organizations need plans for building and evolving core assets and products. Later, in the "Operations" practice area (Section 6.7), we'll see that a product line's operational concept must define a process for building and evolving core assets and products. Assuming that we are not prescribing the same activity in two different places, what do you suppose the difference is between the output of Technical Planning and the output of Operations?
2. How do you think a technical plan should be validated? Who are its stakeholders, and how should they be involved?
3. One can imagine a detailed technical plan for all phases of a project or a less detailed plan that refers to other plans (such as a testing plan) for detail as appropriate, rather like calling a subroutine. What are the advantages and disadvantages of each approach?
4. Make a list of the practice areas whose execution you think should entail the creation of a technical plan.

5.7 Technical Risk Management

Risk management is the practice of managing risks within a project, an organization, or a team of organizations. A complete risk management program should provide processes, methods, tools, and an infrastructure of resources and organizational responsibilities to identify and assess what could go wrong (the risks), determine what to do about the risks, and implement actions to deal with the risks. We distinguish between the practice areas of *technical* risk management and *organizational* risk management based on the scope and extent of the risks they address and the people likely to carry them out. Like other technical management practice areas, technical risk management addresses project-level concerns.

A risk is defined as the possibility of suffering a loss. Therefore, a risk has an associated probability that an event will happen and an associated negative impact or consequence if the risk is realized. When a risk is realized, it is no longer a risk, it is a problem. A problem is a certainty rather than a possibility.

Having a standard way of stating and communicating a risk provides clarity and consistency and is a critical component of risk management, serving as a basis for future risk-mitigation planning. There are two parts of a risk statement: the condition and the consequence (see Figure 5.4). The condition should be based on fact and provides the reader with the anomalous condition or circumstance that causes concern. At least one possible consequence should be noted so that future readers of the risk statement will better understand the original concern of the author.

For example, consider the following risk statement:

> *The commercial off-the-shelf (COTS) high-speed data link selected by the project team was never envisioned by the vendor to be used in a hardened environment; it may not perform as needed, causing rework and integration slips.*

The condition causing concern is the program selection of a component unproven in the target environment. One possible consequence is rework and schedule slips. Risk statements that are fact-based and actionable allow the project team to begin to reason about the risk constructively. To help in the risk-mitigation process, the context under which a risk statement was generated is typically added to the statement. The context is simply additional information regarding the circumstances, events, and interrelationships within an organization (or, in the case of product lines, among the various products) that may affect the risk. The context description captures more detail than can be captured in the basic risk statement. The risk statement with its associated context helps identify the true source of the risk.

There are several risk management paradigms [Boehm 89, Charette 89]. The Continuous Risk Management (CRM) paradigm developed by the Software Engineering Institute (SEI) is representative and is illustrated by the CRM icon in Figure 5.5 [Dorofee 96]. In this paradigm, risks are first *identified* and then *analyzed* to determine their probability of occurrence and impact (risk exposure) on the organization, the interrelationships between individual risk statements, and which related risks (risk areas) are most important to mitigate. Mitigation *plans* are developed for the most important risk areas. Individual

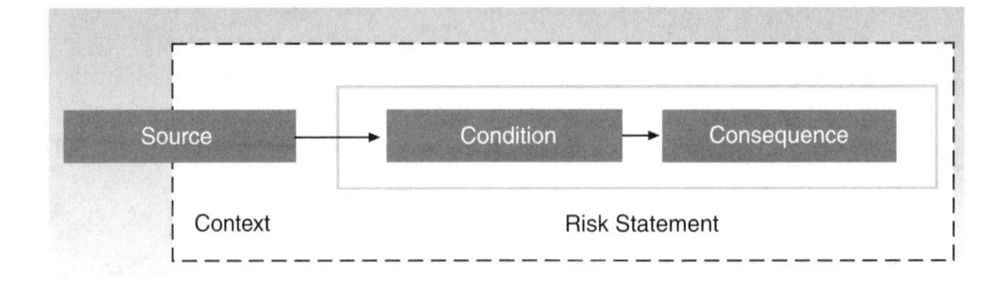

Figure 5.4 The Risk Statement with Context

Figure 5.5 Continuous Risk Management (CRM) Paradigm

risks, mitigation plans, and the risk process are all *tracked* to determine the effectiveness of mitigation actions and the risk process. *Control* decisions (for example, close, replan, continue tracking) are made and documented. The diagram is circular to emphasize that effective risk management should be a continuous process. This is in contrast to a risk management program that might only identify risks once at the start of a project and never revisit them.

Communication is represented as an encompassing activity to emphasize that the flow of information throughout the project or organization is essential to successful risk management.

5.7.1 Aspects Peculiar to Product Lines

In product lines, risks most often involve more than one product, so the overall consequences are more far-reaching. While standard risk management paradigms can be applied to product lines, the challenge will be in tailoring the program to the organization and to product line issues. A risk management program is implemented most effectively as an integrated part of organization or project management rather than as a separate activity.

Second, in a product line approach, some sources of risk may be different or may have different emphases. This could affect the process of risk identification. If you use a risk method that comes with its own taxonomy of risk areas or directed questioning techniques, be prepared to modify it in order to stimulate thought about the more common product line risks, such as those identified under the heading Practice Risks for each practice area.

Finally, as with all projects, the timing of risk management activities is critical. Since many important decisions are made early in the life cycle of a product line, include risk management in the plans at the start of the effort (that is, when the product line effort is launched).

5.7.2 Application to Core Asset Development

The application of risk management to a product line approach is fundamentally the same whether one is developing core assets or developing products from those assets. If there is a significant difference, it may be with respect to the importance of a rigorous risk management program. Because problems in core asset development have a ripple effect throughout the product line organization, risks in that area should be managed with particular care.

5.7.3 Application to Product Development

As noted above, the application of risk management to a product line approach is fundamentally the same whether one is developing core assets or developing products from those assets. Additionally, the product development risk management program must be coordinated with the risk management program for core assets.

5.7.4 Specific Practices

It is useful to treat the installation of a risk management program as a technological change project. Technological change practices recognize that there are predictable patterns in the needs of the organization and the people within the organization as a new practice or technology is introduced [Myers 92]. Full coverage of this subject is beyond the scope of this document. However, an important principle is to start small and learn how the new practice works in the organization's context before expanding the effort. This minimizes disruption and allows the incorporation of lessons learned for a smoother widespread installation of the practice.

An approach to installing a risk management program consists of the following steps adapted from the approach described by Dorofee et al. [Dorofee 96]:

1. Build the initial awareness and infrastructure.
2. Establish a risk baseline and mitigation plans.
3. Develop a risk management plan that is adapted to existing structures and practices.
4. Install risk management in a pilot project.
5. Improve and expand the risk management implementation.

These steps, which view risk management from somewhat of a project focus, are described below. As mentioned previously, a product line approach requires an intimate association between core asset developers and product developers. Thus a more comprehensive approach to risk management that crosses organizational boundaries may be desirable. Such an approach is team risk management, as described in the "Organizational Risk Management" practice area (Section 6.9).

Step 1. Build the initial awareness and infrastructure: In this step, management is made aware of risk management benefits and implementation requirements. A management commitment is required before the project can proceed. Initial awareness training, including motivation, is conducted within the organization, and an implementation team is established.

Step 2. Establish a risk baseline and mitigation plans: In this step, risks are examined in a comprehensive fashion, and an initial set of risk mitigation plans is created. One technique for establishing a risk baseline is described by Dorofee et al. [Dorofee 96]. A key element of this step is risk identification. For example, the SEI Risk Taxonomy-Based Questionnaire (TBQ) has been used successfully to stimulate thought about sources of risk [Williams 99]. Use of the TBQ supplemented with risks from software product line practice areas is one approach. Other sources of risk are described by Boehm [Boehm 81] and Fairley [Fairley 94]. Once a basic set of risks has been established, it should be analyzed for probability, impact, and time frame; this analysis will help to prioritize the risks. Risk mitigation plans should be built for the highest-priority risks. Responsibility for mitigation plan execution should be assigned.

Step 3. Develop a risk management plan that is adapted to existing structures and practices: A risk management plan should detail the processes and organization that will address risks. As mentioned previously, continuous risk management should be integrated into existing practices. Thus, the first step is to analyze existing structures, functions, and processes. The following types of questions should be addressed:

- What meetings and reviews are already in place?
- Who is involved?
- What tracking and control mechanisms are already in place?

This analysis can help you discover opportunities for inserting the basic risk management practices (that is, identify, analyze, plan, track, and control) or uncover the need to add additional practices or functions. The risk management plan will address how these functions will be incorporated into standard operations [Loveland-Link 99].

Step 4. Install risk management in a pilot project: This is the trial implementation of the risk management plan. The project chosen should be representative of the organization and supported by project management. The project must capture any lessons learned and work collaboratively with the risk implementation team.

Step 5. Improve and expand the risk management implementation: In this step, lessons learned from the pilot project are applied to improve the risk management practices. Implementation is then expanded more widely throughout the organization. Depending on the organization, this expanded use may be instituted in phases. The continued improvement of risk management practices should be ongoing.

5.7.5 Practice Risks

An ineffective risk management program will result in problems catching management by surprise and can lead to decreased morale, low product quality, missed deadlines, and failure to perform. Some of the risks associated with the introduction of a risk management program, which include the risks common to any improvement effort, are as follows [Radice 94]:

- Insufficient senior management sponsorship
- Resistance by middle managers
- Termination of activities before the practice is institutionalized
- Lack of sustained focus on improvement

The biggest risk related to risk management is failure of the existing organizational culture to encourage and reward risk identification. In such a "risk-averse" organization, people are pressured not to raise risks, either overtly or implicitly. Without broad participation in risk identification and management, a risk management program cannot succeed. Table 5.3 shows some barriers that exist in a "risk-averse" organization.

5.7.6 For Further Reading

Foundational references for risk management include Boehm's IEEE tutorial on software risk management [Boehm 89]; Charette's book, *Software Engineering Risk Analysis and Management* [Charette 89]; and the SEI's Software Risk Evaluation (SRE) method description [Williams 99].

5.7.7 Discussion Questions

1. All of the practice risks associated with software engineering and technical management practice areas are prime targets of a technical risk management approach. Pick some risks from each of these practice areas, and discuss how risk management could be used to head off each risk.
2. How does the "Technical Risk Management" practice area (Section 5.7) relate to the "Technical Planning" practice area (Section 5.6)?
3. In your organization, whom would you choose to carry out various technical risk management activities? Would you expect any of these same people to work on technical planning? Why or why not?

Table 5.3 Potential Communication Barriers [Dorofee 96]

Potential Barrier	Description
"ready, fire, aim" approach	People provide solutions to a problem before they have assembled and understood the underlying facts and context of the problem.
"don't tell me your problem" attitude	People require a solution before they even discuss an issue: for example, a manager says, "Don't bring me problems, bring me solutions."
"shoot the messenger" attitude	A project member who intends to inform others or who is seeking help suffers negative consequences because he or she is communicating unpleasant information.
liar's poker approach	Project personnel identify risks but fail to communicate them to others. Instead, they wait until the risks become serious problems that impact project schedules and product quality.
mistrust	Individuals do not trust each other for a variety of reasons (such as past history and preconceived biases). This lack of trust can destroy any credibility in the acquired risk data which, by its nature, is subjective and speculative.
hidden agendas	Situations create individual preferences for results: individuals or groups may promote facts or arguments based on their own goals rather than for the common good.
"placing blame" approach	Risk information is used to place blame on project personnel.

4. If the staff fails to see that the first risk management exercise resulted in any improvement, they may lose patience or confidence in the approach and not be nearly so forthcoming in the second exercise. Discuss ways to make sure this doesn't happen.

5.8 Tool Support

Software development organizations use tools to support many of the activities necessary to transform a set of identified customer needs into a useful product. A multitude of CASE (computer-aided software engineering) tools are available to help automate the analysis, design, implementation, and maintenance of software-intensive products. The challenge is to choose and use tools wisely to support the business goals of the organization and the technical needs of the product developers.

Typically, a range of tools is used over the life of the project. The degree to which they interoperate and support the development process can have a large effect on the productivity of the development team and the quality of the resultant products [Bruckhaus 96, Low 99]. Standards have emerged to provide guidance in the evaluation, selection, and adoption of CASE tools [IEEE 98a, IEEE 95, ISO 95a], and several authors have described approaches to the problem of CASE tool integration and results of CASE tool adoption studies [Brown 94a, Brown 94b, Bruckhaus 96, Low 99, Powell 96, Vollman 94].

5.8.1 Aspects Peculiar to Product Lines

If you're building a software product line, it's a good bet that a variety of tools will be brought to bear because there is no single tool that addresses the needs of all product line practices. While many of the practices supported by CASE tools are applicable to product lines, the product line context brings some of its own particular needs and risks.

This practice area does not address the related issue of choosing and using technologies (such as distributed object technology) that may be new to a product line organization and for which tool support may be required. The focus here is on applying familiar tools to practices in a product line context.

The critical aspect of this practice area is support for concurrently creating, maintaining, and using multiple versions of product line artifacts, both core assets and products. This requires a development environment that facilitates the coordination of asset development and product development teams and processes and the sharing of assets among teams.

A Tool for Software Product Line Production

Tools for software product line development are almost nonexistent, but as the practice spreads, help may be on the horizon. An example of up-and-coming technology is provided by BigLever Software, Inc. (http://www.biglever.com). BigLever's founder and CEO, Charles Krueger, saw that a lot of companies were building and fielding many versions of almost-identical systems without exploiting what they had in common—indeed, without even realizing that they had a software product line (in the sense that this book uses the term). What they did realize was that the complexity of maintaining all of the versions of all of the parts of all of those systems was eating their lunch. Trying to manage large code segments littered with spaghetti bowls of interdependent #ifdef's, pages-long Makefiles and build scripts, arcane runtime configuration files and code conditionals, and (worst and, ironically, most common of all) many cloned and modified source copies, was causing midnight oil to be burned by the gallon. And they could only look forward to worse. These companies viewed themselves as being in the clutches of a configuration control monster, and they couldn't understand why traditional CM tools weren't helping all that much. Krueger knew that source-code-level artifact management was where the complexity of a software product line hit home on an operational day-to-day basis. He also realized that the traditional main-trunk-and-branch model of vanilla CM tools only exacerbated the problem: once a branch is formed, it takes on a development and maintenance life of its own and can never be brought back into the fold. Traditional CM tools are meant to handle variation over time, but they are not as good at handling simultaneously supported variations.

Enter BigLever's tool, called the Product Line Platform. Suppose your company produces e-commerce software for a number of retailers. One of your customers sells bicycles, one sells wedding rings, and one sells pianos. Among them, they sell in Europe, the United States, and Canada. Your customers want you to build each of them a Web site where buyers can order and pay for products. One of your customers wants his Web site to offer a "shopping cart" service where buyers can temporarily "store" purchases between sessions; others do not. Some companies will deliver their products to a dealer for pickup; others offer factory pickup.

The first thing you do is enumerate your products and the ways in which they differ. Say you've got six customers who want you to build their Web sites. The sites vary in terms of the merchandise they sell (bikes, rings, pianos), their business locations (Europe, United States, Canada), whether they offer a shopping cart (yes, no), and what their delivery arrangements are (dealer, factory). To build these systems, you must have, say, 20 or so different components. Most are common across all your applications, such as the component that manages an on-line credit card transaction, but five components exist in different versions depending on what product they're used in: Delivery, Main, Models, Selection, and Title. The second thing you do, then, is list all of the common components and all of the versions of the varying components and define which is used in which product.

The figure that follows shows a screen-shot of the BigLever Product Line Platform. On the right are the dimensions of variation (and the possible values of each) for the product set. An "enumerated" variation means that one value is selected; a "set" variation means that zero or more values can be chosen. On the left are the inventory of products and the software components they comprise. The six products are Bikes Europe to Rings US. The five components that come in different versions are marked with a gear symbol. Main is expanded, showing that it comes in two versions; the logic file contains the simple expression that associates each version of the component with the combination of

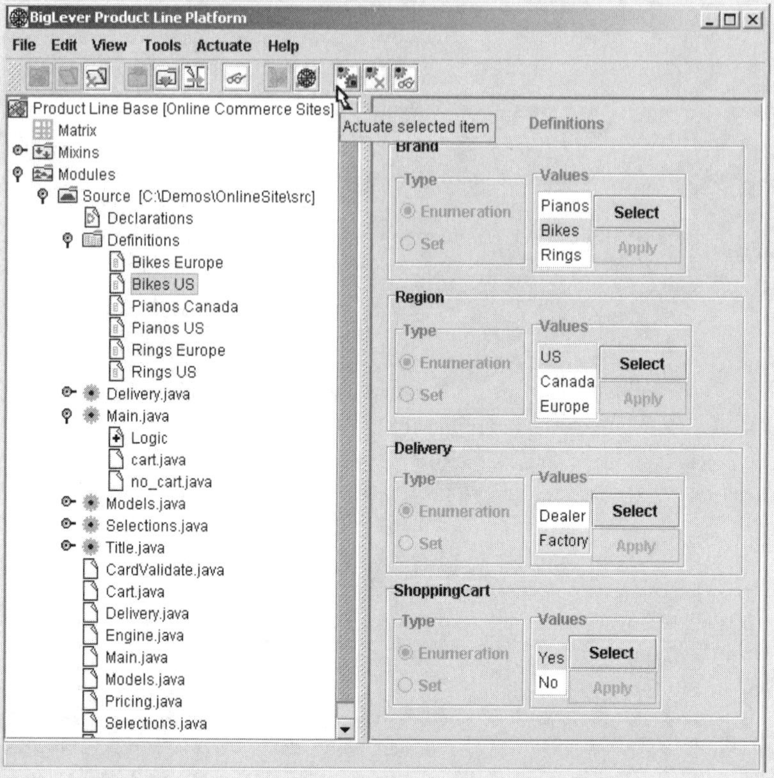

Definitions Screen

variations that causes it to be selected for a product. The complete list of components that constitute a product are in the list at lower left.

In the figure, "Bikes US" is chosen, and we see that the "Bikes US" product—that is, the Web site that we're going to build for them—is going to sell bikes, in the United States, from the factory, and offers a shopping cart.

When the "Actuate selected item" button is pressed, the tool makes the versions of all the components appropriate to "Bikes US" available in a workspace from which the product can be built.

The following figure shows what happens when the actuation occurs. The tool tells us which variants have been selected; here, for example, the version of the Delivery component named "factory.java" has been selected, and so forth. The "Bikes US" product is now ready to be built.

The tool is independent of a company's build process; it just supplies the "right" files to the build tool, which now can be greatly simplified because it no longer has to be concerned about version selection. It is also independent of any CM tool because it doesn't know or care where the file versions come

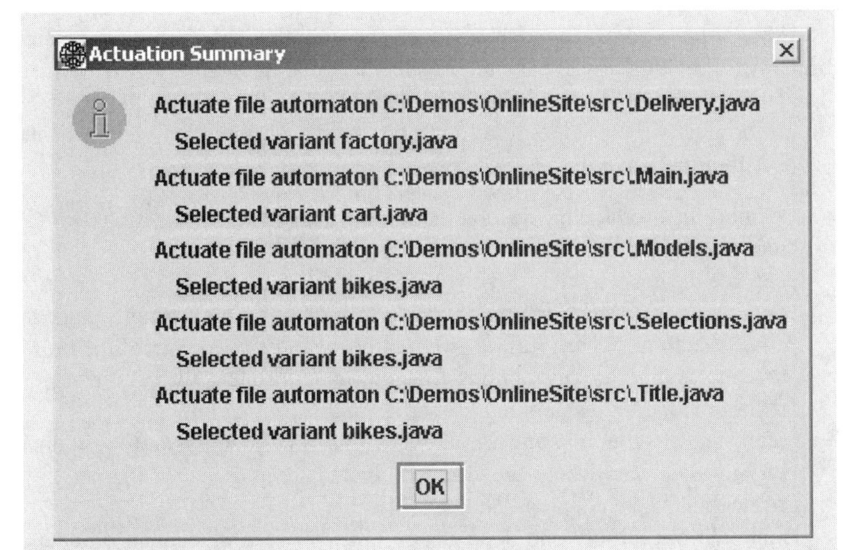

Actuating the Product Choices

from. It is language-independent; it never modifies or even examines the source code. In fact, the "components" don't have to be software at all—they could be chapters in a product line requirements specification, for instance. Our story could, with almost no changes, have been about generating the requirements document for the "Bikes US" system.

Notice how a product line tool imbues product line thinking. A company using this tool cannot help but think of itself as building variations of a single product (see "E Pluribus Unum," sidebar). It's the singular product line that evolves over time, by adding new variation capabilities. Nor can a company help but lay out the product line scope by enumerating all of the products that it builds and all of the ways they vary from each other. The tool also gives companies a splendid strategy for building a product line by means of reengineering legacy assets. To begin with, each of the components might be very large, and the versions might differ from each other in small, unstructured, or even completely unknown ways. It will be more maintenance-efficient in the long run to factor out the differences into small files and leave the remainder in a large file that will go in all products. That refactoring can wait, though, until the product line is up and running. Nevertheless, this tool makes it obvious what reengineering should occur, and it's a small step indeed from that knowledge to an action plan.

BigLever's motto is from Archimedes: "Give me a lever big enough and I will move the world." Krueger believes that software product line production, supported by solid product line technology, is a combination powerful enough to let his customers at least move a few markets.

—PCC

Tool support for a product line is therefore more than the sum of the capabilities of individual tools that support specific software engineering activities. The interoperability of a chosen set of tools is critical for the automated production of products in a product line from core assets. An integrated product line support environment will

- support the product line development process and the organizational structure that implements it.
- enforce the conceptual integrity of the product line based on the definition, obtained from the "Scoping" and "Requirements Engineering" practice areas (Sections 5.5 and 4.6), of what it means to be a member of the product line, including any options for tailoring a product to specific needs without violating the defining properties of the product line.
- represent the common and variant capabilities of products in the product line in all places where they are articulated: requirements, architecture, components, testing, plans, and elsewhere.
- maintain traceability and dependency links between assets and products, for product line maintenance and evolution, through a configuration management capability that covers the entire product line.
- support an architecture-based development process with multiple views of the product line architecture that permit reasoning about architectural qualities.
- support the "steady-state" operation of the product line by providing for the production of specific products from a specification of their desired capabilities.
- provide insight into the business and technical decisions for the product line by supporting technical management practices such as scoping and metrics.
- evolve with the product line to incorporate new technologies and new production strategies and processes as the organization's needs change.

Together these items represent a vision of an integrated product line tool environment. You can expect reality to fall somewhat short of this vision, but it's helpful to remember the ideal so we can nudge the real in that direction.

Establishing tool support for a product line involves the following activities:

- **Identification of needs:** When choosing tools to support a product line effort, be clear about which specific needs the tools are to address, including the expectations of the various people who will install, use, and maintain them. Don't overlook the essential need for documentation of the product line—for example, describing the business case for the product line, describing the variation points in the product line architecture, and describing how a product engineer creates products from assets. The future needs of the product line are also a consideration: investigating how new technologies might support the product line, identifying emerging tools in these new technological areas, and communicating future needs to tool vendors.

- **Selection:** Base tool selection on well-defined criteria rather than on market literature or anecdotal evidence of suitability. The specific practices suggested below offer a variety of criteria.
- **Evaluation:** Ideally, when assessing a tool for fitness of purpose, conduct a trial use before making a final commitment. A tool may look promising because of its claimed ability to, say, support architecture variability, but a trial use may find its representation of such variability to be incompatible with the needs of architects to reason about a product's structural properties. Similarly, interoperability and process-support considerations may nullify any gains in the satisfaction of particular needs.
- **Insertion:** Insertion includes adaptating tools to the environment within which they will operate, training tool users and maintainers, and adapting or adopting the development or business processes and practices that are necessary for the effective use of the tools.
- **Measurement:** The benefits and limitations of tools can be determined only by systematically tracking the effects of their use on an organization's productivity and product quality. The appropriate data should be collected and compared with prior experiences to determine the tools' value in practice.
- **Maintenance:** The environment provided by tools needs to evolve with the product line to incorporate new technologies and new production strategies and processes. The capabilities for evolving a tool, or the receptivity of its vendor to the idea of making such changes, can be a significant issue in choosing the right tools.

5.8.2 Application to Core Asset Development

Tool support for asset development focuses on the commonality and variability of the core assets from which product line instances will be created. An ideal tool set for core asset development supports the development of both core assets and mechanisms for using them to construct products.

Tools are needed for developing all sorts of core assets, including those for constructing documents, code, test support, and installation. This means having tools that support adopted product line practices. For example:

- Product line scoping practices are facilitated by tools that capture and represent the common and variant capabilities of products in the product line.
- Product line requirements engineering practices require tools for describing the requirements for products in the product line.

- Product line architecture definition practices require tools for describing the structures of products in the product line, consistent with the associated commonality and variability assumptions.
- Product line component development practices require tools for creating and testing components that are consistent with commonality and variability assumptions and can be used to construct products.
- Production plan practices require tools for creating mechanisms that support the performance of product development projects.

5.8.3 Application to Product Development

The exact role of tool support in product development depends on the degree of automation involved in the construction of individual products. The development of products may be partially or wholly automated; in the extreme, the products may actually be generated by tools that are specific to product lines. In these cases, tool support is extensive; the software engineering environment is a production constraint that must be factored into the architecture design and component development for product developers and is a significant element of the production plan.

The means of product development are specified in the production plan. Tool support for product development is an issue of particular consideration in developing the production plan for the product line, to ensure that the chosen practices and tools are compatible. The nature of the production plan can differ substantially depending on the degree to which product development activities are to be automated.

5.8.4 Specific Practices

Current tool support for product lines is based on a variety of tools used in the software engineering activities of conventional development efforts and then "stretched" to accommodate product lines [Bass 00]. Using these tools successfully in a product line context requires practices that emphasize the fitness of the tools' purpose (both individually and collectively), the quality of the software produced using the tools, the effect of the tools on the product line development process, and the business benefits accruing from use of the tools.

The practices discussed below are all based on established practices for tool support for computer-aided software engineering and are adapted to the product line context.

Identification of needs: In addition to tools needed for direct support of software development, product line tool support is essential for configuration management, planning, and documentation of all varieties. All of these activities are good places to begin identifying specific needs.

Selection: A comprehensive checklist list of tool selection criteria for software product lines appears in the report by Bass et al. [Bass 00]. Examples of criteria include tool features, cost, vendor stability, training, interoperability with other tools, and process implications. Powell et al. describe an evaluation process that generates selection criteria from a checklist of issues [Powell 96], and the longest section of ISO standard 14102 [ISO 95a] deals with the characteristics of tools by which they can be selected and evaluated. Other authors advocate tying the selection and integration of tools to the development process to be used [Brown 94a].

Evaluation: Brown advocates an evaluation approach based on the desired quality attributes of the entire tool-support environment, not just the individual tools [Brown 94b], and Garlan et al. describe integration woes that have particular relevance for product lines [Garlan 95]. The evaluation process described by Powell et al. [Powell 96] and IEEE standard 1348–1995 [IEEE 95] includes guidelines for the pilot use of a tool.

5.8.5 Practice Risks

Tool support makes some tasks more convenient but makes other tasks (such as extensive unit testing or configuration management) practical where they otherwise would not be. Inadequate or inappropriate tool support will have a devastating effect on productivity in all parts of a project where tooling could be applied. Specific tool support risks include the following [Bass 00]:

- **Lack of tools appropriate for product lines:** The lack of true support for product lines often results in frustration at least, and longer development cycles at worst. For example, if tools cannot coherently represent information about multiple products (especially their commonalities and variabilities), the entire concept of creating multiple products from the same core asset base is undermined. Users may be forced to extend existing tools until they become a heavy maintenance burden. New releases of a tool may invalidate the previous extensions, thereby risking time-consuming rework that will further lengthen the development cycle.
- **Lack of support for variabilities:** Controlled variability is essential for creating a product line that is flexible enough to accommodate changing customer needs. If your tools cannot help you represent and reason about variability early in the life cycle, then you may not be able to express variability in the architecture, particularly in graphical form; trace requirements variability to architecture variability; trace component variability to architecture variability; trace testing variability to component variability; and so forth.
- **Lack of appropriate configuration management tool support:** Product lines require sophisticated configuration management practices and robust tool support. Insufficient configuration management support (especially for capturing and correlating data about changes across multiple products) will chip away at an organization's ability to field products quickly and respond to requests for changes. Releases of the core assets that are not synchronized

with product releases are another source of disruption to the overall product development schedule.

- **Lack of tools supporting specific practice areas:** If adopted tools fail to support adopted practices, the effort required to perform those practices may be excessive.
- **Incompatibility between tools and practices:** If an organization chooses tools and practices separately, their use may conflict, resulting in duplicated effort or failure to use the tools or to carry out the practices properly.
- **Incompatibility between asset development and product development:** If product development uses tools or practices that are different from what asset development anticipates, the provided core assets may not fit properly for use with the tools and practices actually used.

5.8.6 For Further Reading

Both IEEE and ISO have issued comprehensive standards for CASE tool selection, evaluation, and adoption. The IEEE standard [IEEE 95] views CASE tool adoption as more than just the selection of CASE tools; adoption requires the planning and implementation of an entire set of technical, organizational, cultural, and management processes to achieve desired improvements in software development. In addition to the steps for defining CASE needs and evaluating and selecting CASE tools, the practice also includes guidance for conducting a pilot and fostering the routine use of adopted tools. Annexes to the standards provide additional information on aspects of the practice, including defining: the organizational CASE goals, needs, and expectations; approaches to developing an adoption strategy; and evaluation criteria for a pilot.

The ISO standard [ISO 95a] provides guidance on identifying organizational requirements for CASE tools and mapping those requirements to the characteristics of candidate tools to be evaluated. It also describes a process for selecting the most appropriate tool from a candidate set based on the measurements of the defined characteristics. An appendix discusses the advantages and disadvantages of three kinds of selection algorithms. (The ISO standard ISO/IEC 14102 has been adopted by the IEEE as IEEE Std 1462–1998 [IEEE 98a].)

Finally, to see what a group of select product line practitioners had to say about tool support for product lines, see the report by Bass et al. [Bass 00].

5.8.7 Discussion Questions

1. Choose one of the practice areas not normally associated with tool support—"Structuring the Organization," for instance—and hypothesize a tool that you think might help you carry it out.
2. Choose one of the practice areas in which tool support plays an important role—"Technical Planning," for example—and describe differences between

a tool designed to help in that area for single systems and a tool designed to help in that area for a software product line.

3. What does the "Tool Support" practice area (Section 5.8) have in common with the "COTS Utilization" practice area (Section 4.4)? What does it have in common with the "Training" practice area (Section 6.12)?
4. What measures would you take to see if a tool your organization selected was a good idea?
5. Where in your organization would you assign the responsibility for the various dimensions of tool support?

6

Organizational Management Practice Areas

Organizational management practices are those practices that are necessary for the orchestration of the entire product line effort. They correspond to the "Management" part of Figure 6.1, whose scope transcends that of individual product production. In alphabetical order, the practice areas in organizational management are as follows:

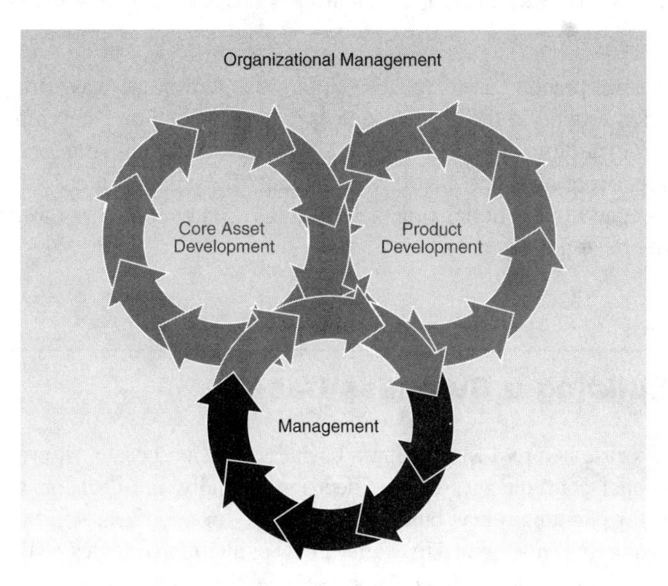

Figure 6.1 Organizational Management

- Building a Business Case
- Customer Interface Management
- Developing an Acquisition Strategy
- Funding
- Launching and Institutionalizing
- Market Analysis
- Operations
- Organizational Planning
- Organizational Risk Management
- Structuring the Organization
- Technology Forecasting
- Training

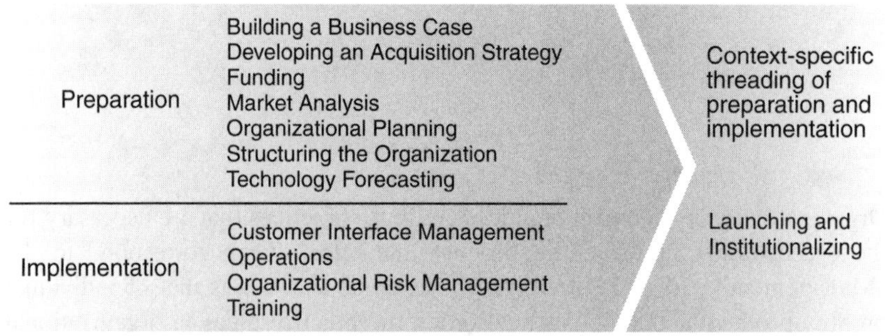

Preparation	Building a Business Case Developing an Acquisition Strategy Funding Market Analysis Organizational Planning Structuring the Organization Technology Forecasting	Context-specific threading of preparation and implementation
Implementation	Customer Interface Management Operations Organizational Risk Management Training	Launching and Institutionalizing

Figure 6.2 A Relationship Among Organizational Management Practice Areas

How are these practice areas related? Figure 6.2 shows one way. Bringing an organization around to the product line approach is not a one-step process but requires preparation and planning and then execution and implementation. Launching a product line involves both, but the practice areas other than "Launching and Institutionalizing" (Section 6.4) can be thought of as applying mostly to one or the other.

6.1 Building a Business Case

A business case is a tool for making a business decision because it predicts the organizational consequences of that decision. Initially, the decision will be a go/no-go for pursuing a new business opportunity or approach. After initiation, the business case is maintained to examine new or alternative angles on the opportunity. As an important communications vehicle, the business case identifies the goals and measures for tracking the move to the new business or approach. It includes the methods and rationale used for quantifying the benefits and costs and lists the critical success factors and contingencies that must be managed in order for the predicted results to appear [Schmidt 97]. By documenting the expected costs, benefits, and risks, the business case serves as a repository of the business and marketing data. In this role, management uses the business case to determine possible courses of action.

A business case addresses the following key questions that an organization faces when planning major changes in its current ways of doing business:

- What are the specific changes that must occur?
- What are the benefits of making the change?
- What are the costs and risks?
- How do we measure success?

An effective business case must convince management that the investment is financially sound, is realistic for the organization, is aligned with other business strategies, and has a clear course of action for putting the change into effect. Business case results are often summarized using several well-defined financial metrics such as net cash flow, discounted cash flow, internal rate of return, and payback period [Schmidt 97].

The need for a change is often precipitated by a market analysis that tells an organization what it needs to do in order to stay competitive in a particular mission or market area. The market analysis begins the process of defining the change. The business case then determines the best approach to meeting the market needs coming from the market analysis. A business case may consider multiple alternatives or look at one proposed solution. In either case, it contrasts the business opportunities offered by a proposed course of action with current ways of doing business.

The business case documents how closely aligned the opportunity is with established business goals for such things as

- reduced time-to-market
- reduced cost
- higher productivity
- improved quality
- increased customer base or bigger market share
- ease of upgrades

It reinforces the motivation for making the change by offering a broad, quantifiable assessment of the opportunity. The goal is to provide management with a sufficient understanding of the approach and adequate data to determine if the return on investment (ROI) is sufficient to justify the proposed venture.

The business case should be maintained as a separate document. There is no standard organization for a business case, but it should address the following [Humphrey 00]:

1. Deciding what to do: list any assumptions (market conditions, organizational goals, and so on), develop alternative approaches, and then either choose one or decide to build a comparison.
2. Estimating the likely costs and potential risks of all alternatives.
3. Estimating the likely benefits contrasted with the current business practice.
4. Developing a proposal for proceeding.
5. Closing the deal: how to make final adjustments and proceed to execution.

6.1.1 Aspects Peculiar to Product Lines

A business case in a product line context can serve one of two purposes. The first is to justify the effort to adopt the product line approach for building systems. The second is to decide whether or not to include a particular product as a member of a product line.

A software product line effort represents an investment in resources and technology. Any organization that adopts a product line approach should have sound business reasons, backed up by data and experience, for doing so. Specific time-to-market improvement, product quality goals, cost targets for product development and delivery, new market growth, and product risk reduction are factors that are often included in the business case. The business case should identify the customers for the products that will be part of the product line, as well as the costs and benefits to those customers and the organization producing the products. Also, it should be directly supportive of higher organizational and/or corporate goals and vision. The business case should be agreed on, documented, communicated to the entire organization, and then validated by market analysis and organizational experience and expertise. Included in the business case will be the product line goals that will in turn drive the data to be collected and the measures to be tracked.

Business case practices for product lines differ only in the nature of the changes being considered and analyzed. The organization is making an economic case built on the current costs of doing business versus a product line approach. Here, the initial go/no-go decision answers the question: "Do we build the set of products we're considering as a product line or not?" As part of the business case analysis, the organization determines how many products are likely to be built in the product line over a certain time, who the customers will be, and whether a product line approach compares favorably with other business opportunities [Reifer 97].

Other Voices: Does It Pay?

Value-based software engineering (VBSE), a process created by a group of Oregon researchers, is based on the simple, obvious, and almost completely overlooked truth that software engineers are not the best people to decide what software to engineer. In a software product line, this translates into the need to assign that responsibility to someone who knows how to build a business case [Faulk 00].

> *First, the ability to make rational decisions over the course of product line development depends on being able to answer the question: "Does it pay?" Does it pay to develop software product P as a product line? Does it pay to include feature F in the scope of the product line? Does it pay to automate production of work-product W for the product line? Indeed, does it pay to use product line technology at all in my company?*
>
> *Second, the issue of whether or not something pays is ultimately a business (rather than software engineering) question. To determine whether it pays to develop software product P as a product line, one must estimate how many members of the family will be developed and what the market is for each. To determine if it pays to include feature F in the scope of a product line, one must be able to compare the return on investment from a product that includes F with one that does not. To determine if it pays for a company to adopt product line technology, one must understand how a product line approach addresses the company's strategic business goals and be able to determine the expected return on adopting a product line process.*
>
> *In short, making sound software engineering decisions about product lines requires understanding both the technical and business implications of those decisions. The advantage of a product line approach is that it takes a strategic view of software development (i.e., addresses the question "what pays?") that goes beyond the scope of a single product development . . . .*
>
> *. . . In a recent customer-value study of three software firms by the authors, a severe disconnect was found between software developers, marketers, and customer service personnel. Although all three groups had at least some contact with customers, the perceptions of their company's ability to create customer value varied widely by function. Software developers, who had the least customer contact, shared marketers' optimism about the customer value that was being delivered. In contrast, customer service personnel, who had to work with unhappy customers every day, took a much dimmer view of their company's customer-value successes.*
>
> *In all these firms, software developers were convinced they were delivering good value to the customers. Their development process, however, failed to provide methods for acquiring and disseminating information about the customers' value requirements to all of the organizational entities responsible for a product.*

The business case reflects the facts and assumptions from the examination of relevant domains, the product line scope, and the market analysis. The business case answers the following ancillary questions:

- Do we have the right capability and resources to launch a product line?
- Can we leverage our domain understanding to provide a unique opportunity and create market demand for our product line?
- What are the financial and business consequences of adopting a product line approach?

The business case may determine that product lines are not a viable approach. For example, if the market is small for future products or won't support more than a very few product variants, there is little incentive to invest in a product line for those products. Predicting future products may be difficult if the market is unstable, and so the business case may also propose alternatives. For example, investment in generator technology may be recommended if a large number of very similar products is likely, or in manual composition if the market forecast is for smaller numbers of products. Developing alternative product line approaches helps assure management that all the options have been considered and that a single strategic reuse decision is not being forced on them. The business case may also propose a business model, such as fielding an architecture and components that system developers from other organizations will use for their products. In any of these product line situations, management will still expect the business case to define the change being proposed, how it differs from current practice, why it's better, what its financial consequences are, and how management will know whether the goals are being met.

Beyond answering the initial go/no-go question for product lines, however, a business case can be used to determine whether a subsequent or envisioned product should be built using the core assets of an already established product line—that is, whether that product should join that family—or be constructed separately (if at all). In this case, the same questions apply, suitably modified:

- Do we have the right capability and resources to build this product as a member of our product line?
- Can we leverage our domain understanding to provide a unique opportunity and create market demand for this product?
- What are the financial and business consequences of including this product in our product line?

Both applications of business case reasoning include financial as well as nonfinancial considerations. Both seek to clarify the organization's position relative to its marketplace, its customers, and its strategic plans. For example, a strong business case can be made for a product that (by itself) will not be profitable, but which will give the organization a toehold in a new application area.

6.1.2 Application to Core Asset Development

First of all, as is often the case with practice areas that produce artifacts, the business case for the entire product line is itself a valuable core asset that should be documented, maintained, and periodically revisited to make sure that the organization's goals are still being adequately served. The business case will inform the product line's scope (see the "Scoping" practice area, Section 5.5) and so will need to be available and current. Second, the business case for an individual product can be reused with some variation when the next product decision has to be made.

Beyond being a core asset in its own right, the business case for the product line is used to justify the effort to build other core assets. Figure 6.3 illustrates the role of the business case in core asset development associated with a product line launch. The development of the initial business case occurs during an early cycle of product line activity, dedicated to making the initial go/no-go decision. If the business case proposals are accepted and product line development gets underway, the business case supports core asset development as a living document designed to reflect changing market conditions, reflect the coordinated product line response, and measure the achievement of desired results. In this later cycle, the organization may develop a business case to determine whether to extend the product line scope, add new components, pursue new customers, or address other new opportunities related to the product line.

Based on the initial scope of the product line, you can estimate and compare likely costs and potential risks of each alternative approach. Figure 6.4 is an example of the cumulative cost estimates for three successive projects, both with and without taking a product line approach. The cumulative cost of the three projects *without* taking the product line approach is shown by the

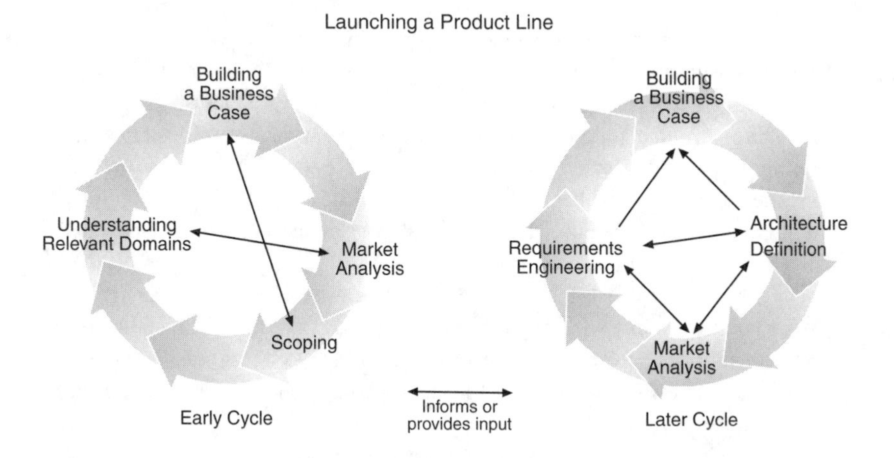

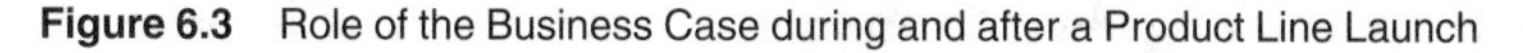
Figure 6.3 Role of the Business Case during and after a Product Line Launch

columns. The sloping lines show the cost *with* the product line approach, as follows:

- There is an initial start-up cost (shown in the figure as 30 units of effort) for moving to a product line approach. In addition to costs for developing core assets, the business case must include the cost of adopting processes for product lines, including the costs of training, incentives, and tool development or procurement. In the figure, this cost is shown as accruing even before the launch of the first project.
- With each successive project, core assets must be maintained and enhanced, and new core assets added. Thus the cumulative cost for developing assets increases over time (as shown by the lower line in Figure 6.4).
- In Figure 6.4, the "Production Cost with Assets" line represents the cumulative effort of developing all three projects shown. Project cost includes start-up cost, the cost of enhancing the asset base for that project, and the cost of project-specific development.

It Takes Two

People considering the move to a product line strategy usually get around to asking some form of the question, "So how much is this going to cost us in the short term?" A time-based version of this question is, "How many days/months/years will it take for my up-front investment to be recouped by cost savings?" As you can imagine, it's a difficult question to answer because of the enormous variations among organizations, products, and markets. The answer is an unsatisfying "It depends."

But that is only if the questioner insists on an answer given in dollars or in days/months/years. It so happens that there is a very satisfying way to reframe the question that normalizes the answer across all of the variables.

The figure that follows (adapted from Weiss [Weiss 99]), illustrates the cost model for product lines versus one-at-a-time systems. Without a product line, the cumulative cost begins at zero and rises steadily. With a product line, the cumulative cost begins with the initial cost of the core assets and then climbs at a shallower rate as projects are turned out. The point at which the two lines cross (and at which the one-at-a-time cost curve becomes higher) is the payoff point. That crossover point can be expressed in terms of the number of systems built. Thus the question becomes how many systems must be fielded before the savings from reuse pay for the up-front investment in building the core asset base.

Surprisingly, the answer to this question does not seem to vary much across organizations, products, or markets. What do you imagine it is? Five or six?

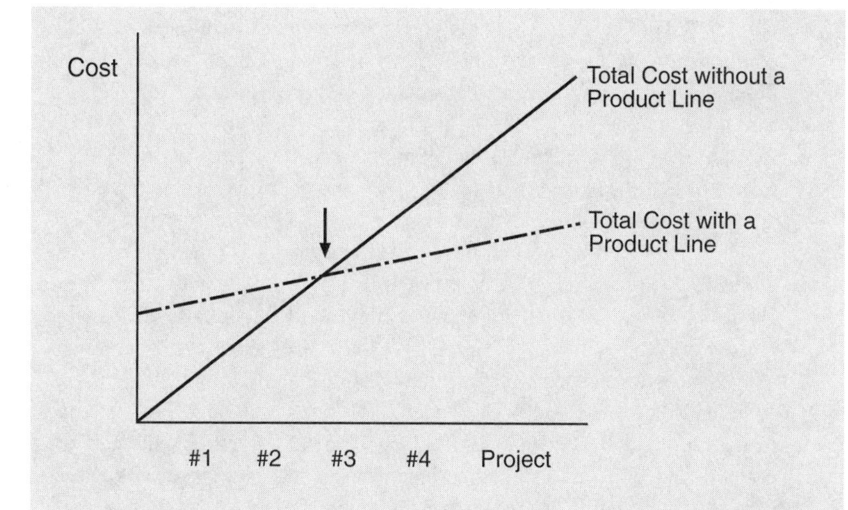

Software Product Line Payoff Point

Ten? Well, it turns out that for the product line approach to pay off, experts agree that the number of systems you need to build is. . . .

Two. Maybe three.

And that's a very good answer indeed, because it's hard to imagine a product line without at least two or three family members. This means that, practically speaking, every single product line can be expected to reap cost savings when compared with building and maintaining its constituent products separately.

Who says so? Apparently, just about everyone:

- In their book, *Software Product-Line Engineering,* David Weiss and Robert Lai wrote that the FAST process of product line engineering produces a payoff after about three systems are fielded [Weiss 99]. Subsequent to the book's publication, Weiss reported new data from Lucent Technologies suggesting that the payoff point is usually between two and three systems. Audris Mockus and Harvey Siy confirmed this with excellent data showing that for a FAST-based product line at Lucent called AIM, "the first nine months of applying AIM saved around three times more effort (61/21) than was spent on implementing AIM itself" [Mockus 99]. (Savings were $6 to $9 million.)
- Jacobson et al. report in *Software Reuse: Architecture, Process, and Organization for Business Success* [Jacobson 97] that a component used three to five times in application projects will recover the initial cost of creating it and the ongoing cost of supporting it. It costs 1.5 to 3.0 times as much to create and support a reusable component as it does to implement a similar component for a single application (suggesting that the payoff point

is 1.5 to 3.0 projects). It costs only one quarter as much to utilize a reusable component as it does to develop a new one from scratch. It takes two or three product cycles, they say, before the benefits of reuse become significant.

- In *Measuring Software Reuse,* Jeff Poulin writes that large-scale strategic reuse (the essence of the product family) becomes worthwhile after the assets are used in a total of three applications [Poulin 97]. Other reuse experts seem to agree. Don Reifer says that the cost recovery point is three in *Practical Software Reuse* [Reifer 97], as do Will Tracz in *Confessions of a Used Program Salesman* [Tracz 95] and Ted Biggerstaff (reported by Tracz in a reuse workshop summary [Tracz 98]). The data of Jacobson et al., cited above, are completely consistent with this estimate.
- John Gaffney and Bob Cruikshank of the Software Productivity Consortium published data in 1992 about SPC's Synthesis method of domain and application engineering. Their data, ranging across three application domains, showed that the payoff point for product-line-style reuse was between 1.67 and 4.86 systems [Gaffney 92]. They also showed that return on investment is based on the payoff point: ROI = $(N/N_0 - 1)100\%$, where N is the number of systems built and N_0 is the payoff point.
- A major American aerospace company told us that they believe the payoff point for their product line of avionics systems comes after about two major block upgrades. A block upgrade is a new, substantially revised version of one of the avionics systems in their family—in essence, a new family member.

These reuse figures would not seem to take into account the overhead of organizational change that is inherent in adopting a product line approach and so might seem a little low—at least at first glance. But organizations that are aggressive and disciplined about reuse (even if they don't call what they're doing a "product line") must have worked out responsibilities for building the reusable assets and ensuring their reuse in a disciplined way, and so their payoff points reflect the organizational restructuring necessary to achieve that. So accepting their payoff points at face value will probably not take us too far off the mark. And to reinforce this, the Lucent, SPC, and aerospace examples did indeed take the organizational costs into account, and their payoff points are even a bit lower.

This result is very encouraging. It's almost a certainty that if you're planning a product line, you're planning to have at least three products in it. So a slightly different version of our opening question is, "Will I save money by adopting a product line approach?" And the answer is a very reassuring "Almost certainly."

Now we aren't promising that you'll *make* money. People actually have to buy your products for that to happen, and even the most breathtakingly efficient production process can't guarantee that you'll make a profit. Instead, we're talking about the relative cost of building a set of products as a product line compared with building the same set as unrelated one-of-a-kind products. The point here is that if you're planning to build three or more related systems—not a particularly burdensome requirement for a product line—then building them from a common set of core assets is almost guaranteed to be the more economical way to turn them out.

—PCC

The graph in Figure 6.4 shows that in this example the third project represents the payoff point for the product line approach because the cumulative cost of the third project without the product line approach exceeds the cumulative cost of the third project with the product line approach. (See "It Takes Two" sidebar for a closer examination of the payoff point for software product lines.)

If cost reduction is a key business driver and the cumulative cost of production with assets is greater than the cost without assets at some desired break-even point, the organization will likely make a no-go decision. Figure 6.4 represents only the cumulative production costs, however. If other factors, such as time-to-market or market share, are drivers and those goals can be met through the product line approach, the organization may forgo an early break-even point on costs in favor of the other factors.

Organizations also estimate anticipated benefits based on market and historical data. This may include factors such as productivity increase, defect reduction, time-to-market, or integration. The business case may propose alternative

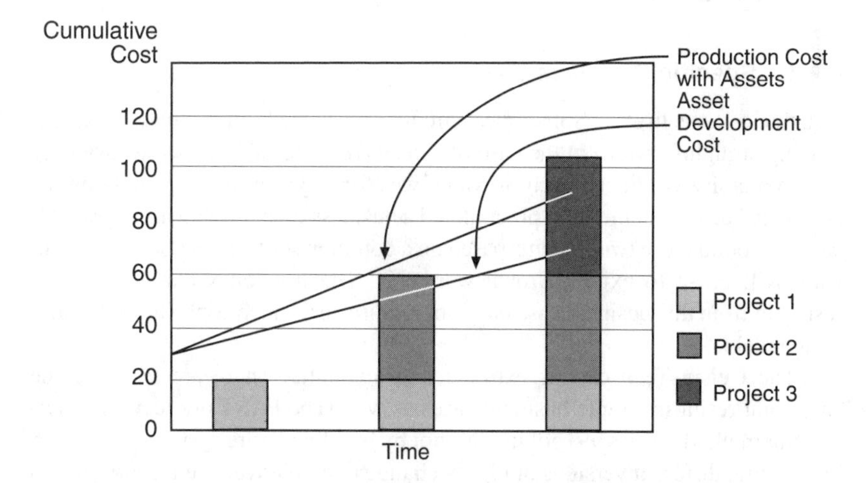

Based on Weiss, et al., *Software Product Line Engineering*

Figure 6.4 Cost Basis for Business Case Assessment [Weiss 99]

approaches and prioritize them on the basis of relative cost versus benefits and risks. In making specific recommendations, the analysis included in the business case looks at the approaches in terms of meeting or exceeding criteria established by the organization.

6.1.3 Application to Product Development

As product line products are developed, the role of the business case evolves within the organization to become a more tactical document. The business case supports decisions to direct or redirect resources during the product development and sustainment phases for

- further requirements analysis to extend the asset base
- core asset refinement in response to product development
- new architectural aspects/development
- product development in new areas
- continuing analysis of market conditions

To support the development of cost data, the business case must consider the financial and other business consequences of the production plan. There will be alternatives in how the organization will produce products. Factored into the business case are cost, benefit, and risk consequences. Another business case decision considers assets users who will be producing the products. The organization developing the business case may be funding assets for internal development or for multiple external development organizations. These approaches may also lead to alternative considerations in the business case.

6.1.4 Specific Practices

"Business case lite": Sometimes circumstances make a business case extremely straightforward. In the case of CelsiusTech, the simultaneous awarding of two massive contracts (each of which was for a system beyond anything the company had ever attempted) precipitated a business case roughly as follows: "If we don't build these two systems based on a common set of core assets, our company will cease to exist" [Brownsword 96]. The implicit go/no-go decision resulting from this business case does not require very much sophisticated analysis to resolve.

The CelsiusTech case is extreme, but authentic. There are less extreme cases that result in simple business cases as well. The FAST product line engineering method [Weiss 99] got its start not by building entire systems, but rather by building different versions of highly changeable, relatively small subsystems restricted to a single domain (electronic message switching). The business case for a small number of small products is simplified because the risk and required early investment are also small. In the case of FAST, early costs included the overhead of the commonality and variability analysis plus the cost of designing a generator language and producing the corresponding generators, all of which were easily measured in person-days.

Estimating the likely costs and addressing potential risks: For each alternative, the organization makes reasonable cost estimates. These costs may be accrued at different times:

- **Initial costs:** When the product line's assets are developed and the initial products are fielded.
- **Incremental costs:** Whenever the product line is extended with new assets. The extensions include improvements within the existing scope or an extension of the scope itself.
- **Product development costs:** Costs associated with using assets in developing products.
- **Annual costs:** Upgrades and annual maintenance costs to fix defects.

The U.S. Federal Aviation Administration, Reifer, and Schmidt provide a variety of techniques for making cost estimates [FAA 95, Reifer 97, Schmidt 97], including:

- Best practices
- Analogy or historical information
- Expert opinion
- Prototypes or pilots
- Parametric cost estimating, such as COCOMO (a well-known empirical cost estimation model)

Developing costs for alternatives may involve simple, back-of-the-envelope estimates or may require more sophisticated cost estimating tools to arrive at cost figures. The organization may exercise more precision by considering other financial factors such as cost discounting, initial rate of return, net present value, and organization-specific techniques.

Each alternative must address the risk element. Because alternatives are a window into the future, they are based on estimates. Management must know not only the estimated costs of each alternative but also its potential risks.

Estimating the likely benefits: The organization must use the cost and risks of the current way of doing business to assess the benefits of switching to the product line approach. A range of metrics can be used to assess the value of proposals to the organization. Some of the factors include

- reduction in personnel required for integration
- reduction in time-to-market
- enumeration of short-term (quarterly cycle) and long-term (two-years or more) benefits

These factors should be contrasted with "as-is" data. In summary, the rationale put forward by the business case must not only show how organizational goals are met but also propose a means of measuring performance against those goals. The business case practice area for product lines can provide example metrics and indicators for assessing performance for each general product line goal.

The developers of the business case should resolve which of these (or other) goals are the primary drivers for making the decision on product line launching. They should then set ways to measure performance against these goals and identify indicators of success. Armed with the goals to be achieved, measures for tracking goals, and the timetable for achieving goals, it is possible to make a reasonable business case.

Table 6.1 lists possible product line goals. Each organization will have its own primary goals—aim for three or four at most—and a second set of less critical goals. Beyond goal setting, however, the organization must set ways to measure whether the product line effort is meeting these goals. Measures should be trackable, although only estimates or projections may be available when the business case is written. The intent of this list is to indicate only the types of measures/indicators an organization should look for; it is not exhaustive. See the "Data Collection, Metrics, and Tracking" practice area (Section 5.2) for more details.

6.1.5 Practice Risks

An inadequate business case (or the lack of any business case at all) can set up a product line organization for failure by inaccurately predicting the outcome of a product line effort or the launch of an individual product within the product line. If the prediction is too optimistic, the organization's investment will not be returned; if it is too pessimistic, the organization will shy away from what might have been a good opportunity. Failure to produce a business case will leave an organization without any way to judge whether the effort was successful or not. An inadequate business case can result from the following:

- **Insufficient data:** It is usually necessary to set cost expectations early and then refine the cost information as the project progresses. An organization needs time to overcome the "sticker shock" that is usually associated with product line adoption. If sufficient cost information is not developed early, the adoption will likely be on hold while the cost/benefit information is scrutinized and validated. This may cause a loss of momentum or possibly even the disbanding of the project.
- **Unreliable historical data:** Most cost development methods rely on good historical data, either from within the organization or from industry. The reliability of the data is essential to justify the approach proposed in the business case. The business case must be able to compare past, current, and projected costs; time-to-market; market share; and competitor information

Table 6.1 Product Line Goals, Measures, and Indicators

Product Line Goals	Typical Measures (raw data)	How to Track/Indicators (status with respect to goals)
• cost savings/cost avoidance • increased productivity	• number of people in development/integration • total product development costs (direct plus share of asset development) • number of products • size of products • number of features per product	• comparison of historical performance with product line performance • ratio of product output relative to cumulative resources to produce it
• time-to-market or time-to-field	• schedule • duration or calendar time of completed projects	• number of projects in the product line and their spacing in terms of completion
• return on investment (ROI)	• estimates of the savings and investments • costs to transition to a product line approach • costs to develop products using the product line approach	• ratio of the estimated savings (or returns) for each dollar invested—that is, the cost of traditional software development versus cost using product line approach/investments to transition
• higher-quality products	• operational availability	• system crashes • outstanding trouble reports
• information and/or business dominance • market satisfaction	• difference between the aggregate of information available to or business captured by competing organizations	• ability to respond to competition • market share • ability to assimilate and exploit new technology
• capturing domain expertise	• timeliness of bringing power to market	• response to threat or anticipated threat

in order to make the case. While it may be possible to estimate prior results, these will tend to weaken the argument.

- **Approaches that fail to work across organizational boundaries:** The business case must be specific as to the organization's goals and mission, as with other business cases developed by the organization, but because product line approaches are new and cover a wide range of organizational, technical, and managerial issues, the business case must draw on cross-functional resources from across the organization. This will require careful planning and intergroup coordination to meet critical milestones, including budget timetables and personnel availability.

- **Uncertain market conditions:** What will be the cost of transition? Who will use the assets? How many products will be needed per year? How long will the product line last? The organization must consider a number of cost factors when developing the business case. While there may be a good basis for estimating the costs of software development, the costs of intangibles, such as changing the process from single-system to product line orientation, will be difficult to predict and measure. The ability to predict "asset value" (the overall benefits of assets to product development) includes making correct assumptions about how product developers will use the assets. If fewer products than expected make use of the assets, the overall cost per use will increase and will affect the positive ROI and time to reach the break-even point. Management is unlikely to provide continued support without achieving these important goals.
- **Management indecision:** The group developing the business case must understand the audience. This audience must include those who can make the final go/no-go decision for proceeding on the proposals contained in the business case. If the business case is presented to the wrong audience, there will be no decision. If the business case does not address the needs of the decision makers, the decision will be no-go. Effective communication requires an understanding of the decision makers' value system in terms of the time-to-market or other financial considerations for commercial organizations. Also, the developers of the business case must determine up front whether the audience wants a range of choices from which to make a selection or a specific decision/policy package on which to base the go/no-go decision. If a decision to adopt the product line approach has been made already, decision makers are more likely to want a set of alternatives from which to choose a specific approach.
- **Shift in organizational goals and needs:** If the goals and needs of the organization have shifted during the preparation of the business case, the results may not be useful or meaningful. If information is presented incorrectly, the business case will have no impact. As a result, there will be either no product line decision or a no-go decision, although facts may justify the business case as presented.

6.1.6 For Further Reading

There is no comprehensive source for assembling a product line business case, but we can draw guidance from several examples. Weiss and Lai present a short but useful section on building a product line business case in their book *Software Product-Line Engineering* [Weiss 99, pp. 45–49]. Reifer's *Practical Software Reuse* provides an excellent set of guidelines for developing a business case to support a reuse effort [Reifer 97]. Topics include scoping the market, developing the business case, and preparing financial data. That book also includes a sample business case and the steps used to prepare it. And Watts Humphrey's article "Justifying a Process Improvement Proposal" provides an example of how to make a business case for process improvement [Humphrey 00]. It assumes that management is thinking strategically and will consider investments that may take a few years to pay off.

6.1.7 Discussion Questions

1. Sketch a business case for switching your organization to the software product line paradigm. Invoke goals that will be meaningful to upper management.
2. A business case for a software product line will need to address the cost of building the core assets and how to amortize that cost over the first and subsequent products. What information do you need to estimate the payoff point—that is, the number of products for which the savings will exceed the investment cost?
3. Sketch a business case for conducting a formal domain analysis of a software product line you can envision or with which you are familiar. Contrast the costs and benefits with doing an abbreviated analysis or simply relying on the expertise of in-house domain experts.
4. How does a business case relate to a make/buy/mine/commission analysis?
5. How does a business case relate to product line scoping, and how do they inform each other?
6. What part does understanding relevant domains play in the construction of a business case?

6.2 Customer Interface Management

In the development of complex systems, there are sets of dependencies and commitments among the producers of products (including products in intermediate stages of production) and the consumers of those products. The consumers may be broadly considered as customers of the producers. Thus, customers include such groups as systems engineers relying on a software group to produce certain software, buyers who purchase products on behalf of end users, and the end users themselves.

All of these customers share in the fact that they have requirements and expectations of what the producers will provide. These requirements and expectations may be highly structured, as in the case of a formal requirements document, or highly informal, such as when an interdisciplinary integrated product team has producers and customers working side by side. In the case of a commercial product for end-user consumption, the only "agreement" may be the one between the vendor and the perceived demands of the marketplace.

In all these cases, there is a need to understand and manage the commitments between producers and customers. As a result, managing the customer interface will require your organization to

1. identify the groups or individuals who are responsible for interfacing with customers. What defines the customer interface and whom does it involve? Who is the customer?
2. define clearly the roles and responsibilities of the designated customer representatives.
3. ensure that customer representatives are trained properly in their roles and responsibilities.
4. implement effective processes to govern the organization's customer interactions and ensure clean interfaces among customer representatives.

The major elements of the customer interface that must be managed are as follows:

- What the customer will see
  - Who are the customer representatives, and what are their customer interface responsibilities?
  - What are the standard product offerings and the preplanned feature variability?
  - What are the corresponding cost, schedule, and quality benefits?
  - What is the product line strategy for future features and evolution?
- What the ground rules are for transacting business
  - What protocol must be followed, and what policies and procedures apply?
  - How are customer requirements to be negotiated and managed?
  - How will a disciplined interface with the customer be enforced?

6.2.1 Aspects Peculiar to Product Lines

By "customer interface" we mean the exchange between designated representatives of the product line organization (acting on behalf of the business, the product developer, and the product line) and the customer who takes delivery of the product produced by the product developer. When we refer to "the customer" who takes delivery of the product, we are really talking about a collective group of customer representatives who represent a particular interest of the customer such as legal, financial, technical, operations, training, and so forth. We will refer loosely to these designated representatives of the customer and the product line organization as the "customer representatives."

The customer representatives of a product line organization typically include marketers, a product manager, domain experts, a user's group coordinator, and other individuals explicitly assigned roles and responsibilities that require them to interface with the customer.

Managing the customer interface in a product line operation is significantly different from managing the customer interface in a single-system development environment. In many software organizations, the marketers court customers by promising (and then pricing) any feature that the customer requests. In a product line organization, however, the marketers must behave quite differently. After listening to a customer's requirements, the marketer assigned to that customer must first confer with the product line management. Is the customer's desired product in the planned scope? If so, then all is well, and the marketer can promise delivery with confidence. If not, however, matters take an interesting turn. The marketer now must negotiate with the customer, along these lines:

> *Marketer: "You know, if you were to relax this requirement over here and drop that little one over there and change this one over here just a bit, then we could build you a system that's in our software product line."*
>
> *Customer: "I see. And this matters to me because . . . ?"*
>
> *Marketer: "Because if we build your system from scratch, it will cost you $4 million, take two years to deliver, and your software will be unique. If you take a member of our product line, it will cost you $2 million, be ready in six months, and your software will be the same that is currently running reliably for 16 other customers. But, of course, it's entirely up to you."*

And now the customer has a choice, and knows (probably for the first time) the true cost of those "special" requirements, which may or may not be worth the cost.

A product line organization must institute a protocol for managing customer requirements on a product line (not an individual product) basis and, through training, compel both the customers and the customer representatives to follow it.

From the customer's standpoint, the real distinction is that a software product line is built around the concept of standard product offerings as opposed to custom-built software. In essence, it is a market-driven, customer-oriented approach. The driving factor is the common collective needs of the market that influence the product line offerings, and hopefully these needs have been captured early in the scoping and product line requirements phase. Customers do not start with a clean slate; if they want unique features, they must be prepared to pay for them. Any features that customers want, but the organization is currently unable to deliver, should be captured and managed on a list of future enhancements. This is not to imply that any specialized requirements cannot be accommodated, only that they have to be considered individually and have special cost and schedule implications to which both parties must agree.

Changes in the customer/development organization interface necessitated by a product line approach include the following:

- The interface with customers becomes market driven and no longer focuses on an individual customer's specialized requirements.
- Strict product line organizational interfaces are enforced.
- Customers choose from standard product offerings, relinquishing some flexibility in return for cost and time-to-market advantages.
- Customers may form user groups to give the *market* a voice and drive requirements for product evolution jointly.
- The organization can consistently deliver products of predictable quality at predictable cost and delivery time.

Marketing takes on a different approach for a product line organization. Marketers have the following responsibilities:

- Educate customer representatives and customers to effect different behaviors.
- Inculcate a product-centric focus for negotiating customer requirements.
- Sell according to the product line offerings, much like selling flexible hard goods.
- Set expectations and point out trade-offs accurately as a part of educating the customer.

Establishing a sound customer interface involves the following steps:

1. **Communicate the product line strategy to the customer:** Provide the customer with information and guidance on product features and capabilities, customer-configurable options, and future development goals, objectives, and strategies. By providing useful information to the customer up front, potential misunderstandings may be avoided. Communication involves
   - educating the customer to encourage desired behaviors
   - helping the customer understand the rationale for deferring product requirements in order to reap cost, schedule, and quality benefits
   - ensuring customer awareness of projected product line features
   - moving the customer toward acceptance of a customer relationship that is similar to a commerical off-the-shelf (COTS) supplier model
   - promoting user groups to support the consolidation and coordination of new requirements

2. **Establish an overarching customer interface process for developing work proposals and negotiating new contracts:** At a minimum, this interface should cover roles and responsibilities including marketing, customer negotiations, contracting, customer liaison during product development, delivery of products and product updates, communications and problem resolution, product support, training activities, and other customer support functions. A customer's request for changes in a product may or may not be within the product manager's authority to approve. Minimally, the customer's product manager must first determine if the request could be satisfied through existing product line components. If not, the product manager must determine if the product line manager believes the requested capability is likely to be needed in the future by existing or new customers. If that is the case, the capability can be developed with the rigor necessary for reusable components and added to the product line core asset base. Typically, this kind of unanticipated product decision would require the reallocation of resources or a downstream adjustment in product enhancement planning. The process needs to include safeguards to ensure that the established policies, procedures, and protocol for customer interactions are followed. This process must address issues such as
   - How are potential architectural ramifications of a customer's requirements taken into account in the requirements negotiation process?
   - How are conflicting requirements or priorities reconciled across the products in the product line?

3. **Train product line marketers and product managers:** The roles of product line marketers and product managers in the product line organization differ slightly from their counterparts in the systems organization. This is most apparent in their approach to the market and to the needs of specific customers. Marketing efforts become more product focused, addressing the product needs of the market at large. Two-way communication is primarily for delivering product information, obtaining market requirements, and validating product development strategies. Products are designed to satisfy the needs of the broadest segments of the market. Achieving this capability requires reevaluation of the skills and knowledge of the customer representatives within the product line organization. This means making investments in the development of a capability where none presently exists. These investments are intended to
   - change organizational behaviors both within the marketing organization and across functions comprising the "product team"
   - deliver products within the parameters of the product line
   - continuously raise customer awareness of the product line and planned enhancements
   - coordinate and communicate with user groups

4. **Provide centralized product support to customers:** This support should include coordinating changes in requirements, providing fixes for operational problems, and managing multiple (new) product releases across the customer base. An essential piece of the customer interface management practice is providing ongoing product support to meet the operational needs of the customer. This begins typically with the product line organization that is responsible for assisting the customer in planning the system installation and ensuring that all the required elements are in place. Support is then available for the installation itself. Once the system is operational, ongoing maintenance fixes may be required to stabilize the new system in the customer's operating environment. Ongoing support may also be available to assist customers in installing product enhancements or major upgrades. In the product line organization, some of these responsibilities are centralized so that the efforts to fix, test, and release product updates are not replicated. Fixes for one customer are compiled and released for the benefit of all the customers of that system. Finally, the support organization is in the best position to track customer installations and configurations. This information is useful to the product engineering organization in planning the distribution of new releases, as well as to the marketing organization as a means of identifying opportunities for the sales of upgrades or new systems.

5. **Establish a user's group, or other liaison means, to assist the product line organization in identifying and prioritizing its customers' emerging and long-term future needs:** The product line organization should encourage customers to form user groups to jointly manage the evolution of their products and drive product line requirements so that upgrades can be provided to all of them at a lower cost than would be possible individually. By forming user groups, customers, who were once separate entities with no common interest, have an opportunity to influence and work out requirements for future product upgrades jointly. From the standpoint of the product line organization, the user groups represent an opportunity to maintain a tightly controlled product line capability by providing their customers with a forum for adjudicating their differences and migrating their products as a collection rather than as a set of disjointed products. Both sides benefit: the product line organization can continue to produce products that closely match its product line capabilities, and its customers can acquire their products more economically.

6.2.2 Application to Core Asset Development

Some of the assets in the core asset base are aimed at the customer community, and others come about as a direct result of customer input. The former group of assets includes marketing literature, sales support, product catalogs, feature descriptions, and cost and schedule information. The latter group includes market analysis, requirements specifications (including the common look and feel of the products), and the product line scope. An organization must have a healthy and vigorous customer interface if it is to

- put the customer-targeted core assets to their intended use.
- gather the necessary information from the customer community to build high-quality, customer-sourced core assets.

Other Voices:
The Needs of the Many
Outweigh the Needs of the One

The Fraunhofer Institute for Experimental Software Engineering in Kaiserslautern, Germany, has an active program investigating software product line organizations and methods. Here, four of their researchers share a hard truth about software product lines: sometimes, for the greater long-term good of the company, individual customers' needs and desires should take a back seat [Knauber 00].

> *Typical for SMEs [small and medium-sized enterprises] is their close cooperation with customers. This offers them marketing advantage over larger competitors because they not only know early about their customers' actual and potential needs but they are also able to react more flexibly to these needs. With respect to product lines, however, this factor proves to be a disadvantage. Basic requirements for successful product line development are a clear vision about the future evolution of the company's applications and some domain stability. If these requirements are not fulfilled, the investment in setting up a reusable infrastructure for the product line might not pay. Successful product line development involves some change in behavior: reacting flexibly to customers' needs gains fewer benefits than actively steering these needs in a direction where they would be supported by their own product line.*

6.2.3 Application to Product Development

The organization's customer interface plays the most important role in requirements negotiation for a product or set of products. A healthy customer interface will allow a customer to negotiate in the context of the benefits and limitations that a product line approach can provide. From the organization's side, it should be able to offer high-quality products of demonstrated capabilities and performance with predictable delivery dates and predictable costs.

Moreover, a product line organization is in a better position to produce "whole" products that include accompanying artifacts such as robust training materials, support, and documentation, backed up by standards and procedures, extensive test cases, and a proven operational track record. Because these associated product artifacts come bundled with the customer's product, from a marketing standpoint they are touted as being "products with a pedigree" [Moore 91].

Organizationally, the customer interface must be managed from a multiple-product, multiple-customer perspective as opposed to a single-product, single-customer (or single-customer-base) perspective. This means that the customer representative responsible for a particular customer's product must act on behalf of both the product developer (who is developing the customer's product) and the product line organization at large. This requires the representative to coordinate and synchronize the efforts of multiple interests of the product line organization carefully. For example, a product manager, in conjunction with the program manager and/or a designated advisory group, will have to coordinate and negotiate customer requirements internally with the core asset development group and other product teams to evaluate their potential effects on the product line. The specific charter and makeup of any advisory group, and the sanctioned lines of communication that support a disciplined customer interface, should be documented as part of the product line's operational concept (see the "Operations" practice area, Section 6.7). The advisory group may be a customer product management group, a systems definition team, a core architecture team, a technical steering group, or some combination of these.

Over time, there will be features that customers want and ask the product line organization to add. These features will have to be evaluated from two aspects: the feasibility of implementing the desired changes and the desirability of including them in the current or future development cycles. The product line's scope will address the first aspect, while a business case will address the second. From a strategic perspective, features that have widespread appeal represent tangible opportunities to expand the product line.

Other Voices: CelsiusTech's Customer Interface

One of the most interesting experiences of CelsiusTech Systems, the company we described in the Preface, was how their relationship with their customers changed over time as a direct result of adopting the product line approach [Brownsword 96].

CelsiusTech's marketers and their customers were faced with the need to change the ways in which they carried out their respective roles. The following examples show the scope of changes:

CelsiusTech customer project managers, who provide the primary liaison with customers after contract award, must negotiate with the product line organization for any requested system changes before committing to any actions.

CelsiusTech's marketers must base new work proposals on very different cost profiles for naval systems.

Customers must make trade-offs between required versus desired specialization of devices and functionality.

As part of marketing its naval product line, CelsiusTech has developed numerous presentations to explain the approach and the benefits to customers. Senior technical staff members routinely were asked to assist in customer marketing situations and in new work proposals. As CelsiusTech staff members have increased their ability to explain the product line approach internally, they have become more effective in conveying their message to their customers.

The level of customer sophistication is growing. In 1995 CelsiusTech and their SS2000 product line customers formed a users group, much like the users groups that form for COTS-based products. To the participants, the users group offers the chance to jointly work out future requirements for ship systems and procure them at a lower cost than they could acquire them individually. To CelsiusTech the users group presents the chance to maintain a tightly controlled product line capability because their customers now have the chance to migrate their systems as a collection rather than a set of disjoint products.

Elsewhere, we said that a hallmark of a mature product line organization is that it regards its mission as building a single thing—the product line—rather than a mixed assortment of things—products (see "E Pluribus Unum" sidebar). A user group shows that the customer community has internalized this understanding as well because its goal is to jointly influence the product line's evolution. CelsiusTech did a good job of educating their customers. At one point, one of them discovered a bug in his version of ShipSystem 2000. CelsiusTech offered to send him a source code patch on the spot to fix the error, but the customer demurred. He said he'd rather live with the bug and wait for the next release than run unique software that deviated from the ShipSystem 2000 family. Now *there's* a customer who got the message about product line benefits.

6.2.4 Specific Practices

Table 6.2 identifies a candidate set of product line customer representatives, the typical roles they play, and example artifacts they commonly use in their customer interface role.

Table 6.2 Typical Product Line Representatives Involved in Customer Interface

Interfacing Representative	Typical Roles of Product Line Representative	Example Artifacts
marketing, sales, financial, and legal personnel	• Explain product line offerings. • Explore customer requirements. • Prepare proposals and conduct preliminary negotiations. • Represent the interests of the organization in contract negotiations.	marketing plan, product proposals, product offerings, specifications, and other marketing collateral, requirements input to product management plans, upgrade plans, legal and contractual documents
product manager	• Represent the product developer to the customer. • Be responsible for the customer's product and all liaison with the customer after contract award. • Be responsible for finalizing negotiations and coordinating efforts across the product line organization. • Be responsible for overseeing all the programmatic aspects of the customer interface, including the specification, development, delivery, and acceptance of the customer product.	technical proposals, product specifications, schedule and cost data, work breakdown structure, technical documentation, status/progress reports, action item tracking, issue resolution, product deliverables
program manager	• Be responsible for the business success of the product line.	business case, forecast, cost/pricing models
senior technical staff members (domain and architecture experts)	• Assist marketers, product manager, and customers in defining the technical specifications of product offerings and negotiating trade-offs in requirements affecting cost, schedule, and quality.	domain model, functional specifications, architectural views, quality attributes
systems/software product engineers	• Deliver and install product upgrades. • Assist customers in resolving operational problems and provide training and technical consultation.	product releases, technical advisories, trouble reports, training courses
user group coordinator	• Work with customer groups to collect product requirements that meet the collective and prioritized needs of users.	customer workshops, strategy sessions, customer operational plans

6.2.5 Practice Risks

Poor customer interface management can very well result in an undermine of the integrity of the product line. If customers are not paid enough attention, the products will fail to meet their needs, and the customers will go elsewhere. If the customer interfaced is not managed at the product line level, then the organization will fail to take advantage, in a systematic way, of the customers' inputs. Poor customer interfaces can result from any of the following:

- **Failure to recognize the extent of the customer interface and its effects:** A fundamental risk is that an organization will not fully realize the extent of the interface or the extent of the cultural changes that must occur on both sides to establish a healthy and mutually productive customer relationship. This could lead to a failure to exploit common requirements, customer alienation, and an eroding customer base.
- **Organizational discontent and resistance in transitioning to a new business paradigm:** Shifting responsibilities and the narrowing focus of new positions may not be welcome changes for many individuals in the product line organization. Satisfying individual customers, possibly at the expense of the product line, is a powerful incentive to undermine the new paradigm. The result will be business as usual. Investments in internal promotion and capability development reinforce the organizational commitment to the change and provide team members the opportunity to change with the organization.
- **Marketers promise the world and fail to point out any trade-offs that are involved:** There is no product line sin as serious as promising the world and being unable to deliver it. When pressed by their customers, representatives must learn to point out any key trade-offs that are involved so that the customer can make fact-based, objective decisions. Failure to do so will result in dissatisfied customers and (in turn) unhappy product developers.
- **Marketers and product managers are insensitive to specialized customer requirements:** A product line organization must ensure that the pendulum does not swing too far away from individual customers' needs. This is a key dilemma for the product line organization—that is, how to satisfy the specific needs of one customer without significantly impacting the product development momentum within the development group. This problem requires analysis by a cross-functional team to assess the impact of the requirement and make recommendations to management.
- **Customers fail to recognize benefits properly and see only the loss of flexibility:** Some customers will be unwilling to give up the control that they associate with conducting business with a systems organization. They will continue to demand that systems be built to the full desired functionality, regardless of the cost, schedule, or risk benefits that a product line approach delivers. In the face of this inherent conflict, the product line

organization and the customer will need to make a decision about the viability of their long-term relationship.

- **The product line organization releases a scheduled product upgrade to all customers that includes unannounced changes that cause sporadic problems for customers:** Forcing unwanted changes on customers will alienate them.
- **Failure to enforce the interface:** In organizations with poor product line discipline, customers may have direct access to development staff and may coerce or cajole them into producing specialized features just for them. While such direct connections make those customers very happy and enhance the organization's reputation for responsiveness, they almost always work to the detriment of the larger product line effort because they short-circuit the product planning process and result in work that satisfies small short-term goals at the expense of much larger long-term ones.
- **Improperly trained customer interface staff:** If representatives are not oriented toward product line operations and miss culture changes, or if representatives are not knowledgeable about the product line strategy and specific product capabilities, the result will be a customer community that is not properly indoctrinated into the benefits of the product line paradigm.
- **Customers with their own agendas dominate user group forums so that other users or customer communities are not heard:** If this is the case, the result will be product line requirements that become skewed artificially in the direction of the dominant customer at the expense of the needs of other customers in the installed base.

6.2.6 Discussion Questions

1. A customer interface is one area to which the "Process Definition" practice area (Section 5.4) applies. Sketch a process definition for a customer interface that you would like to see in a software product line in your organization.
2. Discuss some situations in which acquiescing to a single customer's needs might be penny-wise but pound-foolish in the context of a software product line.
3. To many organizations, not all customers are created equal. How might you provide different levels of customer service and yet still maintain product line discipline?
4. How would you go about convincing a customer (or a customer group) whose primary interest is limited to a particular product that buying into your product line is to their advantage?
5. One purpose of customer interface management is to keep customers at an arm's length so that they do not unduly influence any of the development

activities to their own advantage but to the detriment of the overall product line effort. However, another purpose is to provide ways in which the customer can provide focused input where it will do the most good. Discuss customer interface management in the context of requirements engineering, market analysis, and building a business case.

6.3 Developing an Acquisition Strategy

Acquisition is the process of obtaining products and services through contracting [Bergey 99]. This practice area applies to those organizations that are purchasing or commissioning, rather than developing, at least some of the products, or parts of the products, that they turn out. If your organization has limited resources, you can utilize acquisition in a variety of ways, from augmenting your own development effort to commissioning the development of an entire product or group of products. For example, you might acquire specialized assets from a subcontractor or commercial off-the-shelf (COTS) products from a vendor that can save your organization time and money.

If you commission an outside source to provide assets for any part of your operation, you will have to incorporate the means of managing the work performed under contract and of managing the resultant contract deliverables. To be effective in contracting, you will need to develop an acquisition strategy so that you can mitigate the risks associated with acquiring technical products and services from external sources and integrating them into your operations.

Because an acquisition strategy is of great importance to those organizations that primarily acquire rather than develop, this practice area is especially important for government agencies, such as the U. S. Department of Defense (DoD). Although industry may rely heavily on acquisition for obtaining some core assets and COTS products, corporations rarely acquire an entire asset base or products derived from the asset base or sustain both over the life of the deployed systems. For the DoD, this is closer to the norm.

For acquisition-based organizations, a traditional acquisition approach is to have a separate acquisition for each system and to maintain the system independently throughout its operational life. This is a case of *n* acquisitions for *n* system developments followed by *n* maintenance efforts that may require other multiple-of-*n* acquisitions (because maintenance contracts may have to be rebid several times for long-lived systems) to provide ongoing support for the life of the systems.

Developing an acquisition strategy involves analyzing alternative contracting approaches (some of which are offered as specific practices), considering pros and cons, and performing trade-offs. A strategy should include the following:

- establishing the number and types of contracts needed to satisfy the acquisition requirements
- choosing the contract types, funding alternatives, contract options, and source selection procedures
- considering how the continuity of contractual products and services can best be sustained over the projected lives of the product line and participating projects

For each contract, the following questions must be answered:

- What should be specified in the request for proposal (RFP), which is the initial solicitation by the acquiring organization to potential contractors?
- What should be included in the statement of work (SOW), which defines the work and work products that will be provided by the successful bidder?
- What should be the technical evaluation criteria for choosing among competing bidders and for judging the quality of the delivered products?
- What kinds of incentives are appropriate?
- What deliverables should be mandated?
- What data rights should be incorporated?

Multiple contractors may be involved in acquisitions that incorporate competitive runoffs, multiple suppliers, or teaming arrangements.

An acquisition plan is the artifact used to document the acquisition strategy. The plan should also record the costs, risks, and considered alternatives to the adopted strategy.

6.3.1 Aspects Peculiar to Product Lines

Even if your organization does not typically rely heavily on acquisition or if your make/buy/mine/commission analysis returned "commission" for any of the product line's assets—maybe even the architecture—you need an acquisition strategy.

A product line acquisition strategy is a plan of action for achieving a specific product line goal or result through contracting for products and services. In the case of a software product line, the types of software *products* acquired through contracting include core assets and derivative products built from those common assets. Potential software *services* include elements of domain engineering, application engineering, and management. Acquiring services means contractually engaging an identifiable task rather than furnishing an end product.

Acquisition for product lines is typically structured much differently than acquisition for single systems. First, acquisition of core assets is usually the result of a contracting effort apart from the acquisition of products. Second, the fundamental role of architecture in a product line imparts opportunities for contracting flexibility. An umbrella acquisition might provide the entire product line production capability—architecture, infrastructure, and core assets—or the production capability might be acquired in pieces. The architecture itself might be acquired as an independent step. The acquisition of software components (whose interfaces and interoperating requirements will have been specified by the architecture) might be distributed among several suppliers. Products built from the core assets might be acquired individually or under contract for an entire set. A small number of follow-on acquisitions can accommodate ongoing product development and support for sustaining and enhancing the assets and products over the life of the product line.

Plan your acquisitions early. The contracting process is often arduous and can consume a breathtaking amount of time before a contract is in place and operative. Plus, an acquisition strategy cannot be developed in isolation. It exists to serve the product line goals and interacts with the results of other practice areas (named below), some of which tell us exactly what we wish to acquire. Accordingly, you will need to allow sufficient time to coordinate and interact with those carrying out the work of these other practice areas.

If acquisition will fulfill a major role in your product line, you should form a small acquisition team to develop and implement an acquisition strategy. Begin by drafting a charter to empower the team, to define roles and responsibilities clearly, and to ensure the participation of key stakeholders. The team leader should come from the product line organization. Team members should include a contract negotiator, a representative from the product line organization, representatives from participating product groups, individuals with significant acquisition experience, and key product line stakeholders who have vested interests in the acquisition. Make sure that you

- select motivated individuals who have a "can-do" attitude
- keep the team together through contract award and the start-up of operations to ensure the accountability and continuity of effort
- obtain the early buy-in of those responsible for approving the acquisition plan before committing to a particular strategy

The acquisition strategy team should begin by understanding the organization's concept of how the product line will operate and the role that acquisition will fill. Therefore, the team should coordinate with those carrying out the activities in practice areas in which these issues will be decided. These practice areas include

- "Scoping" (Section 5.5), in which the product line is defined
- "Funding" (Section 6.4), in which the strategy for paying for the core assets is determined
- "Architecture Definition" (Section 4.1), in which a large segment of the necessary core assets is first identified
- "Make/Buy/Mine/Commission Analysis" (Section 5.3), in which decisions are made about which artifacts are to be acquired externally
- "Technology Forecasting" (Section 6.11), which may provide insights about what assets might be acquirable in the future

6.3.2 Application to Core Asset Development

There are several roles that acquisition can serve in obtaining all, or part, of the core asset base. They include the commissioning of

- one or more contractors to develop the product line architecture
- one or more contractors to develop other core assets (for example, components and supporting artifacts)
- one or more contractors to mine legacy assets for inclusion in the asset base
- one or more contractors to manage, sustain, upgrade, and enhance the existing asset base and provide asset support to product developers

Core asset acquisition may also involve acquisition of contractor services, such as scoping, domain analysis, configuration management, testing, and training. An acquisition organization can fill these core asset development needs and/or acquire these services through a single acquisition or multiple acquisitions involving one or more contracts (or contract options) that run sequentially, run concurrently, or overlap.

If an organization is going to commission the development of core asset software components, an architecture will have to be specified because the architecture places constraints on the components that will be included in the asset base. The architecture also determines which components are common across all products (or at least across subsets of the product line) and defines the necessary variations among instances of those components. Example acquisition strategy practices for acquiring an architecture are identified under Specific Practices (Section 6.3.4).

6.3.3 Application to Product Development

Acquisition is also an effective means of obtaining new products (or parts of products) in the product line. There are several roles that acquisition can play. They include the commissioning of

- one or more contractors to develop a specific product or a set of new products using the core asset base and following the production plan
- one or more contractors to maintain, upgrade, and enhance a product or a set of products
- one or more contractors to incorporate or evaluate new releases of assets in a product or a set of products to promote product compatibility with the current asset base and the overall integrity of the product line
- one or more contractors to provide new assets (created in the course of product development or product enhancement) to be evaluated as candidates for potential inclusion in the core asset base

Product acquisition may also involve the acquisition of contractor services, such as requirements engineering, configuration management, architecture evaluation, software system integration, and testing.

6.3.4 Specific Practices

Architecture first: One acquisition strategy involves procuring only an architecture in the first stage, procuring other core assets in the second stage, and procuring products (built from the asset base) in the third stage. The first stage would then focus on devising a strategy for acquiring the architecture. Listed below are four potential strategies for acquiring an architecture that are distinguished by the source of the architecture [Fisher 98].

1. **Systems architect:** A contractor is hired to develop the architecture for the system, but the contractor does not build the system or components. The acquiring organization funds, owns, and controls the product line architecture. Another contractor is hired for the implementation of the architecture. This strategy helps to curtail the risk of getting an architecture that does not fulfill program needs because the program retains control over the architectural development. However, there is still a risk in terms of whether the architecture will be implemented correctly when the system is built, as well as other risks in terms of cost and schedule adherence.
2. **Standards group:** An architecture that is built by a "standards group" or conforms to established standards is acquired. Industry and/or government collaboration creates a public architecture. The acquiring organization influences but does not control or own the product line architecture.
3. **Single contractor:** A single contractor is commissioned to develop the architecture. The contract is put up for bids, and contractor selection is based only on the architecture portion of the system design, although the same contractor may also end up developing components and/or the system under the contract. The contractor supplies the architecture and ownership, and control is negotiated.
4. **Collaborating contractors:** A contract is developed that requires a group of contractors to collaborate on developing an architecture that they all can use later. In addition, each of the contractors is given a contract to develop and maintain some of the system's components. Ownership of the architecture is usually shared among the development contractors, with the acquiring organization holding the licensing rights. The acquiring organization funds joint development and manages the architecture requirements.

Other acquisition strategies: There are several other acquisition strategies for moving toward a product line capability. They are distinguished by the initial product line capability that is desired. They include the acquisition of

- a software architecture for the product line (discussed above)
- a system architecture (similar to that discussed above)
- an architecture and set of components (and related artifacts) that conform to it
- a product and some set of reusable assets

The last strategy, listed above, which focuses on product development, also results in the acquisition of an architecture, a set of components, and a product built using these assets. This strategy is an extension of the third strategy listed above, which reduces the risk of architectural and component incompatibilities. The quality of the architecture and components is demonstrated more thoroughly by building an actual system based on the assets. Also, this strategy aligns with the natural iterative learning that takes place in establishing a product line. By proving that the assets can be used to build a system, you provide valuable credibility for the core assets.

A significant variation on this "assets plus product" strategy is to acquire an additional system—a second product—that will reuse the core assets. This approach allows the program to reap the benefits from the investment in building the reusable assets.

6.3.5 Practice Risks

Introducing acquisition into the equation clearly provides an organization having limited resources with an effective means of pursuing a product line approach and tapping skills and resources that would otherwise be unavailable. However, acquisition also has its attendant risks by virtue of introducing a new, and sometimes arduous, paradigm for managing the products and services that are acquired through contracting. A poor acquisition strategy will result in contracts being let that are not in the best interests of the acquiring organization. In the worst case, the goods delivered do not meet the needs for which they were acquired, and the resources (not the least of which are the time and effort spent on the contract and the time spent waiting for the goods) are wasted. Deadlines will be missed as the organization scrambles to recover. A poor acquisition strategy can result from any of the following factors:

- **Failure to accommodate iteration:** Iteration is a handmaiden to product line practice. It occurs throughout the operational picture, especially during a product line's start-up and evolution phases. Contracting, however, is not designed to be iterative. Thus, creative means that indicate a prescribed protocol for managing contracts and accepting contract deliverables must be preplanned and included in contracts. Such means include specifying interim or partial deliverables, conducting technical interchange meetings (TIMs), including in-progress development checkpoints for events such as architecture evaluations, specifying *services* to enable contractor participation in configuration management (CM) control board meetings, software integration efforts, and technical consultations to assist product development groups.
- **Limited management visibility:** Contracting results in a division of management responsibilities that often reduces visibility into the progress and

status of the work being performed under contract. Formulating a suitable set of product line metrics to monitor the progress of asset and product development efforts is one means of obtaining the needed visibility. Visibility and insight into the progress of the work and the underlying technical problems are more critical in a product line approach because they involve more than just an "end-product view" of systems development.

- **Failure to account for evolving requirements:** The nature of a product line is to manage the commonality and variability of products by means of a requirements-engineering-change management process. Contracting, by nature, works best when the requirements are fixed. Again, creative techniques can be employed to accommodate management of "evolving requirements" and to mitigate the impact on the contractual tasks. This is especially important in the asset sustainment and process refinement phases of product line operations.
- **Failure to account for liability:** In a typical single-system acquisition, the contractor is totally responsible for ensuring that the system complies with the contractual requirements. A product line approach often involves multiple contractors, which raises the question of how liability issues involving the efficacy of an architecture and other core assets will be handled. This can be especially acute if flaws (including documentation errors) are not discovered until much later in product development.
- **Failure to pin down organization roles and responsibilities:** For what things should the acquirer be responsible? For what things should the contractor be responsible? Does the summation of these responsibilities constitute a cohesive approach that covers all the aspects of product line operations? Letting responsibilities fall through the cracks will result in lost time and increased expense to recover when the oversight is discovered.
- **Failure to consider ownership and data rights:** If the prescribed data rights are not consistent with the envisioned product line operations and adoptable by the acquirer and contractor, the product line may well be prevented from growing and evolving.
- **Failure to mandate architecture compliance:** What form will the architecture take, and is there a contractual means of verifying that product development is compliant with the prescribed architecture? Failure to ensure architectural compliance in delivered components may result in a set of core assets that in fact will not support a product line.
- **Failure to consider asset sustainment:** Is there a contractual means of sustaining and evolving the architecture and other core assets? Failure to account for evolution will cause the premature death of the product line.
- **Failure to consider product development support:** Is there a contractual means of providing core asset customization and technical assistance to product developers? If not, the core assets may not be usable in practice.

- **Failure to consider product development:** Will there be a contractual means in place for projects to commission a product line contractor to develop a product, *or* is there a means whereby a project's own contractor can obtain core assets and technical assistance for product development?
- **Failure to consider coupling of contract deliverables:** Is there a contractual means of accommodating product upgrades as changes are incorporated in the common asset base? If not, the product line may produce products that are in fact one-of-a-kind systems that drift out of alignment with the core assets.
- **Failure to ensure continuity of support:** Is there a means of ensuring the continuity of acquisition support over the life of the product line?

6.3.6 For Further Reading

Bergey et al. give a nice overview of the U.S. Department of Defense acquisition environment interpreted for software product lines [Bergey 99].

6.3.7 Discussion Questions

1. Who in your organization is best suited to develop an acquisition strategy? Why? What skills does such a person need? How would you staff the acquisition team?
2. How does an organization's acquisition strategy relate to its business case for building a product line?
3. Suppose you decided to acquire (commission) the architecture for your product line, thus effectively outsourcing the architecture definition practice area. What then, would you do with its partner, architecture evaluation? Would you assign it to the same contractor, assign it to a different contractor, or perform it in-house? What are the advantages and disadvantages of each?
4. Generalize the preceding question to decide how to handle the validation (testing, for example) of any product that you acquire.
5. Suppose you decided to commission the implementation of a major software component. How would you go about making a list of the contractors that you believe could handle the assignment? If you were to advertise for bids, where would you advertise?
6. For the preceding question, what deliverables would the contract specify? What would the contract specify that you provide to the contractor? What quality provisions would you put in the contract?
7. Suppose you decided to acquire (commission) the architecture for your product line, and suppose that three contractors submitted bids for the

contract. How would you decide which one to award the contract to? What deliverables would you require of the winning contractor?

6.4 Funding

The activities involved in any software development effort have to be financed; this practice area addresses how. Funding sources and models vary according to organizational culture and the nature of the software product being developed. If multiple copies of the software product are to be marketed, the organization usually appropriates development funds to a business unit, or the business unit appropriates its own funds. New products often get funded initially out of research and development allocations. If a product is being made specifically to serve the needs of one customer, the customer usually provides the funds. The funding of product maintenance is often dealt with separately and may come from a different source than that of the development financing. Whatever the source, somehow the funds are procured to support what it takes to develop and then to evolve the software product. Good estimates are required so that an adequate amount is allocated, thereby providing a stable funding source through product completion.

6.4.1 Aspects Peculiar to Product Lines

The key funding question for a product line organization is how to fund the core assets (which will be used across several products, most of which will probably not come into existence until long after the assets are initially put in place).

A software product line requires an investment to get it off the ground. This investment is used to establish the core asset base, to perform initial analysis (such as achieving an understanding of the relevant domains, scoping, requirements engineering, architecture definition, and so on), and to establish a production infrastructure. This funding must be sufficient so that the core assets can be of high quality and have the appropriate applicability. Once the product line is up and running, it must be sustained and evolved. The core assets must be kept current; the analysis must be updated; the infrastructure must be modernized. Funding must be stable and enduring so that the assets can be maintained and the associated product line practices and tools can be supported and improved.

The magnitude of the funding required should be defined in the business case for the product line. Since a business case explains how the organization will make money by adopting the product line strategy, it must also explain what the organization must put on the table before that payoff can occur. (See the "Building a Business Case" practice area, Section 6.1.) Therefore, we can think of the "Funding" practice area's goal as planning how the funds that are needed to develop and sustain the product line will be obtained once a business case has been established. Funding involves deciding what strategies can be employed to share/distribute equitably the cost of developing a product line capability and sustaining (and evolving) its ongoing operation.

The "up-front" work on a product line often has to be accomplished in parallel with ongoing operations because few organizations have the luxury of stopping either in-progress or planned developments while they change course to adopt a product line approach. As a result, new or innovative sources of funding for the organization are often required for the product line launch.

Although funding may seem to be a pedestrian or esoteric practice area, it has far-reaching consequences in an organization that is just launching a software product line. In Chapter 9, you'll read about a funding model at Cummins Engine Co. that resulted in the adoption of core assets by business units perhaps not otherwise inclined to participate in the product line effort. And in a struggling product line organization that we know, one of the sources of major frustration and deep-seated resentment is a funding model that lets recalcitrant parts of the organization continue on their one-product-at-a-time way, effectively undercutting the efforts of the struggling and under-resourced core asset group.

6.4.2 Application to Core Asset Development

During core asset development, the focus is on obtaining and managing funds for the following tasks:

- Develop an initial set of core assets and a production plan for building the first product and other future products that fall within the scope of the product line family. Determine the scope and establish the requirements. Define and evaluate the product line architecture. Make, buy, mine, or commission the software components, and test them.
- Define product line processes and procedures. Develop the product line operational concept (see the "Operations" practice area, Section 6.7). Define the data collection program. Institute risk management. Establish test plans.
- Develop or acquire a software engineering environment and related tools that will be part of the production infrastructure for core asset development.

Once the collection of core assets has been established, the focus is on obtaining and managing funds for the tasks listed below:

- Maintain, refine, and evolve existing core assets and perform configuration management on the entire asset base. Test, evaluate, and certify candidate core assets for compatibility with new asset/product requirements. Develop new core assets (software components, for example) that have applicability to products across the domain (as a result of negotiations with projects or as part of a preplanned strategic initiative for evolving the product line).

- Refine and evolve product line practices, processes, and procedures to enhance core asset development, sustainment, and evolution.
- Provide documentation and ongoing technical support to those projects (that is, product engineering groups) that are building derivative products using the core assets.

6.4.3 Application to Product Development

Once the product line has been established and products are being produced on a steady basis, funds must be obtained and managed for the following tasks. These tasks correspond to funding a particular product development group.

- Develop a product (or a set of products) using the existing core assets in accordance with the production plan. Among the activities to be funded are
  - adapting the product line requirements, architecture, and other core assets.
  - developing product-specific assets (software components, for example) that are not part of the core assets but are needed for the finished product. (These project-specific assets may be evaluated for their potential as future core assets.)
  - performing software system integration and testing.
  - developing system and user-oriented documentation.
  - coordinating the entire development effort with the product line support group for core assets.
- Provide ongoing product support (that is, product sustainment and evolution) to customers and users, and coordinate the sustainment efforts and follow-on product developments/enhancements with the product line support group for core assets.

Typically, these product development activities are funded predominantly out of product-specific funds. Consequently, the development costs are often not included in estimates of the funding required for developing a product line capability. This does not mean that these estimates are unnecessary or unimportant. On the contrary, funding estimates are a very important (and essential) element in developing a business case for adopting a product line approach and determining the projected return on investment (ROI). Occasionally, the cost of developing the "first product" is considered (and paid for) as part of the cost of developing a product line. In any event, participating projects need a cost (and schedule) estimate so that they can submit a budget for the funds they will require for their product development based on the product line approach.

Similarly, managing and obtaining funds for sustaining and evolving the actual products once they are operational are considered to be the responsibility of the individual product development groups. The benefit that these groups (or projects) realize is that the sustainment costs are substantially lower because the individual products are part of a family of products that share a large number of common assets that are sustained (and enhanced) by the product line organization. Moreover, because the reliability of these core assets is improved as a result of this centralized sustainment effort, the cost of sustaining an individual product is lower.

6.4.4 Specific Practices

Funding strategies and sources depend on the fiscal infrastructure of the product line enterprise. This infrastructure includes the organizational structure, the mission and functions of the organizational units, the amount and type of funds allocated to these units, and the policies and procedures they must follow to plan and obtain funding. There may be instances in which an existing fiscal infrastructure may not be sufficiently flexible to accommodate unique funding requirements for product lines. Table 6.3 identifies potential funding strategies and sources that may be employed to share/distribute equitably the cost of developing a product line capability and sustaining its ongoing operation. These strategies and sources are a representative set that, when adapted and taken in combination, can effect a complete funding infrastructure for a product line initiative.

The X's in Table 6.3 indicate how applicable an identified strategy is to funding of the indicated activity. Three X's indicate that the strategy is considered highly suitable; two X's indicate that it is moderately suitable; one X indicates that it may be only marginally suitable. The applicability (suitability) of a particular strategy in a given organizational setting depends on that organization's culture, fiscal infrastructure, and strategic goals and objectives. Use this table as a starting point for your organization.

Each funding strategy listed in Table 6.3 is summarized below.

Product-specific funding (individual customer, for example): In this strategy, each product project provides the funding that is needed for the identified product line activities. While product-specific funding is the predominant means of funding product development, it may be used for funding of asset development as well. Although product projects are often viewed (and properly so) as a primary source of funding, they may be reluctant to pay for aspects of product line operations that they feel are the responsibility of the parent product line organization. As indicated in Table 6.3, this funding reluctance may extend to elements of general product line planning and analysis, infrastructure support, and sustainment because they will also be of direct benefit to other projects involved in the product line. In these areas, other funding strategies are often more effective and should be considered carefully.

Table 6.3 General Applicability of Funding Strategies to Product Line Activities

Activities to Be Funded ➡ Funding Strategies ⬇	Product Line Development				
	Planning and Analysis	**Develop-ment**	**Asset Develop-ment**	**Sustain-ment and Evolution**	**Develop-ment Sustain-ment**
1. Product-specific funding (individual customer, for example)			XX		XXX
2. Direct funding from corporate sponsor/ program	XXX	XX	XX		
3. Product line organiza-tion's discretionary funds	X	XXX	X	X	
4. First product project funds effort	XX	XX	XX	X	XXX
5. Multiple projects banded together to share costs	XXX	XX	XXX	XX	X
6. Taxing of participating projects		X	X	XXX	
7. Product-side tax on customers			X	XXX	
8. Fee based on asset usage				XXX	
9. Prorated cost recovery		X	XX	X	X

Direct funding from corporate sponsor/program: This strategy is based on having the corporate-level/program sponsor selectively fund elements of the product line, especially those in the launch of the product line, that are related to planning and development of an initial set of core assets and the necessary production infrastructure.

Product line organization's discretionary funds: This strategy involves using discretionary funds, such as research and development monies, that are directly under the control of the product line organization to offset the greater up-front costs of developing a product line. If the organization responsible for managing and implementing the product line does not have its own discretionary funds (apart from the sponsoring or parent organization), this strategy, in effect, is no different than the "direct funding from corporate sponsor/program" strategy.

First product project funds effort: In this strategy, the first product project, in addition to funding its own product development, agrees to provide the funding for other designated activities such as product line planning and analysis, infrastructure establishment, core asset development, sustainment, and evolution. Under this strategy, the extent of the funding provided by the first project may be limited to establishing an initial product line capability, after which other sources of funding are used to sustain and evolve the product line.

Multiple projects banded together to share costs: In this strategy, multiple product development groups (projects) agree to form an alliance and fund jointly the cost of developing a product line capability that may potentially extend to funding all product line operations including product line sustainment and evolution. Even in this approach, however, each project is usually responsible for funding its own product development part of the effort. This is similar to the approach that CelsiusTech took in its product line development initiative: they pooled contract monies from individual customer projects and collectively developed a family of products [Brownsword 96].

Taxing of participating projects: This strategy involves funding of selected elements of the product line by levying a tax on each participating product development group (project). This taxing strategy can use a flat tax or a prorated tax that is based on some particular product attribute (such as product funds, project size, or estimated number of lines of code). The "product-side tax on customers" and "fee based on asset usage" strategies described below can be viewed as special cases of a taxing strategy.

Product-side tax on customers: In this strategy, a surcharge is assessed to fund selectively designated product line activities other than product development. This surcharge is then budgeted into the total estimated cost of developing a product for the customer, based on a product line approach.

Fee based on asset usage: This strategy involves charging projects a fee proportional to their usage of the core assets in their product development and/or end products. This is similar to enacting a license fee for using a commercial off-the-shelf (COTS) product. In fact, in cases in which there are multiple instances of the same product (for example, an application that is operational in many different aircraft), the product line organization may charge a set fee for every copy made. This is one possible means of obtaining funds for sustaining product line operations.

Prorated cost recovery: The object of this strategy is to have the projects that have benefited from the product line pay back their fair share of the costs of any software development efforts or services that the product line organization performed on their behalf. This strategy could be extended to include prorating all of, or just elements of, the total cost of sustaining product line operations among the participating project/product developers.

6.4.5 Practice Risks

Inadequate attention to the funding model for a product line will result in a core asset base and products whose owners compete in unhealthy ways for the finite resources available. This will result in poor quality on both sides and probably will foster resentment across the divide. A poor funding model can result from any of the following factors:

- **Inflexibility of the organization's fiscal infrastructure:** Each organization's fiscal infrastructure may not be immediately adaptable to the funding of a product line approach. As such, cultural and infrastructure changes would have to be planned and implemented. Such an implementation may take an inordinate amount of time and effort to modify, especially if the infrastructure involves regulations and statutes. Because of such financial barriers, the product line approach may not be initiated, or there may be ongoing contention for funds to sustain the product line.
- **Instability of initial management commitment:** It is, of course, key to product lines to obtain the attention of all levels of management and convince them to commit funds and allocate resources to the product line approach. Managers who are distracted with short-term fires or making sales versus strategic investments typically and understandably cannot be convinced that the approach is in their best interest. This risk also extends to convincing key technical people, or their direct managers, that funding of software product line efforts should, within reason, take precedence over current project demands because of strategic business concerns.
- **Waning management commitment:** Obtaining and sustaining management commitment over the life of a software product line is critical if the organization is to reap the benefits of the product line approach. Changes in business goals, organizational structure, and personnel (especially management) are prevalent throughout industry and government. These changes all have a potential impact on the amount of funds planned and committed to the product line approach. Such changes may result in periodic variations in product line funding, with attendant variations in the benefits achieved, if any are achieved at all.
- **Externally imposed fiscal constraints:** Organizational cuts and cost-saving mandates can limit the ability to fund new approaches, such as core asset development. Government agencies are especially prone to the annual "battle of the budget" and changes in fiscal policies, but commercial organizations are not immune. These yearly upheavals bring with them the risk of limiting sustaining funds for a product line.
- **Lack of strategic focus:** Product line initiatives require strategic planning. Organizations have to overcome a "research and development mindset" in which funds are spent on a small exploratory effort over two or three years without having plans for how this will evolve into a way of doing business

that involves everybody. Moreover, key technical people, or their direct managers, need to be convinced of the priority of funded product line efforts.

- **Inadequate funding:** If the funding allocated for a product line approach is insufficient, the funds could be spent with little residual benefits. That is, if an organization values only product development and is only paying lip service to product lines, any effort toward establishing a product line will be wasted. Unfortunately, such an occurrence may forever polarize the organization and the work force against any future consideration of adopting a product line approach.

6.4.6 Discussion Questions

1. Discuss each of the funding strategies listed under Specific Practices (Section 6.4.4) in terms of how applicable it is to your organization.
2. Discuss how a product line's business case and funding strategy are related to each other.
3. Discuss how the "Funding," "Technical Planning," and "Organizational Planning" practice areas (Sections 6.4, 5.6, and 6.8, respectively) are related to each other.
4. Discuss how funding strategies might differ in the case of a software product line built by adapting some similar, already existing systems, as opposed to starting one from scratch.
5. Suppose an organization is encountering resistance to the product line approach. This resistance manifests itself by a deep-seated tendency to continue building products one at a time and ignoring the core assets. Which funding strategy or strategies would you employ in such an organization? Which one(s) would you stay away from?

6.5 Launching and Institutionalizing

This practice area is about systematic elevation of an organization from a given state of product line sophistication to a higher state of product line sophistication. This practice area is relevant whether an organization is starting a product line effort for the first time or is trying to expand and/or improve the scope of an ongoing product line effort. Launching and institutionalizing a product line is somewhat different in that it is a practice area about applying the other practice areas, as appropriate to the needs and capabilities of an organization.

Launching and institutionalizing a product line is a special case of a technology change project. Technology change projects are undertaken to help organizations prepare themselves to adopt a new technology or a new way of doing business and are highly dependent on the context of the organization; an invariant sequence of steps to execute the project is inappropriate. Successful technology change projects take into account not only the specific technology involved but also the nontechnical or human aspects of change.

All technology change involves an assessment of the current state, an articulation of the desired state, and an assessment of the gulf between the two. After that, solution strategies for bridging the gulf can be crafted, tried out, and then scaled up. Lessons learned along the way can help refine your understanding of the current state, the desired state, or the intended solutions.

6.5.1 Aspects Peculiar to Product Lines

Launching and institutionalizing a product line differs in the particulars from launching and institutionalizing other kinds of technology. Launching a product line is about the judicious and timely application of product line practices. By factoring in a characterization of your individual situation, the part of the product line effort you want to accomplish, the groupings of practice areas that meet your individual needs, and a dynamic view of how the practice areas in that grouping interact to help you accomplish your goals, you can bring the practice areas to bear on your situation most effectively. Practice area patterns, introduced in Chapter 7, are about applying practice areas in a way that is most relevant to the organization's situation. Finding (or inventing) the appropriate practice area patterns is in many ways the essence of launching and institutionalizing a software product line.

Other Voices: Launching as a Project

Thomas Wappler of IBM Consulting Group liked our observation that introducing product line concepts to an organization was a kind of technology change project, with a definite emphasis on "project" and all the attending management obligation [Wappler 00].

> *In the product line practice[s] . . . we read that "Launching and institutionalizing a product line can be viewed as a special case of a technology change project." In other areas, organizations talk about a "business transition project," when the organization has to make changes to the way it does its business. The key word here is "project." The term used is not just "action," "initiative," or something similarly vague. So, besides having a clear goal, it is essential that setting up a product line is actually run as a formal project. This includes having a dedicated project team, formal project planning, project control, quality assurance etc. . . .*

It is not unusual that new concepts are first tried out in a normal development project and later applied across the organization. This works well with small specific topics (e.g., introducing a new tool or a specific new process). But a project for setting up a software product line is a totally different task that cannot be covered within a normal development project. A development project cannot carry the necessary expenses and load; neither will it be able to take on the strategic considerations that go beyond the scope of the development project. Therefore, there has to be a separate team for launching and institutionalizing a product line.

6.5.2 Application to Core Asset Development

Launching a product line will, of course, kick off the core asset development effort. In fact, a product line adoption plan may be one of the first core assets that an embryonic product line will develop. For more information on the product line adoption plan, see the "Organizational Planning" practice area (Section 6.8) and the Specific Practices section below (Section 6.5.4).

Institutionalizing a product line involves improving the processes that are associated with building, maintaining, and evolving the core assets and making those processes part of standard organizational practice.

"Lunching" and Institutionalizing

In 1999, a small group of us visited a company that manufactured software-intensive aircraft subsystems. We were interested in the software architecture(s) that they used for their systems and how architecture played a role in their overall culture and development process. We interviewed more than 20 people in six sessions over two days, including developers, senior designers, functional area managers, QA/CM/tool groups, and systems designers. Although architecture was our quarry for this trip, we were delighted to discover a strong product line culture along the way.

The first interview session was with a group of senior designers, each with the title "project engineer." Project engineers are the technical authorities for projects. They drew for us a very detailed picture of the common architecture for their group of products, which we will give the collective (and, to protect confidentiality, fictitious) name of "Aircraft Systems," and which we were to learn was indeed a product line of systems at that company. The project engineers told us that they got projects[1] off the ground by first attempting to reuse,

1. By "project" we mean the organizational unit or team that builds a product.

with as little change as possible, the architectural components from previous projects. In fact, the process started with the software requirements specification (SRS). The Aircraft Systems group maintained a "common" (what we would call a "core") SRS; system-specific SRSs were written as variations of the common SRS. They also told us that the project engineers met weekly to work out common requirements that they could feed jointly to the groups that maintained the major subsystems and associated software.

We asked what prevented a developer from picking up a component from a previous project and changing it at will to meet the exigencies of the product he or she was working on at the time. The answer, they said, was that this was strongly discouraged. The functional area managers would not allow it, and the offending engineer would "have to eat by himself in the lunchroom." Beneath the levity of this comment, a picture of strong product line culture was beginning to emerge.

Subsequent interview groups confirmed this. We learned that their development environment (in this case, Rational's APEX) played a critical role in the sustainment of the product line. For one thing, every project was open to every other project, so that people could straightforwardly search for components that were candidates for reuse. Each component was stored with its history of usage, its own requirements, its test cases, and its Ada spec, so when retrieved for reuse its entire heritage and artifact accompaniment came with it. APEX revealed which components depended on which other components, and they were able to compare versions to quickly discern differences. And APEX automatically sent e-mail to the cognizant functional area manager when a changed subsystem under that manager's purview was checked in. We were learning that the functional area managers were the guardians of the product line.

At this point, we did not know who these mystical functional area managers were, or what role they played, but they were clearly important to the product line and commanded a lot of respect from the engineers and developers. We asked to interview them—they were not originally on our schedule because we did not know they existed—and they revealed the entire product line picture.

About four and a half years ago, this company faced their own version of the CelsiusTech crisis [Brownsword 96]: three major projects, which were expected to be won in a staggered fashion, came in simultaneously. These projects were to supply systems for three different kinds of United States military aircraft. They realized that they needed to exploit the commonality in all of the systems, and the product line was born. There was apparently no leader from above who ordered the architects into a locked closet and forcefully heeled the organization over to a new tack. Rather, the functional area managers simply began to meet (over lunch, we are told) to work out procedures for exploiting the commonality that they knew existed in previous projects and that would be required in the new ones. Projects apportioned the work and shared each other's components.

Today, the functional area managers control the design and evolution of the subsystems. They are like a core asset group, but unlike other core asset groups, this one has no implementation duties. Rather, the functional area managers are like senior designers who (1) approve or reject design changes requested by individual projects, (2) keep track of changes that are needed by more than one project, and (3) find projects that have the money to make the approved changes. (Sometimes changes are made using IR&D money as well.) So this "core asset group" has the vision and the change authority, but changes are made by projects. These managers have teams of people that "work" for them and are farmed out to individual projects as needed. Each functional area team represents a collection of expertise about a particular functional area (subsystem). Thus, the organization is a matrix in which a developer works for both a functional area manager and (while assigned to a project) a project manager. The figure below illustrates.

Improvements are continually made to the subsystems (which are their primary software core assets). The functional area managers are always looking for ways to improve the architecture and then looking for projects that can use (and hence pay for the making of) those improvements. Examples include (1) moving away from direct subroutine invocation as the collaboration mechanism and toward registration; and (2) simplifying the pattern of dependencies (as manifested by Ada "with" statements) among the subsystems, which at the time of our visit was almost incomprehensibly complex.

Some of the conditions that work in this company's favor include the following:

- a relatively small number of projects so far. The number of versions of any subsystem that a reuser has to browse through is no more than 15 to 20, and 6 is a much more likely number. Thus, they don't yet have a runaway version control or component search problem.

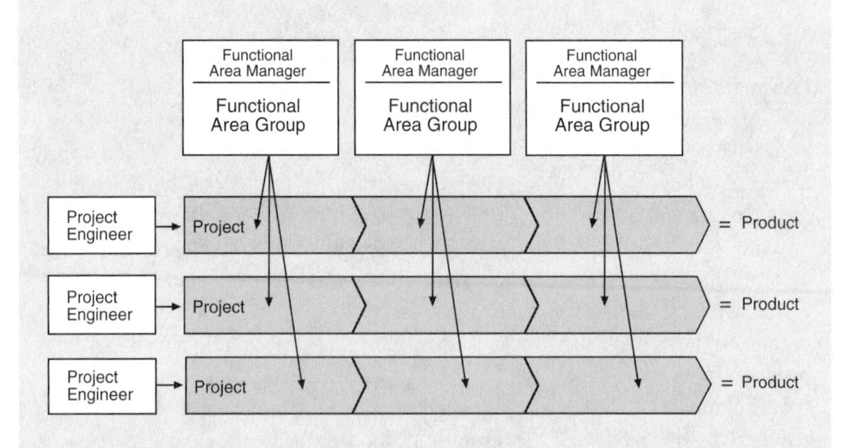

Organization by Functional Area Group

- a domain in which the software architecture naturally mirrors the hardware/system architecture. Most software that they build matches up straightforwardly with electronic boxes that plug into the aircraft, boxes that the company has long manufactured. Other software that doesn't correspond precisely to a box rather naturally falls out and is treated separately.
- deep domain expertise, which is not a surprise.

Also not surprisingly, their architecture supports the product line view by providing changeability and portability qualities. It is strongly layered, and it enforces strict visibility rules among the layers. Subsystems that are present in every product (such as a bus manager that puts messages on the communication bus and pulls them off for other subsystems) are distinguished from subsystems that may or may not be present in a particular product. Subsystems have internal structures of their own; the part that displays information is often changed, but the state machine or controlling part seldom does, and these are well-separated parts of each subsystem. There is an i/o part of each subsystem that communicates with other subsystems via the bus. Overall, the architecture features minimal use of global data, maintains stable subsystem interfaces, and mandates consistent and disciplined interprocess communication protocols. Platform and environmental dependencies, scheduling policies, user interfaces, and message formats are all isolated (encapsulated) in separate software components.

This company clearly has a strong culture of product lines and architecture, and this emerged consistently. Everyone who drew the architecture drew the same picture. Everyone who told how the product line works told the same story. But the culture is an oral one. Nowhere was the product line operation codified in writing. Except for the SRSs, people rather than documents seemed to be the authoritative sources for much of the information necessary in development. But the oral culture has advantages, also. There is a strong and formal mentoring process in place, and it seems to be quite effective. There is also open communication. Developers are free to talk to their project engineers and "argue" with them for changes; they either convince them to make the change or are convinced by them that the change is not needed. The project engineers will not hesitate to lobby the functional area managers for changes. Communication flows freely.

And what does this company have to show for its product line efforts?

- They can port to a new processor in about 8 days and have already ported their software to a PowerPC.
- Reuse numbers as high as 94% were cited, and reuse in the 80% range seemed merely nominal to the groups to whom we spoke, earning only a modest shrug of the shoulders.
- Their tool/environment person (whose tools help collect metrics) estimated that what they used to do in 18 to 38 months they can now do in 8 to 16 months.

So necessity was once again the mother of invention—a product line scenario we have seen more than once. Moreover, under the calm guidance of the functional area managers, who saw what needed to be done and worked quickly and efficiently among themselves to make it happen, the transition to the product line paradigm was accomplished with a minimum of trauma. Besides starting the product line, the functional area managers have been its guardians, have kept it alive and nurtured it, have protected its conceptual integrity, and have instilled a strong sense of product line culture in the entire Aircraft Systems organization. They are its champions.

Not bad for an idea that started over lunch.

—PCC

6.5.3 Application to Product Development

Launching a product line often involves choosing a pilot project or two with which to demonstrate the product line activities. (For information about choosing pilot projects, see the Specific Practices section that follows.) These pilot projects should, if possible, yield marketable products that will enhance the fidelity of the demonstration and subject the core assets used in their construction to real-life constraints. Institutionalizing a product line means making the development of products routine and predictable while still meeting the organization's product line goals. The achievement of this steady state is a signal that product line practice has in fact been institutionalized.

Tiptoe Carefully or Dive Right In?

So you've decided to launch a product line. You're ready to start defining its scope, working on its requirements definition, crafting the architecture, building the core assets, coming up with the concept of operations, unveiling a new organizational structure, and all the rest. You've envisioned how your technical and managerial staff is going to turn out this product line, maintain and grow it on a day-to-day basis, and bring home all the productivity and time-to-market gains that made the business case such a delight to read.

But there's a snag. Presumably your staff is busy doing things now, things that are making your organization a profit or carrying out its mission. Probably they're building products, products with hard deadlines—"hard" having the double meaning of difficult to meet and difficult to change—and products with a targeted market segment and customer base that you can't just breezily dismiss in the name of progress.

So if your staff is busy right now, who's going to build the product line? Put another way, if you redirect your staff to start building the product line, what's going to happen to all those products whose delivery has already been promised?

This problem has two solutions. To solve it, all you need to do is pick one of them. The choice is almost like deciding what to do when faced with a swim in cold water: do you tiptoe in gingerly, submerging one body part at a time, or do you dive in and get it over with?

The "dive in" solution is to say that giving up or delaying products in progress is the price to be paid for all of the business gains that the product line will shower on your organization. During the product line's "incubation" period, while core assets are being built and production plans put in place, the organization conducts no other business, and to the cost of the product line is added the opportunity cost of missing out on the profits, market share, and customer goodwill that other products might have brought in. This solution is fairly draconian, but there are situations where it makes sense, and we have seen it used to good effect by several organizations, both large and small. If your lead time on the planned products is long, or their number is few, then you might be able to turn them out as part of your new product line stable anyway. If you can outsource their production, this might also provide a way out. Or if you have a funding source that will see you through the lean times of product line start-up (such as an R&D budget), then this approach might be viable.

The disadvantages of this approach are, of course, the money and market lost on the interim products. But the advantages are considerable. First and foremost, this approach provides the shortest path to the product line paradigm. Everyone in the development organization comes on board at once, is in sync, and shares in the experience of adopting the product line approach. And the time between product line launch and the first delivery of a member of the product line is minimized. The organizational disruption is broad, but it happens all at once and is over as quickly as it can be.

The "tiptoe gingerly" solution is to stage the adoption of the product line. You can assign a small team to define the product line's scope, craft the product line architecture, plan the construction (or purchase) of the software core assets, and define product line operations and processes. And then, once the planning and design infrastructure are in place, this small team can be augmented to start building or accumulating the core assets. While this is going on, the bulk of the organization is still busy carrying out the organization's mainline business of turning out products the old-fashioned way.

This approach has several advantages. First and most obvious, it lets the organization continue to turn out interim products. Second, each core asset that becomes available is validated by the first few products that adopt it, thus providing every asset with a built-in pilot project or two of its very own; this can increase asset quality. Third, the few-products-at-a-time approach lets the organization adopt the new paradigm in a staged manner so as to not feel so shell-shocked by an all-at-once adoption strategy.

However, there are dangers. First, small teams may produce small results, and expecting a small team to produce all of a product line's core assets and operational processes is unrealistic. Second, if the organization has not fully committed to a product line approach, it is tempting to regard the team as a sideshow set apart from the "real" business of the organization. Product line starvation through neglect is a real possibility. The team needs to be grown, given resources commensurate with its growing responsibilities over time, and staffed with the highest-quality people from the product-building projects—which, of course, will make the product managers shriek in protest. Third, if there is resistance to the product line idea within the organization, this staged effort will prolong the agony of the paradigm shift. It will give the naysayers time to (at worst) entrench themselves in the old ways and find subtly subversive tactics to resist the change. And fourth, there is a danger that the core assets may be designed with only the early products in mind and will founder when applied to subsequent products.

And the "tiptoe gingerly" approach comes with a cost. The cost is delaying the full benefit of the product line approach until the product line has fully blossomed. The cost is lower productivity and higher time-to-market that you could have remedied with a more aggressive approach.

The incremental approach usually works best if the organization has many products in the delivery pipeline with relatively low lead times and cannot afford simply to shut down production until the first product line member is ready to roll out.

So how does the incremental approach work? One organization we know staged their product line adoption as follows:

- They formed a small steering group to define the product line scope and craft the architecture for the product line. The architecture, not surprisingly, was a layered one. The bottom-most layer provided portability across the variety of hardware platforms that were included in the scope. The next layer up provided a set of services that were common across products—that is, every service in this layer would be used by at least two products in the intended scope.
- They identified three upcoming products that would become the first pilots to use the product line's core assets. These products had sequential delivery dates with gaps of six months to a year in between.
- For component design work they staffed the software architecture group with part-time members of those three products' development teams and members from other product groups in the organization.
- They began implementing the software in the lowest layer of the architecture, the portability layer, targeting its completion to accommodate the schedule of the first pilot product, which used it.

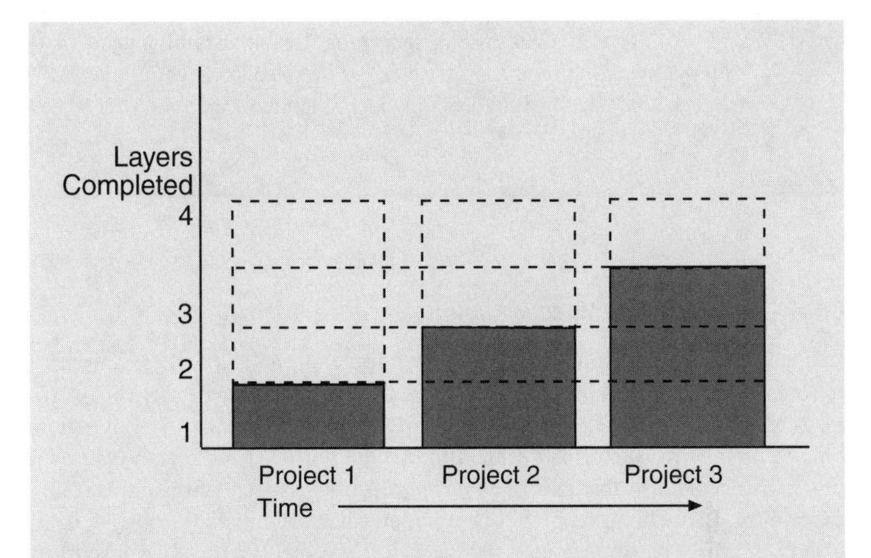

Phasing in a Four-Layer Architecture

- Once this was complete, they began to implement services in the second layer that the second pilot would use. And the second pilot, then, was able to use the entire portability layer and those parts of the common-services layer that they needed and that were ready in time.
- Finally, they completed the common-services layer, and the third pilot was able to use all of that layer.

The figure above illustrates this. This particular organization staffed and resourced its steering group at near-starvation levels, but their fundamental approach was sound. There was some discomfort among product line "purists" that the products weren't really members of the product line because they were not compelled to use the full set of core assets. But, in fact, they were members. Each one used a shared set of core assets—just not the *same* set. But more important than wrangling about definitions is to observe that *each product was better off for using the available core assets than it would have been otherwise.* Even the first pilot product, which used the least of the core assets, gained portability across hardware platforms, something it would not otherwise have enjoyed. And it became a member of the product line family in that the support of that part of its software was the job of the core assets group, and this product joined a supporting community of products using that layer. Once the product line has been established, each of the pilot products is free to reengineer itself to come into full alignment with the product line and adopt those core assets that were not yet ready. It is incumbent on each one to make a business case for either fully joining the product line fold or continuing its prodigal ways.

> Whether you dive in all at once or step in lightly and carefully, deciding how to turn out your first products is one of the first decisions you'll have to make when launching and institutionalizing a product line. Once you're in, the water will feel much better.
>
> —PCC

6.5.4 Specific Practices

Launching and institutionalizing a software product line is a matter of orchestrating the activities of all of the applicable practice areas over time. Your organization's specific launching strategy will be unique. Chapter 7 shows how practice areas can be carried out in *patterns* and how you can create your own practice area patterns that carry you through various aspects of the product line experience. Launching, then, will be a pattern that you create (or borrow from Chapter 7) for your organization. Beyond that, the specific practices discussed below will suggest some additional approaches for bringing your organization up to product line speed.

6.5.4.1 The IDEAL Model

In the technology change domain of process improvement, the IDEAL model has enjoyed wide success [McFeeley 96]. With some generalizations, the IDEAL model is also appropriate for the launching of a product line. As shown in Figure 6.5, the IDEAL model is iterative, allowing the reevaluation of the changing organizational context as the technology change project proceeds. This iteration also makes the model applicable to launching a product line effort from different levels of product line sophistication and to improving or institutionalizing the product line effort. This iterative cycle may be executed as many times as necessary to achieve the desired organizational state.

The model consists of five phases, each providing a basis for the next phase, with the final phase feeding back to the beginning. The five phases, which follow, are initiating, diagnosing, establishing, acting, and learning:

- An organization typically enters the *initiating* phase as a result of some stimulus to change the current way of doing business. In response to this stimulus, the appropriate sponsorship is established, and the appropriate resources are allocated.
- In the *diagnosing* phase, the organization performs a diagnostic activity to baseline the current practices and to probe for improvement opportunities.
- In the *establishing* phase, the recommendations of the diagnostic activity are prioritized; change implementation teams are established; and plans are developed for conducting the activities.
- In the the *acting* phase, the planned activities are carried out.

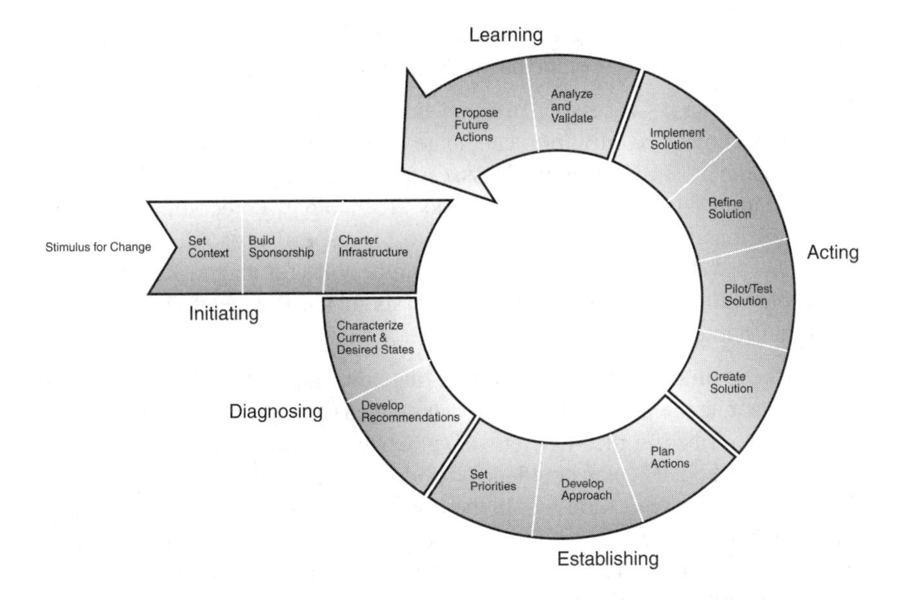

Figure 6.5 The IDEAL Model for Technology Change

- The end of a cycle is represented by the *learning* phase. Here the organization collects lessons learned that can then be applied to subsequent rounds of the technology change cycle.

Some tailoring of the IDEAL model is necessary to guide a product line effort. An organization engaging in its first product line effort should execute at least one IDEAL cycle to see if a product line approach makes sense. Furthermore, in order to guide product line efforts that begin at different levels of sophistication, we must recognize that the phases within a given IDEAL cycle may have different degrees of rigor and formality. In an early cycle, the diagnosis phase might be as simple as a brief review of assets for reuse potential. In a later cycle, it might be much more formal and include a multiday product line technical probe that looks at all the practice areas. Typically, more attention is needed for the *initiating* phase of early cycles than of later cycles. Specific details might be best determined by evaluating the risks associated with each phase, much as in the Spiral development model [Boehm 88].[2]

For a product line launch, the IDEAL cycle entails the following practices:

***Initiating* phase—forming commitment:** Once a product line opportunity has been identified and substantiated (perhaps with early forms of a business case or market analysis), promote management and staff awareness of the

2. Jones discusses how the IDEAL and Spiral models complement each other [Jones 96].

opportunity, obtain staffing and resource commitments, and set product line objectives so as to meet specific business needs.

***Diagnosing* phase—assessing product line conditions:** Evaluate the business and technical viability of a candidate product line opportunity (based on the "Scoping," "Building a Business Case," "Market Analysis," "Funding," "Organizational Risk Management," and "Technology Forecasting" practice areas, Sections 5.5, 6.1, 6.6, 6.4, 6.9, and 6.11, respectively). An organization could also use all the practice areas to determine areas for diagnosing organizational product line practices; this is the basis of the Product Line Technical Probe in Chapter 8.

***Establishing* phase—planning product line adoption:** Develop a transition plan to institute the product line approach defined in product line's operational concept (described in the "Operations" practice area, Section 6.7). As a risk-reduction method, this plan could include pilot projects to prove concepts and to learn about their application within the organization. Such a plan will identify and schedule any actions (with the associated resources) that are needed to improve the organizational capabilities for undertaking a product line approach. Actions include creating an appropriate organizational structure (as described in the "Structuring the Organization" practice area, Section 6.10), providing suitable training (as described in the "Training" practice area, Section 6.12), and creating a supporting infrastructure (as described in the "Tool Support" practice area, Section 5.8). In general, the performance of this practice should adhere to the principles of the "Technical Planning," "Organizational Planning," "Technical Risk Management," and "Organizational Risk Management" practice areas (Sections 5.6, 6.8, 5.7, and 6.9, respectively).

***Acting* phase—monitoring direction and performance:** Utilizing the identified goals and reporting requirements from the plan created in the *establishing* phase, monitor and evaluate the outcomes from its performance and identify any needed revisions in approach to accommodate changes in objectives or opportunities for improvement. The performance of this practice should adhere to the principles set forth in the two "Planning" practice areas (Sections 5.6 and 6.8) and should be based on the results of data collection and metrics activities (see the "Data Collection, Metrics, and Tracking" practice area, Section 5.2).

***Learning* phase—tuning and improvement:** Risk management, planning, and measurement activities will identify any places where the product line effort is not yet a good fit with the organization's own special context. In this phase, the processes and organizational structures are modified to reflect lessons learned and to take advantage of potential optimizations.

Subsequent execution of the IDEAL cycles—promoting institutionalization: Work with other product line efforts in the organization to create shared standards and techniques that provide mutual benefit and leverage or that may aid in the initiation of new product line efforts. Such standards provide proven models and techniques for assessing product line opportunities and achieving success in the initiation and performance of a product line effort. These efforts may also be the basis for the sharing or joint development of training, infrastructure, tools, or product assets that are needed across multiple product lines.

A sample scenario based on the IDEAL model: This scenario is for an initial product line effort based on existing assets. It assumes that an organization is engaged in single-system product development and is moving to a product line approach. Several cycles of the IDEAL model are described. While it is possible that a decision to terminate may be made at any time, it is assumed that the end of each cycle will conclude with a decision to proceed.

IDEAL cycle 0 (concept exploration): A concept-exploration/awareness-building cycle executes the IDEAL model somewhat informally. That is, the phases should not require significant resources and are not always distinguished by a clean separation between phases. Typically, the planning for this cycle is informal:

- ***Initiating* phase:** There is a stimulus to consider a product line approach—that is, shrinking budgets, stronger competition, or mission requirements to develop systems "better, faster, cheaper." Allocate limited resources to investigate.
- ***Diagnosing* phase:** Gather data about product line technology. Informally consider whether the organization might benefit from such an approach. Use consultants or outside advisors if the expertise is not available in-house.
- ***Establishing* phase:** Assuming that the decision is that further exploration is warranted, plan the next cycle and get the authorization needed to proceed.

The *acting* and *learning* phases are typically truncated.

IDEAL cycle 1 (concept refinement and initial implementation): Cycle 1 might proceed as follows:

- ***Initiating* phase:** Build an awareness and advocacy with the appropriate stakeholders. Obtain the appropriate resources to execute this cycle.
- ***Diagnosing* phase:** Perform an initial review of existing assets and organizational readiness to embark on a product line effort. This diagnosis might require consultants if in-house expertise is not available. The purpose of this diagnosis is to determine if a product line approach is viable. Assuming that the diagnosis determines that further exploration is warranted, the next phase can begin.
- ***Establishing* phase:** Based on the results of the diagnosis, create a plan for the initial implementation. Contents of this plan might include activities to
  - develop the organizational vision, goals, objectives, and strategies for the product line effort.
  - develop a business case for product lines.

  - analyze asset commonality and scope the product line.
  - develop a preliminary operating concept.
  - develop a preliminary architecture definition.
  - perform a preliminary mining of existing assets.

  The plan should also contain a preliminary plan for the next IDEAL cycle. Management's approval of this plan signals the end of this phase.
- ***Acting*** **phase:** Execute the plan. Note that if the plan includes the establishment of an infrastructure to sustain the product line effort, this activity effectively overlaps with the *initiating* activities of the next cycle.
- ***Learning*** **phase:** Collect lessons learned, and refine the approach as needed. Unless further *initiating* and *diagnosing* activities are necessary, this phase can overlap with the *establishing* phase of the next cycle.

IDEAL cycle 2 (furthering the implementation):

- ***Establishing*** **phase:** Apply any lessons learned from the preceding cycle to refine the approach. The primary product of this phase should be a product line adoption/implementation plan. The contents of this plan could include
  - a refinement of architecture definition
  - further mining of legacy assets
  - a refinement of the concept of operations (CONOPS)

  The CONOPS will contain a high-level description of the organizational structures for product lines and how business will be conducted. The adoption/implementation plan will describe how the organization will migrate from the current state to the future state described in the CONOPS. The adoption plan might specify further iterations of the implementation in order to reduce risks.
- ***Acting*** **phase:** Execute the plan.
- ***Learning*** **phase:** Evaluate the results thus far and determine if subsequent cycles are needed.

6.5.4.2 Using Pilot Projects

Pilot projects can be an important means of reducing risk and learning more about the organizational and technical issues associated with the product line effort. A successful pilot project can also be an effective means of building advocacy. A pilot should be viewed as a controlled experiment to test specific ideas or concerns.

Other Voices: IBM

Thomas Wappler of IBM Consulting Group writes that a pilot project is an important risk mitigation effort when launching a software product line. A pilot project, he says, serves as quality assurance for the transition project's results, builds confidence in the approach, and provides an initial baseline for future project planning. He counsels the following criteria when selecting a project to serve as the product line pilot [Wappler 00]:

> **Fit.** *In order to be able to provide the desired results, a pilot project should "fit." The architecture that is created as a common base should actually meet the requirements of the project, and the first standard development model should not be "overkill" for a very small project.*
> **Realistic scope and business objective.** *The selected project should have a realistic business objective. A "toy project" will not really challenge the architecture or the development method. Observers may not believe that the architectures will actually scale to the requirements of "real" projects.*
> **Schedule.** *The pilot project's schedule has to meet the schedule of the transition project. If it starts too early, the core assets will not be ready for first tests; if it ends too late, feedback may come too late as well. This also implies that the pilot's size has to be moderate.*
> **Stability.** *A pilot should also be reasonably stable. We know that there are always changes in priorities and plans where projects will get cancelled or put on hold for a period of time. But this should never lead to a situation where there is no pilot project left. If this risk exists then more than one pilot project should be selected.*
> **Room for pilot activities.** *The additional tasks and consequences for the project must be made clear and must be reflected in the pilot's project plan. This may include time for learning, time for specific cooperation with the architecture team, and additional time allocated for providing feedback.*
> **Location.** *Because the pilot has to use incomplete assets, it is essential that the pilot team be located very close to the team that builds these assets. Having these teams in different buildings will be a challenge; working in different time zones will hardly work at all.*

Some criteria to consider when selecting a pilot include the following:

- **Scope:** The pilot should be scoped such that it can be executed in a relatively short time frame with relatively limited resources.
- **Importance and visibility:** The organization should care about whether the pilot is successful. In other words, a success in the "backwater" of the organization is unlikely to generate any enthusiasm. On the other hand, the pilot should not be so important—for example, on a critical path—such that failure has a significant adverse impact on the organization.
- **Probability of success:** Especially for initial pilots, the effort should have a reasonable chance to succeed. If an organization already has success with product lines, more risky pilots might be chosen to test specific concepts.

- **Choice of participants:** Unless the pilot is aimed specifically at testing organizational resistance, the participants in the pilot should be advocates (or at least be open-minded).

6.5.4.3 Lightweight Approaches at First

When initiating a product line effort, some organizations report success with using "lightweight organizational structures" and "lightweight processes" to support them. These lightweight approaches facilitate smoother transitions to product lines that can be changed quickly and nimbly as the organization learns what does and does not work for its particular situation. It is worth noting that this approach is a form of piloting.

6.5.4.4 Product Line Technical Probe

Before an organization can launch and institutionalize a product line capability successfully, it needs to know its blind spots. If it is lacking necessary expertise in one of the practice areas (especially one that tends to manifest itself early in the product line life cycle, such as scoping or requirements engineering), it is unlikely to make a successful (let alone a smooth) transition to sound product line practice. But by recognizing potential trouble spots early, resources can be focused judiciously on shoring up any areas of weakness that, if left untreated, would undermine the product line effort.

An instrument to help an organization identify problem areas is the Product Line Technical Probe. This probe identifies an organization's strengths and weaknesses in each of the product line practice areas. These results provide the grist for an adoption or launching plan, the first part of which will be to rectify any deficiencies in critical skill areas. The probe is described fully in Chapter 8.

6.5.4.5 Development of Product Line Goals, Objectives, and Strategies

Technology change should be initiated not for its own sake but to support specific organizational goals. Thus, an early step in the technology change project is to establish an appropriate set of goals, which are validated by supporting rationale. A set of objectives should also be determined to provide high-level, measurable indicators of progress toward the goals. Given a set of goals and supporting objectives, there are typically a number of different strategies that are appropriate to the achievement of those goals. Presumably, one of those strategies is to initiate (or expand) a product line effort. Another strategy might be to build (or further mature) a software process infrastructure to provide a foundation for the product line effort. An internal workshop is an excellent vehicle for articulating and capturing the goals, objectives, and strategies that will serve as the foundation for building an adoption plan. As the organization progresses with its product line adoption, these should be revisited and updated.

Other Voices: Lucent Technologies

In 1994, Lucent Technologies launched the Domain Engineered Configuration Control (DECC) project to try to standardize software written for the hardware components of Lucent's massive 5ESS telephone switch. The DECC team adopted a product line approach, produced a commonality analysis document for the envisioned family, and wrote tools to help developers, but Lucent was not in a position to compel projects to use their methods. As they put it, "Even if you build it, they may not come." But eventually they did come because the product line advocates took the right steps [Ardis 00].

> *In the summer of 1996 the DECC team found a project that would cooperate in the trial use of the DECC technology. The project was already too far along to switch over to the DECC technology, but they were willing to share their requirements and tests for a side-by-side comparison. The team used the DECC technology to generate software equivalent in functionality to software developed by the cooperating project. They then performed a static analysis and dynamic analysis to show that the two versions had comparable run-time performances.*
>
> *This was an important demonstration of the feasibility and practicality of the DECC technology. Additionally, it provided useful feedback to the domain engineering cycle. After conducting the pilot study, the DECC team revised the commonality analysis document and updated the tools. The total effort spent in performing the pilot project, revising the analysis, and updating the tools was about one staff-year.*
>
> *The first project to adopt DECC appeared a few months later. Again, the DECC team revised the commonality analysis document in light of feedback from this application and made further modifications to the tools. The successful completion of this project has helped to convince other projects to adopt the DECC technology. . . .*
>
> *During the deployment phase the team sought to convince other projects to use their technology. This phase was dominated by a concern with technology transfer issues. The most important lessons of the deployment phase are:*
>
> ***Give demos often.*** *These help to get and keep management support, which is needed to keep resources for the project. These also help convince peers that the technology should be adopted. Put more strongly, demos are concrete indicators of progress, and a project should be managed to produce demos at each milestone. Plan for demos; don't regard them as a distraction.*
>
> *Customer focus is essential to technology transfer. This should start during analysis and continue through design and deployment. Note that learning takes place in both directions. As the team learns more about the customers' needs, they become better able to anticipate the customers' reactions to the technology. At the same time, the cus-*

tomers learn more about the value of the new technology and so become better able to judge its strengths and weaknesses.

If possible, conduct a shadow project to demonstrate value and collect data. This is very important for selling the technology to potential customers. No one wants to be the first user. It may not be as hard to conduct a shadow project as it first appears. On our project we needed access to requirements and tests. These are normal byproducts of our software development process, so they did not impose an additional burden on the other project. We did need to spend some time discussing issues with the other team, but we also contributed to their effort by providing review support.

6.5.4.6 Product Line Adoption Plan

A product line adoption plan describes how product line practices will be rolled out across the organization. Depending on the starting point of the organization, this plan may provide for the definition of processes, the initiation of practices, the selection and implementation of pilots, or the engineering of a product line. If the intention is that the entire organization will eventually adopt a product line approach, the plan should address the entire organization. For example, suppose that a chosen pilot project involves only one part of the organization that eventually will make the transition. That is, after all, one of the benefits of a pilot project: it does not involve the entire organization, and so missteps and early mistakes are confined to a small effort. What, then, do the other parts of the organization do while the pilot is underway? If they do nothing, it's business as usual for them, and in more than one organization we've seen, this has spelled trouble. Those people may feel left out and disenfranchised, and their support for the transition to product lines may suffer as a result. But an adoption plan that applies to the organization (project, business unit, corporation) as a whole may be the solution. Even if a group is not participating actively in the pilot project, they can serve as reviewers, receive training, practice building a business case or scope definition, or be assigned process improvement activities to shore up their capabilities for when they will join the product line. A product line adoption plan, the result of the launching and institutionalizing effort, is the master plan showing how all parts of the organization adopt product line capabilities, perhaps in a highly staged manner.

6.5.4.7 Process Improvement as a Basis for Launching and Institutionalizing

Process discipline provides a foundation for product line practice. It may well be in your organization's best interests to initiate a process improvement effort in conjunction with software product line adoption. If you use the CMMI for

Systems Engineering/Software Engineering (see "Software Process Improvement and Product Line Practice" sidebar) as the basis for your efforts, then the following CMMI *process* areas (not to be confused with the software product line *practice* areas) will bring about the highest payoff first:

- Requirements Management
- Project Planning
- Configuration Management
- Requirements Development
- Risk Management

Depending on your organization, its culture, and its business needs, other process areas also may be important. Risk Management is on the foundational list because it can function as a "safety net" to help make up for the unforeseen. This list implies following a CMMI continuous representation philosophy, as opposed to the staged representation maturity level ordering. If you prefer to strive for a maturity level—the staged representation does indeed provide a proven sequence to follow—then setting CMMI maturity level 2 as your goal will work well to provide a foundation of process maturity that will help a great deal with product lines. Level 2 will prescribe a larger, slightly different set of process areas.

Regardless of the CMMI representation followed, process improvement experience strongly suggests that capability/maturity levels should be implemented in sequence. That is, project level institutionalization (maturity/capability level 2) should be established before organizational level institutionalization (maturity/capability level 3). This sequencing reduces risks associated with premature standardization. Pilot projects operating on a small (less than organization-wide) scale are an effective way to accomplish this.

6.5.5 Practice Risks

The risks of launching a product line relate to misapplying the product line approach by either failing to institute beneficial practices or instituting practices that are not appropriate to the particular organizational situation. A poor launching and institutionalizing strategy will result in failure of the product line to meet its goals, very likely because the staff will fail to accept it as a way of doing business. This can result from

- **No identifiable champion:** Any institutional change requires a strong champion who can effectively communicate the vision, console the troops when things go badly, make sure that the organization is following the new ideas, remind everyone why the organization has decided to embrace the change, and never, ever let enthusiasm wane. A software product line needs such a champion who has the management authority (or has the ear of management authority) to keep the organization on track. An organization lacking an effective champion will have a much more difficult time adopting the product line approach.

- **Approach mismatch:** If the products being developed do not have sufficient commonality to warrant a product line approach, any launching effort will fail. Software product lines should be a strategy that meets specific business goals. In other words, a product line approach to software is a means to achieve an end, not the end itself.
- **Inadequate management commitment:** If management has not been convinced of the viability of a product line approach for their situation, the funding, staffing, and other resources may be inadequate for a successful adoption. Mitigation involves developing additional evidence of the opportunity (perhaps through additional market analyses or narrowly focused pilot efforts) that is aimed at addressing specific concerns. Additionally, efforts may focus on developing the commitment at high organizational levels at which there may be more strategic perspectives on the business situation and future needs.
- **Insufficient staff commitment:** If the technical staff has not been convinced of the viability of a product line approach, they will be likely to torpedo the effort. A major aspect of any product line launch should focus on educating the staff and achieving their buy-in. Involving technical staff in the definition of plans and processes is one mitigation step.
- **Insufficient bounding:** If the planned effort requires too much effort over too long a period of time, the attainable benefits may not be realized soon enough to justify the investment. Mitigation might involve limiting the product line scope to create high-payoff assets or limiting the market focus to address critical or selected work products so that this effort can concentrate on delivering valuable benefits within the needed time frame.
- **Inappropriate application:** If an organization does not have a clear product line charter or has one that is different than the charter that is stated for it, it will probably build products that are too divergent from the planned product line focus to benefit as anticipated from the product line approach. Mitigation involves ensuring that knowledgeable and experienced management, engineering, and marketing staff are involved over an adequate, but not excessive, period of time in resolving the true product line charter to be pursued. Particular effort should be made to ensure that the needed diversity among future products, which must often be avoided with conventional development approaches, is accommodated properly.
- **Premature standardization:** If institutionalization occurs too quickly, inappropriate standards may be instituted, and innovation may be terminated prematurely.
- **Missed or delayed standardization opportunities:** On the other hand, if standardization opportunities are missed or delayed, there may be redundant or unnecessarily divergent efforts and less than optimally effective practices.

- **Insufficient tailoring:** If standardized practices are tailored insufficiently or inappropriately, there will probably be adherence to suboptimal practices or unsupported deviations from the preferred practices.
- **Failure to evolve the approach:** If the approach to software product lines is not continuously improved over time, practices will probably become ineffective, and unsupported deviations will crop up out of necessity.
- **Ineffective dissemination:** If there is an inappropriate level or type of documentation, inadequate training, or ineffective support, the product line launch will not be likely to take effect in the planned form or produce the desired outcomes in the required time frame.

6.5.6 Discussion Questions

1. Successful launching of a product line involves buy-in across the organization. What people or groups in particular need to buy in, and what would you do to ensure their enlistment?
2. Product lines can be launched from upper, middle, or grassroots levels within an organization. Suppose you are promoting the launch from each of these levels in turn. What would you do? How would you enlist the necessary support, and from whom?
3. How does launching a product line relate to the business case for the product line? Think in terms of convincing upper management of the wisdom of adopting the approach.
4. Few companies can afford simply to shut down their product development efforts while they make the switch to a product line approach. Discuss how you would phase in a product line approach even while products continue to be planned, developed, and shipped.
5. Launching a product line approach suggests bringing new products into the product line paradigm. Discuss how you would handle products that are already in the field. Would you try to make them part of the new product line? On what basis would you decide?
6. How do launching and institutionalizing a product line relate to structuring the organization? And how do they relate to market analysis? For both questions, think about using information to decide how to phase in the product line approach.
7. Resistance to adoption of the product line approach can come from almost anywhere, but we observe that it often shows up at the middle management level. Many times the folks in the trenches recognize the benefits of doing things the new way because they're the ones who are tasked with implementing and reimplementing almost identical applications multiple times.

Conversely, senior management tends to have the vision and see the financial bottom lines. Discuss. Do you agree or disagree?

8. Sketch an adoption plan for your organization or for a hypothetical organization adopting the product line approach. Assign a pilot, and give every part of the organization something to do while the pilot is underway. What activities should those on the sidelines be given to ensure their participation?

6.6 Market Analysis

Market analysis is the systematic research and analysis of the external factors that determine the success of a product in the marketplace. It involves the gathering of business intelligence, competitive studies and assessments, market segmentation, customer plans and strategies, and the integration of this information into a cohesive business strategy and plan. For the purpose of this practice area, we will define "market" as the place where people meet for the purpose of trade. Those involved include sellers, buyers, prospective customers, providers of complementary products or services, competitors, and any other party that "participates" in the day-to-day conduct of business transactions.

Organizations conduct market analysis as a means of characterizing quantitatively the business opportunity for their products. From this analysis flows the statement of organizational objectives for cost, quality and productivity, and any associated constraints. Based on this analysis, a business case, strategy, and plan can be developed. The goal of the analysis is to provide sufficient detail to answer the fundamental question: "Does the market represent sufficient economic potential for us to achieve our business goals with this product?"

Even defense organizations considering the procurement of a military system must ask themselves a version of this question. While some commercial market analyses may slip in colorful military metaphors (such as "doing battle with the competition"), these terms are literal for defense groups. For them, a market analysis becomes a "mission" analysis; the competition is referred to as the "threat" or (less obliquely) "the enemy." Time-to-market becomes time-to-deployment, time-to-field, or time-to-operational-readiness. Competing systems are the "counterforce." And whereas return on investment (ROI) is not the overriding business goal, effectiveness and protecting the war fighter are. Such a document may look very different from one produced in a software start-up company looking for venture capital, but the need for it is the same: to answer the question: "Will this product be successful?"

Not surprisingly, market analysis provides a fundamental input to the business case for a product.

Because markets change and evolve, a market analysis should be a living document that guides the decision making throughout the life of the product or products included in its scope. Many organizations couple their ongoing market analysis with an annual planning and budgeting cycle, so that product development and evolution priorities are explicit and integrated into the plan.

6.6.1 Aspects Peculiar to Product Lines

A market analysis is an important ingredient in a decision to shift business strategy from single-system engineering to product line engineering. The market analysis informs the business case, and together these two documents form the basis of the decision package used by management to justify the shift in strategy. Once a product line engineering organization has been established, a market analysis is conducted on a continuous basis to guide the introduction of new products into the product line, to steer the evolution of the product line as a whole, and to oversee the spin-off of related product lines.

The "Building a Business Case" practice area (Section 6.1) relies on business assessments of forecasts, market share, and pricing and highlights the relationship between the market analysis and the organizational need for the business case. This is as true for the ongoing product line operation as it is for the organization making the decision to shift strategy to a product line operation.

In a product line organization, responsibility for the market analysis lies within a strategy formulation or business development function or with the individual responsible for the success of the business unit or product line—whether general manager, product line manager, or product manager.

While engineering and R&D personnel will certainly contribute, they would not normally take responsibility for market analysis. In this way, organizations avoid building products for which there is no market or building elegant solutions before searching for a problem. In a similar way, the sales organization is a significant, but often optimistic, contributor to the analysis because it knows the market. A sales contribution might provide the answer to some key questions, such as:

- "Given a set of products with *these* rough distinguishing capabilities available around *these* dates with a projected price targeted for about *these* amounts, how many of each product in the product line can you sell in Year 1? Year 2? Year 3?"
- "Can you commit to this forecast, and do you agree to be held accountable for its achievement? If not, what level of specificity is required for the capabilities and dates and amounts so that you will agree to such accountability?"

Answering these questions leads the market analyst to the answers to other questions, such as:

- "What customers or market segments will purchase which products?" Or, less concretely, "Which features or feature combinations are important for which customers?"
- "What are the similarities and differences in their buying patterns?"
- "What features are available, and how are they (or how might they be) configured for each product within the family?"
- "Who else offers products that overlap with our product line?"
- "What trends are observable in the market that may affect the answers to any of these questions?"

Armed with quantitative business goals and constraints, a characterization of the market requirement, and known engineering competencies, an organization can make informed decisions concerning the viability of introducing a product line or new products in a product line.

6.6.2 Application to Core Asset Development

Market analysis is one of the early steps that determines the product line scope—that is, what products the product line will comprise, suggesting a first-order approximation of the product line's commonality and variability. This, of course, leads to the architecture, which leads to the software core assets. The result of a market analysis helps provide a customer and product profile around which a focused R&D or engineering program can be designed. Core asset development or acquisition investment decisions are made within the context of customer or market requirements for the product, thus giving the engineering program a purpose.

Beyond this, however, the market analysis is itself a core asset, created when the product line is launched but maintained and updated as new members of the product line are considered, as the product line itself evolves, and perhaps as a new product line is spun off. In the last case, market analysis can be used to identify untapped market areas that a product line's existing core asset base is well-positioned to let the organization exploit.

6.6.3 Application to Product Development

The marketplace is an ever-changing environment, so market analysis needs to be an ongoing activity that continues through the product development phases. Market analysis helps the product developers factor other customer preferences into the product definition. The knowledge of customer preferences drives the decisions about features and feature combinations, as well as quality attributes such as performance, availability, and configurability.

A more detailed knowledge and understanding of the needs of specific customers or customer groups lead to decisions about the number of discrete products within the product line and how these discrete products are defined. Among specific products, there are choices of configuration. What features are selectable or definable by the customer? What is the range of options available for each product within the product line?

6.6.4 Specific Practices

A market analysis can be conducted by executing the following steps:

Identify information sources: The market analysis starts with the identification and location of any information resources that could have an impact or provide insight into the definition of the product line. In identifying these resources, it is important to consider some basic attributes of the resource or information being provided, such as: Is it accessible and reliable? Will it reveal valid needs or simply a fond desire? Is it relevant to the product line at hand? Sources of information include sales calls, meetings, conferences, customer services, newspapers and magazines, past performance, focus groups, surveys, consultants, budgets, published planning data, economic indicators, technology trends, and other intelligence sources.

Other Voices: Customer Value Analysis

Market analysis is about deciding whether or not the market will welcome the introduction of a product or set of products. Predicting what will be a crowd-pleaser is a tricky business that requires a little understanding of the crowd. A group of Oregon researchers provides us with a tool for analyzing the value in a product as perceived by a customer [Faulk 00].

> *Customer value analysis seeks to quantify value drivers that affect a customer's decision to buy a particular product. It seeks to identify and quantify all of the factors that affect a customer's buying decision including tangible attributes like features and price as well as intangible ones like prestige of ownership.*
>
> *The first step in the process [of determining customer value requirements] is to capture internal perceptions of customer-value requirements that are held by the developers, product management, marketers, sales representatives, customer service representatives, and top management. These perceptions are often the ones that end up being designed into the product. It is important that they are captured first to calibrate the development team's initial mindset.*
>
> *The second step is to survey customers. Participants are interviewed about their requirements, reactions to the product concept, competitive options, and price, among other issues.*
>
> *The third stage is to convene a team with representatives of each survey group to reconcile internal value perceptions with those of the*

customers. Because there is often significant divergence between what the design team has conceptualized and what the customers have articulated as their value expectations, this step is critical to aligning the development team's goal with actual customer values.

In our experience, the internal discussion of customer requirements most often focuses on product feature sets, performance specifications, and costs. Often, there is additional discussion concerning whether the product concept would enjoy competitive advantages over similar products. Rarely do internal discussions focus on what benefit the customer will receive or what factors are the most important in the customer's purchase decision.

Customers on the other hand, tend to not be feature driven in their decision making. Competitors often rapidly adopt a "me-too" approach to the feature set. This makes product features a poor candidate for differentiating products. Customers generally are able to form perceptions about how a product may benefit them. In addition, customers are particularly good at identifying the factors that are important to them in deciding which product to buy. It is precisely this perspective that should guide a business's software development decisions.

Gather information: The next step is to gather the information necessary to get a broad market definition, with additional details about specific segments that most closely align with the products within the product line. The analyst should assume that every contact with every customer, potential customer, user, competitor, or other market participant should be exploited for the information it can produce: requirements, a list of features liked/disliked, pricing, competitive trends, business goals and strategies, purchasing plans, budgets, and so forth. This broad market survey provides the product line organization with detailed knowledge and an understanding of the market, their potential customers, and the other market players.

Identify customer segments: Next, the analyst tries to focus on the product usage characteristics of specific customers to understand the similarities and differences. Through this study, distinctions among customers become evident, and generalizations about different classes of customers can be made and categorized. The analysis would show preferences for such things as price, configuration, availability, and technical approach. Other environmental concerns, on a product-by-product basis, would also result from the analysis of these segments: economic potential, the strength of the competition, standards, the rate and direction of technological change, and other key factors critical to the customer's decision to purchase.

Map products to segments: In light of this market information, a comparison can be made between the capabilities of each product or proposed product within the product line and the customer's expectations and requirements within each segment. Based on the degree of alignment between the products in the product line and the segments it was designed to satisfy, the analyst can formulate recommendations concerning the scope, magnitude, and direction of investments in the asset and the product development/acquisition activities of the engineering organization.

Examine the competition: The analyst can compare individual products in the product line with those offered by competitors. The purpose of this comparison is to evaluate similarities, differences, strengths and weaknesses, and competitive differentiators of the product line. Based on the outcome of this analysis, the organization can formulate recommendations concerning product development investments as well as product positioning relative to important competitors.

6.6.5 Practice Risks

If an adequate, thorough market analysis is not done, it is much more likely that the wrong products will be built—wrong in their overall configurations and in how they respond to customer or market requirements. An inadequate market analysis can result from the following factors:

- **Inaccurate forecast of market size:** If the forecast of the market size is inaccurate, the product line organization is likely to be unable to achieve a sufficient return on investment (ROI) from product line development. This could result from an inadequate analysis of the economic potential of the segment or from the organization's inability to penetrate the segment as a result of product weaknesses, unanticipated competitive strengths, or other compelling factors. When this situation occurs, the product organization must face the decision to pull the plug or to increase or redirect investments in the project.
- **Right product, wrong market:** Analyzing the wrong market—for example, by interviewing the wrong market groups—will result in an analysis that appears valid but in reality does not apply.
- **Right product, wrong price:** Having the right product but approaching the market with the wrong price, partners, suppliers, or sales channel can also be a risk. These factors can influence a product line's success or failure as much as the product itself can.

6.6.6 For Further Reading

Porter's *Competitive Strategy* [Porter 80] is required reading for anyone responsible for conducting market analyses. Also worthwhile is "The Core Competency of the Corporation" in *Harvard Business Review* by Prahalad and Hamel [Prahalad 90], in which they make clear the imperative of developing organizational capability to build products that align with market requirements.

6.6.7 Discussion Questions

1. Market analysis is rather like domain analysis in that both rely on first understanding what areas are relevant. How else are the two similar? What techniques from domain analysis can you bring to bear on market analysis?
2. What group in your organization would you assign the responsibility of market analysis? Why? What skills should the people in that group have?
3. Market analysis, scoping, and the business case for a software product line are intimately related to each other. Sketch a process model that shows how the groups carrying out these activities would interact with and inform each other.
4. The "Testing" practice area (Section 4.8) counsels that all core assets should be validated. How would you validate a market analysis?
5. How does a market analysis relate to the "Organizational Risk Management" practice area (Section 6.9)?

6.7 Operations

This practice area is about how business gets done; it is the engine that makes the organization run. Without it, the organization is mostly just a collection of staffed units, poised and willing to do the right thing, but unsure of precisely what that is. Any organization in the business of developing products operates under the aegis of its organizational and/or management strategies and policies, business processes, and work plans. Operations puts all of these items together into a coherent unified corpus of policies and practices. The vehicle for documenting these policies and practices is an *operational concept* [ANSI 92]. The operational concept

- describes the processes for fielding and maintaining the products from an operational perspective
- describes how the organizational units work together to execute these processes
- defines the role that acquisition will play and points to defined acquisition strategies and policies
- facilitates a common understanding among members of the organization as to how products are fielded and how the production capability is evolved and maintained
- serves as a baseline when the organization considers alternatives in its approach as warranted by changing conditions

6.7.1 Aspects Peculiar to Product Lines

With product lines, this practice area spells out how the organizational structure populates and nurtures the asset base and how it uses the asset base to build products. In Figure 3.1, which shows the product line's essential activities, operations tells how the wheels are set in motion, how the right information flows as suggested by the arrows, and how management orchestrates the entire business.

Operations breathes life into the organizational structure that was put into place to carry out product line activities. The "Structuring the Organization" practice area (Section 6.10) will position people in the right work units and assign them broad responsibilities, but without a clear definition of the operational concepts for building and running the product line, those people will flounder—or, at best, perform inefficiently. To borrow an assembly line analogy, structuring the organization is like telling automobile workers, "Stand right here and here and here. When parts come along, put them together so that an automobile comes out the end." That's not enough. Operations, on the other hand, will tell the workers how the pieces fit together and in what order, what to do when the right pieces aren't in place or don't fit together, how to report pieces of poor quality, how to make suggestions for improvement, how to interact with workers standing at stations near theirs, and what they are and are not allowed to do (for example, not bending the pieces to make them fit together). Both structure and operations are necessary for the assembly line to roll out quality products.

Operations describes how and which organizational units

- produce and evolve assets according to those assets' work plans and evolution plans,
- define and evolve the production plan, and
- use the assets and production plan to field products.

Someone, usually the product line manager, needs to own the operational concept, make sure it's well documented and effectively communicated, employ appropriately matched staff, and ensure that they are carrying out the product line operations.

6.7.2 Application to Core Asset Development

For core asset development, operations defines what plans, processes, strategies, policies, and constraints the core asset developers will carry out to do their jobs, and how they will be managed. Therefore, the operational concept for core asset development captures the decisions made by the organization in the following areas:

- The organizational elements and the role each of them plays relative to the core assets

- The core asset development activities moving from scoping through requirements engineering, architecture definition, component development, commercial off-the-shelf (COTS) utilization, mining of assets, testing, and software integration
- The strategy for maintaining the core asset base: the process for creating new assets, modifying existing assets (including changing the architecture), and declaring assets obsolete
- Specific guidance for supporting the shared responsibilities for core asset sustainment, to guarantee the use of the architecture and assets in producing products and the reflection of that use back into the product line assets for their continued improvement

6.7.3 Application to Product Development

For product development, operations defines what plans, processes, strategies, policies, and constraints the product developers will carry out to do their jobs and how they will be managed. Therefore, the operational concept for product development captures the following decisions that are made and assets that are produced by the organization:

- organizational elements and the role each of them plays in product development
- the product development activities moving from product qualification through requirements engineering, architecture definition, component development, COTS utilization, mining of assets, testing, and software integration that are all necessary for using core assets in the development of individual products
- the strategy for maintaining the products and coordinating that maintenance with the evolution of the core assets, including configuration management policies and processes
- specific guidance for feeding back the results of using core assets in product developments to support their continued improvement

6.7.4 Specific Practices

Creating a product line concept of operations (CONOPS): One way to document the operational concept is to develop a formal product line concept of operations (CONOPS). An organization develops this document to establish the desired product line approach that it wishes to take. The CONOPS documents the decisions that define the approach and the organizational structure needed to put the approach into operation.

Other Voices: Incentives at Toshiba

[Toshiba] management relied on an integrated set of incentives and controls to encourage project managers and personnel to take the time to write reusable software parts and reuse them frequently. At the start of each project, managers agreed to productivity targets that they could not meet without reusing a certain percentage of specifications, designs, or code. Design review meetings held at the end of each phase in the development cycle then checked how well projects met reuse targets, in addition to schedules and customer requirements. At the programmer level, when building new software, management required project members to register a certain number of components in the reuse databases, for other projects. Personnel also received awards for registering particularly valuable or frequently reused modules, and they received formal evaluations from superiors on whether they met their reuse targets. The [development environment tool], meanwhile, monitored reuse levels as well as deviations from targets both at the project and individual levels, and sent regular reports to managers. [Cusumano 91, p. 265]

The more conventional purpose of a CONOPS is to represent the user's operational view for a system under development. This operational view is stated in terms of how a system will operate in its intended environment. In the case of fielding a product line, we are discussing a business process rather than a system; the users of that business process include a wide range of stakeholders for the product line. The CONOPS for that process will accomplish much the same purpose as a CONOPS for a system by describing how the mission or purpose of the product line will be fulfilled, the environment for fielding the product line, and the organizational structure to support product line fielding.

All of the items listed above are essential elements in the operational concept. The CONOPS relates a narrative of the process to be followed in fielding the product line, including the roles of the various product line stakeholders involved in the process. It also provides a forum for the exchange of information among the stakeholders on major technical and programmatic issues related to core asset development. The product line approach is not a case of "one size fits all." A CONOPS should include tailoring and change guidance to stay relevant to the organization's needs when unexpected situations arise.

Cohen provides specific guidance for developing a CONOPS [Cohen 99]. He suggests the following chapters and constituent sections for a CONOPS document:

- **Overview chapter:** The overview chapter of the concept of operations (CONOPS) should identify the product line and its context. It must establish the purpose of the CONOPS document, provide basic product line concepts,

and explain to readers why the organization is adopting a product line approach. This chapter should also establish the readership for the CONOPS and describe the document's organization. Sections include
  - Identification: Identifies the product line and its context
  - Concepts: Provides some basic definitions of concepts behind the approach
  - Product line variation: Discusses parameters of the product line development (how development is accomplished, shared responsibilities, the nature of the product line, balance between new and legacy content, and so on)
  - Readership: Explains the message the CONOPS delivers to each stakeholder and provides an overview of contents
- **Approach chapter:** This chapter of the CONOPS should introduce the product line approach for developing new systems. It should also introduce an organizational structure for developing product line assets and fielding the product line. The CONOPS should explain the role that a product line architecture and components will play in developing new product line products. Sections include
  - Developing new systems: Describes the specific approach the organization will take for fielding the product line assets and products
  - Organizational structure: Organization and basic tasks of product line roles
- **Product line background chapter:** This chapter of the CONOPS should describe the history of the product line and the reasons for moving to the product line approach. This description should identify specific developers of product line products or describe the characteristics of developers or products likely to be using product line assets. Sections include
  - Background of the product line: Activities in fielding the product line leading up to creation of the CONOPS
  - Rationale: Reasons for moving to the product line approach
  - Benefits: Benefits of adopting a product line approach
  - Challenges: Issues that must be addressed for successful introduction of the product line
  - Risks: Areas of risk that should be addressed in fielding a product line
- **Organizational considerations chapter:** This chapter of the CONOPS should describe some of the key organizational management issues associated with fielding a product line. To complete this chapter, an organization will have to address several of the key CONOPS issues. Also, there are specific start-up activities that must be initiated. Sections include
  - Product line champion: Describes identification of a champion who will assume responsibility for managing and facilitating the product line effort
  - Architecture-based development: Establishes a development process centered on software architecture to address common and mission-unique requirements

  - Impact of transition: Addresses the impact of change on organization, management, and acquisition elements
  - Support strategy: Explains roles played in the continued maintenance and enhancement of the product line
- **Technical considerations chapter:** This chapter of the CONOPS establishes the product line approach in detail. There are specific start-up activities that must be initiated, and the CONOPS must provide a recommended set of actions. Sections include
  - Phased implementation: Identifies phases in the process of fielding a product line
  - Roles and responsibilities: Describes roles and responsibilities for domain engineering and the relationship between the domain and application engineering organizations
  - Architecture definition: Establishes the significance of architecture for product line definition, component development, and product development
  - Identification and maintenance of assets: Defines activities required to identify and maintain product line assets, including COTS
  - Development and execution environments: Describes the role of the asset support group in producing environments for development of assets and for application support
  - Working with potential product line users: Describes the process for determining when a system is appropriate for development within the product line
  - Development process: Describes the process used to create assets and use them in developing products
- **Recommendations chapter:** This chapter of the CONOPS recommends the order in which steps should be taken in fielding the product line.

Marathon Man

Product line champions are where you find them, but one person who absolutely has to have a clear, coherent vision of the product line is the product line architect. And beyond having such a vision, the architect must be unwavering in his or her communication of the vision in the face of reactions that may well range from apathy to hostility. Why hostility? Because for pockets in the organization that are resistant to change, the architect will be seen as the vanguard of that change. Management may issue dictums and platitudes about how the product line approach will be good for the enterprise—and who could oppose shorter time-to-market and a fatter bottom line?—but the product line architecture is often the first sign to the product developers that it is definitely not going to be business as usual from this point on.

A sure sign of trouble in an organization striving to produce a product line is when the role of product line architect is unfilled. A second sign of trouble is when that role is filled but its occupant has no nominal authority over the architecture of the product line. And a third sign of trouble is when the role is filled, the occupant has titular authority, but no one is listening.

This story is about one organization that went through all three of these phases. The first phase was preceded by a period in which a loose committee was formed to hammer out a product line architecture. The committee had a chairperson who was a gifted designer but, owing to circumstances beyond his control, lacked the organizational presence to make his vision stick outside the committee (where it was needed to produce products). Both he and management needed to understand that his job didn't end when the architecture was drawn up. What he produced was essentially a restructuring of the organization's application libraries, which product builders, for the most part, weren't using anyway. Management was underwhelmed by the efforts and pulled the plug on the committee, which they had failed to sufficiently empower in the first place.

This organization still thought software product lines were the way to go, and tried again. Their second attempt fared better. Another individual was appointed to the job of designing a minimal product line architecture, which amounted to a set of common platform extensions that all products would be required to use. The goal was simple hardware portability. But unlike his predecessor, this architect grasped the big picture by understanding immediately that the platform extensions alone, while better than nothing, would not achieve the product line vision. He lobbied hard for a single architecture for every product in the product line, whereas at the time of his appointment a product's only obligation was to use the common extensions in whatever manner they saw fit. This architect grasped the essential difference between a true product line and products built with reuse. With a common architecture, products could become interoperable (a rich new capability they lacked before) and exploit application-level commonality among themselves beyond the realm of reusing the extended platform.

First, however, the extended platform had to be designed. The architect formed a design committee consisting of a few of the best designers in the domain plus representatives from several of the key product teams. Buy-in was always in short supply and thus foremost on the architect's mind. And over the course of several months, they produced a detailed design of that platform *that also included a picture of how a standard product that used the platform would be structured.* The architecture was, in it simplest form, layered; the topmost layer (L1) was product-specific; the second layer (L2) was composed of software generic to each of the half-dozen or so classes of products that would populate the product line. That is, a product would choose from one of several available L2 layers, depending on what kind of product it was. Lower layers formed the common platform. Well-defined interfaces and interaction mechanisms connected all the layers. (This is a standard scheme for a product line's software architecture.) The architect began to brief the architecture to management and to the product teams, always explaining the benefits of the grand vision. But he was also careful never to let the grand vision get in the way of the work at hand: after all, he would not be able to achieve that vision if he were removed from his position because short-term deadlines were not met.

Buy-in came gradually, and sometimes not at all. A gain in authority here means a loss of authority there, and those giving it up did not do so easily. Some members of the design committee, instead of assuming ownership of the architecture and becoming its proponents in their home groups, seemed to view their role as reporting to their home groups what that wacky design committee was up to now. The architect realized that his committee was not the group of protagonists they needed to be. He knew that some members were even telling their home groups that they didn't understand the new product line architecture—even though they had helped to craft it. He was dealing with a severe case of organizational inertia, and he tried to remedy it. In a series of meetings and e-mail messages, he tried to impress on the committee and on management the importance of the unified architectural vision. "If you feel we should not have one architectural model for the overall product line," he wrote, "please contact me." In other words, either get on board or step off the train now. "As a group," he wrote to the committee, "we need to be comfortable and confident with the architecture. I am leading this effort but not dictating it. However, I am adamant about having a single architecture (for the entire product line) that we all support and understand. We need to know the architecture like the backs of our hands if it is to work. We created it, and we will be the ones who understand it, teach it to others, and grow it."

Eventually, the overall architecture was embraced by management in the form of a reorganization whose work units reflected the structure of the architecture; the platform group and the project groups were now joined by a group responsible for turning out the L2 layer. However, they omitted a critical part of the equation when they failed to appoint a single individual to have overall architectural authority over products. Conversely, the L2 group was not clearly chartered, and confusion was the result. The new head of the L2 group wrote to the architect, saying, "Our group is starting to think about how to design this thing called L2. Your group seems to be the best place to start to think about such things. I'd like to make a presentation that shows how this work may fit into the overall architecture work being done by the design committee. I'd like to include a slide of the overall architecture in a presentation. Do you have one I could use?"

This *thing*? *Your* group seems to be the best place? *Starting* to think? This work *may* fit? The architect nearly threw a fit, and although his reply was composed, the message was clear: "The work you are describing is overall architecture work that is in the purview of the design committee." And he appended a copy of the design committee's scope to gently refresh the L2 leader's memory, and pointedly invited him to the next design committee meeting.

The reorganization should have been the final word in the adoption of the overall product line architecture. In fact, the wheels nearly came off of the whole effort at about the same time. Delivery pressure from some of the product groups caused management to embrace temporarily an expeditious but purely short-term approach: use as much code as possible from the current product set and get the products out the door. Later products could afford the luxury of the product line approach. And who better to lead this effort than a person of proven accomplishments? The architect was told to delay (or wrap up) his work on the architecture and begin porting code.

This was not the first time this organization had faced a crucible such as this; schedule pressures had previously been used as an excuse to delay implementation of product line practices. The architect would have none of it, because he knew that there would always be schedule pressures, and he knew that a true product line capability could never emerge in fits and starts. Rather than openly rebel against his management, to no good end, he saluted smartly and prepared for his new assignment. In a message to the design committee, product groups, and management, he accepted his new assignment with good graces but made sure the architectural vision did not die.

"As some of you have gathered," he wrote, "my project scope has narrowed considerably with respect to ownership of the overall product line software architecture definition. To this point I have been the lead architect. A meeting was held recently in which I was requested to transfer the responsibility of the overall product line architecture to my replacement. I wish him the best of luck and will implement his vision as it becomes defined. Along with leading the design committee, the following responsibilities accompany the lead architect role and will from now on be transferred to him: (a) lead design meetings; (b) develop and maintain the product line architecture and model; (c) communicate the architecture; (d) develop a training class for the architecture; (e) define the technology roadmap of the architecture; and (f) schedule and release dates of architecture. From this point on all questions pertaining to these issues should be addressed to my replacement. To the best of my ability I will help him transition into his new role."

Later, when the dust had settled, he explained his gambit to me. "As you can probably tell by the e-mail flying around," he wrote, "I have been doing my best to keep my company on one architectural path. I have been in extensive meetings with [upper management] and the [middle-level] supervisors. I could write a book alone on what has transpired here in the last couple of weeks. It all comes down to how we are to migrate to a complete product line and the fact that it does take several years to reach Nirvana. But as we migrate, we need to spit out applications at various stages along the way. The first of these junctures was just encountered in this new generation. Several non-product-line proposals were flying around such that the architecture would become a splintered, hacked in, ugly monster that would remain forever. It got to the point where I was completely out of architecture management for about the next 3/4 year. That is why I relinquished control of the design committee. Obviously the people who wanted to split off did not want to take the baggage of architecture management with them. I wanted to make a point that someone is always responsible for the overall architectural vision and the path to that vision. So I handed off the vision! It was at that point that I believe the lights in the managers' heads started turning on as to what they were about to do. I believe we are back on line, and I will explain more in detail as we unveil the plan. *The plan gives me technical responsibility to get the architecture done through all the layers for the pilots.*"

The architect had finally brought his organization through the three signs of trouble we described at the beginning of this story. The victory was not achieved overnight, but through it all he persevered in keeping his unerring vision for a single architecture—and a single source of architectural authority—for the entire software product line.

I have learned that this architect is a marathon runner in his nonprofessional life. This did not surprise me. Although personally I find the thought of running 26 miles horrifying, I understand marathon runners to be driven, disciplined, goal-oriented people who can see the future clearly, don't mind some temporary pain, and actually do their best when they hit what they call "the wall"—the point at which no sane person could possibly take another step. Clearly this architect had exactly the right qualities he needed to succeed in his task at this organization.

—PCC

Managing the operations: Suggested managerial practices for the product line manager include the following:

- defining and articulating the product line vision and promulgating it throughout the organization consistently and often—in fact, every day. This can be done by posting the vision in a publicly accessible location (such as an intranet Web site), crafting slide presentations to be given by organizational and technical managers, and discussing the vision at opportune times, from brown-bag lunches to management seminars.
- creating and posting both personal and organizational performance objectives that embrace the product line goals and strategies
- establishing promotion and reward structures that provide real benefits to individuals who follow the documented product line approach to build products, to individuals who contribute to the improvement of the product line effort, and to individuals who design and build assets that are in fact reusable

- communicating product line progress early, openly, and often
- removing from the critical path (or from the organization) those individuals who are barriers to product line success because of either a lack of productivity or a consistent lack of alignment with defined product line practices
- learning about technology change management, taking formal training if possible
- championing the product line at higher levels of management
- protecting the product line staff from unnecessary distractions, perhaps imposed by higher management or requested by overfamiliar customers, that do not further the product line effort
- ensuring stable funding for true "operation" of the product line. The funds must cover not only the development and evolution of the assets but also the entire supporting infrastructure.
- integrating efforts across organizational boundaries by relying on support and assets from other parts of the organization or other organizations

Developing scenarios: Scenarios can be provided to gain an understanding of the product line operations. The following tasks are examples for which scenarios may be produced:

- utilizing the product line architecture and other core assets to build a product
- developing product-specific assets
- submitting new or modified components to the asset base
- updating the asset base and migrating the changes into existing or in-development products
- determining whether a candidate product is on or out of the product line scope
- delivering product line systems to customers
- supporting the implementation and maintenance of the development and execution environments for product line systems

We know of one organization that casts these scenarios as a series of "A Day in the Life of . . ." vignettes. These vignettes make product line activities come alive for individuals or small groups of role players because they are focused and not loaded with information viewed as extraneous by any single individual. In some cases, the role players themselves are asked to draft the vignettes; this tests their understanding and encourages more enthusiasm and buy-in than scenarios dropped in from management above.

6.7.5 Practice Risks

An inadequate or inappropriate operational concept will result in the product line staff working at cross-purposes and in conflict with each other. Productivity (and morale) will drop, and (depending on the nature of the problem) core assets might not be used in the way they were intended, products might not be turned out as planned, and the product line will stagnate and die. An inadequate operational concept can result from the following:

- **Lack of management commitment and/or leadership:** Product line operations, most especially during the early stages of a product line effort, require leadership and commitment. A manager who simply dictates that product lines will be built but does not provide the requisite support, guidance, and encouragement will torpedo any product line effort. Similarly, commissioning the creation of operations processes but failing to follow through by endorsing the results and ensuring compliance (both immediate and long-term) is another way that management can kill a product line effort by half-measures. Setting in place an effective product line operational concept often requires culture changes and changes in the organizational structure. Only committed, proactive managers succeed in gracefully leading the organization through change.
- **Lack of the necessary ingredients:** Product line operations rely on the existence of plans, processes, strategies, and decisions relative to organizational structure, lines of authority, metrics to track, and so forth. Without these necessary ingredients, the operations will falter, the core asset and product wheels will not spin, and the information will not flow. We need to emphasize again that operations relies heavily on the outputs of other practice areas.
- **Failure to identify a product line manager:** Success of the product line requires strong visionary management. For most organizations, the nontechnical challenges alone will limit success unless one individual is given and embraces management responsibility. The technical activities involved in fielding a product line, from conceptualization to asset development and the production of the first products, may (in extreme cases) take several years during which the organization will be struggling to find its way along the new path. The manager must maintain the vision and keep the organization aligned with that vision during the period of change. In particular, the product line manager needs to oversee the development of the product line operational concept personally and obtain the buy-in of key stakeholders.
- **Failure to update the operational concept:** Operations will evolve, and so must its documentation. The operational concept must not become shelfware if the organizational engine is to keep churning efficiently. The operations and its documentation should be reviewed and revised constantly as the product line is fielded and the product line evolves. As a document usually produced early in the process of fielding a product line, the operational concept can provide only a starting point for product line development. The lessons learned in asset development, initial product development using assets, and sustainment of the assets must be incorporated. If the operational concept is not maintained, even though the operations may become ingrained, newcomers will not have sufficient orientation, and new managers will have a

tendency to undue what has become effective. Moreover, the product line may not evolve successfully to address new customer needs.

6.7.6 For Further Reading

There is an ANSI standard for preparing operational concept documents [ANSI 92]. Cohen updates the idea and applies it to product lines in a technical report [Cohen 99] that contains a generic product line concept of operations (CONOPS) that can be suitably tailored and adapted by an organization to meet its specific needs and circumstances. This generic CONOPS includes guidelines and scenarios to help an organization that has proposed a product line, provides a nearly complete example of a CONOPS for a product line approach, and details the class of information to be contained in each section of a CONOPS. The one section that an organization must write from scratch is the section that provides the background for its product line.

6.7.7 Discussion Questions

1. What is the relationship between operations and process definition? Between operations and technical planning? Between operations and organizational planning?
2. Who should be involved in writing the operational concept for a product line organization? How would you validate it?
3. Many people can promote the concept of a product line, but in nearly all of the highly successful product line organizations we have observed, there has been a single identifiable champion. What qualities do you think a product line champion should have?
4. Suppose that the product line champion—the most articulate, effective, persuasive spokesperson for the software product line approach—is not the product line manager. Could that work? What relationship should exist between the champion and the manager in that case?
5. It is said that the role of a product line champion is equal parts "cajoling, consoling, and patrolling." What do you suppose this means?

6.8 Organizational Planning

Organizational planning pertains to strategic or organizational-level planning. (For information on the foundations of planning, see the "Technical Planning" practice area, Section 5.6.) Organizational planning relies on these same foundations, but its scope transcends individual projects.

As discussed in the "Technical Planning" practice area, when considering the planning activity, it is useful to distinguish between the *process* by which plans are created and the *plans* that result from that process. The process for generating plans is often very similar regardless of the organizational level at which it is applied. The process should differ primarily by who is involved and the scope of the effort to be planned. For organizational planning, senior and mid-level managers are often primary participants. The scope of the organizational planning process should include planning for cross-project activities or activities that are outside the scope of any project.

Regarding the plans themselves, there are different types of plans for addressing different purposes. Examples of organizational management plans include organizational strategic plans, funding plans, technology adoption plans, and organizational risk management plans.

As discussed in the "Technical Planning" practice area (Section 5.6), a collection of interrelated plans is often more appropriate for accomplishing larger tasks than a monolithic master plan. Because of the broad scope of organizational planning, dependencies among these plans and subordinate project plans should be expected. These relationships should be an explicit part of the plans.

6.8.1 Aspects Peculiar to Product Lines

There is nothing fundamentally different about a planning *process* for product lines. However, there are certain types of organizational management plans that are unique to product lines. These plans include

- **product line adoption plans:** These plans describe how to transition an organization from its current way of development to a product line approach. (See the "Launching and Institutionalizing" practice area, Section 6.5.)
- **core asset funding plans:** Funding of the development and maintenance of the core asset base is likely to be done at the organizational level. (See the "Funding" practice area, Section 6.4.)

Besides these plans, other organizational plans that one might find in any development organization will decidedly take on a product line flavor. Organizational planning is used to facilitate the implementation of any of the technical management or organizational management practice areas that have organizational implementations. The major plans are associated with

- **configuration management:** In a product line effort, configuration management (CM) is more complicated and reaches across all of the core asset and product-building projects and possibly even across product lines. It is usually appropriate to plan configuration management at the organizational level.
- **tool support:** Tools are often considered core assets, and one of the savings a product line organization enjoys comes from using the same tool

environment across all of its product efforts. If common tool support is provided and maintained across products in an organization, it should be planned organizationally.

- **training:** Like tool support and CM, it pays to consider training at the cross-product level. An organizational plan for training should include course content, who provides it, who attends, a schedule, and resource allocation.
- **structuring the organization:** This plan will detail the transition steps and shifts in responsibility, outline any logistical or physical relocation, and assign schedules and resources.
- **risk management:** This plan will assign people to participate in the process, account for any training or other preparation required, and lay out an engagement schedule.

In addition to the plan dependencies that result from being at the organizational level, there will be additional dependencies owing to the product line approach. Organizational plans will have dependencies with project plans. Project plans will have external dependencies among other project plans. Organization-level plans may be necessary to coordinate project-to-project dependencies. In a product line context, the project plans can relate to core asset development, product development, or activities that cross between them.

6.8.2 Application to Core Asset Development

Organizational plans strongly related to core assets include those for

- **funding:** Typically, core asset funding issues must be addressed at the organizational level.
- **priorities for core asset development:** Especially when new assets are being developed, product development projects may have competing needs for when particular core assets become available. Organization-level planning may be necessary to resolve the conflicts.
- **configuration management:** In a multiple-project product line effort, it may be appropriate to plan the configuration management of core assets at the organization level.
- **risk management:** Typically, an organizational risk management process would include risks related to core assets. Mitigation plans might be needed to address some of these risks.
- **product line adoption:** A significant part of a product line adoption plan will be a description of how core assets will be created and maintained initially.

And, as is the case with technical (or project) plans, the organizational plans themselves (or parts of the plans) make fine core assets. Ideally, reusable plans should be tailorable in the same fashion as other core assets—that is, they have defined points of commonality and variability. Cost, effort, and schedule estimates may be useful candidates, particularly for reuse, as are work breakdown structures, goals, strategies, and objectives.

6.8.3 Application to Product Development

Typically, product development planning is handled below the organization level. Organizational planning would primarily provide constraints and priorities to guide project planning. Specifically, this might include

- **product line adoption:** The product line adoption plan should describe what initial product development will be accomplished (for example, which project or projects will serve as pilot efforts for launching the product line). Project-level plans would detail how this would be accomplished.
- **risk management:** Typically, an organizational risk management process would include risks related to product development. Mitigation plans might be needed to address some of these risks.
- **configuration management:** In a multiple-project product line effort, it may be appropriate to plan the overall configuration management at the organization level. Project plans would have to be compatible.

6.8.4 Specific Practices

Some characteristics of a good planning process and good plans are described in the "Technical Planning" practice area (Section 5.6). These characteristics are equally applicable to organizational planning.

6.8.5 Practice Risks

The primary risk is that the organization may fail to identify and effectively plan the activities that require organization-level planning, resulting in a muddled product line effort that will fail to meet its goals and expectations. Other risks cited in the "Technical Planning" practice area (Section 5.6) are also relevant to organizational planning.

6.8.6 Discussion Questions

1. Scenarios are often a good way to help uncover small pieces of a big picture. Discuss how scenarios might help in the creation of an organizational plan.
2. Pick some of the practice areas in which organizational planning practices play an important role, and sketch a plan for each.
3. How would you go about validating an organizational plan? Validate the ones you sketched for the preceding question.

6.9 Organizational Risk Management

Organizational risk management is risk management at the strategic level. A discussion of risk management concepts is presented in the "Technical Risk Management" practice area (Section 5.7), which describes the activities that are necessary for project-level risk management. An organizational risk management process relies on the existence of such project-level risk management and provides mechanisms for surfacing and managing risks that transcend, or are shared across, projects.

The seven principles of risk management are shown in Figure 6.6. These principles are divided into one core principle, three sustaining principles, and three defining principles. An effective risk management program exhibits characteristics of all seven principles.

Core Principle

- **Open communications:** An effective risk management process must encourage the free flow of information at and between all project levels. The process should enable formal, informal, and impromptu communication.

Sustaining Principles

Three sustaining principles allow an active risk management process to sustain its success in an organization.

- **Integrated management:** When risk management is treated as a "bolt-on" or side activity, team members become frustrated because managing

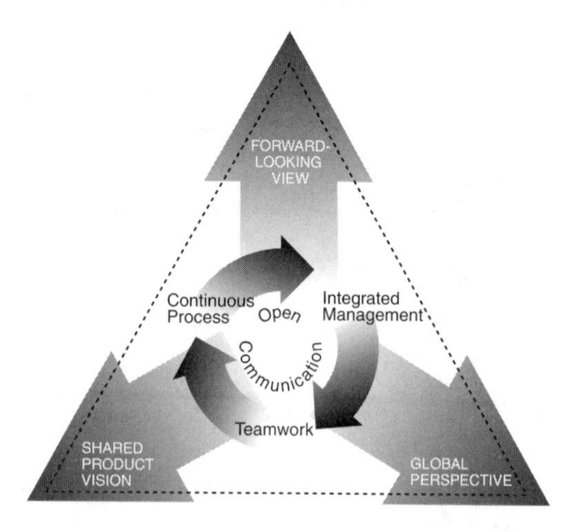

Figure 6.6 Seven Principles of Risk Management

risk is seen as interfering with their "real work." Teams performing risk management must integrate risk identification, analysis, and planning tracking and control into normal product line management activities and forums. As depicted in Figure 6.7, risk management is integral to project management.

- **Teamwork:** The success of any software development project hinges on good teamwork. Team Risk Management (see Figure 6.8) brings together groups with diverse and sometimes conflicting objectives and allows them to discuss risks that cross project boundaries, figure out which risks are most important to mitigate, and pool resources to lower the risk exposure facing all parties.
- **Continuous process:** The risks to an organization change constantly. The key to instituting a continuous process is to maintain surveillance of risks as they change and constantly identify new risks. Warren Keuffel warns against complacency [Keuffel 99].

> *A software development project's environment is constantly changing, as a result of competitive pressures, organizational strategy and personnel changes, and technical challenges. Too frequently, a risk management plan, like a system architecture design, is prepared at the beginning of the project and then shelved. To be valuable, risk management needs to be revisited as frequently as schedule and technical issues.*

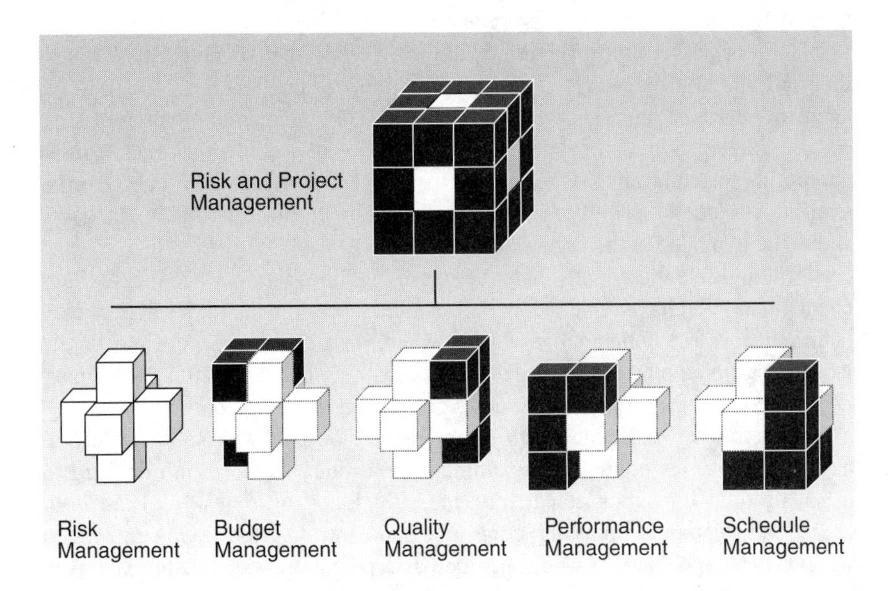

Figure 6.7 Risk and Project Management

Defining Principles

Three defining principles help to ensure success when working in a complex, multiproject environment.

- **Forward-looking view:** Everyone is focused on the same tomorrow. Inevitably, when dealing with multiple, interrelated projects, there will be conflicts in focusing on the same success point. The organizational management will need to keep all parties focused on the same success point.
- **Global perspective:** Everyone has the same definition of success. The definition of success from an organizational point of view may be lower operations and maintenance costs over a 20-year period. It's organizational management's responsibility to articulate the business goals clearly and define success from a global perspective.
- **Shared product vision:** Everyone sees the final capability as the same thing. The entire group of related developers, technical managers, and organizational managers must have a clear vision of where the organization is headed.

6.9.1 Aspects Peculiar to Product Lines

Product line efforts require a great deal of coordination across project boundaries, which makes well-defined organizational risk management practices essential. As the organization orchestrates the product line effort, risks are identified that affect multiple core asset developers and/or product developers.

The core asset and product development teams will manage the risks to their individual projects. (For more information, see the "Technical Risk Management" practice area, Section 5.7.) Each project management team will have cost, schedule, and technical objectives that are peculiar to the task each team is attempting to accomplish. When risks cross multiple projects or affect the organization's successful implementation of a product line approach, the risks should be managed at the organization level.

The multiple viewpoints endemic to product lines will surface in risk management and will have to be reconciled. For example, core asset developers may define success as meeting delivery dates, whereas product developers may define it as integrating the product and delivering capability to the end user. Both viewpoints are valid; the risk management process needs to "hear" both of them.

Sometimes two stakeholders on the same side of the product fence will have different viewpoints. For example, one military organization decided to use a product line approach to provide situational awareness tools to both embedded weapon systems and command and control systems. One embedded weapon system developer was concerned about weapon system safety and performance in a battle environment. This system developer could not accept immature products or products without rigorous testing from the core asset developers. In the course of managing the project, the developer identified the following risk:

> *The core asset development team does not test the situational awareness core assets adequately; we may receive immature products with major defects that can impact the operational effectiveness of our weapon system.*

A command and control development team wanted increased functionality and was willing to accept early deliveries of "beta" version assets. They promised their customer incremental deliveries of new capabilities to support an upcoming operational test. The command and control development team identified the following risk:

> *The development process used by the core asset development team takes too long to support our time-to-field requirements; we may miss critical delivery commitments.*

These two risks, identified by separate product development teams with different project objectives, point to conflicting mitigation approaches. Using a team risk approach, each of these individual risks would be elevated to the product line organization level, and mitigation strategies would be developed to address both concerns. The risk at the product line organization level might be

> *The development process used by the core asset development team is rigid, forcing a "one-size-fits-all" delivery and integration approach; the delivery of core assets to reusers may not support project-level objectives and ultimately fail to meet the user's needs.*

The complexity of managing the delivery of core assets to product development teams requires a management structure with mature methods and tools that can arbitrate conflicting needs and develop win-win solutions for the entire organization. Organizational risk management practices must provide proactive management methods and tools to help solve the complexities associated with implementing a product line approach.

6.9.2 Application to Core Asset Development

Core asset development teams should actively and continuously identify and manage risks associated with developing core assets for the product line. (For more information, see the "Technical Risk Management" practice area, Section 5.7.) When the risks also affect product development teams or other core asset development teams, they should be elevated, using a team risk approach, to the organization level. Core asset development teams need to understand the objectives of the organization's product line approach and work closely with product developers, other core asset development, and product line managers.

6.9.3 Application to Product Development

Product development teams should actively and continuously identify and manage risks on their projects. (For more information, see the "Technical Risk Management" practice area, Section 5.7.) When risks cross project boundaries and affect other product development teams or core asset development teams, they should be elevated, using a team risk approach, to the organization level. Product development teams need to understand the objectives of the organization's product line approach and work closely with core asset development teams, other product developers, and product line managers.

6.9.4 Specific Practices

The success of managing risk across several managed projects[3] depends on the existence of systematic and continuous risk management processes within the individual projects. All projects must work together to manage risk cooperatively throughout the development of the products and core assets. The result is a disciplined environment for proactive decision making among two or more projects. This is accomplished using a structure wherein personnel from multiple projects work together to share information about risks that may affect the other project(s) or the product line itself [Gallagher 99]. Creating such a structure requires a shared product vision, a global perspective, and a forward-looking view.

The organizational management team should develop and implement a risk management process to manage the uncertainties associated with implementing a product line approach. The team must also work closely with the product developers and core asset developers to help mitigate those risks within the control of the management team. At the organization level, the team will need to work with multiple project groups. Most of these projects will have unique project objectives and development processes, including perhaps different risk management processes. Because of these differences, the organizational management group needs to understand the basic principles that are characteristic of an effective risk management process. It is not adequate to understand only the risks facing a project or endeavor; rather, it is essential to couple reasoning about risk with an understanding of the project's ability to manage it. A project or organization with a healthy and mature risk management process is able to undertake more complex endeavors because it is able to recognize, discuss, and mitigate its highest risks.

One cross-organizational approach is Team Risk Management (TRM) [Dorofee 94]. This approach, shown in Figure 6.8, was developed originally to allow individual and shared risk management between a government organization

---

3. For this practice area description, it is assumed that the management of projects (core asset and product development projects) is coordinated at the product line organization level.

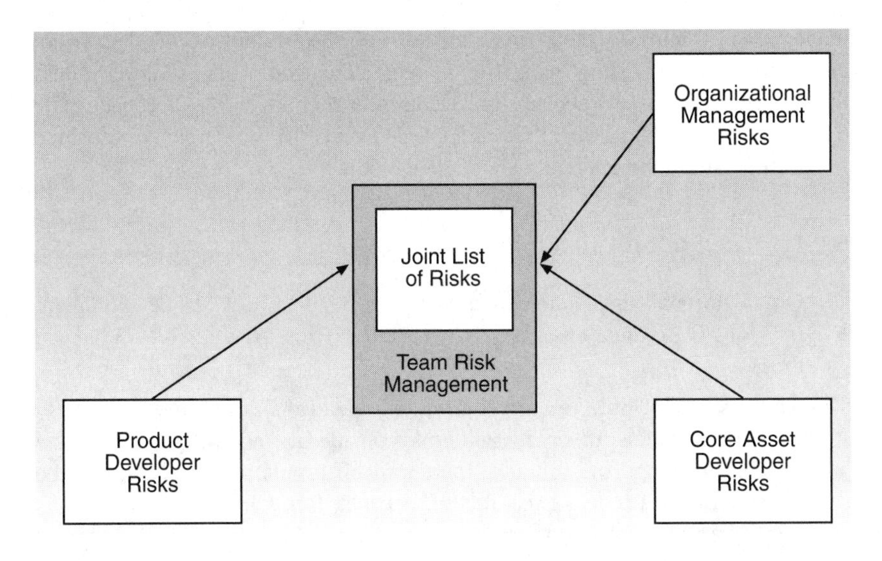

Figure 6.8 Team Risk Management

and a contractor organization. However, the basic principles are applicable to two projects or organizational structures that have mutual interests and shared risks. Simply stated, two projects could install the risk management practices just described. Then an overarching risk management process could be created to share risk management activities where appropriate.

6.9.5 Practice Risks

The biggest risk in managing uncertainties is creating an environment in which team members feel that they can't talk about risks. In his book on software disasters, Glass points out that one shared characteristic of failed projects is the inability of project members to communicate potential problems to the decision makers within a project. Seventy-two percent of failed projects had team members who knew of impending doom, while only 19% of the project managers on the same projects shared their insights [Glass 98]. Risk management allows team members to discuss potential problems in a structured, nonthreatening manner providing insight to decision makers.

The risks highlighted in "Technical Risk Management" (Section 5.7) also apply.

6.9.6 For Further Reading

Glass's *Software Runaways: Lessons Learned from Massive Software Project Failures* [Glass 98] is a wake-up call for those who believe organizational risk management is a luxury they cannot afford. The case studies of failed software engineering projects show what risk management would have averted. Glass imparts lessons learned and abstracts common themes and root causes. The SEI's *Team Risk Management Guidebook* [Dorofee 94] is an essential resource for starting and running a risk management effort.

6.9.7 Discussion Questions

1. Organizational risk management can apply to core asset development, but does it produce any core assets itself? (Hint: Absolutely!) What are they?
2. An outstanding time to carry out an organizational-level risk assessment exercise is when an organization is considering adopting, or has just decided to adopt, the product line approach for its products. This is the essence of the Product Line Technical Probe (see Chapter 8). What risks might be uncovered concerning the organization's ability to forsake old practices and adopt the product line paradigm?
3. In your organization, whom would you put in charge of installing and running an organizational risk management program? Is your answer the same as for a technical risk management program? Why?
4. The core principle of an effective risk management program is open communication. How would you make sure that your risk management efforts obeyed this principle?
5. The three so-called defining principles of risk management (forward-looking view, global perspective, and shared product vision) are all about making sure that everyone in the organization shares a similar mindset about the future. How would you go about establishing and supporting these principles in your organization?

6.10 Structuring the Organization

Organizational structure refers to how the organization forms groups to carry out the various responsibilities inherent in a product line effort. All organizations have a structure, even if it's only an implicit one, that defines roles and responsibilities appropriate to the organization's primary activities. Particular organizational structures are chosen to accommodate enterprise goals and directives, culture, nature of business, and available talent. The organizational structure reflects the division of roles, responsibility, and authority.

In a traditional organization (one that isn't oriented to product lines), individual product teams tend to be fully responsible for technical decisions affecting their products. Specialization might require each product to have its own development group, with no sharing of personnel. The role of the organization's management in this case is to gather and allocate resources and provide high-level oversight, all with the end goal of supporting product teams.

6.10.1 Aspects Peculiar to Product Lines

A product line approach entails new roles and responsibilities related to the creation of core assets and products from those core assets. This practice area deals with placing those roles into the appropriate organizational units to support effectively the product line approach.

Other Voices: People Power in the Japanese Software Factories

As recounted in Cusumano's *Japan's Software Factories* [Cusumano 91], the leader of System Development Corporation's software factory recognized that a core asset group leveraged the skill and experience of his best developers across every product in the family. We don't usually think of people as part of a software product line organization's core asset base—that is short-sighted; they are the most valuable core asset of all.

> *People reusability is almost as important as code reusability. It's clearly true in our business that the second time the same guy solves the same problem, he does it better . . . [W]hat the factory did was keep the people together in one organization. The same people were there the second time it came through, as opposed to doing it here one time, then reconstructing a team somewhere else another time—which is what normally happens with projects. So, in that sense [the factory] created a focus where all the software resources were in place, and therefore the managers managing at that point in time had the ability to reapply the people. They weren't dispersed, off working on somebody else's contract in some other location.*

In a product line context, the dual development of core assets and products dictates an organizational structure that is not product-centric. Beyond that, management must be concerned with identifying the organizational charter and boundaries, identifying functional groupings, allocating and assigning resources, monitoring organizational effectiveness, improving organizational operations, establishing interorganizational relationships, and managing organizational transitions.

Product line organizational structure goes hand in hand with product line operations (see the "Operations" practice area, Section 6.7), because it is the embodiment of the roles, actors, and responsibilities defined there. Both the structure and operations result from an overall vision of how the product line will operate on a day-to-day basis. The job of organizational structure is to make sure that each of the responsibilities and functions of the product line operations has a work unit in which to reside. An organizational structure should be chosen to at least determine which unit or units

- produce and maintain the architecture for the product line.
- determine the requirements for the product line and product line members.
- design, produce, and maintain the product line's core assets.
- assess the core assets for their utility and guide their evolution.
- produce products.
- determine the processes to be followed and measure or ensure compliance with them.
- maintain the production environment in which products are produced.
- forecast new trends, technologies, and other developments that might affect the future of the product line.

6.10.2 Application to Core Asset Development

A first-order choice that must be made when choosing an organizational structure is where to house the people who develop, maintain, and evolve the product line's core assets. Typically, organizations take one of two approaches: either they form a separate unit for the developers and maintainers of core assets, or they house that effort in the same unit or units that build products. [Bass 97, Bass 98b].

Both positions have their advocates. On one hand, having a dedicated component engineering group makes the component engineers one level removed from the pressure of project deadlines, making it more likely for them to produce truly generic components, not ones that are too biased toward the individual product that happens to be under development at the time. Their loyalty is to the product line, not to any one product. However, one of our workshop participants vigorously presented the counterargument: "A dedicated component group," he said, "will produce beauty, but not profit." Having product engineers produce the core software assets ensures that the assets will be truly useful. However, there must be someone with a cross-product perspective and authority who can identify the useful generic components for inclusion in the core asset base, and encourage (if not direct) the appropriate product group to produce that asset for use by other products.

When choosing whether or not to establish a separate core asset group, consider these factors:

- **The size of effort and number of products:** In a product line with many product groups and/or a large number of developers, distributing the core asset task results in an untenably high number of communication channels:

every product group will have to talk to every other one. In this circumstance, a dedicated core asset group will help.

- **New development or mostly legacy-based development:** In product line efforts wherein the core assets are built largely from legacy components, it makes more sense to have product developers (who will probably be more familiar with the legacy assets) be responsible for making the legacy assets more generic to fit the scope of the product line.
- **The funding model:** Funding a component engineering group can be problematic. Who pays for it? When working from legacy systems or when the product line approach matures, it may be hard to justify a separate component group when the product development groups are adding product-specific features to the core assets.
- **The high or low effort for tailoring core assets:** How much development has to be done to get from the core assets to the products? If the amount of tailoring and new development is small, it may make sense to have most people work in a dedicated fashion on the core assets. If producing products requires substantial tailoring and new development, the component engineering job is small by comparison, and integrated groups may be the answer.
- **The volatility of core assets:** Having core assets that evolve frequently and substantially argues for having a dedicated group to manage them, rather than overwhelming the product builders.
- **Parallel or sequential product development:** If products are built sequentially, it makes sense to have an integrated team working on them. When several product development projects are performed in parallel, there is a stronger need for a separate core asset group to avoid the multiple redevelopment of the same functionality.

An evolutionary organizational structure solves this dilemma essentially by having it both ways. The approach starts the product line effort without a core asset group so that the engineers can assume the full responsibility for turning out a real product under the product line paradigm. However, as soon as there are parallel developments in progress, product development is separated from core asset development. Other ways to address the problem include frequent staff rotation and processes that require close communication among the groups.

Whichever way this issue is decided, the product line core assets must be managed to bring long-term benefit to the entire organization, rather than to just one specific application. The organizational structure chosen for product line production must assign the decision-making responsibilities for these functions.

And while the management of the architecture, reusable software components, and component-related assets is an obvious product line responsibility that must be assigned to the right organizational unit(s), the management of nonsoftware core assets must be allocated also to achieve the full benefit of asset reuse. For example, where and how and by whom will product plans, schedules, and budgets be maintained for use across the product family?

6.10.3 Application to Product Development

Product line systems are developed and managed according to a life cycle that differs from the norm. The use of the existing architecture and components places greater emphasis on the integration of components and the testing of interfaces across components. For the unit or units assigned to product development, responsibilities include the following:

- Making sure that each new product uses the core asset base according to the production plan
- Working with the core asset owners to evolve new capabilities if the core assets are deficient in some way for a new product

The product unit(s) may also negotiate customer requirements to situate new products within the scope of the product line to the greatest degree possible, although some organizational structures assign the management of product line requirements to their own units.

The organizational structure must assign responsibility for these roles, as well as for the more traditional product development roles.

6.10.4 Specific Practices

Organizational models from a Swedish product line survey: After studying a number of product line corporations, Jan Bosch has designated four separate organizational models [Bosch 00b]:

- **Development department:** In this model, all software development is concentrated in a single unit. Each of the members is expected to be a jack-of-all-trades in the product line, doing domain engineering tasks or application engineering tasks when and as appropriate. This model appears in small organizations and those that provide consulting services. Although it is a simple model with short communication paths, it has a number of distinct drawbacks. Bosch wrote that it probably works only for units of up to 30 people. But in very small organizations whose product lines are commensurately small, it can be a viable starting-out approach. Figure 6.9 illustrates.
- **Business units:** Each business unit is responsible for a subset of the systems in the product family, which are clustered by similarity. Shared assets are developed by the business units that need them and are made available to the community; collaboration across business units to develop new assets together is possible. This model has variations depending on how

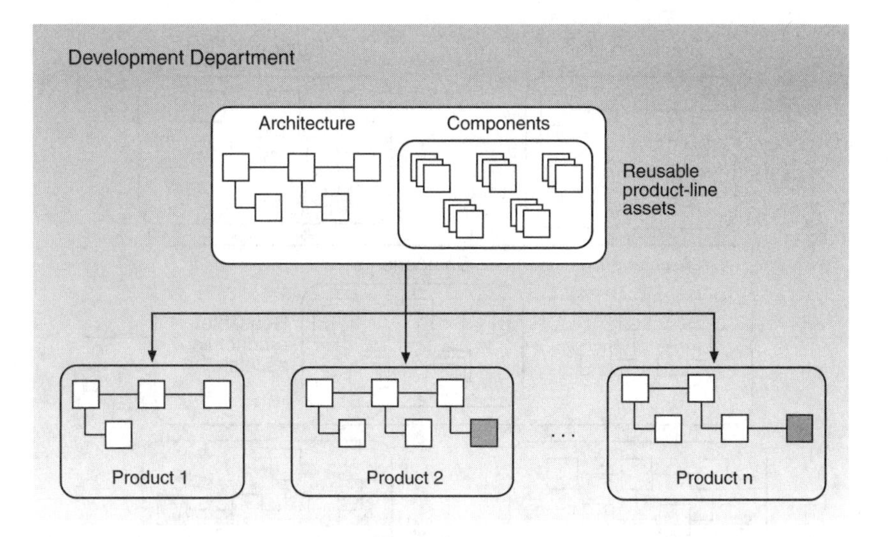

Figure 6.9 Development Department Model

much flexibility a business unit has in developing (or modifying) a shared asset. With no constraints, the products tend to spiral off on their own evolution paths, negating the product line approach. At higher levels of maturity, the responsibilities for particular assets are assigned to specific business units; they are constrained to maintain their assets for the general use of the entire product line, and other business units are required to make use of them. Bosch estimates that this model could apply to organizations with 30 to 100 employees. This model suffers from the obvious risk, mentioned above, that a business unit will focus on its own product(s) first, and the good of the product line will take a back seat. Figure 6.10 illustrates.

- **Domain engineering unit:** In this model, a special unit is given responsibility for the development and maintenance of the core asset base. Business units build the products using those assets. Bosch writes that when organizations exceed 100 employees, the *n*-to-*n* communication channels among separate business units become untenable, and a focusing channel to a central shared asset unit becomes necessary. In this model, a strong and disciplined process becomes much more important in order to manage the communication and ensure that the overall health of the product line is the end game of all parties. Figure 6.11 illustrates.
- **Hierarchical domain engineering units:** In a product line that is very large and/or very complex, it may pay to regard it hierarchically. That is, the product line may consist of subgroups that have more in common with each other than with other members of the product line. In this case, there may be a domain engineering unit to turn out shared assets for the product

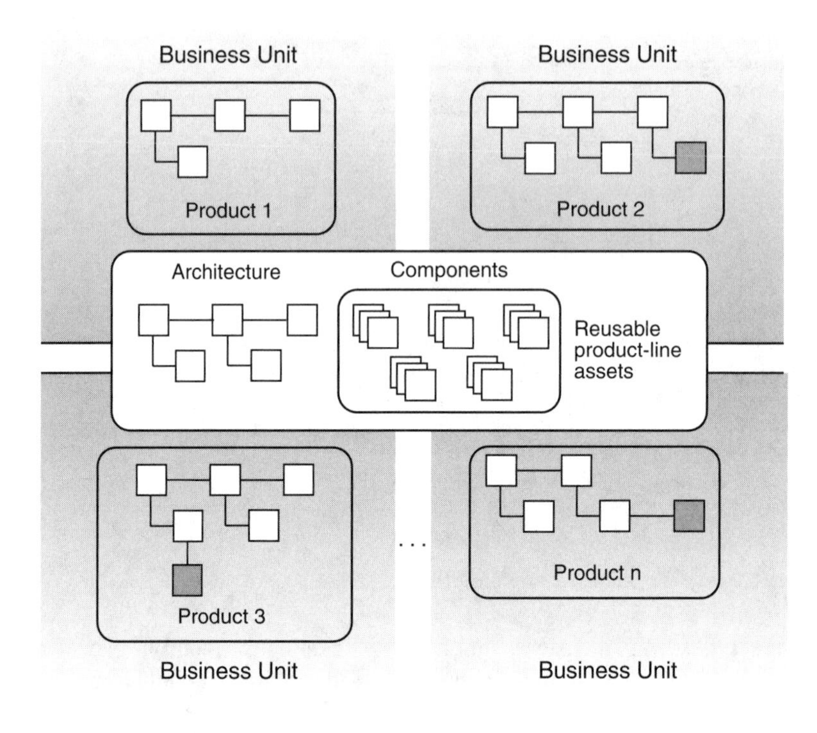

Figure 6.10 Business Unit Model

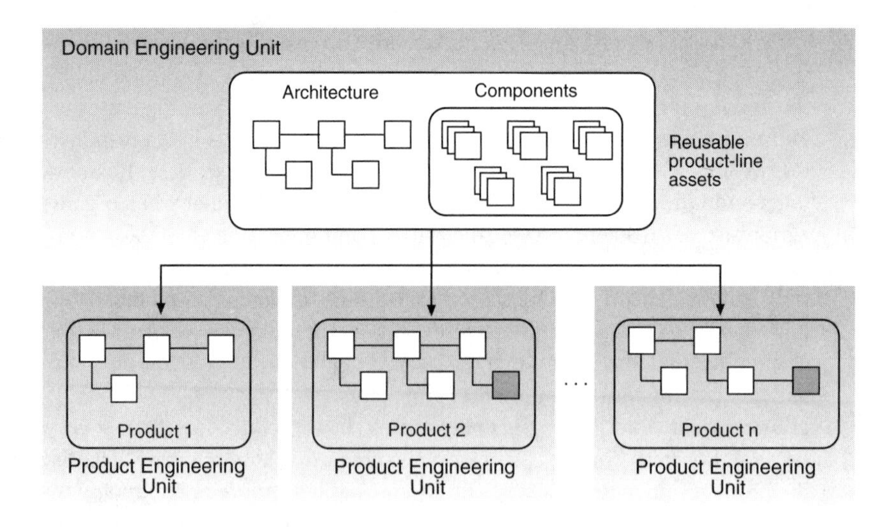

Figure 6.11 Domain Engineering Unit Model

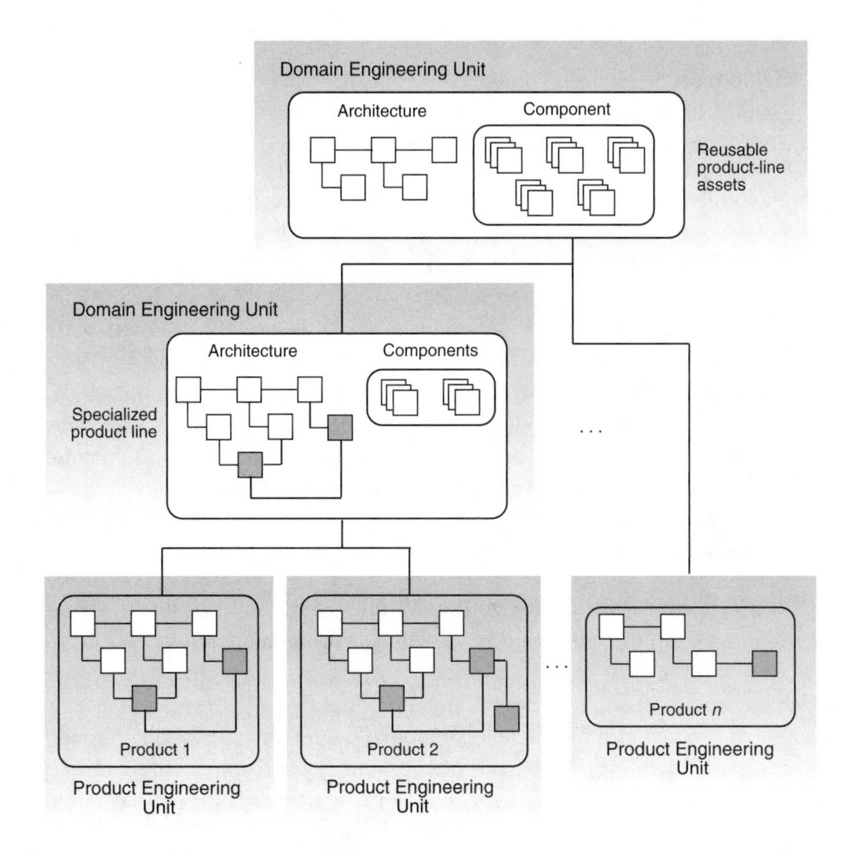

Figure 6.12 Hierarchical Domain Engineering Unit Model

line at large and another domain engineering unit to turn out shared assets for the specialized subgroup. This example has only two levels, but the model could be extended indefinitely if the subgroup had a specialized subgroup within it, and so forth. This model works for very large product lines built by very large organizations. Its main disadvantage is its tendency to bloat, reducing the organization's responsiveness to new needs. Figure 6.12 illustrates.

Organizational structure for a reuse business: Jacobson et al. call for organizing a reuse-based business around a set of competence units, which contain "workers with similar competencies and entity object types that these workers are responsible for" [Jacobson 97, Chapter 9]. They prescribe the following units:

- Requirements capture unit
- Design unit

- Testing unit
- Component engineering unit
- Architecture unit
- Component support unit

The component support unit is responsible for "packaging and facilitating the reuse of component systems, and [is] mostly concerned with maintaining the facades and distributing the component systems so that reusers can access the desired components" [Jacobson 97].

Workers from these competence units are drawn to form an application family engineering team, one or more component system engineering teams, and a group of application system engineering teams. Application family engineering is where product line decisions are made, deciding which applications to develop and when. It also crafts the broad product line architecture. Component system engineering is responsible for the detailed architecture and design of a component system. Application system engineering builds products for individual customers.

Small, distributed core group with component reps: In choosing whether the core asset group is separate or distributed throughout product groups, at least one company we know has opted for a hybrid approach. This company, which has about 50 employees building a product line of information systems, has a set of product groups that revolve around a small but central core group. In this model, the core group is responsible primarily for common support activities, such as configuration management, the maintenance of the core asset base, some process definition, and the like. An architect for the entire product line would also normally reside in this group; but in this company, the architecture is not being evolved, and the architect has been reassigned. In each product group, there is a component representative who has the joint responsibility for ensuring the use of core components and for creating and evolving the software core assets. A strict protocol in which any candidate for inclusion in the core asset base must have at least two component representatives sponsoring it, is enforced. This ensures its reusability across at least two products.

Evolving organizational structures: The CelsiusTech organizational structure evolved as its product line matured and evolved. See "Other Voices: CelsiusTech's Evolving Organizational Structure" sidebar.

Other Voices: CelsiusTech's Evolving Organizational Structure

Here, from the original CelsiusTech case study [Brownsword 96], is how CelsiusTech's organizational structure evolved as their ShipSystem 2000 (SS2000) software product line matured.

Previous Project Organization

The previous development efforts for the naval command-and-control system (Mk2.5) were headed by a project manager who used the services of various functional areas, such as weapons or C3, to develop major segments of system capability. The figure below shows the organizational structure used during the Mk2.5 period. Each functional area was in turn led by a functional area manager who had direct authority for staff resources and for all system-development activities through release to system integration. Functional area managers did not report to the project manager in terms of line responsibility but were lent to the project. CelsiusTech found that this compartmentalized arrangement fostered a mode of development characterized by

- assignment of major segments of the system to their respective functional areas as part of system analysis.
- requirements and interfaces allocated and described in documents with limited communication across functional area boundaries. This resulted in individual interpretations of requirements and interfaces throughout design, implementation, and test.
- interface incompatibilities typically not discovered until system integration, resulting in time wasted assigning responsibility and protracted, difficult integration and installation.
- functional area managers having little understanding of the other segments of the systems.
- limited incentives for functional area managers to work together as a team to resolve program level issues typical of any large system development.

SS2000 Organization, 1986 to 1991

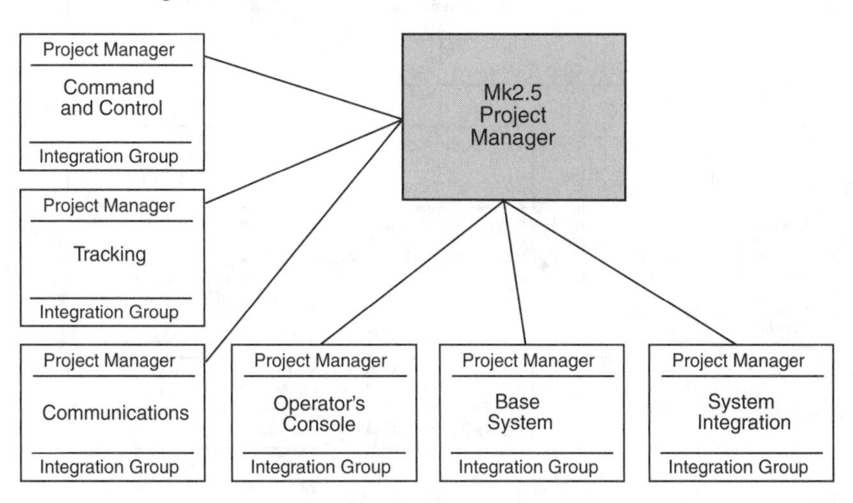

CelsiusTech's Mk2.5 Project Organization from 1980 to 1985

With the advent of the SS2000 product line in late 1986, a number of organizational changes from the Mk2.5 project organization were put into place. The figure below shows the organizational structure that CelsiusTech used from 1987 to 1991 for the creation of the product line. A general program manager was designated to lead the program. He was responsible for both the creation of the product line and the delivery of customer systems built in the product line. CelsiusTech sought to remedy the problems associated with the compartmentalized structure of the past by creating a strong management team focused on the development of the product line as a company asset rather than on "empire building." To this end, functional area managers now reported directly to the general program manager. Developers were assigned to functional areas (weapons, C3, or MMI), common services (used by the functional areas), or the Base System.

A small, technically focused architecture team with total ownership and control of the architecture was created. The architecture team reported directly to the general program manager. CelsiusTech determined that the success of a product line hinged on a stable, flexible, and viable architecture, requiring visibility to and authority from the highest levels of management.

CelsiusTech identified the coordinated definition and management of multiple releases as central to the creation of a product line and determined that high-level management visibility was essential. To improve support for their release management, CelsiusTech combined the software/system integration and configuration management (CM) activities into a new group, reporting directly to the general program manager. Both the architecture team and the

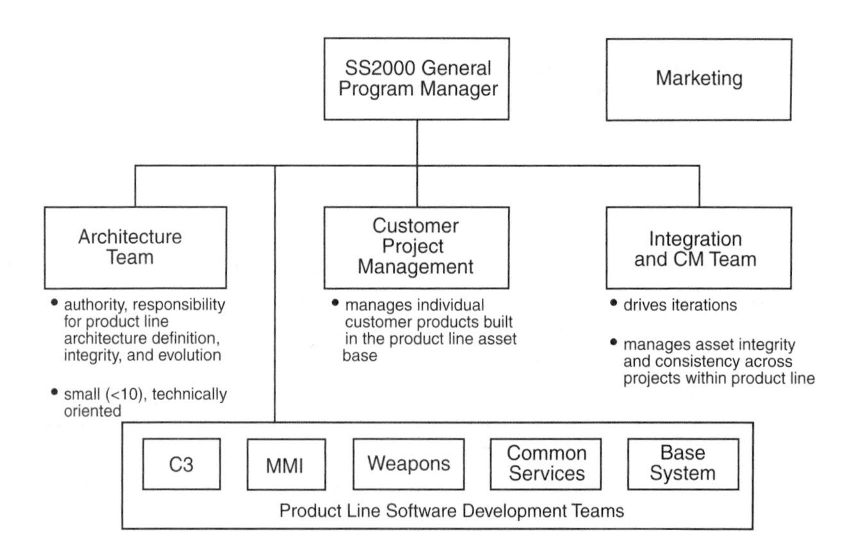

CelsiusTech's SS2000 Organization from 1987 to 1991

integration/CM group were novel approaches for CelsiusTech and factored heavily in the creation of the SS2000 product line. Each is further described below.

The architecture team was responsible for the development of the initial architecture and continued ownership and control of the product line architecture, thus ensuring design consistency and interpretation across all functional areas. Specifically, the architecture team had responsibility and authority for

- creation of the product line concepts and principles
- identification of layers and their exported interfaces
- interface definition, integrity, and controlled evolution
- allocation of capability and system functions to layers
- identification of common mechanisms or services
- definition, prototyping, and enforcement of common mechanisms such as error handling and interprocess communication protocols
- communication to the project staff of the product line concepts and principles

The architecture team was not a committee or an engineering review board. Rather, the team was a small group (10) of full-time senior engineers with extensive domain and engineering experience. The first iteration of the architecture was created by two senior engineers over a two-week period and remains as the [foundation] for the existing product line. The first iteration included the organizing concepts and layer definition, as well as identification of approximately 125 system functions (out of the current set of 200), their allocation to specific layers, and the principal mechanisms for distribution and communication. After completion of the first iteration, the architecture team was expanded to include the lead designers from each of the functional areas. The full architecture team then continued to expand and refine the architecture—in sharp contrast to the past, when functional areas had autonomy for the design and interfaces for their areas.

The combined integration and CM team was responsible for

- development of incremental build schedules (in conjunction with the architecture team)
- integration and release of valid subsystems
- CM of development libraries
- CM of customer release libraries
- development of test strategies, plans, and test cases beyond unit test
- coordination of all tests runs
- creation of software-delivery medium

For the SS2000 program, the integration and CM functions were centralized rather than distributed as in the Mk2.5 systems. The combined integration and CM team was not an organizational artifact in which two functions were "co-located" under the same manager. CelsiusTech redefined these functions into a fundamentally new entity to support the continual integration aspect of its development approach more effectively. Developers no longer controlled the CM of their development artifacts. Rather, the combined integration/CM team managed and controlled development and release libraries. Senior development engineers formed the core of this group. Integration and CM were not merely clerical functions, but a foundational engineering function, and the integration/CM team performed it accordingly.

SS2000 Organization 1992 to 1994

From 1992 to 1994, the emphasis increasingly shifted from the *development* of the architecture and product line components to the *composition* of new customer systems from the product line assets. This trend increased the size and responsibilities of the customer project management group. CelsiusTech modified its organizational structure to assign the development staff to one of the following:

- Component projects that developed, integrated, and managed product line components. The production of components was distributed across component project areas consisting of the functional areas, such as weapons, command and control, and the human-computer interface; common services; and the Base System 2000, which was the underlying operating system. Component project managers were rotated regularly, providing middle management with a broader understanding of the product line. The components are provided to the customer projects.
- Customer projects that are responsible for all financial management, scheduling and planning, and technical execution from requirements analysis through delivery for their customer's product. Each customer system built in the product line was assigned a project manager who was responsible for all interactions and negotiations with the project's customer. Project managers were also required to negotiate customer requirements across all product line users.

The architecture team and the integration and CM team remained. The former became responsible for managing the disciplined evolution of the product line assets; the latter handled all test, integration, and delivery functions.

SS2000 Organization Since 1994

As CelsiusTech completed the basic product line asset base and gained further experience using it, it has moved to the identification of more efficient ways to produce systems and tailor the product line to take advantage of newer technology and changing customer-mission needs. This resulted in the 1994 organizational structure shown in the figure above.

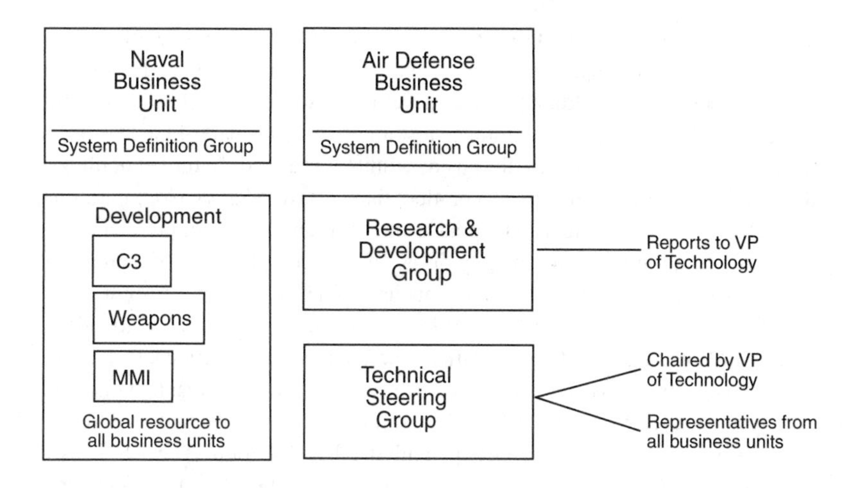

CelsiusTech's SS2000 Organization Since 1994

Each major application domain (naval and air defense) became its own business unit with its own manager. Each business unit has a marketing group, a proposal group, customer projects, and a systems definition group. The business unit owns the components and customer project managers. Each business unit's operations are guided by a set of consistent plans: marketing, product, and technical/architecture. The marketing group is responsible for the marketing plan that describes the business unit's marketing opportunities and value of each market segment. The product plan describes the products that the business unit sells and is owned by the proposal group. The product plan implements the marketing plan. The system definition group is responsible for the technical/architecture plan for its business unit. The technical/architecture plan in turn implements the product plan, outlining the direction for evolution of the business unit's architecture. New project proposals take into account the business unit's product plan and technical/architecture plan. For the naval business unit, this approach keeps the projects aligned with the product line.

Components are supplied by the Development Group. Any customer-specific tailoring or development is managed from the business-unit customer project using development resources matrixed from the Development Group.

The business unit's Systems Definition Group is responsible for the architecture. This group owns and controls the evolution of the architecture and major interfaces and mechanisms. For the Naval Business Unit, the Systems Definition Group is a small group (typically six members) of senior engineers with extensive knowledge of the naval product line. The group remains responsible for overall arbitration of customer requirements and their effect on the product line.

The Naval Business Unit has created a SS2000 Product Line Users Group to serve as a forum for shared customer experiences with the product line approach and provide direction setting for future product line evolution. The users group includes representatives from all SS2000 customers worldwide.

The Development Group provides developer resources to all business units. Integration, CM, and quality assurance resources are also a part of the Development Group and are matrixed to the business units as required. To further optimize the creation of new systems from a product line, a Basic SS2000 Configuration Project was recently formed. The goal is the creation of a basic, preintegrated core configuration of approximately 500K SLOC, complete with documentation and test cases that would form the nucleus of a new customer system.

The Technical Steering Group (TSG) became responsible for identifying, evaluating, and piloting potential new technology beneficial to any of CelsiusTech's business areas. The TSG is headed by the vice president of technology and staffed by senior technical personnel from the naval and air defense business units, Development Group, and the R&D Group. The TSG also ensures that each Systems Definition Group creates and evolves their architecture and technology plan.

6.10.5 Practice Risks

There are two major risks associated with structuring the organization to efficiently turn out a software product line. The first is choosing a structure that is inappropriate for the organizational context at hand. An inappropriate structure—one that doesn't match the talent base and/or the culture of the organization—will cause the organization to fail to achieve the compromise between building overly generic assets that are too general or expensive to serve any specific product and product-specific software that is too customized to serve in a product line. Choosing a reasonable organizational structure and putting in ample feedback and communication mechanisms will go a long way toward working out the generic/specific compromise that will let the product line succeed.

The second major risk is changing the structure in an inappropriate fashion. This will result in a disenfranchised staff, an atmosphere of turmoil and uncertainty, poor product quality, and missed production deadlines. Change requires planning and the execution of change management techniques. Some key success factors in implementing structural change according to Myers and Maher are described below [Myers 90a]. Failure to account for any of these factors constitutes a risk.

- **The current level of organizational stress:** How much stress is the organization currently under as a result of previous changes or other stress-inducing factors?
- **The implementation history:** How effective or ineffective has the organization been in effecting change in the past?

- **Sponsorship:** How effective is the key executive in obtaining commitments to change, communicating the support for change, and managing change?
- **Resistance management:** How will the organization address the inevitable resistance to change?
- **Culture:** Does the proposed change conflict or align with the organization's values, behaviors, and unwritten rules?
- **Change agent skills:** Are the change managers and staff equipped with the skills and motivation needed to implement the change?

A key risk-mitigation approach is to treat changes in the organization's structure as a change management project. This requires the creation and execution of a change management plan. An approach to planning change that includes how to address these success factors is described by Myers and Maher [Myers 90b].

6.10.6 Discussion Questions

1. Using factors from software product lines that you can envision or are familiar with, decide whether your organization would be better off producing software core assets in a separate unit or as part of the product teams. If part of the product teams, how would you decide which team should produce which core asset? And how would you handle the production of nonsoftware core assets, such as a scope definition or the product-line-wide requirements?
2. Do you think it would be better to have a single testing unit to validate both the core assets and the products or a separate unit for each? Why? What about a unit for providing and maintaining tool support for the product line?
3. Product line organizational structures can and do change over time as conditions warrant. What measures would you put in place to tell you when it was time to initiate a change in your organizational structure?
4. Some product lines are structured to divide assets into those that are (a) used in every product, (b) used in only one product, and (c) used in an identifiable subset of products. For example, a maker of diesel engine software might identify software components used in every marine engine, every truck engine, or every mining equipment engine. How would you structure the organization so that responsibility for components such as these was assigned effectively?

6.11 Technology Forecasting

Ironically, one of the most insidious dangers facing any organization is long-term success, for success breeds complacency. While routinely cranking out products and congratulating itself on its stellar productivity figures, an organization is vulnerable to being blindsided by a competitor who is sporting new features, new ideas, and new technologies. To head off such calamities, an organization must institutionalize vigilance, and one way to do that is by practicing technology forecasting. Technology forecasting helps provide strategic market planning—that is, identifying trends and predicting what the relevant markets will bear [Ryans 00]. It spots emerging standards, allowing an organization to position itself early to lead, or at least to react with agility. It reduces risk with respect to innovations, provides the basis for planning and directing investments in research and development areas, and helps set the direction of product migration.

Technology forecasting helps take the pulse of the core technologies on which the products rely, as well as the tools, techniques, methods, and processes used to develop the products and bring them to market. Development techniques and tools are particularly important when time-to-market matters.

Technology is forecast in two areas:

1. Internal development, which includes tools, processes, and methods for producing the software that will end up in products such as
   - development paradigms and notations, such as the Unified Modeling Language (UML)
   - technologies, such as Web-based and wireless, and languages, such as Extensible Markup Language (XML)
   - code development suites and environments
   - analysis tools
   - planning, configuration management, and requirements management techniques and tools
   - process improvement and process management approaches
2. Customer solutions, meaning technology or solutions that will affect (or end up as) features or capabilities embedded in products. These include
   - more efficient hardware platforms
   - better software platforms (such as databases or network and communications middleware)
   - improved user interfaces
   - faster database searching strategies
   - new user-oriented paradigms (such as visual environments and Web-based interfaces)
   - improved architectural solutions
   - better problem-reporting systems

- emerging standards
- new features that enhance the capabilities of users

The rapid pace of technology change makes assessing new technology very challenging [Brown 96] and limits the technology time horizon to no more than three to five years. Consequently, plan to update your technology forecasts periodically.

6.11.1 Aspects Peculiar to Product Lines

For non-product-line development, technology forecasting is performed infrequently. More typically, technology "now-casting" is done, meaning that the best currently available technologies are identified and assessed for their immediate applicability to the situation at hand and likely near-term changes. In product lines, however, technologies are identified and assessed for their potential future applicability and then tracked over time. A technology that shows promise today may find its way into the product line in three years, or it may flicker out before then. On the other hand, a technology deemed much too risky and on the edge today might be the foundation for the next revolution. In product line technology forecasting, time is an ally, and we can afford to be more patient. And because we can amortize the cost over more products, we should also be able to be more thorough.

Technology forecasting for product lines also differs in that the focus is, naturally enough, on technologies that are suitable for product lines and product line environments. Technologies that are not appropriate for multiversion, cooperatively developed, long-lived, robust, changeable systems do not apply.

While all of the investigative areas listed above apply to product lines, a few are especially relevant. They include

- process innovations that make the management, production, and deployment of new products or product releases more efficient and predictable.
- configuration management strategies and techniques that help the product line organization provide better customer services through the ability to recreate and service the "instance" of the product installed and the upgrades that are appropriate for that installation.
- trends within the relevant standards bodies and the migration of the technical basis of the standards that apply to the product line. Ideally, the product line organization exploits the technology forecast to achieve a technology leadership position.

6.11.2 Application to Core Asset Development

Earlier in this practice area, we distinguished between technologies that benefit internal development and those that are customer-focused. While both are relevant for core assets, the technologies that impact development require special emphasis as core assets. Tools and techniques, such as more efficient configuration management or improved tool integration, can be leveraged over a variety of products to improve efficiency and quality; these tools and techniques offer a strong strategic advantage. The architect and developers are primary stakeholders for these types of innovations.

6.11.3 Application to Product Development

Technology forecasting affects the scope of the products that can be produced over time directly. It also affects the usability and utility of the products from the customer's perspective.

6.11.4 Specific Practices

Technology forecasting as continuous improvement. A continuous process improvement paradigm underlies many of the practices of technology forecasting. This paradigm suggests the need to constantly monitor the current technologies, tools, and processes that make up business practices in order to uncover opportunities for improved practices. The challenge is to focus the technology forecast on the areas offering the highest potential return to both the product line organization and the customer. Opportunities for improvement may result from the continuous analysis of defects and trouble reports yielding insights into the areas where the product line could leverage technology improvements. Additional opportunities for improvement may surface as a result of an analysis of changes in the marketplace that have implications on new technology.

Other Voices: Technology Forecasting at Cummins Inc.

Cummins Inc. is the world's largest manufacturer of large diesel engines, in which software plays a large role. Cummins has launched a very successful software product line effort to produce that software across their family of engines. Here, they share the importance of technology forecasting to their success [Dager 00]:

> *Cummins was able to develop multiple products in the 1980s and early 1990s, but not a lasting architecture over this same period. There are many reasons for this, but one major shortcoming was not anticipating the future needs and requirements that were on the horizon. Cummins has proven very capable of doing advanced development to anticipate and prepare for the needs of the future. This advanced development was not, however, cleanly tied to the design processes of current products. The software development team decided that a look beyond the visible horizon was necessary if they were to have any hope of creating an*

architecture that would last. A process known as an environmental scan was established to give the software development teams this look beyond.

The environmental scan polled 25 to 35 of the key stakeholders in the system. Elements for everything the stakeholders saw as incremental capability, now and in the future, were documented in a scenario/context-based style. Approximately 100 scan elements were placed into categories of immediate need, required within the next five years, required within the next ten years, and required in more than ten years. The scan elements were also labeled with a confidence level to help segregate real possibilities from the wish lists. Without a timely look at these future system requirements, Cummins would not have a Core II architecture that had more longevity than its predecessors. In other words, the architecture at Cummins could not be developed solely on the current product requirements or even those of the near term products. Also of significance is that technology is moving faster than our expectations. It is not uncommon that technologies that are labeled as ten years out become reality within five years or sooner.

You can read more about Cummins' software product line for engines in Chapter 9.

Technical steering group. A technical steering group is a proven mechanism for keeping current with technology trends. This type of group comprises of senior technical managers who analyze new trends, customer needs, and technologies. One organization we know also appointed a group of senior engineers as "technology stewards" and tasked them with accumulating and maintaining sufficient expertise in various technical areas so that they could become reliable forecasters.

Technology sources. Once the product line organization has a rationale and focus for conducting the technology forecast, the next task is to identify the sources of technology that are relevant to their needs. Sources include

- centers of technology investigation, such as the Software Engineering Institute (SEI), university laboratories, and corporate research and development establishments that publish their results
- research and development and Object to Object conferences, such as the Software Product Line Conference (SPLC), the International Conference on Software Engineering (ICSE), OOSPLA (Obect-Oriented Systems, Programming Languages and Applications), and others
- networks of professional associations and associates
- journals and periodicals

Validating the forecast. Once focused on the forecast objectives, specific steps include the following:

- Perform sufficient research to isolate the subset of promising technologies.
- Validate the technologies through simulations or models to provide focus on the most promising technology.
- Analyze and quantify the benefits for both developers and customers. Determine any adverse impacts.
- Conduct pilot tests as a proof of concept.
- Integrate the technology with other assets and then test.
- Provide adoption training and rollout.

6.11.5 Practice Risks

Inadequately forecasting technology will result, predictably, in new and promising technologies passing you by. This will result in a product line that is obsolete before its time and will open the door for a more attentive competitor to steal your market. An inadequate technology forecast can result from

- **Wrong technology choice:** The wrong product gets built, and the market turns elsewhere for solutions. This can be a result of investments made in the wrong or obsolete technology or simply choosing "what's good" over "what's popular."
- **Architecture can't support new technology:** Radical changes in technology that the architecture can't accommodate will result in the obsolescence of the product line. The product line organization has a lot riding on its architectural decisions and needs as much advance warning as possible of radical technological changes that will undermine them.
- **Forecasting that is driven by technology rather than by business needs:** Analysts may become enamored by the technology and the search for technology and lose sight of the corresponding business requirements.
- **Ivory tower forecasting:** Technology forecasting can become a "sandbox" or an "ivory tower" so removed from the day-to-day operations that crucial issues, objectives, and priorities get lost.
- **Lack of purpose:** If the problem that the product line organization is trying to solve is unknown, the search for new or emerging technology to maintain product line leadership has the potential to be limitless.

6.11.6 For Further Reading

The book *Winning Market Leadership: Strategic Market Planning for Technology-Driven Businesses* by Ryans, More, Barclay, and Deutscher [Ryans 00] describes a strategic marketing planning approach for technology organizations. The emphasis on adapting to new market conditions and changes in the competitive climate are relevant to this practice area. Examples from Intel, Compaq, Hewlett-Packard, Glaxo-Welcome, and General Electric provide insights from industry leaders. Brown and Wallnau's "A Framework for Evaluating Software Technology" [Brown 96] gives a nice handle for positioning candidate technology in the context of your organization's needs and capabilities.

6.11.7 Discussion Questions

1. Who in your organization should be tasked with technology forecasting? Why?
2. What areas of technology are relevant to the products in your organization?
3. How does technology forecasting relate to understanding relevant domains? Could the same team perform both practice areas?
4. How does technology forecasting relate to scoping the product line?
5. As described here, the technology forecasting practice area does not produce an artifact so much as it ensures an accumulation of corporate knowledge. This leads to two questions:
   - If it did produce an artifact—a technology forecast—what would it look like?
   - How would the people possessing that knowledge pass it on to those who could use it? That is, on what teams and in what processes should the technology forecasters actively participate?

6.12 Training

Training is a core activity of any software development organization. The purpose of training is to provide the skills and knowledge needed to perform software management and technical roles. A training program involves first identifying the training needed by the organization and the entities within it and then developing or procuring that requisite training. Thus, as in many other practice areas, there is an initiation or planning phase followed by an execution phase. Training can be informal through mentoring or other on-the-job mechanisms or formal in-classroom settings or video sessions. Adequate resources and funding are needed if the training is to be effective, and they should be documented in a training plan.

6.12.1 Aspects Peculiar to Product Lines

Training is an element of both the initial product line adoption and the longer-term product line evolution. This practice area focuses on the training practices that need to be instituted by management to ensure that the organizational units responsible for creating, fielding, and evolving the product line have properly trained personnel.

Other Voices: Training in the Japanese Software Factories

Michael Cusumano illuminated many product-line-like practices in *Japan's Software Factories* [Cusumano 91, p. 433]. One of the striking aspects of this book is the comprehensive training provided by the most successful factories.

> *New company entrants in Japanese software factories underwent a minimum of two or three months of classroom instruction and spent several months more in on-the-job training. They then took a sequence of short courses or workshops every year. This training differed from simply providing general education, which many large companies around the world offered their employees, because they taught a common set of methods and tools comprising the company standards, at least for a given product family. [T]his approach . . . increased the possibility of establishing a more predictable and repeatable process while raising average performance levels—thus leveraging whatever skills individuals, and the organization as a whole, possessed. Managers also claimed that training in a standard process facilitated communication among different groups, such as eliminating potential debates over what tools or methods to use, and made it possible to add personnel to late projects without making them later—a practice once thought impossible with software. One might further argue that encouraging young minds to value teamwork, product reliability, or reusability as much as individual creativity provided another way to insure that employees viewed their potential contributions from a larger perspective and adopted organizational rather than merely individual or project-centered goals.*

Management's support of training includes:

- committing to a training plan that provides people with the skills necessary to create a product line from a base of core assets
- ensuring that the plan is implemented and that the training is monitored for effectiveness
- ensuring that the product line training is consistent with and supportive of the overall product line adoption process or any process-improvement efforts

An organization's approach to training in product lines must focus on establishing a core competence in the creation and utilization of core assets. Thus it is not enough, for example, to send people to a course in object-oriented technology or software reuse and then expect them to build product lines. All training must occur within the context of the organization's adoption plan for product line practices and must address the skills needed by people for the new roles they will assume within the organization as the organization moves away from the single-system, project-centered view to the multisystem, product line view.

Product line training must be viewed as a strategic activity that should be planned accordingly. A training plan should be created that complements the overall product line adoption plan and ties training goals to the business goals of the organization. For example, if a business goal is to reduce the time-to-market of products in the product line, any training in software reuse practices must emphasize the creation of reusable assets rather than a reuse library. In the product line context, reuse is a means to an end, not an end in itself, and reuse training must focus on designing for commonality and controlling variability rather than on creating class libraries.

The appropriate product line training also depends on the state and maturity of the organization. An organization already comfortable with following processes will have less of a need to train people to use development processes properly. An organization already fairly sophisticated about architecture and architecture-based design will have less of a need for training in these areas. These two areas cover the majority of developers' concerns. Developers who are used to developing components for a prescriptive architecture will find their work under a product line paradigm familiar.

6.12.2 Application to Core Asset Development

Training for asset development is primarily training in the software engineering practice areas that are described in Chapter 4. Training in domain analysis or software architecture, for example, should be preceded by an introductory course that explains product line concepts in general and the organization's planned product lines in particular. The specific training associated with each software engineering practice (for example, training in a specific domain-analysis method or training in architecture definition) must be tied to the goal of creating a core asset base to support a product line. Similarly, training in the tools for representing and documenting the outputs of a domain analysis or a software architecture definition effort should focus on complementing the analysis and design skills of the asset creators rather than their coding skills.

If commercial off-the-shelf (COTS) components are to be acquired as part of an asset strategy, the training should focus primarily on how to choose and integrate the components that make sense for the product line. Similarly, if legacy software is to be repackaged as an asset for the product line, the training should focus primarily on how to analyze its reusability rather than on how to "wrap" it for inclusion in a current product.

Finally, don't forget that the training materials and plans make first-class core assets themselves.

6.12.3 Application to Product Development

Product development training is the complement of asset development training; its primary goal is to ensure that product developers know how to create products in the product line from the core asset base. The emphasis is on the effective use and reuse of assets such as a domain model and architecture. The architecture for a single system, for example, is derived from (if not identical to) the product line architecture and not built from scratch; the training must emphasize the need to follow the processes that were established for the product line. One of the major "themes" of the product development training should be that asset usage is strategic in nature and that assets that appear to be less than optimal for a particular product may be an optimal element of the overall product line strategy.

Another important aspect of product development training is getting people to follow the process defined for using assets and correcting problems. For example, problems with assets should always be referred to the asset creators. That way, local "fixes" proposed for a particular customer can be assessed against the long-term needs of the product line (for example, configuration management of assets, control of variations).

6.12.4 Specific Practices

Develop a training plan: The most important elements of product line training are the identification of training needs and the creation of a strategic training plan to meet those needs. The plan must identify the current skill gaps and determine the training requirements needed to fill them. It must also address how those skills will be established and maintained in the teams that build product lines: in-house courses, external courses, on-the-job training, mentoring, and so forth. Creating and implementing such a training plan is a key element of the cultural change needed for product line adoption.

Other Voices: Changing Skills at CelsiusTech

Deciding what to train people for depends on what knowledge and skills they need. Here is how CelsiusTech approached the issue of skills and knowledge, beginning with the formative years of their ShipSystem 2000 software product line, launched in early 1986 [Brownsword 96]. First, the technical side:

> *The architecture team was responsible for the creation of the framework and specific building codes (interface standards, design conventions,*

etc.) used in a product line. Team members needed solid domain and customer-usage knowledge. This knowledge was combined with excellent engineering skills and an ability to look and think broadly to find relevant common mechanisms or product line components. Communication and teaming skills were also mandatory.

Developers needed to understand the framework and building codes and how their respective components should fit. During the formative period of the product line, the development staff required skills in the use of Ada, object-based design, and their software development environment, including the target testbed. In addition, broad areas of knowledge were required: product line concepts, SS2000 architecture and mechanisms, creation of reusable components, incremental integration, and at least one functional area domain.

Integration and CM team members required a solid knowledge of the product line architecture, past domain systems experience, the Rational Environment, CelsiusTech's integration and release process, and Ada. Integration and CM were viewed as a single engineering function. The early team members had development experience with the previous systems and the SS2000 system. They were highly skilled, results-oriented engineers. Part of the responsibility of the integration and CM team was to forge an efficient process for development and customer releases. During this time, each customer system had three to five team members with responsibility for all aspects of integration, test, and CM.

Management required a different set of skills and knowledge:

Managers in the formative years of the product line required strong knowledge of the product line concepts, the technical concepts to be applied, and the business rationale for the product line approach. In addition, they needed strong planning, communication, and innovative problem-solving skills.

Management also had to cope with the inevitable discontent and resistance associated with the transition to a new business paradigm and attendant technology. Substantial effort was made to help personnel understand the new business strategy and rationale. People who did not subscribe to or could not grasp the product line approach either left the company or found assignments on maintenance or other projects. This caused loss of domain knowledge that took time to redevelop.

From 1992 to 1994 was a period when the product line was finding its legs. Launching was behind them; four systems were in development, and a growing core asset base was available. This is the point when personnel changes began. Fewer developers but more integrators were needed. Because of the plurality of projects, management staffing remained constant.

With greater emphasis on the composition of systems from the product line assets, developers needed stronger domain and SS2000 product line knowledge than during the creation of the product line. The use of Ada, object technology, and the development environment had become more routine. The integration group focus turned to the integration and release management of many parallel systems. Increasing emphasis was placed on reusing test plans and data sets across customer systems. With integration and release management now routine, more junior staff could augment and start replacing the more skilled engineers used in the formative years.

The architecture team had to maintain a solid knowledge of the product line and factor in the growing set of current and approaching customer-mission needs. Communication skills with customer project managers (for negotiation of multiple customer needs) and developers (desiring to optimize major interfaces and mechanisms) continue to be extremely important. Engineering skill to balance new needs yet preserve the overall architectural integrity are vital for team members.

As more of the product line was available, less emphasis on technology maturation and training was required of management. With more customer systems existing, the coordination of changing customer (existing and new) requirements across multiple customers emerged as a major management focus and priority. Requirements negotiation involved not only customers but also other customer project managers and the product line architecture team. Customer project managers required increasing skill in negotiation and knowledge of the existing and anticipated future directions of the product line.

The period after 1994 has been the "sweet spot" of CelsiusTech's software product line, in which they have enjoyed the full benefits of the approach. Staffing levels have shrunk from over 200 to less than 50, even though dozens of ShipSystem 2000 products have been turned out. Integration of these massive systems is a nonevent. Knowledge and skills valued the most now at CelsiusTech are those that address the overall domain, and the future.

Developers continue to need strong domain and SS2000 product line knowledge with the emphasis on composing systems rather than building systems.

The architecture team now must maintain a solid knowledge of the product line, current and approaching customer-mission needs, and advances in relevant technology. This knowledge must then be balanced with engineering skill as the architecture and its major interfaces and mechanisms continue to evolve. For example, CelsiusTech is currently in the process of upgrading its user-interface technology to exploit X-Windows and Motif. The architecture team has been involved in technical evaluations, prototype development of new interfaces (both for the external user and for application developers), and assessing the effect of the new technologies on the product line.

Management focus continues on the coordination of changing customer (existing and new) requirements across an increasing number of customers. Negotiation skills remain vital for customer project managers. Managers must also not only retain a current knowledge of the existing requirements but must increasingly be aware of anticipated future directions for the product line.

Expect many things to change throughout the life of your software product line: your organizational structure, the product line's scope, perhaps its architecture. The skills and knowledge of your staff should evolve as well.

Train people for the transition to the product line approach: Training to prepare people for the transition to product lines includes such elements as:

- an introductory course on product line concepts and terminology.
- an overview of the organization's current and planned product lines.
- an overview of the proposed development process, including changes in existing processes, organizational structure, and roles.
- a presentation of the concept of operations (CONOPS) for the product line to explain the goal state of the organization and the role of training in achieving that state.
- training in specific product line practices or concepts. Here, software architecture deserves a special mention as a concept whose role and use should be emphasized, especially among the product builders. A familiarization course on the particular architecture being used as the foundation of the product line (including the ways it supports variability) is often most useful.
- training in supporting technologies (such as tools for representing and documenting the core assets).

Other Voices: CelsiusTech's Training Curriculum

CelsiusTech's training regimen was cited as a major success factor for their software product line [Brownsword 96], and its evolution over the years tracks the evolution of the skills and knowledge required for successful management of ShipSystem 2000 (see "Other Voices: Changing Skills at CelsiusTech" sidebar). Its depth and breadth compare favorably with the training offered by the most successful of Japan's software factories (see "Other Voices: Training in the Japanese Software Factories"). Together, these suggest that (1) software product line training, like software product lines, involves more than just a technological dimension, and (2) training is not the place where you want to skimp.

At CelsiusTech, training was used as a risk-management strategy for the transition of new technology and the creation of a new development and management culture supportive of its product line business approach. CelsiusTech's training was substantial by industry norms. Training was a management priority for all development staff and technical supervisors.

The initial training approach was typical at the time, consisting of

- *a one-week Ada course with small hands-on programming exercises focused on the introduction of Ada syntax and constructs and the terminology and concepts of object-based design*
- *a three-day object-based design course composed of lecture and case studies*
- *a three-day hands-on software-development environment course*

Courses were taught by external consultants. Both the courses and the instructors were well regarded by the participants. Several groups of the early developers attended the suite of courses and began development of the lower-level common services. Early analysis of the resulting designs and code found limited use of key software engineering principles that were essential for a flexible, robust architecture and resulting product line. The developers still had a limited understanding of the architecture and associated concepts. The initial training was found suitable for transmitting concepts, features, and mechanisms but did not help students learn how to put into practice the software engineering and object-based concepts and principles. What was needed was an education approach. CelsiusTech also found the traditional classroom performance an unreliable predictor of posttraining performance on projects.

In response, the training was rapidly changed to a reeducation approach that included

- *classroom instruction for Ada and the development environment (similar to the original training strategy)*
- *an introduction to the SS2000 product line architecture and concepts*
- *a six-week practicum in software engineering using Ada*
- *on-the-job mentoring*

While the new practicum went a long way toward bridging the gap between theory and practice, mentoring was found necessary to continue and reinforce the new paradigms. One of CelsiusTech's early goals was to develop an in-house training and mentoring capability. The initial practicums trained the key designers and project leaders. External consultants provided the initial training and mentoring to this core group. As the core group's experience grew, the group in turn provided the mentoring to the next groups. CelsiusTech instructors were trained and "certified" by the external consultants through a phased train-the-trainer program. This bootstrapping approach leveraged scarce resources and helped in rebuilding a common development culture.

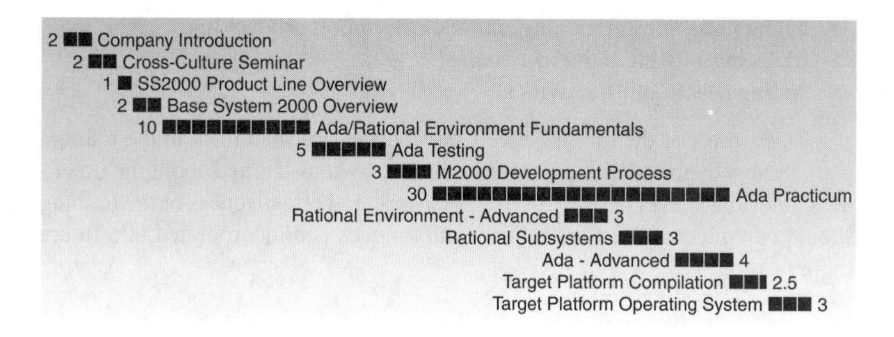

CelsiusTech Training Curriculum

A summary of the 70-day curriculum is shown in the above figure. And CelsiusTech has continued to expand its training scope, concentrating on higher-end concerns. With the emphasis shifting to the composition of new systems and the potential for building new product lines, CelsiusTech has created a 300-hour architects training program that aims to develop future product line architects.

Note that the first four items above are really about education rather than training and that even experienced practitioners may need to be reeducated about how their skills and roles apply in the product line context.

Training needs to be tailored to the specific processes and skills of the organization and to the product line adoption plan. Establishing a core competence in asset creation and utilization means understanding and applying new concepts, not getting high marks in a training class.[4] Any training in, for example, domain analysis, software architecture, object-oriented technology, design patterns and frameworks, specific programming languages, or specific development environments must be planned and implemented as part of the product line strategy and not as ends in themselves.

Implement the training plan: Implementing the training plan includes making decisions about the most effective way to deliver the training: classroom training, hands-on training, tutorials, workshops, pilot projects, mentoring, and so forth. An important decision in this regard is the scope of any planned in-house training and mentoring capability and the extent to which external courses and instructors will be used. In general, implementing the product line training plan involves some or all of the following choices:

---

4. CensiusTech found traditional classroom performance to be an unreliable predictor of post-training performance on real projects [Brownsword 96, p. 62].

- augmenting current training activities to support product lines
- replacing existing training activities
- adding new training activities

To ensure that the training meets the goals established for it in the training plan, it must be monitored and measured. Any lessons learned about the timeliness, relevance, level of difficulty, deficiencies, and effectiveness of the training should be collected from the trainers and trainees and incorporated into future training.

6.12.5 Practice Risks

An inadequate training program will result in a staff that is ill-prepared in any of a number of ways to perform their jobs efficiently and effectively in the product line organization. Component developers, for example, who are not trained to create truly reusable assets will probably not do so and will consequently undermine the quality of the core assets. Inadequate training can result from

- **Inappropriate focus:** Too much time spent training people on the tools, programming language, or development environment without the requisite product technology foundation will only succeed in helping to automate the wrong operation.
- **Lack of strategic investment:** Sacrificing vital training in order to meet current customer schedules and deliverables will in the long run result in staff who are ill-equipped to handle the needs of the product line operation.
- **Lack of big picture:** If insufficient time is spent on communicating the product line vision and on building an awareness and acceptance of the product line, the rest of the product line training will fail to have a meaningful context.
- **Inadequate training resources:** A lack of the necessary instructors, funding, classroom facilities, hardware, or software can derail any training plan.
- **Lack of coordination:** If the training plan is not coordinated with the overall product line adoption plan or process-improvement plan, the staff will probably become frustrated and overwhelmed.
- **Lack of training assessment:** If the effectiveness of the training is not monitored or measured, there will be no basis on which to predict the results or to improve the training.

6.12.6 For Further Reading

Goldberg and Rubin devote two full chapters of their book, *Succeeding with Objects: Decision Frameworks for Project Management* [Goldberg 95], to training in object-oriented technology. Chapter 18 describes what a training plan is and discusses it in terms of both training and educating the entire team.

The discussion covers subject areas, proficiency levels, and training formats (for example, classroom, mentoring, and self-study). Chapter 19 describes how to set up a training plan and provides several examples of real training projects.

Chapter 16 of *Managing Software Reuse: A Comprehensive Guide to Strategically Reengineering the Organization for Reusable Components* [Lim 98] is devoted to staffing software reuse projects. It includes an identification of the key roles and responsibilities for implementing reuse and a description of the elements of a core curriculum in reuse.

6.12.7 Discussion Questions

1. How would you validate a training plan? This means, among other things, how would you verify that the training you are planning to provide is the training that is needed?
2. Sketch a training curriculum for your organization. Identify the courses and prepare an outline for each course. Estimate their durations, who should attend, and who you would have teach them.
3. Managers are sometimes reluctant to give people time to attend training sessions, especially if product deadlines are looming. What metrics would you propose to convince management that training was paying off for the organization and was worth the investment of time?
4. Training is an excellent candidate for make/buy/mine/commission analysis. Sketch a business case for each of the alternatives as it applies to your organization.

PART III

Putting the Practice Areas into Action

Part II of this book laid out 29 areas of expertise, which we call practice areas, for establishing a successful software product line. Part III will show how to put those practice areas to use in your organization.

You work for a Fortune 100 company with offices in 64 countries throughout the Americas, Eurasia, and Africa. Your company employs 105,000 people at 32 mines, 54 manufacturing plants, 148 storage and shipping facilities, and more than 12,000 retail outlets. Your company is organized into six major divisions, corresponding to lines of business. Some of the retail outlets sell products from a single line, some from more than one. Similarly, the storage and shipping facilities are aligned with one or more divisions. Each division is responsible for its own software, and to date there are about 1100 software systems being maintained or in development across the company. Predictably, with software developed independently, there is enormous unexploited commonality. Workflow, business rules, security protocols, credit checking, customer account management, commodities brokering, retail support, inventory tools, accounting, supply chain management, and a host of other repeated functionality all exist in dozens of varying incarnations across the corporation. The pace is too rapid for you to call a time out. The only thing that's constant is that nothing is constant, and the pressure to build more systems is relentless. There is an undercurrent of uneasiness throughout all the IT departments: the present madcap rush to build so many systems cannot be sustained, and a disaster can be seen brewing on the horizon. Clearly everyone would be better off if a way could be found to take advantage of all of the commonality by merging the similar systems across business units into software product lines, but how? "Congratulations," your CTO says to you one day. "Your job is to make it happen." What do you do? Where do you begin?

Alternatively, suppose *you* are the CTO of your company. You're also the CIO, the Chief Architect, the Vice President of Testing and Quality Assurance, the Vice President of Product Development, and every other Tuesday it's your turn to clean out the company fridge. Your employee roster is exactly the same as your stockholder roster, and both are just 16 entries long. You're trying to hire more people, but so is everyone else in Silicon Suburbs, and competition is keen. You're aiming your first product at a particular market segment, but the people you're getting venture capital advice from are telling you that you need to be nimble and agile and able to quickly target other market segments as well. Certainly you'll be turning out multiple versions of your product stable in the near future. You recognize that if you don't start out with a good handle on the product variations on day one, then in the not-too-distant future you're going to be swamped by the inability to manage the complexity. Your tiny, barely growing staff will never be able to turn out even the modest family of products you have in mind, let alone provide reasonable support over the long term. And never mind trying to achieve the "mass customization" capability your VC people are clamoring for. You need to launch a software product line. What do you do? Where do you begin?

No matter if you're in the top management of a large corporation, managing a small unit in a big company, or running a tiny e-business start-up, a paradigm that comes with 29 more things (practice areas) you have to manage and assign scarce resources to is not at all appealing.

And yet organizations of all sizes are succeeding handsomely with the software product line concept. At the large end, the experiences of companies such as Lucent Technologies, Philips, CelsiusTech, and others are mentioned time and again throughout this book. The experience of Cummins Inc. and the U.S. National Reconnaissance Office together with Raytheon are case studies in upcoming chapters. At the small end of the spectrum, the Market Maker case study in Chapter 11 is the model example in this book, but there are others. No company—large, small, or in between—adopts the product line approach by assigning one person the job of establishing 29 new practices or by hiring 29 new people and assigning each one a practice area. So how do they do it?

Part III is about answering that question. How do they do it? How do they apply finite resources to orchestrate a coordinated attack on 29 activity-rich practice areas?

The answer has four pieces. The first piece is straightforward, and we will dispense with it here. The other pieces merit their own chapters in this part of the book.

First, they recognize that most of the practice areas do not precipitate *new* work but rather call for a change in the way that people do the work *they would be doing anyway*. Then it becomes a simple matter of finding people in the organization who are natural choices to be assigned responsibility for one or more practice areas. Large or small, you have component developers; the "Component Development" practice area gives them new ways to do what they would be doing anyway. Large or small, you had better have one or more architects; the "Architecture Definition" practice area gives them new ways to do what they would be doing anyway. Large or small, you have marketers and maybe market analysts; who better to take care of the "Market Analysis" practice area? Large or small, you have someone who figures out the organizational structure and signals when it's time for a new one; let that person be guided by the "Structuring the Organization" practice area.

Second, they use a divide-and-conquer strategy. Based on an understanding of your organizational context, they divide the product line effort into chunks of work to be done, together with the associated practice areas required to do that work. They then assign responsibility for each chunk to appropriate individuals or teams. This is a more manageable approach because it allows them to deal with several groups of related practice areas rather than with 29 individual ones. For example, suppose you know that you need to determine what to build, provide the requisite organizational support, set up the production support system, develop the assets, field products, and monitor the effort. Then,

- a product planning team could *decide what products to build.*
- the product line manager could *provide the requisite organizational support.*
- a software support team could *set up the production support system.*
- the architecture team together with the software developers could *develop the assets.*
- product development teams could *field the products.*
- one or more project-level managers could head the asset development and product development teams, and together they could *monitor the effort.*

But in order to succeed with a divide-and-conquer product line strategy, you still need to identify which practice areas apply to each of these functions. It isn't sufficient to characterize the bodies of product line work you need to accomplish and assign responsibility. You must know which practice areas relate and how you will get practice area coverage. This could be painful and risky if you are new to product lines and have to proceed without assistance. Chapter 7 holds the key to success. There we describe a number of *software product line practice patterns* that give common product line problem/solution pairs, where the problems are product line work to be done and the solutions are the groups of practice areas necessary to apply in concert to accomplish the work.

Third, they apply their resources where they will do the most good. By understanding its own inherent strengths and weaknesses, an organization with product line ambitions can quickly identify areas needing a concentrated dose of remedial attention and take action early to address trouble spots. Until now, sniffing out these trouble spots has been an exercise in management intuition at best and guesswork (or neglect) at worst, but Chapter 8 offers something more dependable. A Product Line Technical Probe is a diagnostic exercise that uses the practice areas as the basis for both data collection and analysis. It will identify which of the practice areas appear to be in good stead and which have the potential to derail the product line approach.

And fourth, they learn from others. Examples are often much more instructive than principles. Chapters 9 through 11 provide three complete examples. Cummins Inc., the U.S. National Reconnaissance Office with Raytheon, and Germany's Market Maker Software AG are in very different businesses and very different circumstances; each made the conscious decision to adopt a software product line approach. The case studies will take you through the experiences of each, from their critical early decisions through the present day.

This is how we answer the question: "How do they do it?" We hope Part III will let *you* answer the question: "How do *I* do it?"

7

Software Product Line Practice Patterns

7.1 The Value of Patterns

In Part II we provided a comprehensive encyclopedia of practice areas. We wanted you to appreciate the spectrum of practice areas and to understand the characteristics of each. Recall that the 29 practice areas introduced in Part II were grouped into three categories: software engineering, technical management, and organizational management. These categories, we said, reflect the different bodies of knowledge required and are roughly indicative of the skill sets of the people needed to carry them out. Practice areas in the same category share a relation that might be described as "requires the same kind of knowledge as" or "requires the same kind of skill set as."

There are also very general relations among the categories, as illustrated in Figure 7.1. The technical management practice areas serve to manage and support the software engineering practice areas. The organizational management practice areas serve to enable and orchestrate the totality of the other practice areas.

These practice area categories are useful because 29 things are too many to keep track of separately and because the software engineering, technical management, and organizational management groups constitute a simple classification intended to permit you to focus on understanding the landscape of practice areas.

But now you understand the landscape, and you want to apply your knowledge. You need to put the practice areas into play. You aren't going to attack all

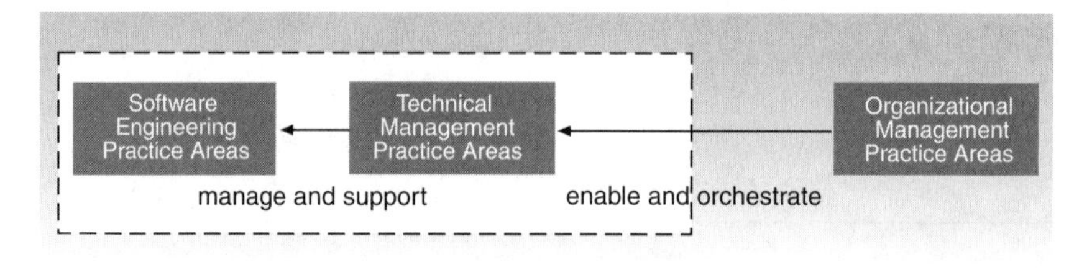

Figure 7.1 Relations among Practice Area Categories

of the areas at once. You need to follow a divide-and-conquer strategy that permits you to divide the product line effort into chunks of work to be done. You can then assign responsibility for each chunk to appropriate individuals or teams. The three categories we provided would not meet your needs because, given a complete, static body of knowledge with very general relations, it is not intuitive how you should put that knowledge to use. Four things are missing:

1. a characterization of your individual situation
2. the part of the product line effort you want to accomplish
3. the grouping of practice areas that meet your individual needs
4. a dynamic view of the practice areas in that grouping

It may be that your organizational situation and what you want to do in terms of software product lines are unique, but that is actually quite rare. Even more rare is for the practice area solution you arrive at to be completely distinct from other similar situations. What we see in practice is familiar chords played again and again. We see *software product line practice patterns.*

Patterns are a way of expressing common contexts and problem/solution pairs. They have been found to be very useful in architecture [Alexander 79], in economics [Etzioni 64], in software architecture [Buschmann 96], in software design [Gamma 95], in software implementation [Coplien 94], in software engineering [Beck 94], and in dealing with just about any kind of problem or social interaction [Newell 72]. In his book, *The Timeless Way of Building,* the architect Christopher Alexander states:

> *Each pattern is a three-part rule, which expresses a relation between a certain context, a problem, and a solution.* [Alexander 79, p. 247]

Alexander used patterns to show how particular architectural challenges could be met by using specific spatial configurations whenever the situation made them relevant. Architecture and design pattern names have become part of the standard lexicon for software architects. We routinely use terms such as "Publish-Subscribe," "Bridge," "Facade," and "Model-View-Controller," among others, to both describe and identify common design-problem solution pairs [Gamma 95, Krasner 88].

Alexander's definition of patterns fits our needs nicely. For software product line practice patterns, the context is the organizational situation. The problem is what part of a software product line effort needs to be accomplished. The solution is the grouping of practice areas and the relations among those practice areas (and/or groups if there is more than one) that together address the problem for that context.

Buschmann et al. provide a fine list of reasons why patterns for software architecture are particularly helpful to the software architect [Buschmann 96]. We adapt this list to show how practice area patterns will help you. Software product line practice patterns

- address recurring product line problems that arise in specific software product line situations and present solutions to them.
- document existing, well-proven software product line experience.
- identify and specify abstractions that are broader in scope than single practice areas.
- provide an additional common vocabulary and understanding for software product lines.
- are a means of documenting new software product line efforts.
- help manage the complexity inherent in software product line approaches.
- can be combined to build complex product line solutions.

This is a compelling list that more than warrants use of the pattern concept. But software product line practice patterns will not do all your work. They provide neither detailed nor complete solutions. The patterns will list practice areas, a practice area grouping, and relations. They will not provide a fully specified method or process model. They may focus on particular practice areas and ignore others entirely. You will need to address the ignored practice areas individually or in another pattern because in Part II you learned that mastery of all the practice areas is necessary for product line success. Even so, the software product line practice patterns provide a helpful handle for selecting and applying the appropriate practice areas to meet your individual needs.

In Sections 7.3 through 7.14 we describe a collection of software product line practice patterns that characterize common product line contexts and problem/solution pairs that we have observed. We don't pretend that our collection is complete. In fact, it is our hope that the community will add to this collection as experience with software product lines grows. However, before we introduce our pattern collection, we need to agree on our pattern language. Section 7.2 gives a template for describing each pattern.

7.2 Software Product Line Practice Pattern Descriptions

If the point of software product line practice patterns is to help you apply software product line practices, then the patterns must be described in a way that you can easily understand. They need to come with sufficient detail to permit you to recognize the pattern context and problem and to implement the solution. The descriptions should also be consistent over the entire pattern collection so that you can compare, contrast, and build on the set. The context-problem-solution pattern schema is illustrated in Figure 7.2. You can see that the solution really has two pieces:

1. a *static* description that simply shows the grouping (that is, one or more groups of practice areas)
2. a *dynamic* description that shows relations among the practice areas and/or groups

We look to the patterns community, active across many disciplines, for guidance on how to describe software product line practice patterns [Gamma 95, Buschmann 96]. So the template we will use is based on our context-problem-solution pattern schema but also includes other information. We present each software product line practice pattern using the following template:

- **Name:** A unique and intuitive pattern name and a short summary of the pattern.
- **Example:** One or more scenarios to help illustrate the context and the problem.
- **Context:** The organizational situations in which the pattern may apply.
- **Problem:** What part of a product line effort needs to be accomplished.

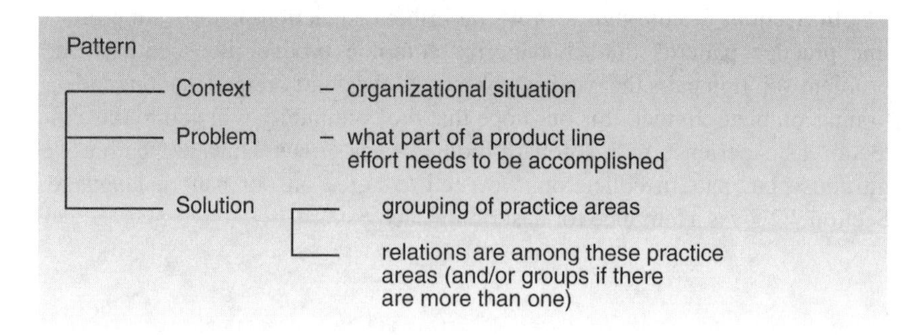

Figure 7.2 Software Product Line Practice Pattern Schema

- **Solution:** The basis for the practice area pattern grouping underlying the pattern.
- **Static:** The grouping that lists the practice areas in each group.
- **Dynamics:** A table, diagram(s), or possibly scenario(s) describing the relations among the practice areas in each group and/or among the groups if there is more than one.
- **Application:** Any suggested guidelines for applying the pattern.
- **Variants:** A brief description of known variants or specializations of the pattern.
- **Consequences:** The benefits the pattern provides and also any known limitations.

Before we use the template, we need to underscore how the iterative essence of software product lines colors the relations we depict in the Dynamics section of each pattern description. Recall from Part I that the three essential software product line activities—core asset development, product development, and management—are intrinsically continuous and highly iterative. Likewise, the practice areas, which together support those three essential activities, are exercised, and exercised again, iteratively. Consequently, any relation that shows dynamic interaction between two practice areas also has to be iterative.

The actual relations will vary depending on the pattern. A relation between two practice areas might be "can be usefully practiced at about the same time as" or "produces artifacts or knowledge used by." Whatever the stated relation, assume it is iterative. Often we will depict a relation as an arrow from one practice area to another, but the arrow will never mean a strictly linear completion sequence. So,

```
practice area A → practice area B
```

will never mean "do A and then, when A is complete, do B," because in reality you will work on A and then B, and then B and then A, and so on. Interpret the arrows as denoting a shifting of active emphasis but by no means exclusion.

Given that blanket assumption about practice area dynamics, we are now ready to unfold our practice area pattern collection. We will begin by showing that some practice area groupings that we have already introduced are useful to describe as patterns. We will then introduce new software product line practice patterns that span various ranges of abstraction, scale, and purpose. The context for some of the patterns will be universal—that is, they apply in all situations. The context for others will be particular to specific organizational conditions. There may be relationships among patterns, where each pattern solves a part of the overall product line approach and where a pattern hierarchy makes sense.

Let's start by revisiting our discussion at the beginning of this chapter and by treating the practice areas in their three categories—software engineering, technical management, and organizational management—as a practice area pattern. We will repeat some of that discussion to couch it in the pattern perspective and to demonstrate use of the pattern template.

7.3 The Curriculum Pattern

Name: The *Curriculum* pattern groups all of the 29 product line practice areas required to succeed with software product lines into three categories that are based on the skill sets of the people who would be needed to carry them out.

Example:
Scenario 1: The CTO of an organization that builds Web-based on-line ordering systems for individual businesses has now deployed 30 very similar but separate systems and is expecting orders for at least another 20. His organization is already struggling to handle the 30 existing configurations. He has read that software product lines have helped other organizations get control of multiple similar configurations and at the same time have expanded their product sets. He would like to learn all of the practices that would be required for his company to turn their product set, past and future, into a successful software product line. And he would like to understand the knowledge and skills his employees would need to achieve product line success.

Scenario 2: An individual has been appointed software product line manager and is charged with creating a successful product line operation in the division of his organization that produces the software for automotive audio systems. He has launched a product line initiative but has limited understanding of what is really needed to succeed. He needs comprehensive knowledge to determine what practices he might be currently lacking, what practices he needs to improve, how he can use the skills of his current staff, and what additional talent he might need.

Scenario 3: A software architect working for the product line manager described in Scenario 2 is responsible for creating a product line architecture for the family of audio systems. He is new to the whole software product line concept. He needs to understand what is required of him, what will be going on around him, and how his work will fit into the entire software product line effort.

Context: Any individual or organization interested in software product lines.

Problem: To learn the practices required to succeed with software product lines as well as the bodies of knowledge and approximate skill sets of the people needed to carry them out.

Solution: Because the problem involves acquiring a comprehensive understanding of all product line practices, all 29 practice areas are included in the solution. To communicate what knowledge bases are necessary, the practice areas are divided into three groups that we have already referred to as categories: software engineering, technical management, and organizational management.

Static: Table 7.1 describes the static structure of Curriculum by giving the three groups and the practice areas in each. (Note that this is just a reprise of the practice areas as they appear in Part II.)

Dynamics: Practice areas in the same group (or category) share a relation that can be described as "requires the same kind of knowledge as" or "requires the same kind of skill set as." There are also very general relations among categories, as illustrated in Figure 7.3 (which is identical to Figure 7.1 but is repeated here to illustrate how it fits as part of the Curriculum pattern description) and explained below. The technical management practice areas serve to manage and support the software engineering practice areas. The organizational management practice areas serve to enable and orchestrate the totality of the other practice areas.

Table 7.1 Static Structure of the Curriculum Pattern

Software Engineering Practice Areas	Technical Management Practice Areas	Organizational Management Practice Areas
Architecture Definition	Configuration Management	Building a Business Case
Architecture Evaluation	Data Collection, Metrics, and Tracking	Customer Interface Management
Component Development	Make/Buy/Mine/Commission Analysis	Developing an Acquisition Strategy
COTS Utilization	Process Definition	Funding
Mining Existing Assets	Scoping	Launching and Institutionalizing
Requirements Engineering	Technical Planning	Market Analysis
Software System Integration	Technical Risk Management	Operations
Testing	Tool Support	Organizational Planning
Understanding Relevant Domains		Organizational Risk Management
		Structuring the Organization
		Technology Forecasting
		Training

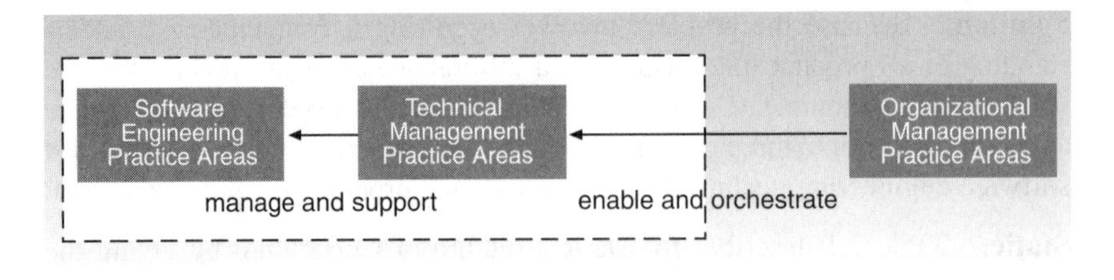

Figure 7.3 Dynamic Structure of the Curriculum Pattern

Application: Curriculum is intended for learning about product lines. An individual can read all three categories to get encyclopedic knowledge or read only the grouping that matches his or her skill set or interests. The CTO in Scenario 1 would use the groupings to match the knowledge and skills of the people in his organization against the practices they would need to master. The product line manager in Scenario 2 would also want to educate himself in all three categories. Given that he already has a product line effort underway, he would certainly want to learn about those practice areas he has not addressed. He would also note how those he has already addressed could be worked more effectively. He would also use the groupings to match the knowledge and skill sets needed with those of the people who work for him and to identify new positions he may have to create. The software architect in Scenario 3 would study carefully all of the software engineering practice areas because those are practices for which he would be responsible or in which he would be directly involved or that would most affect or be affected by his architecture. He might scan the technical management and organizational management practice areas to get an appreciation of what others in the organization must do.

Variants: One could imagine another pattern that includes all 29 practice areas for the purpose of learning about them but that uses another classification scheme and hence has different groups.

Consequences: Curriculum provides a comprehensive picture of the 29 practice areas that must be mastered in order to succeed with product lines. The three groups are helpful because 29 things are too many to learn without any classification scheme and because the software engineering, technical management, and organizational management groups provide a simple classification readily understandable by anyone in the software business. Curriculum provides a handy reference to all of the practice areas, but it is purely educational, and so the pattern is primarily static. The dynamics provide general relations but no real insight into how to prioritize the 29 practice areas for a given organizational context or how to make them operational. Curriculum is not helpful in terms of putting the practice areas into play.

7.4 The Essentials Coverage Pattern

Name: The *Essentials Coverage* pattern gives a mapping of each practice area to each of the three essential product line activities: core asset development, product development, and management.

Example:
Scenario 1: A product line manager has read all of the practice area descriptions and has an appreciation of the skill sets needed to succeed with his product line effort. He knows he needs to develop core assets, develop products from those assets, and manage the entire operation. He would like to determine which practice areas provide the strongest support for each of these essential activities.

Scenario 2: A student studying software product lines has absorbed all of the practice area descriptions and would like to see how each relates to the essential activities and prove that they do in fact cover the "essentials waterfront."

Context: Any individual or organization interested in software product lines.

Problem: To determine how the practice areas map to and provide coverage of the three essential product line activities.

Solution: All 29 practice areas are included in the solution. Although every practice area is supportive of the essential activities in one way or another, some provide stronger support than others.

Static: The structure of Essentials Coverage has three groups of practice areas, named for the three essential activities. Table 7.2 lists the practice areas in each of the three groups. Some of the practice areas are included in more than one group.

Dynamics: Practice areas in the same group are related by a relation that can be described as "strongly supports the same essential activity as." Practice areas can be in more than one group because they strongly support more than one of the essential activities. Several of the management practice areas directly support either core asset development or product development or both, rather than management itself. For example, "Tool Support" is a technical management practice area, but it is in both the "Core Asset Development" and " Product Development" groups. Tool support is what management provides, but it doesn't support management activities as much as it supports the core asset development and product development activities.

Table 7.3 shows these relations and the practice areas' coverage of the essential activities explicitly. The rows are the practice areas in their Curriculum groups. The columns are the primary outputs or dimensions of the three essential activities. A √ in a column denotes the relation "strongly supports the creation or performance of."

Table 7.2 Static Structure of the Essentials Coverage Pattern

Core Asset Development Group	Product Development Group	Management Group
Architecture Definition	Architecture Evaluation	Building a Business Case
Architecture Evaluation	Component Development	Configuration Management
Building a Business Case	Configuration Management	Customer Interface Management
Component Development	Data Collection, Metrics, and Tracking	Data Collection, Metrics, and Tracking
Configuration Management	Developing an Acquisition Strategy	Developing an Acquisition Strategy
COTS Utilization	Operations	Funding
Data Collection, Metrics, and Tracking	Requirements Engineering	Launching and Institutionalizing
Developing an Acquisition Strategy	Software System Integration	Make/Buy/Mine/ Commission Analysis
Make/Buy/ Mine/Commission Analysis	Technical Planning	Market Analysis
Market Analysis	Technical Risk Management	Process Definition
Mining Existing Assets	Testing	Operations
Operations	Tool Support	Organizational Planning
Process Definition	Training	Organizational Risk Management
Requirements Engineering		Scoping
Scoping		Structuring the Organization
Software System Integration		Technical Planning
Technical Planning		Technical Risk Management
Technical Risk Management		Technology Forecasting
Technology Forecasting		
Testing		
Understanding Relevant Domains		

Application: If you are tackling a certain essential activity, you may want to begin by studying those practice areas that strongly support that activity first. Essentials Coverage is exactly what the product line manager in Scenario 1 needs to understand what is necessary to effect each of the three essential activities. If he were to establish a core asset development group, he knows what management practices will be most needed to support that group and what software engineering practice areas they will need to be equipped to handle. The student in Scenario 2 now has a traceability matrix that shows how the essential activities are addressed.

ble 7.3 Dynamic Structure of Essentials Coverage Pattern

	Output of "Core Asset Development" Essential Activity			Output of "Product Development" Essential Activity	Dimensions of "Management" Essential Activity	
	Product Line Scope	Core Assets	Production Plan	Products	Technical Management	Organizational Management
Software Engineering Practice Areas						
chitecture Definition		√				
chitecture Evaluation		√		√		
mponent Development		√		√		
TS Utilization		√				
ing Existing Assets		√				
quirements Engineering	√	√		√		
ftware System Integration		√	√	√		
sting		√		√		
derstanding Relevant Domains	√					
Technical Management Practice Areas						
nfiguration Management		√	√	√	√	
ta Collection, Metrics, and Tracking			√	√	√	
ke/Buy/Mine/Commission Analysis		√			√	
cess Definition		√	√		√	
oping	√				√	
chnical Planning		√	√	√	√	
chnical Risk Management		√		√	√	
l Support		√	√	√		
Organizational Management Practice Areas						
lding a Business Case	√					√
stomer Interface Management					√	√
veloping an Acquisition Strategy		√	√	√		√
nding					√	√

(*continued*)

Table 7.3 Dynamic Structure of Essentials Coverage Pattern (*continued*)

	Output of "Core Asset Development" Essential Activity			Output of "Product Development" Essential Activity	Dimensions of "Management" Essential Activity	
	Product Line Scope	Core Assets	Production Plan	Products	Technical Management	Organizational Management
Launching and Institutionalizing						√
Market Analysis	√					√
Operations		√	√	√	√	√
Organizational Planning						√
Organizational Risk Management						√
Structuring the Organization					√	√
Technology Forecasting	√					√
Training		√		√	√	

Variants: None known.

Consequences: The Essentials Coverage pattern shows the explicit mapping of software product line practice areas to the three essential product line activities. That mapping provides both a helpful foundation for anyone attempting a software product line approach and a big picture of the necessary skill sets and practice areas necessary to accomplish each of the three essential activities. Although this pattern is a bit richer in dynamics than Curriculum, there are still too many practice areas in each group to provide much assistance in dividing and conquering a product line effort. It is more pedagogical than operational.

7.5 Each Asset Pattern

Name: The *Each Asset* pattern consists of practice areas that should be used whenever any asset in the core asset base is being developed.

Example:
Scenario 1: A requirements engineer has been charged with leading the team that develops the product line requirements for a software product line of Web-based

systems that provide interactive training on foreign languages. The scope of the product line has already been determined, and domain models have been built for the areas of interactive training/learning, foreign languages, and effective pedagogy associated with learning foreign languages. The engineer would like to know how he should proceed.

Scenario 2: A technical manager is about to task an experienced component developer with writing the code for a "video switch" component that will be included in the core asset base for a software product line of multimedia systems. The product line requirements, including use cases (with variation points), that apply to video capability are in pretty good shape. The product line architecture exists, including the interface specifications for the video switch component. A decision was made to build this component in-house because (1) no commercial products that both satisfy the requirements and address the scope of product to be included in the product line exist and (2) there isn't any legacy code in the company that can really do the job. The manager wants the job to be done in the best way to help ensure the ultimate success of the software product line. He needs to know how to instruct the component developer to proceed.

Context: An individual knows the asset to be developed, has the specifications or other necessary information for the asset, and knows who will complete the task. The person(s) to complete the task is knowledgeable in that area.

Problem: To use the proper set of practices to develop the asset so that it will be an effective member of the product line's asset base.

Solution: The asset needs to be developed in a way that is appropriate for an asset of its type and with the appropriate tools. However, in addition to the production of the actual asset, there are other necessities related to asset development. There should be a work plan for developing the asset. An attached process that indicates how the asset will be used in the actual production of products should be defined. Each asset (and its attached process) should be tested to guarantee that it meets its specifications and then should be put under configuration management. Data about the asset and its development should be collected as dictated by the measurement plan for the product line. Progress against the work plan should be tracked throughout the asset development process.

Static: The practice areas that address the solution and that provide the structure for the Each Asset pattern are

- The practice area that relates to the development of the asset in question, which we designate PA*
- Tool Support
- Technical Planning
- Process Definition

- Testing
- Configuration Management
- Data Collection, Metrics, and Tracking

Dynamics: As shown in Figure 7.4, each practice area in the group for this pattern serves to complete one or more parts of the solution.

- PA* provides the practices needed to develop the individual asset. For example, PA* would be "Architecture Definition" if the asset in question were the product line architecture, "Component Development" if the asset were a component, "Requirements Engineering" if the asset were the product line requirements, "Developing a Business Case" if the asset were the business case for the product line, and so on. The contribution of PA* to the solution would be the asset itself.
- "Tool Support" contributes the automated support needed to develop the asset.
- "Technical Planning" contributes the work plan by providing the practices needed to develop a technical plan.
- "Process Definition" gives the practices necessary to define a process suitable to a product line environment and yields the attached process for the asset.

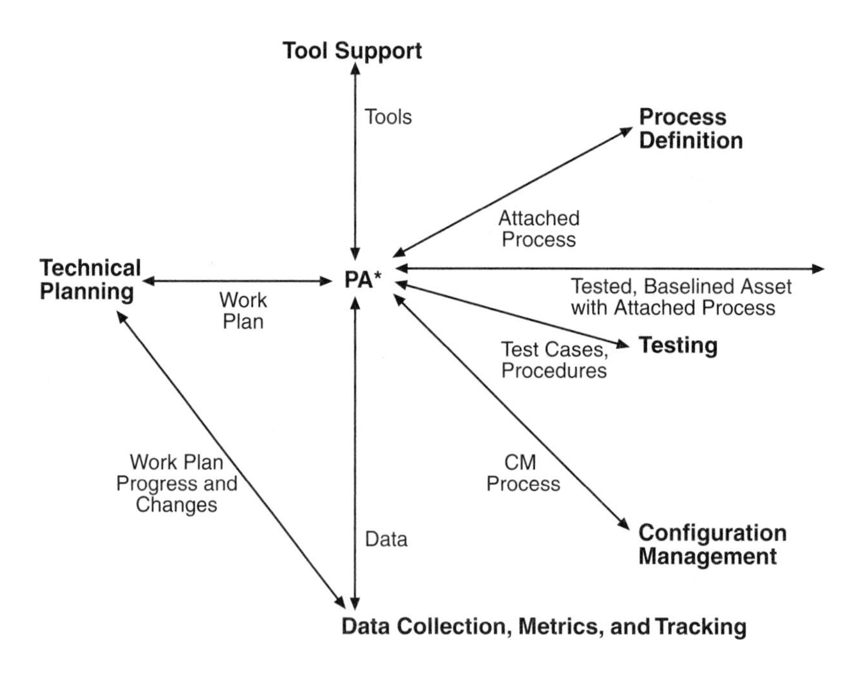

Figure 7.4 Dynamic Structure of the Each Asset Pattern

- "Testing" provides the practices necessary to build test case(s) and testing or validation procedures for the asset and to conduct the test.
- "Configuration Management" practices contribute the configuration management process and tools and show how to incorporate the asset in the asset base and keep it under configuration control.
- "Data Collection, Metrics, and Tracking" practices show how to define the measures appropriate for the asset and its development process and the corresponding data to collect. In addition, these practices track the progress of the asset development and trigger a change in the work plan if necessary.

Of course, these relations, like all of the dynamic relations for the software product line practice patterns, are iterative. For example, there will be a back-and-forth flow between "Testing" and PA* as problems and risks are surfaced during the testing process, and likewise between PA* and "Process Definition" because the definition of the attached process will often bring to light potholes that need to be repaired before the asset is baselined.

Application: Each Asset is an atomic pattern that you can use for the development of each and every asset that is included in the core asset base.

The requirements engineer in Scenario 1 would select practices from "Requirements Engineering" to develop the requirements and identify the tools to use as provided by "Tool Support" practices. With this knowledge as his guide, he would use the practices in "Technical Planning" to build a work plan. The work plan would include tasks to

- use the identified tools and requirements engineering practices to develop the product line requirements;
- employ practices from "Testing" to test the resultant requirements against the scope and domain models he has in hand, as well as any standards that have been set up for the product line requirements;
- define an attached process using "Process Definition" practices to show how the product line requirements should be tailored for a specific product; and
- apply "Configuration Management" practices to add the product line requirements, their test cases, the attached process, and even the work plan to the asset base.

The requirements engineer would then put this plan into effect. Throughout, he would collect the appropriate data according to "Data Collection, Metrics, and Tracking" practices, track progress against the work plan, and initiate any changes to the plan as required.

Variants: The *Each Asset Apprentice* pattern is a variant of Each Asset. Each Asset Apprentice has the same problem and the same context as Each Asset with one minor exception. The condition "The person(s) to complete the task is knowledgeable in that area," is replaced with "The person(s) to complete the task lacks knowledge in that area." The solution (both the static and the dynamics) is similar to Each Asset except that the "Training" practice area is added. Training (in the form of formal instruction or mentoring) will contribute to as many of the other practices as necessary. There is also likely to be more iteration among practices in Each Asset Apprentice because that's just the way it is when you are new on the job.

Evolve Each Asset is another variant that would be used to evolve any asset in the core asset base. The context and the problem of Evolve Each Asset differ in that the word "develop" from Each Asset is replaced with "change." The solution (both the static and the dynamics) is the same as for Each Asset except that PA* would be used to change the asset and "Process Definition" would be used to change the attached process.

We also note that Each Asset is really a family of patterns where each member of the family has a specific practice area associated with PA*.

Consequences: Each Asset is a very handy pattern to have. Not only can it be used to point the way in the development of each and every core asset, but it also shows how the technical management and software engineering practice areas are blended to perform the essential activity of core asset development. This pattern demonstrates clearly that both software engineering and technical management skills are needed, and those skills might very well be resident in the same individual. So, for example, the requirements engineer, who is a use case expert and a domain modeler par excellence, would appeal to his technical management knowledge to develop and track the work plan and to define the attached process. Or perhaps, if he really doesn't have any technical management skills, he would make sure that a person with those skills works with him to complete the management-related tasks.

Each Asset assumes that you know which asset you are responsible for developing and that you have the specifications or other necessary information (ideally as output from one or more other practice areas). If the specifications come in the form of a "mandate from on high," you may need to bring into play the other practice areas that were neglected. For example, in Scenario 1, suppose that the requirements engineer was tasked but had neither a domain model nor a product line scope to work from. Then practices from "Scoping" and "Understanding Relevant Domains" might need to be included as part of his requirements engineering task to compensate for the lack of better information.

Each Asset also assumes the existence of the requisite knowledge to develop the type of asset. If that's not the case, use the Each Asset Apprentice variant. Finally, if it is not clear who is responsible for developing a given asset, Each Asset won't help. Practices from "Structuring the Organization" and/or "Operations" would be necessary first.

7.6 What to Build Pattern

Name: The *What to Build* pattern consists of practice areas that help an organization determine what products ought to be in its software product line—what products to build.

Example:
Scenario 1: A three-year old company develops Web-based registration systems for conferences. They currently have contracts with three major computing conferences, and these systems are in place. They have leads for another six conferences and think the demand could become even greater. They have decided to adopt a product line approach for their systems because there is considerable commonality among the three they have fielded and because maintaining them separately has become a configuration nightmare. They don't want to limit themselves to the systems they have already developed, but it isn't clear to them what other systems ought to be in their product line. On the other hand, they are a small organization, so they really need to target a niche that's narrow enough to limit the complexity of the assets they need to build. Because they don't know what products to build, they can't generate product line requirements or begin the development of the other core assets.

Scenario 2: A well-established company that makes automotive components has decided to begin a new product line of "integrated dashboards" that incorporate many of the individual products they currently market and some they don't, all accessible by the driver from the dashboard interface. There is considerable software and hardware involved, and they will use a product line approach for both. They are new to the integrated dashboard product area. They want to determine what products to include in their product line.

Context: An organization has decided to field a software product line and knows the general product area for the set of products.

Problem: To determine what products should be included in the product line.

Solution: Determining what to build requires information related to the product area, technology, and market; the business justification; and the process for describing the set of products to be included in the product line.

Static: The practice areas that address the solution and that provide the structure for the What to Build pattern are

- Market Analysis
- Understanding Relevant Domains
- Technology Forecasting
- Building a Business Case
- Scoping

Dynamics: Figure 7.5 illustrates the relations among the five practice areas that structure the What to Build pattern.

- "Market Analysis" practices contribute an understanding of the market climate—that is, what products are in demand, what the competition offers and is planning to offer, the size of the market, and the window of opportunity.
- "Understanding Relevant Domains" practices provide a sketch or model of the chosen product area, the features of systems in this area, and the variabilities and commonalities that are present in such systems.
- "Technology Forecasting" practices give predictions of what products might become feasible in the near future.
- "Building a Business Case" practices provide justification for the choice of products and the product line approach to build them.
- "Scoping" practices yield the description of which products will and will not be included in the product line.

There is considerable iteration among the practices in these five areas, most especially between "Building a Business Case" and "Scoping" until the scope is defined clearly enough so that the product line can proceed.

Application: The practices from "Market Analysis," "Understanding Relevant Domains," and "Technology Forecasting" could be conducted in parallel by separate groups. All of the information and output from these three practice areas would be fed to those building the business case and defining the product

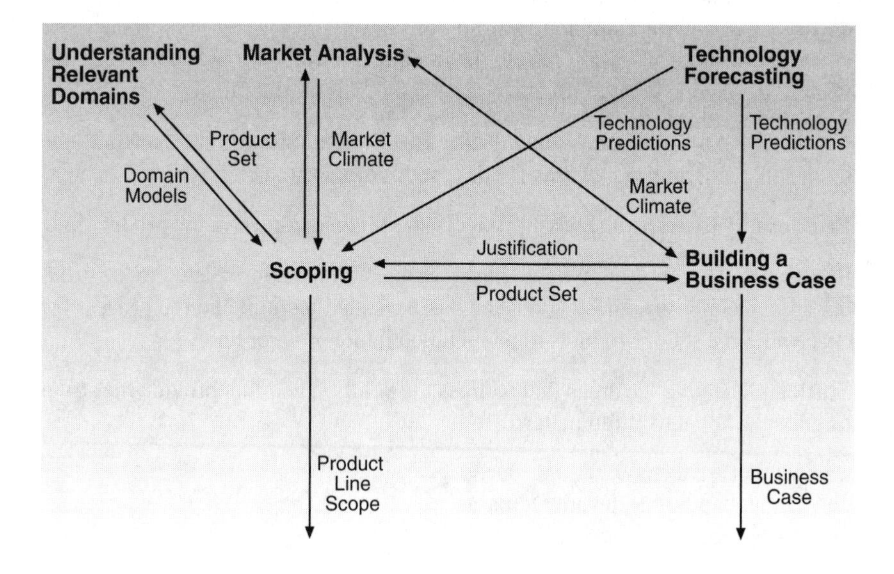

Figure 7.5 Dynamic Structure of the What to Build Pattern

line scope. More information may be requested from either area to get a clearer picture. As a preliminary scope is defined, a preliminary business justification is created (or vice versa), and then the two processes work in tandem until a scope definition for which there is a solid business justification exists.

This pattern is especially applicable to those who are well versed in the marketplace and are able to describe it in its current form and to predict trends and future directions. However, What to Build can be carried out by a small organization that doesn't actually have specialists in each of the five practice areas included in this pattern or by a large organization that does. The large organization would no doubt apply the practices more rigorously, but some degree of each practice area should be applied regardless. Thorough scoping is a must in any case.

What to Build is precisely what the organization in Scenario 1 needs. Because they are small, they may not have market analysis expertise on board. They would either hire a consultant or rely on the business development people in their organization. They would extract the necessary domain information from the three existing systems together and from the systems for which they have leads. They would rely on their sharpest technologists to do the technology forecasting or, again, hire a consultant. The team (or the individual) in charge of product planning would work back and forth between defining the scope and building the business case until they arrived at what products would (at least initially) constitute their product line. The product line scope definition that results from What to Build is used to drive the product line requirements and the product line architecture. The resulting business case is input to "Data Collection, Metrics, and Tracking," "Organizational Risk Management," and "Funding" practices, among others.

The What to Build pattern can also be applied after a product line is already in existence and new market demands, new technology, or the presence of revenue data precipitates a reexamination of what to include in the product line. In fact, the What to Build pattern ought to be an ongoing solution as long as the product line is alive. Periodically revisiting the scope definition is healthy for any product line. One of the benefits available to software product line organizations is the ability to move into new business areas that are close to what they are already producing (see "Past, Present, and Future" sidebar). The What to Build pattern allows for the purposeful expansion or reorientation of an existing scope to efficiently enter potentially lucrative nearby markets.

Variants: The *Analysis* Pattern has a broader context, problem, and solution than What to Build. Analysis determines the locus of trade-off options among approaches—options and strategies that relate not only to what to build, but also to the requirements for the product line, the architecture, and the way individual assets will be developed. The following practice areas are comprised by Analysis:

- Market Analysis
- Understanding Relevant Domains
- Technology Forecasting
- Building a Business Case
- Scoping
- Requirements Engineering
- Architecture Evaluation
- Make/Buy/Mine/Commission Analysis

It could be the case that you have many products in the field that all are very similar. The sheer number of them coupled with the single-system approach with which they are handled has created a situation that has gotten out of hand and spells imminent disaster (like the Fortune 100 company described in the introduction to Part III). You have been told to create a product line from the systems already in the field and get a handle on the situation. What to Build is not appropriate because you already know what market you are in and you don't need a business case; your management has ordered you to construct a software product line from the systems at hand. In this case, the *Forced March* pattern is appropriate.

Forced March is a variant of What to Build that solves the problem "what to look for in the legacy systems that exist" in the context "organization has been directed to create a product line from an existing set of legacy systems." The practice areas in Forced March are just three:

- "Understanding Relevant Domains," which will help you survey the systems in your company's stable and distill out commonalities and variations, and also tell you if there are other related systems that you might expect to add to your product line some day.
- "Technology Forecasting," which will tell you in what directions you should expect products in this area to go in the future.
- "Scoping," which crystallizes the results.

Consequences: What to Build provides a handle on which practices are needed to figure out what is in the product line. Although you may think that knowing what to build has to be the first step, there are many organizations that begin to develop requirements, or worse yet start with the architecture, before they have formulated at least an initial picture of what products are to be in the product line. Although knowing what is architecturally possible is always a good idea, defining an architecture without knowing the product line scope is not. Building assets that target the universe of possible products is an investment that rarely pays off. Organizations, large or small, need to identify a market for their product line, and then, if the market expands, so can the product line. What to Build is a pattern that can help get the product line off to the right start.

What to Build is not useful if organizational management has already dictated what is going to be in the product line (in that case, use the Forced March variant instead) or if the developing organization has been commissioned to build a product line that has already been defined.

7.7 Product Parts Pattern

Name: The *Product Parts* pattern is a composite pattern. It consists of practice areas and other patterns that should be used to develop the core assets that will be part of the products in the product line.

Example:
Scenario: A company that develops medical systems has decided to use a product line approach for its brain scanner products. The company has a rich legacy of such products in its inventory to draw from. The initial scope for this product line has been determined. No commercial products are available for this product area, and outsourcing component development is not an option. Architecture, core component development, and core test teams have been established and staffed with knowledgeable individuals. The architecture team is responsible for the product line requirements, the definition and evaluation of the product line architecture, and the determination of the source of components. The core component development team is responsible for seeing that components are developed. The core test team is responsible for integrating and testing the assembly of the components prescribed by the architecture. The product line manager would like these organizational units to use the best practices to accomplish their tasks.

Context: An organization knows what products are to be included in the product line and has designated knowledgeable individuals or groups to develop the core assets that will be used to develop the products.

Problem: To develop the core assets that will be joined together to form the products in the software product line.

Solution: The core assets of interest to Product Parts are the product line requirements, the product line architecture, the components, and their test-related artifacts that will be included in the asset base. Each of these core assets needs to be equipped with an attached process that describes how it will be used in the construction of products. The best source for each component needs to be determined. Individual components could be built in-house, mined from something the organization already has, bought if commercially available, or contracted out to someone else to build. Each core asset needs to be tested, and the suite of core assets needs to be integrated and tested.

Static: There are four product line practice patterns and seven practice areas that address the solution and provide the structure for the Product Parts pattern. The patterns are

- Each Asset for requirements
- Each Asset for architecture
- Each Asset for components
- Each Asset for test-related artifacts

The practice areas are

- Architecture Evaluation
- Make/Buy/Mine/Commission Analysis
- Mining Existing Assets
- COTS Utilization
- Developing an Acquisition Strategy
- Software Systems Integration
- Testing

Dynamics: Figure 7.6 illustrates the relations among the patterns and practice areas that structure the Product Parts pattern.

- Each Asset for requirements yields the product line requirements that drive the product line architecture and component definition along with the attached process for using the requirements to build products.
- Each Asset for architecture delivers the product line architecture that specifies the components and its attached process.
- Each Asset for components provides components and their attached processes.
- Each Asset for testing provides the reusable test plans, test cases, and other test-related artifacts, along with their attached processes.
- "Architecture Evaluation" provides a careful analysis of the product line architecture.
- "Make/Buy/Mine/Commission Analysis" practices determine the best source for each component.
- "Mining Existing Assets" practices reveal which assets in the legacy base could be rehabilitated for inclusion as core assets and deliver components from the legacy base.
- "COTS Utilization" practices reveal which components are commercially available and buy selected ones for the asset base.
- "Developing an Acquisition Strategy" practices set up the machinery necessary to commission component development. (The organization so commissioned then uses Each Asset for component development.)
- "Software System Integration" practices assemble the components as dictated by the product line architecture.

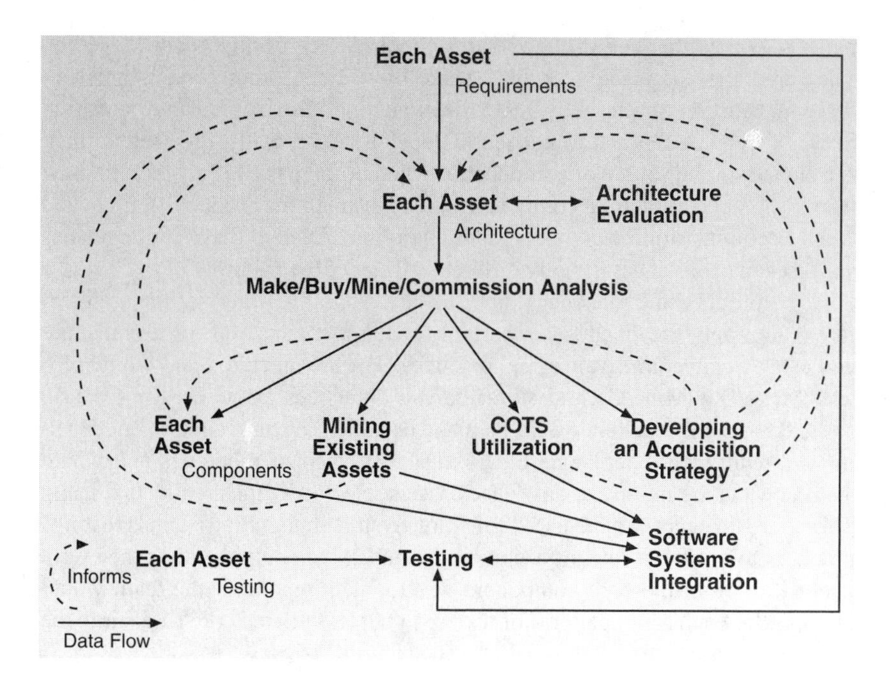

Figure 7.6 Dynamic Structure of the Product Parts Pattern

- "Testing" practices test individual assets (within the Each Asset pattern) and the assembly of components as dictated by the product line architecture.

Product line requirements are themselves product parts, but they also can be thought of as the bridge between What to Build and the rest of the product parts that are in the asset base. Every product needs an architecture, and it should be evaluated. Once the architecture has defined the components that will compose the products, the source of those components must be determined, and they must be obtained. The third tier of Figure 7.6 ("Make/Buy/Mine Commission Analysis") accounts for that determination, and the tier below that takes care of obtaining them. System building (integration and testing) is ongoing as components are completed. The relations are not unidirectional as the figure illustrates. The availability of components (either on the open COTS market or in an organization's own vaults) may well influence the architecture.

Application: Product Parts is a composite pattern with practices that require individuals and teams with a combination of software engineering and technical management skills. The practices will get parceled out depending on the way the product line organization has been structured and the way the roles and responsibilities are defined. In small organizations or in the case of a relatively simple product set, one team might be responsible for all of the practices in the pattern. At the other end of the spectrum, multiple teams might work together. The practices associated with "Make/Buy/Mine/Commission Analysis," "Mining Existing Assets," "COTS Utilization," and "Developing an Acquisition Strategy" may or may not be needed. It depends, respectively, on whether there is a choice for the source of components, whether there is a legacy base to draw from, whether commercial components are relevant to the product solution, and whether commissioning components is an option. (Each of these contingencies suggests an obvious but trivially different variant of the pattern.)

The product line manager in the scenario would require that the architecture team apply the Each Asset pattern for requirements and for architecture and use "Architecture Evaluation" practices. The architecture team would also use "Make/Buy/Mine/Commission/Analysis" practices, but under the scenario as stated, the only options would be make or mine. The core component development team would apply the Each Asset pattern for components and would also carry out the mining of any legacy assets selected by the architecture team. The core test team would use "Software System Integration" and "Testing" practices to gradually integrate and test assemblies of components as they were handed off from the core component development team, but the team would also use the Each Asset pattern for testing to put test-related core assets into the asset repository.

Variants: If the individuals or groups designated to build one or more of the core assets to be included in products do not have the knowledge or skills required to carry out their roles, then the appropriate Each Asset pattern should be replaced by the corresponding Each Asset Apprentice variant.

Green Field is a variant of Product Parts that makes the context more restricted by adding the phrase "has not built products of this type before and will develop or buy all assets." (For this variant, the example scenario would be changed by deleting the phrase "a rich legacy of such products in their inventory.") The static structure of Green Field is the same as for Product Parts except that "Developing an Acquisition Strategy" and "Mining Existing Assets" are deleted.

Barren Field is a variant just like Green Field, applied when the scope has not yet been determined. It consists of the Green Field variant with the What to Build pattern added.

Plowed Field is another variant of Product Parts that similarly makes the context of Product Parts more restricted by adding the phrase "but will use existing products in the product scope as the source of as many assets as possible." The static structure of Plowed Field is the same as for Product Parts except that "Developing an Acquisition Strategy" is deleted. However, in the case of Plowed Field, the dynamics are quite different, as illustrated in Figure 7.7.

"Mining Existing Assets" practices would dominate and would be performed before and after any requirements were defined or practices from

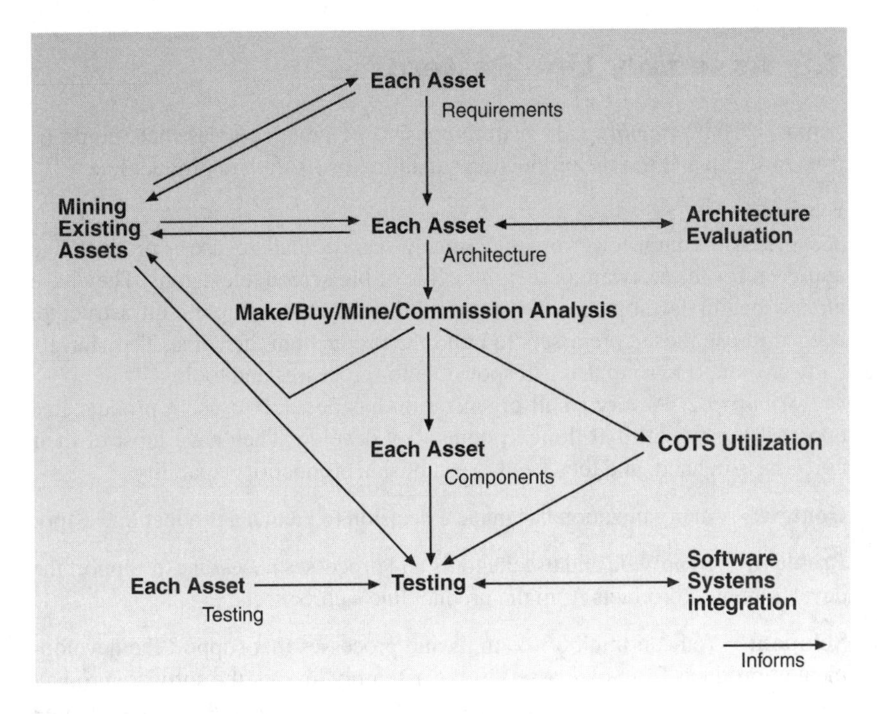

Figure 7.7 Dynamic Structure of the Plowed Field Pattern

almost all of the other practice areas were carried out. Existing assets would be candidates for all that would become product parts, including the product line architecture.

One could also imagine other variants that would make the context more specific. For example, the context might be "An organization knows what products are to be included in the product line, has designated knowledgeable individuals or groups to develop the core assets that will be used to develop the products but will commission all component development to an outside organization." In this case, the structure of the variant would probably eliminate the practice areas "Make/Buy/Mine/Commission Analysis," "Mining Existing Assets," and "COTS Utilization."

Consequences: Product Parts links together the practices that design and provide the parts that will roll down the product line assembly line to be joined together to form products. It provides a handy road map for core asset development. Product Parts assumes that you know what products are going to be included in the product line and that assignments within the organization have been made to develop the core assets. These are two big givens without which the pattern will not be effective.

7.8 Assembly Line Pattern

Name: The *Assembly Line* pattern consists of practice areas that should be used to set up and run the production capability of a software product line.

Example:
Scenario 1: A large electronics company has decided to use a product line approach for the software in their new line of big screen televisions. They have already begun developing core assets and they want to set up the infrastructure needed to use those core assets to build the products in their line. They have a software support group that is responsible for processes and tools.

Scenario 2: A very small organization has decided to use a product line approach for the utility billing systems they develop. They have most of their core assets in hand, and they need to establish a production capability.

Context: An organization has made a decision to launch a product line effort.

Problem: To provide and use the tools and processes necessary to support the development of products from the product line's core assets.

Solution: You can think of the tools and processes that support the development of products from core assets as the assembly line for the software product line; they provide the production capability to build products. The assembly line dictates how to assemble the products from their core asset parts. It also specifies which asset versions to use and where to find them, the schedule for the assembly, how to use automated tools to speed up the process, and how to coordinate all of the activities involved in the assembly operation.

Static: The practice areas that address the solution and that provide the structure for the Assembly Line pattern are

- Configuration Management
- Process Definition
- Tool Support
- Operations
- Technical Planning
- Organizational Planning

Dynamics: Figure 7.8 illustrates the relations among the six practice areas that populate the Assembly Line pattern.

- "Configuration Management" practices ensure that the assembly line and all of the assets to be used in products are up-to-date and that the right versions are used.
- "Process Definition" provides the expertise necessary to craft the production plan, which is the blueprint for how the assembly line will work.

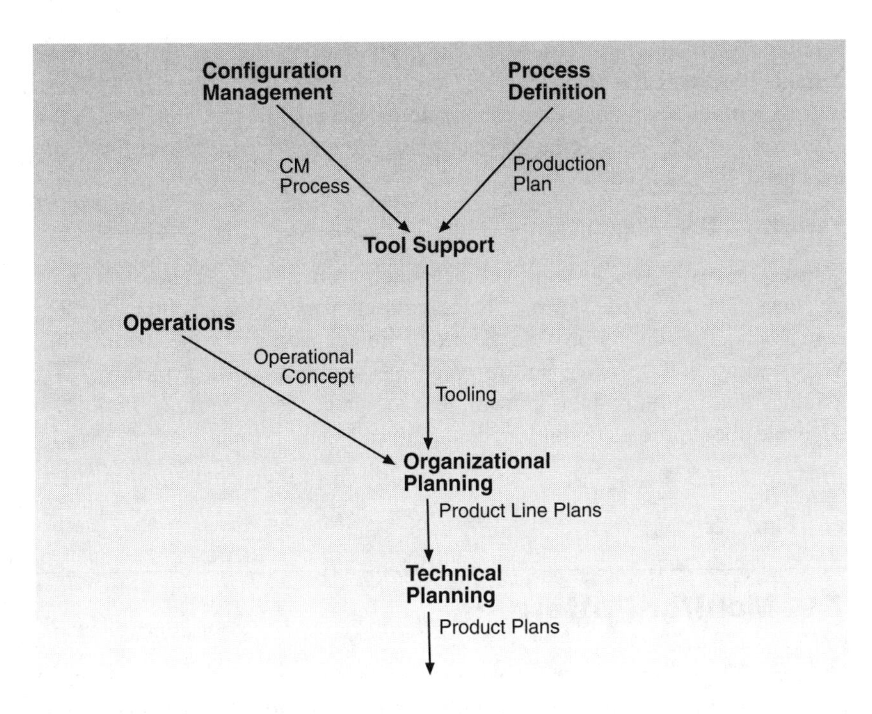

Figure 7.8 Dynamic Structure of the Assembly Line Pattern

- "Tool Support" provides the tooling for the production process.
- "Operations" dictates the flow of all activites in the assembly line.
- "Technical Planning" and "Organizational Planning" practices yield product line and individual product plans that enable the organization to forecast resource needs and product delivery dates and to provide for both in a timely manner.

Application: A large organization might charter a software support group. Such a group would be responsible for carrying out some of the technical management practices that make up the Assembly Line pattern. For example, the software support group of the company from Scenario 1 would be tasked with defining and implementing both the configuration management process and the production plan as well as selecting and administering the appropriate tool support. They would also assist the product managers and the product line manager in the development of product plans and the operation concept. The tools that are chosen should always support the processes and plans and not dictate them.

In a small organization such as the one in Scenario 2, the product line manager and one or two developers would perform the Assembly Line practices. Processes, plans, and tool support for the production capability are important for small organizations because they determine the efficiency with which products can be assembled. Only those tasked to carry out the practices are capable of defining processes and plans.

As with the dynamics for all the patterns, the relations are iterative. In this case, for example, as specific product plans are developed, product line plans may need to be revised.

Variants: None known.

Consequences: The Assembly Line pattern provides the handle on those practices that are needed to use the core assets routinely and efficiently. The core assets alone do not provide the production capability for the product line. You need a rapid, reliable, and repeatable assembly process. Assembly Line assumes that the individuals carrying out the practices are sufficiently knowledgeable about process definition, planning, and support tools.

7.9 Monitor Pattern

Name: The *Monitor* pattern consists of practice areas that all serve to monitor an ongoing product line effort and apply course corrections to keep activities on track.

Example:
Scenario 1: A company has a software product line of flight simulator video games. They have a core asset base. They have fielded five different games, all still being sold, from the set of assets. They need to keep a watchful eye on the organization to guarantee that all of the product line processes are being followed, existing plans are realistic, their products are being well received in the marketplace, and their staff is performing according to expectations. They also need to be nimble in changing plans and processes to fine-tune their operations or to become more responsive to their market.

Scenario 2: TelecomPlus recently launched a software product line effort for their new line of mobile phones. The product line architecture has been developed, and component development is nearing completion. The first product to be built from the assets is being actively marketed, and development has just begun. Their schedule to get this first product to market is tight. They need to ensure that their product line effort will get them to market on time *and* will poise them for the second product, which is to appear close on the heels of the first.

Context: An organization has a software product line effort in play.

Problem: To monitor the product line operation and apply course corrections when needed.

Solution: Monitoring a product line operation requires routinely performed practices that keep a pulse on the organization by collecting and analyzing process and product data, communicating with customers, and identifying and analyzing risks. It also requires routinely performed practices that precipitate needed changes in product line operations.

Static: There are two groups of practice areas that address the solution and provide the structure for the Monitor pattern:

1. The Listen Group includes
   - Data Collection, Metrics, and Tracking
   - Technical Risk Management
   - Organizational Risk Management
   - Customer Interface Management
2. The Response Group includes
   - Technical Planning
   - Organizational Planning
   - Process Definition

Dynamics: Figure 7.9 shows the relations between the two groups in the Monitor pattern. The practice areas in the Listen Group keep a pulse on the organization and provide recommendations to the Response Group. Specifically,

- "Data Collection, Metrics, and Tracking" practices yield the raw input needed to assess progress, operational well-being, adherence to defined processes, and the need for course correction.
- "Technical Risk Management" and "Organizational Risk Management" practices identify, analyze, mitigate, and track risks at multiple levels in the organization in an effort to avoid the pitfalls associated with software product lines.
- "Customer Interface Management" practices keep a watch on the customers of the product line, ensuring that they are satisfied with the products in the product line and that their feedback is received and acted on if necessary.

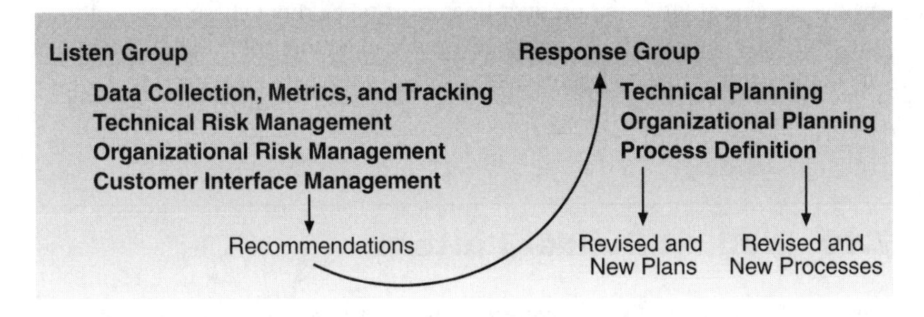

Figure 7.9 Dynamic Structure of the Montior Pattern

The practices in the Response Group precipitate changes. Specifically,

- Both "Technical Planning" and "Organizational Planning" practices adjust the many work and other plans that plot the product line activities and provide the marching orders for those involved in the product line operation.
- "Process Definition" practices provide needed or advantageous improvements in existing product line processes as well as new processes to address risks or problems that have surfaced.

Application: Monitor, as its name suggests, is an ongoing pattern that needs to be applied for the life of the product line. Managers at both the technical and organizational levels do the work associated with the Monitor pattern. They employ practices from "Data Collection, Metrics, and Tracking"; both risk management practice areas; and "Customer Interface Management" to gauge progress, efficiency, appropriateness of plans and processes, and quality of both assets and products. They use practices from the planning practice areas and from "Process Definition" to instigate needed changes.

Monitor applies to the companies in both Scenarios 1 and 2, even though these companies are at different stages of their product line operations. The video game company in Scenario 1 is in a product line steady state. Most likely this organization has already identified people to carry out most of the Monitor practices. They might actually have a product line steering group that reviews the data and risks collected by groups involved in the product line and makes recommendations for changes in plans or processes. On the other hand, TelecomPlus from Scenario 2 might need to define roles and responsibilities to apply the Monitor pattern.

Variants: None known.

Consequences: Monitor is especially useful for an organization in the early stages of a product line effort because it identifies the practices on which they need to keep a watchful eye. These are practices that might be neglected in the heat of getting the assets built and that first product or two out the door. More mature product line organizations can also benefit because metrics, customer interface, and risk management programs are typically quite Spartan in their early years and grow as the product line effort takes root. These organizations will often have the luxury of applying Monitor in a more robust and less urgent way than their less mature counterparts.

7.10 Product Builder Pattern

Name: The *Product Builder* pattern consists of practice areas that should be used whenever any product in the product line is being developed.

Example:
Scenario: A medical electronics company has launched a software product line of heart monitors. They have established their production capability and are in the process of building the core assets and creating the production plan. They have selected the first product to be part of the product line and the team that will build the product. The team wants to understand the practices that will be part of their product-building effort.

Context: An organization has already established the production plan, the production capability, and the core asset base and has designated knowledgeable individuals or groups to develop a product that has been determined to be in the product line.

Problem: To develop a product from the core assets using the production plan.

Solution: The production plan is followed using the established production capability to create an instance of the product line. Any additional components are developed and integrated into those assembled from the asset base. The components are integrated and tested according to the production plan.

Static: The practice areas that address the solution and provide the structure for the Product Builder pattern are

- Requirements Engineering
- Architecture Definition
- Architecture Evaluation
- Component Development
- Testing
- Software System Integration

Dynamics: Figure 7.10 illustrates the relations of the practice areas in Product Builder.

- "Requirements Engineering" practices yield product-specific requirements based on the product line requirements and the attached process for tailoring them for specific products.
- "Architecture Definition" practices create an instance architecture for the new product from the product line architecture according to its attached process.
- "Architecture Evaluation" practices evaluate the product architecture.
- "Component Development" practices deliver the components for the product.
- "Testing" practices test individual parts of the product as well as the assembled whole.
- "Software System Integration" practices assemble the components.

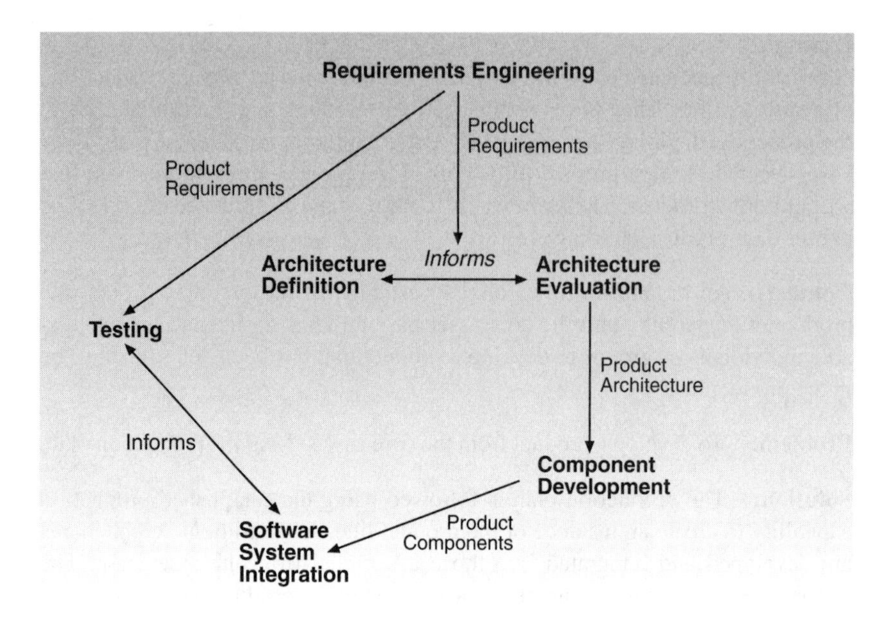

Figure 7.10 Dynamic Structure of the Product Builder Pattern

Application: Building products is a matter of following the production plan, which includes an attached process for the major product artifacts. You generate the product requirements, following the attached process for the product line requirements. You create an architecture instance for the product, following the attached process for the product line architecture. You should evaluate the product architecture. The evaluation can be abbreviated if the product architecture does not differ in quality-attribute-affecting ways from the product line architecture. Otherwise, you need a separate and thorough evaluation. Components can be used directly from the asset base, used directly after binding in the built-in variabilities, used after modification or adaptation, or developed specifically for the product. Testing is done as the product is developed to verify that each part of the product is correct and suitable. Test cases, test scripts, and test data from the asset base are used according to their attached processes. These test artifacts will need to be developed if components were developed specifically for the product. Testing is also done to validate the product against its requirements. Software system integration follows the tested integration scheme for all the products in the product line and so is usually quite simple unless new components have been created for the product. This is the course that the product team in the scenario would follow.

Variants: Road Race Plus decided to use for their software a product line approach that handles the timing, placement, and statistics for road races of all sorts. They have the core assets and have an established production capability. They use a system generation approach to production, have developed two products in the product line, and they are about to develop a third. They have already determined that the third product fits within the product line scope and have designated a software engineer to be responsible for the new product. He has not been involved in either of the previous product efforts and would like to know the practices he needs to complete his assignment.

This scenario seems to fit Product Builder. However, Road Race Plus's system generation approach gives a slightly different twist that makes a variant of Product Builder more appropriate. *Product Gen* is a variant of Product Builder that applies if the production plan for the product line takes a system generation approach. In that case, the requirements for the product are needed; then, to integrate the system you just provide appropriate values for the necessary parameters and launch the construction tool. Finally, you test the result.

Therefore the following practice areas structure Product Gen:

- Requirements Engineering
- System Integration
- Testing

Product Gen would be appropriate for the given scenario. The software engineer in this scenario follows the production plan, which would probably have him develop the product requirements by selecting appropriate variations for the variation points given in the product line requirements. He would then determine the corresponding parameter values, launch the construction tool to generate the system, and test the result.

Consequences: Product Builder collects those practices that are needed to construct products. It assumes that you have a production capability, an existing asset base, and knowledgeable product developers. If any of these are missing, the practices in Product Builder will have to be performed in harmony with those for Assembly Line and Product Parts.

7.11 Cold Start Pattern

Name: The *Cold Start* pattern consists of practice areas that should be used whenever any organization is launching a software product line for the first time.

Example:
Scenario: A company that develops software for engine control systems has decided to use a product line approach for the software it builds. This is the first software product line the company has considered. The director of the engine

control business unit wants to know what he needs to do to get the effort started, and then he wants to do it.

Context: An organization is launching its first software product line.

Problem: To effectively prepare the organization for its first software product line production.

Solution: The organization must shape itself so that it can effectively use a product line approach to turn out products. The person(s) in charge must fund the effort; put in place an organizational structure that designates core asset developers, product developers, assembly line builders, and so on; provide training for the people involved; prepare customers for the new approach; develop an acquisition strategy for any suppliers that will be involved; develop a concept of operations; establish an organizational risk management program; and create a product line adoption plan. All of these tasks are about launching the software product line.

Static: The practice areas that address the solution and provide the structure for the Cold Start pattern are

- Launching and Institutionalizing
- Funding
- Customer Interface Management
- Developing an Acquisition Strategy
- Operations
- Organizational Planning
- Organizational Risk Management
- Structuring the Organization
- Training

Dynamics: Figure 7.11 illustrates the relations among the practice areas in Cold Start.

- "Launching and Institutionalizing" practices suggest how the other practice areas in the pattern are threaded for the particular organization and prepare the organization for the technology adoption experience that embracing a product line approach brings.
- "Funding" provides the means by which the asset development, production capability, and launching tasks will be financed.
- "Structuring the Organization" determines the needed organizational units and puts the right people in the right positions.
- "Operations" practices yield a product line operational concept that identifies the roles and responsibilities of the individuals and groups involved in the product line effort.

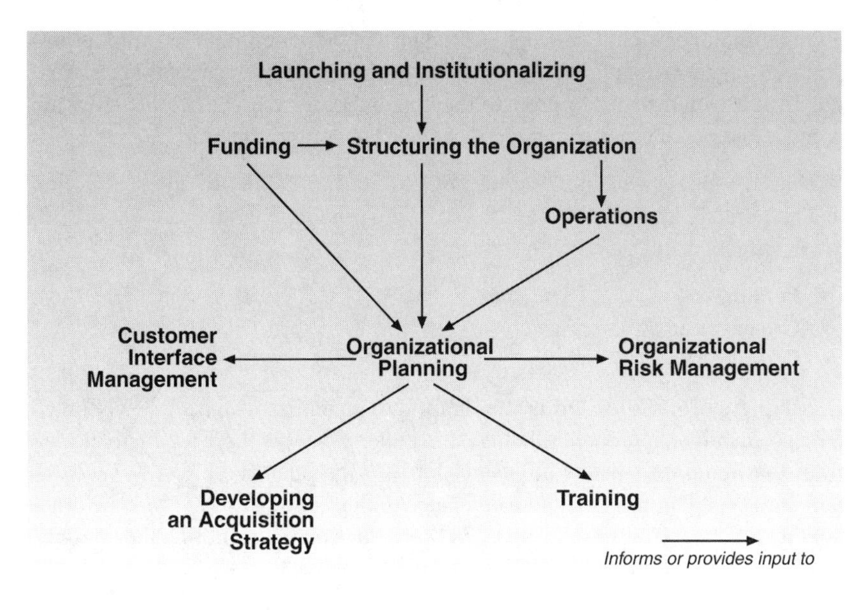

Figure 7.11 Dynamic Structure of the Cold Start Pattern

- "Organizational Planning" practices provide a product line adoption plan that the organization will follow in launching the product line.
- "Customer Interface Management" prepares the customer community, and the organization's interface with it, for the product line approach.
- "Developing an Acquisition Strategy" determines how the organization will interface with any suppliers of assets.
- "Training" practices will institute a training program to prepare personnel to use product line practices.
- "Organizational Risk Management" practices will put in place a risk management program that will identify, analyze, and track risks that threaten the entire product line effort.

Application: People in charge apply Cold Start; organizational management skills and authority are required. The person(s) in charge would begin with launching practices as a way to frame the other practices. The engine control director of the company in the scenario would use launching practices to learn what needs to take place in his organization to make the technology shift to product lines and to make sure that it happens. He would determine a way to finance the effort. He would set up organizational units that would accomplish the product line tasks, ensuring that there were individuals or groups responsible for determining the product line scope, developing and evolving the assets, setting up the production capability, monitoring the effort, and building products. Either he or someone (or some group) he designates would develop a product line operational concept, a product line adoption plan, a training program, an organizational risk management program, and an acquisition strategy. Finally, he would begin to prepare the customers for the shift to the software product line paradigm. Leadership is required to apply Cold Start.

Variants: *Warm Start* is a variant of Cold Start; it applies to an organization that has already launched at least one software product line. In this case, the following practice areas are involved:

- Funding
- Organizational Planning
- Operations

Consequences: Cold Start is very helpful to managers who have newly opted for a product line approach. It helps them understand that there are many necessities that require their attention in order for a product line effort to succeed. Software product lines cannot be delegated to the technical staff; there are practices that managers must take on. Cold Start relies on the authority, the commitment, and the organizational skills of whoever applies it.

7.12 In Motion Pattern

Name: The *In Motion* pattern consists of practice areas that keep a product line effort going after it has been launched. In Motion is really a variant of Cold Start but is described separately because it plays a major role in product line efforts.

Example: A robot manufacturer has launched a product line for the software in its line of warehouse robots. Funds have been secured, groups have been set up and tasked, a product line manager has been appointed, and a product line adoption plan has been developed and is now being implemented. The product line manager has developed an operational concept, a training program, a risk management program, and an acquisition strategy. She has also prepared customers for the new approach being taken to develop the software for warehouse robots. The groups that have been set up to do the product line work are functioning. The product line manager now wants to know what practices she needs to adopt in order to keep the effort in motion.

Context: A product line effort has been launched.

Problem: To keep the product line effort going.

Solution: The organization must continue to stoke the product line fire. The person(s) in charge must ensure that funds to operate the effort are sufficient, operations are running smoothly, personnel are adequately prepared for their tasks, and both customers and suppliers are in close communication and in tune with the product line effort. Changes in the organizational structure are made as necessary.

Static: The practice areas that address the solution and provide the structure for the In Motion pattern are

- Customer Interface Management
- Developing an Acquisition Strategy
- Funding
- Operations
- Structuring the Orgnanization
- Training

Dynamics: Figure 7.12 illustrates the relations among the practice areas in In Motion.

- "Funding" supplies a steady source to finance operations.
- "Operations" practices play out the operational concept, implementing the defined processes and following the defined plans. The parts of the processes that accommodate feedback and improvement are especially relevant to In Motion.
- "Training" implements the training program that prepares the players in the product line effort for their roles.
- "Customer Interface Management" practices provide ongoing connection with the customers—keeping them informed, receiving their feedback, and making sure they are on board with the product line effort.

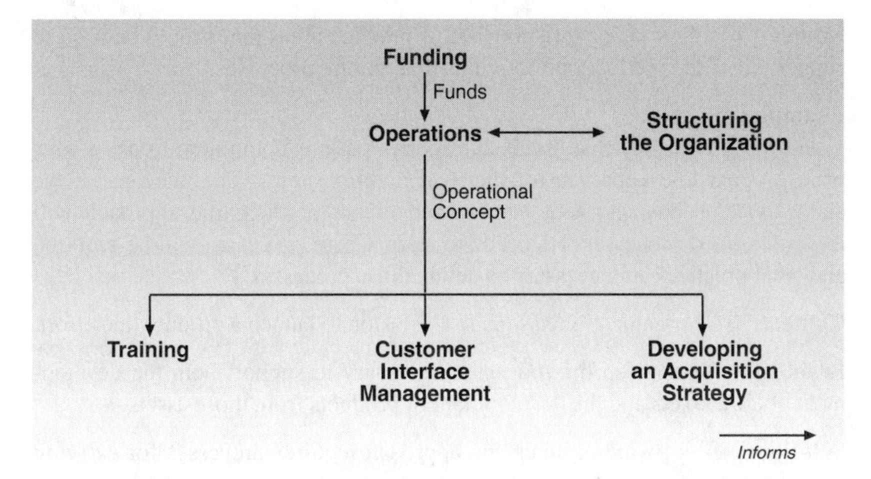

Figure 7.12 Dynamic Structure of the In Motion Pattern

- "Developing an Acquisition Strategy" practices follow the acquisition strategy to ensure that suppliers perform their roles in the product line effort according to defined processes and plans.
- "Structuring the Organization" practices refine the original staffing and structure decisions based on feedback from customers, those who monitor the operations, trainers, and suppliers.

Application: People in charge apply In Motion; organizational management skills and authority are required. Generally, a product line manager is assigned. For example, the product line manager in the scenario would keep a close watch on her budget and financials to ensure that funds for the product line effort are stable and adequate. She would do all that is necessary to see that everyone involved is operating according to defined processes and plans. She would guarantee that customers and suppliers are being included in the loop and that the personnel are adequately trained. And finally, she would make changes in organizational structure or reassign tasks and/or roles when needed. Leadership is required to apply In Motion.

Variants: None known.

Consequences: In Motion is a wonderful guide for product line managers. It provides the set of practices that should be the focus of the person(s) in charge.

7.13 Process Pattern

Name: The *Process* pattern consists of practice areas that should be used to support all of the product line activities that require processes.

Example:
Scenario: A company that builds automotive parts is committed to use a software product line approach for their car audio systems. The manager of the audio systems business unit has learned that a product line approach will require defined processes. He needs to learn where processes will be required and what practices are necessary to define those processes.

Context: An organization has made a decision to launch a product line effort.

Problem: To develop the processes necessary to support both the development of core assets and the development of products from those assets.

Solution: A software product line approach requires processes for carrying out an assortment of activities so that those activities are performed routinely and with predictable results by one or more teams operating harmoniously. An organization that decides on a product line approach must have foundational skills in process definition and must ensure that those skills are applied to defining the required processes.

Static: There is a single group that contains practice areas and patterns that addresses the solution and provides the structure for the Process pattern. The pattern in Process is

- Each Asset for all the assets in the asset base

The practice areas in Process are

- Configuration Management
- Data Collection, Metrics, and Tracking
- Process Definition
- Operations
- Organizational Planning
- Organizational Risk Management
- Technical Planning
- Technical Risk Management

Dynamics: Figure 7.13 shows the relations among the practice areas in the Process pattern.

- "Process Definition" practices provide the capability to define and document processes.
- Each Asset yields an attached process for each asset in the asset base.
- "Configuration Management" practices provide the configuration management process(es) that will be followed for core assets, for products, and for the two in concert.
- "Data Collection, Metrics, and Tracking" practices yield a process for data collection as well as the analysis and tracking of the resultant measures.

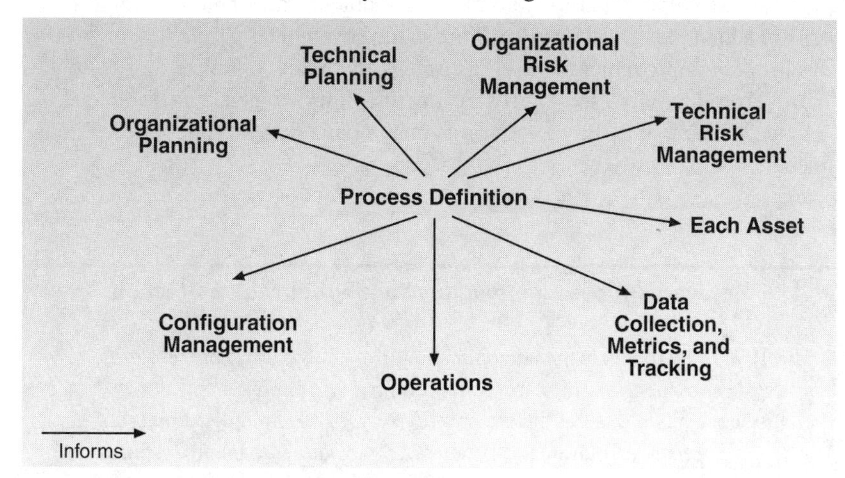

Figure 7.13 **Dynamic Structure of the Process Pattern**

- "Operations" practices deliver the overall process that keeps the product line effort operating smoothly.
- "Organizational Planning" and "Technical Planning" offer planning processes that create the many plans needed in the product line organization.
- "Organizational Risk Mangement" and "Technical Risk Management" provide the risk management processes to be followed at various levels in the product line organization.

Application: In a medium-sized to large organization, there is often a group dedicated to process definition and improvement. Such a software process support group has the resident expertise in defining and documenting processes. Either they define the processes needed by the product line organization or they work with (or coach) other individuals or teams to do so. They are likely to be the maintainers of the processes for the product line organization.

In a small organization, there is probably no dedicated process support group, but then the processes can be of lighter weight. Nonetheless, even a small organization must have someone with process definition capabilities because defined processes are important regardless of the size of the organization.

Process will show the product line manager in the scenario that processes are needed throughout the product line organization and where the process definition capability is essential.

Variants: *Process Improvement* is a variant of Process with the following context/problem pair:

Context: An organization has an ongoing product line effort.

Problem: To improve the processes necessary to support both the development of core assets and the development of products from those assets.

The "Launching and Institutionalizing" practice area and the Monitor pattern are added to the structure for Process Improvement.

Process improvement is itself a strategy that many organizations follow to improve productivity (see "Software Process Improvement and Product Line Practice" sidebar and "Process Improvement Gains with a Product Line Focus" sidebar).

Software Process Improvement and Product Line Practice

The 1990s saw the widespread application of manufacturing process principles to the development of software. Software process improvement, based on the quality concepts pioneered by Crosby [Crosby 79], Deming [Deming 86], and others, has resulted in dramatic benefits. Organizations typically report return on investment (ROI) figures of 5:1 to 8:1 for successful software process improvement. Additional quantified benefits include productivity gains, improved time-to-market, significantly improved project planning estimations, and reduced defect rates. Other observed benefits include improved employee morale, less employee turnover, and increased customer satisfaction.

Process improvement has a significant relationship to product line practice. Product line practice is strategic in nature. A strategic effort requires more coordination, discipline, and commonality of approach than a more independent effort. Dependencies within an organization are greater, and predictability and quality become even more critical. Process discipline can provide the basis for a strategic effort and has proven that it can provide better predictability and quality. Thus, an organization with a culture of process discipline is much better poised for product line success.

Many organizations have had success by basing their improvement efforts on the Capability Maturity Model (CMM) for Software [Paulk 95]. The CMM is a model that contains the essential elements of effective processes for software development. The most recent descendant of the CMM is the CMMI (Capability Maturity Model Integrated) for Systems Engineering/Software Engineering, which additionally incorporates essential elements for systems engineering [SEI 00]. The wide acceptance of this model is evidenced by large annual Software Engineering Process Group (SEPG) conferences in both North America and Europe, as well as by the more than 100 Software Process Improvement Network (SPIN) chapters worldwide. While the CMM is not the only model for software process improvement, its widespread acceptance makes it a de facto standard. Because the CMMI models are scheduled eventually to replace the CMM model, the rest of this discussion will focus on the CMMI models.

Structurally, there are two representations for CMMI models, the *staged representation* and the *continuous representation*. A major organizing element for both representations is the *process area*. A process area is a group of related activities that are performed collectively to achieve a set of goals. In the context of these models, processes refer to "what to do" rather than "how to do it." A process area specifies goals that describe the result of successful application and practices that prescribe activities to achieve those goals. Some goals and practices are specific to the process area; others are generic and apply across all process areas. The generics describe essential ways a process can be *institutionalized*. Institutionalization refers to the degree of repeatability, standardization, and sophistication of control of a process.

The staged representation has the additional major organizing element of the *maturity level*. A maturity level is an indicator of the extent to which a set of processes is institutionalized. The degree of institutionalization of an individual process area in the continuous representation is referred to as the *capability level* of that process area. Maturity levels recognized by the CMMI are

1. *Initial:* The organization has informal process control; no process areas are institutionalized.

2. **Managed:** Here, in the level of basic project management, processes are standardized within individual projects.
3. **Defined:** This level is characterized by process standardization across projects.
4. **Quantitatively Managed:** Quantitative management of processes is the hallmark of this level.
5. **Optimizing:** Continuous process improvement occurs at this level.

Maturity levels also provide a recommended order for implementing processes within an organization. Continuous representation models do not contain a recommended implementation order. While in theory this implies freedom of implementation order when using a continuous representation, key associations among the process areas preclude arbitrary implementations. Experienced implementers often take advantage of the strengths of both representations. For example, while relying on a staged ordering as a "first cut" prioritization, you might vary the basic implementation ordering based on business needs or "where it hurts most."

How do the CMMI's 22 process areas compare with the 29 practice areas for product line practice described in this book? While both cover many similar subjects, the emphases are different. Roughly speaking, a CMMI process area describes where an organization should have *processes,* whereas a product line practice area describes where an organization should have *expertise* (which sometimes includes process expertise). Having said that, the table below draws some tenuous associations between practice areas and process areas. This table notwithstanding, bear in mind that any comparison between a CMMI process

Associations between Product Line Practice Areas and CMMI Process Areas*

Product Line Practice Areas	CMMI Process Areas
Software Engineering Practice Areas	
• Architecture Definition	Technical Solution
• Architecture Evaluation	Verification
• Component Development	Technical Solution
• COTS Utilization	Supplier Agreement Management
• Mining Existing Assets	(none)
• Requirements Engineering	Requirements Development
• Software System Integration	Product Integration
• Testing	Verification Validation
• Understanding Relevant Domains	(none)

Product Line Practice Areas	CMMI Process Areas
Technical Management Practice Areas	
• Configuration Management	**Requirements Management** **Configuration Management**
• Data Collection, Metrics, and Tracking	**Measurement and Analysis** **Project Monitoring and Control** **Integrated Project Management**
• Make/Buy/Mine/Commission Analysis	**Decision Analysis and Resolution** Supplier Agreement Management
• Process Definition	Organizational Process Definition
• Scoping	(none)
• Technical Planning	**Project Planning**
• Technical Risk Management	**Risk Management**
• Tool Support	(none)
Organizational Management Practice Areas	
• Building a Business Case	(none)
• Customer Interface Management	(none)
• Developing an Acquisition Strategy	Supplier Agreement Management
• Funding	(none)
• Launching and Institutionalizing	(none)
• Market Analysis	(none)
• Operations	(none)
• Organizational Planning	Project Planning
• Organizational Risk Management	Risk Management
• Structuring the Organization	(none)
• Technology Forecasting	(none)
• Training	**Organizational Training**

* Process area names in bold provide fairly direct support for the corresponding practice areas, while others are less strongly related. The CMMI process areas of Process and Product Quality Assurance, Organizational Process Focus, Organizational Process Performance, Quantitative Project Management, Causal Analysis and Resolution, and Organizational Innovation and Deployment do not correspond to any product line practice areas.

area and a product line practice area is weak. Practice areas and process areas are fundamentally different. Even where at first glance they appear to cover the same topic, similar names do not mean that they cover the same ground. Practice areas also extend the realm of their coverage into the situation where product lines are the goal, and this is not a focus of the process areas. Just because, say, your organization has institutionalized the CMMI process area of Configuration Management, it does not mean that you have mastered the practice area of Configuration Management for product lines. Moreover, while the CMMI is probably best known in its staged representation, the product line practices do not constitute a maturity model. There is no predetermined sequence for attacking the practice areas; that depends on your goals and context. Neither is a substitute for the other, but the CMMI and the product line practices together can help guide an organization to the state necessary to achieve product line success.

—LAWRENCE G. JONES

Process Improvement Gains with a Product Line Focus

John D. Vu, Technical Fellow and Chief Engineer from the Boeing Company and longstanding process improvement zealot, has collected and shared impressive data about the benefits of software process improvements in software projects [Vu 97]. More recently, he has focused on higher-maturity organizations, specifically on improvements that take an organization from level 3 to level 4 of the Capability Maturity Model for Software (CMM) [Vu 00]. His recent data show that when an organization with a single project/product focus moves from level 3 to level 4, the productivity gain is minimal because most of the improvements that can affect a single product or project will have already happened at level 3. In other words, the benefits you can achieve from process improvement approach a limit if you have a single-product focus.

However, when the process improvement from level 3 to level 4 includes a shift to a product line focus, the productivity increase is very significant. Vu's data indicate as much as a 70% productivity improvement as well as highly satisfied employees. He attributes this dramatic increase to a more systematic approach to the way products are built, including a strong focus on architecture, greater customer involvement and end-user participation, and disciplined reuse of artifacts. All of these factors contribute to reductions in defects, cycle time, cost, required testing, and rework. In Vu's opinion, product line management with a focus on architecture is the key to a level 4 that has real business benefits. The statistical data practices advocated for level 4 then result in business data rather than technical data, and the focus shifts from just process to a profitable process-and-product harmony.

—LMN

Consequences: Process is a foundational or building-block pattern that is required to support the product line operation. You can think about it as the scaffolding for the assembly line. Without this scaffolding it is impossible to master product lines. This is the place to start for organizations that have low process maturity, and for them, applying this pattern will take considerable time—as long as two years.

7.14 Factory Pattern

Name: The *Factory* pattern is a composite pattern that describes the entire product line organization.

Example:
Scenario: The CTO of a company (a subsidiary of a major car manufacturer) that builds computer simulations for testing auto designs before they are moved into prototyping and production has a problem. The simulations save vast amounts of engineering time and therefore result in faster time-to-market for new auto designs. However, now the multitude of simulations that this CTO's organization has built have become a configuration nightmare. He has read about the software product line approach and realizes that it offers great potential for his organization. In fact, it may be his only salvation. He would like a blueprint of how his organization would look if it had that capability.

Context: An organization considering (or fielding) a product line.

Problem: To map the entire product line effort.

Solution: Fielding a product line can be thought of as accomplishing six things:

1. deciding what products you wish to build;
2. building and running the production capability (the assembly line, if you like) to build those products;
3. preparing the organization to effectively use the assembly line;
4. designing and providing the parts that will roll down the assembly line to be joined together to form the product;
5. running the assembly line and building products from those parts; and
6. monitoring the process, keeping a pulse on the operations, and applying course corrections as necessary to keep the organization on course.

Static: Factory consists of the following other patterns:

- Assembly Line
- Each Asset

- Cold Start
- In Motion
- Product Builder
- Product Parts
- Monitor
- What to Build

Dynamics: Figure 7.14 illustrates the relations among the patterns in Factory.

- What to Build yields the set of products to be included in the product line.
- Each Asset provides individual core assets and their attached processes.
- Product Parts supplies the core assets that will be part of the product.
- Assembly Line provides the production capability.
- Product Builder constructs the products.
- Cold Start prepares the organization for the product line operation.
- In Motion keeps the product line organization running.
- Monitor keeps watch on the organization and responds with any needed changes.

Application: Factory can be applied as a road map for the entire product line organization. The CTO in the scenario can visualize the entire setup and then can apply Factory's individual patterns.

Variants: One can imagine variations of Factory based on variants of the patterns it contains.

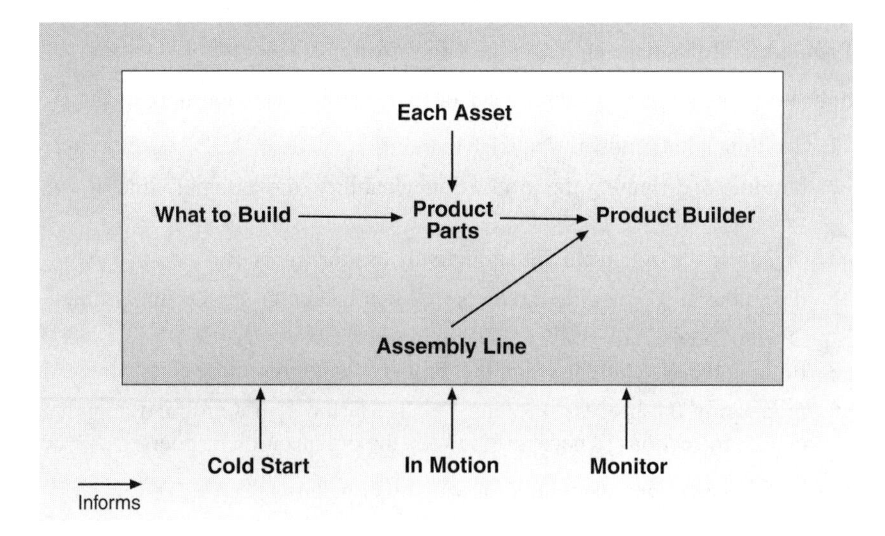

Figure 7.14 Dynamic Structure of the Factory Pattern

Consequences: Factory is a top-down view of the product line organization and a blueprint for a divide-and-conquer strategy. It is the granddaddy of the product line practice patterns. Such a top-down view is usually more intuitive after there have been a few bottom-up approaches; that is, organizations will usually not have the up-front vision to start with Factory, but it does provide a great organizational support system for visualizing the product line road ahead.

7.15 Other Patterns

We have presented a total of 22 patterns, including variants. Table 7.4 provides the entire set, in alphabetical order.

Without a doubt there are many other patterns that we did not include, but we feel that the collection in this chapter provides a useful guide to applying product line practices for many common situations you are likely to encounter. If your context and the product line work you are trying to accomplish do not appear to match any of the patterns or variants we have given, try to analyze

Table 7.4 List of Software Product Line Practice Patterns

Pattern	Variants
Assembly Line	
Cold Start	Warm Start
Curriculum	
Each Asset	Each Asset Apprentice Evolve Each Asset
Essentials Coverage	
Factory	
In Motion	
Monitor	
Process	Process Improvement
Product Builder	Product Gen
Product Parts	Green Field Barren Field Plowed Field
What to Build	Analysis Forced March

what is different and see if you can come up with a variant we haven't described. Or perhaps you have discovered the need for a new pattern. In either case, use the pattern template to describe your pattern so that you can see the relations among the practice areas involved, which will guide your application of the corresponding practices.

7.16 Practice Area Coverage

One final note before we conclude our discussion of software product line practice patterns. Using any of the patterns we have described or any other one that you write does not give you a waiver to exclude any of the 29 practice areas. All of the practice areas are essential to a mastery of software product lines. When practice areas are skipped, we have learned that most likely those practices are carried out anyway under the guise of another practice area. If you create your own patterns or map your own trajectory through the practice areas, be aware of this, and make sure that the right work gets accomplished. For example, suppose that you are defining the product line architecture from the product line scope, but no actual product line requirements have been written. You will need to do requirements engineering; there is no way around it. But you may end up doing it under the guise of architecture definition. This may make sense, but be aware of what you are doing, and make sure you document the requirements and include variation points.

7.17 Discussion Questions

1. Demonstrate how the Each Asset pattern would be used to solve the problem given in Scenario 2 of that pattern's description.
2. Create a scenario to which Each Asset Apprentice would apply. Complete the rest of the template for Each Asset Apprentice.
3. It was noted that Each Asset is a family of patterns. Could it be considered a product line?
4. Demonstrate how What to Build applies to Scenario 2 in that pattern's description.
5. Provide the description of the "Dynamics" and "Consequences" sections of the Analysis pattern, which is described as a variant of What to Build.
6. Provide a complete pattern description for Forced March.

7. One could argue that "Operations" ought to belong to the Response Group of the Monitor pattern. State your position. One could also argue that "Customer Interface Management" does not belong in Monitor. State your position.
8. Create a second scenario for the Product Parts pattern.
9. Describe the dynamics of the Green Field Pattern.
10. Why isn't the scenario in Product Parts a better candidate for Plowed Field?
11. There were no variants given for the Assembly Line pattern. Can you think of any?
12. Write the pattern description for Evolve Each Asset.
13. Should there be an Evolve Parts pattern? If so, provide the context, problem, and solution with both static and dynamics. If not, defend your position.
14. There are many plans that are required in a product line operation. Do you think there should be another building block pattern called *Plan* that does for plans what Process does for processes? If so, what would its structure (static and dynamics) look like?
15. Provide the dynamics for the Process Improvement pattern.
16. There is some overlap between Assembly Line and Process. Why is this so? Is there any problem with the overlap?

8

Product Line Technical Probe

The software product line practice patterns require you to characterize your organizational context and identify what part of the product line effort you need to accomplish so that you can recognize what patterns apply. What if you can't? Or what if there isn't a pattern that fits? Or what if you are in the throes of a product line effort, know that the effort is not going as well as it should, but can't determine why? Or maybe you would just like to know if you could be doing something better. Maybe you want to know if you should even begin a product line effort.

If any of these situations applies, you are not alone. Many organizations have been in similar quandaries. To get their product line efforts off the ground or back on track, organizations can use the Product Line Technical Probe.

8.1 What Is the Product Line Technical Probe?

The Product Line Technical Probe is a diagnostic method for examining an organization's readiness to adopt, or ability to succeed with, a software product line approach. The probe consists of a series of structured interviews of small peer groups within the organization, followed by data analysis. The 29 practice areas serve as a reference model for the probe in both the data collection and the data analysis. The probe follows a structured process based on proven mechanisms and principles of software process capability, technical risk evaluation, and earlier product line evaluations. The results include

- a set of findings that characterize the organization's strengths and challenges relative to its product line effort
- a set of recommendations

These results can serve as the basis for developing action plans to help make an organization more capable of achieving product line success. The probe is applicable when an organization has already initiated a software product line effort or is seriously considering a product line approach.

You can think of the probe as a checkup on the product line health of an organization. At the risk of making you queasy, we will pursue this medical analogy. If you go to your family doctor for a medical checkup, he has a standard set of areas he examines—your heart, blood, lungs, ears, eyes, and so on. Medical knowledge tells him what healthy body parts look like and how they perform. He assesses your parts against that body of knowledge and his own professional experience. He reports his findings to you, part by part, and then he gives an overall picture of your health.

That's exactly what happens with the Product Line Technical Probe. The examiners check your organization against the essentials of any product line operation—the practice areas. They do this by conducting a series of interviews with tiers of individuals within the organization. They ask questions that are structured by our body of knowledge about those practice areas—the descriptions provided in Part II. And they analyze the responses against that same body of knowledge. As with any checkup, you get a report on the health of all the parts (practice areas) and, based on that report, an overall picture of your organization's product line health. And as with any checkup, you have to act on the findings. If there are problems, you may have to take corrective measures to fix specific areas, or you may have to change your organizational life style. If your organization is not the picture of product line health, you are in charge of correcting the situation.

Using the Product Line Technical Probe to analyze a product line effort has several benefits. The probe takes a baseline snapshot of the product line (or the potential product line) organization. It is then possible to chart a course from where you are to where you want to be, presumably enjoying the benefits of product line success. This baseline can also be a very useful benchmark against which to gauge progress. The probe also serves as a reality check. Very often organizations ignore certain ailments, hoping they will go away, and sometimes they just don't know that they have problems or that they might have them in the future. The probe identifies weaknesses, which helps the organization avoid common product line pitfalls. Some of those weaknesses might be problems that need to be addressed immediately, and some are risks that should be mitigated so they don't become problems later.

The probe also identifies strengths. Sometimes an organization already knows its strengths, but sometimes not. There are at least two positive aspects of knowing your strengths. Strengths are areas that you don't have to fix and can feel good about, and strengths are areas that you should exploit. So if your architecture practices are exemplary, you should continue in the same direction and rejoice in the knowledge that you are doing well in an area that is pivotal to your product line success. If the probe reveals that you have an exceptional customer interface, you should exploit that relationship by involving the customer in evaluations to gather as much feedback as you possibly can and by setting up opportunities for the customer to sing the praises of your product line to others. One more word about strengths: you shouldn't take any positive report as permission to slack off in that area. If your heart rate and blood pressure are stellar for a person of your age because you run 30 miles a week, you don't want to stop your running program. Instead, you want to feel good about yourself and begin to address other areas that might need attention.

There is one other aspect of the probe that results in profound, albeit unquantifiable, benefits: the probe is a social exercise. It begins and ends with a gathering of the stakeholders in the product line effort. During the course of the probe, peer groups of stakeholders are interviewed together. Just getting the important players together to be heard and to hear each other's answers does wonders. Clogged communication paths are opened, and individuals who are not quite on board or in the mainstream of the effort become involved. Often it's this social benefit that makes the probe exercise worthwhile.

8.2 Probe Interview Questions

Because we want the probe to be a repeatable diagnostic service with repeatable results, there is a predefined set of interview questions for each of the 29 practice areas. These questions get at the heart of the practice areas and are designed to gather as much pertinent information as possible. There are no questions that evoke simple "yes" or "no" responses. Many are of the form, "Would you please describe . . . ." Many of the questions have "listen for" annotations. The "listen fors" give the questioner a checklist against which to evaluate answers to particular questions.

For example, the set of probe questions for "Architecture Definition" is as follows:

1. Who is the chief architect for the product line? What are his/her responsibilities? What experience does he/she have in architecting systems? What experience does he/she have in architecting product line systems?
   Listen fors: the architect's prior training and experience in architecting systems in the domain of the intended product line
2. Is there a defined process for architecture definition? If so, please describe it.
   Listen fors: attention to functional and quality requirements; architectural drivers identified; process steps, sequencing, and system building and support accounted for; validation and refinement included

3. Please describe how variation points are handled in the architecture. How are they documented? How will they be communicated to component developers? How will they be communicated to product developers?
   Listen for: some sort of an attached process that describes how the variation points get exercised
4. How are the component interfaces defined and specified?
   Listen for: more than a "signature" description
5. What styles and patterns that might apply to the product line have been used before in architectures at this organization?
6. Are there any architectural frameworks that apply to the product line?
7. Are there any existing architectures from other products or systems in the same or related domains? What are those domains? Have those architectures, or lessons learned from them, been incorporated into the product line architecture definition process?
8. What traceabiliy is established between architectural decisions and the architectural drivers (requirements) that precipitated them?
9. What standards are in place for architecture documentation? Are those standards any different for the product line than they are for single-system architecture? What mechanisms are in place to keep the documentation up to date?
10. Where is the rationale for architectural decisions captured? How comprehensive and up-to-date is it? What plans are there to keep it up-to-date?
11. What notations or languages are used to represent architectures and to convey understanding to others? How do those notations or languages accommodate the needs for product line architecture?
12. What architecture design tools are available? Who uses them? How often and for what? Do the tools contain the authoritative version of the architecture(s)? Are the tools used to capture variation mechanisms?
    Listen for: "official" versions residing elsewhere, and for what purpose
13. What processes or checks are in place to ensure that product developers actually use the product line architecture when they build products and use it in the way it was intended? NOTE: This question also relates to the "Operations" practice area.
14. What training or familiarization was done to allow product builders to become knowledgeable about the product line architecture? NOTE: This question also relates to the "Training" practice area.

Because the probe can be applied to an organization with an ongoing product line effort or to one that is about to launch a product line effort, many of the practice areas have two sets of questions—one for each context. For example, the set of probe questions for "Requirements Engineering" is as follows:

If a product line effort is already underway:

1. Please describe how requirements engineering activities for the product line are planned.
2. Do you have a documented requirements engineering process for the product line effort? If so, please describe it.
3. How are commonalities and variabilities in the requirements identified and modeled?
4. How are requirements communicated to the architects and the component developers?

If a product line effort has not begun:

1. How are requirements engineering activities typically planned?
2. How are changes in requirements typically handled?
3. How do you plan to tailor your existing requirements engineering process to address the following items:
   - Product line requirements
   - Commonalities and variabilities in the requirements
   - Product-specific requirements
   - Requirements changes
   - Communications of changes in requirements
   - Traceability of requirements to relevant core assets

Obviously, not all of the questions can be asked of each set of interviewees. Question sets are pared down in two ways that do not degrade the validity of the diagnostic. First, before the probe interviews, the probe team preselects the practice areas that most relate to the individual interview peer groups. For example, the architects would certainly be asked the "Architecture Definition" questions but probably not the "Organizational Planning" questions. However, all practice areas are covered, with very few exceptions (for example, if the organization does not do any outsourcing, then "Developing an Acquisition Strategy" can be ignored). As part of the preselection process, there is an initial check to ensure that the questions for each practice area are asked of at least two groups. The probe team needs to get coverage of the practice areas and responses from at least two groups to balance out biases.

Second, some questions in a given practice area might not be asked explicitly because answers have been given as part of responses to previous questions. In this latter case, some of the questions spontaneously become "listen fors," but coverage is still achieved.

8.3 Probe Participants

There are two sets of individuals involved in the probe: the probe team and representatives from the organization's product line stakeholder groups. The probe team typically consists of four product line experts. One member serves as the team lead. The lead is responsible for the orchestration and the logistics. The team members are not only armed with the bank of product line practice questions but are also experts in software product lines. Because software product lines require a range of technical and managerial practices, the team composition must be selected to ensure both breadth and depth of product line expertise. In addition, each team member must have interviewing and facilitation skills. The organization's product line stakeholders include all those who are involved in the product line effort as well as those who have vested interests in the fruits of the product line. The stakeholder groups may vary with the organization, but typically they consist of the following:

- senior managers/executives
- middle managers
- project managers
- technical team leads
- architects and/or senior designers
- systems engineers
- requirements analysts
- developers
- testers
- marketers
- internal customers
- support groups (quality assurance, configuration management, training, tool support, process group)
- external customers
- end users

Representatives are selected from the designated stakeholder groups to fill eight peer group interview sessions. In selecting the interview groups, it is important that there be no reporting relationships among the individuals selected for any one group and that there be no more than eight individuals in any one group. It is important that no one feels threatened or intimidated and that everyone gets an opportunity to provide answers. Just as the probe team must have expertise that covers the entire range of practice areas, the chosen stakeholders should as well. The idea is to get a complete picture of the product line organization through candid answers to the probe questions for all practice areas.

8.4 Probe Process

The process consists of three phases: the *Preliminary Phase,* the *Technical Probe Phase,* and the *Follow-On Phase.*

Preliminary Phase

The primary purpose of the *Preliminary Phase* is to gather some initial information that provides a sketch of the organizational context before the probe is conducted and to plan for the probe. This phase begins with a preliminary meeting that typically occurs one month before the probe. The probe team spends a day with key members of the organization, including the management sponsor(s) (for the first 2½ to 3 hours), the point of contact, and a few people who are deemed knowledgeable to help the probe team understand the basic context. Typically, three to five people will be there for the entire meeting, but this depends on the organization. During this preliminary meeting, the probe team explores a set of context-setting questions. These questions (see "Preliminary Phase Questions" sidebar) are supplied to the organization in advance, but not with the intent that someone prepare answers. The questions are supplied to enlist for the meeting those people who are the most qualified to answer them. This first round of data to be gleaned includes the following:

- the goals for the product line effort
- the status of the product line effort (how far along the organization is in its product line activities)
- what the organization hopes to learn from the probe
- the current organizational structure
- any terminology particular to the organization
- the organization's level of process maturity
- a list of available, relevant documentation
- the organization's product line stakeholder groups

Preliminary Phase Questions

A. Overall context

1. Are you launching a product line effort, or have you already done so?
2. What is your motivation for using a product line approach?
3. What are your business goals for adopting a product line approach?
4. Do you have a product line vision? If so, please describe it.

5. What are your strategies for achieving your product line goals?
6. What is your timeline for carrying out this effort?
7. Is there more than one product line under consideration/implementation?
8. Please describe the nature of your product line by answering the following questions:
   - What are the intended products?
   - Where will they be used?
   - Does your product line have any distinguishing characteristics?
   - Are your customers different from the end users?

B. Probe context

1. What are your goals for the product line probe?
2. Do have particular concerns that you would like us to investigate?
3. What will your organization do with the results of the probe?
4. Please describe any other efforts (such as feasibility studies or pilots) you have taken to evaluate your organizational readiness to embark on a product line approach.
5. If your product line effort is already underway:
   - Has a market analysis been performed?
   - Is there an established business case?

C. Terminology mapping

What alternative terms (if any) does your organization use for the following:

- core assets
- architecture
- product line
- products
- production plan

D. Process maturity context

1. Are any process or quality initiatives underway? If so, how are they proceeding?
2. Has the organization been assessed? If so, what was the result?
3. Is there an established process improvement infrastructure? If so, what is its relationship to the product line effort?

E. Legacy context

1. How long have you been building systems similar to those in the product line?
2. Do you intend to use legacy artifacts as part of your asset base?
3. Do you intend to migrate legacy systems to your product line?

F. Management and structural context

1. What is your current organizational structure, including job titles, roles and responsibilities, organization chart, and qualifications of personnel?
2. Please identify the organizational entity or entities responsible for the product line effort, specifically,
   - product line manager(s)
   - component developers
   - software or system architects
   - requirements specialists
   - product developers
   - configuration management personnel
   - testers
   - customer interface specialist (such as marketing or internal customer interface)
   - training personnel
   - management steering group
3. Is there any concept of distributed engineering? Across different organizations/geographical locations?
4. Who is the highest-level sponsor? What is the level of this sponsor?

G. Implementation context

1. Do you have a plan for moving to and/or executing the product line approach? If so, please answer the following questions:
   - What does it contain?
   - What is the anticipated schedule and other drivers?
   - Are things going according to plan?
2. Please briefly describe any work that has been done in the following areas:
   - Commonality analysis and scoping of the product line
   - Development of an operating concept
   - Definition of the product line architecture
   - Inventory of legacy assets
   - Mining of existing assets

H. Documentation context

If available, please provide copies of the following documents:

- Product Line Concept of Operations (or existing pieces)
- High-level product line architecture description
- Product line feasibility studies
- Product line business case
- Product line scoping documents
- Descriptions of organizational structures
- Product line pilot result reports
- Domain model(s)
- Product line requirements
- Product line adoption plan
- Any other documents you might think are useful

This information provides a framing of the organization and its product line effort, which allow the probe team to identify the following:

- the appropriate range of questions (product line underway or not, any practice areas that don't pertain) to be used in conducting the probe
- which groups within the organization to interview
- what supporting documents to review
- the logistical details and schedule for the Technical Probe Phase

The probe team then selects practice areas to cover with each interview group and reviews all documents to steep themselves in the organization's domain, culture, and approach. The organizational culture plays a major role not only in how the practices will play out, but also in how to conduct the interviews. Organizational culture is both a unique and a defining factor of a product line organization (see "Cooperative Culture at Hewlett-Packard" sidebar). There is no single product line culture, and the specific culture will dictate which practices within the practice areas will be the most effective for that organization. For example, certain cultures can thrive with a core development/product development group separation (see "Pas de Deux: Making the Two-Part Organization Work" sidebar), whereas others would wither under it. The probe team must have a handle on the product line culture before the Technical Probe Phase in order to assess the appropriateness of the practices they hear about during the interviews.

Cooperative Culture at Hewlett-Packard

A theme of *culture* has emerged as a factor that ties successful product line organizations together. All three of the case studies in this book (Chapters 9, 10, and 11) include observations about how preexisting corporate culture gave those organizations a big jump-start for their product line efforts. Cummins has a deeply ingrained history of doing the right thing for the long-term health of the company. Market Maker Software AG succeeds by nourishing a close and abiding relationship with its customer base, making mass customization the natural course. The mutual comfort of Raytheon and the U.S. National Reconnaissance Office with processes and crosscutting teams has made their orchestration of product line activities seem natural and familiar.

A common cultural aspect specific to product lines is the ability to regard the entire product line, rather than individual products, as the heart of the company's business (see "E Pluribus Unum" sidebar). However, even some of the most successful companies, while they exhibit this singular outlook, aren't always conscious of it. But we know of one company that is not only aware of its product line culture but has consciously used that culture to take its product line organization to the next level. That company is Hewlett-Packard (HP).

HP already enjoys a strong reputation as a product line company. Their family of printers and how they developed it play a central part in Meyer and Lehnerd's *The Power of Product Platforms* [Meyer 97], which is a testimonial to the power of the product line approach in the nonsoftware arena. But the firmware that drives that printer family is also a product line—a software product line. One of the projects that produces that software is called the Owen[1] Firmware Cooperative [Toft 00].

Owen produces firmware for printers and so-called "all-in-one" devices that support printing, copying, scanning, and faxing. Unlike many software product line projects, which feature ponderous organizational structures with heavyweight operational processes, Owen takes a different approach. There is no central monolithic core asset team. Rather, the core assets are developed exclusively by product teams. There is a platform team (to use their term), but it is very small, and its charter is just to ensure that the platform code is robust and that the product teams know how to use it. This means that the product teams depend on each other for the core assets, and this quickly gives rise to the notion of a cooperative—an informal organization in which participants work together for the common good. Participation in the Owen cooperative is not compulsory; rather, projects that wish to join do so voluntarily. Projects join because they can expect (on average) to get 70% of their product by reusing

1. This name is fictitious to preserve confidentiality. It was chosen by HP when they wrote about the project to honor Robert Owen, the founder of the Cooperative Movement.

Owen core assets verbatim, 20% by making small modifications to core assets, and only 10% by writing new code. The new code represents new functionality, which is often turned into a new core asset that the project contributes back to Owen. Projects have responsibilities to the cooperative that are explicitly laid out. Projects must make their code available in the central repository. They must get permission from other projects before making an interface change in a repository asset. Any new code they write must be compliant with the Owen architecture. If they change a component by more than 25%, they agree to take over its ownership. If someone else changes a component of theirs by 5% or less, they agree to try to continue to support it. (For changes between 5% and 25%, the two projects negotiate about ownership.)

"The Owen team has invested in generating a sense of community across the whole cooperative," write the authors. "As the cooperative experiences ongoing success in helping to meet the goals of its members, it also fosters an increasingly strong sense of community and shared responsibility." One of their eight operating principles is "Value the community and get value from the community." Another is "People matter," which is elaborated as follows:

> *The Owen cooperative relies on interpersonal relationships and individual cooperation as much as it does on the Owen technology and processes. Give community members the opportunity to meet face-to-face and get to know one another.*

The organizational structure behind Owen is unique and innovative:

- The Owen Steering Group guides the strategy and direction of the cooperative "to establish and institutionalize its culture and values." It explains the cooperative to division managers and resolves internal conflicts. All projects in the cooperative are represented on the steering group. The team meets about once every six weeks.
- The Firmware Architect adapts and extends the Owen architecture to meet new requirements of new products as they arise. There is one or more firmware architects for each division that has membership in the cooperative. Each is the first point of contact for assets owned by that division. The Owen architecture (HP actually calls it a "framework") is a confederation of loosely coupled components. Each component is carefully specified, with special attention paid to its interface. Clear guidelines and principles—for example, "the services structure of the system is a hierarchy of components in client-server relationships"—guide the evolution of the architecture and the use of components on each project.
- The Firmware Asset Lead in each division makes Owen assets available to Owen teams in that division and makes local developments and modifications available to other divisions in the cooperative.
- The Owen Cooperative Steward convenes steering group meetings, acting as the first point of contact for potential new subscribers and representing

the work of the cooperative to management and others outside. The steward empowers members to make decisions and is the one who judges when the architecture or operating models have become overextended and need revisiting. HP describes this role as "vital to maintaining the health of the community" and stresses the interpersonal aspects of the job. Part of the steward's job is to offer encouragement and make community members feel valued.

The results? The usual set of breathtaking numbers: Owen products have been built with 75% fewer people, 67% less time, and 96% fewer defects compared with earlier products.

Most companies are delighted just to be able to build a software product line, but an elite few want to extend their knowledge to a deeper level—to understand not just their product line but software product lines in general. Hewlett-Packard was clearly in this latter camp when, a few years ago, they participated in one of our product line workshops. Their presentation, unlike most, was not just a summary of what they did and why, but a fascinating inquisitive introspection about how their experiences fit into product line practice in general. For their product line, they claimed a fourfold increase in productivity. This was measured, not in some vague manner, but by "normalized feature density per product shipped per engineer per unit time." At this, a murmur of admiration ran through the crowd. We weren't so much impressed with the magnitude of the number as we were with its pedigree: HP clearly was *very* interested in its product line abilities if it collected such detailed data to produce such a definitive measure.

Owen would probably not have worked if there hadn't been a strong product line culture in place at HP. It's what made the subscribers believe that they would get real value and real savings by joining the cooperative. Owen may represent the first example of the next level of product line culture.

—PCC

Technical Probe Phase

The *Technical Probe Phase* begins with a kickoff meeting during which the probe team leads gives a brief introduction to software product lines and to the Product Line Technical Probe. The probe team then performs repetitive cycles of data gathering as well as data analysis followed by results consolidation and reporting.

The primary data gathering technique is structured interviews of small groups designated as representatives of the product line stakeholders. These peer groups are chosen to have similar job responsibilities and no reporting relationships. The team follows a rule of strict confidentiality and nonattribution of any remarks in order to promote the free flow of information. The interview questions are derived from the practice area probe question set, as tailored on the basis of the information gathered during the Preliminary Phase. Each interview lasts 1½ hours, with one probe team member asking the interview questions and the others recording the responses. The probe team members rotate the questioning responsibility to exploit each member's area of expertise and to mitigate any exhaustion that might set in.

Directly following each interview session, the probe team gathers to analyze the interview data practice area by practice area. The practice area descriptions in Part II, as modified by the context gleaned during the Preliminary Phase, are used as the basis of the analysis. Responses (data) are labeled as strengths or weaknesses, and areas requiring further information or clarification are noted. This ongoing data consolidation provides the basis for determining the results, which are characterized as general observations, strengths, weaknesses, and recommendations. Strengths and weaknesses are reported for each relevant practice area and then are rolled up to form overall strengths and weaknesses. Recommendations are proposed and prioritized by the probe team. The software product line practice patterns (from Chapter 7) are helpful in identifying recommendations for typical contexts and challenges. For example, if the "Requirements Engineering" practice area is a weakness, the solution for the Each Asset or Each Asset Apprentice pattern for requirements engineering can be recommended.

The probe team prepares and delivers a Final Findings Presentation at the conclusion of the on-site Technical Probe Phase and responds to questions. The probe results are also documented formally in a written report that is prepared and delivered several weeks later.

The Technical Probe Phase tends to be a productive but draining experience for the probe team. There is a heavy load of data gathering and analysis condensed into a four-day period, as illustrated in the "Typical Probe Schedule" sidebar. But the burden on the organization is not unreasonable because no advanced preparation is required for any of the interviews; and any one stakeholder participant is only present for the kickoff meeting, one interview session, and the Final Findings Presentation.

Typical Probe Schedule

A typical probe schedule is as follows:

Day 1:
8:00–8:40 Kickoff meeting—ENTIRE GROUP PRESENT
8:40–8:50 Break
8:50–10:20 Interview Group #1—Senior Managers

10:20–10:30 Break
10:30–12:00 Interview Group #2—Project Managers
12:00–12:45 Data consolidation, interview preparation, and working lunch
12:45–2:15 Interview Group #3—Architects and Senior Designers
2:15–2:30 Break
2:30–4:00 Interview Group #4—Developers
4:00–5:30 Data consolidation and interview preparation

Day 2:
8:30–10:00 Interview Group #5—Technical Support Groups
10:00–10:30 Break
10:30–12:00 Interview Group #6—Testers
12:00–1:15 Data consolidation, interview preparation, and working lunch
1:15–2:45 Interview Group #7—Customers/End Users
2:45–5:30—Data consolidation and interview preparation

Day 3:
8:30–10:00 Interview Group #8—Marketers
10:00–10:15 Break
10:15–11:45 Interview Group #9 (optional—depends on the organization)
11:45–12:30 Data consolidation and working lunch
12:30–5:30 Data consolidation, briefing preparation, and start final report

Day 4:
8:00–10:00 Complete preparation of briefing
10:00–11:30 Present overall results—ENTIRE GROUP PRESENT

Follow-On Phase

The *Follow-On Phase* is optional, but it is useful for organizations that need help in proceeding with the recommendations. For example, if "Technical Planning" and "Organizational Planning" are among the challenges for the organization in question, it is unlikely that they will be able to plan a course of action to address these challenges without some assistance. The Follow-On Phase consists of

- the development of one or more action plans using the SEI's Product Line Planning Workshop to address the probe findings. The action plans work toward surmounting the challenges while at the same time exploiting identified strengths.
- tailored assistance in executing appropriate portions of the action plans.

The Product Line Planning Workshop is a tailored, facilitated work session in which a planning team works with a customer team to build action plan(s) to address the findings of the Product Line Technical Probe. The customer team should consist of the group responsible for implementing the plan(s).

Two broad types of plans that are critical to product line success are

- a product line adoption plan that orchestrates and coordinates the overall strategies to address the recommendations of the Product Line Technical Probe; and
- technical plans that flesh out the details of how to achieve one or more of the goals specified in the product line adoption plan.

The Product Line Planning Workshop can address each kind of plan. Each workshop lasts 1½ days. The workshop includes tailored instruction on product line plans and facilitated construction of those plans. Participants create skeleton plans using a defined planning process. Once learned, this process can be used by the organization to build additional product line plans or to revise the plans as the product line effort progresses.

8.5 Using the Probe Results

Of course, the organization does not have to opt for the Follow-On Phase. They could instead review the probe findings carefully and devise their own "get stronger" action plan. The plan should put into effect strategies to overcome weaknesses and exploit strengths. The software product line practice patterns are most helpful in identifying problem/solution pairs, and then the practice area descriptions can be used to assist in applying the pattern solutions or adopting them as strategies.

8.6 Conducting a Mini Self-Probe

Although they say, "A doctor who treats himself has a fool for a patient," you could safely conduct your own self-probe. Walk through the practice areas and determine how your organization's practices stack up against the basic essentials. Keep track of your own strengths and weaknesses. For example, in the "Structuring the Organization" practice area (Section 6.10), the unavoidable questions are: "Who is going to produce your core assets and, who is going to produce your products?" You can't fail to decide that, so you may as well decide it conscientiously. In the "Architecture Evaluation" practice area (Section 4.2), the questions are: "Do you evaluate your architecture? For what? How do you address the results?" In small organizations, such a mini self-probe would probably be adequate. It could also serve as a checklist for a quick-start or a "mini-launch" strategy for an organization of any size. Although definitely not scientific or guaranteed, this technique could give you a quick breadth-first approach to examining and possibly applying the practice areas. You could actually put the essence of each practice area (the most important facets) into play first, and leave details and options for the next iteration.

You could also use the practice patterns to help with your analysis. Use the Essentials Coverage pattern to see where you are weak in addressing the three essential activities. Use other patterns to identify solutions to common context/problem pairs. Or use the Factory pattern, which covers an entire product line effort, to provide a top-down view of a product line organization. Then work your way down, identifying on the basis of your self-examination, where you will have difficulties in applying the patterns within Factory.

8.7 Discussion Questions

1. Two versions of probe interview questions for the "Requirements Engineering" practice area were given. Choose the one that applies to your situation. Ask the questions of your organization, and then record your own strengths and weaknesses. See if applying the Each Asset practice pattern for requirements would help address your weaknesses, if you have any. If you don't, go out for ice cream.
2. Develop a mini-self-probe instrument by listing what you believe to be the three most important questions to ask for each practice area.
3. Tag the practice area questions you just wrote as to where they would be used in the Factory pattern solution.

CASE STUDY

Cummins Inc.: Embracing the Future

Change is a way of life. An industrial company should seize upon change as opportunity. It should look forward to change; it should thrive on change; but most of all, it should create and force change rather than react to change created by others. . . . Change is healthy. Creating and forcing change is the prime job of any management, no matter what the institution or group, no matter where the location.

—HENRY B. SCHACHT

Obsolete your own products.

Grow or die.

—J. IRWIN MILLER

9.1 Prologue

Adopting the software product line paradigm is about embracing change. One of the "constants" we've observed about organizations that move to the product line approach is that none of them does it on a whim or because it simply seems like the fun, trendy thing to do. Rather, all of them are faced with an oncoming crisis or challenge. But all of the *successful* organizations have something else in common: optimism. While eluding the clouds of disaster, they can see a silver lining—a better future. While running from disaster, they are simultaneously running toward success.

This chapter tells the story of the software product line experience of Cummins Engine Inc., the world's largest manufacturer of commercial diesel engines above 50 horsepower. It is the story of a company with a long and rich culture that meshed perfectly with the organizational and managerial changes a software product line imposes. It is the story of leadership and paying attention to the people issues that come with product lines. It is the story of making a two-part organizational structure for product lines (in which core asset development and product development are separate groups) work. And it is the story of a company that thrives on embracing change while never forgetting who and what they are.

All successful software product line stories have their own breathtaking litany of results, and those achieved at Cummins are as eye-catching as any. Whereas it used to take them a year or more to bring the software for a new engine to the test lab, now they can do it in less than a week. The product line approach has enabled them to augment their command of the automotive diesel engine market by expanding vigorously into the industrial diesel market, where just 20 software builds provide the basis for more than a thousand separate engine products, and has also enabled them to offer a mix of feature and platform flexibility that otherwise would require almost four times their current staff. The flexibility afforded by the product line approach has allowed them to enter whole new markets aggressively. (These and other results will be detailed in Section 9.7.) And they are making new and even more ambitious plans for the future.

9.2 Company History

On a crisp day in the autumn of 1908, the fates were with 19-year-old Clessie Cummins. Clessie, a self-taught mechanic and inventor, was applying for a job as a driver and mechanic for William Glanton "W.G." Irwin, a wealthy banker-investor in Columbus, Indiana. W.G. wanted someone to drive and maintain the family car, at a salary of $85 per month. Many wealthy owners of these newfangled automobiles hired their own driver/mechanics, and the job would suit young Clessie perfectly. But first he had to demonstrate that he could start the car.

Like all cars in 1908, Irwin's big Packard sedan was started by rapidly turning the crank in front, a feat requiring considerable strength, and it was completely unimpressed and unmoved—literally—by the efforts of the 110-pound teenager. Clessie thought a moment and then dipped a rag in the gas tank. He dripped some gasoline in the primer cups of the engine, jostled the car to work the fuel and some air into the cylinders, and fired the ignition spark. Years later, when he knew much more about engines than he had that Indiana autumn, he realized that the odds against that trick working were astronomical, but work it did. The big Packard coughed to life, and Clessie got the job.

His work for the Irwins soon branched out to odd jobs in the various family-run businesses, and his ties to the family grew. Clessie had a flair for invention, most of which involved automobiles, engines, or both. In 1911, to demonstrate a possible alternative for cars to the then-terrible roads throughout the country, Clessie put railroad wheels on Irwin's Packard and, amid great publicity and fanfare, drove W.G. and a carload of railroad officials along 19 miles of Indiana track. He averaged a jaw-dropping 60 miles per hour on the round trip, stopping only once when the railroad general manager's hat blew off. In 1913, W.G. set Clessie up in business for himself as an auto mechanic, letting him start out in the stable behind the Irwin mansion. Clessie christened this enterprise "The Cummins Machine Works." Here, he could indulge his urge to invent things, some as whimsical as a propeller-driven bobsled, and earn a living. Throughout World War I, Clessie's machine shop fulfilled government contracts. By this time, he was well aware of a new kind of engine invented by the German Rudolf Diesel. Gasoline was in short supply, and Clessie immediately grasped two things about Diesel's engine. First, it had great advantages over the gasoline internal combustion engine in terms of economy and durability. Second, Diesel's design was far from perfected; it would need a lot of work before the engine could be made practical.

By 1918, Clessie's company employed 50 men. The end of the war brought an end to government contracts, and Clessie had to choose a new direction. He decided to enter the diesel engine business and secured the manufacturing rights from an American licensee of a Dutch variant of the technology. Fourteen weeks after the end of World War I, in February of 1919, Cummins Inc. was born, with W.G. Irwin providing the necessary capital. Clessie and his engineers made improvements on the Dutch design, mainly involving better delivery of combustible fuel to the cylinders. In 1921 the company was able to patent a new fuel delivery method that let it jettison the Dutch design, with its limiting license, and start fresh as the owner the new technology. Throughout the 1920s the company grew steadily. Their main line of business became diesel engines for boats, especially fishing trawlers and yachts.

The Great Depression put an end to that market, as well as others in which Cummins had been gaining share—construction equipment and railroad locomotives. On December 15, 1929, W.G. called Clessie to his office to tell him that it was time to liquidate the company and close the doors. The Cummins history on the company's Web site at <http://www.cummins.com> picks up the story at this point:

> *But Clessie's creativity averted bankruptcy. He mounted a diesel engine in a used Packard limousine and—on Christmas Day, 1929—took W.G. Irwin for*

> *a ride in America's first diesel-powered automobile. This gamble saved the company. With a new infusion of Irwin capital, Clessie was determined to popularize the notion of the automotive diesel. He set a diesel speed record with the Duesenberg at Daytona Beach, then piloted a Cummins-powered truck coast-to-coast on a mere $11.22 worth of fuel. In 1931, a Cummins team set a new endurance record—a grueling 13,535 miles—at the Indianapolis Motor Speedway. Impressed with the economy and durability of these prototypes, a small number of truckers and fleet operators began to repower their vehicles with Cummins engines.*

Throughout the 1930s, Cummins gained a foothold in the automotive diesel market, just in time to greet a nascent trucking industry, and reinvigorated its foray into diesel locomotive engines for the railroads. In the 1940s they went to war along with the rest of the American manufacturing industry. In the postwar economic boom of the 1950s, America's new interstate highway system brought commercial trucking to new levels of importance, and the economics of engine operation loomed large. By the 1960s, Cummins owned the lion's share of the automotive diesel market. Cummins rode the ups and downs of the American and global economies throughout the last few decades of the 20th century. They went through internationalized expansion, recession-induced downsizing and industry consolidation, mandated reductions in engine emissions, grueling labor struggles, and a massive restructuring and belt-tightening; and they fended off takeover attempts in the buyout- and merger-crazed 1980s. Through it all, Cummins remained a remarkably stable company that maintained a clear vision of what they were about: building high-quality diesel engines.

One reason for the company's stability is that their leadership has been stable. Clessie Cummins played an active role in the direction of the company through the 1950s, and his presence was felt until his death in 1968 and beyond. J. Irwin Miller (the grandson of W.G. Irwin) was brought on board in 1934 as the company's second general manager. He stayed with Cummins in a role of undisputed leadership until his retirement 60 years later. Much of the Cummins culture can be traced to the colorful Miller, who in 1968 *Esquire* magazine said "should be the next President of the United States." Miller imprinted the company with his own values and style. "Grow or die" was his business mantra, which imbued the company with an indefatigable competitiveness. But equally evident was his uncompromising sense of business ethics, and this, too, he imprinted on the company. Some call Miller the "father" of the company, not in the sense of a founder but in the sense of a patriarchal leader whom you would rather die for than disappoint. In 1969, Miller elevated a young executive and Harvard Business School graduate named Henry B. Schacht to president. A painful strike in 1972 cost the company market share and forced them to reevaluate their direction. Under Schacht, the company tried branching out into some unrelated ventures such as manufacturing skis, but this was a short-lived diversion. Schacht brought on James A. Henderson, another Harvard Business School graduate, to take over the day-to-day operation of the company. From the late 1970s through the mid-1980s, Schacht and Henderson oversaw the introduction of new technologies and effected a painful restructuring of the company, trimming thousands of jobs and cutting costs. They refocused the company on issues of cost, quality, and responsiveness. This effort consumed a full decade and culminated with total investments of $1.3 billion in new plants, equipment, and engine designs. In 1994, Henderson succeeded Schacht as CEO.

In the 1980s, electronics began to play an important role in Cummins products. The first forays were into electronically controlled fuel injectors and onboard electronic recording devices. The Cummins Electronics Company, Inc. was formed to concentrate expertise in this expanding business area, which was perceived by Cummins to be a new core competency. Electronics was soon seen as the way to give an engineer the utmost control over an engine's emissions, performance, and fuel economy through precise control of when fuel was injected, and how much was injected, into the combustion sequence. This was the vision. But in the interim, electronics was viewed as expensive, and the reliability of electronic components in the harsh operating environments of diesel engines was an unknown. Cummins began by introducing electronics for speed governors and cruise control, where failures would be noncritical. The full-authority electronic controllers would come later, beginning in the early 1990s. Cummins Electronics was folded back into the company to keep the newfound expertise in electronic controls as close to home as possible, while yielding to Motorola the responsibility for manufacturing the electronic control modules themselves.

At about this time, Cummins brought in Ronald H. Temple (among others) from Ford to learn from the automaker's experience in integrating electronics throughout their engines and vehicles. Temple was made vice president of the Electronics Technical Organization; it was his job to deliver the hardware and software—a relatively new word at Cummins—for an ever-expanding family of engines.

This is where our software product line story begins.

9.3 A Product Line of Engine Software

In late 1993, Ron Temple was a man with a problem. Six engine software projects were underway in his group, with another 12 planned. These software projects were critical to the delivery of new models of Cummins diesel engines, for as surely as engines drove trucks, software was now driving the engines.

Modern internal combustion engines have not changed in basic theory since their invention more than a century ago, but they have changed radically around the edges. They rely on high-speed electronics to control their ignition and fuel delivery, so that the engines can deliver an optimum mix of high power, high fuel economy, and low emissions. These three goals are plainly in high tension with each other, and their target values come from the marketplace as well as from regulatory statutes. To make matters more complex, the target values change dynamically as a function of driving conditions: temperature, load, road incline, and so on. The engine must be able to sense its environment and respond to the driver's needs immediately and efficiently. The software that controls the engine must be robust and highly reliable: a bug that puts the family pickup truck out of commission, let alone a $200,000 highway truck or a multimillion-dollar mining excavator, will not be tolerated. In Cummins's case, these programs are in the 130 KSLOC range, a mix of C, assembler, and microcode.

The array of products that is powered by diesel engines is staggering: automotive, industrial, power generation, marine, mining, railroad, agriculture, and military applications just scratch the surface. The range of features is commensurate; Cummins engines range from 50 to more than 3500 horsepower, have from 4 to 18 cylinders, and operate with a wide variety of fuel systems, air-handling systems, and sensors. The engines operate all over the world, requiring different operator interfaces and communication/datalink capabilities, and must be serviceable by vastly differing distribution and service infrastructures. As electronics was poised to make its wide-ranging contribution to all of these engines, it was going to be terribly difficult to keep all the variations under intellectual control.

As Temple surveyed the projects under his purview, he saw that each group was using its own process, developing to its own architecture, and even selecting its own language. One or two groups were trying to use object-oriented methods to build their products, eager to bring this modern technology in-house. There was no plan in place to manage the variability inherent in the domain. Delivery of feature-rich individual products, even if developed under a bad process with no thought to downstream maintenance, was rewarded. Temple realized that although some of the projects underway were likely to succeed (some were nearing completion), this was no way to do business for the future. Not even the very near future. The twelve projects that were planned could not possibly be pulled off using this ad hoc approach. For one thing, the available staff and resources were far from sufficient. They would need to hire some 40 more experienced software engineers just to keep up, which was out of the question.

Thus, in May of 1994, Temple made a bold and courageous decision. He called a halt to all of the projects. This move astonished and dismayed many, not the least of whom were the people working on those projects. Temple split the project that was leading the pack into two parts. To one part he assigned the responsibility of building generalized core assets that all of the products—both in progress and planned—could use. Toward this end, the product line scope was laid out, and it encompassed systems for many engine products, serving many markets, running many applications, and executing on many platforms (which in this domain are called electronic control modules or ECMs). Temple ended the promising but ultimately diversionary foray into object-oriented technology; his staff didn't know enough about object technology to make it work. He established a standard Controls Software workflow process, formed a standard hardware process group, and launched a dedicated development environment team chartered to establish common development and configuration management (CM) tools and processes.

The project that had been farthest along, and the one that was split into two halves, served as the focal point for these activities: this was their pilot project. In late 1994, customer testing began, and in 1995 the project was launched on time (relative to the revamped schedule) and proved to be of high quality.

Then it was merely a matter of building on that auspicious beginning. The other projects used the core assets, and they also delivered on time with high quality. As new needs were identified, more core assets were added to the mix, and the organizational infrastructure supporting the interdependence between the project groups and the core asset group was fine-tuned and grew more robust.

9.4 Getting off the Ground

Not everyone was entirely pleased at the work stoppage decreed by Ron Temple. Some 10% of the developers, including those keenly disappointed that the company was not going to pursue object technology, left. In retrospect, it was Temple's leadership and vision that seem to have played the largest role in the success of the product line's launch and the formative early part of its life. Someone would say, "Here's a problem we didn't foresee, so let's fall back to the old way of doing things," or "My schedule has changed, and I just can't wait for the core assets, so I'll just go ahead and build without them." These and other deviations needed to be handled by the product line manager in a way that preserved the overall, long-term vision. The first order of business, however, was to show those who stayed that there was a light at the end of the tunnel. Building a business case and training both played large roles.

Making the Case

The business case for the software product line at Cummins was pretty straightforward: they couldn't deliver to the existing product plan without it. It was as simple as that. Nevertheless, accentuating the positive, they undertook a communication effort to make everyone aware of the tremendous potential that the product line approach afforded the company, especially in terms of bringing new products to fruition quickly. The business case spoke of productivity gains to be had, which would allow the massive growth called for in the product plan and by the feature requests that were coming in. The productivity gains would need to compensate for the 40 new software engineers that Cummins was not going to get. The business case spoke of cycle time reductions—of setting a target of shaving an entire year off the complete engine cycle. It spoke of product quality improvements through elimination of high-risk development and through cross-product testing of core assets. And finally, it spoke of enhancing customer satisfaction by delivering not only more features, but features with a common look and feel to them.

Accompanying the business case in the effort to win over the organization was training to familiarize the staff with product line ideas. Courses included product line concepts and terminology, gave an overview of planned product lines, and introduced the operational concept for the product line. As Cummins refined and expanded the common workflow for their product line operations, and as they built a toolset to support it, training was expanded to include courses in both.

Building the Core Assets

To "bootstrap" the product line, one of the legacy systems under development was chosen as the starting point for the product line's core assets. The system chosen had demonstrated the necessary reliability and stability and had an architectural structure that was modular enough and sufficiently well documented to serve as the embryonic core asset base.

Cummins made a conscious decision about what to outsource and what to keep in-house. For them, the make/buy/mine/commission question took on an extra dimension: could they acquire the whole system using one of the four methods or only components of it? Fresh-start development (making) of either was out of the question because of time pressures. Buying and commissioning were also discarded because Cummins's policy is not to rely on outside vendors for strategic work—that is, for work that enables Cummins to meaningfully differentiate their products from those of their competitors to gain competitive advantage. That left mining, which is what they did. Because the legacy systems had been built under different architectures, it was not possible to mine components from those systems, which is why they decided to start with an entire legacy system as the starting point for the product line.

Cummins used a combination of traditional requirements analysis and lightweight domain analysis to establish the product line requirements. "Features" (customer-visible capabilities of the software) were the unit of discourse in requirements. Domain experts in different market segments were interviewed individually. Once a feature was identified, it was denoted as common or unique, and its likelihood, delivery timing, and relative priority were established. Common features were implemented by the core asset group, with the domain analysis providing information about the necessary degrees of variation they had to provide. Product-specific features were farmed out to the appropriate product teams. Market experts contributed by adding new-feature forecasts to the mix on the basis of their analysis of market trends, and the requirements engineers were careful to account for nonoperational and quality attributes. The process was all-encompassing, with participation from all of the product teams (who were, during this time, all focused on developing the same common product line) and domain experts.

Cummins used wrapping and generators as the heart of its software system integration strategy. Build tools automated some of the build-time configuration settings and helped handle declarations, hardware configurations, tool interfaces, and file selection. On the whole, it was felt that the build tools more than paid for themselves by removing human error from tedious, time-consuming work. They also provided a structure to enforce the use of the architectural variability mechanisms.

Systems in this domain have a rich and textured variability. "Basic" or coarse-level variability includes the engine on which the software will run (one of nine types), the number of cylinders (from 4 to 18), the displacement (from 3.9 to 164 liters), the kind of ECM(s) on board (any of 12), the range of microprocessors available (5), the number of fuel systems with which the software must interact (10), and the fuel type of the engine (either diesel or natural gas). Software components used #ifdefs—some 2600 of them—as the basic build-time mechanism for selecting implementation versions for different applications. On top of this, Cummins provided thousands of parameters that controls engineers can use to configure and tone the controls to the application, plus some 300 parameters, such as idle speed, that could be set by the customer after delivery. The requirements had to capture all of the variabilities and when each one was available for binding. And the architecture had to provide the appropriate mechanisms.

The architectural vision for the software product line, it must be said, differed from the architectural reality. In the vision, the architecture would consist of two groups of reusable components, tied together by common interaction mechanisms. One group would provide an encapsulated hardware interface, thus allowing the application software (the other group) to be portable across platforms. On top of this two-layer architecture would be added system-specific or system-group-specific functionality, such as all the software that ran with a particular fuel system. In reality, that functionality was sometimes at odds with the core components, which would then be changed by the product teams. As a result, there was no standard, communicated, enforced architecture, and the vision (which was never very strong to begin with) began to deteriorate. The architecture, such as it was, was documented using data flow and logical views, but the documentation did not always match the mined code, let alone the modified code. If there is a weakness in this product line story, this is it. In retrospect, the product line group now realizes that their product line at that time consisted of a loose collection of reusable components. While their achievements under those conditions were laudable, they now understand that they failed to reap the benefits that a strong architecture would have afforded them. Therefore, they are now launching what they call the Core II architecture, which will be described later.

Launching

Cummins thus saw their launching process as a six-step affair:

1. Establish and implement the core asset implementation plan. This consisted of selecting the core group and laying out their work.
2. Select the legacy software for the starting point, and demonstrate its modularity.
3. Establish core asset and development teams, and modify the software to meet the core architecture (principally by making it conform to the modularity imposed by that architecture).
4. Establish the workflow (process) and toolset to be used; establish the detailed project plans.
5. Pilot the first application, and use the experience to improve the workflow and toolset.
6. Roll out subsequent products, and continue to incorporate improvements in the process and tools.

The organizational structure implied by step 3 and institutionalized in step 4 adds an extra dimension to this product line story.

9.5 An Organization Structured for Cooperation

Any analysis of Cummins's success soon reveals the importance of organizational structure issues. The structures in place both reflect and reinforce the Cummins culture of doing what's right cooperatively.

At Cummins, engines are roughly divided into automotive, industrial, and power generation categories, but the business units for the various kinds of engines are assigned responsibilities that consciously prevent them from becoming stovepipe operations. For instance, the core asset unit is part of the industrial business unit, whereas the automotive business unit controls some of the resources for manufacturing commonality. The business units have to cooperate, because none is self-sufficient, and intentionally so. The idea of letting somebody else handle common tasks across the board is thus ingrained by design; the business unit managers are comfortable with the concept of a "core asset" capability that is housed outside of their shop. This acceptance transfers to the product groups and helps make the software core asset group successful.

The cooperation is more than pro forma. As it was described to us, the business unit managers "have personal commitments to one another," and that phrase speaks volumes about the company. No manager can do his job without the others, and each has given his word that the common asset group under his control will deliver on time to the other groups. This policy works because each manager understands that his unit cannot succeed unless all the units succeed. This view that "the needs of the many outweigh the needs of the one" is an aspect of Cummins's culture that does more than any other to make this software product line story so compelling.

As the software product line was taking off, all of the controls groups (including the separate core assets group) reported to a single vice president, who was, of course, Ron Temple. Cummins was a case where, happily, the product line champion was also the product line manager. Temple was able to ensure that each of the product teams was following the product line approach and personally to oversee progress and help circumvent obstacles. And he was able to make the organizational structure featuring a separate core asset group work (see "Pas de Deux: Making the Two-Part Organization Work" sidebar).

Pas de Deux: Making the Two-Part Organization Work

The "Structuring the Organization" practice area (Section 6.10) lays out a few basic strategies for compartmentalizing product line work. One of the most common strategies is to have a separate core asset group that provides core assets to the product-building groups, and this is the strategy that Cummins chose.

In a 1947 speech to the House of Commons, Winston Churchill said, "Democracy is the worst form of government, except all those other forms that have been tried from time to time." Sometimes the two-part organization for product lines seems to deserve that sentiment. Cummins has made it work where other organizations have failed to do so. But not without some hard lessons. Those lessons are worth a closer look.

The two-part organization certainly has a lot going for it. A separate core asset group provides a focused setting wherein the product line as a singular entity can be managed and evolved. It provides a central repository for the commonality and variability knowledge that is essential to running a product line. It is the first place where a new product idea can be explored for feasibility by seeing how many of the core assets it would use. It's the place where cross-product commonality can be identified and exploited. It provides core assets that are generic across the entire family and not tilted toward any particular project.

However, it can be tricky to run. For one thing, a product line manager has to staff a core asset group carefully. At one of our software product line workshops, a speaker rose to say that he could not entice any of his people to work in the core asset group because they felt it was too far removed from the real business—product delivery. But the next speaker rose to say that in his shop, everybody wanted to work in the core asset group because the software they wrote was used many times over, and that's where they could have the biggest impact on their business. The core asset group generally requires the most talented designers and implementers, who are of course the most coveted by the project teams that will probably have to give them up.

Morale is a big issue with the two-part structure, but it is almost always overlooked. The core asset group forms a very convenient target when things go wrong for the product builders, but they don't always seem to share in the warm spotlight of success when things go right. Members of the core asset group at Cummins told us of the time when a couple of errors were found in a delivered product; this was very bad news. E-mail flying around at the time accused the core asset people of being the culprits. It turned out not to be so, but somehow the retraction (if it appeared at all) was not circulated with the same enthusiasm or at the same shrill volume. And they said, a little wistfully, that when things do go right, it's the product team that gets the tickets to the Indy 500 as a reward, not the core asset group. Among organizational issues for product lines, Ron Temple lists team morale as an area of high concern:

> *A crucial challenge is maintaining team structure and morale. The "kudos" for product delivery will tend to go to the team closest to the end user customer in terms of customer and management visibility. The pressure and the "recriminations" for perceived delivery issues will tend to be aimed at the central team who are working to balance implementation, and therefore delivery, across multiple BUs. This tension can be ameliorated several ways—rotation of members between both types of teams, either on a temporary or long term basis, is one good answer. Living in your supplier's or customers' shoes for a while has very beneficial effects on your appreciation of the other person's challenges.*

Finally, the core group people must be careful not to engender resentment by being perceived as dictators attempting to impose their own standards, processes, and tools on the product groups. At Cummins, "core" was sometimes treated as a four-letter word. This can be very frustrating for a group trying to juggle the concerns of a multitude of project teams and trying to keep everyone's attention on the big picture.

What made the two-part organization work at Cummins? In our view, there were four things: (1) having the product line champion (Temple) in a place of authority, (2) a culture of cooperation within the company, (3) an effective funding model, and (4) a product-based consensus on priorities. We'll discuss the last two here.

Recall that the "Funding" practice area (Section 6.4) is concerned with who pays for the core assets. It may have seemed to be an esoteric, possibly dry little practice area, but funding at Cummins is not only what gets the core assets built but also what gets them *used*. Funding is used to drive the proper behavior and establish a healthy organizational tension among the groups. Here's how it works. The budget for the core asset group is established. Each business unit is billed a portion of that budget in proportion to that business unit's overall sales. Thus, each business unit has every incentive to use the core assets because they're charged for them whether they use them or not. Once again, the tendency to rely on cross-organizational sources is reinforced by policy. A funding model such as this is a sure sign of whole-hearted endorsement from top-level management of the concept of core assets and therefore of product lines. It's more than lip service; management is voting with their pocketbooks. A by-product is that business units (or, for that matter, individual projects) are strongly discouraged from bypassing the core asset group by building their own software. No project manager wants to stand up in front of his peers and admit to having the resources to commission duplicate work. That's a sign of a project that apparently has too much money—a situation that can be quickly remedied.

This brings us to the fourth factor that makes the system work. There are weekly technical planning meetings between the core asset group and all of the product groups. These meetings are held to discuss new feature requests and to trade information, and are invaluable as opportunities to find new areas of commonality. And it is at these meetings that the project managers put in their bids for what they need from the core asset group. They do this by prioritizing the change requests and problem reports that are in the core asset group's queue. The elegance of this approach is twofold. First, it relieves the core asset group of having to decide what's important to the product groups and thus prevents them from being perceived as legislating product priorities, something that would surely be resented. Second, it compels the product groups to work out among themselves what the actual priorities are. No project manager will stand before his peers and claim that all of his change requests are critical. The meetings force consensus among the product groups, and once again the "needs of the many" culture is reinforced by organizational policy. The net effect is that it lets the core asset group be responsive to the product groups as a whole. The product groups regard the core asset group not as alien outsiders forcing assets down their throats, but as a service group driven to be as responsive as they can to the wishes of the product groups. "Having actual meetings is critical," one of the participants told us, "because you have to look the other managers in the eye when you say what your project's priorities are."

What if a product group really does need a core asset, but the core asset group is at capacity and the need isn't deemed high priority by a concensus of all the product groups? Does the product group build it? No. If the need is really for something common, and the product group has the resources to build it, then those resources are reallocated to the core asset group.

Cooperation between the core asset providers and the product builders has made the two-part organization succeed at Cummins; the Cummins people called it "concept alignment"—the sense that all groups are working toward common goals for the common good. How they work is defined in the operational concept that must be communicated to all those involved.

The two-part organization is not right for every software product line, but Cummins has found the key to making it work.

—PCC

9.6 Running the Product Line

As described in the sidebar "Pas de Deux: Making the Two-Part Organization Work" the product line at Cummins grows and evolves by virtue of the weekly project meetings where the product groups prioritize and agree on the work to be done by the core asset group. This work is defined in terms of change requests and problem reports. Change requests that add new features are not uncommon; in this way the product line's scope is continuously evolving. The weekly meetings are also at the heart of the technical planning process, providing input to a dedicated technical planner who keeps track of new program starts, new and changing product plans, feature plans, core asset releases, and maintenance status, and who tracks change requests and problem reports.

All core artifacts—especially requirements—are naturally kept under strict configuration control. A CM plan guides CM activities. Change requests and problem reports for all configuration items are initiated, recorded, reviewed, approved, and tracked according to a documented procedure. Product creation and release are done according to documented procedures, as are recording of configuration item status, report generation, and any changes in baselines. Cummins made a significant investment in an integrated tool environment that helped them with CM, requirements and traceability management, architecture definition, a data dictionary, system builds and configurations, testing, parameter tuning, and software release and distribution. Through this toolset, all projects have access to all other projects' problem reports and change requests, which helps people (especially those on the core asset team) spot potential commonalities that can be raised at the weekly meetings.

The data collected focus mainly on the core assets: time required for development, which assets are used by which products, and bugs found in core assets by product developers. However, cost and effort data are also collected on the individual products.

As would be expected in a real-time embedded domain, Cummins pays a great deal of attention to software and system testing, including unit testing, subsystem integration testing, system testing, regression testing, deployment testing, and acceptance or field testing. The core asset team performs generic testing, whereas the product teams perform product testing. Both use a common test environment and toolset that, among things, provide automated unit and regression testing, which are essential in Cummins's view because of the large number of builds they produce. Test artifacts (such as test procedures, test cases, and automated tests) are first-class core assets in the Cummins product line. Recently, the core asset group acquired a dedicated engine (and a truck to put it in) so their software can be tested under real end-user conditions. The effect of this is twofold. First, the quality of the core software benefits because of the more extensive tests that previously were not possible. Second, the quality of the core software is *perceived* to be high by the product teams: there's nothing quite like watching software drive a real truck down the road or around the Cummins parking lot to make doubters of the core concept change their minds.

Unlike most organizations, Cummins practices explicit and ongoing architecture evaluation. They use unstructured reviews; but what they lack in method, they make up for in enthusiasm and frequency. In addition to the weekly meetings to track and prioritize changes, Cummins also holds frequent monthly design reviews to assess whether the architecture is still suitable. The focus is on algorithm suitability and parameterization variability, but one suspects that these reviews will take on more of a structural tone and play a larger role in the stringent Core II architecture planned for the future. At the meetings, technology forecasters and market analysts bring their knowledge of future trends to the architect's attention, and verbal scenarios are used to play out change cases to see if the design will stand up to future challenges.

Risk management is a standard part of Cummins's practice. Each contract includes risk management in its stated activities, and they use a standard "Identify, Analyze, Plan, Track, Control" model. Risks are addressed during technical reviews, during management reviews, and when contracts are let; they are discussed in the weekly coordination meetings. The risks that are identified, and how they are handled, are communicated throughout the organization.

9.7 Results

What benefits has the product line approach wrought for Cummins since Ron Temple called a halt to the non-product-line projects in 1994? Just these:

- More than 20 product groups have been successfully launched, which, when counting build-time and customer-managed variation, have produced more than 1000 separate engine applications.
- On average, more than 75% of all product software now comes from the core assets.
- The product cycle time has been slashed, reducing "time to first engine start" from 250 person-months to just a few person-months. One prototype for a new product was built over a weekend.
- Software quality is at an all-time high, which Cummins attributes to the broad testing, extensive use, and common fix implementation gained from the product line approach.
- Customer satisfaction is high. The product line productivity benefits enabled a significant number of new features to be developed (more than 200 to date) and easily built and integrated by a staff that now has more time to do feature exploration. In addition, Cummins products now have a more common look and feel to them, something that was lacking before.
- Projects are more successful. Before the product line approach was adopted, only three of ten projects were on track. Four were failing or had failed, and three were teetering on the brink. In 1997, 15 of 15 projects were on track.
- There is a widespread feeling that developers are now much more portable across projects because their knowledge is applicable across the board. Use of core assets and common workflow has shortened the learning curve (from one product to another) from many months to a few weeks. This simplifies technical planning and lets the organization respond effectively to situations in which a project needs help quickly.

One way to summarize all of this is to say that the capacity of the organization to deliver products is skyrocketing. Table 9.1 quantifies this effect; it is a measurement of how broad the product line's scope is. Notice how it took off in 1995 and beyond, once the product line was in place. The last row in the table is telling because it indicates the breadth of the product line's scope and also shows a flavor of the path not taken at Cummins. It would take more than 360 software engineers to produce the separate software systems with the feature/ECM mix that Cummins achieves today with only 100. This is a productivity

Table 9.1 Scope of Cummins's Product Line

Supported Components	1992	1993	1994	1995	1996	1997	1998
Electronic control modules (ECMs)	3	3	4	5	5	11	12
Fuel systems	2	2	3	5	5	10	11
Engines	3	3	5	5	12	16	17
Features/ECMs	60	80	180	370	1100	2200	2400

improvement of 3.6:1—not a gain of 20% or 30%, which wouldn't be bad, but *360%*.

Software product lines have two kinds of beneficial effects. The first, outlined above, is that they let you carry out your business with impressive gains in efficiency. But the second is even more exciting: they let you gain entry into new areas of business that might otherwise have been off limits. At Cummins, software product lines let the company leap into the industrial engine market. While automotive diesels come in a bewildering variety of sizes and features, their variability pales in comparison to that of the industrial market. Table 9.2

able 9.2 Partial List of Industrial Applications for Cummins Engines

Aerial platform 4B	• Milling machine K19
Asphalt/concrete 6B	• Mixer 4B, L10
Backhoe/loader 4B, 6B	• Mower 4B,
Blower 6B	• Oilfield equipment L10, N14, K19
Carrier 4B, 6B, L10, N14, K19, K38, K50, V903	• On-/off-road vehicle 4B, 6B, C, N14, K19, V28
Chipper N14, K19	• Paver/finisher 4B, 6B, L10
Cleaner 4B, 6B, N14	• Planer 4B, 6B, C, K19, K38
Compactor 4B, 6B	• Power unit 4B, 6B, L10, N14
Compressor 4B, 6B, V903, L10, N14	• Pump 4B, 6B, C, N14
Conveyor 6B, C	• Refuse collector 6B, C, L10, N14
Crane 4B, 6B, C, L10, N14, K19, V28, K38, V903	• Roadmaking equipment 6B, C, K19, K38
Crane carrier L10, N14, K19	• Rough terrain 4B, 6B, N14
Crash tender N15, V903	• Saw 6B, N14, K19
Crusher 6B, C, L10, N14	• Screening unit 4B
Chipper 4B, 6B, C, L10, N14, K19, V28,	• Skidder 4B, 6B, C, L10, K19
Drilling equipment 4B, 6B, C, L10, N14, K19, K38	• Slurry/chip spreader 4B, 6B, C
Dumper L10, N14, K19, K38, K50, V28	• Snow equip 4B, 6B, C, L10, N14, K19, V903
Excavator 4B, 6B, C, L10, N14, K19, K38	• Special vehicle 6B, C
Firefighting equipment 4B, 6B, C, L10, N14	• Sprayer 4B, 6B, C, L10
Forklift 4B, 6B, L10	• Sweeper 4B, 6B, C
Grader 4B, 6B, C, L10, V28	• Tractor 4B, 6B, C, L10, N14, K19, V903
Harvester 4B, 6B, C, N14, K19	• Trencher 4B, 6B, C
Hoist 6B, N14	• Truck 4B, 6B, C, L10, N14, K19, V28
Loader 4B, 6B, C, L10, N14, K19, K38, K50, V28	• Welder N14
Locomotive 4B, 6B, N14, K19	• Winch 4B, 6B
Maintenance equipment 4B, 6B, C, N14, K19, K38,	

shows some industrial applications and the engines that Cummins supplies to each one. If you count the software versions and configurations and calibrations that populate the engines in this market, Cummins builds well over 1000 different variations, based on just 20 software builds. Before this foray, 80% of Cummins engines were for automotive applications. Now the figure is 40%, with the slack taken up by industrial and power generation applications.

The industrial market is a perfect fit for the software product line approach because it's a low-volume, high-variation proposition. Not many of each version will be sold, but the number of versions is enormous. If each version had to be hand-tooled from scratch, it wouldn't be feasible to try to gain market share, but because quickly turning out versions is what a software product line does best, it's a perfect match.

Cummins is certainly not afraid of change, but they are careful about what changes they undertake. Naturally, they want to target improvement areas where the benefit will outweigh the cost—and the more the better. In their estimation, process improvement brings home a benefit-to-cost ratio of 2:1 to 3:1—not bad—and we know that process improvement and product line practice go hand in hand, as described in "Software Process Improvement and Product Line Practice" sidebar. However, they estimate that software product line practice brings with it a benefit-to-cost ratio of about 10:1.

9.8 Lessons Learned

The people at Cummins shared with us the many lessons they had learned about software product lines. Foremost was the fact that product line development is much more complex than single-system development, presenting a challenge even for a mature software organization. Without the discipline to follow the concepts, especially in the face of schedule pressures or (in their delightful phrase) a "creative workforce," they believe an organization will fail.

Cummins credits much of their success to an effective, well-placed champion who guided them through the formative phase and kept them on track. They believe the champion has to be a visionary, able to convince other senior managers and the affected organizations of the need to change the way the company does business. The champion, they said, must be able to take the long-term view and to make a long-term commitment to make the ideas stick. Every product line seems to have a point early in its development when the organization reaches a crucible: unforeseen difficulties emerge, and the pain of change is greater than Cummins anticipated. At that point, the "good old days" of business as usual look warm, familiar, and very inviting. This is when the champion is needed the most.

In retrospect, the people at Cummins realize that they made the leap to product lines because of the critical situation they faced. Other organizations have shared this experience—product lines are attempted because the alternative is failure. In fact, the people with whom we spoke doubted that any company would adopt the product line approach on the basis of financial considerations alone. Avoiding a clear and present danger is usually a much more compelling motivation. They felt that the business case for software product lines, while qualitatively compelling, lacked the numbers to make it concrete. Many people were skeptical that the savings would materialize, which suggests that top Cummins management supported Ron Temple's plan as a leap of faith.

In the case of Cummins, launching the product line was an all-or-nothing proposition; they didn't think that tip-toeing into the product line world would have worked. The eventual large-scale changes in organizational structure, workflow, culture, rewards, economics, measures of success, and overall mindset would not, they believe, have been possible if attempted piecemeal.

Other lessons of note include the following:

- **Mining:** Reusing small functions or other code-level assets is often the most feasible, but that is not where the big payoff is. Reusing architectures, large-grained components, requirements statements, tests, and toolsets should be (and for Cummins, was) the goal. However, unmanaged legacy assets often have too many interactions to be feasibly extracted, and so mining often presents a conflict: very large chunks of mature software are the most desirable and reliable but are also the most difficult and expensive to salvage.
- **Configuration management:** Although a software product line is more than just a component library (see "What Product Lines Are Not," Section 1.2), a component library is the backbone of a software product line because it provides the central core asset repository for product builders. Product teams need to know what has changed since they last used an asset in a build and what versions of what assets were used in what previous builds. They rely on disciplined CM processes to make that information available. The Cummins developers felt strongly that the library should store traceability information among the artifacts—tying requirements to design to test, for example.
- **Product builder's guide:** Cummins knew that a product builder's guide was needed to help development teams turn the core assets into products, so they wrote one. It was hundreds of pages long; it was descriptive rather than prescriptive; it was called a "Guide" instead of something more authoritative, such as a "Standard"; and compliance with it was not checked, required, or enforced. The result was predictable: it wasn't routinely used. The four shortcomings listed above suggest four clear lessons

about product builder's guides. Besides the obvious ways to fix these four factors, Cummins felt that a solid, integrated build tool would go a long way toward making the product-building process repeatable and compliant with a standard process.

- **Release management:** There is a balance to be struck between changing the core assets (to achieve new-feature capability) and freezing the core assets (to reduce downstream maintenance costs). Each core release will find its way into a set of products, which then obligates the company to maintain that version for an indeterminate period of time. Cummins felt that the fewer releases they could get by with, the better.
- **Data collection:** They felt that data on tracking cost, reuse, and concept adherence were important and useful; this allowed them continually to take the pulse of the organization with respect to the product line concepts and the promises made for them. "Metrics are a challenge," they told us. "Institutionalize them up front."
- **Requirements engineering:** The people at Cummins felt strongly that product line requirements must be established and coordinated via a process spanning the entire product line organization. Because the Cummins software product line crosses major business units, this means a corporate effort. They prescribe involving all the markets within the scope, both current and future. They make sure to elicit nonoperational and quality-attribute requirements as well as functional and feature-based requirements. Only in this way can true commonality and variability begin to be identified. Cummins kept in place a strong trace between requirements deemed common and software core assets; this gave them a handle for managing and evolving the core asset base. They felt that strong scrutiny of unique requirements was always in order because "unique" requirements often turn out to be common when viewed in the correct light. But a top domain expert has to be available to shine that light. Finally, they said, make sure you challenge designs that are just masquerading as requirements.
- **Understanding relevant domains:** Domain analysis must be performed by domain experts, and the architect must also be a domain expert. The goal of domain analysis is to understand (and document) the major commonalities and variations so as to let the architecture and core asset definition begin on a solid footing. Thus, for Cummins, the architect and the core asset developers were consumers of a documented domain model.

The major lesson learned deals with architecture. Cummins created their original core asset base by making architectural improvements in legacy software. It was mature, reliable software but did not have or conform to any documented architecture. The focus was on making each component generic with respect to its envisioned scope of usage by adding parameters or embedding alternative implementations (chosen at build time by means of #ifdefs) within the same file. Time and resource constraints did not permit architectural reengineering beyond this. Cummins now characterizes what they did as component reuse, and they feel that component reuse alone will not gain them the tenfold productivity improvement promised by an architecture-based product line approach. Lacking a central architectural vision that is effective and well communicated, product developers could and did interconnect components at will. Sometimes the components weren't meant to be connected in a particular way, which invited the developers to make unilateral changes in the assets in order to shoehorn them into the ad hoc scheme. During the first phase of the product line, product developers were not required to report when they tailored the core assets. The result was, effectively, different architectures that were used by different product groups, and this resulted in some functionality being coded multiple times (once for each architecture). In addition, this multiple implementation approach resulted in slight to major differences in functionality. This prevented Cummins products from having a common look and feel to their customers.

Looking back, the core asset group feels more strongly than ever that a well-defined architecture is critical to a software product line; one gets the feeling that the pride in their accomplishments is tempered by regret that they did not achieve all that a strong architecture would have given them. They are firm believers in patterns and styles because they reduce risk. And for software product lines, they counsel architects to consider the number of components (not too many and not too few), to make sure to handle the needed variability in each component and across the architecture as a whole, to make the variability mechanisms explicit and managed, and to minimize the number of #ifdefs and other mechanisms that limit testability. Above all, they say, the architecture must be well documented and scrupulously maintained.

To ameliorate the problems with their architecture (or lack of it), Cummins is now launching an effort called Core II. Core II will feature a strong, well-documented architecture with core components that comply with it. The architecture will be built on the foundation of a three-month-long domain analysis effort that has already been completed. They are changing their workflow to eliminate the opportunities for unilateral tailoring of the core assets, and they are introducing workflow audit procedures for enforcement. They are trying to improve their requirements efforts by producing pure software requirements, whereas previously the effort was centered around system requirements. Under the old architecture, features not needed in a product were loaded but turned off. Under the Core II architecture, if a feature is not needed in a product, it will be omitted. This will make more room for other features, allow more flexibility, simplify maintenance and testing, and ease the configuration control problem as products are released into the maintenance stream. The Cummins-built operating system will be retooled to emphasize platform portability and standard i/o interfaces.

9.9 Epilogue

In 1993, as the people at Cummins were celebrating the company's seventy-fifth anniversary, they hired Jeffrey Cruikshank and David Sicilia to research and write a history of the company. Their effort, which took more than three years, resulted in *The Engine That Could: 75 Years of Value-Driven Change at Cummins Engine Company* [Cruikshank 97]. Their 600-page close-up portrait[1] tells the story of a company that has always had an unshakable vision of what it was and where it was going, through good times and bad. In summarizing what they found to be the essential aspects of the Cummins story, Cruikshank and Sicilia listed five factors that resonated loudly with us. All five are important qualities for a software product line organization to have, and we found them in abundance at Cummins. They are as follows:

1. **Cultivate and preserve organizational competence:** Cummins managed to avoid the conglomeration and diversification craze of the 1960s and 1970s. Except for a couple of ill-advised and quickly jettisoned side businesses, they were founded as and have remained to this day a manufacturer of commercial engines and related products, period. Even so, core competencies tend to shift with technology. Basic metal machining had to make room for advanced metallurgy, fluid dynamics, computer-aided design, and (as of late) onboard electronics and hard real-time embedded software engineering. Cummins realized, perhaps unconsciously, that the ability to produce highly varying software systems quickly and efficiently was going to be a business enabler and would put the company squarely within the realm of core expertise in which it should hold competence. Of more immediate import, consciously maintaining core competence is what gives them a deep understanding of the relevant domains, and it also gives them the impetus to embrace change when doing so will maintain that competence.
2. **Compete in the long term:** "At Cummins," write Cruikshank and Sicilia, "this perspective is captured in the phrase 'patient capital.' The patient-capital tradition at Cummins was established by the members of the founding Irwin-Sweeney-Miller family, who infused money into the business continuously for twenty years (including the most trying years of the Great Depression) before their diesel-making venture finally managed to turn a profit." This attitude was exemplified when Ron Temple halted the independent projects so that he could launch the product line. Making short-term sacrifices for long-term benefits is the way the company does business.

1. This book and the Cummins Web site were the sources of the historical information about the company in this case study.

3. **Embrace change:** "Nowhere is Cummins's willingness to embrace change more apparent than in its encounter with Japanese diesel competition in the 1980s," wrote Cruikshank and Sicilia. "When Detroit realized belatedly that Japanese imports represented a mortal threat, the industry sought protection through trade barriers. As a result, the industry wound up surrendering market share in exchange for short-term profits. When Cummins's time came—that is, when the Japanese began making exploratory forays into the U.S. heavy-duty diesel market in the early 1980s—the Engine Company tightened its belt and cut its new engine prices by 20 and 40 percent. The immediate result was a flood tide of red ink at Cummins. But in the medium term, the Japanese challengers decided that they could not compete on Cummins's home turf." Meanwhile, Cummins was learning a great deal about manufacturing practices from its Japanese competitors. When pollution regulations and the Clean Air Act were passed, Cummins worked with regulators instead of stonewalling them and hoping they would go away. In the software realm, the product line paradigm brought fundamental change. However, it was greeted not with fear, but with a sense of confidence: "Yes, that makes sense. We can do that." And the way they're running the product line now shows their comfort with change: weekly meetings to handle change requests and monthly meetings to see if the architecture needs to change. This is extraordinary. Most companies would rather not know if their architecture is decaying; they would rather just hunker down and hope for the best. At Cummins, one gets the feeling that they're happiest when they discover a need for change.

4. **Identify and build relationships with all stakeholders:** At the corporate level, this means community, labor, government, vendors, distributors, customers, and shareholders. It is no coincidence that "community" comes first. Cummins has long had a social conscience and is known for an extensive program in corporate philanthropy. In the product line venue, building stakeholder relationships means paying attention to how all involved parties will interact and cooperate with each other to the mutual benefit of all, and it brings the team-based work ethic that Cummins is known for to bear on the production of high-quality software.

5. **Use values to drive the business:** In the 1970s, Cummins decided not to build a plant in South Africa because the apartheid government would have imposed conditions, such as white-only supervisors, that were repugnant to Cummins's ethical standards. This effectively forfeited the entire South African market for diesel engines to one of their less concerned competitors, but it took the board of directors just five minutes to make the decision. Cummins has always had a sense of trying to do the right thing and a faith that business rewards would follow. In the case of the software product line, this resulted in a launching that was intense and all-encompassing

and avoided the even more painful melodrama that some companies suffer when they know that they need to change but do so only grudgingly and in small steps. Adopting the product line approach was clearly the right thing to do, and the organization did it. Having made that determination, they could do nothing else. We asked Ron Temple why he thought top management supported him when he made the eye-popping decision to halt production. "They trusted me," he said with a no-big-deal shrug of the shoulders. "It's why they brought me in."

Finally, Cruikshank and Sicilia's account of how their book came to be rang true with us. The company had tried to commission a history of itself on the occasion of earlier anniversaries, but the results were never satisfactory. "Straight advertising style," grumbled J. Irwin Miller about one fluffy attempt. He didn't want a whitewash but a full and accurate accounting of the company's history, which he knew was rich and strong enough to withstand a full disclosure. No subject was off limits to Cruikshank and Sicilia, with three small and inconsequential exceptions based in legality. "Dig deeper," they were told. "Tell it all." This is typical of the tough-minded honesty we found at Cummins. For our case study we were told what few areas were off limits and why, but we were otherwise given free rein. And we were surprised and delighted by the amount of studied introspection our hosts had already done, cataloging practices used and lessons learned about every one of the 29 practice areas in Part II of this book. Cummins is a company that does the right thing as they see it, and they aren't afraid to talk about it.

Clessie Cummins never heard of software product lines, but he wasn't afraid to try new things. His favorite kind of innovation was the kind that commanded attention, from mounting a propeller on the back of a bobsled to putting a Packard on railroad wheels. No software product line can match the flair of a propeller-driven bobsled, but a 10:1 benefit-to-cost ratio, a 3.6:1 productivity gain, and the capacity to get an engine running over a weekend are just as attention getting in their own way. It's a good bet that Clessie would have approved.

9.10 Practice Area Compendium

The product line practice areas discussed in Part II are a distillation of common activities that companies engage in when building a software product line. But no company engages in all of them to the same degree or as a set of 29 discrete and easily identified activities. Each organization finds its own path through the product line activities, often blending the practice areas into patterns (as in Chapter 7) that are sometimes unique to the organization.

Rather than try to tell the Cummins story as a dissonant 29-part harmony, we decided to tell it in its own terms with its own natural flow. Nevertheless, we wanted to ground the story in the practice areas so that all of the case studies would share a common frame of reference. Table 9.3 recounts the major sections of the Cummins story and lists the practice areas that played starring roles in them. A few practice areas are unaccounted for in this table. The Cummins product line uses no COTS products or commissioned software, so "COTS Utilization" and "Developing an Acquisition Strategy" are absent. And in a few other cases, a practice area was applied in a completely predictable way, the description of which added nothing to the telling.

Table 9.3 Practice Areas and the Cummins Product Line

Section	Software Engineering Practice Areas	Technical Management Practice Areas	Organizational Management Practice Areas
Getting Off the Ground	Architecture Definition Mining Existing Assets Requirements Engineering Software System Integration Understanding Relevant Domains	Make/Buy/Mine/Commission Analysis Scoping	Building a Business Case Launching and Institutionalizing Market Analysis Training
An Organization Structured for Cooperation		Technical Planning	Funding Operations Structuring the Organization
Running the Product Line	Architecture Evaluation	Configuration Management Data Collection, Metrics, and Tracking Scoping Technical Risk Management Tool Support	Organizational Risk Management Technology Forecasting

9.11 For Further Reading

Cruikshank and Sicilia's book about Cummins Inc. is an interesting study of an American industrial icon [Cruikshank 97]. A compelling aspect of the company's culture is its tradition of high ethical standards in the conduct of its business.

9.12 Discussion Questions

1. The story of how Cummins made the two-part organization work is the story of a practice area pattern. Write a Pas de Deux pattern that shows the interaction among the practice areas mentioned in that sidebar (page 427). Include "Structuring the Organization," "Funding," "Technical Planning," "Organizational Planning," and "Operations." Which other ones do you think are relevant?
2. One of the lessons that Cummins learned about architectures for product lines is that architecture, workflow (which we would call "process" or "operations"), technologies, and the tool environment all affect each other and must be considered as a system. To that list we would add the product line's scope, as manifested by a statement of the commonalities and variations that the architecture must support. Practice areas working in concert in this way constitute a practice area pattern. Give this pattern a name, and write it.
3. Requirements engineering at Cummins took on the flavors of several of the practice areas. Does their approach match any of the patterns or variants in Chapter 7? If not, write such a pattern or variant.
4. Embedded in the "Pas de Deux" sidebar was a profile of a core asset developer. Write a checklist that you would use to interview a candidate for a core asset developer position.

10

Control Channel Toolkit: A Software Product Line That Controls Satellites

with Sholom Cohen and Patrick Donohoe

In October 1957, the Russians launched Sputnik I, the first artificial satellite to orbit the earth. In the years since, our world has become satellite-dependent. Today there are about 750 active military, commercial, and civilian satellites. Commercial satellites are widely used for a range of wireless communication, including Internet and television transmissions, for weather forecasting, and for geographic positioning. The United States military forces and intelligence agencies rely on satellites to guide weapons, pinpoint the enemy, navigate, communicate, and eavesdrop. According to the U.S. Space Command, the United States has slightly more than 300 active satellites, of which 60% are commercial, 20% are military, and 20% belong to civilian government agencies.[1]

We have now seen that it is possible to field engine control systems successfully using a software product line approach. Is it possible to do the same for satellite command and control systems? Space is the new frontier of great promise and great challenge, and yet we've heard satellite experts say again and again, "Satellite command and control is . . . well, command and control." They

1. Source: http://www.usatoday.com/news/washdc/ncswed05.html

say this because although there is plenty that is challenging about the software associated with satellites, much of the command and control software isn't very challenging and is not unique. In fact, so much is the same from one command and control system to another that the United States National Reconnaissance Office (NRO) decided to take advantage of that commonality and build a product line asset base for their ground-based spacecraft command and control software.

Early results show that they made a fine decision. The first system in their product line is enjoying, among other benefits, 50% reductions in overall cost and schedule, and nearly tenfold reductions in development personnel and defects. These are impressive results for a first foray into software product lines. How did they do it?

The case study we are about to unfold tells their story—the story of the Control Channel Toolkit (CCT), their software asset base for a product line of ground-based spacecraft command and control systems. We begin by characterizing the CCT context and then we chronicle the history of the effort, describing the justification for CCT, the CCT team's organizational structure and influences, the software artifacts that were developed, and the practices and processes that were used. We also describe the results that were achieved and the lessons that were learned, including the measurable benefits the government has already reaped in the initial use of CCT on a specific spacecraft command and control system. Throughout, we underscore software product line practice area coverage and patterns as well as how the CCT effort uniquely addressed many of the practice areas.

10.1 Contextual Background

Let's begin with an overview sketch of CCT. CCT is a software asset base commissioned by one organization (the NRO) and built under contract by another (the Raytheon Company). This acquirer/contractor arrangement adds a bit of a twist to some of the software product line practice areas and also introduces some interesting economic motivations. Raytheon hopes to use the CCT experience to secure future spacecraft command and control system business. The NRO hopes to persuade other government spacecraft ground system projects to subscribe to the product line effort that it commissioned, thus defraying some of the CCT development and sustainment costs.

CCT is neither a complete software system nor a complete software product line; it is a software product line asset base. The asset base consists of generalized requirements, domain specifications, a software architecture, a set of reusable software components, test procedures, a development environment definition, and a guide for reusing the architecture and components. CCT users build products. CCT users are individual government contractors commissioned by a government office to build spacecraft command and control systems using the CCT software assets. CCT is currently being used to field several government systems. Those systems constitute the actual product line. The NRO is currently funding Raytheon to maintain the CCT for current and future users. Figure 10.1 annotates our software product line signature diagram to illustrate. You can see from this illustration that in this case the product development and the core asset development are split among potentially different contractor organizations, and Raytheon, the NRO, and CCT users share the management responsibilities. If we are to understand how this all works smoothly, we need to know something about the two key organizations—the NRO and Raytheon.

10.1.1 Organizational Profiles

The NRO designs, builds, and operates defense reconnaissance satellites. NRO intelligence products, provided to an expanding list of customers such as the U.S. Central Intelligence Agency (CIA) and the U.S. Department of Defense (DoD), can warn of potential trouble spots around the world, help plan military

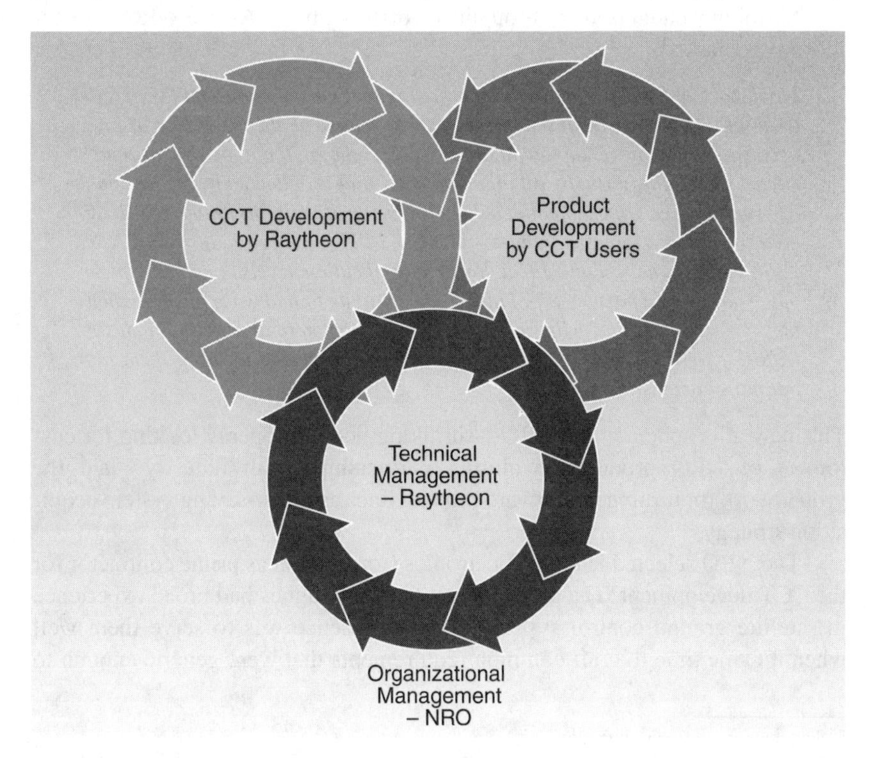

Figure 10.1 The Three Essential Activities and CCT

operations, and monitor the environment. As part of the 13-member Intelligence Community, the NRO plays a primary role in achieving information superiority for the U.S. Government and Armed Forces. The NRO is staffed by both Dod and CIA personnel. It is funded through the National Reconnaissance Program, part of the National Foreign Intelligence Program. The U.S. Assistant Secretary of the Air Force for Space also serves as the Director of the NRO.

In the past, the very existence of the NRO, let alone its software projects, was classified information. In recent years, the NRO has implemented a series of actions declassifying some of its operations. The organization's existence was formally declassified in September 1992, followed by the location of its headquarters in Chantilly, Virginia, in 1994. In February 1995, CORONA, a photoreconnaissance program in operation from 1960 to 1972, was declassified, and 800,000 CORONA images were transferred to the National Archives and Records Administration. The declassification of the satellite generation following CORONA is currently planned. In December 1996, the NRO announced for the first time, in advance, the launch of a reconnaissance satellite. This new policy of openness is, among other things, intended to increase the NRO's customer and contractor base.[2]

Shrinking budgets have brought all of this about. As the NRO director recently remarked,

> *I look back at former NRO Directors, having had tons of money and very little oversight, and they achieved great results. I look at them with great envy because now I have an awful lot of oversight and not nearly as much money. . . . Today, virtually all of the imagery that is collected by the National Reconnaissance Office is collected [as] non-sensitive information. It's delivered to military forces around the world. . . . [T]he large majority of NRO information can be handled at lower classification levels, opening up the opportunities for partnership. Finally, we continue to find ways of strengthening our partnerships with industry. As the commercial satellite industry matures, we're looking at industrial practices and trying to bring them into our major acquisitions.*[3]

This new atmosphere at the NRO—shrinking budgets, openly looking for customers of NRO products, exploring partnerships with industry—laid the groundwork for turning to software product lines as a cost-saving system acquisition strategy.

The NRO selected Hughes Electronics Corporation as prime contractor for the CCT development. The development team at Hughes had broad experience in satellite ground control systems. This experience was to serve them well when it came time to craft common requirements that were generic enough to

2. Source: http://www.nro.odci.gov.

3. From remarks by Keith Hall, Director of the National Reconnaissance Office, to the National Space Symposium, Colorado Springs, Colorado, 9 April 1998. Source: http://www.nro.odci.gov/speeches/nss-498.html.

serve the first three different satellite projects, yet specific enough to be useful to each of them. They were already knowledgeable in areas such as orbit dynamics, coordinate system transformations, vehicle configuration variability, and other technical aspects that would need to be mastered before they could build any single satellite ground control system, let alone an asset base for an entire family of systems. Furthermore, the Hughes team was accustomed to following defined processes for both software project management and software development. The process discipline required for software product line efforts was not a stretch for them.

Hughes Electronics subsequently merged with the Raytheon Company. The consolidation of Hughes into Raytheon also brought together related operations formerly called Raytheon E-Systems, Raytheon Electronic Systems, and the Texas Instruments divisions earlier acquired by Raytheon. Overall, the Raytheon Company operates in both the defense and commercial sectors in the area of electronics, aircraft systems, and engineering and construction. Raytheon is one of the largest American defense contractors, with $20 billion in sales and more than 92,000 people. Their products include missiles, radar systems, sensors and electro-optics, reconnaissance, surveillance, air traffic control, and aircraft integration systems.[4]

When Hughes was merged with Raytheon, CCT became a Raytheon project, although the development team remained unchanged. There were 20 to 25 employees on the Raytheon development team who took CCT from domain analysis through its architecture creation and implementation. The team peaked at 45 people during component engineering. With the exception of a very small number of subcontractors, all technical work was done at the contractor's site in Denver, Colorado. But who conceived the idea for CCT in the first place?

10.1.2 Project History

Recall from the introduction to this case study that experts already knew that there was much in common among satellite command and control systems. In fact, the Control Channel Toolkit project actually emerged from earlier efforts to produce common software for satellite command and control. In 1993, an Air Force program office began the acquisition of a replacement command and control system for a classified satellite program. The contract for the Distributed Command and Control System (DCCS) began in 1994. The DCCS is designed to fly a specific type of space vehicle. Its design is for the most part object-oriented with some wrapped legacy code that provides highly specialized numerical algorithms.

In 1996, the Air Force Space and Missile Center (SMC) began an effort for a Standard Spacecraft Control Segment (SSCS) that brokered several other satellite

4. Source: 1999 Raytheon annual report, http://www.raytheon.com/finance/1999/ray_annual.pdf.

program office requirements into a single specification. The SSCS goal was to exploit DCCS to produce a common core capability for use by these other program offices, thus offering development and maintenance savings for SMC. The SSCS technical approach was to modify the DCCS design and code artifacts to meet new (common) requirements. Shortly after development began, it was recognized that the approach was faulty: DCCS had not been designed to address the new requirements. In short, DCCS had not been designed for reuse. All major SSCS schedule milestones were missed. The effort was redirected to work on common human machine interfaces as a way of standardizing business processes.

At this point, the Air Force and the NRO met to determine a common development path for SSCS and DCCS that would offer reduced cost and effort in both development and maintenance phases. There was yet another government project, which we will call the Spacecraft C2 System, that had also planned on modifying the DCCS artifacts to meet their requirements. This project was early in its requirements phase. The Air Force requested a revised program plan for all three systems to determine how they could realistically take advantage of the commonalities found in all three and potentially in others as well.

A two-month feasibility study was approved and commenced in May 1997. Six working groups were formed to explore architecture definition, process definition, operations and maintenance definition, cost analysis, schedule assessment, and risk assessment. Learning from the flawed reuse approach of DCCS/SSCS, the NRO initiated the Control Channel Toolkit (CCT) project to reengineer DCCS from an architecture perspective. The Spacecraft C2 Program became the first user of CCT. The Software Engineering Institute (SEI) became involved with the CCT effort at the request of the NRO in October 1997 and continued the collaboration until CCT completion.

CCT was originally conceived to be a "toolkit" that would consist of:

- a set of reusable software components
- tools to help integrate them into complete systems

As we shall see, the toolkit concept evolved into something much more sophisticated and much more usable—namely, a software product line asset base. While a product line asset base certainly includes components and tools, we have seen (and so did the CCT team) that much more is required to achieve strategic, predictable, and measurably beneficial reuse. But before we spin much more of the CCT story, we need to continue with our context description. We need to know at least the underlying principles that are operative in the domain of spacecraft command and control.

10.1.3 Control Channels

Command and control software is employed throughout the life cycle of a space vehicle project. Typically, each satellite project develops and maintains a separate software system for the purpose of commanding and controlling the spacecraft vehicle. As the complexity of satellite systems has increased over the years, so have the requirements of the ground systems necessary to command and control them. Typical command and control systems exceed 500,000 lines of code.

The CCT supports a product line of ground-based spacecraft command and control systems (also referred to as "control channels"). Satellite control channels provide ground processing support to spacecraft, allowing operations staff to monitor spacecraft functions, configure spacecraft service and payload systems, manage spacecraft orbits and attitudes, and perform mission planning. Control channels receive clear (unencrypted) telemetry data from the front-end processing equipment and release spacecraft and ground system commands. Within a control channel, telemetry data are used to assess spacecraft health and perform payload functions. The telemetry may be provided to external clients as well; these clients may in turn provide command data to the control channel. Control channels also exercise control of the ground antenna system, uplink transmitter operations, and downlink receiver control. These monitoring and command capabilities combine to allow real-time control of the spacecraft and its payload.

The execution of these real-time functions requires connectivity between the control channel software functions and the spacecraft. The period of time and system configuration used to achieve connectivity describe a *contact*. Contacts normally include a preplanned set of tasks, such as assessing state of health, commanding the spacecraft into a new configuration, or executing an orbit or attitude maneuver. Since contacts require line-of-sight visibility from a ground antenna to the spacecraft and use ground resources as well, they are scheduled events determined by the scheduling activities of a spacecraft mission. Unplanned contacts may also be required to perform anomaly resolution for the spacecraft.

Control channels perform orbit and attitude maintenance through processing of tracking and telemetry data and generation of orbit estimates and maneuver data. These data are used to determine the need for future contacts and command parameters as well as the times required to execute the maneuvers. Special consideration is given to launch and early-orbit operations, which often place the spacecraft into unique configurations or impose unique requirements.

Some control channel processing is real time or near real time and is called *execution* processing. The remainder is batch or off-line and is called *planning*. During a contact, the control channel primarily executes capabilities associated with the receipt of telemetry and the release of command data to the ground equipment and spacecraft. The control channel receives raw telemetry from the spacecraft and the antenna ground system through its front-end processing equipment and converts it into client-usable form. The control channel distributes the telemetry to client processes, often with graphical user interfaces (GUIs) provided for operators to make real-time assessments of the spacecraft's health. Client processes may also initiate command requests that cause formatting and transmission of command data to destination services such as the spacecraft or to ground equipment such as the antenna. In many systems, traditional operator functions are automated through the use of special client processes that use rule-based processing.

Control channels archive telemetry and command data as well as other systems data such as operator actions and tracking data. These data form key inputs to the planning functions and provide a historical log for analysis and bookkeeping. Historical data are available for trend analysis and anomaly resolution.

Modern spacecraft use on-board processors to control both platform bus and mission payload functions. Control channels model the on-board processor instruction and data loading and its execution in order to anticipate spacecraft state and behavior.

In off-line processing, the control channel performs planning functions to estimate and propagate the spacecraft orbit and attitude, calculate maneuvers to change orbit or attitude, and schedule future contacts and resource needs. These functions include both launch and early-orbit support for the spacecraft as well as on-orbit operations.

10.2 Launching CCT

From our description of the "Launching and Institutionalizing" practice area (Section 6.5) and from the Assembly Line pattern (Section 7.8), you already know that launching a product line means putting into play a number of practice areas. So it was with CCT.

The primary motivation for adopting a product line approach is economic—the promise of long-term savings in return for some extra short-term effort. Thus, business issues often dominate any discussion about a particular product line. The resolution and handling of those business issues may determine the success or failure of the product line effort, as measured by its long-term costs and savings. The feasibility study team, which was already steeped in the understanding of the domain we just summarized, analyzed both business and technical issues. In getting started, they and the initial CCT team that followed exercised practices in the following software product line practice areas:

- Developing a Business Case
- Developing an Acquisition Strategy
- Funding
- Structuring the Organization
- Technical Planning
- Organizational Planning
- Operations

And it was the combination of practices from these areas that accomplished the "Launching" part of the "Launching and Institutionalizing" practice area.

10.2.1 Developing a Business Case for CCT

The business goals for CCT were to reduce life-cycle costs and development risks, promote interoperability, and provide flexibility. For the government spacecraft community, flexibility translates into accommodating multiple implementation contractors and enabling the integration of both commercially available and legacy assets. The strategy was to develop a toolkit once and have the three candidate programs share the development and maintenance costs.

The study team examined an array of government and commercial spacecraft command and control systems, including the three under primary investigation. They objectively examined the life-cycle cost data of the DCCS, the SSCS, and the Spacecraft C2 Program. Original program estimates were used; the validity of these estimates was not challenged, although the estimates were considered by the study team to be lower than the actual costs. Based on a domain requirements analysis, cost estimates were derived for implementing the three candidate systems using a product line approach. The commonality of requirements across these systems ranged from a low of 49% to a high of 89%, and the cost-benefit analysis showed significant life-cycle savings. The team also conducted a thorough risk identification and analysis activity. Mitigation strategies were defined for identified risks.

The feasibility study concluded the following:

- There was a credible CCT development schedule that contained a supportable staffing plan and no staffing impacts to DCCS and that was timely enough to meet Spacecraft C2 needs.
- CCT would ensure significant cost savings for these three programs over a ten-year period.
- Risks that could preclude CCT's success were manageable.
- CCT supported the overall government reuse vision.

The business case for CCT, as expressed in the original CCT statement of work, described cost savings over multiple programs that were partially attributable to maximized reuse of DCCS assets and exploitation of DCCS experience. Interestingly, the cost analysis did not show major savings for CCT's three candidate systems in terms of development; program sponsors were sold on the vision of greatly reduced risk and the promise of cost savings in the future. The concept of recruiting additional subscribers to the product line—that is, finding new satellite programs that could be built using CCT—was always a key part of the business strategy behind CCT.

10.2.2 Developing the Acquisition Strategy and Funding CCT

Typically a command and control system is acquired as part of a larger procurement that includes whatever is being commanded and controlled. The contract for the entire procurement is usually awarded to a single prime contractor. In the case of CCT, three government programs formed a partnership to acquire software that could be used across those three programs, as well as others. The CCT acquisition strategy required that the government assume some responsibility for development because spacecraft software systems are becoming too complex to be acquired as stand-alone, one-of-a-kind systems. Otherwise, both the cost and the risk are too great.

Asset ownership was a key product line issue because the product line was commissioned by one organization but developed by another. In the CelsiusTech example we described in Part I, a defense contractor developed a product line on its own initiative and successfully sold it to many governments around the world. In that case, CelsiusTech made sure to retain all intellectual rights to the product line.

In the case of CCT, however, the product line was commissioned by the U.S. Government, which wanted to recover its up-front investment in building the assets by realizing savings across other programs, some of which had not yet been identified. Therefore, it retained the rights to the asset base. In both the CCT and CelsiusTech cases, intellectual rights resided with the organization that (1) paid the up-front cost to build the asset base and (2) took it upon itself to find more customers for the product line to recoup that cost.

Although the NRO commissioned Raytheon for development of product line assets, the assets may be used by other government organizations. These organizations will commission contractors to build specific spacecraft command and control systems. The U.S. Government retains total rights to the CCT architecture and the components. However, Raytheon has full freedom to develop commercialized derivations that they can then bring to the marketplace.

10.2.3 Structuring the CCT Organization

There are four organizational groups or stakeholders in the CCT effort; the NRO (the sponsoring customer) and Raytheon (the commissioned developer) have already been mentioned. The third set of stakeholders consists of the organizations charged with developing the systems for which the product line was launched: the Spacecraft C2 System, DCCS, and SSCS. The fourth set of stakeholders includes future CCT users—those organizations that may subscribe to CCT as a basis for building or reengineering their own systems in the future. Only the organizational units that the NRO and Raytheon structured for CCT were important to the initial CCT effort.

Raytheon's CCT Program was divided into the organizational units shown in Table 10.1 to accomplish the CCT development tasks. CCT development was structured into six overlapping increments with an integrated development team responsible for each. The members of the integrated teams came from a cross section of the organizational units listed in Table 10.1 with the exception of the

Table 10.1 Raytheon's Organizational Structure for CCT Development

Organizational Unit	Responsibilities
Contractor program office	Technical management of development effort; accountable to the NRO's CCT Program Office
Program support	Technical management support functions—for example, configuration management, quality assurance, business operations
Domain engineering and architecture	Requirements engineering; architecture definition
Component engineering	Component development
Application engineering	Testing of architecture that demonstrates the ability to build products from CCT
Test engineering	Component and assembly testing
Training	Training materials and internal training of CCT personnel
Sustainment engineering	Fixing and enhancing of CCT baseline; working with application engineers and users to refine, deliver, and maintain the CCT assets

first increment, which involved only the Domain Engineering and Architecture group because this increment was primarily dedicated to scoping the CCT product line. The phases and the integrated teams make explicit the iteration we talk about as inherent in core asset development.

The NRO's organizational unit for CCT was the CCT Program Office, which consisted of a small team of government management and technical personnel who managed CCT development at the organizational level. The CCT Program Office was augmented by a small number of technical personnel from two government research and development centers, the SEI and the Aerospace Corporation.

Every product line effort is dependent on strong communication among the stakeholders. To ensure effective communication and to guide CCT's development over the extended life cycle—creation, usage in an initial product set, usage in a future product set, and evolution—the CCT Program Office created a variety of working groups. The main CCT working group coordinated project-level decisions for the CCT program and ran the stakeholder working groups. In turn, the stakeholder working groups provided direction for the CCT component and sustainment engineering groups. An architecture group advised the main working group on issues relating to the CCT architecture.

Raytheon's integrated teams and the NRO's working groups were a unique aspect of the CCT organizational structure that permitted productive cross-pollination and communication among the stakeholders.

10.2.4 Organizational and Technical Planning

The NRO and Raytheon partnered in the planning of CCT. CCT development was scheduled to begin in August 1997 and end on December 31, 1999. Plans were developed that spanned this time period. These plans carefully addressed the organizational management needs of the CCT Program Office for reviews and incremental deliveries, Raytheon's technical management needs for plotting and tracking the development processes, and Spacecraft C2's needs for requisite CCT assets for their system development effort. In addition, configuration management, risk management, and quality assurance plans were developed. There was also a transition plan to be used by developers of CCT-based systems, which describes the process for delivering and installing the CCT assets for use by developers of target systems. The formal process of maintaining the CCT assets was documented in a CCT Sustainment Plan.

All of these plans were accessible at the CCT Web site, and all were updated as the CCT effort progressed to depict the current status of the CCT development and integration process. The CCT effort scored high in the two planning practice areas; the development of the plans, the plans themselves, and their practice of religiously keeping the plans visible, accessible, and up-to-date make CCT an exemplar in these practice areas.

10.2.5 Operations

Operations for core asset development were governed by the plans set in motion. The integrated teams for each of the six development increments carried out the development tasks. The systematic reuse approach adopted by the CCT effort was process-driven and took advantage of what was available—legacy assets, proven algorithms, and commercial off-the-shelf (COTS) products. Value-adding operational processes included frequent technical interchange meetings, weekly status meetings with the CCT program office, and use of the CCT Web site to post all artifacts and documentation. The government designated more than 20 documents as deliverables in addition to supporting documents created to aid developers and users. Baselined versions of all deliverable documents and links to the CCT models and software development folders were available on the CCT Web site. The site also hosted the CCT master schedule, archives of reviews, and project status information.

The integrated teams and the working groups promoted sufficient community and stakeholder involvement to make traditional long, drawn-out government reviews unnecessary. The CCT Program Office established a modest number of review points at which increment deliverables and the status of development and technical management activities were reviewed. Metrics were defined and the corresponding data were collected to track and evaluate progress. A proof-of-concept prototype was developed to show how long it would take to mine assets and integrate them with the architecture.

As for how the CCT effort would connect with the software product line it was to support, the NRO developed the CCT Program Concept of Operations, which documented operations for coordination with CCT users (those organizations developing products from the CCT assets). This concept of operation contained the following:

- the strategies, tactics, policies, and constraints that describe processes to be used to field products
- the organizations, activities, and interactions involved in fielding the products
- the specific processes, in overview fashion, that provide a process model for fielding a product in terms of when and in what order these processes take place, including dependencies and concurrencies

Also defined are three stages for using CCT to support the envisioned spacecraft command and control product line: asset development, asset sustainment and process refinement, and product line sustainment and improvement.

1. **Asset development:** Development activities, performed by the CCT contractor, translate the set of common user command and control requirements into software components that provide the needed capabilities. The six developmental increments of CCT that were already described were all part of asset development.
2. **Asset sustainment and process refinement:** Delivery and installation of CCT assets as increments are completed by the CCT Contractor to CCT users, including assistance with installing and transitioning these increments into the user's development environment.
3. **Product line sustainment and improvement:** Coordination of continuous improvement of CCT and its attached processes. As use of CCT increases, it is expected that members of the CCT user community will participate in a CCT users group. The sustainment effort will be coordinated by means of the chief CCT working group processes and procedures.

The CCT Concept of Operations called for a Senior Management Panel to provide "corporate oversight" of the product line and to guide its evolution by setting strategic goals (such as attracting particular new customers). The CCT Program Office was to take the lead in evaluating new subscribers. The sustainment costs were to be shared equally by all future partners, although it is easy to imagine variations on this allocation should all parties agree.

The *Business Plan: Asset Development Phase,* an addendum to the concept of operations, established procedures and criteria for working with potential CCT users. These procedures were designed to support evaluation of the ability of the CCT assets to accommodate the technical and programmatic requirements of new users. Also identified are organizational responsibilities, coordination processes, and timelines for conducting these evaluations and establishing agreements with new users. Specifically, the business plan addressed the qualification of new subscribers. A preliminary assessment evaluates a prospective new program that inquires about using the CCT product line assets. This assessment was designed to determine the answers to the following questions:

- Does the candidate user fit into the CCT vision?
- Will the candidate user's needs alter the scope of the CCT domain?
- Is the candidate user's concept of system operation compatible with the CCT architecture?
- Does the CCT schedule satisfy the candidate user's needs?
- Would there be a potentially significant impact on existing users if the candidate user were to be added to the CCT user community?
- Does the CCT asset base benefit from accommodating the candidate user?
- Are there any significant contracting issues associated with supporting the candidate user?

If the preliminary assessment were favorable, then a detailed evaluation would take place, based on the following criteria:

- Technical
  - extent to which CCT currently satisfies candidate user's requirements
  - benefits to CCT from enhancing capabilities to encompass a greater portion of candidate user's requirements set
  - fraction of candidate user's proposed requirements that fall outside the scope of CCT assets (and user must pursue independently)
  - potential for technology infusion from user to CCT assets and expected functionality improvements
  - compatibility of CCT architecture with candidate user's system concept of operations, including computing platforms, development tools, and operations skill mix and staffing profiles
- Schedule
  - feasibility of CCT program office meeting candidate user's schedule requirements
  - impact of candidate user's requirements on schedule commitments to existing CCT users
- Cost
  - feasibility of identifying and allocating costs for added development work required by candidate user
  - acceptability of cost sharing provisions to candidate user and existing users
  - potential for overall cost savings
- Risk (technical performance, cost, and schedule)
  - level of risk for meeting commitments to candidate user
  - increase in level of risk associated with meeting commitments to existing users

- Contract issues
  - extent to which accommodating the needs of candidate user falls within defined CCT contract scope
  - issues regarding sole-source vs. competitive selection for any additional required development work

CCT also developed a concept of operations for the sustainment phase that contains the following:

- the strategies, tactics, policies, and constraints that describe how the product line assets will be sustained and used to field future products
- the organizations, activities, and interactions that describe who will participate in sustaining the product line and what these stakeholders do in that process
- the specific operational processes, in overview fashion, that the CCT program will apply to sustain the assets and maintain CCT user collaboration.

The concept of operations documents developed for CCT provide rich examples for organizations that will not be the product developers of the products in their product lines.

10.3 Engineering the CCT Core Assets

CCT development consisted of six major software engineering processes:

1. Domain engineering and architecture
2. Component engineering
3. Application engineering
4. Test engineering
5. Sustainment engineering
6. Training

These processes incorporate many of the practices of Jacobson's incremental and iterative reuse-based approach [Jacobson 97] and Kruchten's "4+1 view" model of architecture [Kruchten 95], complemented by the test engineering process. As we have already noted, the engineering processes proceeded through six increments, delivering successively more complete versions of CCT assets. These processes map to the product line practice areas, but we will be faithful to CCT terminology for our description.

The domain engineering and architecture processes were responsible for defining and specifying the product line and creating the product line architecture.[5] The component engineering process created the components of the toolkit. Application engineering was an internal reuse process designed to create a spacecraft command and control application for testing, deriving the application from the reusable assets delivered by the other processes. In particular, the application engineering team created demonstration architectures from the CCT assets and, with the test engineering group, created detailed test procedures for validating the reusability of the asset base after each increment was complete. The sustainment engineering process managed the maintenance and evolution of the CCT assets once they were baselined following delivery during each CCT increment.

The domain specification, reference architecture, and components addressed the common core functionality for systems in the product line. Together with the architecture model and Reuse Guide aimed at users of CCT assets, they comprised the major deliverables of the CCT project. The processes for creating and validating assets, the process outputs, and the process interactions evolved during the course of development. An example of this evolution was the addition of an architecture evaluation step to the architecture-creation process, and the creation of the architecture model as a separate deliverable. To a large extent, the documents produced during the CCT creation were a reflection of the processes.

10.3.1 Domain Analysis

Although a formal domain analysis method was not used, the essential tasks of domain analysis were performed. They

- captured and analyzed common requirements and their variation across several systems
- synthesized them into a set of common requirements for the product line
- captured the essential terminology

The CCT domain analysis began with an analysis of the requirements of the three satellite command and control systems for which CCT was built: DCCS, SSCS, and the Spacecraft C2 System. This activity defined the scope of the product line and created a set of generalized common requirements for CCT. The final phase of the domain analysis created a specification of satellite ground-based command and control requirements, applying a use-case-driven approach to describe the commonality and variability across the product line.

---

5. In CCT parlance, domain engineering is distinguished from architecture creation, whereas elsewhere the creation of an architecture is regarded as being part of domain engineering. In this narrative, the process activities relating to the definition and specification of the domain will be described as domain analysis and the architecture-creation activities will be treated under the heading of software architecture. In addition, the term "reference architecture" was used in the CCT effort to describe what we have called the product line architecture.

The domain definition process classified product line requirements into the two domains: execution (the real-time or near-real-time activities that occur during a contact with a satellite) and planning (the non-real-time activities that occur before or after a contact). Within these two domains, the process identified categories of components to be provided by the toolkit (for example, handling of telemetry streams and orbit estimation) and the common services that support these categories (for example, persistent storage services and event notification services). This partitioning of the problem domain provided the basis for the logical view of the CCT architecture: a planning part and an execution part. Raytheon partitioned the requirements on the basis of the consensus of the domain analysts and the contractor's own experience in building previous spacecraft command and control systems.

The domain definition process produced three documents that described the scope and general requirements of the product line:

1. The **Domain Definition Document** provided an overview of the product line. It described the common features of related systems and defined the scope of the CCT assets for supporting those systems. A glossary of product line terminology was also provided. The scope of CCT was defined in terms of the mission and system characteristics that CCT supports, organized in terms of component categories. For example, CCT will support up to two simultaneous telemetry streams per spacecraft, but users have to provide their own persistence and archiving solution since CCT does not provide a standard database solution.
2. The **Generalized Requirements Specification** documented the contractual requirements for CCT. To create this document, requirements from three different customer bases were examined: DCCS, the Spacecraft C2 System, and SSCS. The document captured common capabilities to be provided by the toolkit. Each requirement was briefly described and was classified as being in one of the domains identified by the domain definition process—execution or planning—or categorized among the common services. Variability in the common requirements was expressed in terms of variation points that were more fully described in the Domain Specification Document. This initial requirements process was supported using Rational's Slate tool to create and maintain a matrix of requirements and textual descriptions mapped to unique identifiers and to the component categories. To maintain traceability from the generalized requirements back to their origins in the three analyzed systems, an additional document was created using Slate.
3. The **CCT Domain Specification Document** contained use-case diagrams and descriptions for the common requirements. Variability was incorporated into the use cases as explicit variation points. This document also provided the design for each use case in terms of sequence diagrams that show

the interactions among the blocks participating in the use case. It provides the top-level analysis model to be used by the subsequent domain engineering, component engineering, and application engineering processes.

10.3.2 Architecture

Prior to initiating the architecture activity, the architecture group conducted a survey of architecture techniques to provide early input to the architecture creation process. They decided to follow the "4+1 view model" of Philippe Kruchten [Kruchten 95] and to use UML to represent it. The process for defining the software architecture evolved considerably during the development of the CCT assets; they were a bit late in getting "architecture religion." During the early increments, the architecture group considered the component categories as fully embodying the architecture. As their understanding matured, the group developed and maintained a CCT architecture model. They also agreed to two architecture evaluations—one for each of the execution and planning logical entities.

10.3.2.1 Architecture Definition

There were two key documents that described the CCT architecture and its use:

1. The **CCT Architecture Model** provided a complete description of the architecture. This model provided the philosophical underpinnings of the approach, architectural drivers and concepts, and architectural and design patterns.[6] It also included the architectural views: the logical view, which consists of the static object model; the development view, which showed layers; the dynamic view, which consisted of the component interaction model; and the process view, which depicted process interaction. UML, as supported by the Rational Rose tool, was used.[7]
2. The **CCT Reuse Guide** documented the CCT assets that could be used to build a product in the product line. The audience for this document was software engineers responsible for selecting and utilizing CCT assets when building a product. The Reuse Guide helps compare capabilities of CCT with program requirements for a new command and control system. This was to assist product builders plan their use of CCT assets and determine modifications and extensions that would be needed. For extensions at variation points, the Reuse Guide provided and described the implementing

---

6. A notable feature of CCT architecture is an abundant use of architectural and design patterns, which provide a vocabulary for describing and reasoning about the architecture.

7. The tool didn't support the capture of additional CCT architectural representations. Layer diagrams, use-case maps, and overall execution and planning architecture diagrams were created, but were captured on the CCT Web site pages and other documents delivered to the NRO.

mechanisms. The CCT Reuse Guide was the production plan for building products in the product line.

Architecture definition and component engineering were closely coupled. The architecture imposed constraints on the design of the components and their interactions. In particular, the less-is-more approach of successful architectures, which seeks to limit the number of different design elements and the permissible interaction mechanisms, was used. The CCT architecture definition process addressed these issues by explicitly listing permissible component interaction mechanisms (such as publish-subscribe, callback, event notification, and so on) in the Architecture Model. The model discussed their rationale and the constraints of these mechanisms as part of the description of the reference architecture concepts. The Reuse Guide provided the implementation view that explicitly identified the programming approaches associated with architectural components.

The Common Object Request Broker Architecture (CORBA) was chosen as the basis for the architecture's intercomponent communication infrastructure. Mission-unique modification and feature extension could happen in several ways. Product builders could replace components at the architectural level by wrapping the new (or legacy) components with Interface Description Language (IDL) specifications and using the Object Request Broker (ORB) to integrate them into the runtime system. They could also use ORB common services to add their components to the architecture transparently by using common events or data. Finally, they could extend CCT component implementations at designated variation points using inheritance or parameters [Hollander 99].

Common services corresponded to CORBA services and facilities. These included naming and event services, object persistence services, and event notification and callback services. Other services included those for creating data-driven displays, printing, manipulating and translating time values, manipulating coordinate systems, activity logging, and managing application event loops. Services are also provided for controlling multiple threads in an application. CCT also provided wrappers for device drivers.

The CCT architecture organized software components into component categories; a category supported development of a specific subsystem within the product line. Within each component category lived related components that users might integrate together to achieve higher-order functionality. Components in different categories might use each other in well-defined ways, so that many system functions would be accomplished through the operating and interaction of components across different categories.

There were two primary subsystems in the CCT architecture: planning and execution. The planning architecture referred to the non-time-critical component categories that, for example, produced commands to send to a satellite at some future time. The execution architecture referred to the time-critical component categories that facilitate communication of commands to and reception of telemetry from a satellite. Component categories across these two subsystems did not interact except by reading data from and writing data in shared files. The most common form of interaction would occur when an execution component reads (and transmits to the satellite) a command sequence produced by a planning component.

Execution Architecture

Figure 10.2 shows the data flow view of a product architecture using the CCT architecture's execution subsystem. The shaded area covers components provided by CCT. The arrows indicate control and/or data flow. Variation is supported by the addition of the components outside the shading. The CCT components within the five component categories provided common features and also supported variation as follows.

Status Component Category

Status referred to the processes needed to receive telemetry data streams from either ground equipment or the spacecraft, perform integrity checks on the data stream, and decommutate the data into last recorded values (LRVs), which represent the latest and best estimate of the parameter's raw value. Variation points included how the status component would recognize and respond to format changes as well as how the component would perform validity checks.

LRV Component Category

LRV received raw decommutated telemetry data from status processes. Processes in LRV then performed predefined conversion operations to generate engineering values for the decommutated data, performed limit checks on the data, generated alarms in response to undesired telemetry states, and provided LRV data to other processes. The logging of LRV data formed the key interface for providing data to the planning part of the system. A key variation point was the ease with which new LRVs could be defined and integrated into existing LRV

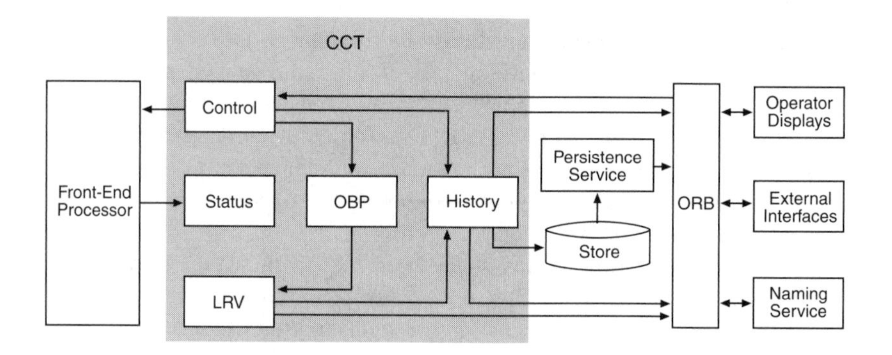

Figure 10.2 CCT Execution Architecture: Data Flow View

processing. CCT provided LRV processing components that performed basic conversions, limit checking, and alarm generation and supported various forms of customization through parameters and inheritance.

- New algorithm definitions were allowed, and a distribution service was provided.
- Definition of new LRVs was supported.
- LRVs could be defined in terms of other LRVs, providing the ability to define higher-level state information.

Control Component Category
Processes in the control component category encoded client commands to external devices (ground equipment or spacecraft) into data packets or streams with appropriate formatting. CCT provided a command request interface to process and release regular and time-critical commands. Basic formatting algorithms could be parameterized or replaced. Unique verification logic could be added. CCT also provided a procedural control language that can be used to automate complex commanding sequences.

On-Board Processing Component Category
On-board processing referred to processes that model and help manage computer processor memory on board the spacecraft. Common capabilities included providing state information to clients and comparing the predicted memory map with telemetry-based snapshots of the actual memory map. CCT provided a memory map model with interfaces to support product extensions.

History Component Category
History referred to the processes that log and retrieve data received or generated during contact with a spacecraft. CCT provided common logging and retrieval from short-term storage to flat files. Product builders would be responsible for providing alternative persistence strategies, such as database logs and data replication.

Planning Architecture
Figure 10.3 shows the data flow view of a product architecture using the CCT architecture's planning subsystem. The shaded area covers components provided by CCT. The arrows indicate control and/or data flow. The CCT components within the six component categories of planning provided common features and supported variation as follows.

Orbit Component Category
Orbit referred to processes that estimate a spacecraft's orbit parameters based on observed data (state determination) and then propagate the orbit through time. CCT provided a standard family of estimators and propagators, including those commonly used by systems for spacecraft command and control missions. Variation points permitted product-specific tools to generate orbit data or use outside sources to provide orbit data.

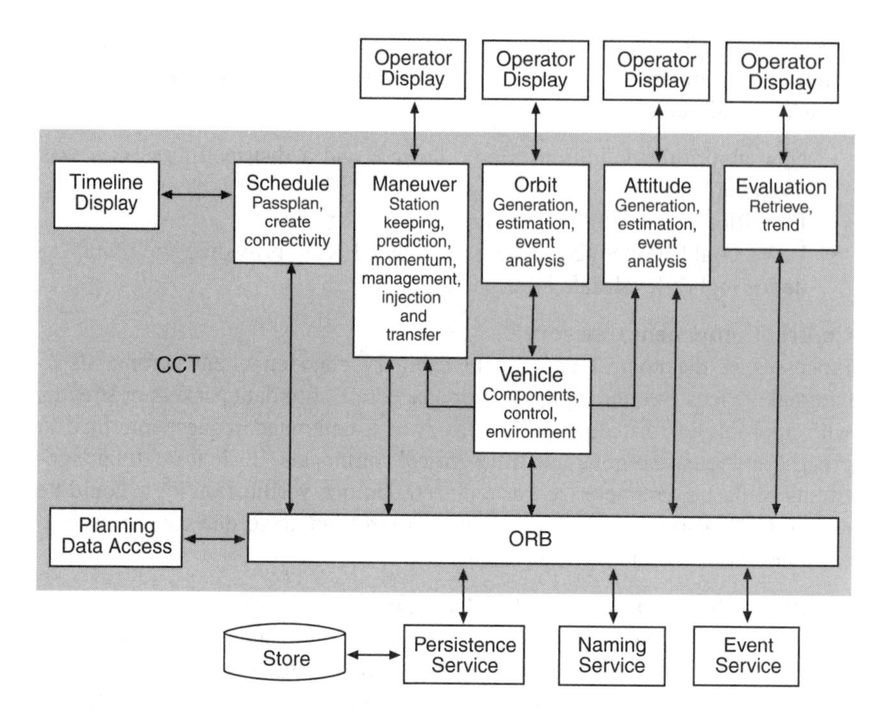

Figure 10.3 CCT Planning Architecture: Data Flow View

Attitude Component Category

Attitude referred to processes that estimate a spacecraft's attitude (orientation) based on observed sensor data and then propagate the attitude through time to accomplish prediction. CCT provided attitude estimators and propagators for spin-stabilized and three-axis-stabilized spacecraft. Products could integrate their own tools to generate attitude data or sources to provide attitude data.

Maneuver Component Category

Maneuver referred to those processes that plan and generate maneuver sequences. These sequences use thruster (jet) firings to change a spacecraft's orbit, attitude, or momentum rate. Maneuver is key to orbit and attitude maintenance, taking orbit and attitude information, along with vehicle-specific propulsion system models, and generating the necessary plan to maintain or achieve the desired orbit or attitude. Maneuver planning depends heavily on the specifics of the spacecraft and its mission. Since the variation in this area is so wide, CCT provided general component frameworks for developing maneuver-planning processes. CCT implemented a common solution for spin-stabilized and three-axis-stabilized spacecraft. These implementations could be further generalized as the product line matures.

Vehicle Component Category
Vehicle referred to components that provide mission-unique spacecraft models to other components. The vehicle component captured several common interfaces of a spacecraft, with each parameter requiring user definition and implementation. These parameters included the following spacecraft characteristics:

- A unique identifier
- Mass properties as determined by the positions and mass properties of the spacecraft subsystems and appendages
- Orbit, attitude, and time state

The vehicle component category provided extensibility so that users could capture their mission-unique spacecraft features. Users could freely extend the given vehicle model for their spacecraft by defining new spacecraft components and component relations.

Schedule Component Category
Schedule referred to processes that plan spacecraft and ground system activities. The scheduling process results in a chronological set of scheduled activities from which plans are generated. The CCT architecture provided an extendable framework and a default implementation that accepted inputs through a timeline display, scheduled the activities, and then generated plans for a satellite pass. Variation points included selection (or addition) of scheduling and conflict resolution algorithms as well as mission-unique requirements and data.

Evaluation Component Category
Evaluation referred to the processing of previously collected telemetry and control data. This processing could generate trending or unit history data or be used to play back archived data through the execution telemetry and control component categories. Evaluation was performed in support of the needs of component categories in both the execution and planning subsystems. Variation points included inserting new algorithms for controlling playback speeds and processing data.

Variation Summary
Within each of the CCT subsystems, use of individual components could vary, according to mission-unique requirements. Variation points were identified during domain specification, propagated through analysis and design, and were supported by the CCT architecture. Depending on the type of variation point, CCT provided one of six standard mechanisms:

Dynamic attributes	Parameterization
Template	Function extension (callbacks)
Inheritance	Scripting

Table 10.2 provides a summary of the breadth of variation CCT can accommodate [Shaw 00].

Table 10.2 Component Variation across CCT

Domain	Component Category	Components	Variation
Execution	Status	4	1
	LRV	4	1
	Control	6	14
	On-board Processing	3	2
	History	5	7
	Other (playback)	1	1
Planning	Orbit	7	19
	Attitude	4	9
	Maneuver	5	12
	Vehicle	3	5
	Schedule	3	13
	Evaluation	4	3
Object services		10	13
Infrastructure		42	11
TOTALS		101	111

The process of starting with the architecture and reusable components and building specific applications included the following steps:

1. Determine COTS and legacy usage in the end system.
2. Identify real-time user interface products and database implementations.
3. Select a CORBA vendor to provide the intrasystem communication infrastructure.
4. Address security needs by adding security layers or secure gateways.
5. Determine how to extend and vary the CCT components by means of inheritance or the use of parameters. Replacement components may take the form of COTS products, legacy code, or hardware.
6. Package the components into executable applications and allocate them to the nodes of the end system's physical network.

10.3.2.2 Architecture Evaluation

Both the planning and execution architectures underwent explicit evaluation led by the SEI using the Software Architecture Analysis Method (SAAM)

[Bass 98a]. SAAM gathers together stakeholders of a system and lets them brainstorm scenarios of usage and modification that the software architecture of that system should support with little or no change. For CCT, SAAM produced scenarios of usage for ground-based spacecraft command and control systems. The scenarios that the CCT architecture supports conveyed an idea of the scope of the product line for which CCT should prove useful. Some of the scenarios were aimed at illuminating the production plan by which systems are built from the CCT architecture and components.

Neither the planning nor the execution architecture evaluations revealed any modifiability (extensibility, variability) problems with CCT. That is, no scenario adopted by the evaluation group revealed any problems that would require the CCT program or a user more than a few person-months to correct. Most scenarios either were already accommodated by CCT variation points or would require only minor changes to support.

For the planning subsystem architecture, the scenarios are as follows:

- A user wants to include mission management (payload planning, for example). How would CCT planning interact with and support mission management?
- The database is replaced with a new database technology for which the existing abstract interface is insufficient.
- The network and/or some computers go down, but users want the planning processes to continue operation.
- A user wants to manage a constellation of satellites (for example, global positioning system [GPS], communication satellite). Replace the vehicle model with an abstraction to represent a constellation.
- A user chooses to integrate another orbit package to replace one provided by CCT. More specifically, a user integrates a proprietary orbit package with different inputs (for instance, orbit packages are frequently optimized for a particular orbit).
- A user adds a new vehicle and associated "stuff" to existing system (for example, to go from a spin-stabilized to a three-axis-stabilized vehicle). Use CCT to support up to six different vehicle families simultaneously from the same installation.
- Add continuous orbit management to component categories in the planning domain.
- How well will CCT support flexible scheduling using more on-board intelligence? Suppose some kind of request for service comes from the satellite to CCT (for instance, a message that says a data buffer is full).
- A user requests testing of a legacy database for inclusion in CCT.
- How will a CCT component utilize a service that didn't exist when it was built?

For the execution subsystem architecture, the scenarios are as follows:

- Integrate an inference engine to perform constraint analysis.
- Inhibit commands.
- Change the computer platform, operating system, ORB, ORB version, operating system version, implementation language, or methodology. Change from a relational database management system to an object-oriented database management system.
- Add a new command source.
- Add telemetry-command synchronization (closed-loop control).
- A software routine called "via callback" hangs up (perhaps becomes stuck in an infinite loop). How does the system recover?
- The operator reconfigures a set of components dynamically.
- Add more automated, finer control to component categories in the execution domain.
- Increase the number of simultaneous telemetry streams.
- Send high-priority emergency commands to save a spacecraft (support command prioritization).
- Build a minimal execution application and add to it incrementally.
- A user evaluates a CCT component with respect to dependencies. A system architect assesses CCT architecture. An application architect assesses CCT status components.
- Have the telemetry stream update the on-board processor's memory map in real time.

Future users of the CCT assets would benefit from the evaluations and the increased attention paid to the architecture. The inclusion of software architecture evaluations in the CCT development process highlighted the need for a shared architectural vision; the creation of the Architecture Model and the Reuse Guide was a response to that need to document the architecture to make it more comprehensible to the stakeholders. The CCT architecture working group watched over the growth of the CCT architecture, and members continue to provide guidance during asset evolution.

CCT processes, as robust product line processes should be, are centered on the architecture. The Architecture Model and Reuse Guide emerged as focal points for the integration of the development processes for CCT assets and for target systems derived from those assets. The architecture focus for the development processes greatly improved the documentation of the architecture for both developers and users alike and did much to dispel the original notion that CCT is "just a toolkit."

10.3.3 Component Engineering

Component engineering produced the components within the various component categories. These categories were identified in the Domain Definition Document and specified in the Domain Specification Document. The reusable components created by component engineering constitute the development view of the 4+1 view model. Component engineering was also responsible for unit testing of the components. There were two potentially conflicting goals related to component engineering:

1. The reuse of DCCS components: CCT sought to use components from this legacy system as a starting point.
2. The creation of reusable CCT components: CCT assets could not be limited to capabilities of any individual system.

Coupled with these goals, the CCT program needed to provide components to support the first real CCT user, the Spacecraft C2 System, and to do so in line with that project's schedule. They took a number of measures to achieve these goals. To the best of their ability, they strictly adhered to their development plan in the planned increments so that the Spacecraft C2 Project would not fall behind schedule. They built components that were capable of handling the variation points in the domain specifications and that met the interface specifications dictated by the architecture. DCCS code that was used was wrapped, reengineered, or thoroughly reviewed to ensure that it would work in the CCT context. The Spacecraft C2 team was involved in the review of all component development work. The Web access to all of the CCT artifacts gave Spacecraft C2 early visibility into the progress of the component development effort.

The components in each component category were implemented to have the interfaces and interconnection mechanisms called for by the software architecture. However, component interaction in products was still a concern: the interconnection mechanisms provided were so rich that product builders could easily assemble components into a configuration not envisioned by the CCT architects. To prevent this, the Reuse Guide established restrictions on mechanisms that product builders should use for component interaction. The descriptions of component interfaces were included in the Architecture Model. The Architecture Model also contained use-case maps to illustrate how components should interact during a scenario.

10.3.4 Testing: Application and Test Engineering

Application engineering and test engineering together built the system test architecture and executed detailed test procedures. The test engineers validated CCT reusability, including the architecture and other assets.

Recall that for CCT, application engineering was an internal reuse process that assembled a spacecraft command and control application from the reusable assets delivered by the other processes. For each CCT increment, this application was called a system test architecture. Test engineering used the system test architecture to perform the formal testing of CCT components. The formal testing complemented the informal testing done during component and application engineering.

CCT defined four levels of testing:

- Level 0: Unit testing of components (informal, performed by component engineering)
- Level 1: Requirements verification of components and component categories (formal, performed by test engineering)
- Level 2: Integration testing—the test architecture was used to test the integration of CCT into an application development effort and to exercise the variation points defined in the use cases (informal, performed by application engineering)
- Level 3: System-level performance requirements verification (formal, performed by test engineering)

Level 3 testing, in particular, was the formal test engineering effort used to demonstrate to both the quality assurance staff and the customer that system and performance requirements had been met. Specific performance goals (for exaxmple, the ability of the architecture to handle some specified number of LRVs) were levied by satellite programs such as the Spacecraft C2 System.

The application engineering team was, in effect, the first user of the CCT assets. Their validation of the assets complemented the activities of the domain engineering group. For each defined CCT increment, the application engineering process attempted to create a "complete" spacecraft command and control system from the CCT assets. The testing process facilitated the exercise of the defined variation points and tested system-level requirements (such as overall system-level runtime performance). Figure 10.4 represents the process of using assets first for building the system test architecture, then for building the first operational system. After testing the assets created for that increment, the production plan provided the steps for producing the appropriate increment of the Spacecraft C2 System. The CCT approach repeated this step for each increment.

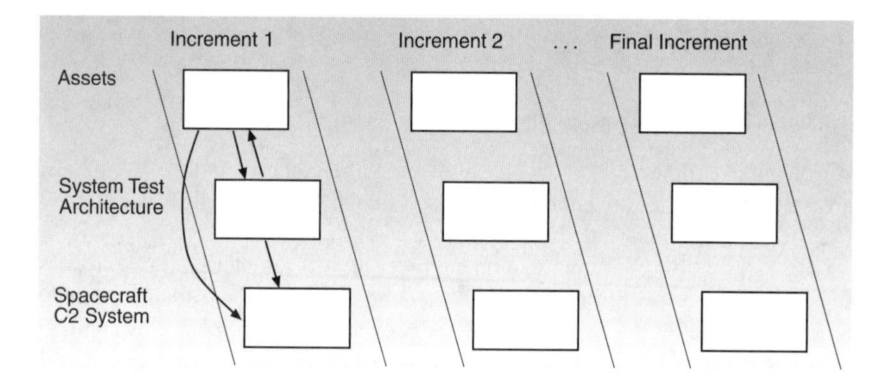

Figure 10.4 Production Plan for Building Test and Operational Systems from Assets

The Test and Integration Plan described the test methodology in generic terms for the first increment and then in more specific terms on a per-increment basis. The test engineering team created test plans and procedures based on the use cases in the Domain Specification and demonstrated the portability of the CCT assets across several platforms. They created test cases (high-level preliminary descriptions of how requirements were tested) and test procedures (elaboration of test cases in terms of specific inputs and steps) for the formal tests. The component engineering team created level 1 test drivers, whereas the application engineering team created the executable test system for level 3 testing. CCT used a discrepancy report process to document problems that occurred during testing. The discrepancy reports documented and tracked all problems discovered during testing. This process was documented in the Test and Integration Plan. As part of the testing process, peer groups reviewed and prioritized test cases and procedures.

The test engineering process validated CCT's reusability. The process integrated CCT assets into a spacecraft command and control application. It also exercised the variability of the components by adding mission-unique extensions to CCT just as a real-world user would. The test engineering group participated throughout the CCT development cycle and in all the standing meetings. There was a conscious effort to ensure that CCT testing for each increment was not an after-the-fact process.

10.3.5 Sustainment Engineering: Product Line Evolution

The sustainment engineering process included tasks to maintain and evolve the CCT assets. A sustainment engineering team was the primary point of contact after an increment was delivered. Their work began after formal testing and delivery of an increment. The input they received included the following:

- Requirements that could not be met during initial component development were communicated. The team oversaw the process to consider these as inputs for inclusion in later increments of CCT.
- Postdeployment problems (discrepancy reports) on assets. Specific CCT review boards determined the impact of proposed changes in the CCT software baseline and determined the action that the sustainment engineers should take.
- Issues raised by potential use of CCT assets by targeted users. Many of these issues were taken up by the Architecture Group but were not addressed during the CCT development.

The CCT Sustainment Support Plan documented the process for sustainment engineering.

The sustainment engineering team continues to deal with discrepancy reports to this day. In this maintenance role, sustainment engineering is building a community of CCT users that depend on CCT for a significant portion of their control channel needs. Multiple satellite programs have different, and possibly conflicting, requests for modifications of the CCT baseline. The sustainment activity continues to determine which modifications to support and which modifications may affect the architecture.

10.3.6 Documentation

Because it created assets for reuse, the CCT program produced some documents that are not found in typical government procurement cycles. Documents that exist because CCT was a product line effort include the following, some of which have been mentioned earlier but are collected here to highlight the special role documentation plays with software product lines.

- **CCT Domain Definition:** This document described the boundaries of the command and control product line and the functions that CCT addresses. The Domain Definition also included a glossary of terms and acronyms used within the CCT products.
- **Generalized Requirements Specification:** This document captured common capabilities to be provided by the toolkit. It was produced by examining requirements from three different customer bases: DCCS, the Spacecraft C2 System, and SSCS.
- **CCT Domain Specification:** This document provided a requirements analysis, employing use-case-driven methodologies and documented using the Unified Modeling Language (UML).
- **CCT System Test Architecture:** This document described a test system architecture (design and implementation) used to verify CCT functionality. Users could use this document as a starting point for their designs, as an ad hoc implementation for factory testing, and as an example of CCT component integration.
- **CCT Portability Demonstration Plan:** This document contained an assessment of portability to selected nonsupported operating systems.
- **CCT Sustainment Support Plan:** This document detailed maintenance and evolution management for the CCT assets. Users who wish active involvement in the CCT's management would participate through the described plan.
- **CCT Program Concept of Operations:** This document described the life cycle of the CCT product line, the stakeholders who have an interest in the product line over its lifetime, and business concerns such as qualifying a new subscriber (user) for the product line.
- **CCT Architecture Model:** This model provided a complete description of the architecture. Future product developers could use it to evaluate CCT capabilities with respect to target program requirements, to determine how

to plan their use of CCT assets, and to evaluate what changes and extensions they need to provide.

- **CCT Reuse Guide:** This document described and provided examples of the steps necessary to build a product line application from CCT assets. It was the CCT production plan. The CCT Reuse Guide did not prescribe a development process, but rather provided the process basis for reuse analysis and design. Users could determine how best to incorporate this basis into their own development standards and practices

10.4 Managing the CCT Effort

The management of a product line effort, especially when the effort marks a departure from the standard approach to software development, requires sophisticated management skills and well-honed leadership qualities. In Part II, we laid out a healthy collection of technical management practice areas and an even larger collection of organizational management practice areas. We have already described the CCT practices for a good number of these areas. The technical management practices and the management style are most notable.

First, there is technical management. Raytheon's process sophistication and discipline resulted in superb execution of CCT's technical management activities. Processes for technical planning, configuration management, technical risk management, process definition, data collection, metrics and tracking, make/buy/mine/commission analysis, scoping, and testing were stitched into the fabric of the CCT development process. There were very few process snags throughout the entire CCT development process, and none that wasn't handled—which brings us to the management style of those at the helm of CCT.

During the feasibility study prior to the CCT official launch, the entire NRO management chain responsible for CCT supported strategic reuse. They could all be described as visionaries. They all recognized the unnecessary duplication and risk involved in stand-alone efforts for similar spacecraft systems. They all were open to the changes that a product line approach would necessitate in terms of the organizational and technical practices to which they were accustomed. They stayed the course and provided unwavering support.[8]

In particular, the CCT Program Office manager, John Ohlinger, was deeply committed to the success of a product line approach. He maintained a loose, relaxed management style, providing sufficient direction while being flexible

8. Near the completion of the CCT effort, those in the NRO chain of command above the CCT Program Office moved on, one by one. As others filled their ranks, support for the effort diminished.

enough to hear ideas, bring in experts, and respond midstream to perceived needs. For example, early on he became convinced of the need for a greater focus on the architecture in order for CCT to succeed. He altered the original plan to incorporate two architecture evaluations despite some dissention within his office and the contractor team. He then formed the CCT Architecture Group to address the evaluation findings and to continue to shine a light on architectural issues and their resolution.

His counterpart, Jeff Shaw, Raytheon's CCT program manager, was a high-energy individual and a firm believer not only in software product lines but also in the ability of his team to deliver the CCT asset base. His enthusiasm was contagious. His support was obvious in the way he treated his staff and handled their needs. He was structured and well organized, a superb communicator who made others in his organization into CCT believers. Both he and Ohlinger had a great deal of technical savvy and experience in the spacecraft command and control domain. Ohlinger's and Shaw's styles were complementary; together they provided a protective shield and a supportive environment for the CCT development team. They didn't just manage; they led.

Close to CCT completion, Jeff Shaw was reassigned. His deputy assumed his responsibilities and applied her own leadership skills to complete the CCT effort on time and within budget.

10.5 Early Benefits from CCT

The CCT story continues to unfold; user systems are still in development and the CCT sustainment processes are still relatively immature. Nonetheless, there are early benefits to herald. First and foremost, CCT is a ground-breaking effort within its government communities. It broke down organizational and cultural barriers to garner support for a product line approach, and it achieved its objectives. CCT was completed on schedule and within budget in December 1999 with no outstanding risks and no outstanding actions. Few software efforts in its class can boast such a track record. Moreover, CCT is being used successfully to build the Spacecraft C2 System.

The initial NRO business case for pursuing a product line approach sought benefits in several areas. These included the following:

- reduced development costs
- increased quality in the form of continuous improvement and evolution
- decreased time-to-field
- savings in sustainment costs

This business case attempted to quantify cost savings over a ten-year life cycle, including CCT development, use, and sustainment. The NRO determined that costs during the period of intense CCT development (1997–2000) would be higher than normal, in spite of near concurrent use with the Spacecraft C2 System. However, when forecasting was done over the longer term (1997–2009), it was determined that for systems using CCT overall cost savings would accrue as follows:

Development	18.2% savings in anticipated total government development-related expenditures
Sustainment	27.8% savings in anticipated total government sustainment-related expenditures

Savings in both cases are in comparison with expected costs using a non-product-line approach.

10.5.1 First CCT Product

The Department of Defense has already enjoyed specific, measurable benefits in the initial use of CCT on an actual operational system—namely, Spacecraft C2. Because of CCT, the Spacecraft C2 Program is enjoying reductions in development costs, schedules, work force, and product risk, as well as increased product flexibility. Table 10.3 summarizes these benefits.

Interviews with the Spacecraft C2 developers also revealed other, less tangible benefits. Program staff attrition is unusually low, at two staff members in three years. After initial training, these developers were very satisfied with the CCT approach and praised the selection of and support for the variation points. They reported greater professional satisfaction with the product line approach. They expressed a sense that the pedestrian tasks had already been done and the focus was on the interesting, mission-specific capabilities. The risks of system failure were felt to be fewer, and the tension on the program to be substantially lower.

10.5.2 Benefits beyond CCT Products

The government and Raytheon have achieved the intended benefits from CCT. Spacecraft C2 has achieved measurable benefits, and there are other users beyond Spacecraft C2. The government has already met three of its first four goals: reduced development costs, increased quality, and decreased time-to-field. It is too soon to calculate the savings in sustainment costs.

Raytheon is also capitalizing on the CCT experience by using CCT assets in other of its systems and by using the CCT processes and tools on other efforts.

Other commercial organizations will have access to CCT products and may use similar approaches for launching their own product lines in spacecraft command and control. The Software Object Technology Group, a joint government and industry group led by NASA and the NRO, has applied the CCT architectural concepts to the definition of an object/interface standard for space-related applications.

Table 10.3 Summary of Measurable Benefits Attributed to Use of CCT

Factor	Benefits to Spacecraft C2 System
Quality	One-tenth the typical number of discrepancy (defect) reports for a system of this type. The problems identified were all local ones, with localized fixes, having no ripple effects, and no effect on the architecture.
Performance	Use of CCT improved performance over results predicted without CCT. In identified places where reuse may lead to timing problems, CCT variation points can be exercised to apply mechanisms that circumvent CCT software and apply faster algorithms.
Integration time	Incremental builds completed in weeks rather than months, as was the case for non-CCT portion. This approach is a direct carryover from the incremental approach to development.
Code volume	The number of design objects for subsystems using CCT is lower than planned by 34% to 88% with similar reduction in actual source code size. Total SLOC developed by Spacecraft C2 is 76% less than planned.
Productivity	Smaller development staff required (15 versus 100 for other similar systems) Overall costs cut by 50% Overall schedule cut by 50% Documented flexibility in meeting requests for modifications by the Spacecraft C2 System customer CCT treated like a COTS product (initial training required, then development proceeded on the basis of domain specification, interface definitions, and Reuse Guide)

10.6 Lessons and Issues

With asset development complete, CCT offers its users a set of tested assets to support development of new ground-based spacecraft command and control systems. Many lessons were learned during the CCT effort, and several major challenges still face the CCT program as it evolves from an effort primarily focused on asset development to one dedicated to product development by external organizations. The use of CCT for development of the system test architecture and the Spacecraft C2 System brought many nagging issues to the surface. Future development and collaboration with external users will shed light on others. We conclude the CCT story with a brief tour through some of these lessons and outstanding issues.

10.6.1 Tool Support Is Inadequate

Tools for adequate support of software product lines lag behind the adoption of product line approaches, so it's no surprise that the tools for support of CCT processes were not ideal.

In common with many domain analysis efforts, the CCT domain analysis used existing object-oriented analysis and design tools to capture and represent domain-level concepts. The outputs of the domain analysis process were spread over a number of documents that incorporate text, outputs from the Rational Rose tool, and outputs from the Slate tool. Collectively, these documents comprise the requirements database for CCT; there is no single, easily maintainable model. Maintenance is painful, which may pose a risk for long-term use of the assets. The same is true for the Architecture Model, which contains the layer model diagrams, use-case maps, and overall execution and planning architecture diagrams. Owing to a lack of tool support, these diagrams exist separately. The distribution makes maintenance awkward and time-consuming and increases the risk that changes will not be incorporated consistently.

Lack of consistent tool support for traceability among the CCT assets continues to hamper ongoing CCT maintenance. The CCT team documented a complete set of generic requirement specifications based on the initial analysis and subsequent understanding achieved through design and implementation. A formal, tool-supported mechanism should record issues and decisions and feed them back into the domain model and other analysis results. Unfortunately, the tool support doesn't yet exist, and the resultant manual efforts are cumbersome.

10.6.2 Domain Analysis Documentation Is Important

The CCT domain analysis products did not contain a record of issues and decisions regarding the presence or absence of particular domain features, nor a record of trade-offs that might influence subsequent design decisions. Such information would have been useful to CCT developers. It would also be useful now to targeted CCT users as they try to decide whether or not to use CCT for their products and to determine how CCT could be used.

10.6.3 An Early Architecture Focus Is Best

A software product line approach relies on a strong product line architecture that is used to structure all of the products in the product line. The architects need to take great care to ensure that the product line architecture is accessible to and understandable by all future product builders. Because of the acquisitional nature of this product line effort, even greater care was needed; the product builders will not be members of the CCT development team and probably will not belong to the Raytheon Company, nor will the CCT Program Office commission them. In order for the NRO to benefit fully from the product line that CCT is intended to support, the CCT architecture documentation and its attached process must be of exceptionally high quality. Moreover, the NRO would like some means to ensure that product architectures (called target architectures by the CCT effort) actually conform to the CCT architecture. They want to ensure that the CCT assets are used in the intended way and not simply to feed some ad hoc reuse of components that would undermine the true potential of CCT.

Unfortunately, the CCT effort was not architecture-centric from the start. Remember that the original vision called for a toolkit. The architecture and architectural knowledge were in the heads of the CCT architects, who did a fine job and remained involved in every aspect of the CCT development and its initial use. Although this involvement was a plus, it didn't really permit the architecture documentation to be exercised to the fullest by the development team. Team members could always go ask the architects, and for that matter, so could the first product builders.

Early on, the SEI was concerned about the architecture and its documentation and advocated two architecture evaluations and the development of the Reuse Guide. The CCT Program adopted these suggestions but had to insert these efforts into the schedule after the project was well under way. It is to the Raytheon team's credit that they embraced both activities even though architecture evaluations weren't in the original contract.

During the first software architecture evaluation, it was apparent that there was a lack of architecture documentation that could stand on its own. The CCT Architecture Group was established to address this need. This group advocated creation of the Architecture Model and was a strong proponent of the Reuse Guide. Both documents attempt to communicate CCT architectural concepts and decisions to CCT users who would build future products. These documents, however, were not in the original plans and suffer a bit from their late start. They are not as user-friendly as they should be, and in their current format it is more difficult to determine architecture conformance.

10.6.4 Product Builders Need More Support

The CCT effort focused on the creation of a set of assets for spacecraft command and control and much less on the integration of those assets. There were two outcomes that have proven to be disadvantageous to future product builders:

1. Crafting of an end-to-end production plan, which starts with product requirements and ends with a plan for system integration, was never part of the CCT agenda.
2. More emphasis was placed on evaluating the functionality of the assets, in stand-alone fashion, than on testing their integration.

The Reuse Guide is the CCT production plan, and its very existence is positive. It provides extensive documentation on the use of individual component categories, their variation points, mechanisms, and tailoring—what we might call the attached process for components and what they call component categories. However, other information is less well organized and in some cases missing. Critical architectural information regarding the range of overall qualities (for example, runtime performance and reliability) of the systems built from CCT assets is either difficult to locate or missing. There really is no attached process for creating an instance of the architecture and no attached process for system integration and testing. A decision was made to leave the process up to the builder, which might be fine, but a product builder wants to get a system perspective first, and the Reuse Guide offers no direct support for such a perspective. The product builder has to glean this in a bottom-up fashion. The Reuse Guide is also missing any sort of CCT primer that explains basic concepts and assumptions and helps a potential user mount the CCT learning curve.

Production capability was tested in two ways: by having an internal application engineering team (the system test architecture developers) act as early users of CCT, and by having the first real user—the Spacecraft C2 System—cooperate in the CCT development effort. Both were positives for CCT. However, the end-system perspective wasn't pervasive enough during the creation of the test system, despite the involvement of domain experts and architects: the test cases were in some instances too simple to address the kinds of issues involved in integrating CCT assets into the development of an operational system. Integration and other systemwide issues, such as meeting a range of real-time performance requirements, were not adequately tested. The CCT component-level requirements were met, but it was not entirely clear from integration-level testing that the needs of real, full-up command and control applications would be met. The first user was successful, but was intimately involved in the entire CCT development process and so is not a typical future user, who will need more support. These key reuse aspects were not addressed early in the program to the same extent as were the technical requirements [Ohlinger 00].

10.6.5 CCT Users Need Reuse Metrics

There are two types of CCT users: those who would commission systems to be built from CCT (acquirers) and the contractors who would be doing the building. The acquirers are interested in knowing that the systems built by their contractors do in fact use the CCT architecture and do in fact take advantage of CCT as a product line asset base. They want to measure architecture conformance. The CCT Architecture Group developed conformance guidelines to support this user need. The conformance guidelines define six conformance levels. The Architecture Group applied these guidelines to the system test architecture to determine its level of conformance. The SEI conducted a conformance analysis of the system test architecture and the CCT architecture at the component category level. Both results provided useful metrics and also led to some recommendations on architecture enhancement.

There was no metrics program that identified specific measures for analyzing the reusability of the CCT assets or the benefits that would accrue from their reuse. Full tracking of the extent and remediation of defects provided some measures, but these measures were not preplanned. Since CCT completion, there has been an effort to collect data that speak to the reuse potential and the inherent benefit of using the CCT assets. These benefits were reported earlier and are now included in a business case being developed by the NRO. Such metrics are essential for attracting new users (acquirers) and convincing their contractors of CCT's merits; they both need to know the benefits and the costs in quantitative terms. Data should have been proactively collected from the beginning. There were potential users who rejected CCT because of the lack of such quantitative information.

10.6.6 It Pays to Be Flexible, and Cross-Unit Teams Work

True to its name, CCT was conceived as a "toolkit" development effort. The increments were created on the basis of staged delivery of component categories. The incoming assumption was that a rich set of highly flexible class categories could support the requirements of future spacecraft command and control systems. Significant effort was applied to understanding and documenting the variation points for support of variability and to the mechanisms for implementing the variation points, but the focus was on the functionality and availability of components.

The shift to an architecture-based approach came about as a result of the first architecture evaluation and a subsequent decision made by John Ohlinger and other key CCT players to form the CCT Architecture Group. The Architecture Group had representatives from the entire spectrum of major players in CCT development, including the contractor, technical support consultants to the CCT Program Office, the SEI, the Aerospace Corporation, and end-user organizations. Its chartered purpose was to guide the evolution of the CCT product line architecture, and its functions were to

- investigate and assess the architectural impacts of design issues and new technology insertion
- oversee any proposed inclusion of major enhancements in the CCT
- promote the interoperability of CCT components with other component environments, commercial products, platforms, and other customer architectural environments

- promote the extensibility of CCT components by recommending architectural solutions that are reusable and customizable
- seek reductions in life-cycle costs through improvements in technology, methodology, specifications, and tools

The Architecture Group was the major influence in moving CCT from a component-based effort to an architecture-based effort. The lesson that was learned is really twofold: (1) structuring the organization is an ongoing process that requires organizational flexibility, and (2) a permanent crosscutting architecture group has great benefits.

10.6.7 A Real Product Is a Benefit

The Spacecraft C2 System was really the first to test the reusability of CCT. This program consisted of two major subsystems:

- Spacecraft command and control partially built using CCT
- Payload operations entirely independent of CCT

The program integrated CCT assets into its spacecraft command and control application, and it also exercised the variability of the components by adding mission-unique extensions. The Spacecraft C2 System supported CCT by providing essential feedback in two areas:

- **Test engineering:** The program evaluated system tests.
- **Sustainment engineering:** The program provided feedback on actual component use.

Spacecraft C2 was a major influence on CCT and a factor in CCT evolution since the initial increment. This real product demonstrated the strategic intent of CCT—to show that satellite programs could use CCT as the basis for their spacecraft command and control solutions—and that demonstration was critical. Here is the lesson for organizations that commission a product line asset base: commission or develop a product in concert with the asset base development. The schedules and the demands of the product team have to be managed carefully, but the advantage of having a real product to provide valuable feedback and prove the usability of the assets outweighs any extra management required.

10.7 Summary

The development of the Control Channel Toolkit provides an illuminating software product line case study, an exciting advancement in satellite software development, and a major stride for software product lines within the U.S. government. The

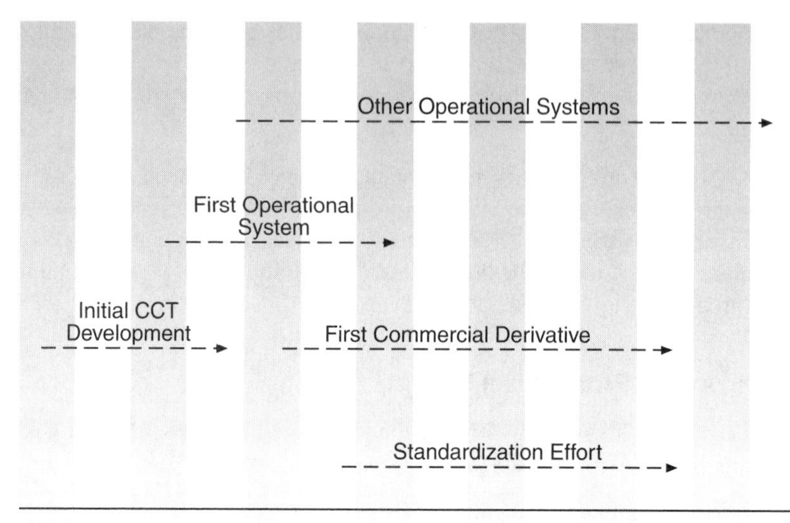

Figure 10.5 Growth in Use of CCT Assets

NRO established both the product line assets and an organization to support and sustain their use, and they succeeded in their goals. The following themes, which pervade other successful product line efforts, were echoed in the CCT story:

- Deep domain experience resident at Hughes/Raytheon and at the NRO
- A legacy base from which to build
- Process maturity
- A dedicated champion (in this case, two) throughout asset development
- Strong architectural vision
- An incremental development and refinement approach

CCT is still in its infancy. The CCT Concept of Operations calls for multi-year phases after development to improve both the assets and the process as they are applied in satellite programs. In spite of its relative immaturity, the accomplishments of CCT should provide guidance to other organizations intending to field software product lines. Figure 10.5 shows the expected growth in the application of CCT in government and industry.

10.8 For Further Reading

John Ohlinger and Jeff Shaw have both written papers and given presentations about the development of CCT [Hollander 99, Ohlinger 00, Shaw 00].

10.9 Discussion Questions

1. Map each of the CCT core asset development engineering processes to the appropriate software engineering practice areas. Did they miss any of the software engineering practice areas?
2. Can you identify the application to CCT of any of the product line practice patterns that we described in Chapter 7?
3. The role of the NRO as the acquirer of CCT and the role of Raytheon as the contractor complicated the product line operations considerably. Discuss in what way(s) and why.
4. What effect might a buy-out or merger during a product line start-up have on the developing organization, as happened when Hughes and Raytheon merged? Think about what technical and organizational management practice areas might be affected, and in what ways.

11

CASE STUDY

Successful Software Product Line Development in a Small Organization

with Cristina Gacek, Peter Knauber, and Klaus Schmid

11.1 Introduction

Software product lines may be fine for large organizations, but not for small ones. Small companies can't afford the start-up cost. Further, the burdensome processes, the strict organizational roles, and the tedious planning all run completely counter to a small organization's lean, nimble, leap-out-of-the-starting-gate culture.

So goes the conventional wisdom in many parts of the software engineering community—and it is not without a certain understandability. Many of the best-known and most publicized software product lines come with pedigrees written in large script: Nokia, Motorola, Hewlett-Packard, CelsiusTech, Philips, and others. These organizations boast hundreds of developers, with budgets more than ample enough to cover an experiment or two with a new and untried paradigm. And if it fails, well, there's always a bit of a risk with an R&D project, isn't there? It's not as though the company will be in peril.

For small companies, R&D is an unaffordable luxury. Experiments are for laboratories, not for lean, need-it-now production shops where every product has to strike market gold for the company to survive. No wonder the conventional wisdom views software product lines as a game only for the heavyweights.

For the record, the conventional wisdom is wrong.

In fact, software product lines offer many small companies their last, best hope for success. Time-to-market and economy of production are two of the strongest benefits of a product line, and both are many times more critical for a small company. Of course, even the largest software house would like to cut costs and get products to market sooner, but the large companies enjoy reputations that help them entice customers to wait for an announced product. After release, large volume helps pay for large development staffs. Small companies, for the most part, have neither a global reputation nor the expectation of global-sized volume to provide a cushion. Their road to success lies through navigating the tricky waters of turning out products that are impossibly customized, in an impossibly short time, using an impossibly small staff.

We know of many small companies that have used software product lines to increase (or even establish) their viability, and in more than one case the results have spelled the difference between life and death. This chapter is about one such company—Market Maker Software AG of Kaiserslautern, Germany. In the late 1980s, a university student who liked to program in his spare time noticed that there was no software available to help private individuals track the stock market. This student, whose father was a bank chairman, recognized a business opportunity. In 1989, the student founded Market Maker, and soon thereafter released the first product, a program that ran under the DOS operating system. The program could maintain a user's watch list and display various charts and data about selected stocks. On a weekly basis, the company sent its subscribers diskettes full of data typed in manually from newspaper stock quotations.

From a single programmer in 1989 to almost 60 in early 2001, Market Maker has enjoyed steady growth. Its data subscription service provides a dependable revenue stream because its customers recognize that its data are higher in quality and more reliable than the data available from other sources, even from the markets themselves. And other products have replaced the old DOS program. A Windows version of the Market Maker product for individual users was released in 1998. Along the way, the product was picked up and marketed by a large German media company under its own publishing house brand, resulting in the sale of more than 150,000 copies and making it Europe's most popular stock market software. Then, in 1999, Market Maker decided to launch an Internet-based version of its product.

The idea behind the Internet version was that the company could use the fundamental 1998 product functionality as the engine to power other companies' financial Web sites. But that functionality would be only one part of the total product. The total system would, depending on the customer, have to integrate with other databases and other content-producing software, run on who-knows-what kind of computing platforms and servers, satisfy human-user performance requirements, and be tailored to show exactly the kind of data, in exactly the kind of charts, in exactly the kind of form required by each particular customer's Web site. That is to say, the product had to be flexible, widely tailorable, deliverable in a very short amount of time, and producible by a very small development staff. In other words, it had to be built as a software product line.

And so it was. The result is a 520-KSLOC system that meets all of those requirements and more. Six people (two of whom were part-time) worked for about a year to produce the core system, from which instantiated products are turned out. Each version of the system—that is, every product—must be built to the client's specifications and installed and tested on the client's own platform. Visit http://www.diba.de/wpinfo/fs_info.html, and you'll see a member of Market Maker's Internet software product line running on the Web site of one of Germany's leading direct brokers. And how long does it take Market Maker to put up a system like this? As little as *three days*.

So much for the conventional wisdom.

11.2 The Early Years

In the late 1980s, a university student named Axel Sellemerten noticed that there was no available software that would let private individuals track stock market data. The only options at the time were systems produced by such giants as Reuters and Bloomberg. They were designed strictly for the large professional market houses, were difficult to use, and were prohibitively expensive (about $10,000 or more per year). Recognizing a business opportunity, Axel decided to fill the void. Programming gradually supplanted his university studies, until in 1989 he founded his own small company. In 1990, he released a DOS version of a program that could track stock prices, show historical charts of stocks, and compute some technical market indicators. Sales the first year were about DM 300,000 (about $135,000 at January 2001 exchange rates). In 1992 Axel renamed the company after that first product: Market Maker Software GmbH. Soon, a second computer science student, Christian Hank, joined Axel to help with the programming tasks. Except for a short hiatus, Christian was to stay with the company for quite some time: today he is its CEO.

Software that tracks stock market data is no good without data to track, and so hand-in-hand with the software came a data service that provided the latest stock quotes. In the beginning, the data went out by mail on floppy diskettes, on a weekly basis. The data were typed in from the financial pages of various newspapers. One of the first jobs the new company offered was a data entry position, because the availability of data was so crucial to the company concept.

The data service was an important part of Market Maker's business for two reasons. First, it provided a dependable revenue stream because people came to recognize that Market Maker's data were more dependable and more accurate than data from other sources. Just as important, it instilled a sense of identity within Market Maker: they were not just a provider of shrink-wrapped software systems, but a *service provider,* with a vital, direct, and ongoing link to each and every one of their customers.

Soon Market Maker started to acquire, merge, and repackage data from other data sources. While the diskette service stayed around for quite some time, on-line downloading of the data files became the dominant method for bringing daily data to the customer. Customers could subscribe to different data packages (such as those for German markets, American markets, European markets, Asian markets, and various indexes). The data grew to include bond markets and tracking of other securities. Soon, data provision became Market Maker's major source of revenue.

The DOS-based Market Maker software needed to be able to handle all these different subscription packages transparently. A second, more important source of variability was introduced in 1990. Already at this early stage, an additional package called "technical indicators" was developed, which was a separately chargeable package of functionality that at the same time was strongly integrated into the core functionality of the system. Thus, early on the company had to face the challenge of developing and maintaining their software as a set of different variants.

This, then, was Market Maker's phase 1. Their DOS product was quickly accepted by private consumers, but to the delight of the fledgling company, they found that small asset managers and investment advisors also liked it. It was highly capable and carefully engineered to show useful information quickly. Moreover, it was affordable; the price ranged from DM 500 to DM 4000, depending on the version.

As their reputation grew, Market Maker was also able to sell this software to banks, which equipped their investment advisors with it. But this introduced another source of variability; the system also needed to be able to work with bank-specific data. Over time, more and more packages of functionality were added to the DOS version, such as depot management,[1] trend analysis, and option strategies. This, however, led to increasing complexity of the product and a rapidly growing set of variabilities. This second phase of the company, informally defined, lasted until about 1997.

During this second phase, the company's developer ranks swelled to five. These developers started in 1995 to work on a new version of the software, later to be named Market Maker 98, shown in Figure 11.1. This project aimed at a complete reimplementation of the software that would support all the previous

1. A depot account is analogous to a portfolio account in America.

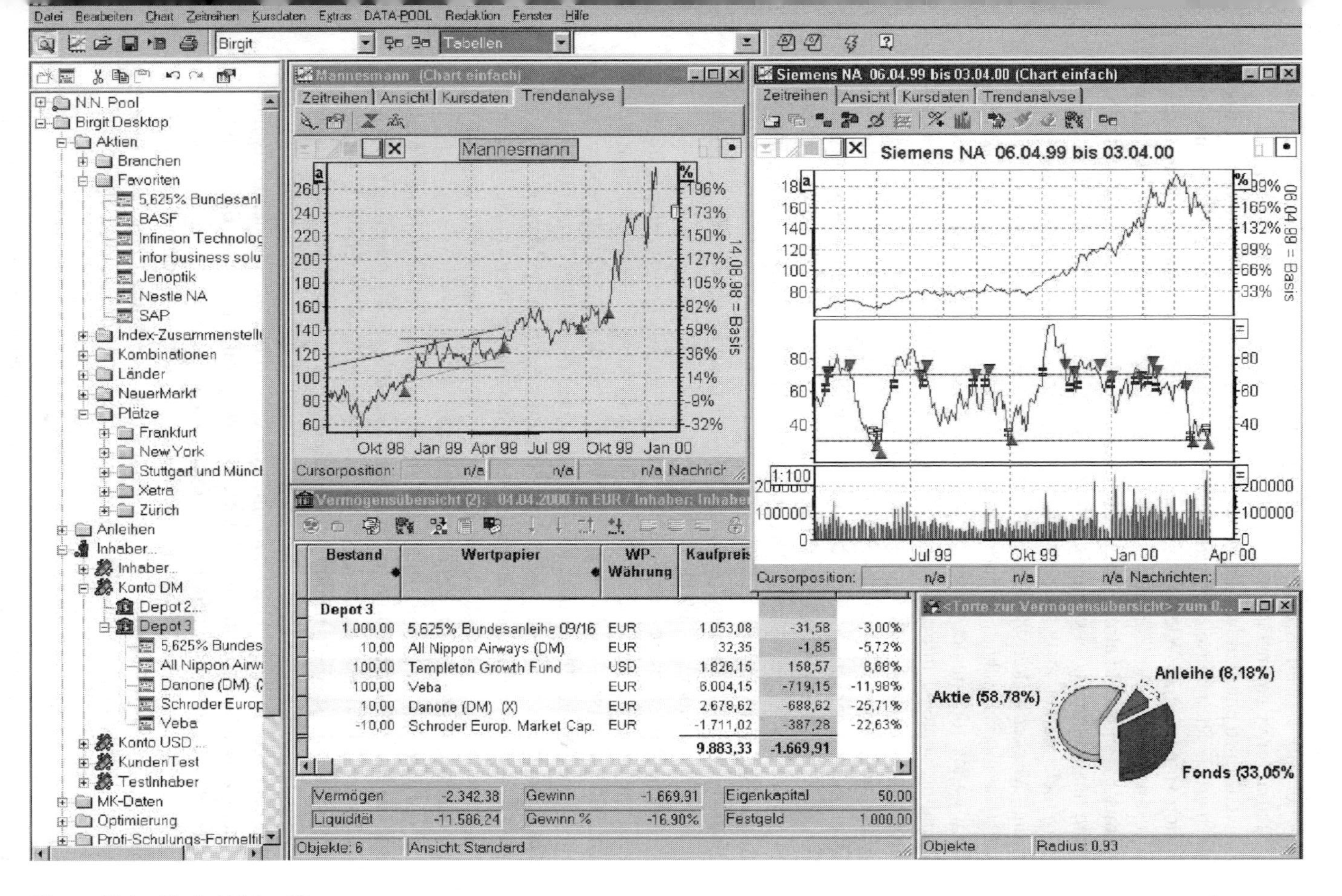

Figure 11.1 Market Maker 98

functionality as well as future variability and would take full advantage of the potential for visual metaphors that the new Windows environment provided.

The third phase of Market Maker can be characterized as broad exposure to the market. The release of Market Maker 98 got the attention of a German television show named WISO, which focuses on financial issues (such as taxes, investments, and the like) and is presented by the ZDF TV network. The name of this TV show had already been used successfully to market specialized software (tax solutions, for example). Now the idea was to use this label for branding stock market analysis software. A candidate for this venture was soon found: Market Maker 98. However, the software was actually too powerful for what the marketers had in mind. Thus, a new offspring of the Market Maker 98 family took form under the name of *WISO-Börse*. Soon, with the help of this branding strategy, more than 150,000 copies were sold, making it Europe's most popular stock market software. As a result of this wide exposure, Market Maker now enjoys a solid reputation for producing a quality product with a high level of customer satisfaction. The success of WISO-Börse led to more offspring products, such as WISO Fondsmanager, Telebörse,[2] and Telebörse Trader. Figure 11.2 is a screen shot of Market Maker's Web page giving order information for Market Maker 98 as well as the original DOS version of Market Maker. Both show the rich variety of functionality that can be ordered by a customer and provided modularly by the company.

All of this software was based on the concept of daily stock data, with only six data points per day. But in 1996 the company introduced another new product: MMLive! (see Figure 11.3). This product was developed independently of the Market Maker 98 product line and addressed the market of real-time data. However, the product was never a success compared with the Market Maker 98 products, nor could it form the basis of a product line of its own. Nevertheless, the existence of this product was still instrumental in the development of the product line that is the subject of this case study.

Around that time (mid-1997), the first cooperation between Market Maker and the Fraunhofer Institute for Experimental Software Engineering (IESE), a German industrial/academic research consortium, was established. Together with five other small- to medium-sized enterprises, Market Maker joined a project run by IESE called "Software-Variantenbildung" (software variant building) that centered on adapting product line concepts to the specific needs of small organizations and transferring those concepts in pilot projects. Based on this experience, a strong cooperation was established.

In 1998, an important business decision was made. The company ownership structure was now based on stocks, a structure that in Germany is not as common as it is in the United States. In 1999, the publisher of the major daily financial

---

2. Telebörse is a daily TV news magazine focusing on the private stock investor.

MARKET MAKER ---- Schaufenster - Microsoft Internet Explorer

Adresse C:\IESE\MM-Preise.htm

Charts	498,- DM
Profi-Charts mit Indikator-Optimierung (NEU!)	1.198,- DM
Fundamental-Analyse *	498,- DM
Trend-Analyse mit Kauf- und Verkaufsignalen aus der Formationsanalyse	~~798,- DM~~
bis 31.12.2000 nur	498,- DM
Report-Writer für individuelle Auswertungen und Listen (NEU!)	398,- DM
Optionsstrategien *	798,- DM
Quantitative Analyse zur Berechnung und zum Vergleich von Kennzahlen	498,- DM
Depotmanagement 'privat' zur Verwaltung von zwei Depots	498,- DM
Depotmanagement 'multi' zur Verwaltung von beliebig vielen Depots	998,- DM
Depotmanagement 'professionell' mit konsolidierten Auswertungen etc.	1.998,- DM
Verwaltung für einen Investment-Club *	398,- DM
Nachträgliche Erweiterung von Charts auf Profi-Charts (NEU!)	700,- DM
Nachträgliche Erweiterung von Depot 'privat' auf Depot 'multi'	500,- DM
Nachträgliche Erweiterung von Depot 'multi' auf Depot 'professionell'	1.000,- DM

Startseite

~ Impressum

MARKET MAKER 4.80 DOS — Bausteine Bestellen Sie jetzt!

Charts	498,- DM
Profi-Charts mit Indikator-Optimierung	1.198,- DM
Fundamental-Analyse	498,- DM
Trend-Analyse mit Kauf- und Verkaufsignalen aus der Formationsanalyse	798,- DM
Report-Writer für individuelle Auswertungen und Listen	398,- DM
DTB-Optionsstrategien	798,- DM
Quantitative Analyse zur Berechnung und zum Vergleich von Kennzahlen	498,- DM
Depotmanagement 'privat' zur Verwaltung von zwei Depots	498,- DM
Depotmanagement 'multi' zur Verwaltung von beliebig vielen Depots	998,- DM
Depotmanagement 'professionell' mit konsolidierten Auswertungen etc.	1.998,- DM
Verwaltung für einen Investment-Club	398,- DM
Nachträgliche Erweiterung von Charts auf Profi-Charts	700,- DM
Nachträgliche Erweiterung von Depot 'privat' auf Depot 'multi'	500,- DM
Nachträgliche Erweiterung von Depot 'multi' auf Depot 'professionell'	1.000,- DM

DATA-POOL — Abonnements Bestellen Sie jetzt!

Deutschland	49,- DM / Monat

Figure 11.2 Some Products from Market Maker's Current Palette. You can visit the current product list at: http://www.market-maker.de/Schaufenster/Preise/.

newspaper in Germany, the Verlagsgruppe Handelsblatt GmbH, bought 35% of Market Maker's shares. This investment provided the company with a potential for future growth and sufficient financial backing for major undertakings.

Over time, the company had grown steadily and strongly. In 1999, they had about two dozen people; their average age was about 30. Flush with success, Market Maker knew that the time had come to orient its products more toward big businesses. The banking climate of the time was (and still is) tilted toward

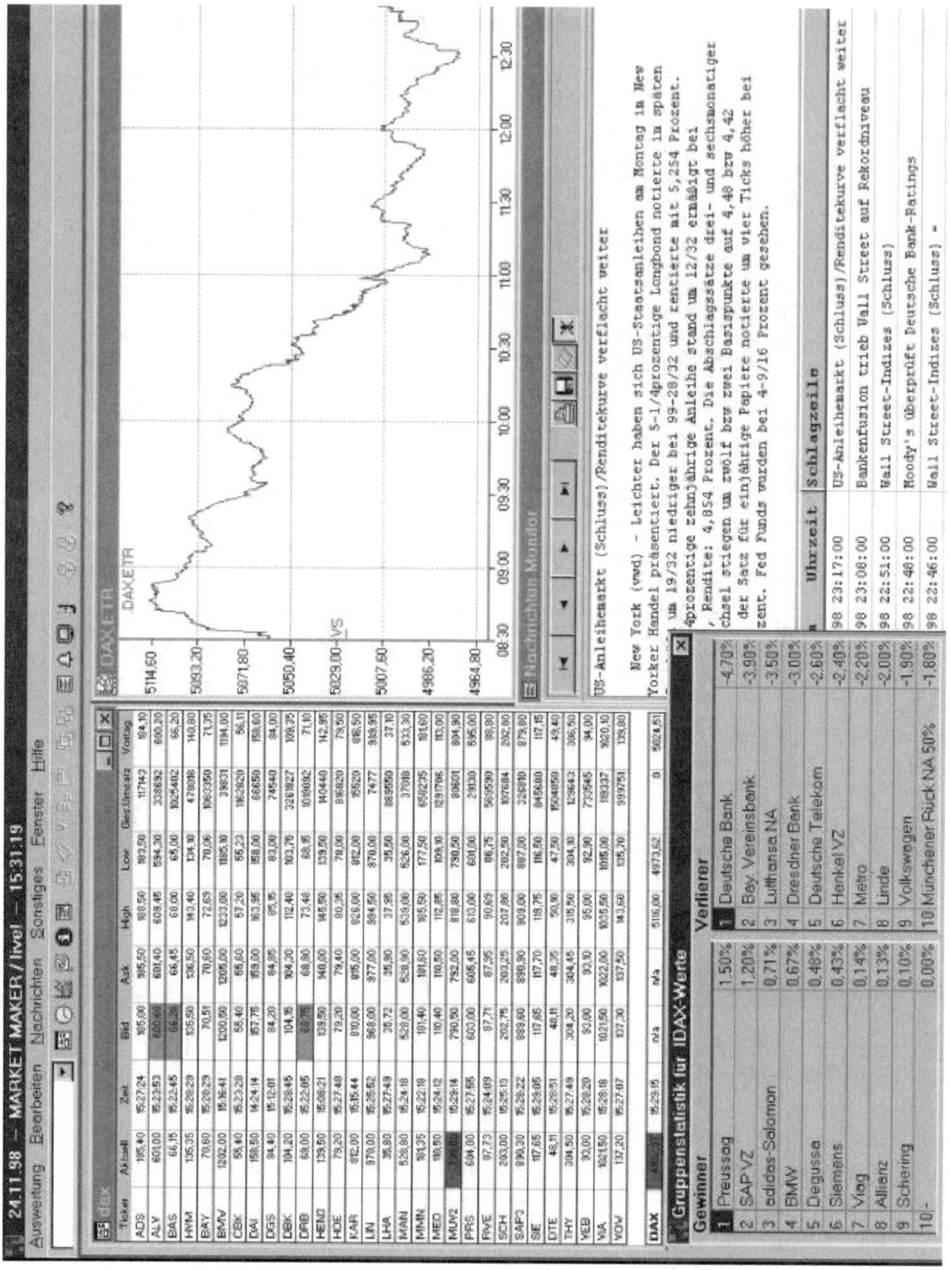

24.11.98 – MARKET MAKER / live! – 15:31:19

Auswertung Bearbeiten Nachrichten Sonstiges Fenster Hilfe

dax

Ticker	Aktuell	Zeit	Bid	Ask	High	Low	Ges.Umsatz	Vortag
ADS	185,40	15:27:24	185,00	185,50	188,50	183,50	117143	184,10
ALV	601,00	15:23:53	600,60	601,40	609,45	594,30	338692	600,20
BAS	66,15	15:22:45	66,20	66,45	68,00	65,00	1025402	66,20
HVM	135,35	15:28:29	135,50	136,50	143,40	134,10	478016	140,80
BAY	70,60	15:28:29	70,51	70,60	72,69	70,06	1060350	71,35
BMW	1202,00	15:16:41	1200,50	1205,00	1233,00	1185,10	39831	1194,00
CBK	55,40	15:23:28	55,40	55,60	57,20	55,23	1162820	56,11
DAI	158,50	14:24:14	157,75	159,00	163,95	158,00	66650	158,60
DGS	84,40	15:12:01	84,20	84,85	85,15	83,00	74540	84,00
DBK	104,20	15:28:45	104,15	104,30	112,40	103,75	3261827	109,35
DRB	69,00	15:22:05	68,75	68,90	73,48	68,15	1018092	71,10
HEN3	139,50	15:08:21	139,50	140,00	145,50	139,50	140440	142,95
HOE	79,20	15:27:48	79,20	79,40	80,35	78,00	816820	79,50
KAR	812,00	15:15:44	810,00	815,00	826,00	812,00	15520	816,50
LIN	970,00	15:25:52	968,00	977,00	994,50	970,00	7477	989,95
LHA	35,80	15:27:49	35,72	35,90	37,95	35,50	869550	37,10
MAN	528,80	15:24:18	528,00	528,90	539,00	526,00	37018	533,30
MMN	181,35	15:22:18	181,40	181,60	185,50	177,50	658235	181,60
MEO	110,50	15:24:12	110,40	110,50	112,85	109,10	1291706	113,00
MUV2	[illegible]	15:29:14	790,50	792,00	818,80	790,50	80601	804,90
PRS	604,00	15:27:55	603,00	605,45	613,00	601,00	29130	595,00
RWE	87,73	15:24:09	87,71	87,95	90,69	86,75	569590	88,80
SCH	203,00	15:25:13	202,75	203,25	207,80	202,50	107684	202,80
SAP3	890,30	15:28:22	889,60	890,90	909,00	887,00	326810	879,80
SIE	117,65	15:29:05	117,65	117,70	118,75	116,50	845680	117,15
DTE	48,11	15:28:51	48,11	48,35	50,90	47,50	1504850	49,40
THY	304,50	15:27:49	304,20	304,45	316,50	304,10	123643	306,50
VEB	93,00	15:28:20	93,00	93,10	95,00	92,90	733545	94,00
VIA	1021,50	15:28:18	1021,50	1022,00	1035,50	1015,00	119337	1020,10
VOW	137,20	15:27:07	137,30	137,50	143,60	135,70	999751	139,80
DAX	[illegible]	15:29:15	n/a	n/a	5116,00	4973,62	0	5024,51

DAX.ETR

DAX.ETR

5114,60 5093,20 5071,80 5050,40 5029,00 VS 5007,60 4986,20 4964,80

08:30 09:00 09:30 10:00 10:30 11:00 11:30 12:00 12:30

Nachrichten Monitor

US-Anleihemarkt (Schluss)/Renditekurve verflacht weiter

New York (vwd) - Leichter haben sich US-Staatsanleihen am Montag im New
Yorker Handel präsentiert. Der 5-1/4prozentige Longbond notierte im späten
um 19/32 niedriger bei 99-28/32 und rentierte mit 5,254 Prozent.
4prozentige zehnjährige Anleihe stand um 12/32 ermäßigt bei
, Rendite: 4,854 Prozent. Die Abschlagssätze drei- und sechsmonatiger
chsel stiegen um zwölf bzw zwei Basispunkte auf 4,48 bzw 4,42
der Satz für einjährige Papiere notierte um vier Ticks höher bei
zent. Fed Funds wurden bei 4-9/16 Prozent gesehen.

Uhrzeit	Schlagzeile
98 23:17:00	US-Anleihemarkt (Schluss)/Renditekurve verflacht weiter
98 23:08:00	Bankenfusion trieb Wall Street auf Rekordniveau
98 22:51:00	Wall Street-Indizes (Schluss)
98 22:48:00	Moody's überprüft Deutsche Bank-Ratings
98 22:46:00	Wall Street-Indizes (Schluss) -

Gruppenstatistik für IDAX-Werte

Gewinner			Verlierer		
1	Preussag	1,50%	1	Deutsche Bank	-4,70%
2	SAP VZ	1,20%	2	Bay. Vereinsbank	-3,90%
3	adidas-Salomon	0,71%	3	Lufthansa NA	-3,50%
4	BMW	0,67%	4	Dresdner Bank	-3,00%
5	Degussa	0,48%	5	Deutsche Telekom	-2,60%
6	Siemens	0,43%	6	Henkel VZ	-2,40%
7	Viag	0,14%	7	Metro	-2,20%
8	Allianz	0,13%	8	Linde	-2,00%
9	Schering	0,10%	9	Volkswagen	-1,90%
10	-	0,00%	10	Münchener Rück NA 50%	-1,80%

more centralized computing services with thin, low-cost clients running identical software (mostly browsers). Branches with high-powered PCs doing specialized computing at each location were viewed as too expensive and not cost-effective. Therefore, network solutions were, and still are, preferred.

Moreover, Market Maker had to realize that at a time when everybody was talking about the Internet, the company did not have anything like an Internet strategy. In fact, the investment market was a major contributor to the network-based push. Although private German investors had lagged behind their American counterparts in rushing to private stock market investment, German banks knew that the wave would soon be upon them. In 1997, German banks opened the first Internet-based brokerage houses and are now investing to try to prepare their branch offices for high-volume asset account management. Widely accessible information is now the watchword. Web sites have sprung up offering a multitude of different information and content, in which financial markets appear next to daily news, sports, and weather, for example.

It was in this climate that market Maker had the strategic insight that all those new markets could be addressed by means of an Internet/intranet-based line of products that would leverage the existing technology of the Market Maker 98 line of products. It is this Internet/intranet line of products that is the subject of this software product line case study.

11.3 The MERGER Software Product Line

In early 1997, Martin Verlage of Kaiserslautern, Germany, was going to be a father. Like other parents-to-be, he attended a variety of classes in the care and feeding of newborn babies. Sharing bonds of impending parenthood, Martin soon struck up a friendship with another man in the classes, Christian Hank. Christian happened to be the CEO of a small Kaiserslautern company called Market Maker Software AG. Martin was at the time a researcher and project manager at the Fraunhofer IESE. His work was focused mainly in the software process area.

Discovering their mutual interest in technology, Martin and Christian began discussing ideas for new products. Martin was interested in Christian's domain, and Christian was interested in Martin's knowledge of state-of-the-art software system technology and ideas about how to apply it. For the next year and a half, these two held informal discussions as they walked in the woods (presumably pushing baby carriages). Christian offered Martin a job in July of 1999, and Martin accepted.

Martin was brought on board because of his expertise in technology, but he did not wish simply to run studies and provide internal consulting. He wanted to contribute to the company's cash flow. At the time, on-line products were forming (in concept) a whole new business area for the company. Martin immediately recognized the business drivers for the new product line, although they were formulated informally and imprecisely. The need to bring out a tailored product "as early as possible" topped the list. Martin chose the year 2000 as the goal for the new product. He knew that Market Maker 98 was going to serve as the engine for the new product and that rewriting its 400,000 lines of code was out of the question. Yet it was written in Delphi, which is a Pascal-based environment for Windows user applications and not a viable choice for the rest of the system. Martin's first job was a technology investigation designed to solve this mismatch and other problems. The solutions would find their way into the architecture for the new product.

At about the same time, Market Maker got an opportunity to perform an in-depth analysis of their competition, such as it was. The Verlagsgruppe Handelsblatt GmbH publisher group, which had purchased 35% of the stock of Market Maker Software AG, asked them to perform a comparison of Internet-based financial tools. They chose Market Maker because of their expertise in financial tools; the part about the tools being Internet-based was purely serendipitous. Christian helped a great deal in this exercise. As the two men visited, evaluated, and critiqued financial Web sites, Christian pointed out to Martin places in which the software had obviously been (as he put it) "created by technicians" and not by someone fluent in the nuances of the financial industry.

As the vision for the new product took form, the management at Market Maker made a conscious decision to hire new people to build it. They reasoned that their existing work force, with their experience and background, was sorely needed to keep maintaining and updating Market Maker 98. This worked both ways; the new developers would not have to have their attention "polluted" by streams of phone calls and trouble reports on the existing system. Also, the Internet product was going to require skills and technological expertise not readily available among the current staff. And so hiring began, but not at what one would call a frenetic pace. The first developer was hired in October of 1999, and in November of that year the first lines of new code were laid down for the product. The second and third new developers came in January and April of 2000; the latter was part-time. Another joined in April, and two more (one of whom was part-time) rounded out the new team in August 2000.

The first order for the new product was signed in February of 2000. Throughout late 1999 and early 2000, the vision for the product line, which was christened MERGER, crystallized. It had to reuse Market Maker 98, but the architects thought more in terms of reusing the vast domain knowledge embodied in that package than of simply reusing the code. Time-to-market was absolutely critical for systems in the product line. The products had to be easy to produce and eminently flexible in preplanned ways. The system had to be open, in that it would need to work with commercial and third-party products of unknown variety and run on a wide range of systems, servers, and platforms. Finally, low maintenance effort was a requirement, and this flowed directly from a business philosophy: Market Maker wanted to use its small cadre of personnel to expand their customer base and not have them spend time on maintaining what they already had.

Figure 11.4 summarizes the business drivers for the MERGER project. Even a nonspeaker of German will recognize "Schnelles Time-to-Market" and "Flexibilität" as critical drivers. After 12 calendar months (and roughly 36 person-months[3]) of development activity, the first product was deployed. As of this writing, the product line has ten products in service, and many more are planned.

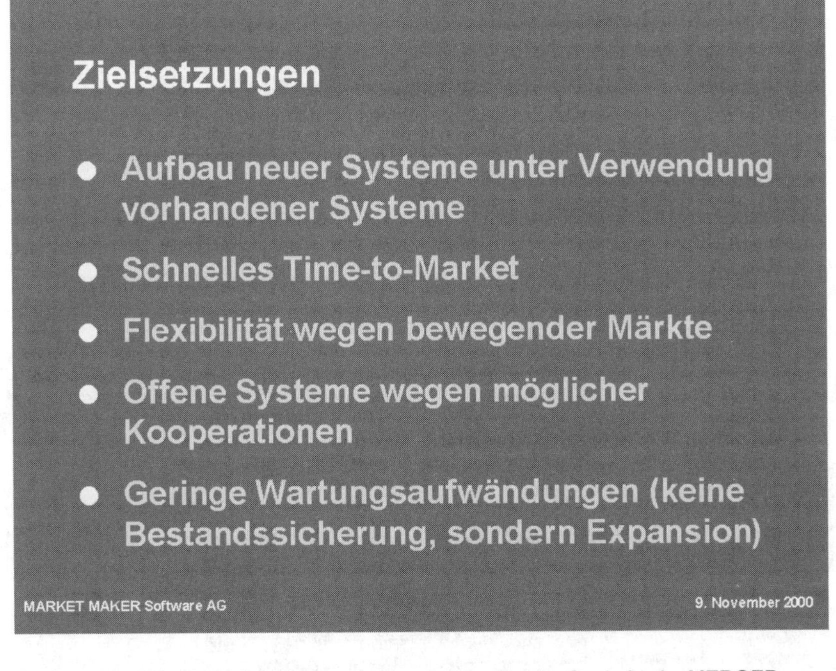

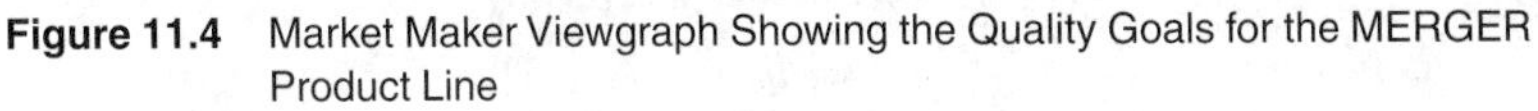

Figure 11.4 Market Maker Viewgraph Showing the Quality Goals for the MERGER Product Line

3. This number assumes eight-hour work days, although the norm was closer to 12 hours.

11.4 Market Maker Software Product Line Practices

11.4.1 Architecture Definition

The design of the architecture of the MERGER product line started in October 1999 when Martin Verlage went through in-depth discussions with the first developer hired for the MERGER project. Based on their different ideas and experience, they discussed possible ways to build the new product line and eventually defined the architecture as it is sketched in Figure 11.5. The current size of the MERGER product line is about 120,000 lines of Java code in addition to the 400,000 lines of wrapped Delphi code salvaged from Market Maker 98.

Figure 11.5 shows the different possible data sources for the MERGER product line. The data access layer can process data from real-time feeds (reusing parts of the MMLive! product), from external (that is, customer-specific) data sources, and from Market Maker 98. All these data sources are accessed using the Java RMI (Remote Method Invocation) technique. Only for external (customer-specific) applications do specific interfaces have to be built; these applications are then accessed directly. The data access layer passes the data to the application layer to perform computations on them. The resulting data objects are passed on to servlets (using RMI again) that generate respective

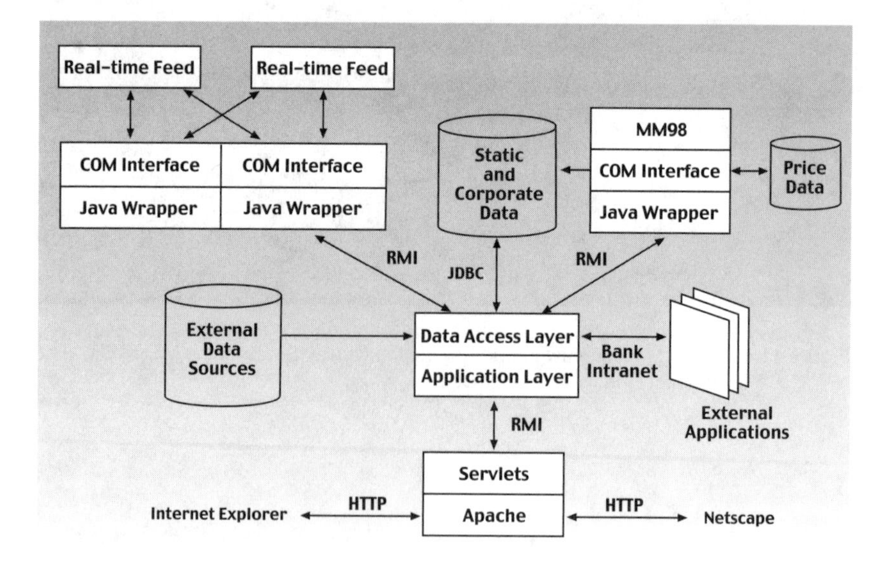

Figure 11.5 Architecture Overview of MERGER

HTML pages. These pages are made available by an Apache Web server[4] and can be accessed using standard Web browsers such as Netscape or Internet Explorer.

The two most important requirements for the systems to be built were performance and 24/7 reliability. The approach taken was to add abundant redundancy to the architecture by means of a varying number of servers and to provide extensive caching for achieving good performance. Other important aspects to be considered were as follows:

- Although functionality of Market Maker 98 had to be reused, Market Maker 98 could not dictate the architecture of the new product line. To achieve this, the 400,000 lines of Delphi code from Market Maker 98 were encapsulated as COM components for access in black-box fashion.
- Similarly, the MMLive! product needed to be integrated. The reuse of this otherwise peripheral product (compared with the success of Market Maker 98) provides MERGER with the ability to process tick-by-tick data, whereas Market Maker 98 works with historical data only.
- The MERGER products must be open, in that they need to work with commercial and third-party products and run on a wide range of systems, servers, and platforms. This requirement led to the use of standardized approaches wherever possible—standard (not enhanced) Java virtual machines, standard (not extended) SQL, and other established standards such as RMI, COM, and HTTP for communication and JDBC/ODBC (Java Database Connectivity/Open Database Connectivity) for accessing external databases.
- The MERGER products have to be integrated in different customer environments, implying that they have to be able to access external data sources present in the target environment. This was achieved by separating data handling in a layer different from the application layer. The data access layer manages the handling of different key sets used in the applications and databases, and caches data. It may interact with existing external data sources and applications to retrieve and deliver data.
- The application layer is responsible for representing/visualizing the data. Here, servlets are used, allowing for separation of data visualization from internal data representation. This technique enables easy customer-specific design of GUIs, making each customer's site look unique and different from those of competitors, while being based on the same product line.
- The application layer holds complex objects (such as dynamic tables) and performs computations on the data. The objects managed by the data layer

4. The Apache Project is a collaborative software development effort aimed at creating a robust, commercial-grade, featureful, and freely available source code implementation of an HTTP (Web) server.

are passed to servlets that generate HTML pages for presentation to the user. The servlets also manage sessions to overcome the deficiencies of the stateless HTTP (Hypertext Transfer Protocol).

- No code changes are permissible for adapting to local environments. All instances must be fully derivable from the code base.

The concept of building a system from components is well known and well liked at Market Maker. The first DOS version of Market Maker was constructed from components in order to be able to develop one component at a time (bowing to resource constraints) and to sell partial functionality to customers (achieving a marketing strategy). That strategy has been applied even more to the MERGER products by making them internally customizable. Each box in Figure 11.5 is subject to tailoring (but not recoding) when delivered to a customer.

Customization of the system is (mainly) done by changing property files. These files control the system behavior in various ways while avoiding the need to change any code (as far as the adaptations have been planned and realized). Examples of possible customizations are the services available at a customer site, the external data sources used, the external applications to communicate with, or the platform on which the system runs. "My vision is to have one common code for all our customers and to have all information necessary for the installation of a customer-specific version on one floppy disk," Martin Verlage said. "That means, the code should not be changed in order to be adapted to a local environment."

To realize configuration by property files, the Java reflection mechanism is used: on demand, the (versions of) classes needed are instantiated and used in that particular system. Sophisticated makefiles are no longer needed. Currently, 8 to 12 property files have to be adapted per customer. According to Martin, "An installation manager that would generate these property files would help to make the installation even easier."

11.4.2 Component Development

From the beginning, the development of the software was driven by the vision of a product line. This is apparent in the implementation as well as in the architcture. Throughout development, a product line vision has always been a major driver for decision making. Even when delivery pressures made it necessary to take shortcuts, Market Maker was always careful to analyze implementations to look for (and extract) new opportunities for commonality and variation. Each product in the product line, rather than being a bulk piece of code, consists of individual services that are actually started at initialization time from a master. This requires that each of the service implementations be actually quite self-contained.

During analysis and implementation, a small number of services was identified that are present in nearly every system but are subject to specific tailoring (caching, for example). These services were implemented in a very generic manner using Java abstract interfaces. For each service, a single class implements all interfaces (for example, access to cached objects, refreshing objects, removing objects, controlling the service, and monitoring). The class is instantiated by using Java's reflection mechanism. A string specifying the class is read from a configuration file and used as a parameter for java.lang.Class.forName(<string>). The result is input to a java.lang.Class.newInstance(<class>) method call. While the current implementation looks quite simple, a considerable amount of effort had to be expended to come up with such an elegant (and small) solution. Market Maker was able to achieve high reusability through the use of modern programming mechanisms.

Although carefully handcrafted implementations were used in the cases described above, generator-based approaches were used in some areas of functionality. A specific example of this is the design of Web pages. Here, a third-party generator package is used to describe the to-be-generated Web pages in an abstract manner: the page layout can be described in the form of a template instead of programming the format explicitly. A similar approach is used for generating reports. The introduction of this implementation approach even has organizational ramifications. In this case, it is now possible to delegate the design of the Web pages to a designer, who does not need to have a true programming background. The pages that are designed are later turned into templates.

The strongest usage of generation is in the area of chart generation, which can even serve as a template for the future development of the implementation approaches. Although charts can also be generated using Market Maker 98, it was decided to reimplement this functionality and to make this reimplementation strongly configurable, anticipating the needs of customers who want strong diversification in the look and feel of their Web sites. It is now possible to configure the look and feel of the charts using an additional customization tool, to see how the charts will look, and to generate the corresponding configuration file with a mouse click. This reduces the customization time from days to minutes.

One other piece of replicated functionality is portfolio management. The intention here was to offer a less sophisticated version of the Market Maker 98 features to whet the appetites of MERGER users. The high-end functionality of Market Maker 98 would be available for a higher price, but with no extra development effort.

11.4.3 Structuring (and Staffing) the Organization

Martin Verlage was hired to create a new line of products. In fact, he started with the in-depth analysis of competitors in the market (the first project for Handelsblatt) and in another project where he did some technology evaluation.

Both topics helped him to understand the domain and the opportunities offered by new technology concepts such as Web development with Java and its abstraction mechanisms.

For the development, new people were hired, which proved to be an advantage because they were not involved in existing Market Maker products—that is, they could concentrate on their new tasks and learn about new technology without being distracted by the old products. Moreover, all of them were hired for development in a product line context, which helped to instill among them a common understanding of the products, the development style, and the philosophy.

The team is now moving toward division into two organizational units: development and installation. The development group will handle the more strategic planning of the product line as a whole and the development of generic (customizable) components. The installation group (currently only one person) will be concerned with adaptation of these generic components to the needs and wishes of specific customers, including installation at the customer's site. These two tasks require (at least partially) different skill sets but also offer different opportunities for the people performing them.

Recently, two people with experience in the banking domain were hired, mostly for testing purposes from a domain (that is, not a component) point of view.

One thing Martin emphasizes about company organization is the importance of working closely with new people to integrate them from the beginning and to communicate the product line concepts to them.

11.4.4 Testing

For testing, Market Maker follows a two-fold strategy. First, the developers themselves test single components. All components are enhanced with special code that also enables later testing at runtime, independent of the runtime environment. After successful component tests have been performed, integration testing is done in the Market Maker environment. Then property files[5] are set up to adapt the system to the customer's (runtime) environment, and the system is installed there.

Second, the system can be tested at runtime using the special test code in each component. If the components (that are instantiated using the property files) still adhere to their specifications, then the entire system is running properly. Otherwise, the source of the error—that is, the misbehaving component—can be identified directly.

Testing of the system from a domain perspective becomes more and more important in comparison with testing of single components. For that purpose,

5. These property files control the system behavior in various ways while avoiding the need to change any code.

people from the Market Maker 98 group with experience in the domain of funds management have sometimes been engaged.

Components are not tested in their full flexibility—that is, with respect to all possible instantiations in the family—but only with respect to the next product to be instantiated.

According to Martin, the documentation of the product line architecture is kept too generic to be evaluated directly. Instead, Market Maker always talks about example systems—product line instances. Thus, the architecture is at least partially instantiated before it is evaluated using scenarios. That is, testing of the architecture as well as of the code is done for (partial) instances only.

11.4.5 Data Collection and Metrics

Until recently, Market Maker did not perform any detailed measurement, relying instead on the experience of their developers to predict the effort required. However, they are searching for a more disciplined and repeatable method of estimation. They would also like to pay more attention to measurement in the future to be able to tell precisely when investment in the product line pays off. Recently, they started an ambitious measurement program, not only aiming at a detailed analysis of their costs, but also trying to identify the factors influencing their costs and the benefits they achieve through reuse. For measurement, Market Maker distinguishes among development *for* reuse, development *with* reuse, and *system-specific* development:

- Development for reuse comprises the creation of new components or integration of new features in existing components.
- Development with reuse is basically the instantiation of existing generic components for new systems to serve the needs of certain customers and to add customer specifics.
- System-specific development aims at the development of customer-specific needs.

The difficulty at Market Maker (and at most organizations) is that there were no data available on effort spent for "traditional" development—that is, before the product line concepts were introduced with the MERGER product line. Given this fact, they cannot tell at which point in time the product line reaches its break-even point, but Martin's intuition tells him that they will reach that point by the middle of 2001.

11.4.6 Launching and Institutionalizing the Product Line

Based on the success of the previous Market Maker products, it was possible to carefully plan and construct the MERGER product line without being forced to make money from the beginning by developing for a particular customer. This way, the MERGER platform was not built as an extension of a "first MERGER product," but it was possible to consider more than one single product for planning from the beginning. Here, the comparison of different existing systems that was ordered by the Handelsblatt publisher group came in handy. In addition, technology feasibility studies were performed.

Of core importance for defining a successful product line is identification of the right requirements and market segments that are to be addressed. This is possible only if one already has an adequate understanding of the market. After initial development had been performed, the MERGER concepts were shown around at trade fairs as a kind of customer study to get ideas, comments, and other feedback from potential future customers for evaluating the initial concepts.

After delivery of the first product, the visibility of MERGER suddenly became quite high. This created a lot of market pressure, forcing Market Maker to release new MERGER products very quickly. At this point in time, it was impossible to do careful planning and generic development for potential future requirements; instead, many products had to be derived from the existing platform in a very short period of time. Sometimes this resulted in subsequent needs for reconsolidation of the platforms. But the important thing is that these reconsolidations were actually performed. This path of development of the product line is actually one expression of the vision of all the MERGER systems together as *one product*.

Martin believes that having some kind of quiet planning and development phase before the actual delivery of a product was the only way to plan and create MERGER as a sound platform for the development of customer-specific products later on. This avoided the strong influence of a "reference customer" from the beginning.

11.4.7 Understanding the Market

Knowledge of competing systems is part of the job description of the company's chief marketer. The people at Market Maker say, "Good knowledge about the market is a prerequisite for success." They view their systems as providing higher-quality information and unique and more valuable services than those of their competitors. To achieve this, they work very hard and very conscientiously to establish and maintain close contact with their customers and to know what they want, how they use the information, and what their jobs entail. Information about their domain flows in by various means.

The company makes it easy for customers to contact them. For example, Market Maker 98 customers can call a free hotline to ask questions, voice complaints, report problems, or ask for new features. Some customers call more than 150 times a year. Once, a customer called to say that the software was computing a technical stock indicator incorrectly. The indicator was one that was not all that well defined in the economic community to begin with, and it would have been easy to sidestep the problem. The company responded, however, by mobilizing a small research force. Some people went to libraries to pore over economics books, others scoured the software to make sure they understood the nuances of what it was computing, and all worked with the customer to make sure they understood the problem. In the end, the software was modified, the company was more knowledgeable, and the customer was delighted.

The company holds seminars for its users. Classes for beginner investors, classes on portfolio analysis, classes on chart analysis, and others are held regularly. Asset managers are invited to gather to talk about their desires for future versions of the company's products. The people at Market Maker say, "You know your customers well, or you're out of the market."

Over the years, Market Maker has come to know their customers well using these and other means, and the comparatively small size of the company has helped to make customer awareness a pervasive feature throughout the organization. This knowledge was an important prerequisite to defining the product line right and defining the right product line. A simple example may illustrate this. Over the years, Market Maker came to know their customer group of independent investment advisors (typically, independent two- to three-person agencies offering investment advice) very well. They knew that the customers of these advisors liked to check on the status of their current investments over the Web. On the other hand, the investment advisors would certainly not like to set up and run their Web servers. Thus, it was a requirement for the MERGER products addressing this market segment to support Web-hosting. In this way, the customers of the investment advisors could get their investment account information from the Market Maker Web site, where the information was always automatically updated by the MERGER copy running at the offices of the advisors. These ideas were present from the start of product definition. Thus, there was no need to retrofit these key distribution requirements into the MERGER architecture at a later time, perhaps compromising the architectural integrity of the system.

11.4.8 Technology Forecasting

Besides knowing as much information about your market as possible, you also need to know what you don't know. Market Maker knows that at most they can plan for the next three to five years. Beyond that, the uncertainties are too great. Thus, they are committed to using this time frame well.

Martin indicated that, "As a small company, we can't afford the resources to run our own research department. Instead, we use Fraunhofer IESE as kind of an external research department." Based on the experience from past cooperation, there exists enough trust within Market Maker to rely on IESE expertise when questions about issues such as product lines, security, and documentation standards are discussed.

Most of the necessary domain-related technology know-how was acquired during the first project for Handelsblatt. In this project, competitor products already present on the Web were analyzed, with special emphasis on the way they presented information and their support for interaction with the user.

11.5 A Few Observations

In this section, we will try to highlight some of the interesting facets of the Market Maker experience.

11.5.1 Effects of Company Culture

Throughout this book, we have pointed out situations in which a company's culture—that intangible way it has of viewing the world and conducting itself and its business—has played a large role in its success with software product lines. With Market Maker, we have another example.

When trying to extract lessons from the Market Maker experience, one cannot help but be impressed by two aspects of the company's culture that have conspired to breed success. The first is an abiding, almost cherished, relationship with their customers and the customer community, and the second is a long tradition of, and faith in, the idea of a few products tailored for many customers.

Market Maker saw itself early on as a customer service company; its high-quality data distribution service cemented that vision from the earliest days. We have already seen how Market Maker works hard to cultivate customer relationships, but the watchword at Market Maker is expansion of the customer base, not just maintaining the status quo. Deep insight into customer needs allows them to do this. During Martin and Christian's forest strolls, they often talked about new capabilities. "Suppose our client wanted to work while sitting in his garden on a Saturday morning, sipping tea," they might say. "He wouldn't want to drag his laptop out with him, and he certainly wouldn't want to scan the newspaper to try to extract the blend of information he wanted. Wouldn't it be nice if we could fax him the information he needed? He could just pick it up on his way out of the house." Detailed and somewhat offbeat scenarios such as this reflect both a deep understanding of who their customers are and a deep commitment to providing an outstanding level of customer service. The latter is not possible without the former.

Market Maker's relentless drive to satisfy its customers led right away to the concept that different customers require different capabilities. The DOS version of the tool started out as a core product, with new functions added modularly over time to meet the needs of a growing market. Market Maker 98 has highly modular functionality: customers can purchase the features that they need and yet not be burdened with what they don't need. In both of these cases, a software tailoring capability flowed directly from a marketing decision. But the extra idea here, the intellectual coup that leads to a software product line, is the realization that *it is possible to serve different needs with the same product.* In the case of Market Maker 98, every customer receives exactly the same software, no matter what functions he has purchased. Some features are simply disabled. There is a breathtakingly elegant vision in place in the company, and, although it has not quite been realized yet, the vision sets the stage for the unshakable institutionalization of the software product line paradigm. The vision is that every time a new version of the software is released, say four times a year, new CDs are burned. Every customer gets a CD with the precompiled binaries appropriate for his operating system (Web servers, database drivers, and installation routines) and a floppy disk containing keys that allow the functions he ordered to be accessed. At installation time, the customer loads the CD and the floppy, and the system auto-installs itself. This epitomizes a product line culture.

To reinforce this admittedly abstract notion of product line culture, we note that during our initial conversations, Martin kept referring to "the product." A product line is, of course, a set of products. When we asked for clarification, Martin told us that the Market Maker culture is to produce "one product to serve many customers." Then everything became clear, and we knew that the product line culture was strong. As we have said before, mature product line organizations refer to what they do in the singular: they build and maintain and nurture the *single* entity that is the product line. By contrast, immature or struggling product line organizations think of themselves as being in the business of turning out *products,* albeit tightly coupled ones.

11.5.2 Cost Issues

As we have seen with other software product line examples, cost is conspicuously absent from the list of driving forces behind the Market Maker effort. "Reducing cost" simply doesn't give one a foothold from which to make progress. Or, as Martin put it, "You can't reduce cost by thinking about cost." But certainly cost is in the back of everyone's mind, and savings from the rapid introduction of a multitude of mass-customized products will undoubtedly satisfy the implicit goals.

Market Maker expects their Internet effort to pay for itself by the middle of 2001—about two years after the project's inception. If the price of the products were not artificially low to gain market entry, the payoff would occur about six months sooner. There is certainly every reason to believe that for each product deployed subsequent to the break-even day, the payoff will be substantial. And the market outlook is optimistic: Market Maker can field more flexible products at lower cost than its competitors, which gives it the freedom to price flexibly in order to execute market strategies.

11.5.3 The Customer Paradox

A product needs a customer—but not too soon. For its Internet product, Market Maker "had the luck not to have a customer at first." In fact, in retrospect, another six months without a customer would have been welcome. Although this sounds heretical, a customer waiting anxiously for a product induces delivery and specialization pressures that can derail long-term goals. Developing in the absence of such pressures helps ensure more generic (and therefore more broadly useful) designs.

However, developing in a vacuum is not a good idea, either. A customer presents you with absolutely authentic needs and requirements. Without these, your product may be elegant but useless.

Market Maker balanced these conflicting goals by gathering feedback from early presentations, by showing prototypes at trade fairs, and by keeping their existing customers informed. But they resisted the strong temptation to promise delivery of those prototypes, even when faced with eager buyers.

11.5.4 Tool Support

Product line development in general requires not only changes in the development process but also changes in tooling. Proven approaches to coping with complexity might become less usable when you adopt a product line approach. Setting up an environment prior to launching was not an issue at Market Maker. Time did not allow for it; cost did not allow for it. Although they had experience in instantiating products by switching on components in Market Maker 98, these instantiations were somewhat limited in the set of possible instances. MERGER is much more complicated, and therefore more need exists for tools to handle the complexity. When asked about the tools he wished he had, Martin's answers were all about instantiation:

- An instantiation tool: This would allow them to generate the property files for adaptation of the products to the target environment.
- A tool for document management: This would allow them to develop (technical and user) documentation of the products in a generic way, like the software. This way, customer-specific documentation of the software could be instantiated like the software itself.
- A tool for testing: This would check the correct installation of the software in the environment target and, at runtime of the system, the correct behavior of the instantiated system components.

Of course, the absence of tools has consequences in quality but more so in time. Instantiating a product by changing dozens of lines in configuration files is burdensome, error-prone, and annoying. Nevertheless, learning from these painful lessons is what allows precise requirements for automated support of a product line process.

Martin's advice about tool support is characteristically to the point: "Don't expect perfect environments," he says. "Just do it."

11.6 Lessons Learned

Martin shared with us what he would do differently if he could. The list is a short one and includes concerns that would not be surprising to any manager.

- *Produce more and higher-quality documentation.* In the beginning there was too little staff and hardly any need to communicate information beyond the inner circle of developers of this information; later there was just no time for systematic documentation, given the numerous contracts.
- *Give his team more time before the first delivery—ideally, about six more months.* Time is needed to design and develop the platform right, from the start. However, at some point you just have to get started. This is hard to balance, even in retrospect.
- *Spend more time with his team, to better understand their satisfaction drivers.* All the team members were new people, just entering the company. If you want to work successfully over a long time with a team, you have to get to know them.
- *Pay more attention to data collection, to better understand where effort is being expended.* Data analysis would help to build models for a second product line. This would help to guide project managers through the process of defining the product line, architecture analysis, and instantiating first products.
- *Install an error-reporting system to better track problems and problem fixes.* Because the team was working on architecting the system instead of programming, their attention was pulled away from small functional flaws that resided in the software for some time afterwards.
- *Pay more attention to the environments in which the products are to be installed, to better understand the needs and requirements of the operators, the installers, and so on.* These stakeholders are not particularly impressed that the software they're getting is a product line, but are impressed by ease of use and understandability of the configuration files.

11.6.1 Drawbacks

The Market Maker story is one full of pleasing results, but of course not all is perfect. Martin shared these weaknesses of the software product line approach:

- There is no clearly defined archetypal product. It is therefore easy to promise a customer just about anything. For example, in the Market Maker demo, the customer sees the full version, with all the features enabled, and is often unpleasantly surprised when something less is delivered. Reminding him of the contractual specifications he signed does not usually diminish the disappointment. This problem should diminish as more installations are completed, providing more products to show.
- Some changes must be made in certain ways simply to maintain architectural integrity, causing them to take longer than they might otherwise. Such changes are hard for a customer to understand. Any given customer will want his system delivered (or fixed) right away, and has no desire to wait longer for changes that will benefit the company or other future customers in what is to him a very abstract way.
- Changes in the core assets require more time. In particular, they require group thinking because the goal is to arrive at the best solution for the whole family. Sometimes the core group spends the better part of a day in a meeting to work out one change. Their strategy is to ask, "What is the more general problem behind this special-case change?"
- The software product line endows flexibility, but only in limited (that is, predefined) ways. Not every change or customer whim can be satisfied. This underscores the need for careful design and deep domain expertise, so that the predefined avenues of variation are the right ones.

11.7 Conclusions: Software Product Lines in Small Organizations

Why did Market Maker adopt a software product line strategy for its Internet product? It was, we were told, "the obvious solution." Market Maker was operating with an extremely small cadre of developers, who could not hope to produce code for each customer's Web site. Even if they had employed a brigade of coders and testers, the time-to-market requirements precluded one-at-a-time product development. The software product line approach added a layer of complexity to an already (technologically) complex situation, but it removed complexity as well. As Martin put it, it is analogous to cars of today versus cars of 30 years ago. Today, they are vastly more complicated, but that complexity is hidden in the components, making things much simpler for the people who assemble and drive them. So it is with software product lines. The ability to generate code adds complexity, but once accomplished, the instantiation step is orders of magnitude simpler.

In addition to the expansion plans highlighted in Section 11.2 (including, for example, completion of the electronic interface to banks), Market Maker has plans to pursue other market segments. For example, they understand the need to stay ahead of security issues. Some Internet customers do not wish to maintain their own servers, nor do they wish to be exposed to the risk of hackers breaking in and stealing or corrupting resident data. Market Maker therefore is building up a new service as an application service provider for financial advisors, in which data are stored confidentially and clients may retrieve the files via the Internet.

In our experience, there are several necessary ingredients for a software product line. The first is a champion, someone who has a vision of the software product line and has the communication skills and management attention (or power) to induce others to share that vision. Clearly, the MERGER product line has a product line champion in Martin. He is articulate and likeable, and his understanding of the approach and why it is supremely important for Market Maker to follow it is utterly unshakable. The second ingredient is some sort of pressure to drive the organization away from traditional development paradigms. In other case studies, the software product line approach was adopted because the company's clear alternative was annihilation (see, for example, the CelsiusTech experience [Brownsword 95]). Circumstances were not so dire for Market Maker, and yet there was a clear sense that the company *could not* operate traditionally. It was more than a matter of product lines being a good idea that would bring about efficiencies. The third essential ingredient is, in our view, long and deep expertise in the relevant application domains. Market Maker has this in spades and has gone to great lengths to gather it explicitly and bring it to bear on their product designs. It is in large part what makes their products successful. The fourth ingredient is an emphasis on, and expertise in, architecture. Market Maker excelled in this area. The fifth ingredient is management commitment. Because Market Maker is a small company, management is not distant from the working organization. In fact, it was the management that championed product lines—an ideal situation. The last essential ingredient is the ability of an organization to exercise process discipline. Here, to be candid, Market Maker is not an exemplar. And yet, they do follow strong processes. When new versions of older products need to be hacked to meet, say, a Christmas marketing deadline, they always recapture the rogue version by realigning it with their mainline release tree. No one in the Internet group would dream of covertly cloning a piece of the core architecture to shortcut a product development task. And Market Maker enjoys the advantages of being a small organization, in which oral cultures can effectively take the place of written process definitions.

Now we come to our last point. We began this chapter by pointing out that small companies are not always considered the best candidates for launching software product lines. Throughout our information gathering, we listened for advantages and disadvantages that small organizations could expect to encounter when launching and fielding software product lines. Advantages of a small company over a large one include the following:

- It is much easier to articulate a vision in a small organization and make it stick. This is true of *any* vision, but it is especially true of a product line vision. Product lines are typically sold to management because they hold the promise of lower cost and quicker turnaround. In a large organization, those goals are fairly abstract to the troops grinding out code. But in a small company, the developers are much more tuned in to the company's economic picture; there is a short distance from economics to developers. Nevertheless, Martin felt it was important to explain the rationale for the product line approach in terms that were meaningful to developers. He simply pointed out that a software product line approach would let them spend more time doing the things they wanted to—working on new features and improving existing ones—instead of spending mountains of time on repetitive tasks such as bug fixes, code patches, and installations. It worked. There was never any formal training in product lines at Market Maker. The developers simply "got it." Of course, it didn't hurt that the average age of the developers was around 30. This tends to preempt arguments of the form, "But we've never done it that way before."
- A corollary to the previous point is that it is much easier in a small company to find places where the vision needs reinforcing. An example is in forming effective development teams. As Martin told us, "I think that —— and —— are working very well together and complement each other's skills. The same is not true of ———."
- A small organization can get by with lightweight product line processes because they are used to lightweight processes anyway. For example, Market Maker does not have a strong CM process, which is a concern. But their small size allows them to get by for now because word-of-mouth is an effective means of CM protocol, especially when (as in Market Maker's case) only two people are allowed to touch the code. This is not by any means to be recommended, but it must be acknowledged that informal processes work in the small and allow a company such as Market Maker to phase in stronger processes as they grow. Project and organizational planning are similarly less burdensome, which is helpful, because it is hard to make detailed plans involving a new approach that is employing new technology.
- A small organization's developers can more easily acquire useful domain knowledge.
- Managers in a small organization typically apply their hand at many tasks, including development, so they know firsthand where the approach is falling short.

Disadvantages of small companies are as follows:

- A small organization just starting out and struggling to survive may be sorely tempted to "sell its soul" to its first customer, promising anything and taking any shortcut to make it happen. And when the second customer comes along, survival pressures may make hacking the first product a tempting idea. As Martin put it to us, a small organization "always has a sense of urgency, and it is easier to induce pressure." Clearly, Market Maker could resist this pressure in part because it had another source of revenue—but so do many small companies these days, at least until the tidal wave of high-tech venture capital dries up. But Market Maker also could resist because it knew the difference between short-term expediency and long-term profitability. What, after all, was going to happen when the third customer came along, or the fourth? The hacking, one-at-a-time approach would lead to unmanageable complexity and, in the not-too-distant future, disaster.

- A small organization has more risk exposure to personnel loss—but this is a risk that is not limited to software product lines.

We began this chapter by repeating the conventional wisdom that small organizations are not well suited for software product lines. We conclude by observing that, all in all, small organizations appear to be exceptionally well poised to adopt the software product line approach. If product flexibility, short time-to-market, high staff productivity, and low maintenance are important business drivers, we now have existence proofs across all parts of the organizational spectrum that software product lines represent a viable approach.

11.8 For Further Reading

Fraunhofer IESE works with several small and medium-sized companies to help them adopt the software product line approach; Market Maker was one of them. A paper by Knauber et al. summarizes some of the lessons they've learned along the way [Knauber 00].

11.9 Discussion Questions

1. Although we didn't specifically mention several practice areas, Market Maker addressed them handily. For example, what role did Mining Existing Assets play, and what practices did Market Maker use? Name other practice areas not called out by name but implicitly addressed in this case study, and describe the associated practices. Will any of these practices need to be altered as Market Maker expands its product line operation?

2. A conspicuous part of Market Maker's success stems from its close and abiding relationship with its customers. This has given them a deep understanding of relevant domains, has helped them with technology forecasting, has made market analysis much easier, has simplified building a business case, and has driven their customer interface. Write a product line practice pattern that captures the relationship among these practice areas at Market Maker. Is this pattern a variant of the patterns we presented in Chapter 7?
3. Small organizations tend to be more nimble and flexible than large ones, but even large ones can spin off small groups and give them a certain amount of autonomy and freedom to innovate. If you belonged to a large software organization, what small-company advantages would you try to instill in a small group? What parts of your large-company culture would you try to keep?
4. What metrics and measurements do you believe Market Maker should begin to track?

12

Conclusions: Practices, Patterns, and Payoffs

A software product line is a set of software-intensive systems sharing a common, managed set of features that satisfy the specific needs of a particular market segment or mission and that are developed from a common set of core assets in a prescribed way.

This is where we began in Chapter 1, with a fundamental idea that software organizations of all shapes and sizes are using to achieve remarkable improvements in the way they develop and field systems. Software product lines epitomize the concept of strategic, planned reuse as opposed to accidental, haphazard, opportunistic reuse, which study after study discredits. We have tried to show that the product line concept is more than just a set of products built with extraordinary efficiency. It is about the purposeful reinvention of an organization, a disciplined way of thinking about the way one does business. This new way of thinking comes with a keen awareness of an organization's position with respect to its customers, its market, its own capabilities, and its future.

And the time is right. There are global trends sweeping today's software community that are coming together to make software product lines a viable proposition for almost any organization. These trends include the following:

- **Rapidly maturing, increasingly sophisticated software development technologies:** Sophisticated communication and coordination infrastructures are available off the shelf in the form of commercial middleware. Object technology has matured and is the default design paradigm in many quarters. Stand-alone components of extraordinary functional capability are available from vendors in scores of domains. All of these contribute to repeatable, predictable, reliable assembly of systems.
- **A global realization of the importance of architecture:** All of the high-powered components in the world will not work together in the absence of

a suitable, well-defined, and communicated architecture. The community is coming to understand that it is the architecture that imbues a system with its nonbehavioral quality attributes and spells the difference between a running system that does what it is supposed to do and is maintainable, and one that consists of a bag of expensive but mismatched components.

- **A universal recognition of the need for process discipline:** The world is waking up to the fact that cowboys belong on horses and not at workstations. Organizations whose focus is getting a system out the door using any means available and with no thought for tomorrow tend to reap the future they sow. Process discipline, like software technologies, has grown up and matured and is no longer a take-my-word-for-it proposition. Solid industrywide data translate the judicious use of process into a fatter bottom line.
- **The role models and case studies that are emerging in the literature and the trade journals:** Once there were pioneers, and now there are role models and case studies that not only show how other organizations tackled the problems but are bona fide existence proofs that it can be done. They give advocates the courage to be the impetus for change in their own organizations.
- **The conferences, workshops, and education programs that are now including software product lines in their agendas:** Product lines used to be something that we "heard" other companies were doing. Now, they're coming into the light, where their motivations, methods, approaches, and results are shared and are part of the community's body of knowledge.

We know that leaps in technology occur when the foundational support is in place and there is a pressing need to be met. For software product lines, both conditions are now present. The need for software is escalating at a rate far exceeding our capacity to provide it, unless we change the way we go about our craft.

12.1 The Practices

We introduced concepts that provide foundational underpinning: core assets, a production plan, attached processes, product line scope, product line practice patterns, and others.

Three essential activities comprise software product lines: core asset development, product development, and an overarching management to orchestrate and coordinate it all. That's all there is to it. If your organization can master these three things, it can master software product lines.

But these are three very large bites to swallow, and mastering these three things involves becoming expert at solving a whole host of issues. The 29 product line practice areas catalog those issues. Practice areas represent areas of expertise in software engineering, technical management, and organizational management that are needed to carry out the product line approach. Nearly all of the practice areas simply layer new aspects onto subjects familiar to any software engineer or program manager: requirements engineering, software architecture, testing, risk management, configuration management, planning, training, and so on. Some practice areas are so product-line-centric as to be effectively brand new: scoping and funding, for example. For each practice area, we told you what it was about in general, what it was about in the context of a software product line, examples of how real-world organizations go about it, and what can go wrong if you're not careful.

We tried to illustrate the practices, not with convenient invented examples but through the real-life experiences of organizations that have not only succeeded but excelled at developing software product lines. We shared lessons about the practices that we gathered along our path and let "Other Voices" tell you in their own words the lessons they've learned. We let you see software product line practices through the eyes of as many practitioners as we could.

12.2 The Patterns

Practices are one thing; practicing them is another. Our studies of product line organizations make one thing unmistakable: no two organizations are the same. No two organizations' goals, contexts, starting points, abilities, predilections, or cultures are the same. Trying to teach someone about product lines by giving them a simple catalog of practice areas, no matter how comprehensive, would be like trying to teach them to garden by handing them a picture book of flowers.

Product line practice patterns are there to assist you in applying the practice areas that are right for *your* organization and *your* context. And the language for describing the patterns gives you a tool for creating your own, as befits an organization facing a unique situation, as all organizations do.

The Product Line Technical Probe is a good tool for providing insight into practice area selection. The probe is a diagnostic instrument that uses the practice areas as the basis for both data collection and analysis, to identify which of the practice areas appear to be in good stead and which have the potential to derail the product line effort.

Finally, we have tried to show how practices and patterns occur in "nature" by giving three comprehensive case studies that follow organizations from the start of an idea to its fruition.

12.3 The Success Factors

Of the many software product line organizations we have studied, the successful ones stand out in particular ways. We see several key themes that repeat themselves over and over:

- **A pressing need that addresses the heart of one's business:** No organization we examined entered the product line arena on a whim. Panic, of course, is counterproductive, but a little healthy urgency can actually help. In fact, it was a big help to some of the organizations we surveyed: it gave them a clear sense of why they were doing what they were doing, which gave them measures of success. They knew they had to quadruple productivity, for example, to continue their market presence, and that put in place a very concrete goal that everyone could strive for. It also gave the champion(s) of the approach an unassailable position when the going got tough and the fainthearted wanted to turn back: "We can't turn back. Turning back is not an option." Which brings us to . . .
- **A strong and effective product line champion:** Necessity may be the mother of invention, but determination is its midwife. Every successful product line organization we have ever seen had someone who understood the concepts, who could see the bright future for the organization if they would adopt the concepts, and who was in a position of authority or leadership to make the change happen. In one or two cases, the champion was a group of people who brought their respective parts of the organization to the product line table together, but more often it was a single, articulate individual who commanded the technical and personal respect of the organization. It has been a leader. We like to say that a champion has to be equal parts cajoler, consoler, and patroller: he cajoles people to go along with the concept, he consoles them when the going gets tough, and he patrols to make sure people don't fall back to the old ways.
- **Strong and unswerving management commitment:** Getting a product line off the ground can be stressful for an organization. If management does not play the champion's role, they must give the champion their unqualified support, including whatever empowerment is necessary for success. There's an old joke about contribution versus commitment: in a ham-and-eggs breakfast, the chicken contributes, but the pig is *committed.* Management needs to support the product line by actions as well as words. They can give all the supportive all-hands presentations they want—and those are good—but if they allow project after project to forsake the approach to meet deadlines, or if they continue to give bonuses to workers who make customers happy by short-circuiting the process, or if they fail to empower the champion—well, they've laid an egg.

- **Comfort with a high degree of process discipline:** Software engineering is about cooperation, about many people coming together to create something more complex than any of them could have managed by himself in the time allotted. Software product lines take cooperation to the next level, with even stronger role definitions and stakeholder recognition. The extra dimension imposed by software product lines—multiple products all evolving cooperatively over time—makes it imperative that people rely on their colleagues to do the right thing. And "the right thing" is defined in a process that spells out the responsibilities and obligations of each role-player. When we survey product line organizations, we like to ask "What prevents a programmer building a product from checking out a core asset and unilaterally changing it?" Often the people we ask look at each other with a bewildered look on their faces, as if to say, "Who would think of doing such a bizarre thing?" When we see that, we know we're in a shop where the people are comfortable with process.
- **Long and deep experience in the relevant domains of one's products:** This experience tells them what variations to expect, and what not to expect, over the lifetime of their product lines. It informs the architecture, which must account not only for those variations, but also for the inevitable nuances and idiosyncrasies that make each domain unique. No organization we've seen enters an application area cold. Product lines, as we've seen, give them the ability to enter new business markets, but in highly related domains. And as product line organizations mature, they find that the people in highest demand are not just programmers or testers, but domain experts. In a product line, building a new product is not a problem. Deciding what products to build in the first place is. Domain experts help an organization see the future.
- **Architectural excellence:** Product line organizations require a solid, robust product line architecture as well as competence in using architecture as a product blueprint. Architectural excellence includes formal evaluation using a repeatable method. It includes disciplined documentation of component interfaces beyond the mere API or syntactic "signature." It includes obligating the necessary resources to produce and maintain up-to-date documentation. And it includes the understanding that architectures need to evolve over time.
- **Loyalty to the product line as a singular entity:** We called this aspect of product line culture "E Pluribus Unum" sidebar—thinking of many as one. The best product line organizations we've seen do not think of themselves as producing products, but as maintaining and growing *the product line* to which they show a palpable loyalty. If a particular product is good for the health of the product line, they'll build it. If it isn't, they won't. This outlook is anathema to old single-product-oriented organizations that can't imagine saying "no" to any customer. But product line organizations know that what

they're building and preserving is a way to serve *more* customers in *better* ways than was ever possible before.

12.4 The Payoff

To principles and practices, we add payoff. Time-to-market slashed from years to days, productivity increased not by tens of percentage points but hundreds, a small staff doing the work of an army, higher quality, increased customer satisfaction, unequalled product flexibility, the ability to achieve mass customization, and an unparalleled opportunity to move boldly and successfully into brand new markets—these are some of the results that companies that have taken the software product line path have shared with us.

Many organizations have succeeded in ways they never anticipated. CelsiusTech, our pioneer example, moved from ship systems to air defense systems and on *day one* had 40% of their system in hand. Cummins moved emphatically into the industrial engines market, which previously had been too small-volume and idiosyncratic to warrant a strong presence. Raytheon took satellite control systems seamlessly from the government to the private sector.

From ship systems to medical systems, from e-business engines to diesel engines, from satellites to telephone switches, from small Internet start-ups to century-old industrial giants, from government agencies to government contractors to private enterprise: all have their individual stories to tell, but in the end, all tell the same story—software product lines work.

12.5 Finale

Our goal in writing this book was to provide you with a map for your product line journey and encouragement along the way. We have laid out the three essential activities and the practice areas that are necessary to accomplish those activities. We have offered you patterns, role models, and a diagnostic tool that can guide you in putting those practice areas into play in your organization. And we have tried to illustrate the application of the concepts with real examples at every turn.

There is one other thing that, in our observation, successful product line organizations have in common: confidence and optimism about the future. While adopting product lines was a way to move away from impending doom, theirs was not a disorderly retreat but rather a purposeful march in a new direction toward a better way. They believed that they could overcome the obstacles along the way and that they would ultimately prevail. They believed in themselves, and they believed in the future.

The optimism and confidence shown by these successful organizations is infectious and in no small way influenced us. We believe that software product lines are here to stay. And as you start the journey to bring them to your organization, we believe that you'll be infected with optimism and (we hope) confidence as well. We wish you a prosperous journey.

Glossary

Acquisition The process of obtaining products and services by contract.

Acquisition plan The artifact that is typically used to document the acquisition strategy.

Acquisition strategy A plan of action for achieving a specific goal or result through contracting for products and services.

Application engineering An engineering process that develops software products from partial solutions or knowledge embodied in software assets.

Attached process The process associated with a core asset that tells a product builder how to instantiate it or otherwise put it to use in a specific product.

Business model A framework that relates the different forms of a product line approach to an organization's business context and strategy.

Commission To contract with another party to build a product or provide a service.

Concept of operations A document describing an organization's structure, roles and responsibilities, processes, and policies that all detail the way the organization operates.

Core asset A software artifact that is used in the production of more than one product in a software product line. A core asset may be an architecture, a software component, a process model, a plan, a document, or any other useful result of building a system.

Development A generic word used to describe how software comes to be.

Domain An area of knowledge or activity characterized by a set of concepts and terminology understood by practitioners in that area.

Domain analysis A process for capturing and representing information about applications in a domain, specifically common characteristics and reasons for variability.

Domain engineering An engineering process that develops software assets for one or more domains.

Economies of scale The condition wherein fewer inputs such as effort and time are needed to produce greater quantities of a single output.

Economies of scope The condition wherein fewer inputs such as effort and time are needed to produce a greater variety of outputs. Greater business value is achieved by jointly producing different outputs. Producing each output independently fails to leverage commonalities that affect costs. Economies of scope occur when it is less costly to combine two or more products in one production system than to produce them separately.

Mining Resurrecting and rehabilitating a piece of an existing software system to serve in a new system for which it was not originally intended.

Platform A core software asset base that is reused across systems in the product line.

Practice area A body of work or a collection of activities that an organization must master to successfully carry out the essential work of a software product line.

Product line A group of products sharing a common, managed set of features that satisfy specific needs of a selected market or mission area.

Product line approach A system of software production that uses software assets to modify, assemble, instantiate, or generate a line of software products.

Product line architecture A description of the structural properties for building a group of related systems (that is, a product line), typically the components and their interrelationships. The inherent guidelines about the use of components must capture the means for handling required variability among the systems (sometimes called a reference architecture).

Product line scope A description of the products that will constitute the product line.

Product line system A member of a software product line.

Production plan The guide to how products in the software product line will be constructed from the product line's core assets.

Project An undertaking typically requiring concerted effort that is focused on developing or maintaining a specific product or products. Usually, a project has its own funding, accounting, and delivery schedule.

Software architecture The structure or structures of a system, which consists of software components, the externally visible properties of those components, and the relationships among them.

Software product line A set of software-intensive systems sharing a common, managed set of features that satisfy the specific needs of a particular market segment or mission and that are developed from a common set of core assets in a prescribed way.

Software product line practice pattern A description of an organization's context, the product line problem it is trying to solve, and the set of practice areas to use in concert to solve the problem.

Bibliography

[Abowd 96] Abowd, G.; Bass, L.; Clements, P.; Kazman, R.; Northrop, L.; & Zaremski, A. *Recommended Best Industrial Practice for Software Architecture Evaluation* (CMU/SEI-96-TR-025). Pittsburgh, PA: Software Engineering Institute, Carnegie Mellon University, 1996.

[Alexander 79] Alexander, C. *The Timeless Way of Building*. Oxford University Press, 1979.

[America 00] America, P.; Obbink, H.; van Ommering, R.; & van der Linden, F. "CoPAM: A Component-Oriented Platform Architecting Method Family for Product Family Engineering," Donohoe, P., ed., *Software Product Lines: Experience and Research Directions.* Denver, Colorado, August 28–31 2000. Boston, MA: Kluwer Academic Publishers, 2000: 167–180.

[Anastasopoulos 00] Anastasopoulos, M. & Gacek, C. *Implementing Product Line Variabilities* (IESE-Report No. 089.00/E, Version 1.0), Kaiserslautern, Germany: Fraunhofer Institut Experimentelles Software Engineering, November 6, 2000.

[ANSI 92] American National Standards Institute. *Guide for the Preparation of Operational Concept Documents* (ANSI/AIAA G-043-1992). Washington, DC: American National Standards Institute, 1993.

[Arango 94] Arango, G. Ch. 2, "Domain Analysis Methods," 17–49. *Software Reusability*. Hemel Hempstead, England: Ellis Horwood, 1994.

[Ardis 00] Ardis, M., Dudak, P., Dor, L., Leu, W., Nakatani, L., Olsen, B., and Pontrelli, P. "Domain Engineered Configuration Control," Donohoe, P., ed., *Software Product Lines: Experience and Research Directions.* Denver, Colorado, August 28–31 2000. Boston, MA: Kluwer Academic Publishers, 2000: 479–494.

[Bachmann 00] Bachmann, F.; Bass, L.; Chastek, G.; Donohoe, P.; & Peruzzi, F. *The Architecture-Based Design Method* (CMU/SEI-00-TR-001). Pittsburgh, PA: Software Engineering Institute, Carnegie Mellon University, 2000.

[Basili 84] Basili, V. R. & Weiss, D. "A Methodology for Collecting Valid Software Engineering Data." *IEEE Transactions on Software Engineering SE-10,* 6 (November 1984): 728–738.

[Bass 97] Bass, L.; Clements, P.; Cohen, S.; Northrop, L.; & Withey, J. *Product Line Practice Workshop Report* (CMU/SEI-97-TR-003). Pittsburgh, PA: Software Engineering Institute, Carnegie Mellon University, 1997.

[Bass 98a] Bass, L.; Clements, P.; & Kazman, R. *Software Architecture in Practice*. Reading, MA: Addison-Wesley, 1998.

[Bass 98b] Bass, L.; Chastek, G.; Clements, P.; Northrop, L.; Smith, D.; & Withey, J. *Second Product Line Practice Workshop Report* (CMU/SEI-98-TR-15). Pittsburgh, PA: Software Engineering Institute, Carnegie Mellon University, 1998.

[Bass 00] Bass, L.; Clements, P.; Donohoe, P.; McGregor, J.; & Northrop, L. *Fourth Product Line Practice Workshop Report* (CMU/SEI-2000-TR-002). Pittsburgh, PA: Software Engineering Institute, Carnegie Mellon University, 2000.

[Beck 94] Beck, K. & Johnson, R. "Patterns Generate Architectures," pp. 139–149. *Proceedings of ECOOP '94,* The Eighth European Conference on Object-Oriented Programming. Bologna, Italy, July 4–8, 1994. Germany: Springer-Verlag.

[Beizer 90] Beizer, B. *Software Testing Techniques*. Boston, MA: International Thompson Computer Press, 1990.

[Bergey 99] Bergey, J.; Fisher, M.; & Jones, L. *The DoD Acquisition Environment and Software Product Lines* (CMU/SEU-99-TN-004). Pittsburgh, PA: Software Engineering Institute, Carnegie Mellon University, 1999.

[Boehm 81] Boehm, B. *Software Engineering Economics*. Englewood Cliffs, NJ: Prentice-Hall, 1981.

[Boehm 88] Boehm, B. "A Spiral Model of Software Development and Enhancement." *Computer 21,* 5 (May 1988): 61–72.

[Boehm 89] Boehm, B. *IEEE Tutorial on Software Risk Management*. Piscataway, NJ: IEEE Computer Society Press, 1989.

[Boehm 00] Boehm, B. ". . . And Very Few Lead Bullets, Either." *Proceedings of Impacts 2000: The 2000 Software Engineering Symposium*. Washington, DC, Sept. 18–21, 2000. Pittsburgh, PA: Software Engineering Institute, Carnegie Mellon University, 2000.

[Booch 94] Booch, G. *Object-Oriented Analysis and Design with Applications*. Reading, Ma.: Addison-Wesley, 1994.

[Bosch 00a] Bosch, J. *Design and Use of Software Architectures: Adopting and Evolving a Product-line Approach.* Reading, MA: Addison-Wesley, 2000.

[Bosch 00b] Bosch, J. "Organizing for Software Product Lines," *Proceedings, 3rd International Workshop on Software Architectures for Product Families (IWSAPF-3).* Las Palmas de Gran Canaria, Spain, March 15–17, 2000. Heidelberg, Germany: Springer LNCS, 2000.

[Brooks 87] Brooks, F. "No Silver Bullet: Essence and Accidents of Software Engineering." *Computer 20,* 4 (April 1987): 10–19.

[Brown 94a] Brown, A. W.; Carney, D. J.; Morris, E. J.; Smith, D. B.; & Zarrella, P. F. *Principles of Case Tool Integration.* Oxford, U.K.: Oxford University Press, 1994.

[Brown 94b] Brown, A. W. "Why Evaluating CASE Environments Is Different from Evaluating CASE Tools," 4–13. *Proceedings of the Third Symposium on Assessment of Quality Software Development Tools.* Washington, DC, June 7–9, 1994. Los Alamitos, CA: IEEE Computer Society Press, 1994.

[Brown 96] Brown, A. & Wallnau, K. "A Framework for Evaluating Software Technology." *IEEE Software 13,* 5 (September 1996): 39–49.

[Brownsword 96] Brownsword, L. & Clements, P. *A Case Study in Successful Product Line Development* (CMU/SEI-96-TR-016). Pittsburgh, PA: Software Engineering Institute, Carnegie Mellon University, 1996. Available http://www.sei.cmu.edu/publications/documents/96.reports/96.tr.016.html.

[Bruckhaus 96] Bruckhaus, T.; Madhavji, N. H.; Janssen, I.; & Henshaw, J. "The Impact of Tools on Software Productivity." *IEEE Software 13,* 5 (September 1996): 29–38.

[Buschmann 96] Buschmann, F.; Meunier, R.; Rohnert, H.; Sommerlad, P.; & Stal, M. *Pattern-Oriented Software Architecture: A System of Patterns.* New York, NY: John Wiley & Sons, 1996.

[Carney 98] Carney, D.; Brownsword, L.; & Oberndorf, T. "The Opportunities and Complexities of Applying Commercial Off-the Shelf Components." *Crosstalk 11,* 4 (April 1998): 4–6.

[Charan 99] Charan, R. & Colvin, G. "Why CEOs Fail." *Fortune,* June 21, 1999: 69–78.

[Charette 89] Charette, R. *Software Engineering Risk Analysis and Management.* New York, NY: McGraw-Hill, 1989.

[Chastek 01] Chastek, G.; Donohoe, P.; Kang, K.; & Thiel, S. *Product Line Analysis: A Practical Description* (CMU/SEI-2001-TR-001). Pittsburgh, PA: Software Engineering Institute, Carnegie Mellon University, 2001.

[Clemen 91] Clemen, R. T., *Making Hard Decisions: An Introduction to Decision Analysis.* Boston, MA: PWS-Kent Publishing Co., 1991.

[Clements 00a] Clements, P. *Active Reviews for Intermediate Designs* (CMU/SEI-2000-TN-009). Pittsburgh, PA: Software Engineering Institute, Carnegie Mellon University, 2000.

[Clements 00b] Clements, P. & Northrop, L. *A Framework for Software Product Line Practice.* Available http://www.sei.cmu.edu/plp/framework.html.

[Clements 01] Clements, P.; Kazman, R.; & Klein, M. *Evaluating Software Architectures: Methods and Case Studies.* Reading, MA: Addison-Wesley, 2001.

[Cohen 92] Cohen, S. G.; Stanley, Jr., J. L.; Peterson, A. S.; & Krut Jr., R. W. *Application of Feature-Oriented Domain Analysis to the Army Movement Control Domain* (CMU/SEI-91-TR-28). Pittsburgh, PA: Software Engineering Institute, Carnegie Mellon University, 1992.

[Cohen 98] Cohen, S. & Northrop, L. "Object-Oriented Technology and Domain Analysis," 86–93. *Proceedings of the Fifth International Conference on Software Reuse.* Victoria, BC, June 2–5, 1998. Los Alamitos, CA: IEEE Computer Society Press, 1998.

[Cohen 99] Cohen, S. *Guidelines for Developing a Product Line Concept of Operations* (CMU/SEI-99-TR-008). Pittsburgh, PA: Software Engineering Institute, Carnegie Mellon University, 1999.

[Coplien 94] Coplien, J. O. *The Counted Body Idiom,* Pattern Mailing List Reflector, February 1994.

[Coplien 98] Coplien, J.; Hoffman, D.; & Weiss, D. "Commonality and Variability in Software Engineering." *IEEE Software 15,* 6 (November/December 1998): 37–45.

[Crosby 79] Crosby, P. B. *Quality Is Free.* New York, NY: McGraw-Hill, 1979.

[Cruikshank 97] Cruikshank, J. L. & Sicilia, D. B. *The Engine That Could: 75 Years of Value-Driven Change at Cummins Engine Company.* Boston, MA: Harvard Business School Press, 2001.

[Curtis 92] Curtis, B.; Kellner, M.; & Over, J. "Process Modeling." *Communications of the ACM 35,* 9 (September 1992): 75–90.

[Cusumano 91] Cusumano, M. A., *Japan's Software Factories,* Oxford: Oxford University Press, 1991.

[Dager 00] Dager, J. "Cummins's Experience in Developing a Software Product Line Architecture for Real-time Embedded Diesel Engine Controls," Donohoe, P., ed., *Software Product Lines: Experience and Research Directions.* Denver, Colorado, August 28–31 2000. Boston, MA: Kluwer Academic Publishers, 2000: 23–45.

[Davis 90] Davis, A. M. *Software Requirements: Analysis and Specification.* Englewood Cliffs, NJ: Prentice-Hall, 1990.

[DeBaud 00] DeBaud, J. & Schmid, K. "A Systematic Approach to Derive the Scope of Software Product Lines," 34–43. *Proceedings of the 21st ICSE.* Los Angeles, CA, May 16–22, 1999. Los Alamitos, CA: IEEE Computer Society, 1999.

[Deming 86] Deming, W. E. *Out of the Crisis.* Cambridge, MA: MIT Center for Advanced Engineering, 1986.

[DISA 93] DISA/CIM Software Reuse Program. *Domain Analysis and Design Process, Version 1.* Arlington, VA: Defense Information Systems Agency Center for Information Management, 1993.

[Donohoe 00] Donohoe, P., ed., *Software Product Lines: Experience and Research Directions.* Denver, Colorado, August 28–31 2000. Boston, MA: Kluwer Academic Publishers, 2000.

[Dorfman 97] Dorfman, M. & Thayer, R. H. *Software Requirements Engineering*. Los Alamitos, CA: IEEE Computer Society Press, 1997.

[Dorofee 94] Dorofee, A.; Walker, J.; Gluch, D.; Higuera, R.; Murphy, R.; Walker, J.; & Williams, R. *Team Risk Management Guidebook.* Pittsburgh, PA: Software Engineering Institute, Carnegie Mellon University, 1994.

[Dorofee 96] Dorofee, A.; Walker, J.; Alberts, C.; Higuera, R.; Murphy, R.; & Williams, R. *Continuous Risk Management Guidebook.* Pittsburgh, PA: Software Engineering Institute, Carnegie Mellon University, 1996.

[Ecklund 96] Ecklund Jr., E.; Delcambre, L.; & Freiling, M. "Change Cases: Use Cases That Identify Future Requirements," 342–358. *Conference Proceedings of the OOPSLA 96*. San Jose, CA, October 6–10, 1996. San Jose, CA: ACM Press, 1996.

[Etzioni 64] Etzioni, A. *Modern Organizations.* Prentice-Hall, 1964.

[FAA 95] FAA Office of Information Technology Integrated Product Team for Information Technology Services. Ch. 6, "The Business Case," *Business Process Improvement (Reengineering) Handbook of Standards and Guidelines.* Washington, DC: Federal Aviation Administration, 1995. Available http://www.faa.gov/ait/bpi/handbook/.

[Fairley 94] Fairley, R. "Risk Management for Software Projects." *IEEE Software 2,* 3 (May 1994): 57–67.

[Faulk 97] Faulk, S. R. "Software Requirements: A Tutorial," 128–149. *Software Requirements Engineering.* Los Alamitos, CA: IEEE Computer Society Press, 1997.

[Faulk 00] Faulk, S., Harmon, R., & Raffo, D. "Value-Based Software Engineering (VBSE): A Value-Driven Approach to Product-Line Engineering," Donohoe, P., ed., *Software Product Lines: Experience and Research Directions.* Denver, Colorado, August 28–31 2000. Boston, MA: Kluwer Academic Publishers, 2000: 205–224.

[Finkelstein 94] Finkelstein, A. et al. *Software Process Modeling and Technology.* Taunton, England: Research Studies Press Ltd., 1994.

[Finnegan 97] Finnegan, P.; Holt, R.; Kalas, I.; Kerr, S.; Kontogiannis, K.; Muller, H.; Mylopolous, J.; Perelgut, S.; Stanley, M.; & Wong, K. "The Software Bookshelf." *IBM Systems Journal 36,* 4 (November 1997): 564–593.

[Fisher 98] Fisher, M. *CECOM Architecture for Practitioners Course.* Pittsburgh, PA: Software Engineering Institute, Carnegie Mellon University, 1998.

[Gaffney 92] Gaffney, J. E., & Cruickshank, R. D. "A General Economics Model of Software Reuse," 327–337. *Proceedings of the 14th ICSE.* Melbourne, Australia, May 11–15, 1992. New York, NY: ACM, 1992.

[Gallagher 99] Gallagher, B. P. *Software Acquisition Risk Management Key Process Area (KPA)—A Guidebook Version 1.02* (CMU/SEI-99-HB-001). Pittsburgh, PA: Software Engineering Institute, Carnegie Mellon University, 1999.

[Gamma 95] Gamma, E.; Helms, R.; Johnson, R.; & Vlissides, J. *Design Patterns: Elements of Reusable Object-Oriented Software*. Reading, MA: Addison-Wesley, 1995.

[Garlan 95] Garlan, D.; Allen, R.; & Ockerbloom, J. "Architectural Mismatch: Why Reuse Is So Hard." *IEEE Software 12,* 6 (November 1995): 17–26.

[Glass 98] Glass, R. L. *Software Runaways: Lessons Learned from Massive Software Project Failures*. Upper Saddle River, NJ: Prentice-Hall, Inc., 1998.

[Gleick 87] Gleick, J. *Chaos: Making a New Science.* New York, NY: Penguin Books, 1987.

[Goldberg 95] Goldberg, A. & Rubin, K. S. *Succeeding with Objects: Decision Frameworks for Project Management*. Reading, MA: Addison-Wesley, 1995.

[Grady 92] Grady, R. B. *Practical Software Metrics for Project Management and Process Improvement.* Englewood Cliffs, NJ: Prentice-Hall, 1992.

[Graham 98] Graham, I. *Requirements Engineering and Rapid Development: An Object-Oriented Approach.* Essex, England: Addison-Wesley, 1998.

[Griss 95] Griss, M. "Software Reuse: Objects and Frameworks Are Not Enough," (HPL-95–03). Palo Alto, CA: Hewlett-Packard, 1995. Available http://www.hpl.hp.com/techreports/95/HPL-95-03.html.

[Griss 98] Griss, M. L.; Favaro, J.; & d'Alessandro, M. "Integrating Feature Modeling with the RSEB," 76–85. *Proceedings of the Fifth International Conference on Software Reuse.* Victoria, BC, Canada, June 2–5, 1998. Los Alamitos, CA: IEEE Computer Society Press, 1998.

[Hammond 99] Hammond, J. S.; Keeney, R. L.; & Raiffa, H. *Smart Choices: A Practical Guide to Making Better Decisions.* Boston, MA: Harvard Business School Press, 1999.

[Harel 98] Harel, D. & Politi, M. *Modeling Reactive Systems with Statecharts: The STATEMATE Approach*. Reading, MA: Addison-Wesley, 1998.

[Hofmeister 00] Hofmeister, C.; Nord, R.; & Soni, D. *Applied Software Architecture*. Reading, MA: Addison-Wesley, 2000.

[Hollander 99] Hollander, C. & Ohlinger, J. "CCT: A Component-Based Product Line Architecture for Satellite-Based Command and Control Systems." Proceedings of Workshop on Object Technology for Product-Line Architectures. Lisbon, Portugal, June 15, 1999. Bilbao, Spain: European Software Institute, 1999.

[Huff 96] Huff, K. E. "Effect of Product Lines on Current Process Technology," 5–7. *Proceedings of the 10th International Software Process Workshop*. Dijon, France, June 17–19, 1996. Los Alamitos, CA: IEEE Computer Society, 1996.

[Humphrey 92] Humphrey, W. & Feiler, P. *Software Process Development and Enactment: Concepts and Definitions*. (CMU/SEI-92-TR-04). Pittsburgh, PA: Software Engineering Institute, Carnegie Mellon University, 1992.

[Humphrey 00] Humphrey, W. "Justifying a Process Improvement Proposal." *SEI Interactive,* March, 2000. Available http://interactive.sei.cmu.edu/Columns/Watts_New/Watts_New.htm.

[IEEE 87] Institute of Electrical and Electronics Engineers. *IEEE Guide to Software Configuration Management* (IEEE Std 1042–1987). New York, NY: Institute of Electrical and Electronics Engineers, 1987.

[IEEE 90] Institute of Electrical and Electronics Engineers. *IEEE Standard Glossary of Software Engineering Terminology* (IEEE Std 610.12–1990). New York, NY: Institute of Electrical and Electronics Engineers, 1990.

[IEEE 95] The Institute of Electrical and Electronics Engineers, Inc. *IEEE Recommended Practice for the Adoption of Computer-Aided Software Engineering (CASE) Tools.* IEEE Std 1348–1995. New York, NY: IEEE Computer Society Press, 1996.

[IEEE 98a] The Institute of Electrical and Electronics Engineers, Inc. *Information Technology—Guideline for the Evaluation and Selection of CASE Tools* (IEEE Std 1462–1998). New York, NY: IEEE Computer Society Press, 1998.

[IEEE 98b] Institute of Electrical and Electronics Engineers. *IEEE Standard for Software Configuration Management Plans* (IEEE Std 828–1998). New York, NY: Institute of Electrical and Electronics Engineers, 1998.

[ISO 95a] International Organization for Standardization. *Information Technology—Guideline for the Evaluation and Selection of CASE Tools.* Reference number: ISO/IEC 14102:1995(E). Geneva, Switzerland: International Organization for Standardization, 1995.

[ISO 95b] International Organization for Standardization & International Electrotechnical Commission. *Quality Management—Guidelines for Configuration Management* (ISO 10007:1995 E). Geneva, Switzerland: International Organization for Standardization/International Electrotechnical Commission, 1995.

[Jackson 00] Jackson, M. *Problem Frames and Methods: Structuring and Analyzing Software Development Problems.* New York, NY: Addison-Wesley, 2000.

[Jacobson 97] Jacobson, I.; Griss, M.; & Jonsson, P. *Software Reuse: Architecture, Process, and Organization for Business Success.* New York, NY: Addison-Wesley, 1997.

[Jandourek 96] Jandourek, E. "A Model for Platform Development." *Hewlett-Packard Journal 47,* 4 (August 1996): 56–71.

[Jones 96] Jones, L.; Kasunic, M.; & Ginn, M. *Using the SEI IDEAL Model in a Less Than Ideal World.* Salt Lake City, UT: Software Technology Conference, 1996.

[Jones 99] Jones, L. & Northrop, L. *Software Process Improvement Planning,* European Software Engineering Process Group Conference. Amsterdam, Netherlands, June 7–10, 1999. UK: European Software Process Improvement Foundation, 1999.

[Kang 90] Kang, K. et al. *Feature-Oriented Domain Analysis (FODA) Feasibility Study* (CMU/SEI-90-TR-021). Pittsburgh, PA: Software Engineering Institute, Carnegie Mellon University, 1990.

[Kang 98] Kang, K.; Kim, S.; Lee, J.; Shin, E.; & Huh, M. "FORM: A Feature-Oriented Reuse Method with Domain-Specific Reference Architectures." *Annals of Software Engineering 5,* 5 (September 1998): 143–168.

[Kazman 98] Kazman, R. & Carrière, S. "View Extraction and View Fusion in Architectural Understanding," *Proceedings of the 5th International Conference on Software Reuse,* Victoria, BC, Canada, June 2–5, 1998. New York, NY: IEEE Computer Society Press, 1998.

[Keuffel 99] Keuffel, W. "Planning for and Mitigating Risk." *Software Development Magazine 7,* 9 (September 1999).

[Knauber 00] Knauber, P., Muthig, D., Schmid, K., & Widen, T. "Applying Product Line Concepts in Small and Medium-Sized Companies." *IEEE Software 17,* 5 (September/October 2000): 88–95.

[Krasner 88] Krasner, G. E.; & Pope, S. T. *A Cookbook for Using the Model-View-Controller User Interface Paradigm in Smalltalk-80,* Journal of Object-Oriented Programming, 1(3), pp. 26–49, August/September 1988, SIGS Publications, New York, 1988.

[Kruchten 95] Kruchten, P. "The '4+1' View Model of Software Architecture," *IEEE Software 12,* 6 (November 1995).

[Kruchten 98] Kruchten, P. *The Rational Unified Process: An Introduction,* Reading, MA: Addison-Wesley, 1998.

[Kuusela 00] Kuusela, J. & Savolainen, J. "Requirements Engineering for Product Families," 61–69. *Proceedings of the International Conference on Software Engineering*. Limerick, Ireland, June 4–11, 2000. New York, NY: ACM, 2000.

[Lee 00] Lee, K.; Kang, K.; Koh, E.; Chae, W.; Kim, B.; & Choi, B. "Domain-Oriented Engineering of Elevator Control Software," Donohoe, P., ed., *Software Product Lines: Experience and Research Directions.* Denver, Colorado, August 28–31 2000. Boston, MA: Kluwer Academic Publishers, 2000: 3–22.

[Lim 98] Lim, W. C. *Managing Software Reuse: A Comprehensive Guide to Strategically Reengineering the Organization for Reusable Components.* Upper Saddle River, NJ: Prentice-Hall PTR, 1998.

[Loveland-Link 99] Loveland-Link, J.; Barbour, R.; Krum, A.; & Neitzel, A. *Rollout and Installation of Risk Management at the IMINT Directorate, National Reconnaissance Office* (CMU/SEI-99-TR-009). Pittsburgh, PA: Software Engineering Institute, Carnegie Mellon University, 1999.

[Low 99] Low, G. & Leenanuraksa, V. "Software Quality and CASE Tools," 142–150. *Proceedings of the Ninth International Workshop on Software Technology and Engineering Practice (STEP '99)*. Pittsburgh, PA, August 30–September 2, 1999. Los Alamitos, CA: IEEE Computer Society Press, 1999.

[McFeeley 96] McFeeley, R. *IDEAL: A User's Guide for Software Process Improvement* (CMU/SEI-96-HB-001). Pittsburgh, PA: Software Engineering Institute, Carnegie Mellon University, 1996.

[McGregor 99] McGregor, J. D. "Validating Domain Models." *Journal of Object-Oriented Programming 12,* 4 (July/August 1999): 12–17.

[McGregor 00] McGregor, J. D. "Building Reusable Test Assets for a Product Line" tutorial, First Software Product Line Conference. Pittsburgh, PA: Software Engineering Institute, Carnegie Mellon University, 2000. Available http://www.cs.clemson.edu/~johnmc/conferences/ProductLine Tutorial.html.

[Meyer 97] Meyer, M. H. & Lehnerd, A. P. *The Power of Product Platforms: Building Value and Cost Leadership,* New York, NY: The Free Press, 1997.

[Mockus 99] Mockus, A. & Siy, H. "Measuring Domain Engineering Effects on Software Coding Cost," 304–311. *Proceedings of Metrics 99: Sixth International Symposium on Software Metrics,* Boca Raton, FL, November 1999. New York, NY: IEEE Computer Society Press, 1999.

[Moore 91] Moore, G. A. *Crossing the Chasm, Marketing and Selling Technology Products to Mainstream Customers.* New York, NY: Harper Business Publishing, 1991.

[Moszkowski 86] Moszkowski, B. *Executing Temporal Logic Programs.* New York, NY: Cambridge University Press, 1986.

[Muller 88] Muller, H. & Klashinsky, K. "Rigi—A System for Programming-in-the Large," 80–86. *Proceedings of the 10th International Conference on Software Engineering (ICSE).* Raffles City, Singapore, April 11–15, 1988. New York, NY: IEEE Computer Society Press, April 1988.

[Musa 99] Musa, J. *Software Reliability Engineering.* New York, NY: McGraw-Hill, 1999.

[Myers 90a] Myers, C. R.; Maher, J. H.; & Deimel, B. L. *Managing Technological Change (Version 1.92, Software Engineering Institute Workshop).* Pittsburgh, PA: Software Engineering Institute, Carnegie Mellon University, 1990.

[Myers 90b] Myers, C. R. & Maher, J. H. *Managing Technological Change: Implementation Plan* (CMU/SEI-90-SR-20). Pittsburgh, PA: Software Engineering Institute, Carnegie Mellon University, 1990.

[Myers 92] Myers, C.; Maher, J.; & Deimel, B. *Managing Technological Change, Course Materials.* Pittsburgh, PA: Software Engineering Institute, Carnegie Mellon University, 1992.

[Newell 72] Newell, A. & Simon, H. A. *Human Problem Solving.* Upper Saddle River, NJ: Prentice-Hall, 1972.

[Oberndorf 98] Oberndorf, P. *COTS and Open Systems.* SEI Monographs on the Use of Commercial Software in Government Systems. February 1998. Pittsburgh, PA: Software Engineering, Carnegie Mellon University.

[Ohlinger 00] Ohlinger, J. "CCT Lessons Learned What We Did, Why We Did It, and What We Would Do Differently." Presentation: GSAW 2000. http://sunset.usc.edu/GSAW/GSAW2000/pdf/Ohlinger.pdf.

[OMG 97] Object Management Group. *The Common Object Request Broker: Architecture and Specification, Revision 2.0* (97-02-25). Object Management Group, 1997. The World Wide Web site for the Object Management Group is located at http://www.omg.org.

[Park 96] Park, R. E. et al. *Goal-Driven Software Measurement—A Guidebook* (CMU/SEI-96-HB-002). Pittsburgh, PA: Software Engineering Institute, Carnegie Mellon University, 1996.

[Parnas 71] Parnas, D. "Information Distribution Aspects of Design Methodology," 339–344. *Proceedings of the 1971 IFIP Congress*. Ljubljana, Slovenia, August 1971. Amsterdam, Netherlands: North Holland Publishing Company, 1971.

[Parnas 85] Parnas, D. & Weiss, D. "Active Design Reviews: Principles and Practices," 132–136. Weiss, D., & Hoffman, D., eds., *Software Fundamentals: Collected Papers By David L. Parnas.* Reading, MA: Addison-Wesley, 2001.

[Paulk 95] Paulk, M., et. al. *The Capability Maturity Model®: Guidelines for Improving the Software Process.* Reading, MA: Addison-Wesley, 1995.

[Porter 80] Porter, M. *Competitive Strategy.* New York, NY: The Free Press, 1980.

[Poulin 97] Poulin, J. S. *Measuring Software Reuse: Principles, Practices, and Economic Models.* Reading, MA: Addison-Wesley, 1997.

[Powell 96] Powell, A.; Vickers, A.; Williams, E.; & Cooke, B. Ch. 11, "A Practical Strategy for the Evaluation of Software Tools," 165–185. *Method Engineering: Principles of Method Construction and Tool Support (Proceedings of the IFIP TC8, WG8.1/8.2 Working Conference on Method Engineering).* Atlanta, GA, August 26–28, 1996. London, UK: Chapman & Hall, 1996.

[Prahalad 90] Prahalad, C. & Hamel, G. "The Core Competency of the Corporation." *Harvard Business Review 68,* 3 (May–June 1990): 79–92.

[Pressman 98] Pressman, R. *Software Engineering: A Practitioner's Approach.* 5th ed. New York, NY: McGraw-Hill Book Company, 1998.

[Pronk 00] Pronk, B. J. "An Interface-Based Platform Approach," Donohoe, P., ed., *Software Product Lines: Experience and Research Directions.* Denver, Colorado, August 28–31 2000. Boston, MA: Kluwer Academic Publishers, 2000: 331–352.

[Radice 94] Radice, R. & Garcia, S. "An Integrated Approach to Software Process Improvement." Tutorial presented at the Software Technology Conference. Salt Lake City, Utah, April 1994.

[Ramesh 97] Ramesh, B.; Stubbs, C.; Powers, T.; & Edwards, M. "Requirements Traceability: Theory and Practice." *Annals of Software Engineering 3,* 3 (September 1997): 397–415.

[Reasoning 00] Reasoning Systems. "Code-Based Management System for Transformation Software." Available http://www.reasoning.com.

[Reifer 97] Reifer, D. J. *Practical Software Reuse: Strategies for Introducing Reuse Concepts in Your Organization.* New York, NY: John Wiley and Sons, Inc., 1997.

[Rigg 95] Rigg, W.; Burrows, C.; & Ingram, P. *Ovum Evaluates: Configuration Management Tools.* London, UK: Ovum Limited, 1995.

[Robertson 98] Robertson, D. & Ulrich, K. "Planning for Product Platforms." *Sloan Management Review 39,* 4 (Summer 1998): 19–31.

[Ryans 00] Ryans, A.; More, R.; Barclay, D.; & Deutscher, T. *Winning Market Leadership: Strategic Market Planning for Technology-Driven Businesses.* New York, NY: John Wiley & Sons, 2000.

[Schmidt 97] Schmidt, M. J. *Solution Matrix White Papers.* Boston, MA: Solution Matrix, Ltd. 1997–99. Available http://www.solutionmatrix.com/kb.html.

[SEI 00] Software Engineering Institute. *CMMI℠—SE/SW, v1.0 Capability Maturity Model—Integrated for Systems Engineering/Software Engineering, Staged Representation, Version 1.0* (CMU/SEI-2000-TR-018). Pittsburgh, PA: Software Engineering Institute, Carnegie Mellon University, 2000. Available http://www.cmu.sei.edu/cmmi/products/v1-staged.pdf.

[SEI ATA] http://www.sei.cmu.edu/ata/ata_init.html

[SEI CBS] http://www.sei.cmu.edu/cbs/index.html

[SEI PLA] http://www.sei.cmu.edu/plp/pl_analysis.html

[SEI REENG] http://www.sei.cmu.edu/reengineering

[Shaw 96] Shaw, M. & Garlan, D. *Software Architecture: Perspectives on an Emerging Discipline.* Englewood Cliffs, NJ: Prentice-Hall, 1996.

[Shaw 00] Shaw, G. "Control Channel Toolkit: Open Architecture-Based Product Line Development." Presentation: GSAW 2000. http://sunset.usc.edu/GSAW/GSAW2000/pdf/shaw.pdf

[Slater 98] Slater, R. *Jack Welch & The G.E. Way: Management Insights and Leadership Secrets of the Legendary CEO.* New York, NY: McGraw-Hill, 1998.

[Smith 90] Smith, C. *Performance Engineering of Software Systems.* Reading, MA: Addison-Wesley, 1990.

[Smith 99] Smith, C. & Woodside, M. *System Performance Evaluation: Methodologies and Applications, E. Gelenbe edition.* Boca Raton, FL: CRC Press, 1999.

[Smith 01] Smith, C.; & Williams, L. *Software Performance: Engineering for Object-Oriented Systems.* Reading, MA: Addison-Wesley, 2001.

[Sommerville 97] Sommerville, I. & Sawyer, P. *Requirements Engineering: A Good Practice Guide.* West Sussex, England: John Wiley & Sons, Ltd., 1997.

[SPC 93] Software Productivity Consortium. *Reuse-Driven Software Processes Guidebook* (SPC-92019-CMC, Version 02.00.03). Herndon, VA: Software Productivity Consortium, 1993.

[STARS 96] Software Technology for Adaptable Reliable Systems (STARS*). Organization Domain Modeling (ODM) Guidebook Version 2.0* (STARS-VC-A025/001/00). Manassas, VA: Lockheed Martin Tactical Defense Systems, 1996.

[Svahnberg 00] Svahnberg, M. & Bosch, J. "Issues Concerning Variability in Software Product Lines," 50–60. *Proceedings of the Third International Workshop on Software Architectures for Product Families.* Las Palmas de Gran Canaria, Spain, March 15–17, 2000. Heidelberg, Germany: Springer LNCS, 2000.

[Szyperski 98] Szyperski, C. *Component Software: Beyond Object-Oriented Programming*. Harlow, England; Reading, MA: Addison-Wesley, 1998.

[Thiel 00] Thiel, S., & Peruzzi, F. "Starting a Product Line Approach for an Envisioned Market: Research and Experience in an Industrial Environment," Donohoe, P., ed., *Software Product Lines: Experience and Research Directions*. Boston, MA: Kluwer Academic Publishers, 2000: 495–512.

[Tichy 89] Tichy, N. and Charan, R. "Speed, Simplicity, Self-Confidence: An Interview with Jack Welch." Harvard Business Review, September–October 1989, Number 5: 112–121.

[Tilley 98] Tilley, S. R. *Discovering DISCOVER* (CMU/SEI-97-TR-012). Pittsburgh, PA: Software Engineering Institute, Carnegie Mellon University, 1998.

[Toft 00] Toft, P.; Coleman, D.; & Ohta, J. "A Cooperative Model for Cross-Divisional Product Development for a Software Product Line," Donohoe, P., ed., *Software Product Lines: Experience and Research Directions.* Denver, Colorado, August 28–31 2000. Boston, MA: Kluwer Academic Publishers, 2000: 111–132.

[Tracz 95] Tracz, W. *Confessions of a Used Program Salesman: Institutionalizing Software Reuse,* New York, NY: Addison-Wesley, 1995.

[Tracz 98] Tracz, W. "RMISE Workshop on Software Reuse Meeting Summary," 41–53. *Software Reuse: Emerging Technology.* Los Alamitos, CA: IEEE Computer Society Press, 1998.

[TreeAge 99] TreeAge Software, Inc. DATA Interactive White Paper [online]. Available (1999): http://www.treeage.com/products/activex.htm.

[van Zyl 00] van Zyl, J.; & Walker, A. J. "Strategic Product Development: A Strategic Approach to Taking Software Products to Market Successfully," Donohoe, P., ed., *Software Product Lines: Experience and Research Directions.* Denver, Colorado, August 28–31 2000. Boston, MA: Kluwer Academic Publishers, 2000: 86–111.

[Vollman 94] Vollman, T. "Standards Support for Software Tool Quality Assessment," 29–39. *Proceedings of the Third Symposium on Assessment of Quality Software Development Tools.* Washington, DC, June 7–9, 1994. Los Alamitos, CA: IEEE Computer Society Press, 1994.

[Vu 97] Vu, J. Keynote. Proceedings of SEPG 97 (Software Engineering Process Group). San Jose, CA, March 17–20, 1997. Pittsburgh, PA: Carnegie Mellon University.

[Vu 00] Vu, J. Keynote. "Findings of the Managing Software Innovation and Technology Change Workshop." Proceedings of SEPG 2000 (Software Engineering Process Group). Seattle, WA, March 20–23, 2000. Pittsburgh, PA: Carnegie Mellon University.

[Wallnau 97] Wallnau, K.; Weiderman, N.; & Northrop, L. *Distributed Object Technology with CORBA and Java: Key Concepts and Implications* (CMU/SEI-97-TR-004). Pittsburgh, PA: Software Engineering Institute, Carnegie Mellon University, 1997. Available http://www.sei.cmu.edu/publications/documents/97.reports/97tr004/97tr004abstract.html.

[Wappler 00] Wappler, T. "Remember the Basics: Key Success Factors for Launching and Institutionalizing a Software Product Line," Donohoe, P., ed., *Software Product Lines: Experience and Research Directions.* Denver, Colorado, August 28–31 2000. Boston, MA: Kluwer Academic Publishers, 2000: 73–84.

[Wartik 92] Wartik, S. & Prieto-Diaz, R. "Criteria for Comparing Reuse-Oriented Domain Analysis Approaches." *International Journal of Software Engineering and Knowledge Engineering 2,* 3 (September 1992): 403–431.

[Weiderman 98] Weiderman, N.; Northrop, L.; Smith, D.; Tilley, S.; & Wallnau, K. *Implications of Distributed Object Technology for Reengineering* (CMU/SEI-97-TR-005). Pittsburgh, PA: Software Engineering Institute, Carnegie Mellon University, 1998.

[Weiss 99] Weiss, D. M. & Lai, C. T. R. *Software Product-Line Engineering: A Family-Based Software Development Process.* Reading, MA: Addison-Wesley, 1999.

[Wijnstra 00] Wijnstra, J. "Supporting Diversity with Component Frameworks as Architectural Elements," 50–59. *Proceedings of the International Conference on Software Engineering*. Limerick, Ireland, June 4–11, 2000. New York, NY: ACM, 2000.

[Williams 99] Williams, R. *Software Risk Evaluation (SRE) Method Description (Version 2.0)* (CMU/SEI-99-TR-029). Pittsburgh, PA: Software Engineering Institute, Carnegie Mellon University, 1999.

[Withey 96] Withey, J. *Investment Analysis of Software Assets for Product Lines* (CMU/SEI-96-TR-010). Pittsburgh, PA: Software Engineering Institute, Carnegie Mellon University, 1996.

[Xerox 99] Xerox PARC. *Aspect-Oriented Programming Home Page*. Menlo Park, CA, 1999. Available http://www.parc.xerox.com/csl/projects/aop/.

[Yacoub 00] Yacoub, S.; Mili, A.; Kaveri, C.; & Dehlin, M. "A Hierarchy of COTS Certification Criteria," Donohoe, P., ed., *Software Product Lines: Experience and Research Directions.* Boston, MA: Kluwer Academic Publishers, 2000: 397–412.

[Zhao 99] Zhao, J. "Bibliography on Software Architecture Analysis." *Software Engineering Notes 24,* 3 (May 1999): 61–62.

[Zubrow 00] Zubrow, D.; Campbell, G. *Basic Metrics for Software Product Lines* (CMU/SEI-00-TN-012). Pittsburgh, PA: Software Engineering Institute, Carnegie Mellon University, 2000.

Index

Note: Page numbers followed by the letters *f* and *t* indicate figures and tables respectively

D

E

M

P

The SEI Series in Software Engineering

Evaluating Software Architectures

Methods and Case Studies

Paul Clements, Rick Kazman, and Mark Klein

This book is a comprehensive, step-by-step guide to software architecture evaluation, describing specific methods that can quickly and inexpensively mitigate enormous risk in software projects. The methods are illustrated both by case studies and by sample artifacts put into play during an evaluation: view-graphs, scenarios, final reports—everything you need to evaluate an architecture in your own organization.

0-201-70482-X • Hardcover • 240 Pages • ©2002

Software Product Lines
Practices and Patterns
Paul Clements
Linda Northrop

Software Product Lines

Practices and Patterns

Paul Clements and Linda Northrop

Building product lines from common assets can yield remarkable improvements in productivity, time to market, product quality, and customer satisfaction. This book provides a framework of specific practices, with detailed case studies, to guide the implementation of product lines in your own organization.

0-201-70332-7 • Hardcover • 608 Pages • ©2002

The People Capability Maturity Model

Guidelines for Improving the Workforce

Bill Curtis, William E. Hefley, and Sally A. Miller

Employing the process maturity framework of the Software CMM, the People Capability Maturity Model (People CMM) describes best practices for managing and developing an organization's workforce. This book describes the People CMM and the key practices that comprise each of its maturity levels, and shows how to apply the model in guiding organizational improvements. Includes case studies.

0-201-60445-0 • Hardback • 448 Pages • ©2002

Building Systems from Commercial Components

Kurt C. Wallnau, Scott A. Hissam, and Robert C. Seacord

Commercial components are increasingly seen as an effective means to save time and money in building large software systems. However, integrating pre-existing components, with pre-existing specifications, is a delicate and difficult task. This book describes specific engineering practices needed to accomplish that task successfully, illustrating the techniques described with case studies and examples.

0-201-70064-6 • Hardcover • 432 pages • ©2002

CMMI℠ Distilled

A Practical Introduction to Integrated Process Improvement

Dennis M. Ahern, Aaron Clouse, and Richard Turner

The Capability Maturity Model Integration (CMMI) is the latest version of the popular CMM framework, designed specifically to integrate an organization's process improvement activities across disciplines. This book provides a concise introduction to the CMMI, highlighting the benefits of integrated process improvement, explaining key features of the new framework, and suggesting how to choose appropriate models and representations for your organization.

0-201-73500-8 • Paperback • 336 pages • ©2001

The CERT® Guide to System and Network Security Practices

By Julia H. Allen

The CERT Coordination Center helps systems administrators secure systems connected to public networks, develops key security practices, and provides timely security implementations. This book makes CERT practices and implementations available in book form, and offers step-by-step guidance for protecting your systems and networks against malicious and inadvertent compromise.

0-201-73723-X • Paperback • 480 pages • ©2001

Managing Software Acquisition

Open Systems and COTS Products

B. Craig Meyers and Patricia Oberndorf

The acquisition of open systems and commercial off-the-shelf (COTS) products is an increasingly vital part of large-scale software development, offering significant savings in time and money. This book presents fundamental principles and best practices for successful acquisition and utilization of open systems and COTS products.

0-201-70454-4 • Hardcover • 400 pages • ©2001

Introduction to the Team Software Process℠

Watts S. Humphrey

The Team Software Process (TSP) provides software engineers with a framework designed to build and maintain more effective teams. This book, particularly useful for engineers and students trained in the Personal Software Process (PSP), introduces TSP and the concrete steps needed to improve software teamwork.

0-201-47719-X • Hardcover • 496 pages • ©2000

CMM in Practice

Processes for Executing Software Projects at Infosys

Pankaj Jalote

This book describes the implementation of CMM at Infosys Technologies, and illustrates in detail how software projects are executed at this highly mature software development organization. The book examines the various stages in the life cycle of an actual Infosys project as a running example throughout the book, describing the technical and management processes used to initiate, plan, and execute it.

0-201-61626-2 • Hardcover • 400 pages • ©2000

Measuring the Software Process

Statistical Process Control for Software Process Improvement

William A. Florac and Anita D. Carleton

This book shows how to use measurements to manage and improve software processes within your organization. It explains specifically how quality characteristics of software products and processes can be quantified, plotted, and analyzed, so that the performance of software development activities can be predicted, controlled, and guided to achieve both business and technical goals.

0-201-60444-2 • Hardcover • 272 pages • ©1999

Cleanroom Software Engineering

Technology and Process

Stacy Prowell, Carmen J. Trammell, Richard C. Linger, and Jesse H. Poore

This book provides an introduction and in-depth description of the Cleanroom approach to high-quality software development. Following an explanation of basic Cleanroom theory and practice, the authors draw on their extensive experience in industry to elaborate the Cleanroom development and certification process and show how this process is compatible with the Capability Maturity Model (CMM).

0-201-85480-5 • Hardcover • 416 pages • ©1999

Software Architecture in Practice

Len Bass, Paul Clements, and Rick Kazman

This book introduces the concepts and practice of software architecture, not only covering essential technical topics for specifying and validating a system, but also emphasizing the importance of the business context in which large systems are designed. Enhancing both technical and organizational discussions, key points are illuminated by substantial case studies.

0-201-19930-0 • Hardcover • 480 pages • ©1998

Managing Risk

Methods for Software Systems Development

By Elaine M. Hall

Written for busy professionals charged with delivering high-quality products on time and within budget, this comprehensive guide describes a success formula for managing software risk. The book follows a five-part risk management road map designed to take you from crisis to control of your software project.

0-201-25592-8 • Hardcover • 400 pages • ©1998

Software Process Improvement

Practical Guidelines for Business Success

By Sami Zahran

This book will help you manage and control the quality of your organization's software products by showing you how to develop a preventive culture of disciplined and continuous process improvement.

0-201-17782-X • Hardcover • 480 pages • ©1998

Introduction to the Personal Software Process

By Watts S. Humphrey

This workbook provides a hands-on introduction to the basic discipline of software engineering, as expressed in the author's well-known Personal Software Process (PSP). By applying the forms and methods of PSP described in the book, you can learn to manage your time effectively and to monitor the quality of your work, with enormous benefits in both regards.

0-201-54809-7 • Paperback • 304 pages • ©1997

Managing Technical People

Innovation, Teamwork, and the Software Process
By Watts S. Humphrey

Drawing on the author's extensive experience as a senior manager of software development at IBM, this book describes proven techniques for managing technical professionals. The author shows specifically how to identify, motivate, and organize innovative people, while tying leadership practices to improvements in the software process.

0-201-54597-7 • Paperback • 352 pages • ©1997

The Capability Maturity Model

Guidelines for Improving the Software Process
By Carnegie Mellon University/Software Engineering Institute

This book provides the authoritative description and technical overview of the Capability Maturity Model (CMM), with guidelines for improving software process management. The CMM provides software professionals in government and industry with the ability to identify, adopt, and use sound management and technical practices for delivering quality software on time and within budget.

0-201-54664-7 • Hardcover • 464 pages • ©1995

A Discipline for Software Engineering

The Complete PSP Book
By Watts S. Humphrey

This book scales down to a personal level the successful methods developed by the author to help managers and organizations evaluate and improve their software capabilities—methods comprising the Personal Software Process (PSP). The author's aim with PSP is to help individual software practitioners develop the skills and habits needed to plan, track, and analyze large and complex projects, and to develop high-quality products.

0-201-54610-8 • Hardcover • 816 pages • ©1995

Making the Software Business Case

Improvement by the Numbers

By Donald J. Reifer

This book shows software engineers and managers how to prepare the *business* case for change and improvement. It presents the tricks of the trade developed by this well-known author over many years, tricks that have repeatedly helped his clients win the battle of the budget. The first part of the book addresses the fundamentals associated with creating a business case; the second part uses case studies to illustrate cases made for different types of software improvement initiatives.

0-201-72887-7 • Paperback • 304 pages • ©2002

Beyond Chaos

The Expert Edge in Managing Software Development

Larry L. Constantine

The essays in this book, drawn from among the best contributions to Software Development magazine's Management Forum, reveal best practices in managing software projects and organizations. Written by many top names in the field—including Larry Constantine, Karl Wiegers, Capers Jones, Ed Yourdon, Dave Thomas, Meilir Page-Jones, Jim Highsmith, and Steve McConnell—each piece has been selected and edited to provide ideas and suggestions that can be translated into immediate practice.

0-201-71960-6 • Paperback • 416 pages • ©2001

Component-Based Software Engineering

Putting the Pieces Together

By George T. Heineman and William T. Councill

This book provides a comprehensive overview of, and current perspectives on, component-based software engineering (CBSE). With contributions from well-known luminaries in the field, it defines what CBSE really is, details CBSE's benefits and pitfalls, describes CBSE experiences from around the world, and ultimately reveals CBSE's considerable potential for engineering reliable and cost-effective software.

0-201-70485-4 • Hardcover • 880 pages • ©2001

Software Fundamentals

Collected Papers by David L. Parnas

By Daniel M. Hoffman and David M. Weiss

David Parnas's groundbreaking writings capture the essence of the innovations, controversies, challenges, and solutions of the software industry. This book is a collection of his most influential papers in various areas of software engineering, with historical context provided by leading thinkers in the field.

0-201-70369-6 • Hardcover • 688 pages • ©2001

Software for Use

A Practical Guide to the Models and Methods of Usage-Centered Design

by Larry L. Constantine and Lucy A. D. Lockwood

This book describes models and methods that help you deliver more usable software-software that allows users to accomplish tasks with greater ease and efficiency. Aided by concrete techniques, experience-tested examples, and practical tools, it guides you through a systematic software development process called usage-centered design, a process that weaves together two major threads in software development: use cases and essential modeling.

0-201-92478-1 • Hardcover • 608 pages • ©1999

CMM Implementation Guide

Choreographing Software Process Improvement

by Kim Caputo

This book provides detailed instruction on how to put the Capability Maturity Model (CMM) into practice and, thereby, on how to raise an organization to the next higher level of maturity. Drawing on her first-hand experience leading software process improvement groups in a large corporation, the author provides invaluable advice and information for anyone charged specifically with implementing the CMM.

0-201-37938-4 • Hardcover • 336 pages • ©1998